ROUTLEDGE HA.
HUMAN SECURITY

This handbook will serve as a standard reference guide to the subject of human security, which has grown greatly in importance over the past twenty years.

Human security has been part of academic and policy discourses since it was first promoted by the UNDP in its 1994 Human Development Report. Filling a clear gap in the current literature, this volume brings together some of the key scholars and policy-makers who have contributed to its emergence as a mainstream concept, including Nobel prize winner Amartya Sen and Sadako Ogata, who jointly chaired the 2001 Commission on Human Security. Drawing upon a range of theoretical and empirical analyses, the handbook provides examples of the use of human security in policies as diverse as disaster management, arms control and counter-terrorism, and in different geographic and institutional settings from Asia to Africa, and the UN. It also raises important questions about how the concept might be adapted and operationalised in the future.

Over the course of the book, the authors draw on three key aspects of human security thinking:

1 Theoretical issues to do with defining human security as a specific discourse
2 Human security from a policy and institutional perspective, and how it is operationalised in different policy and geographic contexts
3 Case studies and empirical work

Featuring some of the leading scholars in the field, the *Routledge Handbook of Human Security* will be essential reading for all students of human security, critical security, conflict and development, peace and conflict studies, and of great interest to students of international security and IR in general.

Mary Martin is a Research Fellow at the Civil Society and Human Security Research Unit, London School of Economics, UK.

Taylor Owen is the Research Director of the Tow Center for Digital Journalism at Columbia University, USA. Research and writing can be found at www.taylorowen.com.

ROUTLEDGE HANDBOOK OF HUMAN SECURITY

Edited by Mary Martin and Taylor Owen

Routledge
Taylor & Francis Group

LONDON AND NEW YORK

First published 2014
by Routledge
2 Park Square, Milton Park, Abingdon, Oxfordshire OX14 4RN

Simultaneously published in the USA and Canada
by Routledge
711 Third Avenue, New York, NY 10017

Routledge is an imprint of the Taylor and Francis Group, an informa business

First issued in paperback 2015

British Library Cataloguing in Publication Data
A catalogue record for this book is available from the British Library

Library of Congress Cataloging in Publication Data
Routledge handbook of human security / edited by Mary Martin and Taylor Owen.
pages cm
Includes bibliographical references and index.
1. Human security--Handbooks, manuals, etc. I. Martin, Mary, 1957-
JC571.R772 2014
355',033-- dc23
2013012769

ISBN 978-0-415-58128-8 (hbk)
ISBN 978-1-138-18368-1 (pbk)
ISBN 978-1-315-88592-6 (ebk)

Typeset in Bembo
by Fakenham Prepress Solutions, Fakenham, Norfolk NR21 8NN

CONTENTS

Contents

FOREWORD

In the globalizing world of today, the concept of security has evolved from the traditional state-based context to cover a whole range of economic, social and technological factors. The end of the Cold War and the decolonization process resulted in new state building among diverse groups of people. Advancement in communication and information technology accelerated economic growth and brought new opportunities. While interdependence benefited people in general, it also made them vulnerable to developments outside their immediate circles. In parts of the world undergoing decolonization and decentralization, diverse groups – ethnic, religious and indigenous – began fighting over contested rights and resources. The international community was short of effective tools to deal with the diverse claims of people and states.

At the 2000 UN Millenium Summit, Secretary-General Kofi Annan stressed that people should be assured of their "freedom from want" as well as their "freedom from fear". He emphasized the importance of responding to social and economic needs of the people as well as political and military threats that had dominated the security fields. At the time, Prime Minister Obuchi of Japan, during his visit to Southeast Asia, had also advocated the need to protect people threatened by survival and announced his commitment to promote human security. His understanding of "human security" was fundamentally developmental, to protect people from "threats to human lives, livelihoods and dignity". The Japanese government announced its readiness to establish the UN Trust Fund for Human Security, and promoted the establishment of the Commission on Human Security. The Commission was mandated to develop the concept of human security as an operational tool for policy formulation and implementation.

I was invited to co chair the Commission on Human Security with Nobel Prize economist Amartya Sen. The Commission took a broad view of human security, focused on the security of people living under critical and pervasive threats, victims of conflicts, refugees and displaced persons, people living in abject poverty, hunger and disease. After two years of research, field visits and public hearings, the report of the Commission, *Human Security Now* was published.

The Commission proposed a framework of action that promotes the protection and empowerment of people. Rather than viewing people as passive recipients of care and assistance led by the state, the Commission regards people as the primary initiators to determine their own fate. By empowering people through education, social mobilization and participation in public life, they themselves are better able to cope with misery and threats surrounding them. It is a "bottom up" approach that regards people as active initiators as well as operators.

The main role of the state on the other hand is protection of its people. Through improving law and order, strengthening judicial institution and ensuring access to basic human needs, the state on its part has to ensure people fair and effective management of public life. The state also holds responsibility over relations with foreign states, ensuring proper and beneficial economic and political relations. The debates and decisions at the Commission caused wide repercussions in policy making and academic circles.

The UN Trust Fund for Human Security was established at the United Nations and operated under an advisory board with a unit in the United Nations Secretariat. It was designed to promote multi-sector aid projects in line with the principles of human security. Primarily funded by Japan, the Fund has provided community development projects in Afghanistan, refugee integration in Zambia and early post-conflict community reconstruction projects in the Congo, among others. The promotion of projects through the Human Security Trust Fund attests to the significance of the concept of human security as the operational tool to protect people and elevate human lives and dignity. The projects are primarily implemented by UN agencies together with local ministries and agencies, and embody the essential ingredients of human security principles. Bilateral development agencies, notably, the Japan International Cooperation Agency, adopted "human security" as its fundamental policy principle.

Lastly, the adoption of the resolution (A/Res/66/290) on Human Security by the General Assembly in September 2012 stands as a major breakthrough. It attests to the growing recognition by member states of the relevance of "human security" on key policy discussions at the United Nations. It also provides concrete steps for the United Nations and Member States to act on threats and issues that threaten the security of member states and the people.

This *Handbook of Human Security* is further demonstration of the impact of this concept in stimulating thinkers, decision-makers and practitioners. The chapters show some of the many ways in which human security has become an important framework for shaping how states behave and how people can enjoy not just security but also dignity. The book tells us how far we have already travelled in adjusting ideas of security for a global era, but also reminds us that there are many areas of policy which still require us to adjust our thinking, for example in arms control, in fighting terrorists or in making sure people do not go hungry. We should see it not only as an important reference of what the concept of human security has achieved but as an agenda for change going forward.

Sadako Ogata

LIST OF ABBREVIATIONS

APEC	Asia-Pacific Economic Cooperation
AQ	Al Qaeda
AQAP	Al Qaeda in the Arabian Peninsular
ASEAN	Association of Southeast Asian Nations
ATT	Arms Trade Treaty
AU	African Union
CA	Constitutive Act
CFSP	Common Foreign and Security Policy
CCW	Convention on Certain Conventional Weapons
CHS	Commission on Human Security
CIDO	African Citizens' Directorate
CIS	Commonwealth of Independent States
CPA	Coalition Provisional Authority
CSS	Critical Security Studies
CoP	Copenhagen School
CTC	Combating Terrorism Center
CWC	Chemical Weapons Convention
DDR	Disarmament, Demobilization and Reintegration
DFAIT	Department of Foreign Affairs and International Trade (Canada)
DPS	Department for Peace and Security
DRR	Disaster Risk Reduction
ECOSOC	Economic, Social and Cultural Council
ESDP	European Security and Defence Policy
ESS	European Security Strategy
ETA	Euskadi Ta Askatasuna
EU	European Union
EULEX	European Rule of Law Mission
FAO	Food and Agriculture Organization
GA	General Assembly
HD	Human Development
HDR	Human Development Report

HFA	Hyogo Framework for Action
HLP	High Level Panel on Threats, Challenges and Change
HS	Human Security
HSN	Human Security Network
IASC	Inter-Agency Standing Committee
ICC	International Criminal Court
ICISS	International Commission on Intervention and State Sovereignty
ICRC	International Committee of the Red Cross
IDP	Internally Displaced Person
IGC	Interim Governing Council
IHL	International Humanitarian Law
MDGs	Millennium Development Goals
NATO	North Atlantic Treaty Organization
NGO	Non-Governmental Organization
NHDRs	National Human Development Reports
NPT	Nuclear Non-Proliferation Treaty
OAU	Organization of African Unity
OCHA	Office for the Coordination of Humanitarian Affairs
ODA	Official Development Assistance
OSCE	Organisation for Security and Cooperation in Europe
PDA	Department for Political Affairs
PoA	UN Programme of Action on Small Arms and Light Weapons
R2P	Responsibility to Protect
ROTC	Reserve Officers Training Corps
SG	Secretary General
SIPRI	Stockholm International Peace Research Institute
START	Strategic Arms Reduction Treaties
UNDP	United Nations Development Programme
UNOCHA	UN Office for the Coordination of Humanitarian Affairs
UNRCA	UN Register on Conventional Arms
UNSC	UN Security Council
WTO	World Trade Organization

CONTRIBUTORS

Lloyd Axworthy, President and Vice-Chancellor of the University of Winnipeg, served as Canada's Minister of Foreign Affairs from 1996–2000. In the Foreign Affairs portfolio, Minister Axworthy became internationally known for his advancement of the human security concept, in particular, the Ottawa Treaty – a landmark global treaty banning anti-personnel landmines. He has served on the boards of the MacArthur Foundation, Human Rights Watch, the Educational Policy Institute, the Canadian Landmines Foundation and the University of the Arctic, the Conference Board of Canada among others. In 2010, he was made an honourary member of the Sagkeeng First Nation in Manitoba and was given an Ojibwe name – Waapshki Pinaysee Inini, which means White Thunderbird Man.

Robert Bailey is a Senior Research Fellow at Chatham House, leading the institution's research on food and environmental security. Current research projects include work on improving the responsiveness of governments and humanitarian agencies to early warnings of slow onset food crises, opportunities to address the impacts of biofuel mandates on food price volatility and policy options for food and water insecure countries. Before joining Chatham House, he worked at Oxfam in a variety of roles and authored a number of publications including the report *Growing a Better Future: Food Justice in a Resource Constrained World*. He was based in West Africa during the 2010 Sahel food crisis, and was responsible for Oxfam's policy and advocacy response to the emergency.

Deepayan Basu Ray is a Policy Adviser on Arms Control and Development at Oxfam. His work is focused on ensuring that the Arms Trade Treaty adequately reflects the impact of armed violence, corruption, excessive military expenditure and unaccountability on processes of development. He has a background in international relations and political science with expertise in human security, conflict, disarmament, arms control and aid effectiveness in fragile contexts. He has a diverse policy and analytical background, and has worked for NGOs, think tanks, consulting companies, academic institutions and government agencies. Deepayan has also published extensively on human security, arms control, aid effectiveness in fragile states, security and development, and non-traditional security threats.

Aybüke Bilgin is a doctoral candidate at Salve Regina University, focusing on women's development and rights

Ryerson Christie is a lecturer of East Asian Studies in the School of Sociology, Politics and International Studies (SPAIS) at the University of Bristol. His research touches on issues of post-conflict reconstruction and the relationship between the humanitarian industry and developing states. As a past Canadian Consortium for Human Security doctoral fellow he has explored the critical value of human security, and has testified to the Canadian Senate on how it might reframe national security issues. Current research is exploring the implications of representing language and food policies as security concerns. His recent publications have addressed Provincial Reconstruction Teams (PRTs) in Afghanistan, globalizations, and peace-building and NGOs: State-Civil Society Interactions, for the Routledge Studies in Peace and Conflict Resolution.

Martijn Dekker is a political anthropologist and lecturer at the University of Amsterdam. His main research interests are human security, civilian initiatives in war situations, armed conflict, humanitarian intervention and the interaction between foreign troops and a local population.

Paul Evans is a professor at the Institute of Asian Research and the Liu Institute for Global Issues at the University of British Columbia in Vancouver. A specialist on international relations in Asia Pacific, he served as the Co-CEO of the Asia Pacific Foundation of Canada (2005–2008) and was the founding director of the Canadian Consortium on Human Security in 2001–2002.

Mient Jan Faber is a mathematician by training and was the head of a Peace Institute in the Netherlands for almost three decades. Currently he is emeritus professor at VU University Amsterdam and visiting professor at the University of Houston, teaching wars and human security (from below).

Andrew A. Gallo is a US Army Infantry officer currently serving as the Regimental Operations Officer for 3d Cavalry Regiment in Fort Hood, Texas. He has a BS from the United States Military Academy at West Point (2000) and an MPA from the Woodrow Wilson School at Princeton University (2009). He previously served as an Assistant Professor in the Department of Social Sciences at West Point (2009–2012).

Des Gasper works at the International Institute of Social Studies in The Hague (Netherlands), as Professor of Human Development, Development Ethics and Public Policy. His research in recent years has been on theorizing well-being, human security and development ethics, with applications particularly in areas of migration and climate change. Recent publications include: 2011: *Trans-National Migration and Human Security* (co-editor; Springer); 2012: 'Climate change – the need for a human rights agenda within a framework of shared human security', *Social Research*, 79(3); (2013) 'Climate change and the language of human security', in *Ethics, Policy and Environment*, 16(1).

Dorothea Hilhorst is Professor of humanitarian aid and reconstruction at Wageningen University. She specializes in aidnography of conflict, disaster, humanitarian aid and reconstruction and manages research programmes in several disaster and/or conflict-affected countries. She has published widely on these topics, and, amongst others, is author of *The Real*

World of NGOs (ZedBooks) and editor of *Mapping Vulnerability* (Earthscan) and *Disaster, Conflict and Society in Crises: Everyday politics of crisis response* (Routledge).

Cindy R. Jebb is Professor and Deputy Head of the Department of Social Sciences at the United States Military Academy Westpoint. She teaches courses in Comparative Politics, International Security, Cultural Anthropology, Terrorism and Counterterrorism, and Officership. She has authored/co-authored three books: *Bridging the Gap: Ethnicity, Legitimacy, and State Alignment in the International System*; *Mapping Macedonia: Idea and Identity*, co-authored with P. H. Liotta; and *The Fight for Legitimacy: Democracy Versus Terrorism*, co-authored with P. H. Liotta, Thom Sherlock, and Ruth Beitler.

Sir Richard Jolly is Honorary Professor and Research Associate of the Institute of Development Studies at the University of Sussex. He is on the Council of the Overseas Development Institute and from 2001–2006 was a Trustee of Oxfam and Chairman of the UN Association of the United Kingdom. He was an Assistant Secretary General of the United Nations holding senior positions in UNICEF and UNDP for nearly 20 years. From 1996 to 2000 he was Special Adviser to the Administrator of the United Nations Development Programme (UNDP), and architect of the widely acclaimed Human Development Report. Professor Jolly has written or been a co-author of some 20 books including four of the volumes on UN history.

Mary Kaldor is Professor of Global Governance and Director of the Civil Society and Human Security Research Unit at the London School of Economics. She is the author of many books, including *The Ultimate Weapon is No Weapon: Human Security and the Changing Rules of War and Peace, New and Old Wars: Organised Violence in a Global Era* and *Global Civil Society: An Answer to War*. Professor Kaldor was a founding member of European Nuclear Disarmament and of the Helsinki Citizen's Assembly. She was also convenor of the Human Security Study Group, which reported to Javier Solana.

Denisa Kostovicova is a senior lecturer in Global Politics in the Department of Government at the London School of Economics and Political Science. She is the author of *Kosovo: The Politics of Identity and Space* (Routledge, 2005), and co editor of *Transnationalism in the Balkans* (Routledge, 2008), *Persistent State Weakness in the Global Age* (Ashgate, 2009), *Bottom-up Politics: An Agency-Centred Approach to Globalization* (Palgrave Macmillan, 2011) and *Civil Society and Transitions in the Western Balkans* (Palgrave Macmillan, 2013).

Keith Krause is a professor at the Graduate Institute of International and Development Studies in Geneva, Switzerland, and Director of its Centre on Conflict, Development and Peacebuilding. He is also the Programme Director of the Small Arms Survey, an internationally recognized research centre NGO he founded in 2001. Keith's research interests include the changing character of contemporary armed violence, peace-building and state-building, human security and multilateral security cooperation.

Jennifer Leaning is the Director of the Harvard François-Xavier Bagnoud Center for Health and Human Rights at Harvard University, and the FXB Professor of the Practice of Health and Human Rights at Harvard School of Public Health. As Associate Professor of Medicine at Harvard Medical School, she is a faculty member in the Department of Emergency Medicine at Brigham and Women's Hospital. Her research interests focus on issues of public health, medical ethics, and early warning in response to war and disaster, human rights and international humanitarian law in crisis settings, and problems of human security in the context of forced migration and conflict. She has field experience in problems of public health assessment and human rights in a range of crisis situations (including Afghanistan, Albania, Angola, Kosovo, the Middle East, former Soviet Union, Somalia, the Chad–Darfur border and the African Great Lakes area) and has written widely on these issues.

Peter H. Liotta (1957–2012) was Professor of Political Science and Humanities at Salve Regina University, and former Executive Director of the Pell Center for International Relations and Public Policy. His last book was *The Real Population Bomb: Megacities, Global Security & the Map of the Future*. As a member of the United Nations Intergovernmental Panel on Climate Change, UN's IPCC, he shared the 2007 Nobel Peace Prize.

Mary Martin is Senior Research Fellow in the Department of International Development, London School of Economics. She was previously Director of Communications and Research for Human Security at LSE Global Governance, and co-ordinator of the Human Security Study Group from 2006–2010. Her research focuses on how state and non-state actors including businesses apply human security in post-conflict situations. Her publications include *National, European and Human Security. From Co-Existence to Convergence*, edited with Mary Kaldor and Narcis Serra (2012); 'The second generation of human security' with Taylor Owen, *International Affairs* (2010); and *The European Union and Human Security* (2008) with Mary Kaldor.

Syed Mansoob Murshed is Professor of the Economics of Conflict and Peace at the International Institute of Social Studies (ISS) of the Erasmus University, Rotterdam in the Netherlands, and is also Professor of Economics at Coventry University in the UK. He was the first holder of the rotating Prince Claus Chair in Development and Equity in 2003. He is the author of seven books and over 120 refereed journal papers and book chapters. His latest book published in 2010 is *Explaining Civil War* (Edward Elgar). His research interests span the economics of conflict, political economy and international economics. He is on the editorial board of several journals, including *Civil Wars*.

Erin Michelle Crocetti is an independent researcher who has worked for local and international NGOs, governments and community groups across the Asia Pacific region, specializing in disaster risk reduction for regions of complex emergencies. Her PhD concerns the application of rights-based approaches after the 2004 tsunami in Sri Lanka. Erin is currently based in Papua New Guinea.

Edward Newman is a senior lecturer in the Department of Political Science and International Studies at the University of Birmingham, where he works in the area of security studies. He has published widely – including in *Security Dialogue*, *Review of International Studies*, *Third World Quarterly*, *Contemporary Security Policy*, *Terrorism and Political Violence*, *Journal of Intervention and Statebuilding*, *Studies in Conflict and Terrorism*, and the *Journal of Peacebuilding and Development*, amongst others – and he is currently conducting research on civil war and intrastate conflict in historical perspective. Dr Newman is the editor-in-chief of *Civil Wars* journal and his personal website can be found at www.edward-newman.net.

Gerd Oberleitner is a lecturer at the Institute of International Law and International Relations at the University of Graz, Austria. He was Lecturer in Human Rights at the London School of Economics and Political Science and Visiting Scholar at the LSE's Centre for the Study of

Human Rights, the European Inter-University Centre in Venice and the Université du Québec à Montréal. His publications include *Global Human Rights Institutions: Between Remedy and Ritual* (Cambridge, Polity, 2007).

Taylor Owen is the Research Director of the Tow Center for Digital Journalism at Columbia University. He is the Founding Editor of the Canadian International Council's international affairs platform OpenCanada.org, Director of the International Relations and Digital Technology Project, and Research Director of the Munk Debates. His Doctorate is from the University of Oxford where he was Trudeau Scholar. He was previously a Banting Postdoctoral Fellow at the University of British Columbia, a Fellow in the Genocide Studies Program at Yale University, a Research Fellow at the London School of Economics and a Researcher at the International Peace Research Institute, Oslo. His research and writing focuses on the intersection between information technology and international affairs. Taylor Owen's publications can be found at www.taylorowen.com.

Alpaslan Özerdem is Professor of Peacebuilding and Director of the Centre for Peace and Reconciliation Studies, Coventry University, UK. He specializes in humanitarianism, disaster response, security sector reform and post-conflict reconstruction. He has published extensively and, among others, is co-author of *Disaster Management and Civil Society,* co-editor of *Participatory Research Methodologies in Development and Post Disaster/Conflict Reconstruction* and co-author of *Managing Emergencies and Crises.*

Amartya Sen is Thomas W. Lamont University Professor, and Professor of Economics and Philosophy, at Harvard University and was until 2004 the Master of Trinity College, Cambridge. Professor Sen was co-chair of the Commission on Human Security which reported in 2003. He was formerly Honorary President of Oxfam and is now its Honorary Adviser. His research has ranged over social choice theory, economic theory, ethics and political philosophy, welfare economics, theory of measurement, decision theory, development economics, public health and gender studies. Amartya Sen's books have been translated into more than thirty languages, and include *Development as Freedom* (1999), *Identity and Violence: The Illusion of Destiny* (2006) and *The Idea of Justice* (2009). He was awarded the Nobel Prize in Economics.

Javier Solana served as the European Union's High Representative for the Common Foreign and Security Policy and Secretary General of the Council of the European Union from 1999–2009. Prior to that, Dr Solana was Secretary General of NATO where he negotiated the NATO Russia Founding Act and presided over the establishment of the Euro-Atlantic Partnership Council. He is currently President of ESADE Business School's Centre for Global Economics and Geopolitics, Distinguished Senior Fellow in Foreign Policy at Brookings Institution, Honorary President of the Centre for Human Dialogue, Senior Visiting Professor at the LSE Global Governance, and member of the board of the International Crisis Group and of the European Council on Foreign Relations. Previously, Dr Solana held different ministerial portfolios in the Spanish government, including Foreign Affairs.

Shahrbanou Tadjbakhsh leads the specialization on Human Security at the Masters of Public Affairs (MPA) at L'Institut d'Etudes Politiques (Sciences Po), Paris and is a Research Associate with the Peace Research Institute, Oslo (PRIO). She is author, with Anuradha Chenoy, of *Human Security: Concepts and Implications* (Routledge, 2007) and editor of *Rethinking the Liberal Peace: External Models and Local Alternatives* (Routledge, 2011), in addition to numerous articles on human security, regional security complexes, liberal peacebuilding, Afghanistan and Central Asia. She previously founded a student run, peer-reviewed *Journal of Human Security* (2004 2008).

Yukio Takasu is the Under-Secretary-General for Management at the United Nations. He has served as Permanent Representative of Japan to the United Nations, and senior functions with the United Nations, including Assistant Secretary-General, Controller of United Nations. Mr Takasu has played a pivotal role in advancing a greater understanding of the notion of human security. He launched the International Commission for Human Security and in 2005 was appointed Ambassador in charge of human security. In 2006, as a Special Envoy for United Nations reform, he initiated the formation of the informal Friends of Human Security group. In December 2010 the Secretary-General appointed Mr Takasu as his Special Adviser on Human Security.

Thomas Kwasi Tieku is cross-appointed to the Munk School of Global Affairs and New College in the University of Toronto. His current research focuses on international mediation and negotiation, regional institutions, international organization and foreign policy. A former director of African Studies in the University of Toronto, Professor Tieku has consulted for international organizations such as the World Bank Group and governments. He is the author of *U.S.–Africa Relations in the Age of Obama*, co-editor of *African Journal of Political Science and International Relations*, and editor of a peer-reviewed *Discussion Paper Series* at the Waterloo-based Centre for International Governance Innovation. Some of his articles can be found in *Democratisation, African Affairs, Africa Today, African Security Review, Canadian Foreign Policy Journal* and *International Journal*.

LIST OF ILLUSTRATIONS

Figures

Tables

Box

INTRODUCTION

Mary Martin and Taylor Owen

It is two decades since the United Nations Development Programme included the phrase 'human security' in its 1994 Human Development Report, triggering a long and sometimes fractious debate about this 'new' vision of security, which sought to challenge classic formulations based on state sovereignty, the defence of territory and elite decision making. More than perhaps any other formulation, which sought to reframe security after the end of the Cold War for an age of globalisation, human security provokes strong reactions. At issue are claims that it represents a new paradigm of security, or at least a radical way of addressing problems associated with conflict, crisis and severe deprivation.

Yet for many people, particularly those charged with making policies in these areas, the idea of human security is still hazy. Its overarching policy implications are unclear, and practical examples of its application are relatively few. Far from threatening to overturn established practices, it still competes with traditional approaches, not least the embrace by powerful western states of the 'War on Terror'. Because it sits in the interstices of human rights, human development and security discourses, it sometimes appears marginal to more mainstream debates on these topics, and implementation requires the crossing of policy and disciplinary boundaries. As Keith Krause notes in chapter 6 of this volume, human security did not arise originally from the security establishment, but from development, nor was it part of the new wave of security thinking after the Cold War. It has been specifically removed from a number of key policy tracts, including the 2005 Copenhagen Declaration of Social Development, and it has been shelved by Canada's ministry of foreign affairs, a once enthusiastic proponent of the concept. This suggests that there is something difficult and problematic about human security as a label and as a policy idea.

And yet, as countless journal articles and policy documents prove, as well as UN debates and the creation of international academic and political institutions to promote human security, it exercises an appeal across a wide range of political, geographic, institutional and cultural contexts. It has not evaporated, as those who dismissed it as hot air might have expected (Paris 2001). There have been setbacks, but also many advances. The concept has become embedded in various tracts of UN discourse. It grounded numerous international advocacy campaigns. It was the core of an EU strategic review. Numerous governments continue to use it as a policy framework. It is widely used in the development community. And it is used as both a framing concept for a strain of academic research sitting at the intersection of development and security policy, as well as a theoretical framework for critical security studies.

The aim of this volume is to take stock of what has been written and practised in the name of human security, and capture the flavour of the debates that it has engendered as a topic for scholars and practitioners. These debates range across definitional arguments and conceptualisations of security. They straddle disciplinary boundaries with different epistemological traditions, including specific language and vocabularies, and diverse political agendas and motivations. We have grouped these perspectives into four parts: concepts and contexts, global policy challenges, actors and applications, and lastly methodologies, tools and approaches. Such delineations should not be taken as conceptually or analytically rigid: we have grouped contributions in a way which we believe is logical and at the same time allows the reader to see how human security has evolved as a rounded discourse encompassing not only ideas and values, but practical utility and application. There are overlaps between the chapters and between parts, underlining the fact that there is a circularity to all discussions about human security. They encompass not only conceptual phenomena, but also human security's normative claims, as well as its instrumental attributes, and practical aspects. As is particularly clear in the chapters in Part IV on human security methodology, but also in Part II on how human security has been used in policy and by different national and international actors, the answer to the question 'what is human security?' is to be found not only in definitional debates, but in concrete attempts to apply its ideas in the field. This includes considering what are appropriate tools with which to research human security in the social sciences.

Knowing what human security is when we see it should not be regarded as suggesting that only empirics matter, or a refusal to continue engaging in theoretical discussion. The core tenets of human security – re-imagining security as different from classical state sovereignty, expanding the horizon of potential threats, incorporating a 'worm's eye' of vulnerability rather than a 'bird's eye' or top-down perspective, and empowering individuals – are starting-points on a rich journey of ideas and experience about what makes us afraid, how we respond to those fears and what we imagine as necessary to a secure life, in an era of globalisation.

In elaborating this starting-point, the volume offers not only a retrospective view of human security. It contains some seminal contributions to the discourse, which stand as milestones in a debate, notable for richness of analytical, political and philosophical thought. The chapters also offer insights for the future direction of scholarship and practice – sometimes in original pieces which have been updated by their authors, but also in chapters such as the one by the late, respected scholar Peter Liotta on how human security is relevant to addressing the challenge of urban growth in the twenty-first century, as well as chapters on arms control and terrorism and on the search for appropriate methodologies.

The benefit of revisiting original works on human security alongside new analyses is that they remind us what we have forgotten, and left underexplored as human security ideas and applications have multiplied, diverged and fragmented. For example, there is the clarity of Amartya Sen's insistence that the theoretical underpinnings of human security must contain at least (*inter alia*): an attention to social arrangements for safety, and therefore the avoidance of a socially detached view of individual human predicament and redemption; 'a reasoned concentration on the downside risks of human lives, rather than on the overall expansion of effective freedom in general' and an emphasis on the more elementary rather than the entire range of human rights.

Sen also, in typically modest fashion, argued that human security should not be taken as exclusively important, but as a way of leading us to a set of objectives among many, which may legitimately claim our attention. How to integrate a human security focus so that it complements rather than competes with other types of policy approach or analytical lenses is an endeavour which has been neglected by proponents and critics alike. Although the position of human security in relation to allied concepts such as human development and human rights features regularly in scholarly and policy debates, its compatibility with and relevance to other current security concepts receive less attention.

So the chapters in this book are intended to tell a story which is both familiar and novel. As Sen notes in chapter 1, human security is not in fact a new idea, but it has had a remarkable revival, becoming a 'buzz' expression, for a generation of academics, policy-makers, practitioners and civil society policy watchdogs. This universe of constituencies has also changed in the past twenty years and its breadth and diversity is also part of the story of human security.

Human security is not only about the shift of referent object away from a focus on states and *raison d'état*, towards individuals, groups and communities. It is about cosmopolitan ideas, transnational movements and the idea that a universal humanity should frame decisions about who is vulnerable, and should be protected. While the term 'referent object' has become a useful shorthand to describe the key change in analytical approach represented by human security (Newman 2001: 239), it is not only objects of security, but the nature of subjectivity, as well as the interrelation between providers and receivers of security, which have undergone a transformation as part of this departure from traditional thinking. Human security reflects different assumptions about security provision at the same time as reconfiguring our perception of insecurity. People endangered by risks to health, lack of food and shelter or environmental change require policy responses that no longer emanate only from traditional sources. Security is not the exclusive preserve of those tasked with protecting borders and state assets. It becomes the concern of a broader spectrum of policy and competences, and different kinds of actors, including NGOs, business, religious organisations and other civil society movements. As already noted, active co-operation is required to bring together different capabilities, across disciplinary and practitioner boundaries, to fulfil a vision of holistic, comprehensive security, which can address the everyday needs and fears of individuals and communities.

As Mrs Ogata observes in the foreword, a significant premise of the 2003 Commission on Human Security was that security should give individuals a voice in articulating what makes them fearful and what can be done to make them safe. Even vulnerable people – including refugees, unorganised civilians, the poor, minority groups and victims – should not be relegated to being passive recipients of someone else's decisions. They have agency, and deserve dignity and the opportunity to take charge of their own futures. Thus issues of subjectivity and the interaction between the 'objects' of security and those who deal out the means and resources for safer and more tolerable lives are also key elements in considering what is human security and how it has advanced.

Another narrative thread in the human security debate, observed by Sen, is the danger that in becoming more prolific, the idea of human security risks being summoned too often and too loosely. In the first part, authors trace not only the evolution of human security discourse, but also the ways in which definitional arguments have splintered it. In doing so, they highlight not only the reasons for its popularity but also illustrate some of the discursive traps of human security, including how Sen's warning about overstretch might be justified. These chapters provide the broad contours of human security thinking, as well as finer details. They also situate human security, historically, philosophically and politically within wider security and policy debates. They allow us to view the consequences of a change in mindset and policy practice which sees security in a people-centred way. Here we begin to glimpse the conundrum of human security, what Edward Newman later terms the 'central paradox' of the idea in his chapter about the United Nations. While human security calls for a critique of the structures and norms that produce insecurity, its ontological starting point for scholars and practitioners assumes a perpetuation of just those structures and norms. The 'uncomfortable duality' (Newman this volume) of being intellectually challenging while also practically possible suggests both theoretical as well as operational problems of application.

As Des Gasper observes, human security has displayed an unexpected degree of spread, including into gender studies, environmental studies, migration research and the thinking of various organisations. It has been useful because 'it seems to help in generating unexpected insights, through person-centred attention to the intersections of multiple dimensions of life', as well as being flexible enough to be used to support completely opposing conclusions and interventions.

Gasper sets the scene for the definitional and critical chapters which follow in this part, by reminding us that it is the primary purposes of the users of human security which have determined the various interpretations which have emerged. Whether in elaborating a research programme or in setting a policy orientation, the role required of human security, as well as the nature of the actor using it, become important considerations in deciding its definition and how it will be implemented. In this, human security sits squarely as part of critical security studies and Robert Cox's often quoted remark that 'all theory is for someone and for some purpose' (Cox 1981). Indeed Cox and his contrast between problem-solving and critical theory features throughout this volume. The chapters here demonstrate how human security has reflected both – as opposed to conforming to either one or the other. They also testify to the remarkable pliability it has displayed in the hands of the many who have embraced it.

Thus, the broad versus narrow definitional contest which has become so characteristic of human security debates can be seen in a more specific light: it stemmed from a desire on the one hand by some proponents to move decisively beyond the traditional focus on state security, performed by military actors, because it was deemed insufficient for a new era. Meanwhile others reacted to the UNDP promotion of the idea in its 1994 Human Development Report with a desire to retain a focused view of security, rather than accede to expanding it too far, thus promoting narrow definitions.

Shahrbanou Tadjbakhsh mounts a defence of the broad view of human security, based on the concept's ability to add value to security studies, human development and human rights, as well as being an essential approach for understanding contemporary crises. It represents a turn away from the 'amoral' position adopted by classical IR theorising – another echo of Cox – and turns on highly normative and ethical considerations. This means that the concept cannot be judged solely in terms applied to empirical and positivist theories such as realism, or on whether it is workable. Unlike realism, for Tadjbakhsh human security refuses to succumb to a dominant political agenda, and confronts issues of power relations in international relations. A broad definition is essential to this purpose.

The radical claims made for human security have been a persistent source of contestation by critics, and there are plenty who disagree with this kind of endorsement. On the one hand, the concept is accused of being too vague to represent an alternative paradigm, on the other, that it actively subverts its own transformative potential through attempting to 'securitise' issues in order to solicit interventions, through exaggerating threats, locating them in non-traditional power centres in the developing world, and substituting crisis management for strategic foreign policy visions (Bellamy & McDonald 2002; Duffield & Waddell 2006; Chandler 2008: 428). Tadjbakhsh refutes the criticism that it is too broad and too ambitious as missing the point that it needs to be flexible to account for the myriad sources of insecurity which blight human lives, while the very fact that there are so many different human security approaches, she argues, stimulates necessary critical debates about what constitutes power and legitimacy.

Taylor Owen puts forward his case for seeing human security not as a choice between broad and narrow ranges of threats, but rather as thresholds of severity. He sees a definitional paradox at the core of the human security discourse, that definitions are either narrow, sacrificing conceptual integrity for policy utility, or broad, prioritising a literal referential shift to the individual over the needs of policy-makers. To overcome this, he proposes a threshold-based approach, whereby threats in any one location would be classified as human security threats if they threaten the vital core of the individual from critical and pervasive threats. This, he argues, allows the concept to remain both broad enough to include threats from any cause, but to also remain focused on those harms that cause the most harm.

Mary Kaldor makes the point that how human security is operationalised matters in validating its claims to represent something novel in security thinking and practice. Only if it proves capable of addressing the lived experiences of individuals in dangerous circumstances, can it claim to deliver legitimate new forms of power. Human security has emerged as a result of profound changes in political authority and these provide the context in which its relevance can be understood.

Kaldor's chapter outlines a backdrop of diminished state autonomy, a weakened social contract between states and their populations, the increase in global forms of governance, individual as well as state rights, and the changing nature of conflict amid constraints on states' recourse to conventional forms of warfare. In this context, human security is 'about extending individual rights beyond domestic borders and about developing a capacity at a global level to provide those kinds of emergency services to be deployed in situations where states either lack capacity or are themselves the violators of rights.' The crux of Kaldor's argument is that these changes have not been matched by a profound rethinking on the part of political leaders, nor a change in mindset necessary to implement human security's progressive vision. This point is echoed in Keith Krause's review of the spread of human security discourse, in which he concludes that the critical potential of the discourse is immanent rather than actualised. Whatever it promises, actually existing human security remains a state-centred discourse, which relies on state resources and complicity to produce improved conditions for individuals.

After the 1994 Human Development Report, which proved the springboard for launching human security into policy discussions, the debate moved away from broadening security, and focused more on its application to physical threats and 'freedom from fear'. This, Krause explains, was consistent with a historical idea of security 'intertwined with the struggle to control the institutions and instruments of organised violence' as well as with the ability of the state and the Westphalian system to guarantee the security of its citizens. It also provided further evidence of state entrenchment in international relations, resistant to the advent of new thinking, or to dialogues with non-governmental actors and civil society. It meant that human security itself was prey to the influence of traditionalist foreign policy bureaucrats, and prone to failure in attempting to do any more than superficially rearrange power relations in matters of security.

Krause suggests this central normative paradox of human security is manifest in multiple subordinate contradictions. These include the fact that policy initiatives, especially in the area of security sector reform or post-conflict reconstruction, imply not just a dependence on, but a strengthening of the role and resources of the state, even where the state is regarded as a cause of insecurity. Krause speaks of human security as the 'culmination of the liberal project of building strong, legitimate and representative political institutions', which began with enlightenment ideas of individual rights and personal freedoms. Can it escape its own internal tensions, some of which are highlighted by both Kaldor and Krause, to develop into a discourse of fundamental change? In other words is human security only the end of something old, or the beginning of something new?

Ryerson Christie's chapter turns up the volume on human security as a conundrum by exploring in more detail its relevance to critical security studies; how scholars in this field have sought to utilise the concept, yet they run the risks of engaging with a discourse which has demonstrated the resilience of traditional security actors. Specific debates which are of central importance to liberal scholars, about broad or narrow versions of human security, or the relative importance of freedom from fear versus freedom from want, are less compelling for critical scholars than considerations of power and the chance to change the behaviour of states. Christie shows that here again, whatever the abstract theoretical position, context and conceptualisation have been closely related. Both have shaped the way the human security discourse has developed. After 9/11 some critical scholars saw human security as a way to re-enter policy debates and to attack the 'war-machine' set in motion by the 'Global War on Terror'. Other groups have drawn on Foucauldian analysis to critique human security as a form of biopolitics to control lives in the Global South through security interventions and humanitarian assistance, or to produce certain kinds of knowledge (Duffield and Waddell 2006; Grayson 2008). For many, including feminist scholars, the value of human security has been to advance debates about emancipation and ethics in global politics. Rather than the narrow versus broad view which has dominated our horizon of human security, Christie reveals the multiple sub-currents of academic and political agendas which lie beneath the surface of debates about human security, and which portray dilemmas of seeing it as a radical discourse. Is engagement with the policy community an implicit acceptance of the existing unequal terrain of security practice, and in fact merely 'problem-solving'? Like Krause, Christie wonders whether human security offers critical security studies an appropriate platform for moving security practices forward or is it a dead end? The relative failure of human security as a domestic policy in Western states is one sign for Christie that human security may not represent a new paradigm but simply a tactical and strategic choice in readjusting existing practices, particularly at a time when foreign security policies have been in flux.

The final chapter in Part I suggests ways in which human security could move forward, and assert its relevance by being applied to the increasing problems of troubled megacities, with implications for both domestic and global policy. It offers another reply to critics and critical advocates of human security concerned that it has been irrevocably subsumed in a traditional and hegemonic security discourse. Peter Liotta and Aybüke Bilgin emphasise the idea of vulnerability rather than threats, pointing out that threats tend to generate oppressive reaction by policy-makers, particularly if they take the form of military solutions. They argue that states and the international community will have to focus on 'long-term entangled vulnerabilities' in order to avoid persistent conflicts and crises, and the need for expensive and perpetual ad hoc response mechanisms. Human security, practised within states and regions, rather than as emergency foreign policy agendas, where it is currently predominantly nested, is a conceptual and practical way to deal with the future trajectory of global insecurity, through prevention, tackling privation and social marginalisation in places where they are most inflammatory.

The megacity of the future and the challenge of creating human resilience moves us from the context and conceptualisation of human security, to its policy value. Part II contains an extensive, though far from exhaustive, range of policy applications in which human security has been, or is starting to be used. The idea of the state as the main provider of human security remains pivotal, but as Mient Jan Faber and Martijn Dekker describe, under circumstances of violence, the focus is also on strategies for self-protection by individuals faced with new forms of warfare and 'the chaotic and combustible mixture of identity politics, organised crime, terrorism and other gruesome forms of violence'. This is the fabric of contemporary conflict, as well as some forms of state, liable to both strength and weakness. It is the absence of functioning state level governance that gives rise to human security from below, even though this substitute for effective and legitimate authority may be messy, imperfect and itself ridden with ethical dilemmas.

The search for human security amid conditions of violence will involve such groups as spoilers, competitors and predators, as well as victims themselves. They will be tied together in a complex web of local power relations. However unsavoury some of these groups might be, human security will only serve to stem violent conflict if it is inclusive and co-opts them. It must not become a means for further marginalisation and community divisions, or a form of 'divide and rule of law'.

The same bottom-up imperative is evident in the use of human security in development policies, where rich contextualisation, based on specific experiences in time and location, contributes to its value-added, as Richard Jolly demonstrates with reference to the diversity of analysis and prescription in national human development reports. Here again, there is support for adopting a broad view of threats, in the perceptions of at-risk individuals as they categorise and rank multiple sources of insecurity. A broad perspective helps to direct public expenditures away from traditional policy silos by making visible novel forms of insecurity, it raises public awareness of individual and interrelated threats, and aids more efficient use of resources. Nevertheless, choice and resource allocation are still significant challenges in carrying through this broadening of the security agenda, as Richard Jolly notes. His proposal is to change the practices of security and deepen, rather than simply broaden, analysis at country and regional levels, including conducting more rigorous scrutiny of the way public money is spent on security.

Human security should not only be imagined as an outcome or policy objective. While its finality, and identifiable achievement is conceptually and practically problematic, it should also be seen as a process, which shapes institutions, practices and the terms of debates in international politics. The chapter by Lloyd Axworthy, former Canadian Minister of Foreign Affairs, illustrates this in the case of the Responsibility to Protect (R2P) principle, which emerged from the International Commission on Intervention and State Sovereignty (ICISS) in 2001. The Commission's report redefined classical state sovereignty in terms of states' duty to protect their civilian populations, and permitted intervention by outsiders in case this duty could not be fulfilled. The ICISS report established a trio of responsibilities: prevention, reaction and rebuilding to put civilians at the forefront of decision-making, with (armed) intervention being only one and the most extreme of measures to enforce the protective duty.

R2P has become an embodiment of human security in practice, yet has also become regarded as synonymous with western militarist interventionism (Kaldor 2011). It challenged not only the ends of classical security policy, but reconsidered the means. In Axworthy's phrase: 'the old model of separate state authority simply cannot respond to the current generation of shared challenges' or what Ruti Teitel calls 'humanity's law' – a humanity-based framework for addressing conflict (Teitel 2011). R2P is only one in a number of new international norms and tools which need to emerge around human security. Axworthy concludes that: 'It is the evolving concept of collective security that is unique to understanding human security. The common experiences of individuals across borders and not solely within borders and the opportunity to discover innovative and cooperative solutions to these threats is what makes the concept of security unique in this century.' Whatever the nuances of the ICISS report, dealing with the circumstances of mitigated sovereignty, intervention as a top-down response to crises challenged policy-makers as to how best to address insecurity of affected civilian populations.

Jennifer Leaning's chapter takes the discussion of human security and threats down to the personal and intimate, highlighting the dramatic psycho-social dimensions of conflict. Here again, there is a stark illustration of the differentiation with traditional security, in the need to pay attention to affective elements such as long reparation guilt, anger, humiliation and revenge These pepper the conflict environment and contribute to the recursive dynamics of tension and bitterness which prevent post-conflict healing and often presage further conflict, and are a hallmark of individual experiences of fear and insecurity.

Natural, rather than human engineered disasters, have traditionally appeared to offer less scope for preventive action, instead requiring rapid reactive responses, and triggering a heavy protective agenda. Given new thinking in the field of disaster recovery which combines the idea of vulnerability and hazards and emphasises a more rights-based approach to those affected by disasters, it is perhaps surprising that there has not been more alignment between natural disasters and human security. This is an agenda which is still evolving, but given momentum by recent disasters such as cyclone Nargis and the Haiti earthquake. Dorothea Hilhorst, Alpaslan Özerdem and Erin Smith pose the question whether R2P would be applicable in situations of naturally occurring disasters. The difficulties of engaging in universal preventative protection in the face of the sovereignty concerns of states, as well as the prevalence of geo-strategic international politics, clearly are a hurdle to this alignment with human security. A more practical concern is that, as a rapid disaster response mechanism, UN sanctioned intervention under R2P is too slow and cumbersome, although it may have merits in post-disaster rebuilding, and in helping to mitigate future vulnerability. There are other reasons why human security has not been integrated into disaster management even though it can provide a useful conceptual framework for reducing disaster risks: the regulations governing disaster response including international humanitarian law, humanitarian principles, human rights, codes of conduct and refugee law have been developed in the framework of violent conflict. Applying them in peacetime is ambiguous and sometimes controversial. However, a more rights-based approach to natural disaster management, and the integration of ideas of vulnerability, resilience and prevention, are moving humanitarian relief and rebuilding efforts further onto the terrain scoped out by human security.

In many parts of the world, chronic food insecurity is a major impediment to human security. Although it may sometimes be triggered by environmental and natural disasters, as Robin Bailey argues, it is also the result of governance failures and aggravated power imbalances. The hungry lack the economic power to access affordable food, and to pressure governments. Chronic hunger is concentrated among the poor and marginalised, most of whom are women, and in rural areas. Food and hunger become weapons of war and oppression, where governments deliberately deprive populations of the means to eat. It is not only governments of the Global South whose policies create food vulnerability. The development of biofuels by the US and EU is credited with increasing the volatility of commodity prices and aggravating food insecurity. Not only is human security jeopardised by people being hungry, emergency responses are also often inappropriate, tailored to interest groups in donor countries rather than the vulnerable, and disempowering when they are provided in-kind rather than in-cash, and sourced internationally.

Food security is likely to become a more intense challenge in the decades ahead: population growth, economic development and climate change could combine to trigger regional food crises, commodity price spikes, droughts and floods, and higher incidence of diseases. Almost one person in seven is already hungry and starvation is rising in parts of the world. Human security policies to tackle this aggravated abuse of the most basic of needs should go beyond humanitarian responses, handing out relief supplies. They need to also empower people to act, to reclaim both local and global politics, assert their rights and hold governments to account.

The last two chapters in this part on global challenges deal with a more traditional terrain of security policy. National defence and its contemporary bedfellow, counter-terrorism, reflect the classical prerogatives of the state and a governing elite, in guaranteeing safety from physical attack, whether by foreign enemies or by domestically based groups and individuals. The question of compatibility between human and national security remains an active ingredient in the wider contemporary security debate. Deepayan Basu Ray seeks to explore how the concept of human security can help to develop arms control regimes that are fit for purpose in the twenty-first century, capable of protecting lives and livelihoods. This is no mean task for human security, because it requires arms control architecture to overcome what Basu Ray terms the 'national security barrier'.

In the case of terrorism, Cindy Jebb and Andrew Gallo argue that traditional counter-insurgency strategies, which reify top-down kinetic solutions, miss the point about grass-roots individualised sources of insecurity which fuel terrorist sympathies. While both these policy applications demonstrate the 'problem-solving' approach which critical scholars might reject as sustaining rather than overturning a dysfunctional or illegitimate use of state power, by venturing deep into the traditional sphere of state competence, and showing how it could be recalibrated, these chapters illustrate the contemporary appeal and continuing relevance of human security discourse. They allow us to judge whether new thinking can confront highly traditional conceptualisations of security, to provide creative, innovative policy solutions.

The idea of arms control is appealing to proponents of human security because it sets out to control tools of violence, as well as seeking to curb the dominance of the state in determining the forms of insecurity to which policy solutions must be found. Basu Ray points out that while lethal armed violence accounts for over half a million deaths across the globe each year, the vast majority occur not through conflicts, but as a result of organised crime or gang killings, against which heavy armaments, which soak up so much government spending, are irrelevant. Although some arms control initiatives, such as the Convention on Cluster Munitions, focus on protection of vulnerable civilians, while the UN Programme of Action on Small Arms and Light Weapons forms an important part of peacebuilding policies, other initiatives are framed in the language of hard security. Arms negotiations do not feature expanded notions of human security, and in the words of Basu Ray, they are: 'alarmingly narrow in scope, catering almost exclusively to military and defence policy needs'. Human security offers an alternative conceptualisation of national security, which does not deny the Weberian state's role as the monopoly holder of the legitimate use of force in protecting its population. However, it brings in additional perspectives, reworking the understanding of how legitimate security needs can contribute to, rather than compete with, socio-economic development needs. Thus, far from being outside the discursive field of arms control, human security can help shape the way it is negotiated to produce a consistency between government responsibilities of social protection and service delivery on the one hand, and national security on the other. An individual-centric approach could reframe arms control to include not just development issues, but also human rights, and an emphasis on transparency and accountability.

For Jebb and Gallo, a human security perspective opens up the security aperture in important ways, which can make counter-terrorism more effective. It can also address issues of the contested legitimacy of anti-terrorist activities, which are socially and politically divisive. Their reading of human security is not as the antithesis of counter-insurgency, but as a framework for the use of more effective tools to contain it. Key elements in this framework are the importance of individual, local and holistic perspectives, and the divergence between the agendas of international security actors and the interests of communities where terrorists are based, where (in)security is closely linked to the lack of basic needs and infrastructures.

Jebb and Gallo's focus is on the nature of the insurgency, deconstructing what is required to confront it more efficiently than traditional measures based on force and coercion. They base their presentation of an alternative on the fact that terrorism is a security environment, which presents primarily non-military challenges, and that human security can open an exploration of non-military elements of power, which both feed it and can be used to respond to it.

In Part III, we look at the operationalisation of human security from another perspective, that of policy actors who have taken up the concept and made it part of their security discourse. Here the lens is both conceptual and practice-grounded. Authors writing on Africa, Asia, Japan, the UN and EU show how human security has been taken up within different institutional settings, with policy-makers seeking to apply it as an approach to specific issues.

Policy entrepreneurs, whether operating at national, supranational, transnational or regional level, have been an essential component in the evolution of human security discourse. The concept is notable for the fact that it emerged neither in the non-governmental community, nor in a state, but in international organisations such as the UN and later in the EU. Within these contexts it was individual thinkers and politicians who were pivotal in promoting a different approach to security. Mahbub-ul-Haq and Amartya Sen are among the 'fathers' of human security as a philosophically grounded discourse. In the policy arena there have been equally indispensable pioneers such as Kofi Annan and Yukio Takasu at the UN, Javier Solana and Benita Ferrero-Waldner at the EU and Salim Ahmed Salim at the Organisation of African Unity. State politicians such as Keizo Obuchi, who set Japan on a human security course, and Lloyd Axworthy, who was instrumental in leading Canada's campaigns on land mines and R2P which are described in the policy challenges section. In Costa Rica under Oscar Arias, Switzerland and Austria, there have been similar stories of how human security was promoted as a result of personal or institutional policy initiative.

These accounts reveal not only how the concept has been disseminated and its policy utility increased. They also show how institutional intervention was important in shaping under-standings of human security, and how in turn the concept has helped to define certain global actors. UN forums and thematic debates have been at the forefront of developing not only specific human security practices, but underpinning the concept with a new understanding of state sovereignty, in the context of changing norms about individual rights. R2P began as a human security initiative, and has been endorsed in official reports such as the *High-level Panel on Threats, Challenges and Change* and the 2005 World Summit Outcome document, and UNSC resolutions, notably 1973, of 17 March 2011, authorising armed intervention in Libya. Yet institutional take-up has not been a story of unmitigated progress.

Edward Newman analyses how, despite its role as the originator of human security policy, the UN has declined to take a 'critical' approach, instead attempting to promote human security within existing political, legal and normative constraints. Thus human security has developed alongside UN practices that uphold state sovereignty and a traditional Westphalian view of the world. The UN also uses state forums as the means through which to implement its vision of human security. Neither has the organisation used the concept to develop a consensus normative view on issues of justice and rights, instead tolerating differences amongst states. What has emerged is a state-centric view of human security, which plays down its transformative potential and depends on a trade-off with member states, encouraging their acceptance of its less radical implications in exchange for tolerating it as a generic policy label. Here again we return to the central paradox of human security, that it works inside a given reality of security rather than seeking to change it. The UN's human security initiatives do not question existing structures power, gender and distribution. Indeed UN policies see a strong state as a necessary requirement for individual security, despite the obvious problems in making some states guarantors of a security which they themselves undermine daily. This is evident for example, as Newman points out, in the Secretary-General's 2010 report which observed that governments retain the primary role for ensuring the survival, livelihood and dignity of citizens, and that human security was an 'invaluable tool' helping them to do this (UNSG 2010:1). The experience of the UN as the originator of human security as a policy discourse leads Newman to conclude that it is neither a paradigm-shifting nor emancipatory movement; 'at best, it would be an incremental, contingent process within an imperfect system'.

A similar conservatism, which sees human security in reduced terms as an additional component to existing policy approaches, is to be found in the EU's adoption of human security. In the hands of the External Relations commissioner Benita Ferrero-Waldner, the EU's initiatives were often overtly labelled as human security, but they were much more *sotto voce*, when applied by the EU High Representative Javier Solana who was answerable to EU member states within the intergovernmental dimension of EU foreign policy. The EU turned to human security as not only consistent with its ambitions as a global actor, and its genesis as a peace project without primary responsibility for territorial defence (this was NATO's task), but also because it could provide an identity narrative at a key moment in 2003, when member states faced a deep and damaging schism over the invasion of Iraq. As Javier Solana remembers, human security filled a narrative void in the quest for the EU to develop as a particular kind of security actor: it was available and appropriate in a way which other security discourses were not. If it did not bind the 27 member states together, neither was it going to necessarily drive a wedge between them, providing a backdrop for collective action. For some states – particularly the more powerful such as the UK, France and Germany – it was less acceptable, which explains the difference in enthusiasm with which the EU's High Representative, who was answerable to them, used the term compared with the External Relations commissioner, who was not.

In this part we are able to discern the politics of human security. These consist not only of the fundamental tensions over how the individual as the referent object should reframe security practice. Politics dictate if, when and how human security is used as an approach to security challenges. Human security is controversial because it challenges the relationship between governments and their own population, often making them feel uncomfortable in respect of their obligations to them. It imposes a responsibility and duty of care, which also has repercussions in how states are viewed by other states. In extreme circumstances this norm provides the justification for challenging their sovereignty and territorial integrity. Thus some see human security as an extension of the 'human rights imperialism', linked to a Western attempt to impose 'liberal' values on third party states. The politics of human security mean that rather than being the expression of a universal set of values, as its proponents intended, it is often a calculated attempt on the part of certain actors not to advance a humanitarian agenda but to enhance their relative power and advantage. As well as considering the motives behind state and organisations' sponsorship of human security, we also need to consider the evidence of why certain actors have succeeded or failed in persuading others to accept this as a worldview and policy approach. As the chapters in this part show empirically, the success of policy entrepreneurs depends on a host of factors which are independent of the moral and ethical validity of human security ideas. Without engaging in an extensive theoretical discussion of a core theme in International Relations, the accounts show the presence of a mixture of classic power relations, economic resources, competence in policy entrepreneurship, individual leadership, events and conducive contexts, among others.

How and why human security is operationalised is as vigorous a source of contestation in the debate as the definitional differences which were highlighted in the first part of this book (Debiel and Werthes 2006). Perhaps ironically for a discourse which is predominantly about foreign policy, Japan was one of the earliest proponents of human security. It was prompted by the Asian financial crisis of 1997–8, and the response to crisis which was a domestic politics of austerity, in which financial institutions left people without a social safety net. Japan sponsored and encouraged the setting up of the UN Human Security Trust Fund to help vulnerable people at a global and regional level. Its first beneficiaries were in Japan's neighbourhood.

Japan's approach was collaborative, exemplified by network initiatives which it pioneered, such as the Friends of Human Security. Its priority was to not only ensure that initiatives would be multilateral, but they would also keep a broad view of human security on the table, and provide conceptual, political and financial backing for UN policies to maintain a freedom from fear perspective. For Japan this meant that human security could continue to be used flexibly and across a range of policy requirements, from financial crises, to health epidemics and natural catastrophes. Like the EU, human security was an expression of Japanese identity. As Yukio Takasu explains, it resonates culturally with Japanese attitudes and is notable for being not a source of contention as it is in the case of many other policy actors, but a bipartisan ideal which is shared inside and outside of government.

East Asia remains important in the evolution of human security thinking and practice. Paul Evans' chapter shows how it has served to rein in dominant conceptions of human security as a liberal prescription for a well-functioning security order. It is also an incubator of ideas for dealing with transnational problems. Security co-operation is paramount in Asian versions of the discourse, as is the importance of non-traditional security thinking. Both features are ambiguous about whether the state is the primary or only force capable of addressing regional problems. As the victims of recurrent natural disasters, Asian countries' focus on environmental degradation and the adaptation to climate change also represents a more contemporary working of the discourse, but one which is likely to become more significant in future.

The African Union's motives behind its advocacy of human security stemmed also from need on its doorstep, and the perception that traditional understandings of security had contributed to Africa's security and economic predicament. The AU turned to human security to fill a void which emerged after 9/11, which was ideational as well as political. The African Union became as, Thomas Tieku describes: 'an instrument for the promotion and socialization of human security ideas at the interstate level. Almost all decisions, declarations and protocols that African leaders adopted in the first eight years since the formation of the AU had strong human security undertones.'

Human security served, as with other proponents, to cement the AU's sense of identity as a regional actor, and cohesion among member states. This in turn enhanced its standing in comparison to its predecessor, the Organisation for African Unity. The participation of civil society in co-operation and development programmes, which was part of the human security narrative, also supplied an essential missing link in the development of Pan-Africanism, making it acceptable to elites and grass roots. The AU's use of human security is also an example of the depth of socialisation and codification the concept has undergone: it is not only enshrined in legal instruments applicable at regional and national government level, but the AU has also worked hard to embed it in security practices among continental elites.

In the final part, we analyse human security as a practical approach to security issues and dilemmas. Although the concept has frequently been dismissed as of limited utility because it is too fuzzy, as Parts II and III show, there are widespread thematic and geographic applications, and attempts to implement the ideas which underpin it. This part shows how human security can be viewed as a *method* of security, not only as a desirable end state. Practising it in ways which are, at a minimum, consistent with its defining characteristic as human–centred, and paying more than lip service to its normative proposition, is an essential part of the discursive shift from traditional security approaches. These challenges are as acute for social scientists and the Academy as for security practitioners. The chapters in this part set out to illustrate a selection of some of these, in considering the interrelations between human security and risk analysis, economics and resource allocation, research methodology, and international law. In some respects, this part embodies the stiffest test of the validity of human security, for without adequate tools, or the ability to integrate human security into areas such as law, economics and geography, the concept will wither. It will be little more than an interesting intellectual exercise, rendering moot the arguments in favour of a new approach to security, which has been set out in the preceding parts.

Syed Mansoob Murshed explains how economics is significant to understanding the causes of human insecurity as well as devising policy responses to deliver not only freedom from want, but also freedom from fear. Economic policy for development requires an absence of violent threats. The capacity of conflict to derail growth has also brought economics further into security studies in recent years. Murshed's chapter shows how this gap between security and economic discourses is narrowing, and that human security can help in aligning them more closely.

Gerd Oberleitner shows that the operationalisation of human security through law is often implicit rather than explicit, with recourse to related, but not always synonymous ideas, and through an emphasis on components such as human rights, dignity and empowerment. Where law is more explicitly supportive of human security is in its deconstruction of state sovereignty. It underpins a search to re-imagine a world in which individuals are the focus of efforts at protection, development, assistance and wellbeing, and supports their role as drivers of a cosmopolitan security.

Taylor Owen builds on his threshold definition outlined in chapter 1 to show how human security can be measured and mapped. His method for going from a broad conceptual framework through to threat identification, data collection, mapping and analysis shows how a seemingly boundless concept can be empirically assessed at a local level.

The chapter on research methods and conflict analysis by Mary Martin and Denisa Kostovicova opens up an under-explored front in human security studies, which attempts to find ways of investigating insecurity consistent with the shift away from nation states as the dominant reference point for analysis, focusing on people and groups. Methods are also important in emphasising the multiple interlinked nature of insecurity at this level, and achieving the empowerment, rather than the pathologisation of individuals. Here again, as with law, this is work in progress for human security scholars and practitioners.

It is entirely appropriate that this volume should end with contributions which look forward, and pose new questions of the discourse. The story of human security is, like any other, woven together through historical events, the intervention of individual efforts and institutional innovation. The chapters in this book attempt to capture the flavour of an extraordinary two decades, rich in intellectual endeavour and policy challenge, and hold out a promise that there is still more to learn about human security, what it is and how we deliver it.

References

Bellamy, Alex J. and Matt McDonald (2002) 'The utility of human security: which humans? What security? A reply to Thomas & Tow', *Security Dialogue* 33(3): 373–377.

Chandler, David (2008) 'Human security: the dog that didn't bark', *Security Dialogue* 39(4): 427–438.

Cox, Robert (1981) 'Social forces, states, and world orders: beyond international relations theory', *Millennium: Journal of International Studies* 10(2): 204–254.

Debiel, Tobias and Sascha Werthes (eds) (2006) *Human Security on Foreign Policy Agendas: Changes, Concepts and Cases* (Duisburg: Eigenverlag).

Duffield, Mark and Nicholas Waddell (2006) 'Securing humans in a dangerous world', *International Politics* 43: 1–23.

Grayson, Kyle (2008) 'Human security as power/knowledge: the biopolitics of a definitional debate', *Cambridge Review of International Affairs* 21(3): 383–401.

Kaldor, Mary (2011) 'A decade of the "War on Terror" and the responsibility to protect: the global debate about military intervention', *Social Science Research Council Essay Forum: Ten Years after September 11*. Available online: http://essays.ssrc.org/10yearsafter911/a-decade-of-the-%E2%80%9Cwar-on-terror%E2%80%9D-and-the-%E2%80%9Cresponsibility-to-protect%E2%80%9D-the-global-debate-about-military-intervention-2/ (accessed 10 January 2013).

Newman, Edward (2001) 'Human security and constructivism', *International Studies Perspectives* 2: 239–251.

Paris, Roland (2001) 'Human security: paradigm shift or hot air?', *International Security* 26(2): 87–102f.

Teitel, Ruti (2011) *Humanity's Law* (New York: Oxford University Press).

UNSG (2010) *General Assembly*, 'Human security. Report of the Secretary-General', 8 March 2010, A/64/701, p. 1.

PART I

Concepts of human security

1

BIRTH OF A DISCOURSE

Amartya Sen

Editors' note: This chapter includes excerpts of articles, presentations and an interview recorded between 2000 and 2008. Taken together they trace the emergence of human security as a concept in public communication and discourse, and its growing acceptance as a policy tool and paradigm of security.

It begins with Sen's ideas on how rights and security are linked to development in which education occupies a central place and includes comments following publication of the Commission for Human Security's report 'Human Security Now'.

Theoretical underpinnings[1]

Human security is not a new idea, but it has had a remarkable revival. It is invoked astonishingly often in recent discussions. As a new 'buzz' expression, it is in some danger of being summoned too often and too loosely, as is the fate of many such newly favoured terms, like 'social exclusion' which (in Else Oyen's unflattering portrayal) has been 'picked up' by people who 'are now running all over the place arranging seminars and conferences to find a researchable content in an umbrella concept for which there is limited theoretical underpinning.'[2]

Since that restless fate would be worth escaping, we might as well get straight to the 'theoretical underpinning' of the concept of human security.

In initiating the discussion on 'human security' in Japan and elsewhere, Prime Minister Obuchi Keizo described it as the key idea in 'comprehensively seizing all of the menaces that threaten the survival, daily life, and dignity of human beings and to strengthening the efforts to confront these threats.'[3] He saw this focus as reflecting the 'belief that human beings should be able to lead lives of creativity, without having their survival threatened or their dignity impaired.' Thus seen, human security can be understood as the protection and preservation of human 'survival' and 'daily life' (presumably against premature death, avoidable ill-health, the massive handicap of illiteracy etc.) and also the avoidance of various indignities that can shower injury, insult and contempt on our lives (related, for example, to destitution, penury, incarceration, exclusion, or – again – illiteracy or innumeracy).

Pursuing this line of analysis, it can be argued that the 'underpinning' of the concept of human security must include at least the following distinct elements:

1   a clear focus on individual human lives (this would contrast, for example, with the aggre-
    gately technocratic notion of 'national security' – the favoured interpretation of 'security' in
    the military context)
2   an appreciation of the role of society and of social arrangements in making human lives
    more secure in a constructive way (avoiding a socially detached view of individual human
    predicament and redemption, emphasized in some – but not all – religious contexts)
3   a reasoned concentration on the downside risks of human lives, rather than on the overall
    expansion of effective freedom in general (contrasting with the broader objective of the
    promotion of 'human development')
4   a chosen focus, again, on the 'downside' in emphasizing the more elementary human rights
    (rather than the entire range of human rights).

Human security is important but not exclusively so. The idea of human security identifies one
class of objectives among many others which too may have legitimate claim on our attention.
There is a good deal of complementarity with other foundational notions that have found their
place in global social dialogue: for example, 'human development' (brilliantly championed by
the late Mahbub ul Haq), or 'human rights' (revived in a new conceptual setting that draws
indirectly on the classic championing of the 'rights of man' by Tom Paine, or the 'vindication
of the rights of women' by Mary Wollstonecraft more than two hundred years ago).

The term human security does relate to 'human development' and 'human rights,' and even to
'national security' and to 'individual dedication,' but it is not the same as any of them. It is as
important to be clear about the distinctions involved as it is to see the interdependence and
interlinkages of human security with other important concerns pursued in contemporary global
discussion.

The majority of people are concerned with the security of their own lives and of the lives
of other people like them. This general concern has to be directly addressed, and any understanding of security in more remote terms (such as military security or so-called national
security) can be integrated with it to the extent that this makes human life more secure.

A broader understanding of human security is extremely important precisely because it
affects human lives. The idea of what is called 'national security' is somewhat more remote from
human lives, in the sense that it is often defined in terms of military preparedness and other
features of national policy. Defence can, of course, be important for the lives of people within a
nation, and to the extent that this is so, that consideration can be fully covered within the idea
of human security itself.

The idea behind development as freedom and, by extension, the relationship between
human security and freedom is that freedom is the principal end of development as well as
its primary means. The basic understanding here is that freedoms of different kinds (such as
political liberty, social facilities, economic opportunity, etc.) are each individually important,
but they also complement each other. Each kind of freedom serves as an end in itself and also
as a means to the other freedoms.

The idea of freedom is very broad and deals with freedom from insecurity as well as freedom
to enhance general living conditions and people's ability to do what they value doing and have
reason to pursue. Human security is, thus, connected with one part of human freedom, and
it is that part with which the report of the Commission on Human Security is specifically
connected (CHS 2003). In the context of human security we are especially concerned with
'downside risks'.

Indeed, even when overall progress is very positive, the threat of insecurity may still be
present and serious. For example, even though South Korea had two decades of extremely rapid

economic growth with much equity in the distribution of economic gains, when the East Asian economic crisis came in 1997, it turned out that a proportion of the population had remained extremely vulnerable, despite their having participated in the general aggregative progress in the economy as a whole. The trouble is that when things go up and up, people often move up together, but when the downfall comes, they tend to fall extremely divided.

Thus, the old idea of growth with equity does not provide an adequate guarantee of security when there are inescapable downturns. By focusing specifically on human security, supporters of the concept such as the Commission on Human Security extended the more 'upbeat' pursuit of development, by paying specific attention to dangers of downturns and unantici-pated declines. The idea of human security, thus, fits in well with the broader notion of human freedom, but focuses particularly on the question of vulnerability.

However, all this also built on a notion of human development pioneered by Mahbub ul Haq, who contrasted a GNP-centred understanding of the process of development with a concept of human development which drew on the need to focus on enhancing human freedom and capability in general.

The first decade: human capabilities and vulnerabilities[4]

Mahbub ul Haq could not really have had any complaint that the world took a long time to appreciate the remarkable merits of his brainchild, the *Human Development Report*, as a vehicle of communication, nor to accept the pre-eminence of the idea of 'human development' as an illuminating concept that serves to integrate a variety of concerns about the lives of people and their well-being and freedom. Mahbub's creation received remarkable notice and acclaim in less than a decade. When I recall the telephone calls that came repeatedly from Mahbub in summer 1989, I have a sense of proximity in time that is in some tension with the way the idea of human development and the commanding presence of the *Human Development Report*s have become solid parts of the contemporary landscape of social thinking in the international community. What must have appeared to many in the United Nations system as a rather eccentric plan of an independent-minded Pakistani economist has become a central component of critical attention in the world of communication and public discourse.

Pluralist conception

Why did the *Human Development Report* receive so much attention with such speed in a world where new ideas often take decades, sometimes centuries, to receive the recognition they deserve? Why is the idea of human development such a success in the contemporary world? This is not a question about the profundity of Mahbub ul Haq's creative ideas, which is, of course, absolutely clear and not in any way in dispute. At a very basic level of social under-standing, the *Human Development Report*s had – and have had – much to offer to the discerning public. But the value of new knowledge and understanding is not always   indeed, not often quickly – recognized, and the swift success of the approach of human development has to be judged in that context. For one thing, the *Human Development Report*s have experienced a much more rapid appreciation and general acceptance than any of us (involved in helping Mahbub) had expected. We must ask, why has this happened?

This raises a more elementary question. What does the human development accounting, in fact, do? What is its special feature, its identifying characteristic? This is, at one level, an easy question to answer. Rather than concentrating only on some solitary and traditional measure of economic progress (such as the gross national product per head), 'human development' accounting involves a systematic examination of a wealth of information about how human beings in each society live (including their state of education and health care, among other variables). It brings an inescapably pluralist conception of progress to the exercise of development evaluation. Human lives are battered and diminished in all kinds of different ways, and the first task, seen in this perspective, is to acknowledge that deprivations of very different kinds have to be accommodated within a general overarching framework. The framework must be cogent and coherent, but must not try to overlook the pluralities that are crucially involved (in the diverse nature of deprivations) in a misguided search for some one measure of success and failure, some single clue to all the other disparate concerns. The issue of plurality and openness to multiple concerns is quite central to the success of the exercise.

It is important to distinguish the general idea of a pluralist conception from the more specific proposals on which human development accounting has tended to rely, involving the integration of particular criteria such as life expectancy, literacy and indicators of economic affluence. Mahbub's innovation was, in an important sense, a philosophical departure.

Utilitarianism and single-mindedness

To understand what is involved in Mahbub's innovative departure in the world of traditional development evaluation, it is useful to consider an analogy, involving the hold of utilitarian philosophy over rivals as the dominant form of ethical reasoning, especially in the Anglo-American intellectual tradition. The utilitarian calculus involves a quintessentially singleminded approach to ethical accounting. The one variable on which it concentrates, namely utility, has some plausibility if, for some obligatory reason, we have to choose only one variable – exactly one and no other – for our ultimate focus. Indeed, it cannot be denied that avoiding pain and suffering must be a good thing, or that happiness is an important reward of living. No ethical accounting can really ignore this elementary understanding. But even those who concede this readily may easily identify many other features of human life and social events that are also significant. Why not take note of them, in addition to utilities (in the form of happiness, desire fulfilment or whatever metric the utilitarians advocate)?

There is, in fact, the rub. In the intellectual victory that utilitarian accounting achieved in mainstream moral philosophy, quite a bit of the work was done, often implicitly, by the trumped-up belief that it would be somehow analytically mistaken, or at least ferociously clumsy, to have many different things as being simultaneously valuable.

The victory of utilitarianism not only suppressed the claims of rival theories, it also corrupted and deformed the intellectual basis of the claims underlying these theories by making their advocates opt for a subsidiary route to influence via their effects on utilities.

The utilitarian emperor offered small native kingdoms, under strict viceregal supervision, to advocates of freedom, rights, equal treatment and many other putative claimants to ethical authority.

The rejuvenation of ethics and political philosophy in recent decades, led particularly by John Rawls (certainly the greatest moral philosopher of this century), involved, among many other things, a rebellion against the formulaic and reductionist programme established by the dominance of utilitarianism. Rawls brought many more concerns and a wealth of ideas into the analysis, beginning with his radical insistence on the 'fairness' of processes, and proceeding to the priority of liberty, on the one hand, to resistance to arbitrary privileges, on the other, and finally to an irreducible concern with both efficiency and equity in the distribution of basic resources, as the final part of this complex claim. On the way to a different system, Rawls had to brush off, in effect, the utilitarian special pleading in favour of a monoconcentrationist playing field. Once Rawls opened the door out of the reductionist prison, many rival theories have flourished in contemporary moral and political philosophy, without having to pay homage to the centrality of utility as the one great thing that overshadows all other individual claimants to that pre-eminence.

Development and monoconcentration

What has happened in the field of development evaluation can be better understood in terms of this analogy. Riding initially as a kind of younger brother of utility, the concept of real income had managed to get a very special status in applied work in development economics. The basis of real income evaluation in pure economic theory has almost always been utility (as any serious student of real income evaluation would know). But, in the rugged world of measurement, the concentration shifted from the foundational concern with utilities (often very difficult to reach with measurable data) to a practical involvement with income statistics and evaluations based on this.

It was thus not unnatural that the world of economic evaluation was dominated by concepts such as the Gross National Product (GNP), or perhaps some distribution-adjusted version of aggregate income. If interest was expressed by some sceptic on the possibility that something else could also matter, the prompt response tended to take the form of pointing out how messy the world of plural evaluation must be. The devotees of what is called 'an operational metric' declared victory over all pluralist rivals by insisting that some monoconcentration alternative would be needed. In this playing field, it was not so easy to defeat the dominance of utility and, in practice, of the GNP or other related income-based measures.

Plural concerns in development

It is this faith in monoconcentration that had begun to receive much sceptical attention by the time the *Human Development Report*s were launched. Mahbub took on the leadership of large armies of discontent that were gunning, somewhat sporadically, at the single-minded concentration on the GNP. There were activists arguing for the recognition of 'basic needs'. There were international interventionists lamenting 'the state of the world's children'. There were relief organizations concerned with hunger and epidemics. There were writers focusing on 'disparities' between the actual lives of the rich and the poor. There were humanists voicing the need for social justice in the quality of life. There were advocates of measures of physical quality of life. There were even some philosophically oriented critics wondering about the bigger insights into social ethics provided in the far reaching works of Aristotle, Adam Smith, Karl Marx, and even of John Stuart Mill. It is to the credit of Mahbub's integrating vision that he saw the possibility of harnessing these different discontents into the development of a capacious alternative outlook which would be, at once, both practical and broad, and which could accommodate – however roughly – these different concerns. If the idea of human development had a rapid acceptance, this was made possible by the skill – ultimately Mahbub ul Haq's skill – in coordinating discontent and in weaving them together into a rival and flexible format.

Central to this exercise is enlightened public discussion. Supporting the intellectual basis of well-informed public discussion is one of the main glories of the human development enterprise. The idea of human development won because the world was ready for it. Mahbub gave it what it had been demanding in diverse ways for some decades preceding that. Mahbub's impatience with theory, which (I have to confess) I sometimes found quite frustrating, was a great help in this. He wanted to build on agreement (what Cass Sunstein, the Chicago legal theorist, calls 'an incompletely theorized agreement'). Such agreements may emerge pragmatically, on quite diverse grounds, after a general recognition that many things are important. Mahbub transformed the inquiry into an intensely practical one. He told the world: 'Here we have a broad framework; if you want something to be included in this list, which may deserve a table in the *Human Development Report* (and with incredible luck, may even be considered for inclusion in one of the indices like the Human Development Index, or the Human Poverty Index), tell us *what*, and explain *why* it must figure in this accounting. We *will* listen.' Liberated from the monoconcentrationist shackles, the world of evaluation was open to pragmatic reasoning, invoking different kinds of argument within a broad and permissive framework of reasoned social evaluation.

What lessons, then, do we draw from this reading of the basis of the speedy success of the idea of human development and the soundness enterprise of *Human Development Reports*? I shall briefly point to a few.

First, it would be a great mistake to concentrate too much on the Human Development Index, or on any other such aggregative index. (As, perhaps, the principal author of Human Development Index, I say this with some hesitation, but no less firmly for that reason; it is not a case of infanticide anyway, since the infant has now grown up and can take the rough with the smooth.) These are useful indicators in rough and ready work, but the real merit of the human development approach lies in the plural attention it brings to bear on developmental evaluation, not in the aggregative measures it presents as an aid to digestion of diverse statistics.

Second, the very lack of a general theory allows an openness that is important for this kind of work. Mahbub himself experimented with some departures, such as the inclusion of an index of political freedom. That particular departure was not, I think, a success, but it is important to be open to suggestions, and not to stifle further broadening on any *a priori* ground.

For example, the advocates of human rights have suggested that the enterprise of human development should take them more seriously.

This is a justified demand. Perhaps this will be a good extension, or maybe it will not prove to be so; but it has to be carefully examined and tried out. The same can be said of a variety of ideas that have been proposed for further extending the domain of coverage of human development accounting. The adventure of the decade to come must not be turned into any repeated chanting of mantras, no matter how exalted the mantras may be.

Third, as and when we face new problems, the focus of attention has to be sensitive to the new reality. In the heyday of initiation of human development reporting a decade ago, some countries were doing astonishingly well despite low income, through concentration on particular types of social interventions, such as educational expansion, basic health care and epidemiology, and so on. The *Human Development Reports* duly recorded their success. However, it emerged that some of these economies also had basic problems which had not been adequately addressed, in the form of lack of transparency in business transactions which made them rather fragile.

Perhaps more importantly, there was also the extreme vulnerability in a downturn of those whose economic viability depended entirely on a buoyant market – without any social safety net. While people were united on the way up, they were often very divided as they fell. The importance of this phenomenon, that of human security in general, requires a reorientation of factual concentration and of proper reflection in development accounting.

Fourth, there is the issue of democracy – its acceptance, and its working and practice. This also needs to be more fully taken up in the broad picture of human development. There is, related to this, the issue of accountability and the sharing of social responsibility.

I can, of course, go on (Mahbub often grumbled that I usually did). But, before stopping,

I would just like to note that what we have to build on is not any received and frozen theory from Mahbub ul Haq, but his open-minded approach, his scepticism, and his perpetual willingness to listen to new suggestions. The human development approach assumed the leadership of a pluralist world of multiple concerns, and its intellectual departure has a coordinating function that is quite central to the entire enterprise.

Unfreedoms in the world come in many different forms. Many disparate failings and shortfalls need attention. And, furthermore, the world itself is changing even as we look at it and report on it. It is this diverse and dynamic reality on which the enterprise of human development has to concentrate. It is a stream, not a stagnant pool.

From human development to human security[5]

Why is human security important? Prime Minister Obuchi Keizo of Japan made an insightful observation in a keynote address to the first 'Intellectual Dialogue on Building Asia's Tomorrow' in 1998. Obuchi said: 'It is my deepest belief that human beings should be able to lead lives [without] their survival threatened or their dignity impaired'. It is in this context that he invoked the idea of 'human security' describing it as the key phrase to comprehensively seize all of the menaces that threaten the survival, daily life and dignity of human beings and to strengthen the efforts to confront these threats. I would argue that Obuchi's diagnosis and its far-reaching implications provide a good beginning. Specific aspects of this approach derive from Obuchi's concentration on 'survival, daily life and dignity of human beings'. Anxiety about these diverse concerns have troubled humanity throughout its history, and it may well be wondered what is the reason for thinking that this is a particularly apt moment to confront these issues. We must, therefore, answer two different questions: 'Why these issues?' and 'Why now?'

Security of survival: health, peace and tolerance

The particular reasons for trying to make a concerted effort precisely at this time are both negative and positive. The negative reasons include the fact that each of these problems has received some setback in recent years from new developing dangers and adversities, and these call for specific engagement right now. For example, the prospects of survival have been made less favourable in many parts of the world through problems in public health, including the emergence and spread of particular diseases, such as AIDS, new types of malaria, drug resistant TB and so on. Similarly, in the growing persistence and sometimes accentuation of civil wars and associated killings, there is a continuing and worsening threat to survival of civilians caught in the battle of armies and in sectarian genocide or persecution.

On the positive side, however, there is an enhanced possibility in the contemporary world to put our efforts and understanding together to achieve a better coordinated resistance to the forces that make human survival so insecure. We live in a world that is not only full of dangers and threats. But also one where the nature of the adversities are better understood, the scientific advances are more firm, and economic and social assets that can counter these menaces are more extensive. Not only do we have more problems to face, we also have more opportunities to deal with them.

Daily life and the quality of living

Similar points can be made about the other two concerns captured in Obuchi's visionary phrase. For example, despite the fact that the economic progress of East and South-East Asia had been rapid for many decades, and notwithstanding the fact that daily lives in the region did improve in many different ways, the danger of a downturn affecting the lives of hundreds of millions also remained firmly present (even if concealed in the euphoria associated with high and seemingly invulnerable growth rates) When the Asian economic crisis came, the potential danger – already present – became manifest and fierce, and it ravaged the daily lives of people who had earlier felt falsely secure. On the other side, however, this experience itself has taught the world many different things which can now be put to use in a concerted promotion of security of daily life. Along with the old slogan of 'growth with equity' we also needed a new commitment towards 'downturn with security' given the fact that the occasional downturns are common – possibly inescapable – in market economies. In achieving security under these circumstances, and in trying to guarantee secure daily living in general, we need social and economic provisions (for example, for so-called economic safety nets and the guaranteeing of basic education and health care), but also political participation, especially by the weak and the vulnerable, since their voice is vitally important. This requires the establishment and efficient working of democracies with regular elections and the tolerance of opposition, but also the cultivation of a culture of open public discussion. Democratic participation can directly enhance security through supporting human dignity, but it also helps in securing the continuation of daily lives (despite downturns) and even the security of survival (through the prevention of famines).

The need to confront insecurity of daily lives may arise in other ways as well. When the victims remain severely deprived not because of an economic downturn, but because of persistent neglect of social and economic institutions (such as schools, hospitals etc.) on a chronic basis, what is needed is a better understanding of the failure of governance involved in these long-term lacunae, and a greater determination to make provisions for these vital necessities. Given the globalized nature of politics and public discussion in the contemporary world, this is a matter for international initiative as well as for national and local leadership.

Information and ecology

The role of information technology and communicational revolution must be considered in this context, since they are among the major sources of strength in improving the quality of living across the world.

And yet access to the new technology is severely limited not only through economic penury, but also through educational inadequacy. It is important that efforts – global as well as local – be made to improve and increase the access to these new opportunities that can radically transform human lives.

When we shift our attention from the positive merits of information technology to the negative dangers of ecological neglect, we find a different type of adversity. The preservation of the global environment demands particular attention from those who tend to make the biggest contribution to the fouling of our air, water, temperature balance and other implicit sources of security and happy living – now and in the future. The richer countries are particularly in a position to make a difference in this respect (given the size of their consumption), but even developing economies have a significant influence – increasing more so as the process of economic development proceeds.

Since alternations of designs and technical forms can be expensive once they become widely used, the need to think about the future is a contemporary necessity. Also, the local environment can be very important for the quality of life in a particular region, and it can certainly be severely damaged through territorial neglect. The need to pay attention to ecological and environmental concerns applies to all countries – rich and poor. Since ecological irresponsibility is, at least partly, a matter of ignorance (smugness can be generated by unawareness and not just by a perverse unconcern) there is a potentially constructive linkage between informational access and ecological responsibility.

Dignity, equity and solidarity

Human dignity – to turn to Obuchi's third concern – also faces some new threats today, in addition to old ones that tended to make the lives of so many people so honourless and low over the millennia. For example, just as women's movements have grown and made substantial progress in helping to achieve gender equity in many different societies (attempting to counter long-standing inequities), there has also been resistance to these changes from supporters of traditional inequalities (indeed often from beneficiaries of privileges that inequality gives to some at the expense of many others). There has often been, as a result, stagnation in the reversal of inequities and in some cases, even regression. The most extreme cases of regression may even involve the closing of schools for girls, the raping of helpless and victimized women, and other atrocities. Indignities of other kinds – related to class, caste, ethnicity, social opportunity, economic resources – also call for clearer recognition. Development is not only about the growth of GNP per head but also about the expansion of human freedom and dignity. Indignities survive both through omission and commission and they have to be addressed in a comprehensive way. There are, happily, many different signs that can be seen right now which point to a growing commitment across the world to confront inequality and insecurity with greater global solidarity. The commitment may find 'official' expression in the work of international bodies, or 'anti-official' expression in street protests that criticize the role of one international body or another. But there can be little doubt that in the contemporary world, there is more engagement than ever before to look broadly and jointly at international and global problems. Even protests against globalization themselves now take a globalized form with protesters gathering in Seattle or Washington DC from many different corners of the world. There are differences in outlook and analyses, but we must not miss the commendable unanimity of concern that moves people today beyond their local preoccupations into world issues (*sans frontières*), even though they may not – and do not – individually agree on how these issues should be addressed. The subject of globalization itself arouses passion – both in defence and in opposition. It is not, of course, a new phenomenon. Over thousands of years, globalization has shaped the progress of the world, through trade, travel, migration and dissemination of knowledge. The opposite of globalization is persistent separatism and relentless autarky. There is a terrifying image of seclusion that has been invoked, as a warning, in many old Sanskrit texts in India (I know of four such texts, beginning from about two and a half thousand years ago). This is the story of what is called 'kupamanduka' (in Sanskrit) or the well-frog – a frog that lives its entire life within a well and is suspicious of everything outside it. The scientific, cultural and economic history of the world would have been very limited had we lived like well-frogs. This remains an important issue, since there are plenty of well-frogs around and also attorneys of well-frogs. The benefits of global contact and interaction apply to economic relations, among other relations. The economic predicament of the poor across the world cannot be reversed by withholding from them the great advantages of contemporary technology (including of course information technology), the well-established efficiency of international trade and exchange and the social as well as economic merits of living in open rather than closed societies. There is the twin danger of 'unfair inclusion' on one side and 'exclusion' on the other. It is right to be worried about sweated labour and the unusual power of multinational corporations. But just a withdrawal of global investment would not remove the economic adversities that the poor face in being excluded from economic and social opportunities that the more privileged enjoy.

International arrangements and global architecture

The distribution of global benefits from economic and technological intercourse depends, among other things, on a variety of international arrangements, including trade agreements, patent laws, global health initiatives, international educational provisions, facilities for technological dissemination, ecological and environmental restraints, fair treatment of accumulated debts (often incurred by irresponsible military rulers of the past), and the management of conflicts, local wars and global spending on armament.

Institutionalizing human security[6]

The Commission on Human Security was launched in June 2001 to prepare a report on human security issues and promote public understanding of the concept of human security and its use as an operational tool for policy formulation and implementation. The CHS was co-chaired by former UN High Commissioner for Refugees Sadako Ogata and myself. The CHS's final report was presented to UN Secretary-General Kofi Annan on May 1, 2003. It set out the context for a new attitude to security, and called for human security as 'a response to new opportunities for development, for dealing with conflict, for blunting the many threats to human security.' It referred to the new menaces of the twenty-first century, to the threats of development reversed, to the threats of violence inflicted. With so many dangers transmitted so rapidly in today's interlinked world, policies and institutions must respond in new ways to protect individuals and communities and to empower them to thrive. That response cannot be effective if it comes fragmented – from those dealing with rights, those with security, those with humanitarian concerns and those with development. With human security the objective, there must be a stronger and more integrated response from communities and states around the globe.

Today's global flows of goods, services, finance, people and images spotlight the many interlinkages in the security of all people. We share a planet, a biosphere, a technological arsenal, a social fabric. The security of one person, one community, one nation rests on the decisions of many others – sometimes fortuitously, sometimes precariously. Political liberalization in recent decades has shifted alliances and begun movements towards democracy. These processes opened opportunities for people but also new fault lines. And political and economic instabilities, some involving bitter conflicts with heavy casualties and dislocations, have broken out within states. Thus people throughout the world, in developing and developed countries alike, live under varied conditions of insecurity.

Security centred on people

The international community urgently needs a new paradigm of security. Why? Because the security debate has changed dramatically since the inception of state security advocated in the seventeenth century. According to that traditional idea, the state would monopolize the rights and means to protect its citizens. State power and state security would be established and expanded to sustain order and peace. But in the twenty-first century, both the challenges to security and its protectors have become more complex. The state remains the fundamental purveyor of security. Yet it often fails to fulfil its security obligations – and at times has even become a source of threat to its own people. That is why attention must now shift from the security of the state to the security of the people – to human security.

Human security complements state security, enhances human rights and strengthens human development. It seeks to protect people against a broad range of threats to individuals and communities and, further, to empower them to act on their own behalf. And it seeks to forge a global alliance to strengthen the institutional policies that link individuals and the state – and the state with a global world. Human security thus brings together the human elements of security, of rights, of development.

Notes

1 Taken from *Basic Education and Human Security,* Presentation at workshop organized by the Commission on Human Security, UNICEF, the Pratichi (India) Trust and Harvard University, Kolkata, 2–4 January 2002; and interview with SGI Quarterly *Human Security Now,* July 2003: http://www.sgiquarterly.org/feature2003Jly-1.html (accessed 5 June 2013).
2 Else Oyen, 'The Contradictory Concepts of Social Exclusion and Social Inclusion,' in C. Gore and J.B. Figueirdo (eds) *Social Exclusion and Anti-Poverty Policy* (Geneva; International Institute of Labour Studies, 1997), p. 63.
3 Obuchi Keizo, 'Opening Remarks,' in *The Asian Crisis and Human Security* (Tokyo: Japan Center for International Exchange, 1999), pp. 18–19.
4 From 'A Decade of Human Development', published in *Journal of Human Development* (2000) 1,1: 17–23.
5 Based on a presentation entitled *Why Human Security* to the International Symposium on Human Security in Tokyo in July 2008: http://www.scribd.com/doc/25342431/Why-Human-Security-Amartya-Sen (accessed 5 June 2013).
6 This section is drawn from the work of the Commission on Human Security (CHS), the report by SGI Quarterly (see above) and the Commission's final report.

2

HUMAN SECURITY: FROM DEFINITIONS TO INVESTIGATING A DISCOURSE

Des Gasper

Concepts of human security have been debated and disputed at length for the past twenty years or more. Many lists of definitions exist and various comparative analyses of definitions.[1] These reveal not a single concept but a family with many variants, all of which might be relevant for some audiences and contexts. One core theme is the contrast between human security as the security of persons and state security as the security of a state apparatus or territory – a contrast which highlights the aspect: security for or of whom? We should consider besides that several other aspects, including: security of which goods; security to what extent; security against which threats; security using which means; and secured by whom.

Related to this exploration of notions of 'security', we need to consider meanings of 'human', thereby taking further the examination of 'security of which goods' and of the proposed justifications for securitization claims. In contrast to their relatively refined discussion of 'security', many writers give superficial attention to 'human', using merely a contrast between the individual and the state. Yet for Mahbub ul Haq (1999), perhaps the main founder of current human security discourse, 'for [the] human security approach human beings are the core elements', not simply individuals (Lama 2010: 4). Definitional of human beings is that they are not self-enclosed or isolated individuals but complex beings whose individuality arises through relationships. Apart from referring to human beings, 'human' can also connote both the human species and whatever in human persons and collectivities is considered to be most important, most worthy, most 'human' and at risk, and therefore as requiring to be secured.

One needs thus to explore a complex semantic field. No concept exists in isolation from other concepts, from the social contexts of users and their intended (and unintended) audiences, from purposes within those contexts, and from the accumulated patterns of intended and unintended use. In other words, a complex general concept needs to be explored as part of a discourse, or indeed as part of a family of discourses since there are multiple different contexts of use in which it is taken up and related to or confronted with diverse other concepts, users and concerns, and because even within a given context many differences are possible in emphasis.

Within a given context of use, a discourse is partly constituted by the patterns of implication, complementarity, opposition and tension within a system of concepts. In human security literature one finds claims about the human security concept's links to, even constitution by, a family of other concepts that include vulnerability, securitability and participation. We examine this later. Similarly, the concept as championed in the 1994 *Human Development Report* and the subsequent 2003 UN report *Human Security Now* established a contrast not only with the concept of state security but also, for example, with that of human development.[2] It both adds and narrows as compared to the UNDP (United Nations Development Programme) notion of human development: adding a concern with stability and narrowing to a focus on the securing of basic goods, in which goods include but are not limited to bodily security. It thus served as a prioritizing concept – an updated version of basic needs thinking – within the unlimited scope of human development (Gasper 2005). Consideration of human priorities connects to reflection about the interpretation of 'human'. It carries no implication of a reduction of 'basic need' to only material need; and in practice human security discourse encourages attention to subjectivity and to themes of culture, community and solidarity.[3]

Understanding a concept and discourse requires attention to actual use, distinguishing according to different users and contexts. Observation of human security thinking shows an unexpected degree of spread, including into gender studies, environmental studies, migration research and the thinking of various organizations, despite opposition often from conventional security studies theorists and some national governments, and lukewarm or hostile responses from many users of the sister discourses of human development and human rights. The spread has come because a human security perspective seems to help in generating unexpected insights, through person-centred attention to the intersections of multiple dimensions of life (see, e.g., Jolly and Basu Ray 2006, 2007; Leichenko and O'Brien 2008; O'Brien et al. 2010; Picciotto et al. 2007; Truong and Gasper 2011). The concept has also been cited by some groups in support of conclusions and interventions that many others find objectionable. One needs to ask: what variant of the discourse was used? And are the conclusions necessary inferences from the discourse, or dependent on other factors, and would they have been drawn anyway even in the absence of human security language?

The set of issues now identified could justify a book-length treatment. This chapter will take only some preliminary steps, including reflecting on 'security', 'human' and some partner concepts within the semantic field of 'human security'. The following two sections will discuss the 'human security' concept and some of the characteristic contents and style of the related discourse or discourses, in general terms and with illustrations. The chapter concludes with a brief discussion of some of the possible roles and audiences. The aim is to provide themes with which to understand the debates around definitions better than by only listing and categorizing competing specifications.[4]

The concept and the range of definitions

Dimensions

Discussions since the 1980s have brought forward a concept of 'human security', in contrast to the conventional twentieth-century usages of 'security' to mean national security or state security. The 1994 UNDP Human Development Report (HDR) was a key step in this movement, and the process is ongoing. It involves changes in attention, with reference to, first, the object of security: whose security? In human security discourse the object becomes: all human persons, and sometimes, by implication, the human species.

Second, the concept broadens attention when considering security of what? Human security thinking involves more than only humanizing an existing state security discourse by a concern for just the physical security of persons. The 1994 HDR returned to language used in the 1940s during planning for a new world order after the cataclysmic crises of 1930–45: 'freedom from fear' and 'freedom from want'.[5] Subsequently often added to these banners, including in the 1948 Universal Declaration on Human Rights, is an even more general partner: freedom to live in dignity. The 1994 HDR specified in more detail seven typical major areas of security – economic security, food security, health security, environmental security, personal physical security, security of community life, and political security – but these form a partial checklist rather than a definition of human security.[6] The matching definitions concern areas of reasoned human priority; Hampson et al. (2002) spoke of 'core human values' and the UN's advisory Commission on Human Security of 'the vital core' (CHS 2003). More exact specification of what are considered areas for priority attention and protection will be place- and time-specific.

Next, consequent on this rethinking of the object of security and of security in what respects, human security thought involves a much revised identification of, third, what are security threats and, fourth, what are priority security measures, instruments and activities. Security services cannot, unfortunately, be taken for granted as promoters of security and felt safety. Many people in many times and places have felt less secure thanks to the practices of official security forces.[7] Relevant responses to threats include protection of persons in various ways, but also empowerment of persons and strengthening of their 'securitability': 'the ability to avoid insecure situations and to retain a [psychological] sense of security when such situations do occur, as well as the ability to reestablish one's security and sense of security when these have been compromised' (UNDP 2003: 5).[8] Similarly, the Global Environmental Change and Human Security research program has defined human security as the capacity of individuals and communities to respond to threats to their social, human and environmental rights.[9]

Fifth, the agenda set by the human security concept involves attention to how much has, as a matter of public priority, to be secured; it thus involves more detailed discussion of what is 'basic'. King and Murray influentially defined human insecurity as deficiency in any key area: 'deprivation of any basic capabilities' (2001/2: 594), with reference to specified threshold levels. Their measure of human security is the expected number of years of life without falling below critical thresholds in any key domain of well-being (p. 592). It gives a conceptual structure which can be applied in a situation-specific way that reflects local conditions, ideas, values and political processes; the exact meanings of 'critical' and 'key' will be settled through local specification. But for international comparisons King and Murray proposed – as 'domains of well-being which have been important enough for human beings to fight over or to put their lives or property at great risk [for]' (p. 593) – at least: income, health, education, political freedom, democracy (p. 598). Theirs is an objective measure of conditions in key domains, not a measure of people's judgements or feelings; but its findings can help to inform people's subjective measures.[10]

Sixth, and now taking us (like the issue of 'security by what means?') beyond the human security concept and into the discourse, comes the issue of: secured (provided/protected/assisted) by whom? Implied by the rethinking of the object, components, threats to and instruments for security is also a rethinking and extension – compared to discussions of state security – of the range of relevant actors. We can think of a 'constellation of providers' (UNDP 2003).

So the HDR 1994 concept brought shifts in attention concerning security of whom, security with respect to which types of good, to what extent, and against what threats. The attention to a broad range of types of good, and (correspondingly) of types of threat, is objected to by some authors, epitomised by MacFarlane and Khong (2006). They presume ownership of the term 'security' by conventional 'security studies' which concentrates on deliberate violent threats to physical well-being, and simply assert that threats from environmental change, for example, are not part of the 'human security' field. In effect they defend old-fashioned (state) security studies' established access to privileged funding. They aim to reserve the term 'protection' only for protection of life against violent attack, as if protection of health, and protection of anything else against anything else, is not 'protection'.

Security claims are claims of existential threat, meant to justify priority response. Attempts to limit such prioritisation to one type of threat, such as threats of physical damage from physical violence, and/or one type of referent/target such as the state, are arbitrary. The root and usages of the term 'security' validate no such restriction; indeed according to Rothschild (1995), for centuries the term applied only to individuals. Further, remarked Owen, while authors like MacFarlane and Khong do

> make the shift to the individual in theory [they] ignore it in practice by subjectively limiting what does and does not count as a viable threat … [It] is communicable disease, which kills 18,000,000 people a year, not [military-style] violence, which kills several hundred thousand, that is the [greater] real threat to individuals.
>
> *(Owen 2005: 38)*

Similarly, a combination of climatic movements and planned neglect by colonial regimes left tens of millions dead in the late nineteenth century (Davis 2001); a parallel danger is emerging in the twenty-first century (see, e.g., UNDP 2007; Hansen 2009). MacFarlane and Khong's approach reduces to a 'security studies approach', not a 'protection-based' one.

Purpose

We need to consider for any concept its purpose, or purposes. For the human security concept different users have had different primary purposes, leading to different interpretations. Some relate, as we have seen, to re-focusing discussions of 'whose security?' Two other widespread purposes have involved adding to UNDP's original concept of 'human development' (UNDP 1990): firstly, by a concern with the stability of attainment of the goods in human development; secondly, by including the good of physical security of persons.

The first of these latter two concerns leads to definitions of human security (HS) in terms of the stability of the achievement or access to goods; in particular when coping with 'downside risks', a phrase of Amartya Sen (e.g. Sen 2003). But 'human security', if defined only in terms of that phrase, would concern also the degree of stability with which the super-rich hold their super-riches. His partner phrase 'downturn with security' does not equate security to the stability of everything but rather to the removal of unacceptable risks for weaker groups. Reflecting that security is a prioritizing term, and that Sen here discusses 'human' security, 'downturn with security' refers to securing the fulfilment of basic needs or the ability to fulfil them.

The second of the two concerns – broadening human development thinking by adding 'freedom from fear' to 'freedom from want' – involves the addition of personal physical security, in the sense of freedom from violence, to the list of component objectives within 'human development' (HD). Physical security was from the mid 1990s incorporated into the definition of HD (see, e.g., UNDP 1996: 56). This contributed to a confusion that some people felt in distinguishing between HS and HD.

Some users sought then to limit the meaning of HS to physical security of individuals, as sometimes espoused by the Canadian government and the Human Security Network of like-minded countries. As we saw, some authors even want to limit the concept to the physical security of persons against violent threats or, even narrower, the physical security of persons (especially non-military) during violent conflicts and against organized intentional violence.

31

The purpose of this third answer is to broaden the scope of the security studies concept of security, beyond state and military security, and/or to change the focus, to a concern with the physical security of persons. It reacts against both the UNDP notion of HS, felt to be too broad, and the traditional notion of national security, felt to be increasingly misleading or insufficient in an era when most violent conflict is intra-national and overwhelmingly most of the casualties are civilian.

The answer of the UN Commission on Human Security (CHS 2003) gave more careful attention to the notion of 'human'. It considers what are the requirements of being 'human', in addition to sheer existence. These requirements go beyond freedoms from fear and from want. We may add freedom from humiliation and indignity, perhaps also freedom from despair (Robinson 2003), and, for example, the freedom of future generations to inherit a healthy natural environment. The Commission defined human security as: 'to protect the vital core of all human lives in ways that enhance human freedoms and human fulfilment' (CHS 2003: 4). Human security so conceived concerns the securing of humanity, humankind, which must be ensured before its fuller flourishing is possible. Seen from the side of military security studies and policy, this interpretation represents an extension beyond freedom from fear. Seen from the side of human development thinking, it represents an extension beyond freedom from want, but also a narrowing to concentrate on the highest priorities within each category.

A range of definitions

So, broadly speaking, the concept of 'human security' redirects security discussions in one or typically more of the following ways: from the national/state level to human beings as potential victims; beyond physical violence as the only relevant threat/vector; and beyond physical harm as the only relevant damage. The redirection can be done to different extents, so we encounter diverse 'human security' definitions, as shown in the shaded cells in Table 2.1. The columns concern how wide a range of values is included in the concept. Columns I and II have broad ranges, from Human Development discourse; column V a much narrower range, from conventional security studies; and in between them columns III and IV have an intermediate scope. Picciotto et al. (2007), for example, in column IV cover the aspects of 'freedom from fear' and 'freedom from want', using as a weighting criterion the impact on human survival chances; thus they look at far more than direct deaths from armed violence. These various interpretations of human security can be compared with a base case which is not a concept of human security: a 'pure' capability approach definition of human development as expansion of valued capabilities. The rows bring in whether or not human security is defined or partly defined in terms of stability of achievement of valued or priority goods.

We noted that minimalist definitions fail to respond to the fact that much more premature death and human wounding arise from poverty than from physical violence. The UNDP concept of human security involves a focus on a broader range of aspects of people's security than only physical safety and survival. To keep the concept sufficiently sharp and distinctive but not arbitrarily restricted, the Commission on Human Security formulated the range of aspects to include, in effect, basic needs plus stability, with their specification to occur via reasoned prioritization within the relevant political communities. Given the relevance both of priority needs and stable fulfilment and the advantages of a conception that is neither extremely broad nor very narrow, and neither rigidly universal nor purely local, this formulation constitutes a relatively attractive concept of human security and is now quite widely used (see also Owen 2004).

Hubert (2004) added that, given the development-human security nexus it might though make little difference in the end whether the concept adopted of human security is broad or

Table 2.1 Some alternative definitions of human security (see shaded cells)

	I *Valued capabilities expansion* *(e.g. UNDP 1990)*	II *HD in terms of UNDP's longer list of goods* *(e.g. UNDP 1996)*	III *Basic needs only* *(in terms of types and level)*	IV *Life-preservation against structural violence as well as physical violence*	V *Personal physical security only* *(& civil rights)*
Attention to *level* of some valued variables (snapshot or average over time)	Sen's Capability Approach in minimal form	Human Development Reports' focus (includes physical security)	King & Murray (2001/2)		Canadian & Norwegian government definitions of HS[11]
HS in terms of *stability*		Stability in degree of achievement of a long list of goods	'Downturn with stability [for ordinary and poor people]'		
HS in terms of both *level* and *stability*		Haq (1999) & UNDP's maximal definition of HS. Govt. of Japan definition[12] [GECHS]	Commission for Human Security definition (CHS 2003)	Picciotto et al. (2007); Thakur (2004): avoidance of 'critical life-threatening dangers'	

Source: adapted from Gasper (2010).

narrow, if we realise that human security will not be well achieved without development, nor vice versa. The *Human Security Report* series from Canada (e.g. Mack 2005) considers only armed conflict and organized violence as well as their effects, which in fact ramify into almost everything else. So too may their causes. So while violence appears convenient as a focus for data collection and subsequent model-building, the associated research and policy should extend much further. When we look at the fuller human security discourse, we may then find that the disputation around the concept comes to matter less.

The discourse – concepts in context

Behind the foreground features – a focus on security of individual persons, and a wider scope of the areas considered under 'security' and as contributory factors and possible countermeasures to insecurity – are generative themes. One is a humanist normative concern for the well-being of fellow humans: the proposition that what matters is the content of individuals' lives, including a reasonable degree of stability. It is part of what O'Brien (2010) calls the equity dimension in human security thinking. It is largely shared with the sibling discourses of human rights, human needs, and human development (Gasper 2007b). Much human security thinking contains in particular an insistence on fulfilling basic rights, derived from basic needs, for all.

Second, the focus on threats to basic human values leads to a humanist methodology of attention to mundane realities of life – including exploration of the things that people value and of the diverse but interconnected threats (actual and/or felt) to these values.

Third, then, is a richer picture of being human. Humans are not only individual choosers, but are 'encumbered subjects' who have each a body, gender, emotions, life-cycle, identity and social bonds, including memberships of (multiple) groups and of a common species. Normative priorities for being human include a sense of meaning and identification, and recognition of and respect for others. The vision of humans is as both vulnerable and capable.

Fourth, as part of what O'Brien calls the discourse's connectivity aspects, is a character-istic stress on the interconnection of threats. Elsewhere I have called this feature 'joined-up thinking', and used the term 'joined-up feeling' for the motivating focus on human vulner-ability and on the human rights that flow for all from basic human needs (Gasper 2007b).[13] Besides a generalized concern with interconnections, human security thinking involves, fifthly, attention to the specific intersections of diverse forces in persons' and groups' lives.

A holistic methodology of attention to the lives of real persons

We find in human security thinking an anthropological concern for understanding how individual persons live. People seek bodily, material, psychological and existential security. Risks and insecurities are case- and person-specific, and partly subjective, so human security analysis requires listening to people's 'voices', their fears and perceptions, including the 'voices of the poor' but also of the rich (Narayan et al. 2000; Burgess et al. 2007). The methodology lends itself particularly to surfacing concealed issues of women's security (see, e.g., Hamber et al. 2006). Such insights are of long standing in the humanities, in anthropology, and in the basic needs school in peace and conflict studies (Burton, 1990; Mitchell, 2001), but are frequently forgotten in other fields. Human security thinking has given them a new home. The broader ('UNDP/Japanese') perspective on human security (e.g. CHS 2003; JICA 2006) seems to have advantages here over a narrower ('Canadian' or MacFarlane-Khong) one, in conducing to fuller use of this holistic perspective.

Vulnerability and capability

Humans come in units – as persons. We enumerate humans in terms of integers, whole numbers, not fractions and decimals. And the lives of human persons likewise involve specific threshold levels: one does not live a quarter-fold when one receives only a quarter of one's dietary requirements; one dies, relatively quickly. Being human has various specific requirements. From these needs come socially specific notions of a series of normative thresholds across a range of aspects: the minimum levels required for normative acceptability. 'Human security' issues in the area of health, for example, do not include all health issues, only those up to a normatively set minimum threshold, which is to some degree historically and societally relative. (See, e.g., Owen 2005; Gasper 1996, 2005.) Lack of the threshold concept leads writers like MacFarlane and Khong (2006) to attempt to decree that whole issue areas like health and environment are outside the remit of 'security', in the mistaken belief that this is necessary in order to allow meaningful priority to anything within human security discussions.

Attention to the lives of real persons underlines that vulnerability, not only capability, is a defining feature of humanity. Invulnerability could even make one inhuman, without sympathy. We are more likely to be open to the vulnerabilities of others if we share such vulnerabilities ourselves (Rifkin 2009). A human security approach seeks to manage and moderate vulnerability, and complements the stress on capability found in human development thinking.

At the same time, human security thinking emphasizes capability too, as seen in the concept of 'securitability' and the stress on empowerment as well as protection. To only be protected can be disempowering. It reduces both felt security and objective security because capabilities wither or are never developed and confidence stays low. For the Global Environmental Change and Human Security programme, human security is defined as where 'individuals and communities have the options necessary to end, mitigate or [sufficiently] adapt to threats to their human, social and environmental rights; have the capacity and freedom to exercise these options; and actively participate in pursuing these options' (http://www.gdrc.org/sustdev/husec/Definitions.pdf, accessed 6 June).

Many authors explore the posited necessary conditions for human security outcomes; Kraft, for example, holds that 'Human security by its very nature implies [i.e., requires] a more open kind of society – citizens must be able to voice out to the government their security concerns so that these can be given proper attention in the context of the societal good' (2007: 5). Some authors define human security as including those posited conditions and capabilities. The Commission for Africa's definition included a similar stress on participation, apparently proposed as an inseparable necessary condition: people-centered

> human security becomes an all encompassing condition in which individual citizens live in freedom, peace and safety and participate fully in the process of governance. They enjoy the protection of fundamental rights, have access to resources and the basic necessities of life, including health and education, and inhabit an environment that is not injurious to their health and wellbeing.
>
> *(Commission for Africa 2005: 392)*

Interconnection and nexuses

Analyses of requirements can support claims for policy priority to these requirements if and where the analyses identify a major causal connection, from fulfilment or non-fulfilment of a highlighted factor, through to a qualitatively different set of other things that have clear normative importance. The term 'nexus' captures when such a connection concerns a major link, active at least in some situations, between 'spheres' that are conventionally conceived and administered separately – such as between environment and war. Human security thinking looks at such links: for example between economy, conflicts, distribution, environment and health.

The foundational ideas of the United Nations Charter and its system for collective security highlight freedom from want and indignity in addition to freedom from fear, because of not only the first two's independent importance but also an expectation that freedom from fear will never be attained or stable if freedom from want and indignity are absent. 'Collective security now [is] seen to require the defense of human rights norms and principles' (Quataert 2009: 40). State security is expected to be fragile and expensive – as well as morally empty – if not based on the security of persons. Similar principles can apply within nations: 'unless industry is to be paralysed by recurrent revolts on the part of outraged human nature, it must satisfy criteria which are not purely economic', wrote R. H. Tawney (1926: 284).

Nor are the links only limited bilateral ones. Economic trends can greatly increase the chances of conflict, via mechanisms that have lain outside of the field of attention of businessmen, conventional academic economists and economic policymakers (Collier et al. 2003; Picciotto 2005; Picciotto et al. 2007); the resulting conflicts may then have implications for distribution and health, as well as for economy, crime and further conflict; the distributional changes may impact on the environment; and so on. The 'joined-up thinking' required is feasible to a worthwhile extent, even as we move beyond traditional problem-framings, because we can select the particular interconnections to be stressed according to their importance case-by-case.

Thresholds and tipping points

Human security analysis sometimes centres on a particular, dangerous type of connection, at a particular locus: a flashpoint or tipping point, a stress level beyond which threshold the negative effects dramatically escalate, even leading to collapse or, in the case of persons, death or highly increased chances of death, whether through disease or violence or self-harm, as in the suicides of those broken by harassment or debt. Beneath certain levels of malnutrition small children can suffer irreversible mental deficits. Some types of stress or abuse may produce irreversible emotional harm. Arguably, whole societies too can go over a stress tipping point as in Rwanda in 1994, when bad harvests, economic crisis and extreme externally imposed expenditure cuts were loaded on top of a history of tense inter-group relations and recent armed conflict (Prunier 1997; Uvin 1999).[14] Contemporary literature on climate change is replete with warnings about tipping points in our climate systems, beyond which deleterious change will accelerate markedly and become effectively irreversible (e.g. Campbell et al. 2007; Dyer 2010). Climate tipping points are impersonal; but in human systems tipping points often have a strong normative component, linked to ideas about rightful entitlements and past agreements. When normative thresholds or bottom-lines are felt to have been violated, results can be the same as for breaching of an impersonal causal threshold: eruption or collapse. We should distinguish though between the concept of thresholds, which are points beyond which there is dangerous change, the concept of tipping point, where such change notably accelerates, and the more extreme notion of 'point of no return'. These were conflated in the synthesis report on UNESCO's multi-year human security research programme (2008), perhaps contributing to the resistance that programme findings met from the organization's funders and controllers.

Intersectionality

The theme of interconnection is often formulated at a general level in terms of relations between vast sets of factors, the subject matters of different intellectual disciplines (e.g. Brauch 2009). Applied though through the holistic methodology of attention to the lives of real persons, the theme leads us to the intersections of these factors and to the patterns of impact on diverse individuals, groups and localities – the 'local difficulties' that arise as various stress-factors and vulnerabilities interact.

Leichenko and O'Brien's book *Double Exposure* shows how economic globalization and global environmental change, for example, have additive effects and interactive effects, which trigger further rounds of reactions and consequences. The groups who are most threatened by global environmental changes are often the groups who are most threatened by global economic changes. They are more exposed, for example because of where they live. They are also more vulnerable – more damaged by the same exposure and more damaged by their actual exposure – because they have fewer resources to use in protection. And often they are the least resilient because again they have fewer economic, social, cultural and political resources. Leichenko and O'Brien reveal how we miss these vital combinations and interactions when we work in abstracted disciplinary discourses, whether of social science or of environmental science. We notice them when we instead undertake a holistic analysis of human security that starts by looking at particular people and locations and at the intersecting forces in their lives.[15]

Roles – how can concepts help?

A discourse is inevitably incomplete and underdefined, and thus has multiple potentials. How it becomes actualized, and how it further evolves, depends on its users and contexts of use. In clarifying a concept and discourse we must ask for what tasks they are being used or useful: their roles and with respect to whom; for example, in defining a research programme or in indicating and motivating a policy orientation.[16] In particular, much usage of the human security concept, and the very choice of the label 'human security', can be understood as 'boundary work' (Star and Griesemer 1989) that aims to span between conventionally separated intellectual and political spheres.

Adding to understanding

A human security approach can often generate fresh case-specific understandings and insights, through the holistic methodology of looking at specific people's lives and vulnerabilities with an eye for interconnections and intersections. When Hurricane Katrina struck New Orleans the victims were especially poorer Afro-Americans, poorer people in general since they lived on worse land, and people over sixty. This last group suffered more than 60 per cent of the 1800 deaths. Leichenko and O'Brien (2008) recount how economic change had made the city more vulnerable. Its old industries had declined. Strong lobbies had ensured that many new channels had been cut from the Mississippi river to the sea, which allowed new paths for storm surges from the ocean to reach the city. Privatization and corporatization of municipal and social services meant that coordination was weak and could not cope with emergency demands. Patients in private health care facilities were immediately evacuated after the hurricane, while those in public care were left waiting for five days. Similarly, in the reconstruction phase, for-profit facilities were rebuilt much faster than not-for-profit schools and public housing. By using a human security approach, looking at the particular situation and multiple vulnerabilities of particular groups/types of people, and thus as in storytelling and scenarios becoming aware of and 'emphasizing the dynamic interactions between processes, responses, and outcomes, [Leichenko & O'Brien], elicit new insights and research questions beyond those associated with separate framings and discourses' (2008: 33).

Likewise, reviews of the many national and regional Human Development Reports that have taken a human security approach find that they have produced novel insights and suggestions (Jolly and Basu Ray 2006, 2007; Gomez et al. 2013). The studies look into sources of objective and felt insecurity, without *a priori* restrictions according to disciplinary habits or an intellectual template fixed by a donor organization. Amongst such HDRs, several deserve wide attention, including the reports for Chile (1998), Afghanistan (2004), Costa Rica (2005), the Arab Region (UNDP 2009), Benin (2011), Africa (2012), and not least the earlier Latvia report (UNDP 2003).

Reorienting policy analysis

Extending these insights, O'Brien (2006, 2010) suggests that the debate on global environmental change has been stuck in an inappropriate problem-frame. First, it is dominated by natural science questions and not sufficiently framed in terms of human significance. It is likely then to get stuck in science wars which are inherently endless, since more knowledge often produces more uncertainty not less; whereas we should be thinking about which humans face known dangers and which ones also face the nastier sides of the inevitable uncertainties (Gasper 2012). Second, like conventional security studies, the debate continues to operate with a now partly obsolete national framing of issues, so that policy debate is dominated by again inherently endless disputes over the respective rights and blame that should accrue to nations. She proposes that more fruitful and more pertinent may be to frame discussion in terms of human security: to recognize that many poor persons face high and rising insecurity, and to consider how to respond to this.

Wider attention to contributory factors increases our awareness of vulnerability and fragility, but also of opportunities and resilience. In policy design, a human security perspective raises issues of system re-design to reduce chances of crises, not only palliative responses when crises have hit (Lodgaard 2004), and has served 'as a focal point around which an integrated approach to global governance is emerging' (Betts and Eagleton-Pierce 2005: 7). It increases thinking about prioritization within sectors (as in the MDGs programme) and, if we use broad concepts of human security, also between sectors. Seeking system re-design and intersectoral rebalancing are campaigns for change over the longer term, but may bring eventual large-scale benefits.

Providing an intellectual bridge

Besides human security thinking's promotion of analytical integration, it offers 'boundary work' services in other respects. Consideration of the sources of and threats to human security helps to bring together the different organizational worlds of humanitarian relief, socio-economic development, human rights, conflict resolution and national security (Uvin 2004). Human security discourse also synthesizes ideas from the predecessor 'human discourses' of human needs, human rights and human development (Gasper 2007b). It better grounds human rights and human development work in attention to the nature of being and well-being; focuses them on high priorities; highlights interdependence more than does human rights language, and increases attention to dangers, vulnerability and fragility; and it connects to human subjectivity, which increases its explanatory force and motivating potential.

Promoting solidarity?

Human security analysis recognizes emotions, identifies surprising conjunctures and can give a sense of real lives and persons. The language of 'security' itself touches emotions, which is both a source of strength and of danger (Gasper and Truong 2010). While the 'human security' label aims to reorient security discourse, it carries risks of being taken over by the psychic insecurities and fears of the rich and the military instincts of those with large arsenals and the habit of using them. However, those fears and habits exist already and have long had ways of expressing themselves without requiring 'human security' language in order to do so. The difference made by such a language may be in the opposite direction, gradually helping to promote interpersonal and global sensitivity and solidarity. Human security thinking looks at diverse, situation-specific, interacting threats and how they affect the lives of ordinary people, especially the most vulnerable. It promotes the ability to imagine how others live and feel, and the perception of an intensively interconnected shared world in which humanity forms a 'community of fate'. It thus favours the changes that are needed for global sustainability in respect of how people perceive shared vulnerabilities, shared interests and shared humanity (The Earth Charter; Gasper 2009). A narrow concept of human security does not block such changes, but is less conducive than the broader versions.

Human security thinking has to operate at various levels, just as we see in thinking about say 'well-being' or 'equity'. Research and policy programmes in particular geographical, historical and organizational contexts will each make their own particular definitions. Some of those will be narrow, others broad. At the same time, a broad conceptual perspective is necessary since it can inspire and guide the diverse particular endeavours.

Notes

1 For example, an online depository of definitions at http://www.gdrc.org/sustdev/husec/Definitions. pdf, and the collation and comparative analysis in Tadjbakhsh and Chenoy (2007).
2 One can draw various semiotic squares for a concept of 'human security'. Such a square shows a contrast along the top row, and contradictions along the diagonals. Different contrasts can be drawn: of 'human' with 'state' or 'national'; of 'security' with 'rights' or 'development' or 'growth', etc.
3 Berman (2007), for example, reduces the basic needs aspect mistakenly to basic material needs alone and also obscures the global-wide agenda in 'human-' language, such as seen in human rights law.
4 The chapter builds from and extends arguments presented in Gasper (2005, 2010).
5 In the phrase 'freedom from want', 'want' has its older sense of non-fulfilment of a basic need. In this spirit Eleanor Roosevelt declared, for example: 'The freedom of man, I contend, is the freedom to eat.'
6 The seven securities may overlap. The checklist can also be treated as about potential areas of threats.
7 See, e.g., the Bangladesh Human Security Report and the Latvia Human Development Report on human security (UNDP 2002, 2003).
8 Leaning and Arie's (2000) definition of human security likewise concerns psychological security, and presents this an important resource in dealing with the objective insecurity in a person or group's environment. See also Leaning et al. (2004).
9 See http://www.gdrc.org/sustdev/husec/Definitions.pdf. The UN Trust Fund for Human Security (2007) emphasises too that: 'human security goes beyond protective mechanisms to include the need to empower individuals, identifying their security threats and articulating the means by which they will implement the changes needed' (Alkire 2010).
10 For further work along such lines, see Werthes et al. (2011). For another detailed recent objective index of human security, that groups under three main headings – economic, environmental and social fabric – see the work of David Hastings, for UNESCAP and others, at http://www.humansecurityindex.org/. It involves objective measures of objective aspects. We can also have objective measures of subjective feelings/perceptions, and subjective measures of subjective feelings (like fear) or of objective conditions. (See Gasper 2007a for a more refined vocabulary than only objective/subjective.)

11 The Canadian government and its Human Security Network partners have, however, often added 'freedom from want' content to a 'freedom from fear' centred interpretation. Sometimes the government even declared 'For Canada, human security means freedom from pervasive threats to people's rights, safety or lives.' (http://www.pdh.org/suirdev/hsec/Definitions.pdf).

12 Defined in terms of all the forces 'to threaten human lives, livelihoods and dignity'. This formulation is found in many official Japanese statements, e.g. Govt. of Japan (1999) and JICA (2006).

13 Work for the 2009 European Report on Development, on development-conflict linkages and on diverse causes and consequences of state fragility, adopted the 'joined-up thinking' label.

14 The international Joint Evaluation of Emergency Assistance to Rwanda concluded that:

[Explanatory factor 6 behind the 1994 Rwanda genocide of almost a million people in a few months was:] The economic slump starting in the late 1980s and the effects of the actions subsequently taken by the government in consultation with the international donor community, i.e. the structural adjustment programmes of 1990 and 1992. The economic deterioration, largely due to a sharp decline of world market prices for coffee – Rwanda's prime export earner – as well as to unfavourable weather and economic policies such as increased protectionism, price controls and other regulations, affected the whole society. In US dollar terms, GDP per capita fell by some 40 per cent over the four years 1989–1993 ... The international community, including the World Bank and the International Monetary Fund, overlooked [the] potentially explosive social and political consequences when designing and imposing economic conditions for support to Rwanda's economic recovery. (Eriksson et al. 1996: 15)

15 See also O'Brien and Leichenko (2007), O'Brien et al. (2010).

16 Werthes and Debiel (2006) and Gasper (2010) are two more extended attempts to delineate roles in this field.

References

Alkire, S. (2010) 'Human Development: Definitions, Critiques, and Related Concepts', Human Development Research Paper 2010/01, New York: United Nations Development Programme.

Berman, J. (2007) 'The "vital core"', in G. Shani, M. Sato, M. Pasha (eds), *Protecting Human Security in a Post 9/11 World*. Basingstoke: Palgrave Macmillan.

Betts, A., Eagleton-Pierce, M. (2005) Editorial Introduction: Human Security. *St. Antony's International Review*, 1(2), 5–10.

Brauch, H. G. (2009) Human Security Concepts in Policy and Science. In: Brauch, H. G; Oswald Spring, Ú.; Grin, J.; Mesjasz, C.; Kameri-Mbote, P.; Behera, N. C.; Chourou, B.; Krummenacher, H. (Eds.): *Facing Global Environmental Change: Environmental, Human, Energy, Food, Health and Water Security Concepts* (Berlin – Heidelberg – New York: Springer-Verlag): 965–990.

Burgess, J. P., with A. Amicelle, E. Bartels, R. Bellanova, A. Cerami, E. Eggum, G. Hoogensen, S. Kittelsen, K. Knibbe, M. de Koning, K. Koser, K. Krause and O. Salemink (2007) *Promoting Human Security: Ethical, Normative and Educational Frameworks in Western Europe*, Paris: UNESCO.

Burton, J. W. (1990) *Conflict: Basic Human Needs*. New York: St. Martin's Press.

Campbell, K. M.; J. Gulledge; J. R. McNeill; J. Podesta; P. Ogden; L. Fuerth; R. J. Woolsey; A. T. J. Lennon; J. Smith; R. Weitz, and D. Mix (2007) *The Age of Consequences: The Foreign Policy and National Security Implications of Global Climate Change*. Washington, DC: Center for Strategic and International Studies/Center for a New American Security.

CHS /Commission on Human Security (2003) *Human Security Now*. New York: UN Secretary-General's Commission on Human Security, available http://www.humansecurity-chs.org/finalreport/ (accessed 6 June 2013).

Collier, P., V. L Elliott, H. Hegre, A. Hoeffler, M. Reynal-Querol, N. Sambanis (2003) 'Breaking the conflict trap: civil war and development policy.' World Bank Policy Research Report. Washington, DC: World Bank.

Commission for Africa (2005) *Our Common Interest: Report of the Commission for Africa*. London: Commission for Africa.

Davis, M. (2001) *Late Victorian Holocausts – El Niño Famines and the Making of the Third World*. London: Verso.

Dyer, G. (2010) *Climate Wars*. Oxford: Oneworld Publications.

Eriksson, J., with contributions by Howard Adelman, John Borton, Hanne Christensen, Krishna Kumar,

Astri Suhrke, David Tardif–Douglin, Stein Villumstad, Lennart Wohlgemuth (1996) *The International Response to Conflict and Genocide: Lessons from the Rwanda Experience – Synthesis Report*. Copenhagen: Steering Committee of the Joint Evaluation of Emergency Assistance to Rwanda.

Gasper, D. (1996) 'Needs and basic needs – a clarification of foundational concepts for development ethics and policy'. Pp. 71–101 in *Questioning Development*, G. Köhler, C. Gore, U. P. Reich, T. Ziesemer (eds), Marburg: Metropolis.

Gasper, D. (2005) 'Securing humanity – situating "human security" as concept and discourse', *Journal of Human Development*, 6(2): 221–245.

Gasper, D. (2007a) 'Human well-being: concepts and conceptualizations', in M. McGillivray (ed.), *Human Well-Being: Concept and Measurement*. Basingstoke: Palgrave Macmillan, pp. 23–64.

Gasper, D. (2007b) 'Human rights, human needs, human development, human security – relationships between four international "human" discourses'. *Forum for Development Studies*, 2007/1: 9–43.

Gasper, D. (2009) 'Global ethics and human security', in G. Honor Fagan and Ronaldo Munck (eds), Vol. 1 of *Globalization and Security: An Encyclopedia*. Westport, CT: Greenwood, pp. 155–171.

Gasper, D. (2010) 'The idea of human security', in K. O'Brien, A. L. St. Clair, B. Kristoffersen (eds), *Climate Change, Ethics and Human Security*. Cambridge: Cambridge University Press, pp. 23–46.

Gasper, D. (2012) Climate Change – The Need For A Human Rights Agenda Within A Framework Of Shared Human Security. *Social Research: An International Quarterly of the Social Sciences*, 79(4), 983–1014.

Gasper, D., and T-D. Truong (2010) 'Development Ethics through the Lenses of Caring, Gender and Human Security', pp. 58–95 in *Capabilities, Power and Institutions: Towards a More Critical Development Ethics*, S. Esquith and F. Gifford (eds), University Park, PA: Pennsylvania State University Press.

Gomez, O., D. Gasper, Y. Mine (2013) *Good Practices in Addressing Human Security through National Human Development Reports*. Report to Human Development Report Office, UNDP, New York.

Hamber, B., Hillyard, P., Maguire, A., McWilliams, M., Robinson, G., Russell, D. and Ward, M. (2006) 'Discourses in transition: re-imagining women's security', *International Relations*, 20(4): 487–502.

Hampson, F. O., Daudelin, J.; Hay, J. B.; Reid, H.; Martin, T. (2002) *Madness in the Multitude: Human Security and World Disorder*, Oxford University Press, Ottawa.

Hansen, J. (2009) *Storms of My Grandchildren*. London: Bloomsbury.

Haq, M. ul (1999) *Reflections on Human Development* (2nd edn). Delhi: Oxford University Press.

Hubert, D. (2004) 'An idea that works in practice', *Security Dialogue*, 25(3): 351–352.

JICA (2006) *Poverty Reduction and Human Security*. Tokyo: JICA. Available at: http://www.jica.go.jp/english/publications/reports/study/topical/poverty_reduction/pdf/poverty_e02.pdf.

Japan, Govt. of (1999) *Diplomatic Bluebook 1999*, Tokyo: Ministry of Foreign Affairs.

Jolly, R. and Basu Ray, D. (2006) *The Human Security Framework and National Human Development Reports*. NDHR Occasional Paper no.5. New York: UNDP.

Jolly, R. and Basu Ray, D. (2007) 'Human security – national perspectives and global agendas', *Journal of International Development*, 19(4): 457–472.

King, G. and Murray, C. (2001/2) 'Rethinking human security', *Political Science Quarterly*, 116(4): 585–610.

Kraft, H. J. (2007) 'The human security imperatives', *The New Zealand International Review*, 32(5), September/October, available at: http://www.questia.com/library/1G1-169133564/the-human-security-imperatives-herman-kraft-argues (accessed 9 September 2013)

Lama, M. (2010) *Human Security in India*. Dhaka: The University Press Ltd.

Leaning, J. and Arie, S. (2000) *Human Security: A Framework for Assessment in Conflict and Transition*. Tulane: USAID.

Leaning J., Arie, S. and Stites, E. (2004) 'Human security in crisis and transition', *Praxis: The Fletcher Journal of International Development*, 19: 5–30.

Leichenko, R. and O'Brien, K. (2008) *Double Exposure*. New York: OUP.

Lodgaard, S. (2004) Human Security – concept and operationalization. In M. Muller and B. de Gaay Fortman (eds.), *From Warfare to Welfare*, Assen: Royal van Gorcum, 16–38.

MacFarlane, N. and Khong Y.F. (2006) *Human Security and the UN – A Critical History*. Bloomington, IN: University of Indiana Press.

Mack, A. (2005) *Human Security Report*. Vancouver: Human Security Centre, University of British Columbia Press.

Mitchell, C. (ed.) (2001) 'Special issue in honor of John W. Burton', *International Journal of Peace Studies*, 6(1).

Narayan, D., with R. Patel, K. Schafft, A. Rademacher and S. Koch-Schulte (2000) *Voices of the Poor: Can Anyone Hear Us?* New York, N.Y.: Published for the World Bank, Oxford University Press

O'Brien, K. (2006) 'Are we missing the point? Global environmental change as an issue of human security', *Global Environmental Change*, 16: 1–3.

O'Brien, K. (2010) 'Shifting the discourse: climate change as an environmental issue versus climate change as a human security issue' K. O'Brien, A. L. St. Clair, B. Kristoffersen (eds.) *Climate Change, Ethics and Human Security*. Cambridge: Cambridge University Press.

O'Brien, K. and Leichenko, R. (2007) *Human Security, Vulnerability and Sustainable Adaptation*. HDRO Occasional Paper 2007/9. New York: UNDP.

O'Brien, K., St. Clair, A. L. and Kristoffersen, B. (eds) (2010) *Climate Change, Ethics and Human Security*. Cambridge: Cambridge University Press.

Owen, T. (2004) 'Human security – conflict, critique and consensus', *Security Dialogue*, 35(3): 373–387.

Owen, T. (2005) 'Conspicuously absent? Why the Secretary General used human security in all but name', *St. Anthony's International Review*, 1(2): 37–42.

Picciotto, R. (2005) Memorandum submitted to Select Committee on International Development, www.publications.parliament.uk/pa/cm200405/cmselect/cmintdev/464/5031502, UK House of Commons. Accessed 8 October 2007.

Picciotto, R., Olonisakin, F. and Clarke, M. (2007) *Global Development and Human Security*. New Brunswick, NJ: Transaction Publishers/Springer.

Prunier, G. (1997) *The Rwanda Crisis – History of a Genocide* (2nd edn). London: Hurst & Co.

Quataert, J. H. (2009) *Advocating Dignity: Human Rights Mobilizations in Global Politics*. Philadelphia, PA: University of Pennsylvania Press.

Rifkin, J. (2009) *The Empathic Civilization*. New York: Penguin.

Robinson, M. (2003) 'Protection and empowerment: connecting human rights and human security', http://www.oxan.com/about/news/2003-09-18, accessed 8 October 2007.

Rothschild, E. (1995) 'What is security?', *Daedalus*, 124(3): 53–98.

Sen, A. (2003) 'Human security now', *Soka Gakkai International Quarterly*, July 2003.

Star, S. and Griesemer, J. (1989) 'Institutional ecology, "translations" and boundary objects', *Social Studies of Science*, 19: 387–420.

Tadjbakhsh, S. and Chenoy, A., 2007. *Human Security: Concepts and Implications*. Abingdon: Routledge.

Tawney, R.H. (1926) *Religion and the Rise of Capitalism*.

Thakur, R. (2004) 'A political worldview', *Security Dialogue* 35(3), 347–8.

The Earth Charter. http://www.earthcharterinaction.org/content/ (accessed 14 December 2010).

Truong, T-D. and Gasper, D. (eds) (2011) *Transnational Migration and Human Security*. Berlin: Springer.

UNDP (1990) *Human Development Report 1990*. New York: Oxford University Press.

UNDP (1994) *Human Development Report 1994*. New York: Oxford University Press.

UNDP (1996) *Human Development Report 1996*. New York: Oxford University Press.

UNDP (2002) *Bangladesh Human Security Report 2002: In Search of Justice and Dignity*. Dhaka: UNDP.

UNDP (2003) *Latvia Human Development Report 2002–2003: Human Security*. Riga: UNDP.

UNDP (2007) *Human Development Report 2007–8: Fighting Climate Change: Human Solidarity in a Divided World*. New York: Oxford University Press.

UNDP (2009) *Arab Human Development Report 2009: Challenges to Human Security in the Arab Countries*. New York: UNDP.

UNESCO (2008) *Human Security – Approaches And Challenges*. Paris: UNESCO.

Uvin, P. (1999) 'Development aid and structural violence: the case of Rwanda', *Development*, 42(3): 49–56.

Werthes, S. and Debiel, T. (2006) 'Human security on foreign policy agendas', Introduction to T. Debiel and S. Werthes (eds), *Human Security on Foreign Policy Agendas: Changes, Concepts, Cases*. INEF Report 80/2006. Duisburg: University of Duisburg-Essen, pp. 7–20.

Werthes, S., Heaven, C. and Vollnhals, S. (2011) *Assessing Human Insecurity Worldwide*. INEF Report 102/2011. Duisburg: University of Duisburg-Essen: INEF.

3

IN DEFENSE OF THE BROAD VIEW OF HUMAN SECURITY

Shahrbanou Tadjbakhsh

Almost two decades after its mainstream outing in the 1994 UNDP *Human Development Report* (HDR), the concept of human security continues to be a point of contention between those who favor a broad definition, those who prefer a narrow version and those who reject the notion altogether. What was supposed to be a simple, noble and obvious idea soon became engulfed in a cacophony of political and academic debates centered on its definitions, their advantages and weak points, and on its theoretical and practical applicability.[1]

Can human security be considered a paradigm shift, or is it simply an advocacy agenda, a 'glue that holds together a jumbled coalition'[2] of middle powers and development agencies that want to exist on the international scene? It is oft described as a vague concept with no analytical or practical utility; so broad that it includes everything, and therefore, nothing; and a new nemesis from Northern countries, wrapped in an excuse to launch 'just wars' and interventions in weak states. This chapter sets out to defend the broad approach that defines human security as freedom from want, from fear and from indignities as universal and indivisible components. It argues that as a normative concept, human security embodies a number of added values to the fields of security studies, human development and human rights, and is not a mere attempt to 'securitize' issues in order to solicit interventions in the name of 'enlightened self interest' and 'Responsibility to Protect' (R2P).

Scopes and definitions

As Peter Stoett advances, 'Defining words is a fundamental act ... When definitions are constructed in a closed and limited fashion, alternative thinking can be stifled and orthodoxy reinforced.'[3] Defining the concept of human security serves to delineate reality, framework and priorities for the policy agenda. For the academic one, however, it can also be 'a robust pedagogical process ... pushing academic discourse farther along its path of self-discovery.'[4] Defining is after all an act, performed by an actor, and never something neutral or objective. It is therefore important to bear in mind how the definition of human security emerged from or against past theories, who is defining, for what purposes, and what consequences such an act entails for policy and academic debates.

The word 'security' itself, as Steve Smith puts it, is 'an essentially contested concept.'[5] While Buzan refers to security as ultimately a political process, 'when an issue is presented as

43

posing, an existential threat to a designated referent object', In the *Oxford English Dictionary* (OED) security is defined as 'The condition of being protected from or not exposed to danger; safety … Freedom from care, anxiety or apprehension; a feeling of safety or freedom from an absence of danger.'[7] Buzan's definition takes as point of departure mainstream international relations theories, where the notion of 'security' is primarily codified as the prerogative of states (realism), and of states and institutions (liberalism) to be free from what he calls any danger that presents 'an existential threat.' The Oxford English Dictionary definition instead highlights the subjectivity inherent in security as a 'feeling' for individuals, which has relative connotations in different contexts: for some, insecurity spurs from sudden loss of access to jobs, health care, social welfare, etc. For others, it can stem from violence, conflicts, displacement, etc. From people's perspective, security needs to be defined as a subjective experience at the micro level to gain meaning. This experience may be decidedly different from that of states' concerns for their national security.

I therefore submit that security is, in fact, in the eye of the beholder. By extension, human security as a concept engages with the security of people and communities instead of solely that of states and institutions. Once the referent object and subject of security is moved down to individuals, the notion of 'safety' then broadens to a condition beyond mere existence (survival) to life worth living, hence, well-being and dignity of human beings. Thus, human security, in its broadest form, consists of three components which simultaneously delineate its scope: *freedom from fear* (conditions that allow individuals and groups protection from direct threats to their safety and physical integrity, including various forms of direct and indirect violence, intended or not); *freedom from want* (conditions that allow for protection of basic needs, quality of life, livelihoods and enhanced human welfare) and *freedom from indignity* (condition where individuals and groups are assured of the protection of their fundamental rights, allowed to make choices and take advantage of opportunities in their everyday lives).

In dominant state-centered security theories, the protection of territorial integrity and national sovereignty reigns supreme, and threats are recognized primarily as existential ones posed by the militarization of other states. The human security approach instead proposes that classical security theories (like the security dilemma) fail to address insecurity in a comprehensive manner, and security for the state does not automatically trickle down to that of people. Human security threats include both objective, tangible elements, such as insufficient income, chronic unemployment, dismal access to adequate health care and quality education, etc., as well as subjective perceptions, such as the inability to control one's destiny, indignity, fear of crime and violent conflict, etc. They can be both direct (those that are deliberately orchestrated, such as systematic persecutions) and indirect (those that arise inadvertently or structurally, i.e. under-investment in key social and economic sectors such as education and health care). By putting individuals at the center of analysis, security threats (or in other words, insecurities) are recognized in terms of their ability to hamper people's *survival* (physical abuse, violence, persecution or death), their *livelihoods* (unemployment, food insecurity, pandemics, etc.), and their *dignity* (lack of human rights, inequality, exclusion, discrimination, etc.).

In essence, the human security approach rides on constructivist attempts at rethinking security studies, deepening the neorealist conception by moving down to the level of society and individuals or up to the level of international or global security, and broadening it to recognize a wider range of 'non-traditional' threats.[8] It recognizes that broadened threats can menace states' essence in similar ways to that of individuals: they can hamper states' *existence* (territorial integrity), their *functioning* (whether they have the resources and capacity to function and develop as a state) and their *sovereignty* (legitimacy and recognition).

Human security is not an empirical theory per se. It does not explain nor predict the behavior of states. It is rather a paradigm and a concept that allows recognition of threats and vulnerabilities to the full potential of an emancipated life, much like the concept of 'human development' coined by the likes of Amartya Sen and Paul Streeten came to be propagated through the UNDP HDRs since 1990.[9] Its absence and presence is as much an objective notion that can be measured against quantitative indicators (i.e., crime, violence, employment, freedoms etc.) as a subjective factor that requires qualitative assessment of how people 'feel' secure.

Rather than an empirical or positivist theory like realism or neo-realism, human security does not proclaim to be amoral. With its 'human' accolade, it more comfortably belongs to the field of ethics in International Relations (IR) and normative theory, dealing with what ought to be and how the world should be ordered and the value choices decision makers should make.[10] As such it can be considered as an evaluative framework. If realism is supposed to explain why states compete in a competitive anarchical system, human security could be seen as making value judgments on whether this behavior is morally acceptable, judged against the outcomes for individuals and communities as the 'content' of states. And as all normative theories, its rejection by many scholars in IR is related to the positivist bias of the field. It may be worth taking a detour and considering, as Frost writes in his argument for ethics in IR, that the underlying determining structure (system, unit) that forms the basis of positivist theories is also not independent of norms and is itself largely constituted by sets of normative ideas. The state which features as the primary unit of realists' characterization of the international system is not a 'political reality that exists independently of the ideas and norms which people adhere to. In like manner, a system of states does not exist independently of the ideas and norms of the people involved.'[11] Similarly, the structure of power is not independent of the values and norms which people have, and power is 'intimately linked to specific sets of ideas which constrain what the power may be used for'.[12]

Feminist theoreticians have already come a long way in deconstructing the nature of the state as essentially rational egoists guided by the dictates of *raison d'état*. The state and market, in theory and practice, embody masculinist assumptions and structures, and dominant conceptualizations of politics in male dominated terms ignore women's realities, their active contributions and how male and female identities are shaped through social relations.[13] Their scrutiny since the 1980s has opened up spaces for examining how international politics and core IR concepts such as war and security, are themselves gendered.[14] Yet, the engendering agenda, much like the related attempts to put people at the center of security studies and IR, has seen formidable challenges in fields dominated by the over-focus on what are assumed to be amoral, rational states, as if they were entities devoid of social relations, and acting on the basis of national interest that is supposedly not constrained by the norms and differentiated participation of its citizens.

In defense of the broad approach

The broad definition outlined above is obviously contested, not only by those who altogether reject human security as a valid paradigm shift, but also by those who prefer to limit it to particular types of existential threats to individuals. Three schools of thought have evolved from the debates around human security in academia: a first group argues that human security lacks analytical rigor, and is, consequently, at best a 'rallying cry' and at worst as unadulterated 'hot air' as a mere political agenda.[15] Among the most adamant critics are realist scholars who, in the tradition of Kenneth Waltz, warn against the securitization of what is not, essentially, an existential threat. A second school, while accepting the term, insists on limiting the definitions to 'freedom from fear' and direct threats to individuals' safety and to their physical integrity: armed conflict, gross violations of human rights that lead to fears such as imprisonment and death, public insecurity and organized crime. Proponents of the narrower version argue that a useful and workable definition should be restricted to threats falling under the realm of tangible violence,[16] measured, for instance, by the number of battle-related deaths.[17] As their argument goes, broadening the agenda of threats to include poverty or food shortage, for example, would be the equivalent of making a shopping list of all bad things that can happen, making the concept unworkable.[18] A third school, to which this author belongs, argues for a broad definition as essential for understanding contemporary crises, regardless of whether the concept is 'workable' or not, even though tools and methods have been developed to take a more comprehensive and strategic approach to interventions.

Instead of lamenting the lack of workable definitions, proponents of the broad version believe that research should be concerned with ways in which definitions insisted on by security studies circumvent political, moral and ethical concerns in order to concentrate on relations of power.[19] From this perspective, the lack of an agreed-upon definition is not a conceptual weakness but represents a refusal to succumb to the dominant political agenda. A broad definition is therefore critical to transforming the ethos and engaging in the 'political' act of raising questions that are peripheral to security studies. Even though adopting the narrow definition facilitates the researchers' work, the reality of people's lives means that threats like poverty or disease can have an equally severe impact on people's lives and dignity as does tangible violence. When agency is returned to people, it is the localized, subjective sense of the security of individuals that in the last analysis is of paramount importance.

One way to gauge the academic debate is to consider it as a rift between what Robert Cox has labeled as problem-solving and critical theory.[20] For Paris, a broad definition which includes components ranging from physical to psychological, without a hierarchy of security needs, presents difficulties for policy makers to prioritize among competing goals.[21] From his problem-solving point of view, competing demands present challenges for policy makers who need to allocate attention and resources on specific solutions to specific issues. Andrew Mack warns that a broad definition does not allow for an examination of variables and the analysis of violence and poverty for example as separate issues.[22] Most of these positivist scholars above, who tend to accept the narrow approach, dwell in fact on its practical implications in the guise of taking a shot at the analytical nature of the broad concept. Basing themselves on Buzan and Wæver's conception of security threats as informed by urgency, priority and gravity,[23] they assume that securitizing some issues changes their status in the policy hierarchy, making them worthy of special attention, resources and immediate resolution, including by military means. The so-called problem of lack of prioritization and hierarchy of threats however assumes that responsibility for 'action' rests only with political actors limited by competing demands for their attention and resources. Yet, policy-making is not only a vertical process but can be a networked, flexible and horizontal coalition of approaches corresponding to complex situations. Furthermore, to hierarchize and prioritize among human insecurities may be a futile exercise, as threats are interdependent and the eradication of any one of them in isolation is of little effect.

It is within the critical school that debates about how far human security pushes the envelope become interesting.[24] Shifting focus onto the individual as the referent object and subject of security is by itself a critical exercise in challenging state-based security theories as the only valued view. Yet, a set of critiques from within critical theory laments that by not engaging enough with deconstructing the politics of securitization, and by simply 'grafting on' the need to protect individuals to existing international practices,[25] proponents are missing the opportunity to completely deconstruct or reformat existing security approaches.[26] They are said to act in essence as collaborators of state-based international organizations and mostly Western powers in keeping the *status quo* in international relations and reinforcing dominant power relations and structures within the international system.[27] Given the dominant liberal paradigm under which international institutions currently operate, proponents of a human security approach are supposedly reinforcing hegemonic international liberalism. What's more, they have created a justification for even deeper and more invasive forms of interpenetration as a form of biopower.[28] This particular dialogue is located within two different readings of human security which mirror the narrow/broad debate: a liberal/institutional position and an emancipatory version of human security.

In his critical review of a book that this author published with Anuradha Chenoy in 2007, David Chandler claims that human security was a 'dog that did not bark.'[29] His main contention is that human security advocates do not directly engage with a contestation of power relations, leaving the approach open to co-option by political elites.[30] As a result, it is the 'universalist interest of power, understood in vague terms of biopolitical neo-liberal global governance, rather than the cosmopolitan ethics of empowerment, which drives the discursive practices of human rights regimes.'[31] From this author's perspective, however, Chandler has only a partial reading and fails to distinguish between the different visions and nuances of the different human security approaches. In essence, his critique is to the narrow approach, which has insisted on limiting insecurities to threats to survival, and favors institutional responses often of the liberal/ institutional or realist kind.

He posits three propositions as evidence that human security defenders not only fail to provide a radical alternative to interest-based and state-based security theories but are also co-opted by political elites. First, he claims that human security advocates exaggerate post-Cold War security threats and their independence as a ploy for action and attention, in other words, playing up to 'realist calculations of self-interest' instead of posing an 'ethical normative challenge.'[32] In response, this author wonders why the mere recognition of menaces to welfare, dignity and the everyday life beyond the bare life (survival) is automatically associated with the imperative that something must be done by political elites and existing institutions. Threats to human dignity need to be recognized as such, even if they may or may not solicit action by political elites. If one accepts security as a personal feeling, and not the prerogative of the state, then 'securitization' should not automatically raise alarms to send in the troops so to say. The proponents of the narrow approach who argue for a workable definition restricted to life threatening threats may be the ones automatically accepting the efficacy and interest-based morality-in-disguise of those holding on to power and ready to respond to security/existential (in Buzan sense) threats. Recognizing that factors such as poverty or disease threaten people's everyday lives and dignity as much as tangible violence is not an instrumental ploy to solicit action, but a logical if not an ethical exercise. Engaging with the politics of problem-solving and the powerlessness of power is a worthy, but separate exercise.

Second, Chandler declares that by locating new security threats in the developing world, human security advocates ride the bandwagon with realists and liberals in putting an unwelcomed focus on the so-called dangers of so-called failed states.[33] The human security framework is said to facilitate the 'problemitization of the non-Western state',[34] feeding into the fears of Western elites and further securing the rich consumerist West by containing the circulatory problems of world market inequalities and exclusion within the post-colonial South.[35] In response, it must be noted that human security threats are located in the developing world only by those who believe in a division based on countries that can 'act' (hence project their power) in other spheres, and those that are mere recipients of such benevolence/malevolence. This too may be the narrow view of the liberal human security approach which believes that problems of the developing world can and should be solved through interventions, financial assistance, human rights sanctions, democratization, marketization etc., all precepts for making liberal. The broad emancipatory approach would instead argue for the universal applicability of the subject, conceived in regards to people's daily concerns – no matter where they live geographically. Relational, objective and subjective perceptions of insecurity persist as much, if differently, among inhabitants of Parisian suburbs as they do in Darfur. Urban violence, job insecurities, health epidemics, privatization of social delivery, militarization of societies, etc. that plague industrialized societies of the North are as much human insecurities as famine, wars, poverty and genocides that characterize extreme situations of some countries, notably in the post-colonial world. That is why the broader approach may not agree with some academic attempts to propose a threshold of degree of severity of threats to human life,[36] which would then fail to recognize the insecurity felt by people in Western welfare societies. Contextual analysis instead of quantitative absolute measurements better reflects the full meaning attributed to a life worth living as what people consider vital varies across individuals, societies and cultures.[37]

Third, Chandler claims that discussions around urgency facilitate short-term policy-making and eclipse strategic foreign policy visions. This criticism also mostly addresses proponents of the narrow approach to human security, who, when insisting on a threshold that reveals urgent threats to survival that require immediate action, may forgo strategy for short-term action depending on the currency and will available for politicians to act. Yet, for advocates of the broad approach, the mere recognition of structural violence[38] and threats to dignity require, de facto, strategic planning, root cause analysis, preventive action, etc. Dignity-related threats are certainly not to be dealt with through short-term problem-solving approaches. They invite critical assessment of structural causes.

The misdiagnosis of the ability of the dog to bark is because critiques like Chandler's fail to distinguish between the liberal human security approach and the emancipatory one, as there is no one human security approach in the singular. Such partial reading may stem from bias towards the comfortable materialist/empiricist trend in Anglo-Saxon academia to relegate non-material, ideational factors, such as dignity and emancipation, to intermediary roles. The crosstalk between the various communities also seems to stem from whether human security *explains* or at least *identifies* problems or *proposes* solutions, whether it is a framework for description or prescription. The tendency to conflate these, both by proponents and critics, has arguably added to further conceptual confusion. As discussed above, human security cannot proclaim to be a theory, much less one locating itself in the domain of positivism. It is best approached as an evaluative, ethical and critical framework. The broad emancipatory approach as opposed to the more narrow liberal version could be useful for questioning the asymmetries that exist within and between systems by finding more space for contention and pluralist voices.[39] In evaluating the practice of state building, humanitarian intervention, and even the less tested domain of domestic policy, the broad, emancipatory version can be a useful tool to question the outcome of such power projections from the point of view of those affected.

The broad content

The broad approach introduces new dimensions to the traditional security paradigm, human development and human rights fields while locating itself in the area of convergence between them.

Whose security, from what threat and by what means?

The approach can be considered an ethical rupture with traditional security paradigms (by making the security of people and communities as the ultimate goal), and a methodological one (with the idea that by securing individuals, the security of the state, the region and the international system can also be better ensured). As such, the framework postulates different answers to the three questions that have preoccupied security scholars: security of whom? Security from what? And security by what means?

Security of whom? On this question, proponents of the broad and narrow definition seem to agree. From both perspectives, individuals in addition to the state are the 'referent objects' of security, and by implication, their security is the ultimate goal to which all instruments and peripheral actors are subordinated. It thus poses a moral challenge to realism, for whom the moral argument is the *raison d'état* itself.

Security from what? The answer to this question is differentiated among the narrow and broad school of thought. The narrow approach prioritizes individuals in the direct line of danger. King and Murray for example restrict threats to elements over which people are ready to fight and risk their lives.[40] Taylor Owen proposes a threshold which would take into account only the most serious threats to human lives.[41] The broad approach recognizes menaces beyond violence and concentrates on threats to the survival, well-being and dignity of individuals. It postulates three assumptions about threats: 1) that equal weight has to be given to underdevelopment and human rights violations as threats alongside traditional insecurities, 2) that threats are inter-linked and inter-connected, and 3) that these linkages mean that instead of looking for priorities, the connections have to be sought out in order to make sure than interventions in one domain do no harm in others at worse, and multiply positive externalities at best. Consequently, the answer to 'security from what' can only come from an analysis of the given context and find meaning in subjectivity. Contextual analysis would recognize the relative security of a person living under $4 a day but who is well integrated in family and community, lives in a peaceful environment and disposes of a minimum of social security. On the other hand, it would also recognize the insecurity of a person with income and wealth who lives in a conflict situation, or one whose health insurance relies on his/her job in a volatile labor market.

Security by what means? As the main author of the 1994 Human Development Report, Mahbub Ul Haq saw a simple solution: human security can be achieved through development, not through arms. When the survival, well-being and dignity of individuals become the ultimate goal, constructs such as the state, institutions of political democracy and the market are relegated to secondary status as means to achieve that goal. Hence, insecurity should not be dealt with through short-term military or policing solutions, but a long-term comprehensive strategy that combines protection, provision of welfare and emancipation. The narrow approach to human security, when insisting on prioritizing freedom from fear, may opt for policing strategies and humanitarian interventions to protect individuals in immediate danger. The broad approach advocates instead for a practice of prior engagement by the international community, long before interventions are supposed to take place in front of *fait accompli*. Yet, as the section below will discuss, in international politics, human security shifted from a descriptive and universal concept concerned with global justice and equity in the writings of Mahbub Ul Haq, to a prescriptive tool in international relations, 'for others' and 'by others' through its adoption as foreign policy. The capture by some states and regional organizations metamorphosed the concept into a toolbox that served specific external relations purposes. Ultimately, security should be tackled through comprehensive policies, both at home and abroad, and not only through military means.

Not the same as human development

The development of the human security concept is not only located within the rethinking that sought to deepen and broaden security studies. Within the field of development studies and political economy, it made an international debut in 1994 by the same team that coined the human development approach through the UNDP HDRs in 1990. For its authors, Mahbub Ul Haq, Amartya Sen and others, the distinction was simple: human development refers to the process of widening people's choices to be who they want to be and do what they want to do, in other words, the enhancement of capabilities and functionings. It can be ensured through economic growth strategies that include distribution, equity and enhanced freedoms. Human security, by contrast, refers to the condition that enables people to exercise these choices safely and freely, and be relatively confident that the opportunities they have today will not be lost tomorrow. In essence, human security introduces an element of insurance to the development process and assurance that the process and outcome of development is risk-free. Human development can be summarized as 'growth with equity', whereas human security as 'downturn with security.' As Sen argues, 'When a crisis hits, different groups can have very divergent predicaments. United we may be when we go up and up, but divided we fall when we do fall.'[42]

The human security concept draws attention not just to levels of achievement, but to securing gains made by deliberately focusing on downside risks, such as conflicts, wars, economic fluctuations, natural disasters, extreme impoverishment, environmental pollution, ill health and other menaces. It concerns itself with the 'stability' of goods provided within the human development framework as opposed to their levels or trends.[43] Sakiko Fukuda-Parr highlights the differences by stating that human development focuses on absolute levels of deprivation whereas human security emphasizes the risk of sudden changes for the worse.[44]

In contrast to the 'freedoms to' potentials in the capability approach (freedom to do what one wants to do and be what one wants to be), human security concentrates on 'freedoms from,' which as Des Gasper argues, 'concern definite absences not just potential absences.'[45] In the words of Ul Haq,

> Human security is not a concern with weapons. It is a concern with human dignity. In the last analysis, it is a child who did not die, a disease that did not spread, an ethnic tension that did not explode, a dissident who was not silenced, a human spirit that was not crushed.[46]

Human security also puts additional focus on identification, prevention and mitigation of risks that are often overlooked in development strategies. In a nutshell, the concept refers to the sustainability and stability of development gains.[47]

Human security and human rights: same content, different focus

In the policy world, human rights and human security are the two frameworks that most reinforce each other. The human security approach shares with human rights concerns for protecting freedoms, enhancing opportunities, but additionally puts focus on protection from critical and pervasive threats. As the Commission on Human Security puts it: 'human security helps identify the rights at stake in a particular situation. And human rights help answer the question: How should human security be promoted? The notion of duties and obligations complements the recognition of the ethical and political importance of human security.'[48]

The two frameworks share many similarities. Both are pursuant of human dignity, evoke morality and stress the universality of rights and their indivisibility. They also share content: human security threats in the broad definition – fear, want and indignities – find echo in the first (civil and political rights), second (economic and social rights) and third generation human rights (solidarity rights). If the 1948 Universal Declaration on Human Rights included the broad gamut of rights, Cold War politics saw a division between first and second generation rights supported by the two sides of the bipolar divide. Their reconciliation wasn't official until the Vienna Conference in 1993 which disclaimed any priority of rights by declaring that 'All human rights are universal, indivisible and interdependent and interrelated.'[49] It is therefore not a coincidence that the following year, the flip sides of these rights were coined as threats in the 1994 HDR which took as indivisible, universal and inter-related freedom from fear (first generation rights) and freedom from want (second generation rights). In subsequent years, the added definition of freedom from indignities was reminiscent of the third generation 'solidarity' rights related to self-determination, cultural rights, the right to peace, the right to a healthy environment, etc.

Yet, there are also differences between the two concepts: human rights are rooted in legal norms and international covenants and agreements. Human security raises alarms about threats and potentialities but does not have a normative/obligatory framework. As Gerd Oberleitner sums it up:

> human rights and human security share the same concerns—people matter, sovereignty must know limits, common values are stronger than particular interests, and protection must go hand in hand with fulfilling needs and empower individuals. Yet, in addressing these concerns a (predominantly) normative framework meets with a (predominantly) political world view. Human rights entitle and oblige, whereas human security allows for prioritization.[50]

At the context-specific level, human security helps identify the rights at stake in that particular context. In a simplified nutshell, and at the risk that critics from the human rights field would label this as old wine in new bottles, the human rights framework is the prerequisite and platform for human security, while human security is a condition for human rights to be fulfilled. If convergence is sought, Oberleitner hopes that 'human rights and human security together may be able to (re)discover and convincingly demonstrate that security is a human right, too, and that human dignity must be rooted in both freedom and security.'[51]

The broad human security approach hence combines the security, human development and human rights frameworks by adding elements to them. At the same time, it locates itself as a convergence of the three approaches. Visually, it can be located in the middle of the triangle shown in Figure 3.1.

The abuse of human security in international politics

Within international politics, the 1994 HDR was not the first to use the terms freedom from fear and freedom from want. They had already been introduced in the January 6, 1941 State of the Union Address of President Roosevelt, as part of his vision of a 'world founded upon four essential human freedoms.' Of Roosevelt's plea for four freedoms (freedom of speech, freedom of worship, freedom from want and freedom from fear), the last two became the basis for the foundation of the UN. With the end of the Cold War, the UNDP HDR sought to reconcile these, coining a broad human security definition that would simultaneously encompass both freedom from fear and freedom from war.

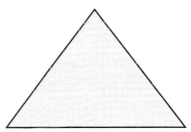

Freedom from fear
HS adds focus on people
What the threat is to: Survival
What it takes: Protection

Human development
Freedom from want
HS adds insurance against risks
What the threat is to: Livelihoods
What it takes: Provision

Human rights
Freedom from indignities
HS adds focus on threats/conditions
What the threat is to: Dignity
What it takes: Empowerment

Figure 3.1 Human security

The 1994 HDR characterized human security as 'safety from chronic threats such as hunger, disease, and repression as well as protection from sudden and harmful disruptions in the patterns of daily life – whether in homes, in jobs or in communities.'[52] It also listed seven interconnected components or seven specific values that needed to be protected: economic, food, health, environmental, personal, community and political security. By 2003, the Commission on Human Security (CHS) in its report *Human Security Now* presented a broader definition:

> To protect the vital core of all human lives in ways that enhance human freedoms and human fulfillment ... It means protecting people from critical (severe) and pervasive (widespread) threats and situations ... creating political, social, environmental, economic, military and cultural systems that together give people the building blocks of survival, livelihood and dignity.[53]

In the past two decades, the concept has seen various institutional lives in international politics, summarized in four stages:

1   The world debut in the 1994 HDR sought to seize the opportunity provided by the end of the Cold War, but was met with skepticism from the G7 during the 1995 World Summit for Social Development in Copenhagen for fear it would lead to violations of state sovereignty. It was subsequently adopted as a foreign policy tool first by Canada and then Japan.
2   Between 2001 and 2003, the concept was revived in the debate on the 'responsibility to protect,' spearheaded by the Canada supported International Commission on Intervention and State Sovereignty (ICISS), and in the discussions on the 'responsibility for development' initiated by the Japanese supported CHS.
3   From 2004 onwards, human security became a topic of reform agendas in the UN. In 2004, the EU adopted a Human Security Doctrine for Europe as a quest to promote its peacebuilding role. In the same year, the UN Secretary General's High-level Panel on Threats, Challenges and Change acknowledged the broadened nature and inter-linkages of new

security threats in its report *A More Secure World: Our Shared Responsibility*. In 2005, Kofi Annan, without making specific reference to the term human security as it had not found consensus in the General Assembly (GA), used the three components of the broad definition as the thematic principles of his Report *In Larger Freedoms*. In the same year, the GA agreed to hold a debate to further define the concept in its Summit Outcome Document.

4 In its current stage, the definitions, scope and 'operationalization' of the concept are being fine-tuned. A Human Security Unit was set up at the UN Office for the Coordination of Humanitarian Affairs (UNOCHA) tasked with disseminating the concept and managing the UN Trust Fund for Human Security, a Japanese initiative set up in 1999.[54]

The GA organized informal Thematic Debates among Member States in 2008 and 2011. The UN SG issued a Report in March 2010 (A/64/701) which was being revised for 2012, and a Special Advisor to the SG on Human Security was appointed, all with the support of the Japanese government. While the Unit at the UN has been pivotal in developing operational tools,[55] as well as trainings for UN staff in different regions, the fact that the burden of dissemination has been centralized within one isolated unit, which also manages a dwindling Trust Fund, puts in question the genuine and durable adoption of the concept within UN agencies. Consensus on the definition may be reached by Member States in the GA, but it is highly possible that given the on-going fears of humanitarian or democracy-imposing interventions, growing fissure between Western countries and emerging powers, and turf politics between the security, development and human rights institutions, may result in consensus on a limited scope of a common minimum denominator rather than a full fledged broad definition.

Institutional politics aside, the adoption of various definitions by states and organizations in the past decade has been a telling sign of the on-going separation and prioritization of rights/ securities/freedoms by political blocs, years after the end of the Cold War and the Vienna Conference which was supposed to have reconciled them. Canada's and the EU's approaches to human security have concentrated on fears and traditional threats, primarily stemming from violations to civil and political rights. If Canada sought to highlight its peacekeeping tradition, Japan, the proponent of the freedom from want approach, instead represented Asian (and emerging countries') preferences for development concerns, which Japan promoted through checkbook diplomacy through its contribution to the UN Trust Fund and its Official Development Assistance (ODA) when the strong Yen allowed for it. If human security, in the original writing of Ul Haq, was supposed to be a convergence of the North/South differences, the subsequent definitional debates and its adoption as foreign policy tool by some states only served to reinforce the divergence.

A second misuse of the concept in international politics has been its adoption, hence relegation, as foreign and aid policy tools. Japan, Canada and the EU for example, by adopting the concept in their external affairs, treated the concept as a functional tool with the premise that the security of people in 'other' states/regions would trickle out to security at home. The 2004 Barcelona Report *Human Security Doctrine for Europe* presented by the LSE study group to Javier Solana as part of his quest for implementing the Common Foreign and Security Policy (CFSP), for example, called on the EU to take on an 'enlightened self-interest' in its 'collective responsibility to intervene' in the 'black holes' outside of the Union which were generating insecurities for the citizens of the EU. Far from Ul Haq's universal and cooperative understanding of global justice, human security as foreign policy tool became a 'good' that some better-off countries could provide for 'others'. First it implied, falsely, that human insecurity was not a problem within industrialized societies, and the concept not adequate enough to be promoted as a domestic strategy. No country in the industrialized world, including Canada and Japan, adopted the concept of human security as a principle for national policy-making. The EU doctrine also failed to talk about the pockets of poverty within its own countries, urban riots, the crisis of multi-culturalism and damning immigration policies.[56] Second, the 'enlightened self interest' approach failed to take into consideration responsibility for causing many of the insecurities that lay in the periphery, ranging from imposing damning conditionality for aid, restrictive trade policies, selective interventions and forced regime changes, the imposition of democracy through military means, the sale of arms, etc. As Hampson puts it, 'Human Security as the North's development establishment understands it, is interventionist when it comes to the policies and practices of states in the South, but essentially *laissez-faire* and status quo regarding the role of the market and global governance arrangements.'[57]

A third misuse, if not abuse, of the concept was the association of its narrow approach with the R2P doctrine which reinforced the North/South divide in international relations. No matter how much the R2P original report of the ICISS sought to put breaks on trigger-happy interventions, its association with the needy's perspective meant that human security, when associated with R2P, has been seen in the South as yet another attempt by the West to impose its liberal values and political institutions on non-Western societies, an excuse for intervention in states' domestic affairs and for conditionality on ODA. The main conceptual criticism to the R2P doctrine is that it stems from a narrow definition of human security which solely emphasizes extreme violations while ignoring other important fears and threats to everyday life. Among the seven categories of the 1994 HDR, only personal, political and community insecurities were considered as threats grave enough to the core of all human lives to justify interventions, while other threats such as poverty, famine, diseases and man-made environmental disasters did not warrant action by the international community. The broad approach to human security, instead of advocating the use of military force for humanitarian interventions, would argue for an *a priori* engagement by the international community to share responsibility for prevention rather than dealing with crises that are already underway.

The criteria set out by the R2P framework ultimately failed to separate the humanitarian from the political rationale, and consequently to alleviate the fears of the motives, i.e., the 'ends' of interventions as well as their means. An ethical, and not political, use of the norm and content of the broad human security would instead seek the end point against which an intervention has to be measured. In other words, actions are not considered right in themselves but are judged against their outcomes. The position echoes Noam Chomsky's 'simple truths': 'The first is that actions are evaluated in terms of the range of likely consequences. A second is the principle of universality; we apply to ourselves the same standards we apply to others, if not more stringent ones.'[58] Human security engagement, instead of R2P, would mean for example putting developing at the core of trade policies, upholding industrialized countries' commitments to the nuclear Non-Proliferation Treaty (NPT) by eliminating their own nuclear arsenals, setting a new code of conduct for arms sales to poorer nations, etc.

Whither human security

Despite the frequent characterization of the human security approach as too broad or ambitious, its essence is ethical: to prevent threats and mitigate their impacts when they materialize. Human security should not be reduced to lists or to a narrow definition, but remain flexible enough to allow for a deeper understanding of the root of insecurities and capacities to address them.

It may seem that in the policy world, terminology consensus would be necessary if a comprehensive human security programme is to be decided on and implemented. Yet, there is little chance that a globally satisfactory definition would be found to genuinely reconcile the concerns of the North and the South, East and West. Critics of the concept include both countries of the North, which would seek an agreement on enforcement mechanisms, and countries from the South or the emerging world, who mistrust the concept out of fear of new conditionality, unwarranted interventions and violations of state sovereignty. Yet, lack of consensual definitions in the political world, such as for example on terrorism, has not hampered action nor inhibited policy-making. Perhaps more important than a global agenda is the need to develop domestic human security policies, which no country has done so far.

Within academia, the variety of human security approaches is a necessity for critical debates. Deliberations help clarify a number of other open questions: the value of normative IR theory, inter-disciplinary convergences, what constitutes power and its legitimacy, the prerogative of states, what dignity means and how it can be measured.

Notes

1 See a summary of the variety of definitions used, critiques and counter-critiques in Chapters 1 and 2 of Shahrbanou Tadjbakhsh and Anuradha Chenoy, *Human Security: Concepts and Implications,* London: Routledge, 2007. By January 24, 2012, Google Scholar gave 44,000 hits when Human Security was entered with brackets.

2 Roland Paris, 'Human security: paradigm shift or hot air?,' *International Security* 26, 2, Autumn 2001: 87–102.

3 Peter Stoett, *Human and Global Security: An Exploration of Terms,* Toronto: University of Toronto Press, 1999, p.3.

4 Ibid.

5 Steve Smith, *The Contested Concept of Security,* Working Paper 23, Institute of Defence and Strategic Studies, Singapore, May 2002, pp. 1–26.

6 Barry Buzan, Ole Wæver and Jaap de Wilde, *Security: A New Framework for Analysis,* Boulder: Lynne Rienner, 1998, pp. 23–24.

7 Gary King and Christopher Murray, 'Rethinking HS,' *Political Science Quarterly,* 2001–2002, 116, 4: 2001.

8 Keith Krause and Michael C. Williams, 'Broadening the agenda of security studies: politics and methods,' *Mershon International Studies Review,* 40, 2, 1996: 229–254.

9 Paul Streeten, 'Human development: means and ends,' *Human Development,* 84, 2, May 1994. 232–237.

10 Paul R. Viotti and Mark V. Kauppi, (eds.), *International Relations Theory,* New York: Macmillan Publishing Company, 1997.

11 Mervyn Frost, *Ethics in International Relations: A Constitutive Theory,* Cambridge: Cambridge University Press, 1996, p. 56 and see Chapter 2.

12 Ibid, p. 62

13 Gillian Youngs, 'Feminist international relations: a contradition in terms? Or: Why women and gender are essential to understanding the world we live in,' *International Affairs,* 80, 1, 2004: 75–87.

14 See J. Ann Tickner, *Gendering World Politics,* New York: Columbia University Press, 2001; Christine Sylvester, *Feminist International Relations: An Unfinished Journey,* Cambridge: Cambridge University Press, 2002.

15 Paris, op. cit. Note 2, p. 91.

16 Taylor Owen, 'Human security – conflict, critique and consensus: colloquium remarks and a proposal for a threshold-based definition,' *Security Dialogue,* 35, 3, 2004: 373–387; King and Murray, 2001–2002 op. cit. Note 7.

17 See for example the Human Security Report Project produced by the Simon Fraser University.

18 Keith Krause, 'The key to a powerful agenda, if properly defined,' in J. Peter Burgess and Owen Taylor (eds),'What is Human Security? Comments by 21 Authors,' Special Issue of *Security Dialogue,* September, 35, 2004: 367–368 at p. 367

19 Kyle Grayson, 'A challenge to the power over knowledge of traditional security studies', in Burgess and Owen (eds), 'What is Human Security? Comments by 21 Authors,' Special Issue of *Security Dialogue,* September, 35, 2004: 357

20 Robert W. Cox, 'Social forces, states and world orders: beyond international relations theory,' *Millennium – Journal of International Studies*, 10, 2, 1981. 126–155.
21 Paris, 2001 op. cit. Note 2.
22 Andrew Mack, 'Report on the Feasibility of Creating an Annual Human Security Report' Program on Humanitarian Policy and Conflict Research, Harvard University, February 2002.
23 Buzan, Wæver and de Wilde, 1998, op cit. Note 6, pp. 21–26.
24 See parts of the debate in Taylor Owen, 'The critique that doesn't bite: a response to David Chandler's "Human security: the dog that didn't bark"', *Security Dialogue*, 39, 4, April/June 2008: 445–453; and David Chandler, 'Human security II: waiting for the tail to wag the dog – a rejoinder to Ambrosetti, Owen and Wibben,' *Security Dialogue*, 39, 4, April/June 2008: 463–469.
25 P. Kerr, W. T. Tow and M. Hanson, 'The utility of human security agenda for policy-makers,' *Asian Journal of Political Sciences*, 11, 2, 2003: 89–114.
26 Jenny. H. Peterson, 'Creating political spaces to promote human security: A solution to the failings of the liberal peacebuilding?' Paper presented at the annual meeting of the International Studies Association, *Exploring The Past, Anticipating The Future*, New York, USA, February 15, 2009.
27 Ibid.
28 Mark Duffied, *Development, Security and Unending War: Governing the World of Peoples*, Cambridge: Cambridge University Press, 2007; O. Richmond, *The Transformation of Peace*, New York: Palgrave McMillan, 2007.
29 David Chandler, ' Human security: the dog that didn't bark,' *Security Dialogue*, 39, 4, 2008: 427–438.
30 Ibid, p. 431.
31 Ibid, p. 488.
32 Ibid, p. 431.
33 Ibid, p. 435.
34 Ibid, p. 435.
35 Duffield, 2007, op. cit. Note 28.
36 See for example Owen, 2004, op. cit. Note 16, p. 374.
37 Commission on Human Security, *Human Security Now*, 2003, p. 4.
38 Johan Galtung, 'Violence, peace and peace research,' *Journal of Peace Research*, 6, 3, 1969: 167–191.
39 Oliver P. Richmond, 'Emancipatory forms of human security and liberal peacebuilding,' *International Journal*, 62, 3: 459–478.
40 King and Murray, 2001, op. cit. Note 7.
41 Owen, 2004, op. cit. Note 16, p. 374.
42 Amartya Sen, *Beyond the Crisis: Development Strategies in Asia*, Lecture at Sustainable Development and Human Security: Second Intellectual Dialogue on Building Asia's Tomorrow, Singapore, 1999, pp. 15–35 at p. 28
43 Des Gasper, 'Securing humanity: situating "human security" as concept and discourse,' *Journal of Human Development*, 6, 2, 2005.
44 Sakiko Fukuda-Parr, 'The new threats to human security in the era of globalization,' in Lincoln Chen, Sakiko Fukuda-Parr and Ellen Seidensticker, *Human Insecurity in a Global World*, Global Equity Initiative, Cambridge, Massachusetts: Harvard University Press, 2003, p. 8.
45 Gasper, 2005, op. cit. Note 43.
46 Mahbub ul Haq, *Reflections on Human Development*, New Delhi: Oxford University Press, 1999.
47 For a more complete comparative table, see Shahrbanou Tadjbakhsh, 'Human security,' *Human Development Insights*, 17, New York: UNDP HDR Networks.
48 CHS, *Human Security Now*, 2003, p. 10.
49 UN General Assembly, Vienna Declaration and Programme of Action, A/CONF.157/23 12 July 1993.
50 Gerd Oberleitner, 'Porcupines in love: the intricate convergence of human rights and human security,' *European Human Rights Law Review*, London: Sweet and Maxwell, 6, 2005: 588–606.
51 Ibid, p. 606.
52 United Nations Development Programme (UNDP), *Human Development Report 1994 – New Dimensions of Human Security*, New York: Oxford University Press, 1994.
53 CHS, *Human Security Now*, 2003.
54 See http://reliefweb.int/sites/reliefweb.int/files/resources/91BAEEDBA50C6907C1256D19006A935 3-chs-security-may03.pdf (accessed 8 May 2013).
55 See, for example, the Handbook on *Human Security in Theory and Practice,* which this author helped produce in 2010, found at https://docs.unocha.org/sites/dms/HSU/Publications%20and%20Products/

Human%20Security%20Tools/Human%20Security%20in%20Theory%20and%20Practice%20English. pdf (accessed 8 May 2013).

56 For an alternative view, see J. Peter Burgess and Shahrbanou Tadjbakhsh, 'The human security tale of two Europes', *Global Society,* 24, 4, 2010: 135–151.

57 Fen Osler Hampson, with J. Daudelin, J. Hay, H. Reid, and T. Martin, *Madness in the Multitude: Human Security and World Disorder,* Oxford: Oxford University Press, 2002, p. 169.

58 Noam Chomsky, 'A Just War? Hardly,' *Khaleej Times,* 9 May 2006.

4

HUMAN SECURITY THRESHOLDS

Taylor Owen

The concept of human security is contested. After nearly 20 years of use, there are dozens of proposed definitions and little consensus on what should and should not be treated as a human security threat. This paper will discuss a threshold-based definition that overcomes the central paradox of human security: that definitions are either narrow, sacrificing conceptual integrity for policy utility, or broad, prioritizing a literal referential shift to the individual over the needs of policy makers. A threshold-based definition attempts to retain conceptual integrity while also being policy relevant.

Towards a new definition of human security

The dozens of existing definitions of human security are ultimately subject to a conceptual paradox: that the greater the conceptual integrity of a definition the less practical the concept becomes. More specifically, the closer to the literal interpretation of the core referential shift of human security a definition becomes, then the more it begins to look like neighboring concepts such as human development and human rights, the more challenging threat identification becomes, and the less useful the term becomes to the field of security studies.

There are four lessons from the literature on human security that are useful in overcoming this tensions: organizing threats in components, allowing political subjectivity, focusing on the 'vital core' of the individual, and using severity as a threat-limiting measure.

First is the importance of using a components-based approach to categorizing threats. Recognizing the need for conceptual order, the original UNDP definition grouped threats into seven categories. This classification provided disciplinary subsets for what is a clearly inter-disciplinary concept, allowing issues to be studied on their own and providing the conceptual differentiation necessary for their interconnections to be analyzed. This allows for the concept to be deep, including a wide range of characteristics, but also coherent, as threats with different attributes are organized into distinct sub-categories.

Second, it must be recognized that threat assessments are ultimately subjective political decisions. Thomas and Tow argue that human security encompasses a distinct class of security problems, separate from those included under the rubric of national security. They argue that this limitation is critical if the concept is going to remain politically salient. Interestingly, political determinants are also at the core of the threat identification process. For example, they suggest that food distribution, gender discrimination and basic shelter are usually best treated as national development concerns. Under their conceptualizations, a threat receives the human security label if its ramifications 'cross a state's borders and assume a truly international significance, affecting other societies and individuals.'[1] These would include threats such as cross-border terrorism, pollution, refugees and genocide. The UNDP definition makes a similar distinction by differentiating between *global* and *national* human security threats – in other words, it was recognized that various scales of threat require various scales of response, and that this decision was ultimately a political one.[2] There is not one single legalistic checklist for determining what is and is not a human security threat. This political subjectivity is important because is allows the concept to remain broad and reflective of threat realities, while still differentiated from neighboring concepts such as human development.

Third is a focus on the vital core of the individual. This is essential in order to differentiate human security from human development, a term which is more appropriately linked with wellbeing than dire emergencies.[3] The Human Security Commission stresses the importance of focusing human security on the vital core of the individual, but defines the preservation of this vital core quite broadly, including threats to the dignity of the individual. While the scope of the vital core is debatable, what is useful is the explicit focus on the ability of the individual to live.[4]

Finally, numerous definitions invoke an assessment of threat severity when developing their criteria for threat inclusion. For example, the UNDP articulated human security as safety from chronic threats such as hunger, disease and repression along with the protection from sudden and hurtful disruption in the patterns of daily life. The point was not to securitize everything, but to shift attention to what was actually killing people.[5] The potential confusion between human security and 'human development' was also clearly addressed in this early articulation. Implying a qualitative difference between the two, human security was said to be a necessary but not sufficient precondition for human development. If human security could cover the most urgent threats, development would then address societal wellbeing. Similarly, for Alkire, a human security threat is anything that threatens the 'vital core' of the individual. The vital core is a subset of human capabilities that one may believe needs to be protected in order to ensure survival, livelihood and dignity. From this a list of threats can then be created based on an assessment of what threats surpass these thresholds.[6] King and Murray likewise envision a line past which a harm should be included as a human security threat, or, as they describe it, would put an individual in a state of generalized poverty. Their measure is universal and could, given the data, assign this value to any country or group. Importantly they introduce the notion that no one human security threat, or generalized poverty-inducing condition, is more severe than any other, removing the need to weight indicators.[7] Finally, Thakur proposes that human security be limited to 'crisis scenarios.' This would imply that a condition could become a threat, should it rise to a pre-determined level of severity[8] All four of these severity-based assessments are critical in allowing a concept to remain open to a wide range of threat causes, but limit the ultimate number included under a human security label.

With these four attributes in mind, a new conceptualization of human security begins to take shape. It must be inclusive, casting a 'broad tent,' it must separate its components into different types of security in order to address causality, it must explicitly focus on the survival of individuals, and it must set a threshold demarcating the line surpassing which an issue becomes a human security threat.

The threshold definition – what is and is not a security threat?

A core challenge in the human security literature is determining which threats should be included and which threats should not. Whereas narrow proponents limit threats to those that are violent in nature, broad proponents cast the net much broader, including a far wider range of harms. What both narrow and broad proponents have in common is that they both use threat categories as the organizing principle for threat inclusion, (i.e. any and all threats in any particular grouping of categories such as physical, health, economic, environment security are included). It is my contention that we should instead use threat severity as the test for inclusion. Human security, therefore, becomes not a universally applicable and finite list of harms, but rather a threshold, past which a condition in any one location, at any one time, may be considered serious enough to warrant the security label.

My proposal for a threshold-based definition of human security is the following:

> Human security is the protection of the vital core of all human lives from critical and pervasive environmental, economic, food, health, personal and political threats.[9]

There are two core components to such a conceptualization.

The first half of the definition has origins in the articulation of the *Commission on Human Security*. In particular, the Commission's reference to threats being *critical, pervasive* and targeting the *vital core* of individuals. First, *critical* places a degree of urgency on potential threats. To be included, a harm must be immanent. Second, the term *pervasive* means that a threat must be widespread. It must affect more than one person in one location. Finally, the conclusion of *vital core* focuses the concept on harms that impede an individual's ability to survive. This could be measured by deaths already caused by the harm, or by the actions taken by individuals to avert death, such as flight. Together, these three metrics constitute a subjective threshold, surpassing which a harm or condition should be considered a human security threat.

The second half of the definition places all potential harms into seven conceptual categories. This grouping of threats serves two purposes. First, it helps in identifying threats. As this conceptualization could potentially include harms from a vast array of causes, it is useful to begin an analysis using categories of harms. For example, one may ask what health threats surpass the threshold in any one location. Second, clustering threats has an analytic utility. Labeling all possible harms as threats to human security with no distinction makes correlative analysis all but impossible. Separating them into categories allows for groupings to be isolated as dependent variables as well as providing a degree of order to a potential unmanageably broad concept including very disparate harms.

The core purpose of establishing human security thresholds is to keep the concept as open as possible to allow for a diverse range of threats to potentially be included, while remaining focused on those that warrant the security label.

Exploring the human security threshold

If we accept that certain conditions surpass a threshold of severity and become not only human rights violations, environmental problems or isolated violent acts, but instead threats to human security, then we must have a very clear idea about what these threats are and where these exist. This, by nature, requires us to define the threshold. Clearly, where the bar is set will have a significant impact on national and international policy. A core aspect of thresholds are that they are subjective – any threat, if severe enough, can be deemed a human security threat in any location and at any time. Three aspects of the concept are key to understanding why this subjectivity is a positive attribute, and not a limiting characteristic of human security: time, space and politics.

First, thresholds are spatially relative. Threats affecting one region will not be the same as threats facing another. Indeed, the principle deficiency with global catch-all measures of human security, such as the Human Security Audit and Global Environmental Change and Human Security Project (GECHS) measure, is that in attempting to include all threats to all people in all places, they either render the threat list unmanageably vast, or they arbitrarily limit threat inclusion based on either data availability or threat category.[10] This spatial relativity functions at any scale. Just as one country's human security threats will be different from another's, one village's will also be distinct. In one region of a country, high levels of malaria, for example, might be linked to large numbers of deaths, and therefore be deemed a human security threat. In another region, perhaps an urban setting, malaria may be low, but violence levels might be extremely high, warranting a human security label. Landmine fields provide another good example. While incredibly hazardous to those living in contaminated areas, they are of little concern to those who do not come into contact with them. Thresholds simply provide the criteria by which to assess what harms should be considered human security threats in any one location.

Second, thresholds are temporally relative. Similar to space, human security threats will also vary over time – a threat becomes a human security issue only when it crosses the threshold. An issue can be important because it is deemed to have the potential to become a human security issue. But until it is causing a critical and pervasive threat, and has crossed the threshold, then it is not one. Kanti Bajpai, in an extensive work advocating for a Human Security Audit, has argued that human security should be defined as an equation between threats and the capability of individuals and groups to mitigate them, both varying in time, and in any one location. As the elements of this equation are both temporally and regionally dependent, he argues, any uniform definition is futile.[11] This is significantly different than Alkire's conceptualization, for example, which argues that potential future impact makes a harm a human security concern.[12] The combination of spatial and temporal relativity serves as a means of narrowing the concept, without arbitrarily limiting threats.

Lastly and perhaps most importantly, thresholds are politically subjective. Although one could conceivably come up with quantitative criteria for the threshold (such as number of deaths), it is more usefully defined as being politically determined. Much as there is no set list for what is and is not a traditional security threat, human security threats would be decided by international organizations, national governments and NGOs. In short, there are a wide range of security actors, and each will ultimately make political decisions on what for them, is and is not a security threat. Human security thresholds should, however, serve to inform relevant actors in any given location and any given time as to what are the principal threats – indeed in any one place and time, these threats will generally be quite clear. That one government, or organization, may have a different list of threats than another is an unavoidable consequence of their independent mandates, capabilities and spheres of influence. Just as national security assessments vary based on the actor conducting the assessment, so too will human security analysis.

In order to show the salience of these three attributes, it is useful to consider how they help separate the concept of human security from neighboring concepts of human development and human rights.

Human development and human rights

First, one of the central ambiguities in the human security literature surrounds the overlap between the concepts of human security and human development. Broad definitions too often incorporate concerns that have a long history within the development discourse, and narrow conceptualizations discount a wide range of harms because they fall under the purview of the development discourse. Thresholds help us move beyond this.

The concepts can be distinguished from one another using thresholds in two ways – threat identification and threat mitigation. First, some threats that traditionally fall within the category of human development have the potential to become threats to human security if they surpass the threshold at any one time and in any one place. The difference between the two concepts, therefore, is rooted in the line which a harm may cross making it something qualitatively more serious and urgent than it once was. Determining this line is necessarily a subjective decision, but in any country or region, the development concerns that fundamentally threaten the lives of large numbers of people are relatively easy to identify. For example, in some countries in Africa, HIV/AIDS is such a large-scale and imminently destructive menace, that it must be tackled with all of the resources and prescience afforded to a security concern. In other countries, the impact of HIV/AIDS may not be as significant, due to an ability to counter the threat, and as such, traditional development mechanisms may be the most appropriate means of addressing the problem. In this construct, certain conditions of under-development, such as environmental, health, economic and human rights abuses, could, however, cross the threshold and become human security threats. Human security is therefore a necessary precondition for human development, but not vice versa.

Second, while most human development issues have the potential to become human security issues, some do not. Issues such as education, for example, even if the education system were non-existent, would never meet the threshold of causing a critical and pervasive threat. However, better education may very well be determined to be a mitigating mechanism for alleviating a human security threat. This same dynamic is true for a host of development issues and practices. A bad road will never be a human security threat. But building a road may help address the threat of high accident rates or for providing access to a village for medicinal supplies or policing. It may be that more or better development is determined to be the best mechanism to address identified human security threats. But identifying the human security threat is a precondition for developing this mitigating strategy.

Part of the difficulty with using the threshold approach is that many harms will not qualify as a security threat in any one place and at any one time. By definition, only those threats that pose a critical and pervasive risk to the vital core are included. Others, while undoubtedly important, should be addressed using existing non-security mechanisms. The case of human rights abuses provides a useful example.

Human rights and human security are very different concepts. While rights signify the basic legal entitlements of individuals, security involves personal safety. Rights generally depict conditions in which all people are entitled to live, while human security thresholds address the very survival of those people. Concepts such as basic rights and the right to life make a similar distinction, but both define the rights of the individual as far broader than simply survival. Henry Shue goes a bit further in narrowing the concept of rights, articulating what he calls the basic right to subsistence, security, and liberty.[13] Human security thresholds seek to identify the line where a human rights concern also becomes a human security threat and can be justified as such.

Following the threshold conceptualization, using the term security has certain pre-conditions.

Security carries with it a level of urgency that should only be used to address immanent disasters. Certainly some human rights abuses would qualify as human security threats, but not all. Mass human rights abuses against a particular group of society are clearly also a threat to human security. Suppression of religious freedom, in and of itself, while a concern, and often the cause of a wide range of harms, some of which may constitute critical and pervasive threats to the vital core, would not in most cases qualify as a human security threat.

The United Nations Declaration of Rights and Freedoms, for example, lists many conditions that while certainly harmful, do not surpass the threshold of severity to be treated as security threats as opposed to criminal, political or legal issues.[14] Instead of demarcating categories of harms, the concept of human security determines which threats, no matter what their cause, constitute a critical and pervasive threat to the vital core. Subsequently, the protection from gross violations of human rights is only one component of ensuring human security. Individuals also need protection from extreme poverty, disasters, conflict and disease. Put another way, protection from gross violations of human rights is a necessary, but not sufficient pre-condition of human security.

Conclusion

When asked to comment on the level of uncertainty, debate, conjecture and outright skepticism regarding the concept of human security, former Canadian foreign minister Lloyd Axworthy responded assertively: 'The world had no idea what sovereignty and the security infrastructure would look like immediately following the signing of the treaty of Westphalia. Norms evolved through decades of debate, thought, action, conflict and compromise.'[15] This is worth considering as we address the current state and future of the concept of human security. There is no doubt that the majority of human vulnerability is not the result of interstate war but rather is caused by disease, extreme poverty, natural disasters, civil conflict and small arms. As the primary threats to individuals have changed, so too must our means of conceptualizing insecurity. But early conceptualizations of human security, all of which shift the referent object from the state to the individual, have run into problems of definitional clarity. While the minimal definition of human security is clear – human security shifts the referent of security from the state to the individual – the maximal definition, describing which threats to the individual should be included, is vigorously contested. This ambiguity has led to a bifurcation of the use of the concept, and a conflation with neighboring concepts such as human development and human rights.

Out of this ambiguity emerges a paradox: that the greater the conceptual integrity of a definition, the more problematic the policy operationalization of the concept becomes. To have conceptual integrity, one must take a broad definition which includes all potential threats to the individual (such as the UNDPs) and to be policy relevant one must use a narrow definition, focused on only one dimension of the concept (such as the Canadian and Norwegian governments' violence-based conceptualizations). To overcome this paradox, it has been proposed here that a threshold-based definition be used to let the actual risks present in a certain location determine what human security is and is not. Recognizing that the point of human security is to bring the resources and prescience of the security infrastructure to a new set of issues, this strategy limits those that are raised to this top priority level. For analytic clarity, it delineates these harms into clusters of threat categories.

This definition of human security is only a tool for threat identification. It does not, in and of itself, specify which policy mechanisms should be used to address the identified insecurities, nor the order in which they need to be addressed, nor the most appropriate actor for dealing with each. What it does do is help policy makers and analysts who want to prioritize human security identify which harms in a given location have crossed a threshold of severity, and should as such be treated with the resources and prescience that the concept of security demands. This lays the groundwork for the policy utility of human security.

Notes

1 Thomas, Nicholas & William T. Tow, 2002. 'The Utility of Human Security: Sovereignty and Humanitarian Intervention', *Security Dialogue* 33(2): 177–192.
2 There are problems with this approach, however. If the referent of human security is the safety of the individual, then why should it matter from where the threat originates and what are it's potential international political implications may be?
3 Ogata, Sadako, and Amartya Sen, *Human Security Now: Commission on Human Security, Final Report*. New York: United Nations, 2003.
4 Ibid.
5 United Nations Development Programme (UNDP), 1994. *Human Development Report, 1994*. New York: Oxford University Press.
6 Alkire, Sabina, 2001. 'A Conceptual Framework for Human Security', CRISE Working Paper 2. Oxford: CRISE.
7 King, Gary, and Murray, Christopher, 'Rethinking Human Security,' *Political Science Quarterly,* 116(4).
8 Thakur, Ramesh, 1997. 'From National to Human Security', in Stuart Harris and Andrew Mack (eds) *Asia-Pacific Security: The Economics–Politics Nexus,* pp. 52–80. Sydney: Allen & Unwin.
9 This definition was first articulated in Owen, Taylor, 'Human Security – Conflict, Critique and Consensus: Colloquium Remarks and a Proposal for a Threshold–based Definition', *Security Dialogue,* 35(3), 373–387. This article expands considerably on the definition and places it within the context or the wider literature on human security.
10 Bajpai, 'Human security: concept and measurement'; Lonergan, 'The Index of Human Insecurity.'
11 Bajpai, 'Human security: concept and measurement'; Bajpai, Kanti, 'An expression of threats versus capabilities across time and space,' *Security Dialogue,* 35(3), 2004.
12 Alkire, 'Conceptual framework for human security,' p. 4.
13 Shue, Henry, *Basic Rights*, Second Edition, Princeton, NJ: Princeton University Press, 1996.
14 UN, 'Universal Declaration of Human Rights,' 1948.
15 Lloyd Axworthy, 'Comments to UBC Human Security Graduate Course,' Liu Institute for Global Issues, Vancouver, BC, November, 2001.

5

HUMAN SECURITY: POLITICAL AUTHORITY IN A GLOBAL ERA

Mary Kaldor

Words like 'security' and 'protection' cannot be disentangled from the concept of authority. It is because we believe that our institutions keep us safe that we trust and submit to those institutions and, by the same token, our trust in institutions depends on the belief that they keep us safe.

Yet both words are deeply ambiguous. Charles Tilly has pointed out that the term 'protection' has two quite different meanings.

> One is comforting, the other ominous. With one tone, protection calls up images of the shelter against danger provided by a powerful friend, a large insurance policy, or a sturdy roof. With the other, it evokes the racket in which a local strongman forces merchants to pay tribute to avoid damage, damage the strongman himself threatens to deliver ... Which image the word 'protection' brings to mind depends mainly on our assessment of the reality and externality of the threat. Someone who produces both the danger and, at a price, the shield against it is a racketeer. Someone who provides a needed shield but has little control over the danger's appearance qualifies as a legitimate protector.[1]

There is a similar ambiguity about the term 'security'. To some, the notion of security services conjures up sinister instruments of repression and surveillance (the dark side of the state) whilst for others, such services are the prerequisite for a well-ordered society. The academic debate about 'securitisation' is an expression of this ambiguity: 'Whenever something took the form of a particular speech act of securitisation, with a securitising actor claiming an existential threat to a valued referent object in order to make the audience tolerate extraordinary measures that otherwise would not have been acceptable, this was a case of securitisation.'[2] In other words there is an analogy between securitisation and protection rackets. The former usually refers to public authorities while the latter is assumed to apply to criminals.

So how does human security fit in this schema? Is it about 'humanising' security or about 'securitising' development?[3] Duffield, for example, argues that the discourse of human security is a form of 'biopolitics', a social mechanism used to maintain stability in what he describes as the uninsured part of the world – a way to maintain the quarantine of rich countries and salve their consciences. The strategic complexes of human security are part of a new paraphernalia of international intervention — a disciplinary technology that preserves the submission of conflict-ridden parts of the world to an unequal world order.[4]

In this chapter, I want to suggest that the validity of this depressing interpretation of the function of human security depends on how human security is implemented. The idea of human security does offer the potential for reconstructing political authority in the context of the process we call globalisation. But whether this form of authority is repressive or emancipatory and whether it is effective depends, as Tilly suggests, on 'our assessments of reality', how human security is operationalised, whether it can address actually existing experiences of danger in the most difficult parts of the world.

Since the end of the Cold War, national security narratives based on the threat of external attacks by foreign enemies have been eroded. The current period is characterised by a plethora of alternative narratives ranging from the 'war on terror' to a new concatenation of notions of risk that seem both vague and lacking in practical implications. This uncertainty about both the way that risk is constructed and the implicit precautionary behaviour is, I believe, linked to a pervasive loss of trust in institutions, especially at the national level. The extent to which human security can offer an alternative basis for legitimate authority depends both on the way that constructions of risk are related to terrifying everyday encounters, and how the concept is put into practice.

In what follows, I start with a broad outline of the various phenomena that we bunch together under the rubric of globalisation; how our understanding of the world has changed in the post-Cold war era and then I discuss the concept of human security and how it might be implemented. I conclude by discussing the implications for political authority.

The global context

The term 'globalisation' refers to many different phenomena. Nevertheless, its widespread use reflects an awareness of some kind of fundamental change in world order, with specific consequences for the character of state sovereignty. The most common factor that helps to explain these different phenomena is technology, especially but not only the spread of communications and information technology. To say this is not to assert a technologically determinist view of history; rather that the emergence and evolution of new technologies can only be understood as the outcome of social interaction – the behaviour of corporations, civil society and other agents of globalisation. So what are the various elements of this fundamental change we call globalisation and what are the implications for state sovereignty?

One interpretation of globalisation is that we have become conscious of a single human community. This is partly the result of global communications, particularly satellite television – we are increasingly aware of human suffering in other parts of the world. Immanuel Kant's argument, made in 1795, that the world community has shrunk to the point where 'a right violated in one part of the world is felt everywhere' is becoming a reality.[5] Pictures of the earth taken from space or global memories like Hiroshima or the Holocaust contribute to this shared sense of consciousness.

This growing human consciousness is reflected in the growth of human rights and norms in the period since the end of World War II. The 1948 Declaration on Human Rights and the various Covenants, and most recently, the Tribunals for the former Yugoslavia and Rwanda and the establishment of the International Criminal Court have created a body of international law that applies to individuals and not states. This law has been backed up and strengthened by an emerging human rights lobby, composed of civil society groups and sympathetic governments.

Growing global consciousness means that it is harder and harder to sustain closed authoritarian states. Even in Bashir Assad's Syria or Muammar Ghaddafi's Libya there were subversive bloggers and mobile footage telling what was happening. The so-called third wave of democratisation in Latin America, Africa, Asia and Eastern Europe and now the Middle East can be understood as an outcome of globalisation – just as in Eastern Europe, links between opposition groups and the outside world, world publicity, and the recourse to international human rights law were important mechanisms for change.

Effectively, these developments imply that state sovereignty is increasingly 'conditional' – dependent both on domestic behaviour and consent of the outside world.

The last decades of the twentieth century witnessed a new wave of migration. Because of the ease of communication and travel, however, the new migrants, unlike the great waves of migration at the end of the nineteenth century, are able to keep in touch with their homeland. The notion of a Diaspora, which earlier applied only to the Jews, has become widespread – these are growing transnational communities based on ethnicity and religion. This also has implications for state sovereignty since the notion of a vertically organised territorially based community congruent to the state is greatly weakened. It is often argued that the cohesion of states depends on the idea of the 'Other' – what Carl Schmitt called the friend-enemy distinction.[6] Yet nowadays, citizens have multiple loyalties, to the state, to their community, which may no longer be congruent with the state, and to humankind. On the one hand, friend-enemy distinctions, as between Israel and Palestine or Serbia and Croatia, are often reproduced within the global cities of the advanced industrial world. On the other hand, such distinctions can be eroded in cosmopolitan communities, undermining securitisation claims.

In the social sciences, globalisation is often defined as interconnectedness in all fields – economic, political, cultural, and social.[7] Effectively, this means that decisions that affect our everyday lives are often taken far away by multinational corporations, international institutions like the IMF, the World Bank or the European Union, or even by powerful foreign states, for example, the United States. Economic policies like 'structural adjustment' or 'convergence criteria', trade and investments agreements, rules about the environment or even international sporting and cultural events, increasingly curtail the autonomy of the state to legislate about developments within its territory. Some authors talk about a 'hollow state' in which civil servants are more often in communication with their counterparts in other countries than their domestic constituencies and in which the task of political leaders is less to rule than to manage complex relationships with international institutions, other states, international companies and NGOs as well as domestic interests and the wider public.

In extreme cases, the difficulty of reconciling all these pressures leads to state failure or state collapse, which is the source of many terrible conflicts happening in the world today. Indeed, the risks or threats we face are less likely to come from authoritarian states but from failing states, although the latter are usually a combination of authoritarianism and state failure.

In the twentieth century, military technology became more destructive, more accurate and more widely available. Some 35 million people died in World War I and some 50 million in World War II. Around half a million civilians died from allied bombing in Germany alone. A million died in the siege of Leningrad. Symmetric war – war between two similarly armed opponents – has simply become too destructive to be fought. The importance of nuclear deterrence in the post-World War II period can be understood as a metaphor for the destructiveness of war in general. This does not mean that such wars will never again take place. The war between Iraq and Iran in the 1980s was just such a war – millions of young men died in trenches rather similar to World War I and the war ended in a stalemate. (We often forget this trauma and the role of our governments in sustaining that war when we discuss Iraq and Iran today.) At the time of writing, there is talk of an Israeli attack on Iran or the possibility of similar occurrences in East Asia, as a consequence of, say, a Chinese attack on Taiwan or a North Korean implosion.

But what the destructiveness of symmetric war does mean is the growing unacceptability of war in general. This happened already after World War I. The notion that war is a legitimate way for states to pursue their interests that held sway in the post-Westphalian period was rejected in the Charter of the League of Nations, in the Kellogg-Briand pact of 1928 and, above all, in the aftermath of World War II when the crime of aggression was enshrined in the Nuremberg trials and in the Charter of the United Nations. As with human rights norms and rules, these prohibitions have been strengthened by civil society pressure, in particular the growth of peace movements, especially in the advanced industrial world.

In other words, the growing destructiveness of war and the growing unacceptability of war mean that states no longer have the option of using war as a policy instrument and therefore have to deal with each other in different ways. Of course, it can be argued that the United States (or China), especially under President Bush, has not respected this emerging principle. But the wars in Iraq and Afghanistan may turn out to be the exception that proves the rule. The main lessons from these wars may well include the difficulty of using the military instrument, that superiority of military technology does not bring decisive victories, and that legitimacy is more important than force.

The destructiveness and unacceptability of wars between states or symmetric warfare does not, of course, mean an end to war. But the new types of war are asymmetric, that is to say violence is primarily directed against unarmed and unprotected civilians rather than against other warring parties; in other words, the increasing use of terror. What I call 'new wars' are wars that have evolved from guerrilla warfare and 'low-intensity wars' as ways of getting around concentrations of conventional force; the warring parties try to control territory politically through fear rather than through militarily attacking an enemy. These wars involve a mixture of warfare (political violence), human rights violations and violations of the laws of war (violence against non-combatants, genocide, massacres, torture and atrocities, mass rape) and ordinary crime (loot, pillage, smuggling and other illegal forms of war finance). They involve state and non-state actors and they blur classic distinctions between combatant and non-combatant, competent political authority and lack of authority, international and external.[8]

These combined changes can be said to amount to a profound restructuring of political authority. States remain the juridical repository of sovereignty; international institutions derive their legal foundation from treaties agreed among states. But in practice, states are hemmed in by a system of global governance, in which they remain key actors, but along with international institutions, regional organisations like the European Union or the African Union, transnational corporations, NGOs and civil society and even individuals. Their capacity to act as autonomous agents is greatly circumscribed and, in particular, the recourse to war as an instrument of policy is now prohibited.

A system of global governance is not the same as a 'global state with a monopoly on the legitimate use of force'[9] and indeed, such a state is probably not desirable since it would have great potential for tyranny. But it is quite different from a world where states act as individuals pursuing their national interests. The Great Divide, as it is known in the International Relations literature,[10] between domestic civil society peopled by individuals, norms, law and politics, and an external state of nature peopled by states that pursue their self-interest, is an expression of the prevailing conception of national security. What is happening today is that the social contract within states is being increasingly supplemented by a social contract at a global level.[11] Rules and laws that apply to individuals as well as states are being negotiated among the family of individuals, groups and institutions that constitute what we call global governance. This is why it is possible to talk about a blurring of the distinction between inside and outside, domestic and external. The Great Divide has not disappeared but it is no longer so clear-cut. The inside can no longer be insulated from an outside of terror, organised crime or ethnic and religious conflict. The outside is increasingly a world where individual as well as state rights apply and where states no longer have the same autonomy to pursue their interests. This is the context in which to understand the relevance of human security.

Human security as a practical concept

The concept of human security is generally defined first in terms of the security of individuals and the communities in which they live as opposed to the security of the state and secondly as referring to both 'freedom from fear' and 'freedom from want' – security from a range of existential threats that include both physical violence as well material deprivation. The debate between the broad and narrow definitions is covered in other chapters of this book, as is the idea of a threshold definition that depends on the extremity of existential threats as a way of overcoming the broad/narrow debate.

In the version of human security that was adopted by the European Human Security Study Group, a third component of the definition was added. This is the link between human security and law. Human security involves a blurring of the Great Divide. Human security is about the kind of security that individuals expect in law-governed societies where law is based on an implicit social contract among individuals. Fundamental to law-governed societies is the assumption of equality before the law. This is different from the idea of a state-based international system in which, even if this system is law-governed as is assumed by the English School of international relations, it is law based on state rights rather than individual rights. In such a system, from an individual point of view nationals are privileged over foreigners. In a law-governed national society, where law applies to individuals, it is assumed that the state will protect individuals from existential threats and emergency services – ambulances, firefighters, police – are part of state provision. In most such societies civil and political rights tend to receive more attention than social and economic rights in practice even though all these rights are enshrined in law.

Human security is about extending individual rights beyond domestic borders and about developing a capacity at a global level to provide those kinds of emergency services to be deployed in situations where states either lack capacity or are themselves the violators of rights. What this means is that national security cannot be assured unilaterally, that the security of any part of the world depends on a global or human security system. Thus instead of defending borders against external attack the security capabilities of states are designed to contribute to global emergency services.

To some extent, this idea is already present in contemporary international interventions. There has been a remarkable increase in international peace-keeping since the end of the Cold War, not only under UN auspices but also regional institutions like the EU, the AU, the CIS or OSCE. Indeed, the Stockholm International Peace Research Institute database of multilateral peace operations includes nearly 600 such missions between 2000 and 2009.[12] Both within international institutions and among governments, there has been a growing effort to mainstream concepts like Responsibility to Protect, stabilisation or human security and to develop or at least to conceptualise appropriate capabilities. Responsibility to Protect was adopted by the United Nations General Assembly in 2005. Since his appointment as Secretary General in January 2007, Ban Ki Moon has said that 'he will spare no effort to operationalise Responsibility to Protect.'[13] It is now standard for United Nations Security Council resolutions to refer to the protection of civilians although the Libya resolution of 2011 was the first to name the protection of civilians as the main goal and almost all current UN peacekeepers are now mandated to protect civilians.

A particularly significant development in the twenty-first century has been the establishment of the International Criminal Court. Indeed, both by enthusiasts and critics, the ICC is increasingly bracketed together with the Responsibility to Protect. The Rome Statute, the legal basis for the Court, was adopted by 120 states on 17 July 1998 and entered into force on 1 July 2002. The establishment of the ICC can be seen as part of the general pressure for humanitarian norms as a result of the war in Bosnia and the Rwandan genocide.[14] The new emphasis on crimes against humanity has generated a whole new machinery of transitional justice.[15]

Alongside these multilateral initiatives, many countries have begun to reconceptualise security as something broader than national defence. There has been much discussion about new or non-traditional threats or risks and the appropriate capabilities needed to complement military force; even countries like Russia and China refer to non-traditional threats. And even the United States has partly begun to move away from classic defence thinking as a consequence of the experience of Iraq and Afghanistan.

Nevertheless there are evidently limits to this shift. First of all civilian protection in practice has been disappointing. In the case of Libya, what began as a mission to protect civilians ended up as a war in which the international community took the side of the rebels; this may have been worthwhile but it has left a legacy of violence and destruction that will make long-term human security difficult. In other places where UN peacekeepers have been mandated to protect civilians, it often has not happened in practice. An independent report on the protection of civilians in UN operations undertaken for the United Nations found that there is still insufficient clarity of mandates, lack of planning, training and preparation, and lack of appropriate structures, resources and tools despite the perseverance of 'many dedicated and creative individuals'.[16] Secondly, in military interventions, rules of engagement are usually based on the laws of armed conflict (international humanitarian law) rather than human rights law or domestic law. Hence the actual experience of civilians in these situations is that their lives have less value than the lives of international personnel. This is evidently the case in Iraq and Afghanistan. Thirdly, for most countries these tasks are often seen as secondary to the core task of defending nations from attack by a foreign enemy. It is argued that the 'high end' of defence spending – advanced equipment and war fighting capabilities – can be applied at the 'low end' but not the other way round. The financial crisis has meant a closing in on core tasks thereby weakening an already fragile capability for the new crisis tasks. Even those directly engaged in international operations, especially the military, recognise the need for change, but few political leaders are ready to embrace new approaches.

What is required is a much more profound rethinking of what is involved in operationalising human security. In the Barcelona and Madrid Reports produced by the European Human Security Study Group, it was proposed to establish human security forces composed of both military and civilian officers under civilian control. This coming together of military and civilians for human security is only possible if they conform to certain principles, which guide the way they are used. These principles are detailed below.

The primacy of human rights

The primacy of human rights is what distinguishes the human security approach from traditional state-based approaches. What this principle means is that the primary goal is protecting civilians rather than defeating an adversary. Of course sometimes it is necessary to try to capture or even defeat insurgents but it has to be seen as a means to an end, civilian protection, rather than the other way round. Torturing suspects who have been arrested is also illegitimate and illegal. So-called collateral damage is unacceptable. At the same time, the application of this principle to saving life directly under threat from other parties may require a greater readiness to use force and to risk the lives of soldiers or aid workers – a shift in the balance between force protection and civilian protection.

In Afghanistan or Libya, NATO air forces made great efforts to minimise civilian casualties and this has been facilitated by the increased precision of contemporary weapons. Nevertheless, these forces still operate under the laws of armed conflict, which do allow civilian casualties in the case of 'military necessity'. Moreover even if civilian casualties are avoided as a direct result of NATO offensives, they occur indirectly as a result of the ensuing fighting. In a human rights framework, where Afghan or Libyan lives are considered equal to Western lives, a very different calculus would have to be made.

Human rights include economic and social rights as well as political and civil rights. This means that human rights such as the right to life, the right to housing, or the right to freedom of opinion are to be respected and protected even in the midst of conflict.

Legitimate political authority

Human security can only be guaranteed by a rule of law that depends on the existence of legitimate institutions that gain the trust of the population and have some enforcement capacity. This applies both to physical security, where the rule of law and a well-functioning system of justice are essential, and to material security, where increasing legitimate employment or providing infrastructure and public services require state policies. Legitimate political authority does not necessarily need to mean a state, it could consist of local government, a city for example, or regional or international political arrangements like protectorates or transitional administrations. Since state failure is often the primary cause of conflict, the reasons for state failure have to be taken into account in reconstructing legitimate political authority. Measures like justice and security sector reform, DDR, extension of authority, public service reform are critical for the establishment of legitimate political authority.[17] As is the involvement of civil society in political debate.

This principle explicitly recognises the limitations on the use of military force. The aim of a human security operation is to stabilise the situation so that a space can be created for a peaceful political process rather than to win through military means alone. It is the political process that is critical.

A huge problem in Afghanistan has been the lack of legitimacy of the Karzai government. This reflects the fact that Western goals were not actually about human security; they were aimed at defeating the Taliban and Al Qaeda. Perhaps the biggest mistake was the incorporation of discredited and deeply corrupt warlords in the Karzai government because they were seen as allies in the War on Terror.

Effective multilateralism

This is related to legitimacy and distinguishes a human security approach from neo-colonialism. Human security means a commitment to work with others, with international institutions, creating or complying with existing common rules and norms and solving problems through rules and co-operation as well as with individual states, regional actors and NGOs. It also means a better division of tasks and agreeing the appropriate means to resolve conflict and build peace.

It is also closely related to international law and the need to operate within an international legal framework. In the current 'strategic complexes' with layers of contracting and numerous agencies, and an internal logic of competition, this may turn out to be one of the biggest obstacles to the implementation of human security. Nowhere was this more apparent than in Afghanistan, where skilled people were absorbed into the international machinery as drivers and interpreters and the international effort had the paradoxical consequence of actually reducing local capacity.

The bottom-up approach

Notions of 'partnership', 'local ownership' and 'participation' are already key concepts in development policy, while soldiers often refer to the 'ground truth' or to knowledge of the 'human terrain'. Decisions about the kind of security and development policies to be adopted, whether or not to intervene with military forces or through various forms of conditionality, and how, will only work if they take account of the most basic needs identified by the people who are affected by violence and insecurity. This is not just a moral issue; it is also a matter of effectiveness. People who live in zones of insecurity are the only ones able to sustain long-term security. There is a tendency among outsiders to focus on those who carry guns. Yet those who carry guns may often be those with a long-term interest in insecurity. Thus communication, consultation and dialogue are essential tools for human security not simply to win hearts and minds nor even to gain knowledge and understanding but to empower those who will have to be responsible for security in the long run. The participation of teachers, doctors, tribal leaders, religious leaders and young people are all critical for both understanding and opera-tionalising human security. Particularly important, in this context, is the role of women. The importance of gender equality for development, especially the education of girls, has long been recognised. The same may be true when managing violence. Women play a critical role both in dealing with the everyday consequences of the violence and overcoming divisions in society. Involvement and partnership with women's groups could be a key component of a human security approach.

Regional focus

The tendency to focus attention on areas that are defined in terms of statehood has often meant that relatively simple ways of preventing the spread of violence are neglected. Time and again, foreign policy analysts have been taken by surprise when, after considerable attention had been given to one conflict, another conflict would seemingly spring up out of the blue in a neighbouring state. The war in Sierra Leone could not be solved without addressing the cause of conflict in Liberia, for example. The war in Afghanistan can only be contained if the neighbouring states, especially Pakistan, are involved.

Clear civilian command

In human-security operations, civilians are in command. This means that the military must operate in support of law and order and under rules of engagement that are more similar to those of police work than to the rules of armed combat. Everyone needs to know who is in charge, and leaders must be able to communicate politically with local people as well as people in the sending countries. It is difficult for civilians to serve under a military command because as happened to the UN in Iraq, they can easily become a target. And it is very difficult for the military to carry out civilian tasks consistently. Perhaps the biggest weakness of the international intervention in Afghanistan was that it was military-led. In 2009, General McCrystal put forward a new strategy that emphasised stabilisation and governance and even used the words human security. But these goals are very difficult for soldiers to carry out, especially given the embedded military culture of defeating enemies. Despite the goals, the emphasis in recent years has been on 'kill or capture' of insurgents.

Fundamental to all these principles is a change of mindset. It is about the equality of human beings. This sounds obvious but in war zones, local civilians are not treated as though they were equal in importance to civilians back home or indeed to the forces themselves.

Northern Ireland is instructive in this regard because, in effect, it was a 'new war' on British territory. The British government could not bomb Belfast. It could not even have sent drones, if the technology had been available. Actually, when British troops were first sent to Northern Ireland, they did not sufficiently appreciate this. They were experienced in colonial counter-insurgencies and they did not understand the difference between Aden, where they had been deployed most recently, and Belfast. As one soldier put it:

> We weren't governed by the same rules that we were in Ireland. The lads over there (Aden) could be a lot rougher, a lot harder because we never had the newspapers there and we never had the Press there or anyone else who could see what we were doing. It made a lot of difference because you were given a freer hand right across the board.[18]

During the first few years, the army failed to protect the nationalist community from house burnings and expulsions, which stimulated the militarisation of the IRA; it used interrogation and intelligence techniques developed in colonial wars, later ruled illegitimate by the European Court of Human Rights; and it used excessive force, most notoriously in breaking up IRA-established 'No-Go' areas and on 'Bloody Sunday', 30 January 1972, when the Parachute Regiment fired on a crowd and killed 13 people.[19] This sparked the bloodiest period of the whole Northern Ireland conflict, accounting for 90 per cent of all deaths. Between 1969 and 1974, some 188 people were killed by security forces and 65 per cent of the deaths were unarmed civilians.[20]

From 1974, a new policy was adopted known as 'normalisation', 'criminalisation' or Ulsterisation. The emphasis was placed on police primacy in dealing with insurgents and captured terrorists were to be treated as criminals rather than enemies. They were to be tried and given the same status in prison as ordinary criminals. The job of the armed forces was to support the police. Army bases were often co-located with police stations, rather like General Petraeus did in Baghdad. This approach lasted until the Good Friday Agreement, in April 1997, which largely ended the conflict.

Of course, there were many weaknesses but the British approach after 1974 did succeed in containing the violence – over the period as a whole, 1969–1997, some 4000 people were killed, 350 by security forces. What made it different was that the people of Northern Ireland were British citizens. A similar example is the Oklahoma City bombing. What if the US government had decided to send a drone against Timothy McVeigh? Could this have escalated to a conflict on American soil?

The reconstruction of political authority

Anne Orford suggests that the emphasis placed by the UN Secretary General on Responsibility to Protect in recent years has to do with efforts by the United Nations to establish executive power. She describes Responsibility to Protect as 'a new basis for justifying and rationalising international rule that emerged at the beginning of the twenty-first century.'[21] I am making a parallel argument about human security. My point is that human security is about the shift from a war paradigm to a law paradigm within the international arena where law applies to individuals rather than states. This shift in the meaning and content of security is a precondition for a more authoritative form of global governance. However, that executive power will always be constrained and perhaps perverted without effective implementation.

Indeed, in the absence of effective implementation, human security could perhaps be interpreted as a form of securitisation, a sort of protection racket. The argument is made that failing states represent 'black holes' which attract and nurture criminality and extremism, thereby threatening the advanced industrial world. That is the argument made for intervention in Afghanistan. It is supposed to make our streets safer. Yet if it is the case that every attack by Western forces against the Taliban and Al Qaeda justifies the recruitment of more desperate young men, then intervention can be better understood as a sort of protection racket. An enemy is constructed that justifies continued attacks, helps to sustain military budgets and a narrative based on a 'we/them' distinction.

Western publics, however, are not convinced – hence the pressure to withdraw troops from Afghanistan. A more nuanced way of putting the securitisation argument is that policies relating to Responsibility to Protect or Human Security are ways that an unequal international order deals with growing human consciousness. It is no longer possible to ignore tragedies happening in different parts of the world. An emerging global civil society, what international relations theorists call the world system, represents the medium through which responses to individual suffering are agreed. However, it is a profoundly unequal global civil society dominated by Northern-based NGOs. The consequence is half-heartedness – just enough is done to satisfy domestic constituencies. Some form of global authority is being established but it lacks executive capabilities.

What this suggests is the necessary link between accountability and human security. Without more equal participation in global civil society it is very difficult to conceive of more effective efforts to implement human security. But without effective implementation the possibilities for broader participation are constrained. And vice versa. The construction of institutions proceeds through changing practice; the extent to which, say, relatively effective intervention takes place in somewhere like the Balkans, the more the responsible institutions, in this case the European Union, establish a degree of executive authority and, of course, part of that relative success may depend on membership in the EU. At the same time, of course, the failure to respond to the insecurity generated by widespread austerity undermines such a scenario.

Finally, it is worth noting the difference between terminologies. One reason for the distrust towards Responsibility to Protect is its top-down character. It refers to the responsibility of states or failing that, of the international community, to protect people from genocide, crimes against humanity or ethnic cleansing. Human security is about the right to be protected. To that extent it necessarily incorporates an element of empowerment, which in turn is a necessary condition for implementation.

Notes

1 Charles Tilly, 'War Making and State Making as Organized Crime,' *CRSO Working Paper 256*, University of Michigan, 1982.
2 Ole Waever, 'Politics, Security, Theory,' *Security Dialogue* 42: 465, 2011.
3 Point made by Jenny Pearce at ESRC seminar.

4 Mark Duffield, *Global Governance and the New Wars,* London: Zed Books, 2001.

5 Immanuel Kant, 'Perpetual Peace' (1795) in Hans Reiss (ed.), *Kant's Political Writing*, Cambridge: Cambridge University Press, 1992.

6 Carl Schmitt, *The Concept of the Political,* Chicago: University of Chicago Press, 1990, p. 33; first published in 1932 as *Der Begriff des Politischen.*

7 David Held, Anthony McGrew, David Goldbatt and Jonathan Perraton, *Global Transformations: Politics, Economics and Culture,* Cambridge: Polity Press, 1999.

8 I have elaborated the character of these wars in *New and Old Wars*, Cambridge: Polity Press, 1999.

9 Michael Walzer, *Arguing about War*, New Haven: Yale University Press, 2004, p. xiv. See also the chapter 'Governing the Globe' with six models of world order. My version is close to what he calls the 'third degree of pluralism'.

10 See Ian Clark, *Globalization and International Relations Theory*, Oxford: Oxford University Press, 1999.

11 See David Held, *The Global Covenant: The Social Democratic Alternative to the Washington Consensus,* Cambridge: Polity Press, 2004; Mary Kaldor, *Global Civil Society: An Answer to War,* Cambridge: Polity Press, 2003.

12 See http://www.sipri.org/research/conflict/pko/multilateral (accessed 15 May 2013).

13 Anne Orford, *International Authority and the Responsibility to Protect,* Cambridge: Cambridge University Press, 2011, p.17.

14 Marlies Glasius, *The ICC: A Global Civil Society Achievement,* Oxford: Routledge, 2006.

15 Iavor Rangelov and Ruti Teitel, 'Global Civil Society and Transitional Justice' in *Global Civil Society 2011: Globality and the Absence of Justice,* Basingstoke: Palgrave Macmillan, 2011.

16 Victoria Holt and Glyn Taylor, *Protecting Civilians in the Context of UN Peace-keeping Operations: An Independent Study Commissioned by the UN Office for the Coordination of Humanitarian Affairs (OCHA) and the UN Department of Peacekeeping Operations (DPKO),* 17 November 2009, p.8. Available online at: http://www.peacekeepingbestpractices.unlb.org/PBPS/Pages/Public/viewdocument.aspx?id=2&docid=1014 (accessed 15 May 2013).

17 See Herbert Wulf, 'The Challenges of Re-Establishing a Public Monopoly of Violence' in M. Glasius and M. Kaldor (eds), *A Human Security Doctrine for Europe: Project, Principles, Practicalities*, Oxford: Routledge, 2005.

18 Quoted in Peter Taylor, *The Brits: The War against the IRA,* London: Bloomsbury, 2001.

19 Peter Pringle and Philip Jacobson, *Those are Real Bullets, Aren't They?* London: Fourth Estate, 2000.

20 Fionnuala Ní Aoláin, *The Politics of Force: Conflict Management and State Violence in Northern Ireland*, Belfast: Blackstaff Press, 2000.

21 Orford, *International Authority and the Responsibility to Protect,* p. 1.

6

CRITICAL PERSPECTIVES ON HUMAN SECURITY

Keith Krause

Introduction[1]

The concept of 'human security' is the latest in a long series of attempts to challenge traditional state-centred conceptions of security. Aside from being the most recent attempt to reformulate or redefine the concept of security, the human security approach is significant because policy-makers in several states, international organizations, and non-governmental organizations (NGOs) have adopted the discourse of 'human security' and have used it to generate important and interesting foreign and security policy initiatives. Actors invoking the language of human security include the European Union, different subsidiary organs of the UN system (including UNDP and the UN Secretariat), states participating in the Human Security Network such as Canada, Norway and Switzerland, and other countries such as Sweden and Japan.

At first glance, scholars who advocate a broadly critical approach to security and security studies (Krause and Williams, 1996, 1997; Booth, 2004; Fierke, 2007; Peoples and Vaughan-Williams, 2010) might be expected to sing the praises of the concept of human security and to engage with (Christie, 2010) or work within what Edward Newman has called 'critical human security studies' (Newman, 2010). But although the emergence of a discourse and practice of human security is politically and intellectually important, there are a number of aspects of the human security debate that have been subject to critical scrutiny, both conceptually and practically. Four major lines of critique can be identified:

1   that the concept is 'normatively attractive, but theoretically weak', (Newman, 2010, 82), that it 'lacks a framework of analysis' (Floyd, 2007, 42), and that its lack of conceptual clarity renders it less useful as a guide to practical policy or action (Paris, 2001)
2   that there is a wide gap between the discourse of human security and the practices of states or international organizations (Muggah and Krause, 2006; Kaldor, Martin and Selchow, 2007; Matlary, 2008)
3   that the emancipatory and critical potential of the concept of human security has been captured and co-opted by states and other international actors, and has 'reinforced, rather than challenged, existing policy frameworks' (Chandler, 2008, 428; Christie, 2010; Browning and McDonald, 2011)

4 that the rhetoric of human security conceals less emancipatory practices of governmentality, biopolitics, intervention and control (Grayson, 2008; McCormack, 2008), including legitimizing the use of force such as in Libya in 2011, 'tak[ing] on the image of the velvet glove on the iron hand of hard power.' (Booth, 2007, 324).

This chapter will not delve deeply into these specific (and often theoretical) debates, but will provide an overview, from a critical perspective, of the emergence and practical or political significance of the concept of human security. It will attempt to answer the following questions:

a what factors contributed to the genesis and diffusion of the discourse of human security? Which states found the idea congenial, and why? What has been the role (if any) of non-governmental actors in promulgating the concept of human security?
b has the concept of human security given rise to innovative political practices, or does it represent little more than clever packaging of foreign policy initiatives based on narrow national interests?
c what are some of the tensions and paradoxes inherent in the concept of human security?

Although this chapter is more focused on the practice rather than the theory of human security, or on the stance critical scholarship should take towards human security (Christie, 2010), these questions also address important debates in contemporary International Relations. These include the role of ideas in constituting the interests and identities of actors, the link between discourses and practices, the transnational diffusion of ideas across states and between states and non-governmental actors, and the relationship between theory and practice in security studies. Ultimately this chapter aims to show that the concept of human security remains salient within the policy world, and that the concept has allowed for new issues to capture the attention of international organizations and states. Despite several confusions within and surrounding the notion of human security, the concept is a useful tool for understanding how certain multilateral responses to twenty-first-century security challenges have been crafted, framed and legitimized. Its critical potential, however, often remains immanent rather than actualized.

The discourse of human security

Articulation

The concept of 'human security' was first explicitly articulated in the 1994 report of the United Nations Development Programme (UNDP). Arguably, its roots are much deeper, and can be traced back to the nineteenth-century work of the International Committee of the Red Cross (ICRC) and 'the notion that people should be protected from violent threats and, when they are harmed or injured, [and] that the international community has an obligation to assist them' (Hampson et al., 2002, 17). But the UNDP's influential definition was much broader, and its version of human security included seven different dimensions: economic, food, health, environmental, personal, community and political security (United Nations Development Programme, 1994). The overall goal was to expand the concept of security, which had 'for too long been interpreted narrowly, as security of territory from external aggression, or as protection of national interests in foreign policy or as global security from the threat of nuclear holocaust.' Human security was thus meant to change the referent object of security 'from an exclusive stress on territorial security to a much greater stress on people's security', and to advocate for 'security through sustainable human development'.

This broad vision of human security was also reflected in the 2003 report of the Commission on Human Security, *Human Security Now*, which focused not just on situations of conflict, but also on issues of fair trade, access to health care, patient rights, access to education, and basic freedoms. A first critical observation is, however, that defining human security so expansively seemed to capture almost everything that could be considered a threat to well-being, falling into the trap that Daniel Deudney describes: 'if everything that causes a decline in human well-being is labelled a "security threat," the term loses any analytical usefulness and becomes a loose synonym of "bad"' (Deudney, 1990, 464; see also Owen, 2004; Newman, 2010). I will return to the definitional problems in human security below. For the moment, however, it is important to note that the context for the UNDP articulation of the concept was the desire to measure and capture the potential peace dividend at the end of the Cold War, and the more immediate attempt to influence the debate leading up to the 1995 Copenhagen social summit (UN Conference on Social Development).

Three other important features of this linking of security to development by the UNDP should be noted. First, it took place outside of the debate on 'new thinking on security', and (almost) completely outside of the traditional security establishment. Although some individuals involved in the 1994 edition of the UNDP *Human Development Report* were linked to security studies, the concept of human security did not develop in response to, or in dialogue with, the contributors to the debate on new thinking on security in the early 1990s.[2] The *Report* does refer to the narrow definition that links security to conflict and the state, but not to any of the other concepts that were floating around at the time (cooperative, common or societal security, for example).[3] As a first critical observation, this counters the arguments of those scholars who argue that theories and concepts in International Relations motivate, animate or influence the discourse and practice of actors in the 'real world'. The tendency in recent security studies scholarship to treat its theoretical debates as somehow significant for political practice reflects a weak (and perhaps rather self-important) understanding of the role of ideas in political life which the human security debate can help illuminate (Eriksson, 1999).

Second, and as well documented by Neil MacFarlane and Yuen Foong Khong (2006), the concept emerged neither in the non-governmental community, nor in a state, but in international organizations. As they note, at different points in the 1990s, key actors in the UN system (notably within UNDP and the Secretariat) embraced the basic ideas of human security, and used them to launch new policy or programmatic initiatives (UN Secretary-General, 2010). This is consistent with the views of many scholars who observe that new norms and ideas, whatever their genesis (in the expert or non-governmental community, in particular), require not only a 'norm entrepreneur' but also an institutional platform in order to be promoted effectively at the global level (Finnemore, 1996; Finnemore and Sikkink, 1998). Much of this literature has focused on issues connected with human rights or environmentalism, however, and has concentrated more on the interaction between external *sources* of ideas and institutional platforms, and less on the potential role of international organizations themselves as a source (and advocate) for new ideas (see, for example, Klotz, 1995; Litfin, 1994; Risse et al., 1999; Price, 1997; Economy and Schreurs, 1997). The articulation of human security within the UNDP represents a potentially interesting example of conceptual innovation *within an international organization* that also challenges those (mainly realists or liberal institutionalists) who argue that international organizations have only limited autonomy or potential for innovation. The rise of the concept of human security shows that international organizations are not only able to 'think for themselves', but have also adapted to the changing global security environment to promote an understanding of the state – and its sovereignty – that makes it responsible for providing security to its citizens.[4] In turn, international organizations become seen as authoritative actors beyond the state that are charged not only with identifying existential threats to individuals (Floyd, 2007: 42), but also with the socialization and the disciplining of states with regard to these threats (Owens, 2011: 3).

Third, the UNDP report effectively reopened the debate about the link between 'security' and 'development' that had been closed since the somewhat sterile polemic around the link between disarmament and development that was conducted in the 1970s and 1980s. The general thrust of this earlier Cold War debate was that the North (i.e.: both sides of the East–West conflict) should disarm, and devote the resources freed up by arms reduction to development in the South. The linking of security and development in the 1994 *Human Development Report* is, however, more nuanced, and argues that security is a pre-condition (or co-condition) for successful social, economic, and political development. More importantly, the concept of human security takes the focus off state-centred security concerns, and draws attention to the ways in which all states are responsible, to varying degrees, for the human security of their citizens. Much effort has been invested subsequently in the development community to explore the practical links between security and development, and the task has proven difficult (Krause, 2013).

Some have even argued that reinforcing the link between security and development is not necessarily a good thing, and that in the contemporary geopolitical environment it represents a new form of suppression and domination of the countries in the global South (Duffield, 2007). Whatever the reality, however, it remains the case that the concept of human security was initially articulated to serve the needs and interests of some actors in the *international development community* in their dealings with countries of the South, and not to redefine security for foreign and defence policy establishments in the North. As Taylor Owen argues, even though there are areas in the developed world that have human security problems (such as indigenous communities, and even some inner city neighbourhoods) the fact that human security threats are most evident in the developing world is an empirical reality (Owen, 2008). Southern resistance to the concept, which most often represents the reaction of state elites and regimes to the possible international oversight of their (putative) sovereign prerogatives, should not, therefore, be surprising.

Diffusion

The importance of a new idea lies not in its articulation, but in whether or not (and why) it is taken up and diffused widely by different actors in world politics, in whether it affects their *practices*, and in whether new ideas empower (constitute) or disempower new actors or constellations of actors. This first step marks only an opening towards a critical evaluation of the concept of human security by asking whether or not an idea was taken up as a discursive theme by a variety of actors, and whether or not it served to *reframe* an issue or debate in order to make particular problems, issues or solutions more prominent.

Measuring the spread and impact of a new idea is, however, an extremely complex enterprise. Should one examine quantitative indicators (the number of times a concept is mentioned by different actors)? Does one have to examine whether actors mean the same thing when they use the concept (and how does one do this)? How can one evaluate the relative importance of the actors who are speaking and practising human security? Obviously, at least some minimal combination of all of the above would be desirable, but within this chapter I cannot present a systematic assessment of the diffusion of the concept of human security. Instead, I can here only briefly trace the way in which human security has been taken up by a variety of non-governmental and international actors, parallel with or prior to its influence on state policies.

First, one should ask why the UNDP articulated a concept of human security, and what interests or purposes were served by the concept. A principal aim of the 1994 UNDP *Human Development Report* was to influence the policies of states in the preparatory phase of the 1995 UN Conference on Social Development (Copenhagen), and a broader goal was to reconceptualise the linkages between development and security. The discourse of human security was thus throughout 1994 and 1995 promoted by several NGOs as a core principle that should be enshrined in the Programme of Action of the 1995 conference, and mentioned in the opening statement of the Conference President. Ultimately, however, reference to human security was dropped from both the Copenhagen Declaration on Social Development, and the Programme of Action of the World Summit for Social Development. The reasons are unclear, but the chairman of the preparatory committee, the Chilean Ambassador to the United Nations, Juan Somavia, declared at an NGO meeting that the concept was dropped to avoid complicating the debate with concepts on which there was no agreement.[5]

But the failure to secure a specific mention of human security in the Copenhagen social summit should not obscure the broader reframing of the discourse of security and development that the concept of human security was catalysing. An illustration of this would be the extensive focus throughout the past decade on 'security sector reform' by major aid donors and international financial institutions, especially in post-conflict contexts.[6] Security sector reform (SSR) initiatives, often justified as promoting human security, include such things as police training, military reform, civilian oversight of the armed forces, and violence prevention and reduction programmes. These domains touch upon the core security concerns of states and ruling elites, and reach deep into the heart of the power structures of fragile and conflict-affected states in ways that are profoundly interventionist (Sedra, 2010).

Such efforts marked a revolution in thinking in the international development community. Throughout the Cold War, debates on how to achieve development were effectively insulated (with some exceptions) from any considerations of security issues, for basically three reasons. First, security policy was deemed an issue of national sovereignty, and thus matters such as defence or military spending were outside of the scrutiny of aid donors or international financial institutions. Second, security policies were often caught up in Cold War conflicts and alliances, and thus a taboo subject for development agencies or institutions. Third, external scrutiny of a state's policies and practices towards its own citizens was deemed to be interference in the internal affairs of a state. Thus development policy concentrated on policy issues such as education, poverty eradication, infrastructure investment, and so forth, while one primary responsibility of a state – the need to ensure the physical security of its citizens – was effectively outside of scrutiny. The result, not surprisingly, was that development efforts were often wasted in states and regions facing endemic insecurities and conflicts. With the rise in attention to intra-state and communal conflicts in the 1990s, it was almost inevitable therefore that the link between development and security should be re-examined. Many major international development actors and agencies, including the World Bank, the OECD, the UK Department for International Development (DFID); the US Agency for International Development (USAID), the Swedish International Development Agency (SIDA), the German Development Institute and others, adopted specific policies to deal with work in conflict-affected or fragile states (Krause, 2013; Klingebiel, 2006) that focused explicitly on the way in which a state provided security and public order for its citizens.

Although little of this work explicitly used the term human security, its programmatic goals were clearly part of its underlying logic. It is also not difficult to find extensive references to the concept of human security in the period since 1994. A nearly-random list of non-governmental or international organizations that have used or promoted the concept of human security (directly or by implicit definition) would include: Oxfam UK, the UN High Commission on Refugees, the Academic Council on the UN System, the UN University, the Arias Foundation, the Worldwatch Institute, the Commission on Global Governance, the Carnegie Commission on Preventing Deadly Conflict, the International Action Network on Small Arms, Pax Christi, the Secretary-General of the United Nations, the Human Security Commission, the Barcelona Report of the Study Group on Europe's Security Capabilities, and so on. Several university-based research centres or study programmes on human security have been established (at the University of British Columbia – now at Simon Fraser University, at the Fletcher School of Law and Diplomacy, at the Ford Institute, University of Pittsburgh, at Tohoku University in Japan and (a short-lived project) at Sciences Po in Paris); a regular *Human Security Report* has been published (*Human Security Report, 2005*, with follow-on publications); and a major international commission also published a report in 2003 (*Human Security Now*). And human security received a specific subheading and reference in the 2005 United Nations World Summit final document, a significant achievement in multilateral terms.

The uses these actors made of the concept was varied, but the unifying theme was the need to frame and evaluate the policy responses of the international community to contemporary challenges in terms of their ability to provide 'freedom from fear' and/or 'freedom from want'. As the World Summit document noted (paragraph 143):

> We stress the right of people to live in freedom and dignity, free from poverty and despair. We recognize that all individuals, in particular vulnerable people, are entitled to freedom from fear and freedom from want, with an equal opportunity to enjoy all their rights and fully develop their human potential. To this end, we commit ourselves to discussing and defining the notion of human security in the General Assembly.

As I will discuss below, these two phrases co-existed rather uncomfortably, and there has been no real definitional consensus on the term since the UNDP 1994 definition.

One can also demonstrate in a crude but clear way the diffusion of the concept of human security by searching for references to it in major news media or Google hits. Using the LexisNexis database for the period from January 1991 to September 2012, Table 6.1 shows the pattern of relatively steadily increasing citations or uses of the phrase 'human security'.

The LexisNexis results are mirrored by Google searches (narrowed by year), which expand exponentially in the past decade.[8] Google scholar citations follow a similar pattern.[9] Although these figures do not indicate anything about the identity of the interlocutors, or the use to which they are putting the concept, it does illustrate clearly that the discourse of human security becomes salient around the time of the UNDP *Human Development Report*, advanced in a more prominent fashion in 1998–1999, coincident with the launching of the Human Security Network (discussed below), took additional 'leaps' in 2003 (the year of publication of the Commission report *Human Security Now*, and the year the European Union officially adopted the human security agenda as a guiding principle in its Foreign Policy) and in 2005 (the year the *Human Security Report* was published), and dramatically increased again in 2007. What this indicates is that despite the claim of some individuals in academia and the policy field that human security is 'dead,' it is clear that the concept has emerged and been widely accepted as one of the key ways of framing and describing the insecurities individuals face both domestically and internationally.

Table 8.1 Use of the phrase 'human security,' by year

Year	Lexis Nexis	Google Search
1991	3	
1992	6	
1993	19	
1994	115	
1995	104	
1996	57	
1997	142	
1998	254	
1999	712	
2000	947	
2001	668	
2002	765	
2003	1047	5,120
2004	1089	7,050
2005	1598	10,100
2006	1649	12,900
2007	2510	18,700
2008	2056	31,000
2009	2195	41,500
2010	2584	56,600
2011	1928	96,300
2012	1316	95,500[7]

The practice of human security

Elaboration

Human security had received a concrete formulation and had begun to circulate widely in non-governmental and international circles by 1997, before (or simultaneous with) it being taken up as a major plank of foreign policy by several states. It is at this point that *practices* re-enter the picture, since from a critical perspective, the influence of an idea is ultimately not measured by the discourse alone. Ideas themselves do not change the world; rather, a concept must in some significant way inform and be linked to particular practices in such a way that new initiatives are undertaken, new modes of acting are developed, and new actors or coalitions of actors are empowered.

The conceptual link between discourses and practices is, however, not straightforward. On some accounts (Bigo, 2011; Pouliot, 2008), and following Pierre Bourdieu, practices emerge out of an almost unconscious internalization of particular norms or ideas in the 'habitus'. Others see the norms as publicly and explicitly articulated and generating particular guides to action as sort of 'best practices' or standards to meet (Navari, 2011). I am using the link between discourses and practices in this second sense, given the clear articulation of human security as a set of norms containing implicit or explicit guides to practice. But matters are still not so simple: to begin, many of the specific practices that are associated with human security – in particular coordinated multilateral action to deal with the problem of anti-personnel land mines, initiatives concerning child soldiers, and the protection of civilians in conflicts – pre-date the elaboration and adoption of the human security discourse. The International Campaign to Ban Landmines (ICBL), for example, was created in 1992, building on existing initiatives by a range of non-governmental organizations. Governments began paying attention to the issue in 1992–1993, originally in conjunction with the review of the Certain Conventional Weapons (CCW) Convention, which was called for by the French in 1993 and held in 1996. Only in 1994–1995 did some states start to accept the idea of a total ban on anti-personnel landmines, and only *after* the successful conclusion of the Ottawa Treaty in 1997 was the entire exercise labelled as an effort to promote human security (see Cameron, 1998; Price, 1998).

Perhaps this is not surprising. Historically, even the constitutive concepts of international relations (such as sovereignty, or key aspects of international law and diplomacy, etc.) emerged as a result of state practices, and the slow crystallization of awareness that a new form of practice was emerging that required a specific label. There is no doubt that sovereignty emerged in this way (Holzgrefe, 1989; Mattingly, 1955). This does *not*, however, mean that the discursive crystallization of a concept is 'mere words', a sort of afterthought or political slogan with no consequences. Rather, once states (and more importantly, bureaucrats within foreign policy apparatuses) come to regard 'human security' as an appropriate label for what they are already doing, the discourse has triumphed.

Beyond noting that 'human security' has become a label to describe significant aspects of the foreign policies of several states and most recently of the EU, one should ask whether or not what states or international organizations 'are doing' today departs from conventional policies and ways of operating of ten or twenty years ago. Here it is possible to demonstrate that the human security discourse *has* captured something novel, that a whole range of issues that would have been low on the agenda of international action now gain high-level policy attention, and that this has had concrete or programmatic consequences. One of the best multilateral examples of this would be the UN operations in Haiti, one of which (UNMIH) was launched in 1993, before the human security language took root, the second of which (MINUSTAH) was launched after (in 2003). One can find clear and practical differences in the way in which the mandate of the operation was framed and undertaken, which reflected the incorporation of human security considerations (such as disarmament, demobilization and reintegration (DDR), and police reform) into the operational practices and programmes of UN actors and agencies (Muggah and Krause, 2006). Similar points could be made about particular aspects of UN peace operations (such as in the Eastern Congo, or Liberia) that place civilians or vulnerable groups at the centre of their concerns, the engagement of states in Timor Leste (Hataley and Nossal, 2004), or the efforts to implement UN Security Council Resolution 1325 on women and peacebuilding (Tryggestad, 2009; *International Feminist Journal of Politics*, 2011).

Most of the practical or policy initiatives that have been associated with the human security agenda have, however, generally adopted a much narrower understanding of human security than the broadest one promoted by the UNDP or the Commission on Human Security. The human security agenda, as pursued by the Human Security Network (HSN) or within the UN system, for example, has generally concentrated on 'freedom from fear': on securing individuals from the threat of violence, especially in conflict and post-conflict environments. This has meant active promotion of the 'civilian protection agenda' (including the emphasis on women in conflict), initiatives to stem the proliferation and misuse of small arms and light weapons, the problem of child soldiers (and children in armed conflict), 'conflict goods' (regulating the trade in such things as diamonds or tropical timber), the establishment of the International Criminal Court, and the enhancement of post-conflict reconstruction and peacebuilding. In all of these areas, new coalitions of states, and of states and non-governmental organizations, have emerged, and have consciously labelled their activities as the promotion of human security (Krause, 2008).

Many of the problems that would come under the UNDP or Human Security Commission understanding of human security have thus fallen by the wayside (for example, health or food security), and the idea of human security has in practical terms narrowed to focus on problems associated with the threat and consequences of organized violence and conflict, at all levels of political, social and economic life. While still broader than the traditional understanding of security (inter-state military conflict), this is still considerably narrower than the UNDP formulation.

This narrowing to focus on 'freedom from fear' and issues related to organized violence is not accidental, because there are particular institutional or political interests *within* states and their foreign policy bureaucracies that would support or promote a more narrow vision of human security (as opposed to the UNDP or Human Security Commission vision). The principal actors translating the security agenda into state policies have not been associated with development agencies, or with human rights work (with some exceptions), but with the foreign policy bureaucracies, including divisions concerned with multilateral relations and the UN, arms control and disarmament, peacekeeping and peacebuilding, and so forth.[10] In many cases, the policy communities associated with these issues have been in transition or even crisis, as their traditional agenda (arms control, for example, or peacekeeping) has either been stalemated, rendered obsolete, or overwhelmed by new problems and issues. Yet the core focus – ameliorating conflicts and enhancing security – remains central to their understanding of their mission. An excellent example of this was provided by a February 1999 'Retreat on Human Security' convened by Canada and Norway, to flesh out the conceptualization of human security that they wished to promote in light of the upcoming meeting of what would become the Human Security Network.[11] Human security was positioned with respect to state security, human rights, and human development. Naturally, it was deemed to be different than each of these three, with the inevitable consequence that those aspects of the UNDP definition that fell in traditional human rights or development areas (e.g.: food security, health security) were considered marginal to the human security agenda.

This is not necessarily a bad thing. Without diminishing the importance of potentially existential issues such as environmental degradation or food and health security, historically the idea of security has been inextricably intertwined with the struggle to control the institutions and instruments of organized violence. This has been central to the emergence of the modern state, and its conception of representative political institutions, civil society and civil–military relations. The successful evacuation of violence from the public sphere is, in many respects, a pre-condition for modern politics. What this implies for the discourse and practice of human security is that it is part and parcel of the ongoing global extension of the logic of the Westphalian system. Parenthetically, the arguments about the 'third wave of democratization' and 'good governance' can also been seen in the same light. The policy objectives of the narrow conception of human security are then a sort of 'negative' focus on the fragilities, failures and pathologies of the Westphalian state, which in the post-colonial period witnessed the emergence of juridical states that had little or no empirical foundations in the territories over which they claimed to rule (Jackson, 1993; Barnett, 1995).

Focusing specifically on institutions of organized violence, the most significant feature of the insertion of post-colonial states into the Westphalian system has been the way in which modern ideas, institutions and instruments of organized violence were transmitted from the North to the South. In many cases, this diffusion of modern military technologies and techniques of organization to post-colonial states resulted in the institutions of organized violence being the only remotely 'modern' institutions in newly emerging states. Yet security forces did not, as early modernization theorists had hoped, play a positive role as an integrative force in fragmented societies, were not a vehicle for the diffusion of modern ideas of development, and did not play a positive political role (e.g.: in promoting respect for human rights and rule of law). Instead, they represented a tremendous reservoir of political power that was often captured by particular groups, and used to impose a particular (and often violent) order on civil and political life. The transplantation of unprecedented means of institutionalized violence and surveillance into political arenas that were empty of the countervailing checks and balances that developed over several centuries in modern European states produced some of the worst forms of political violence in the twentieth century. The practice of human security represents, in particular its emphasis on reforms of the security sector (Sedra, 2010), an attempt to cope with these pathological results by embedding security institutions within a 'modern' language of democratic accountability, transparency, oversight and provision of public goods that is intimately linked to the security concerns of people and their communities.

Institutionalization

The next test of the durability of an idea comes when major actors go beyond the use of a concept to formulate new interests (policy agendas), to the point where it becomes (or not) part of the foreign policy identity of the actors themselves. Questions of 'identity' in international relations are much discussed but seldom studied, and scholars have only now started to come to grips with what it means to attribute an identity to a state or its foreign policy. One important *social* aspect of identity that is relevant for the practice of human security is that one's identity strongly influences with whom one 'feels comfortable' or trusts, with whom one 'can do business' and the kinds of partnerships and activities that can be undertaken. The sole superpower in a unipolar world, for example, can hardly enter equal partnerships with other states without in some way denying what it means to be a superpower.[12] Not surprisingly then, the discourse of human security was monopolized by so-called middle powers or by states promoting a 'soft power' approach to world politics. These included, most prominently, Canada, Norway, Switzerland, Japan, the Netherlands, and Austria. Countless speeches and statements by Foreign Ministers or senior officials testify to the shift in foreign policy that the human security doctrine represented for these states (see Gervais and Roussel, 1998; Behringer, 2005; Edström, 2005).

Perhaps the most important institutional development was formalization of the discourse and practice of human security through the Human Security Network (HSN), which lasted roughly from 1999 until 2009 (when it appears the last ministerial-level meeting was held). This network, which emerged out of a Canada–Norwegian partnership, had 14 participating states, including Switzerland, Jordan, Thailand, Austria, Chile, Slovenia, Mali, Chile, Greece, Ireland, Costa Rica and South Africa (as an observer). They met annually at the Foreign Minister level, and agreed to pursue coordinated initiatives in a variety of formal and informal ways, as a means to influence the international security agenda. The first Ministerial meeting of the HSN, held in May 1999, invoked both 'freedom from fear' and 'freedom from want' understandings of human security, but the subsequent list of policy initiatives or programmatic objectives has mainly reflected an orientation towards the narrow vision of 'freedom from fear'. Over the next decade, the HSN promoted a wide array of initiatives focusing on core topics such as small arms, children in armed conflict, landmines, non-state armed groups, and public security. The agenda was not entirely dominated by 'freedom from fear' concerns though, since issues such as the impact of the HIV/AIDS pandemic on human security, human rights education, climate change and the link between 'security and development' were also discussed. Although many states and international organizations are active in these issue areas, one can say that the HSN network states acted somewhat as agenda-setters in such areas as the proliferation and misuse of small arms and light weapons, conflict goods or child soldiers. The concrete policy activities of the HSN were also only one part of a broader tapestry of initiatives that have been pursued multilaterally over the past decade to promote human security. These initiatives included the Canadian-sponsored International Commission on Intervention and State Sovereignty (*Responsibility to Protect*), support for the publication of the first *Human Security Report* (2005), and the promotion of the human security agenda within the UN.

This partial institutionalization of the human security agenda gives rise to the question of whether or not this collaborative pursuit of common policies can go beyond the narrow pursuit of common interests to implicate a new – and durable – foreign policy identity for these states. Such durable shifts – when (re)definitions of interests become internalized as part of foreign policy identities – are not easy to assess. On a rationalist account, relatively fixed identities *determine* interests in a strong sense, denying any possibility for changing understanding of interests to shape states' identities (or even for interests to change, within a narrow band). On the critical/constructivist account followed here, identity and interests are co-constituted, and interactions with other actors can lead over time to these interests potentially becoming internalized or socialized as part of a slowly shifting identity (McSweeney, 1999).

The verdict to date on human security is mixed. At the outset, the Network was an outgrowth of the informal group of states that had worked together successfully in the Ottawa process on anti-personnel land mines.[13] They had discovered a lucrative set of niche foreign policy issues with strong domestic political resonance, and had an opportunity to champion a 'new diplomacy' that enhanced their roles on the world stage. More importantly, the adoption of human security language can be seen as an adaptive strategy to a foreign policy 'identity crisis' for some of the members of the network. Canada, Norway and Switzerland are outside of the EU, Switzerland is a member of very few multilateral arrangements, and countries like Jordan, Chile or Thailand all struggled to enhance their profile vis-à-vis larger regional neighbours. The same may be true for several other states in the network, at least in the sense that their foreign ministers perceived a short-term advantage to be gained from breaking with traditional patterns of diplomacy. If it were nothing more than this, the Human Security Network would not have been much of an innovation in multilateral diplomacy. It would have been the expected response of relatively weak states to their position in the international system, and remained entirely consistent with their traditional concentration on humanitarian issues.

In addition, some states, such as Canada, that once were strong proponents of the human security agenda, have stepped away from it, despite claims that the promotion of human security was consistent with Canada's longer-term international identity (the Netherlands also left the HSN in 2007). Since the current Canadian government took office in 2006, 'political staffers have worked to purge the language of the previous Liberal government's much lauded "human security" policies from the DFAIT lexicon' (Davis, 2009; Bookmiller and Nakjavani Bookmiller, 2010). Not only has the term 'human security' been black-listed (Martin and Owen, 2010: 211) from working language of politicians and the governmental websites, but key programmes and divisions have also been renamed in order to eliminate the concept from Canada's collective foreign policy memory. The 'Human Security Policy Division' has been re-branded as the 'Human Rights and Democracy Bureau', and the 'Human Security Program' has been renamed to the 'Glyn Berry Program' (after a Canadian diplomat killed in Afghanistan). While the Program still claims to support 'the development of Canadian and international policies, laws and institutions that seek to promote the protection of individuals from violence and armed conflict,' it makes no explicit mention of the concept of 'human security' (DFAIT: Glyn Berry Program).

But this sort of account does not explain the rather stronger commitment to, and internalization of, the specific *content* of human security by the network of actors active on these issues (as distinct from the formal 'Human Security Network'). This looser form of institutionalization has successfully raised the profile of human security issues on the international agenda and become a consistent part of the foreign policy agenda for many states and international actors, as demonstrated convincingly by Charli Carpenter's network mapping (Carpenter et al., 2011). Norway's pursuit of the broad agenda of 'humanitarian disarmament' (the international campaign against cluster munitions, spearheaded by Norway, being perhaps the most recent example) illustrates such a shift from single-issue human security policies to a broader conceptualization that has gained greater traction multilaterally. The renaming of an entire (prominent, and well-funded) division of the Swiss Foreign Ministry the 'Human Security Division' also reflects more than the aggregation of particular issues or campaigns, and suggests at least that it is regarded as a durable aspect of Switzerland's foreign policy *identity*. In addition, some members of the network have been active in spreading issues that are a substantive part of the concept of human security beyond the confines of the group and in a variety of multilateral forums, implying that these states have internalized the substantive commitments of human security even if some of them no longer refer to it explicitly. An excellent example of this is the 'responsibility to protect' agenda (ICISS, 2001; Bellamy, 2009), which ultimately expands the responsibilities states have to prevent the suffering of others. Although this may not lead to the development of a common or collective identity among a particular group of states, the lesser claim – that several states have internalized human security concerns into their own foreign policy identities – can be demonstrated.[14] Similarly, the embedding of the concept of human security within the United Nations, and in particular the follow-up to the 2005 World Summit Outcome, has involved the Secretary-General presenting a report to the General Assembly on 'Human Security' (UN Secretary-General, 2010), and the General Assembly itself voting on a resolution that presented a common understanding of human security, including both freedom from fear and freedom from want (and excluding responsibility to protect!), and placing emphasis on the importance of human security in promoting sustainable development (UN General Assembly, 2012).

Finally, the most important aspect of the institutionalization of human security is probably not the network of states, but the new multilateralism that they claim to practice. This involves developing close working partnerships with non-governmental actors, an emphasis on the role of civil society, and a willingness to work outside established diplomatic (including UN) channels (Krause, 2008; Carpenter et al., 2011). In its pure form, this would represent a democratization of foreign policy. Seldom, however, is the pure form realized. Not only do some states practice the new multilateralism better than others, but individuals in foreign policy bureaucracies differ widely in their responsiveness to non-governmental actors and civil society concerns.

Conclusion: some paradoxes of human security

The use of the concept of human security by states and decision-makers is not a trivial matter of labelling, and it leads states and policy-makers to focus on different issues, to ask different questions, and even to promote different policies. Although these developments have had a positive impact on the contemporary international security agenda, this does not make the concept of human security immune from critical scrutiny.

Somewhat paradoxically, much of the conceptualization of human security, and the elaboration of concrete policy initiatives, have emerged from states and international organizations, rather than from civil society, and it is currently a state-centred discourse. This poses two problems. The first is the inevitable systemic and competitive pressures that states face, which lead them to revert to more traditional foreign and security policy stances when they are perceived as 'getting too far ahead' of the broader international community. Within every foreign policy bureaucracy there exist 'traditionalists' alongside the 'policy entrepreneurs' and the balance shifts between them, depending on the perceived advantages and disadvantages that either approach gives to the state (or its Minister of Foreign Affairs). This sort of bureaucratic pulling and hauling is not surprising, but it can be a long way from the real concerns of human security. Certainly the post-2001 international climate and the 'war on terror' have reinforced the weight of traditionalists in many foreign policy bureaucracies.

The second problem relates to the role of civil society and non-state actors in the practice of human security. In order for human security to be realized, individuals have to be empowered to take control of their environment and to become active participants in the political, economic and social processes that affect them. Yet associating a number of prominent Western scholars or NGOs with the idea of human security, and soliciting their input on a variety of policy questions, does not in itself advance this bottom-up process of social change. Obviously, a more inclusive dialogue between states and civil society is desirable, but in the realm of human security, as in so many other realms, the new multilateralism does not penetrate very deeply, nor are non-governmental actors equal contributors or partners. It is still the case that the people to whom 'freedom from fear' matters are mostly passive subjects in the human security discourse.

The agenda of human security also remains somewhat of a 'donor-driven' process. With only a few exceptions, key human security issues have not been taken up in the domestic political debates of HSN participating states, for example. Similarly, in the study group's *A Human Security Doctrine for Europe* (Barcelona Study Group, 2004; see also Glasius and Kaldor, 2005; Debiel and Werthes, 2006), the promotion of human security was treated as the outward projection of European policies and values onto the international stage. European security would be ensured by promotion of human security abroad, and promoting human security had little if anything to do with domestic European political practice. Most of the activities that attempt to develop the human security concerns of states in the global South have been undertaken through the work of the UNESCO in various regional forums and conferences. Conferences held in Latin America, East Asia, the Middle East and Southern Africa brought together a wide range of scholars to debate and discuss the meaning and relevance of human security for their regions, and their perceptions do not accord easily with the 'freedom from fear versus freedom from want' debate through which much of the debate on human security has been framed (Chourou, 2005; Fuentes and Aravena, 2005; Lee, 2004; Goucha and Cilliers, 2001). These efforts have not, however, been mainstreamed into the broader discourse and practice of human security.

A third critical observation concerns the relationship between human security and sovereignty (non-intervention); and the relationship between individuals and the state in the human security discourse. The promotion of human security is one part of a wider reconceptualization of sovereignty that is underway in contemporary world politics, and while the doctrine of absolute sovereignty and the right to non-interference in domestic affairs has led to some of the most flagrant abuses of human rights and countless humanitarian tragedies, it is not true that all evils will be banished if a generalized right of humanitarian intervention or a responsibility to protect (multilateral or otherwise) is recognized. The selective pursuit of particular issues on the human security agenda – child soldiers, but not military spending; the illicit trafficking in small arms, but not the 'legal' trade or existing state stockpiles – only highlights the dilemmas involved in promoting a people-centred concept of security in a world in which states make the ultimate choices over priorities.

Finally, almost all human security policy initiatives (especially concerning such things as security sector reform or post-conflict reconstruction and rehabilitation) imply strengthening the role and resources of the state. Yet the state has been rightly regarded as part of the problem in the humanitarian and development communities, since states (or rather, the ruling elites) have been responsible for squandering resources, neglecting infrastructures, oppressing or killing citizens, or simply failing to provide minimal security for society. Accepting a policy agenda that has as its ultimate goal the strengthening of the state is thus an ethically problematic position. Disarming the weak without controlling the strong, for example, will not enhance human security in the long run, and may actually exacerbate the situation for many people. Conversely, encouraging security sector reform, economic liberalization, structural adjustment, or lower military spending may actually leave a state prey to lawlessness and anarchy. Perhaps ultimately there are no alternatives to the construction of legitimate and strong states, but from a critical perspective on human security, this normative issue should at least be posed.

Ultimately, promoting an agenda of human security does draw our attention to a number of essential contemporary security challenges. It goes beyond the traditional conflict prevention or conflict resolution agenda, and leads policy-makers to ask some basic questions about how to make people safe and secure in their daily lives. It also shines a spotlight on the links between violence and insecurity, and underdevelopment and poverty, and can help give new direction to the development community. For political actors and activists, human security is also an excellent mobilizing slogan. It generates a coherent set of policy issues, including the problems of post-conflict disarmament and reintegration, the situation of vulnerable groups in conflicts, the problem of armed violence in both war and non-war situations, and the effective and legitimate functioning of the institutions that we have built to provide security and safety in the modern state. In this sense, the contemporary promotion of human security is the culmination of the liberal project of building strong, legitimate and representative political institutions, and has deep roots in enlightenment ideas of individual rights and personal freedoms. This 'liberal bias' manifestly does not make human security stand on its own as a 'critical' political project (Christie, 2010). But as Patricia Owens has argued, today's world of security practices is going through a transformation that blurs the boundaries between public and private, and in which the identification of threats and protection of individual life is no longer the sole prerogative of political institutions associated with the state (Owens, 2011). In such an environment the concept of human security may yet play a critical role in putting the preservation of life at the centre of political analysis and national and international policy.

Notes

1 This chapter is a revised and updated version of 'Critical Perspectives on Human Security,' (in German) in Cornelia Ulbert and Sascha Werthes, eds, *Menschliche Sicherheit: Globale Herausforderungen und regionale Perspektiven* (Baden Baden: Nomos: 2008), 31–50. Thanks to Savannah de Tessières and Jovana Carapic for their assistance in revising and updating the original chapter.

2 The main scholars appear to have been Herbert Wulf (formerly director of the arms trade project at SIPRI, and founding director of the Bonn International Center for Conversion) and Ed Laurance (Monterey Institute, California). For an overview of the various early contributions to the new thinking on security debate, see the special issue of the journal *Arms Control*, 13:1 (April 1992).

3 One exception would be the reference to environmental security, but even here, the UNDP concept did not distinguish between the mainstream work on 'environmental change and conflict' and the more 'ecologically-oriented' contributions.

4 This obviously involves not only the idea of 'responsibility to protect' (R2P), about which a vast amount has been written, but also other multilateral practices such as security sector reform and post-conflict peacebuilding. R2P was a clear offshoot of the human security agenda (ICISS, 2001; Bellamy, 2009).

5 Statement by Juan Somavia to a press conference after the social summit prepcom in New York, as reported in *Econews Africa*, 3:18 (29 September 1994). This is from a paraphrase, not a transcript, and hence I have not used quotation marks.

6 Security sector reform has been the focus of numerous efforts, including that of the British Department for International Development (DFID), the UNDP, the Organization for Economic Cooperation and Development (OECD) and the World Bank. See Krause, 2013.

7 We searched the Lexis-Nexis 'all news – all languages' file. It captures some references to 'human security' that are not related to the topic, but the distribution is likely random over time (perhaps even over-represented in earlier years). Parenthetically, the first international relations mention of 'human security' is a statement by John Kenneth Galbraith, in a 1982 criticism of then-Defence Secretary Caspar W. Weinberger. The first state apparently to use the phrase was Poland – in a letter to the UN Secretary-General in 1984! The first use within an international organizational context was at the UN conference on the decade for women in Nairobi in 1985. Note that for 2012 the search covers only 1 January–30 September.

8 Google citations are unreliable for earlier time periods since they capture more recent citations. It is also possible that the increase in recent years included repeated references to earlier citations. But the trend line is clear.

9 2005–2006: 6,320; 2006–2007: 7,440; 2007–2008: 8,850; 2008–2009: 10,300; 2009–2010: 10,900; 2010–2011: 11,000; 2011–2012: 9,170.

10 This claim can be substantiated for the Canadian, Norwegian, Austrian, Dutch and Swiss cases, but by contrast, it does not apply in the Irish case. I am less sure about other states that have adopted the human security discourse.

11 I was a participant in this retreat. The main author within the Canadian Department of Foreign Affairs was Don Hubert (now a professor at the University of Ottawa).

12 Of course, the creation of NATO and American engagement in several other multilateral arrangements after 1945 were just that, but it is difficult to imagine such developments today, as the American debates over the International Criminal Court, Kyoto Protocol, Ottawa Treaty or the war in Iraq so well illustrated.

13 Canada provided the impetus for the rapid negotiation of the treaty; Austria provided the first draft, Oslo provided the conference venue, and Switzerland, both diplomatically and through the ICRC, was an important hub of pre- and post-treaty activity (with the International Center on Humanitarian Demining).

14 For example, only one of the HSN states – the Netherlands – publicly supported the US-led invasion of Iraq.

Bibliography

The Barcelona Report of the Study Group on Europe's Security Capabilities (2004) *A Human Security Doctrine for Europe*, Barcelona.

Barnett, M. (1995) 'The New UN Politics of Peace: From Juridical Sovereignty to Empirical Sovereignty', *Global Governance*, 1(1): 79–98.

Behringer, R. (2005) 'Middle Power Leadership on the Human Security Agenda', *Cooperation and Conflict*, 40(3): 305–342.

Bellamy, A. (2009) *Responsibility to Protect*, London: Polity.

Bigo, D. (2011) 'Pierre Bourdieu and International Relations: Power of Practices, Practices of Power', *International Political Sociology*, 5(3): 225–258.

Bookmiller, R., Nakjavani Bookmiller, K. (2010) 'Canada and the Human Security Network (1998–2010): RIP?' *British Journal of Canadian Studies*, 23(2): 247–271.

Booth, K. (ed.) (2004) *Critical Security Studies and World Politics*, Boulder: Lynne Rienner.

Booth, K. (ed.) (2007) *Theory of World Security*, Cambridge: Cambridge University Press.

Browning, C., McDonald, M. (2011) 'The Future of Critical Security Studies: Ethics and the Politics of Security', *European Journal of International Relations*, online, DOI: 10.1177/1354066111419538.

Cameron, M. (1998) *To Walk without Fear*, Toronto: Oxford University Press.

Canada, Department of Foreign Affairs and International Trade (1999) *Human Security for People in a Changing World,* Ottawa.

Carpenter, C., Duygulu, S. and Tomaskovic-Devey, A. (2011) 'Explaining the Advocacy Agenda: Insights From the Human Security Network', unpublished paper.

Chandler, D. (2008) 'Human Security: The Dog That Didn't Bark', *Security Dialogue*, 39(4): 427–438.

Chourou, B. (2005) *Promoting Human Security: Ethical, Normative and Educational Frameworks in the Arab States*, Paris: UNESCO.

Christie, R. (2010) 'Critical Voices and Human Security: To Endure, To Engage or To Critique?' *Security Dialogue,* 41(2): 169–190.

Commission on Human Security (2003) *Human Security Now*, New York: Commission on Human Security.

Davis, J. (2009) 'Liberal Era Diplomatic Language Killed Off', *Embassy*, July 1, available: http://www. embassymag.ca/page/view/diplomatic_language-7-1-2009 (accessed 21 September 2011).

Debiel, T., Werthes, S. (eds.) (2006) *Human Security on Foreign Policy Agendas: Changes, Concept and Cases*, Duisburg: Institute for Development and Peace.

Department of Foreign Affairs and International Trade (DFAIT), Government of Canada, *Glyn Berry Program*, available http://www.international.gc.ca/glynberry/index.aspx?view=d (accessed 21 September 2011).

Deudney, D. (1990) 'The Case Against Linking Environmental Degradation and National Security', *Millennium: Journal of International Studies*, 19(3): 461–476.

Duffield, M. (2007) *Development, Security, and Unending War: Governing the World of Peoples*, Polity Press: Cambridge.

Economy, E., Schreurs, M. (eds.) (1997) *The Internationalization of Environmental Protection*, Cambridge: Cambridge University Press.

Edström, B. (2005) 'Japan's Foreign Policy and Human Security', *Japan Forum*, 15(2): 209–225.

Eriksson, J. (1999) 'Observers or Advocates? On the Political Role of Security Analysts', *Cooperation and Conflict*, 34(3): 311–330.

Fierke, K. (2007) *Critical Approaches to International Security*, London: Polity Press.

Finnemore, M. (1996) *National Interests in International Society,* Ithaca: Cornell University Press.

Finnemore, M., Sikkink, K. (1998) 'International Norm Dynamics and Political Change', *International Organization*, 52(4): 887–917.

Floyd, R. (2007) 'Human Security and the Copenhagen School's Securitization Approach: Conceptualizing Human Security as a Securitizing Move', *Human Security Journal*, 5: 38–49.

Fuentes, C., Aravena, F.R. (2005) *Promoting Human Security: Ethical, Normative and Educational Frameworks in Latin America and the Caribbean*, Paris: UNESCO.

Gervais, M., Roussel, S. (1998) 'De la sécurité de l'Etat à celle de l'individu: l'évolution du concept de sécurité au Canada (1990–1996)', *Etudes Internationales*, 29(1): 25–51.

Glasius, M., Kaldor, M. (eds.) (2005) *A Human Security Doctrine for Europe: Project, Principles, Practicalities*, London: Routledge.

Goucha, M., Cilliers, J. (eds.) (2001) *Peace, Human Security and Conflict Prevention in Africa,* Pretoria: Institute for Security Studies.

Grayson, K. (2008) 'Human Security as Power/Knowledge: The Biopolitics of a Definitional Debate', *Cambridge Review of International Affairs,* 21(3): 383–401.

Hampson, F. O., with Daudelin, J., Hay, J., Martin, T., Reid, H. (2002) *Madness in the Multitude: Human Security and World Disorder*, Toronto: Oxford University Press.

Hataley, T.S., Nossal, K.R. (2004) 'The Limits of the Human Security Agenda: The Case of Canada's Response to the Timor Crisis', *Global Change, Peace & Security*, 16(1): 5–17.

Holzgrefe, J. (1989) 'The Origins of Modern International Relations Theory', *Review of International Studies*, 15: 11–26.

Human Security Centre (2005) *Human Security Report 2005: War and Peace in the 21st Century*, New York: Oxford University Press.

International Commission on Intervention and State Sovereignty (ICISS) (2001) *The Responsibility to Protect*, Ottawa: IDRC.

International Feminist Journal of Politics (2011) *Special Issue: Critically Examining UNSCR 1325*, 13: 4.

Jackson, R. (1993) *Quasi-States: Sovereignty, International Relations, and the Third World,* Cambridge: Cambridge University Press.

Kaldor, M., Martin, M., Selchow, S. (2007) 'Human Security: A New Strategic Narrative for Europe', *International Affairs*, 83(2): 273–288.

Klingebiel, S. (ed.) (2006) *New Interfaces between Security and Development*, Bonn: Deutsches Institut für Entwicklungspolitik.

Klotz, A. (1995) *Norms in International Relations: The Struggle Against Apartheid*, Ithaca: Cornell University Press.

Krause, K. (2008) 'Building the Agenda of Human Security: Policy and Practice within the Human Security Network', *International Social Science Journal*, 59(1): 65–79.

Krause, K. (2013) 'Violence, Insecurity and Crime in Development Thought,' in D. Malone, et al (eds.) *Handbook of Development Thought*, Oxford: Oxford University Press, forthcoming.

Krause, K., Williams, M.C. (1996) 'Broadening the Agenda of Security Studies: Politics and Methods', *Mershon International Studies Review*, 40(2): 229–254.

Krause, K., Williams, M.C. (eds.) (1997) *Critical Security Studies*, Minneapolis: University of Minnesota Press.

Lee, S. (2004) *Promoting Human Security: Ethical, Normative and Educational Frameworks in East Asia*, Paris: UNESCO.

Litfin, K. (1994) *Ozone Discourses: Science and Politics in Global Environmental Cooperation*, New York: Columbia University Press.

MacFarlane, S. N., Foong Khong, Y. (2006) *Human Security and the UN: A Critical History*, Bloomington: University of Indiana Press.

Martin, M., Owen, T. (2010) 'The Second Generation of Human Security: Lessons from the UN and EU Experience', *International Affairs*, 86(1): 211–224.

Matlary, J.H. (2008) 'Much Ado About Little: The EU and Human Security', *International Affairs*, 84(1): 131–143.

Mattingly, G. (1955) *Renaissance Diplomacy*, Boston: Houghton Mifflin.

McCormack, T. (2008) 'Power and Agency in the Human Security Framework', *Cambridge Review of International Affairs*, 21(1): 113–128.

McSweeney, B. (1999) *Security, Identity and Interests: A Sociology of International Relations*, Cambridge: Cambridge University Press.

Muggah, R., Krause, K. (2006) 'A True Measure of Success? The Discourse and Practice of Human Security in Haiti', in T. Shaw, et al, (eds.) *A Decade of Human Security: Global Governance and the New Multilateralism*, London: Ashgate, 113–128.

Navari, C. (2011) 'The Concept of Practice in the English School', *European Journal of International Relations*, 17(4): 611–630.

Newman, E. (2010) 'Critical Human Security Studies', *Review of International Studies*, 36: 77–94.

Owen, T. (2004) 'Human Security – Conflict, Critique and Consensus: Colloquium Remarks and a Proposal for a Threshold-Based Definition', *Security Dialogue*, 35(3): 373–387.

Owen, T. (2008) 'The Critique that Doesn't Bite: A Response to David Chandler's "Human Security: The Dog That Didn't Bark"', *Security Dialogue*, 39(4): 445–453.

Owens, P. (2011) 'Human Security and the Rise of the Social', *Review of International Studies*, 38(3): 547–568.

Paris, R. (2001) 'Human Security: Paradigm Shift or Hot Air?' *International Security*, 26(2): 87–102.

Peoples, C., Vaughan-Williams, N. (2010) *Critical Security Studies: An Introduction*, Abingdon: Routledge.

Pouliot, V. (2008) 'The Logic of Practicality: A Theory of Practice of Security Communities', *International Organization*, 62: 257–288.

Price, R. (1997) *The Chemical Weapons Taboo*, Ithaca: Cornell University Press.

Price, R. (1998) 'Reversing the Gun Sights: Transnational Civil Society Targets Land Mines', *International Organization*, 52(3): 613–644.

Risse, T., Ropp, S., Sikkink, K. (eds.) (1999) *The Power of Human Rights*, Cambridge: Cambridge University Press.

Sedra, M. (ed.) (2010) *The Future of Security Sector Reform*, Waterloo: Centre for International Governance Innovation.

Tryggestad, T. L. (2009) 'Trick or Treat? The UN and Implementation of Security Council Resolution 1325 on Women, Peace, and Security', *Global Governance*, 15(4): 539–557.

United Nations Development Program (1994) *Human Development Report*, New York: Oxford University Press, 22–46.

United Nations General Assembly (2012) 'Follow-up to Paragraph 143 on Human Security of the 2005 World Summit Outcome', resolution A/66/L.55/Rev.1, 10 September 2012.

United Nations Secretary General (2010) *Human Security: Report of the Secretary-General to the General Assembly,* A/64/701, New York: UN.

7

THE SIREN SONG OF HUMAN SECURITY

Ryerson Christie

While human security has been the subject of significant critique as an entrenchment of liberal humanitarianism, it has also been adopted and adapted throughout the various approaches to critical scholarship. Despite both orientations to human security being grounded within critical commitments, these positions are seemingly incommensurate. This chapter argues that the tension over its usage – between focusing critical lenses on human security or using the concept to challenge current security practices – reveals the continuing struggle by some to find a basis for political engagement in the 'here and now'. Building on the work of Robert Cox, and his differentiation between critical and problem-solving theory, it is argued that the use of human security has been seen by some as offering a point of entry into specific policy debates. The chapter will lay out the justifications used by various critical scholars, illustrating that there is a common belief that the language of human security offers a basis for limited policy engagement. However, it will then argue that any gains that might be achieved in such a fashion ultimately reinforce the broader state and security practices human security narratives are expected to undermine.

In Homer's *Odyssey*, the crew of the Argonaut come perilously close to ruin on the shoals of Anthemoessa as the Sirens beckon them with their seductive cries. It is only by being forewarned of the risk that they are able to avoid disaster. This can be treated as a cautionary tale for critical scholarship in its desire to engage the traditional security actors, yet the question is whether this should be risked at all. Robert Cox's (1981) distinction between Critical and Problem Solving theories has become one of the touchstones of the Critical Security Studies (CSS) literature. In placing the two in opposition to one another (all the while arguing that there is an important role for addressing 'real world' issues in the here and now), Cox set out a definitional boundary to what constitutes CSS. This has been largely translated into a rejection of engagement with the policy community, with many critical scholars opting to work towards goals that are deemed at odds with the attempt to improve the operation of the present international system. The emergence of the concept of human security has proven irresistible to many, and has been embraced by academics from both sides of the problem-solving/critical divide. While there is substantial literature on the usefulness of human security to traditional approaches of security, and by default to the policy community, what is the draw of the re-centring of security to those who ascribe to a nominally critical label? That a narrative of security has been adopted by both liberals and critical scholars is curious; how can it achieve the aims of both sets of scholars when the rest of their academic and political goals appear to be in conflict? This chapter argues, perhaps controversially, that the appeal of human security is similar for both mainstream traditional *and* critical security studies. Its promise of providing an alternative narrative of security that contests dominant conceptualizations is seductive. While the end goals may be different, the critical advocates of human security have found in the concept a way to re-engage the policy community and to assert their voices on current debates. However, in deciding to adopt this changed referent of security, advocates have chosen to ignore the hidden dangers of engaging in a discourse of security that has been embraced by the policy community. Far from challenging traditional security practices, human security narratives and practices have demonstrated the resilience of traditional actors who, while incorporating some new policy communities (such as development workers) into security practices, have dominated the interpretation and enactment of a human-centred security.

Despite the obvious breadth of appeal of human security to governments and international organizations, numerous critical scholars have used human security as a means of achieving critical aims (in both the short and long term). An examination of the ways in which the various strands of critical scholarship have engaged with the notion of human security reveals an interesting pattern that may demand a re-conceptualization of the intent of critical scholarship, and of its compatibility with problem-solving approaches. The old debate about the theory/praxis divide is once again pushed into the spotlight. The range of critical engagements with a re-centred framework for security share a desire to speak to traditional state and security actors, and subsequently to change their behaviour. Though this is often being done as a means to more fundamentally contest state security activities, it nevertheless involves engagement with those agents. According to Edward Newman, 'human security provides opportunities for non-traditional security ideas to have an impact upon policy, and this should be valued by critical security studies scholars' (2010: 91–92). An exploration of the reasoning behind various critical approaches' adoption of human security reveals as much about the political goals of the academics as it does about the value of human security.

It is useful to begin this chapter with a brief statement about what distinguishes CSS from the traditional forms of security studies. Without falling back on the old adage that one might 'know it when one sees it', it is surprisingly difficult to define the bodies of literature that differ substantially on epistemological and ontological grounds. Robert Cox (1981) tried to define critical work as that which refused to take the world as it is, but rather sought more profound and radical change. While there is significant debate over the precise nature of the world around us and how we can understand it, the critical turn shares a broad commitment that, once again following Cox, theory is never neutral and is always tied up in networks of power – of being for someone and some purpose. As such, as Marysia Zalewski and Cynthia Enloe have argued, rejecting the Weberian imperative that politics should be absent from our analysis, 'theory does *not* take place after the fact. Theories, instead, play a large part in constructing and defining what the facts are' (1995: 299). Critical theorists cannot be content to merely report how the world is, but instead are actively involved in trying to change it.

Any attempt to delineate the boundaries of critical security studies must confront intense definitional debates that are explicit in their normative goals. Rather than siding with a particular form of analysis, I am more interested in the common approaches to human security amongst various strands of critical studies of security. There is a wealth of material that seeks to map what constitutes critical security studies, some of which is quite adamant in support of particular approaches. The divide, for example, between the Welsh school, sometimes written as the capitalized 'C'ritical security studies, and the wider range of small 'c'ritical security studies is perhaps overblown. Though there are important epistemological and normative differences, these cleavages are substantially less severe than between the traditional studies of security and all of the approaches which are variously lumped together under the critical security studies rubric. Following Robert Cox, this chapter has treated critical security studies as incorporating the array of theorizing that rejects as a given the ways in which security practices are constructed and enacted. The point here is, once again following Cox, that 'all theory is for someone and for some purpose'. This entails the recognition that power is implicated in theory, and that the external social world is constructed in a way that privileges some people at the expense of others. Thus, while there are intense debates about how to understand the operation of power, and of the world that we would like to pursue, there is a broadly shared commitment to seeking to empower those who have not been able to have a voice in issues of security. This formulation of what constitutes critical engagement with security goes substantially beyond the simple challenging of realist and neorealist positions. Any conceptualization of critical security studies that relies on such a minimalist notion of 'criticalness' loses substantive value as a challenge to the ways in which the world is ordered. It is within this broad context that an examination of critical scholarship's engagement with human security needs to be considered. We must then ask whether various critical adoptions of it are consistent with the 'critical' label, and if not, then we need to further ask why scholars who profess such orientations have opted to use it.

Conceptualizing human security

Other chapters within this handbook discuss the precise meanings of human security, and trace in detail the emergence of the idea. As the purpose of this chapter is to look at how critical scholars have sought to utilize the concept, providing a detailed reading of the various articulations of it is not essential; rather this chapter works with the basic conceptualization of human security as representing a shift from state-centric to individual-centric security. This draws on Edward Newman's definition: '[i]n its broadest sense, "human security" seeks to place the individual – or people collectively – as the *referent* of security, rather than, although not necessarily in opposition to, institutions such as territory and state sovereignty' (Newman 2001: 239). Despite claims to the contrary (Thomas and Tow 2002), the lack of definitional specificity has in fact been one of its strengths. The variety of possible meanings has facilitated its adoption by critically minded individuals from within policy and academic circles. Furthermore, as will be shown in greater depth, it has served as a bridging concept, providing the means by which scholars, activists, and policy makers, from a broad range of positions, have been able to enter into conversations about how to rethink and reorient the practice of security.

To understand the speed of adoption of human security, and its apparent resilience, the broader practices of international relations must be considered. The post-Cold War era has been largely defined by a supplanting of concerns about state-to-state conflict. At the same time, the era of the liberal peace has seen the emergence of a general consensus of how conflicts in the global South could be resolved. As Mark Duffield argued, 'The idea of *liberal peace*, for example, combines and conflates "liberal" (as in contemporary liberal economic and political tenets) with "peace" (the present policy predilection towards conflict resolution and societal reconstruction)' (Duffield 2001: 11). Just as the old security narratives were seen as insufficient to describe, explain, or understand the apparent expansion of intra-state conflicts, there was an emerging belief that insecurity (no matter how defined) in the South could potentially erode the security in the North. This insecurity in the South was then linked to underdevelopment, making the Global South a space of potential, if not actual, violence. Avoiding a chicken-and-egg debate, the human security idea emerged and gave voice to the linking of development and security. Simultaneously, when NGOs were becoming increasingly important to security, and were taking on leadership roles in development, human security resonated with their humanist perspectives (Tomlinson 2002: 274). The narrative was then ideally situated to provide a basis of communication with the newly expanding rescue industry.

However, it is nevertheless important to at least establish what elements of human security are being picked up, and which aspects of it have been ignored or rejected, by critical scholars. If the liberal human security literature is attempting to respond to dynamics it sees in play, and to push the advocacy of a more individual-centric security policy, there is another position on human security that is simultaneously sceptical of the likely usage of the concept, and at the same time hopeful that it might be used to further a more emancipatory politics. Not surprisingly, the specific policy debates that divided what have been described as the Canadian and Japanese approaches have been largely pushed aside by critical scholars. The debates over prioritization and timing of freedom from fear versus freedom from want have simply not resonated with critical scholars as they are so clearly grounded within a frame of government action that is of little interest to those seeking a more substantive change. The events of 9/11 provided impetus to some critical scholars to push the concept of human security all the more strongly as a means of (hopefully) restricting the scope of the North's over/reaction. At the very least, continuing to advocate for a form of critical human security was hoped to ensure that a calculation of the impact of the subsequent military responses would require an assessment of the costs to the lives of peoples on the ground in Afghanistan and Iraq.

Any attempt to discuss the ways in which critical security studies has engaged with any issue confronts on-going debates about the very nature of critical scholarship, and various efforts to describe and delineate the field. The argument that follows is based on my observation of the nodes of critical scholars and reflects, in large part, communities of engagement and the specific debates that the various groupings are engaged in. In reviewing the existing critical literatures that have opted to use human security, it is possible to distinguish between four common approaches: biopolitics; critical feminisms;[1] emancipatory approaches; and those more centrally concerned with ethical-political considerations. While these divisions are rough, and a great deal of scholarship could readily be placed in any of these categories, they are nevertheless useful for two distinct reasons. To begin with, these reflect perceived boundaries within the corpus of critical scholarship (refer to David Mutimer's (2007) description of the field). Simultaneously, it effectively distinguishes how and why various scholars have used human security, and what they believe it will shed light upon. These four groupings are generally self-referential. This reflects in part the conversations taking place within specific journals and communities.

There has been a remarkable amount of critical engagement with human security and, crucially, rather than merely being a subject of critique (that is the object of critical analysis), it has also been adopted by numerous scholars as a means to critique broader security practices, to advocate alternative conceptualizations of security, and to advance ethical and political debates. The relevance of human security to critical scholars can be seen in Steve Smith's description of the field of international relations:

> the discipline has tended to treat the state as the analytical focus of its enquiry, thereby privileging it. It is the security of the state that matters in International Relations; it is the unit of analysis, and, crucially, it is the moral referent point. The security of individuals is seen as a matter of internal politics, or even of local law and order.
>
> *(Smith 2004: 504–505)*

Following this, many scholars and activists see within human security the potential of enabling profound challenges to the behaviour of states, and how strategic calculations have traditionally been made. However, this does not address the usefulness of turning to a concept that was first articulated by liberal academics and policy makers.

The historical context

It is important to remember that human security began to acquire a small but diverse and active support from within critical scholarship after 9/11. That critical scholars would look for a means of engaging with the policy community should not be surprising. The apparent return of hard forms of state security, and the subsequent wars in Iraq and Afghanistan, have led some critical scholars to seek ways to return to the sphere of policy. This was a call that was in part sounded by Steve Smith (2004) in demonstrating the importance of critical IR to challenging the mainstream of the discipline. I, for one, did not want the debates over what constitutes security to be dominated by the traditional security actors. As a result, I initially saw within human security a means of attacking the traditional state-centric security narratives that saw security threats as being responsive to either the use, or threat of use, of military force. From 2002 onwards we saw an increasing interest by critical scholars in more direct policy engagement, and the pursuit of forms of interaction that might go beyond public critique. In particular there were attempts to intervene in policy debates, with the intent to shape, or at least disrupt, the unfolding war machine. At the time there was general concern amongst scholars that such engagement risked reifying the very structures and discourses that we were trying to resist. It is this difficulty which Cox stressed in arguing that problem solving had an important role to play, but that it had limited critical potential.

Human security, for the reasons discussed in greater detail later, has been seen as providing a means of interaction with the policy community, and the attentive public, on conceptual terrain that is hoped to be advantageous to achieve critical ends. For distinct reasons, the various critical engagements with human security sought to further particular ends, and to alter the policy-making of states, and improve the lives of the subaltern. This is all the more important to highlight given the ways in which human security has proven useful to the broader policy communities. There has been a tired debate about the relevance of human security to the policy community (Maclean *et al.* 2006; Thomas and Tow 2002; Jockel and Sokolsky 2001). Despite the claims by some scholars, particularly from the ranks of traditional security studies, that the concept was far too broad and lacking in definitional rigour to allow policy-making, it has been adopted quite broadly and has proven remarkably capable of supporting decision making (Paris 2001, 2004; Suhrke 1999; MacFarlane and Khong 2006).

Since the initial debates in the late 1990s about conceptual clarity (Paris 2001), the idea of human security has been incorporated by a surprising range of actors. Few, if any, concepts have been as effectively brought into modern security discourse as quickly and completely. In less than two decades it has gone from an invented, and decidedly niche term, to one that is used without hesitation by the breadth of security and development actors. In an era when, as Mark Duffield (2007) has noted, security and development discourses have been merging, human security has been ideally suited. This is in keeping with Annick Wibben's (2008: 458) observations that human security frameworks are consistent with the broadening and deepening of security discourse. That said, the point is whether such narratives have served to expand security considerations beyond the spectrum of strategic studies, and whether such moves (in a reversal of Wibben's argument) actually make individuals and communities *less secure*. This is all the more pertinent today given the ways in which NATO countries are now involved in counter-insurgency operations, and understand a link to exist between individual well-being and the success of the Global War on Terror (GWoT).

With its roots firmly embedded in the era of liberal-interventionism, it is perhaps surprising that the re-centring of security has continued to flourish in the GWoT environment. However, while Northern states have refocused their attention on perceived threats to their own constituencies, this has not supplanted a belief that threats to insecurity arise from spaces of poverty and poor governance. The language of human security provides a means for Northern governments to frame their interests in the Global South. As Duffield has illustrated, combating dangers to the North has come to be seen as requiring the achievement of security in the South. Human security, with its language of threats to peoples in the global hinterland, remains of direct relevance to state and development workers.

Human security as an expression of the biopolitical

Before discussing the modes of critical engagement, it is worth noting the most recent addition to critical engagement with human security. This group of scholars has focused its attention on human security as an artefact to be examined in its own right, rather than as a tool to affect policy change. These scholars have drawn on Foucauldian analysis, particularly the work on biopolitics, as a means of framing the new global interventionism (De Larrinaga and Doucet 2008; Grayson 2008; Youssef 2008; Berman 2007; Richmond 2007; Vankovska 2007). Responding in part to the re/emergence of counterinsurgency operations, worries over global pandemics, and increasingly robust moves to regulate the lives of peoples on a global scale, these authors understand human security narratives to be a natural complement to these other initiatives. It is entirely consistent with moves towards global, regional and local liberal forms of governance. It is also a productive narrative insofar as it both permits and demands Northern interventions in the global South to alleviate suffering in many forms. Human security is then part of a logic of governance that sees the state seeking to expand its influence over the regulation of human life where the population is the problem. The authors working with this framework are seeking to lay bare the ways in which modern security practices, in particular the growth of human security, are not 'new', and are connected to broader practices of power.

Unlike the other forms of critical engagement to be discussed here, these authors have all sought to explore, in a variety of ways, how human security can be understood as an extension of modern forms of biopolitics, using a broadly Foucauldian analysis to understand human security. In their hands, human security becomes an object of analysis, rather than either a tool of analysis or a policy framework. In their work there is a sense that the emergence of human security cannot offer a profound challenge to the norms of international relations, and in fact represents a logical outgrowth of the convergence of security and development narratives (Duffield 2001, 2007)

Feminist literatures on human security

The first body of scholarship that has adopted human security, not just as a subject of study but as a framework for analysis and policy, is the range of critical feminist literature. These authors have all engaged with the notion of human security as a means of highlighting particular forms of insecurities, and of empowering people in the pursuit of dignity (Ogbonna-Nwaogu 2008; Roberts 2008b; Carpenter 2006; Denov 2006; Hamber et al. 2006; Hoogensen and Stuvøy 2006; Chenoy 2005; Fox 2004; Hudson 2005; Agathangelou and Ling 2004; Harders 2003). Amongst those that have opted to embrace the human-centred re/definition of security there is a common sense that this can allow a re-emphasis on the security concerns of women and children and simultaneously undermine the dominant patriarchal definitions of what constitutes security and for whom. As Brandon Hamber *et al.* argue:

> the human security approach represents a significant step forward from the patri-archal statist approach. The human security approach frequently addresses the specific security concerns of particular groups, especially women.
>
> *(Hamber et al. 2006. 489)*

The hope manifested within this statement is that a re-centring of the referent demands an alteration of the security calculation. This is a point that Ann Tickner makes in arguing that 'since feminist perspectives on security take human security as their central concern, most of these definitions start at the bottom, with the individual or community rather than the state or the international system' (Tickner 2001: 62). This in turn provides the opportunity for meaningful debates, not just about the mechanisms of security, but also what constitutes security and questions of trade-offs between security demands.

This position is in part built upon the observation that what has traditionally constituted security has been male (and white) centric, and has privileged the state over communities, and the public over the private sphere. In a variety of ways some feminist scholars have hoped to use the concept of human security not just to reveal the ways in which security practices have affected portions of societies in distinct ways, but to reframe practices in a way that improves the lives of those affected (O'Manique 2006: 175). By commencing from a position that privi-leges the local over the state, it is hoped that the new articulation would alter the grounds on which security calculations are made. Mary Jane Fox, for example, states that, '[i]n spite of the weaknesses of the human security concept, its strengths create a security space in which the gendered insecurities ... can be recognized and addressed' (Fox 2004). This provides insight into the perceived value of the concept.

Some scholars are explicit in seeing human security as emphasizing the specific needs of women and children. David Roberts (2008a, 2008b) argues that the changed referent provides the means of highlighting the distinct forms of threats affecting women and children. This approach is attacked by some feminist scholars as merely replicating and fixing identities (Hoogensen and Stuvøy 2006: 216). In framing the debate around the needs of women and children, the potential is that this would merely return us to a situation where security is enacted on behalf of women and children. In short, the use of human security narratives by feminist scholars may serve to focus attention on issues, such as rape and domestic abuse, previ-ously rendered invisible. Heidi Hudson asserts that '[a] gender-sensitive concept of human security must therefore link women's everyday experiences with broader regional and global political processes and structures' (2005: 164). However, drawing on Cynthia Enloe's work, we must ask whether the highlighting of such issues within the security frame serves to unsettle the 'masculine sphere of life' (Enloe 2000: 4). Instead there is the distinct possibility that the emphasizing of the insecurities of women may only reproduce and reinforce narratives and practices of the security sector protecting women.

Another line of critique against feminist use of the language of human security is its distinct liberal bias (Väyrynen 2004). Human security, with its emphasis on the needs of individuals, and discourse of individual claims *vis-à-vis* communities and the state, cannot provide a corrective on the broader liberal interventionist practices. Indeed it is difficult to determine which aporias in feminist scholarship about security are being filled by narratives of human security. To understand the appeal of this framework, we must instead ask who the audience is. Here, a close examination of the various articles proposing a use of human security within feminist scholarship shows an enduring drive to speak to the traditional security actors. Within the breadth of work on the topic, there are common themes of seeking to articulate the security concerns of women and children, reveal the gendered nature of security discourse and practices, or offer alternative approaches to the topic that should shift the balance away from traditional state-centric (and thus male-centric) conceptions. But these are issues that have long echoed within feminist security studies. The hope is that utilizing the terminology of human security will enable the articulation of security in a way that furthers feminist scholars' short and medium term goals. The question that needs to be asked is why it is important to frame these issues within the rubric of security? All of these scholars have made the deliberate choice to use the word 'security' (with the human qualifier) despite concerns, articulated most clearly by Lene Hansen (2000), about securitizing issues ignored by the state. The use of the language of security, though couched in 'human' terms, appears to be a calculated drive by those involved to *engage* the broader security debates, and to influence policy making.

Security and emancipation

The next grouping of critical scholarship that has sought to utilize the concept of human security is that which has used it to further specific emancipatory goals. While there are a number of such articulations, by giving a voice to the subaltern on security matters, it is hoped that demands for substantive change to the conduct of international politics might be achieved (Ambrosetti 2008). The issue of emancipation remains a central (though not universal) theme of critical security studies (Herring 2009; Aradau 2004; Booth 2007; Alker 2005; Wyn Jones 2005). Indeed, an on-going concern, which echoes the work of some of the feminist scholars, is that security practices have not been enacted on behalf of the weak, but have often been pursued at their expense. As a result, Tim Dunne and Nicholas Wheeler (2004) argue that the core consideration of critical scholars should be to foreground and empower the 'security have-nots'. This has resulted in a call by some scholars for emancipatory goals to be at the core of the critical project (Bourne and Bulley 2011). This has translated into the critical engagement with human security where its focus on individuals, and attention to the insecurities posed by government authority, resonates with attempts to empower people against the state.

Despite the general pursuit of critical ends, there are intense debates about the precise nature of emancipation that should be pursued. For the Welsh School, it is seen as *the* central component of critical security studies, and is accompanied by particular prescriptions of how this should be pursued. Richard Wyn Jones has been one the most consistent advocates of this position, asserting that [C]ritical security studies is 'for "the voiceless, the unrepresented, and the powerless", and its purpose is their emancipation' (Wyn Jones 1999: 159). In many respects, for this grouping of academics, emancipation and security become effectively, if not perfectly, interchangeable concepts (Alker 2005: 207–208). As Columba Peoples and Nick Vaughan-Williams argue, '"Security" thus ultimately has a positive connotation within the CSS perspective when it can be related to the improvement of individual well-being' (2010: 29). However, the position advanced by the Welsh School has not been universally incorporated by the range of critical security studies. One of the main critiques is that, as with the Frankfurt School, this approach to emancipation is constrained by its maintenance of the individual as the referent object. While Richard Wyn Jones was not directly discussing the emergence of human security narratives, his comments in 1995 were prescient:

> by criticizing the hegemonic discourse and advancing alternative conceptions
> of security based on different understandings of human potentialities, one is

simultaneously playing a part in eroding the legitimacy of the ruling historic bloc, and contributing to the development of a counter-hegemonic position.

(Wyn Jones 1995: 313)

As with the feminist scholars, individuals pursuing a broadly emancipatory goal see within the concept the potential of a counter-narrative to the dominant state-centric security narrative. Placing the stress on individuals should, it is hoped, demonstrate the ways in which people are made insecure by state practices (it should be noted that this is generally consistent with mainstream articulation of the concept), but, more importantly, emphasize the needs of those who are rendered invisible by the state. Sunil Bastian (2004) similarly sees human security as offering a potential challenge, not only to states, but also to markets. In their hands human security is thus used to reveal the plight of people/s living on the global periphery, both within and outside the South. In this way the non-state centric discourse may be counter-hegemonic, profoundly challenging the state-ism of the current world order.

It is this last point that needs to be expanded upon: that these scholars see within human security the means to expose the effects of the current world order, and to show the forms of suffering that have been rendered invisible (or have been de-linked from global processes) and to give a voice back to those in the periphery. We must ask why they have turned to this framework when they have been pursuing such goals long before the emergence of human security narratives. In short, what is to be added by the narrative? Why opt for the language of security to do this when we can talk about rights, deprivation, poverty, suffering, and so forth? The point seems to be that in using the language of security, they can accomplish two things. First, as with the liberals who proposed the framework, it can show how state security practices may be part of the problem. At the same time, there is a sense that evoking the security label can shift the debate and capture states' and security practitioners' attention. The scholars are bound together by the belief that the concept might be useful in furthering the interests of those sectors of society that have suffered the greatest. In this way the adoption of the language of human security by some critical theorists has been done because it is seen as providing a guide for strategic action (Cox 1981: 130). This then comes close to Wyn Jones' call for Critical scholars, in pursuing their war of position, to come some way to 'speaking truth to power' (Wyn Jones 1995: 312).

The difficulty in turning to the language of human security in this pursuit is that it ignores the ways in which not all members of communities are able to make calls for security. One only needs to ask against whom these utterances of security are made, to see the bind of this re-articulated security narrative. As Claudia Aradau has argued, 'emancipation is not a privilege of the state, but the struggle is fought against the state's practices of domination and securitization' (Aradau 2004: 404). That human security is ripe for securitization should not come as a surprise. The state remains the dominant security provider, and calls for development and dignity play out within a broader liberal narrative that pre-fixes what constitutes a dignified life. Secondly, by focusing on individual security, the rights of people, on the basis of collective identities, to have their claims heard can be ignored. James Busumtwi-Sam states 'the real problems stem not from ambiguity per se, but from the way the present international institutional structure enables and even reinforces particular interpretations of human security even as it constrains and marginalizes others' (2002: 254). The drive to embrace human security for emancipatory ends resonates within critical security studies as it provides an apparent means to push a security narrative that is in tune with policy makers. The hope is that by shifting the referent that the needs of communities can be put to the fore, and that state security practices can be transformed.

Widening and deepening

Critical security studies has long been seen as at the centre of the widening and deepening of what constitutes security. We have already seen how human security, with its shifting of the referent to the individual, constitutes an obvious deepening of security. In arguing that human security does have critical potential, Newman states that '[d]eepening entails understanding the values within which ideas of security are embedded' (2010: 84). The widening of the security discourse concerns the introduction of new security topics, in particular the recognition of how a range of issues can pose security risks. By shifting our attention away from the state, a host of 'dangers' becomes evident. This involves everything from internally displaced peoples, environmental threats, disease, through to economic hardship. Human security, within this framing, is advocated for its ability to bring a range of issues into focus (Wibben, 2008; Maclean, 2008). Wibben, for one, has been explicit in asserting that the benefit of an altered security referent is its resonance with the expansion of the security discourse. The hope is that by drawing attention to new forms of insecurities, and risks to life that go beyond the traditional concern of security studies (focusing on deliberate violence by foreign forces), that this will not only serve to improve the lives of peoples, but also illuminate the negative impacts of traditional security practices. This clearly echoes the dominant expressions of human security which seeks to reveal the ways in which for many people, it is their own state which poses the most serious source of insecurity.

Unfortunately, this expression of broadening and deepening, reliant on the individual referent, does not seem likely to offer a radical challenge to state-centric security practices. We only need to look at the ways in which studies of human security have been conducted to see that it is not seeking to undermine state security practices writ large, but rather that in practice it targets Southern states. The ways in which human insecurity might exist in the North are simply not subjects of analysis. Secondly, where the broadening debate has led to new issues being framed as security threats, these have tended to be absorbed by the state as something which it needs to act upon. This argument is one that the Copenhagen School (CoS) is particularly well placed to explore. In a simplification, if human security serves to put new issues onto the security agenda, and they are effectively 'securitized', then this will demand state action. This is likely to further entrench the role of the state in acting on such issues, rather than result in any significant change of practice.

The promotion of human security for ethical/political reasons

The final grouping of critical approaches to the study of human security incorporates those that use human security as a means of reinvigorating political debate about issues of security. There are two distinct elements at play in such instances. There is an argument that echoes that of the Copenhagen School which sees human security as challenging the ways in which the state is able to determine what constitutes a security issue. This can be contrasted with the manner in which traditional matters of state security are understood to be beyond the abilities/interests of average people. The necessary grasp of strategic details, and access to highly specialized – and often secretive – knowledge, is deliberately exclusive. As such, debates about security have been remarkably rare, and tend to take place in very limited spaces. Human security might, according to some authors, force a change because its emphasis on the security of individuals rather than the state potentially provides a voice to speak about their security concerns. By claiming a voice for the local level in articulating what is a security concern, the state may be partially silenced.

However, there is another approach which sees human security as potentially ushering in public debate about the very nature of security. According to Kyle Grayson, 'the key to effective security policy in the post-11 September world is that human security should be treated as an *ethos* rather than as an agenda to be slotted into existing security paradigms' (2003: 340). Des Gasper and Thanh-Dam Truong (2005) have also argued in favour of human security as providing a basis for an expanded ethical debate about the nature of international politics and development policies. This position is in part substantiated by the 1994 UNDP *Human Development Report* which argues 'Human security is not a concern with weapons – it is a concern with human life and dignity' (1994: 22). This then effectively stands in opposition to the securitization literature, asserting that re/framing issues through the language of human security will demand not only an alteration of the security calculation of the state, but that it may bring about a change in the very nature of the debate through the shift away from state survival. This can be expressed as a re-framing of the security dilemma along normative lines. A re-articulation of security away from the protection of the state onto individuals demands that policy makers consider how state actions to make its citizenry secure may result in insecurity for others. Matt McDonald (2002) sees such developments as potentially positive precisely because it would demand a consideration of the 'Other' rather than focusing on one's self (or one's state). He writes, 'even a rhetorical engagement with Human Security both presupposes and reinforces a normative context in which Human Security-related concerns are seen to have value' (2002: 292). Human security is then beneficial because it alters the terms of the security debate, and indeed might actually result in substantive debate.

What is interesting is that there is a similar dynamic at play in such calls for action. The debates that human security narratives are expected to initiate are not within academic spheres, but rather within the corridors of power. These authors are the most explicit in their hope that the use of the concept of human security will affect policy decisions. Indeed, the point is precisely that its adoption might lead to public deliberations about state policies and how we in the North should interact with the rest of the world (both within our states and beyond our borders). These arguments are based on the assertion that states will have to respond to the calls for human security. It is thus supported, as with the previous two frames, for its potential to act on the policy community.

The hidden rocks

In all four instances, for the feminist, emancipatory, broadening and deepening, and ethical/ political literatures, the advocates of human security have opted to embrace the narrative of people-centric security out of a desire, in part, to interact with and shape state policies. In so doing, the various works are de-emphasizing Coxian critical analysis in favour of problem solving. Human security is seen as enabling a conversation with traditional actors, and by couching issues that various strands of critical analysis have been long involved with in the language of security, it is hoped that the policy makers will stand up and take notice. The potential of using the language of a de-centred security narrative to facilitate an engagement with traditional brokers of security is compelling. What all of these scholars have argued, in varying ways, is that the very concept of human security emerged from a context where the state was already extending its reach, through humanitarianism and the concomitant rise of the security/development nexus, into the lives of the peoples in the global periphery. These emerging narratives are embedded within networks of power, and to assume that merely articulating a new security referent will silence those voices traditionally empowered to speak security is likely naive. Indeed, numerous authors, both critical and otherwise, have noted the applicability of human security to policy setting.

The call of engagement is enticing, and it may very well yield some short-term strategic benefits. However, there are risks in such strategies, which some scholars have been trying to note. Indeed for some this move is both theoretically suspect, and politically untenable. Keith Krause and Michael C. Williams (1997), and Tara McCormack (2008) have been quite sceptical of the concept's potential to bring about any substantive change to the lives of peoples. Their arguments, that the state will continue to be the dominant voice in security matters (regardless of the referent object), denies any emancipatory potential in the narrative. McCormack goes further and asserts that the framework, and the policies that it ushers in, may actually be undermining the capacity of peoples in the global South to dictate what counts as security, and how it should be achieved. This resonates with the assertions that have been made by Vanessa Pupavac (2005) and Duffield (2001) who demonstrate that the emergence of human security is entirely consistent with the preceding international security policies of the North.

This calls into question the strategic choices of the critical adopters of human security. The struggle over the discourse of what constitutes security might have been won in part, but possibly at the expense of allowing the traditional security actors to dominate the conversations about how this can be achieved. Within Canada's Department of Foreign Affairs and International Trade (DFAIT) human security arrived at a fortuitous time when Canada was seeking to reclaim a leadership role in international affairs, and at a time when issues of development and regional in/security were very much at the fore of policy makers' concerns (Christie 2008, 2010; Crosby 2007; Axworthy 2004; Grayson 2003). Joseph Jockel and Joel Sokolsky (2001) argued that human security discourse provided a means for the Canadian military to justify its mandates and procurements. Oliver Richmond (2007) and Caroline Thomas (2001) have both demonstrated that the new forms of liberal global governance have drawn on the language of human security, and that it has proven remarkably effective in both justifying and demanding liberal interventionism. Similarly, Mary Kaldor, Mary Martin and Sabine Selchow (2007) show how the European Security and Defence Policy (ESDP) has integrated human security into its policy framework. This illustrates how human security has resonated within the halls of power, and how scholars can advocate for a concept and at least indirectly affect policy.

This relevance to the policy community, and the readiness of it to embrace human security, should give pause to the critical security studies movement. What so much of the critical literature that has been discussed here has looked past is the question of power and authority surrounding security discourse. Though it is has clearly been the hope that a re/centring to the individual would result in a significant alteration of security practice, this is dependent on the traditional voices being silenced, so the subaltern can be heard. However, this has ignored the ways in which authorities are able to respond to new claims for security, and are then able to shape the demands and enact policy in a fashion that conforms with broader state action. This is a point that Didier Bigo's (2000) work serves to emphasize. Bigo has shown in detail how the field of security has been the privileged terrain of 'security professionals'. Though his work has focused on the traditional forms of security practices, his arguments clearly extend to the field of human security. The shift of referent has not resulted in a meaning extension of the role of 'security experts' to the new referent, the individual. While it could be asserted that the practice of human security has brought previously excluded experts into the security profession, namely development and health professionals, this has not empowered communities. Rather, it has merely provided new technical lexicons derived from development studies to the privileged sphere of security experts.

Many of us feel an imperative to engage with the policy community. Not doing so risks abandoning the debates to the traditional security agents. Unfortunately, this requires us to act on a terrain that demands foregoing at least some of our critical commitments. The tension over its usage – between focusing critical lenses on human security or using the concept to challenge current security practices – reveals the continuing struggle by some to find a basis for political engagement in the 'here and now'. The point here is not that critical scholars must avoid using human security, rather that we must be aware of the ways in which the discursive terrain of security studies is profoundly unequal. Opting to engage with traditional security actors brings with it considerable risk. Crucially, being heard by them may be more damaging than being ignored. It is this dilemma which has not been adequately addressed, and to which there is no ready answer. However, ignoring the problem is not viable. We must be clearer about who our audience is, more forthright in how the use of human security will further the needs of those who have suffered from state practices, and demonstrate how debates about what constitutes security will change the praxis of security in ways we aspire to.

Does human security represent a break from traditional security studies in a way that is coherent with the desires of critical security studies? If traditional security studies are the study of the use of military force, then the question should in part be whether human security moves past this. In short, human security has not broken free from the traditional security calculation precisely because the new narrative has only added new equations, and has not radically altered who is doing human security. The potential of the call of human security has been seductive, and has captured the attention of critical scholars and activists.

Note

1   The term is used here for the purposes of distinguishing between those forms of feminist analysis that share positivist epistemologies. In this way liberal feminism is excluded.

References

Agathangelou, Anna M. and L.H. M. Ling (2004) 'Power, Borders, Security, Wealth: Lessons of Violence and Desire from September 11', *International Studies Quarterly* 48(3): 517–538.
Alker, Hayward (2005) 'Emancipation in the Critical Security Studies Project', in Ken Booth (ed.) *Critical Security Studies and World Politics*, Boulder, CO: Lynne Rienner, pp. 189–214.
Ambrosetti, David (2008) 'Human Security as Political Resource: A Response to David Chandler's "Human Security: The Dog That Didn't Bark"', *Security Dialogue* 39(4): 439–444.
Aradau, Claudia (2004) 'Security and the Democratic Scene: Desecuritization and Emancipation', *Journal of International Relations and Development* 7(3): 388–413.
Axworthy, Lloyd (2004) 'A New Scientific Field and Policy Lens', *Security Dialogue* 35(3): 348–349.
Bastian, Sunil (2004) 'Human Rights and Human Security: An Emancipatory Political Project', *Conflict, Security & Development* 4(3): 411–418.
Berman, Jacqueline (2007) 'The "Vital Core": From Bare Life to the Biopolitics of Human Security', in Giorgio Shani *et al.* (eds) *Protecting Human Security in a Post 9/11 World*, London: Palgrave, pp. 30–49.
Bigo, Didier (2000) 'Liaison Officers in Europe: New Officers in the European Security Field', in James Sheptycki (ed.), *Issues in Transnational Policing*, London: Routledge, pp. 67–99.
Booth, Ken (2007) *Theory of World Security*, Cambridge: Cambridge University Press.
Bourne, Mike and Dan Bulley (2011) 'Securing the Human Critical Security Studies: The Insecurity of a Secure Ethics', *European Security* 20(3): 453–471.
Busumtwi-Sam, James (2002) 'Development and Human Security', *International Journal* 57(2): 253–272.
Carpenter, Charli (2006) 'Recognizing Gender-Based Violence Against Civilian Men and Boys in Conflict Zones', *Security Dialogue* 27(1): 83–103.
Chandler, David (2008) 'Human Security: The Dog that Didn't Bark', *Security Dialogue* 39(4): 427–439.
Chenoy, Anuradha M. (2005) 'A Plea for Engendering Human Security', *International Studies* 42(2): 167–179.
Christie, Ryerson (2008) 'The Human Security Dilemma: Lost Opportunities, Appropriated Concepts or Actual Change?', in W. Kepner and P.H. Liotta (eds) *Environmental Change and Human Security: Recognizing and Acting on Hazard Impacts*, Dordrecht: Springer, pp. 253–269.

Christie, Ryerson (2010) 'Critical Voices and Human Security: To Endure, To Engage or To Critique?', *Security Dialogue* 41(2): 169–190.

Cox, Robert (1981) 'Social Forces, States, and World Orders: Beyond International Relations Theory', *Millennium: Journal of International Studies* 10(2): 126–55.

Crosby, Ann Denholm (2007) 'Myths of Canada's Human Security Pursuits: Tales of Tool Boxes, Toy Chests, and Tickle Trunks', in Duane Bratt and Christopher J. Kukucha (eds) *Readings in Canadian Foreign Policy: Classic Debates and New Ideas*, New York: Oxford University Press, pp. 265–284.

De Larrinaga, Miguel and Marc Doucet (2008) 'Sovereign Power and the Biopolitics of Human Security', *Security Dialogue* 39(5): 517–538.

Denov, Myriam (2006) 'Wartime Sexual Violence: Assessing a Human Security Response to War-Affected Girls in Sierra Leone', *Security Dialogue* 37(3): 319–342.

Duffield, Mark (2001) *Global Governance and the New Wars: the Merging of Development and Security*, London: Zed Books.

Duffield, Mark (2007) *Development, Security and Unending War: Governing the World of Peoples*, Cambridge: Polity.

Dunne, Tim and Nicholas Wheeler (2004) '"We the Peoples": Contending Discourses of Security in Human Rights Theory and Practice', *International Relations* 18(1): 9–23.

Enloe, Cynthia, (2000) *Maneuvers: The International Politics of Militarizing Women's Lives*, Berkeley: University of California Press.

Fox, Mary-Jane (2004) 'Girl Soldiers: Human Security and Gendered Insecurity', *Security Dialogue* 35(4): 465–479.

Gasper, Des and Thanh-Dam Truong (2005) 'Deepening Development Ethics: From Economism to Human Development to Human Security', *The European Journal of Development Research* 17(3): 372–384.

Grayson, Kyle (2003) 'Securitization and the Boomerang Debate: a Rejoinder to Liotta and Smith-Windsor', *Security Dialogue* 34(3): 337–345.

Grayson, Kyle (2008) 'Human Security as Power/Knowledge: the Biopolitics of a Definitional Debate', *Cambridge Review of International Affairs* 21(3): 383–402.

Hamber, Brandon and Paddy Hillyard, Amy Maguire, Monica McWilliams, Gillian Robinson, David Russell, Margaret Ward (2006) 'Discourses in Transition: Re-imagining Women's Security', *International Relations* 20(4): 487–502.

Hansen, Lene (2000) 'The Little Mermaid's Silent Security Dilemma and the Absence of Gender in the Copenhagen School', *Millennium* 29(2): 285–307.

Harders, Cilja (2003) 'Gender and Security in the Mediterranean', *Mediterranean Politics* 8(2–3): 54–72.

Herring, Eric (2009) 'Historical Materialism', in Alan Collins (ed.) *Contemporary Security Studies*, 2nd edn, Oxford: Oxford University Press, pp. 42–53.

Hoogensen, Gunhilde and Kirsti Stuvøy (2006) 'Gender, Resistance and Human Security', *Security Dialogue* 37(2): 207–228.

Hudson, Heidi (2005) '"Doing" Security As Though Humans Matter: A Feminist Perspective on Gender and the Politics of Human Security', *Security Dialogue* 36(2): 155–174.

Jockel, Joseph and Joel Sokolsky (2001) 'Lloyd Axworthy's Legacy: Human Security and the Rescue of Canadian Defence Policy', *International Journal* 56(1): 1–18.

Kaldor, Mary, Mary Martin and Sabine Selchow (2007) 'Human Security: A New Strategic Narrative for Europe', *International Affairs* 83(2): 273–288.

Krause, Keith and Michael C. Williams (eds) (1997) *Critical Security Studies: Concepts and Cases*, Minneapolis: University of Minnesota Press.

Maclean, Sandra (2008) 'Microbes, Mad Cows and Militaries: Exploring the Links Between Health and Security', *Security Dialogue* 39(5): 475–494.

Maclean, Sandra and David Black, Timothy Shaw (2006) *A Decade of Human Security: Global Governance and New Multilateralisms*, Aldershot: Ashgate.

McCormack, Tara (2008) 'Power and Agency in the Human Security Framework', *Cambridge Review of International Affairs* 21(1): 113–128.

McDonald, Matt (2002) 'Human Security and the Construction of Security', *Global Society* 16(3): 277–295.

MacFarlane, S. Neil and Yuen Foong Khong (2006) *Human Security and the UN: A Critical History*, Bloomington, IN: Indiana University Press.

Mutimer, David (2007) 'Critical Security Studies: A Schismatic History', in Alan Collins (ed.) *Contemporary Security Studies*, Oxford: Oxford University Press, pp. 53–74.

Newman, Edward (2001) 'Human Security and Constructivism', *International Studies Perspectives* 2(2): 239–251.

Newman, Edward (2010) 'Critical Human Security Studies', *Review of International Studies* 36(1): 77–94.

Nuruzzaman, Mohamed (2006) 'Paradigms in Conflict: The Contested Claims of Human Security, Critical Theory and Feminism', *Cooperation and Conflict* 41(3): 285–303.

O'Manique, Colleen (2006) 'The "Securitisation" of HIV/AIDS in Sub-Saharan Africa: A Critical Feminist Lens', in Sandra Maclean, David Black and Timothy Shaw (eds) *A Decade of Human Security: Global Governance and New Multilateralisms*, Aldershot: Ashgate, pp. 161–178.

Ogbonna-Nwaogu, Ifeyinwa Maureen (2008) 'Civil Wars in Africa: A Gender Perspective of the Cost on Women', *Journal of Social Sciences* 16(3): 251–258.

Paris, Roland (2001) 'Human Security: Paradigm Shift or Hot Air?', *International Security* 26(2): 87–102.

Paris, Roland (2004) 'Still an Inscrutable Concept', *Security Dialogue* 35(3): 370–371.

Peoples, Columba and Nick Vaughan-Williams (2010) *Critical Security Studies: An Introduction,* Oxford: Routledge.

Pupavac, Vanessa (2005) 'Human Security and the Rise of Global Therapeutic Governance', *Conflict, Security & Development* 5(2): 161–181.

Richmond, Oliver P. (2007) 'Emancipatory Forms of Human Security and Liberal Peacebuilding', *International Journal* 62(3): 458–477.

Roberts, David (2008a) 'The Intellectual Perils of Broad Human Security: Deepening the Critique of International Relations', *Politics* 28(2): 124–127.

Roberts, David (2008b) *Human Insecurity*, London: Zed Books.

Smith, Steve (2004) 'Singing Our World into Existence: International Relations Theory and September 11', *International Studies Quarterly* 48: 499–515.

Suhrke, Astri (1999) 'Human Security and the Interests of States', *Security Dialogue* 30(3): 265–276.

Thomas, Caroline (2001) 'Global Governance, Development and Human Security: Exploring the Links', *Third World Quarterly* 22(2): 159–175.

Thomas, Nicholas and William T. Tow (2002) 'The Utility of Human Security: Sovereignty and Humanitarian Intervention', *Security Dialogue* 33(2): 177–192.

Tickner, J. Ann (2001) *Gendering World Politics: Issues and Approaches in the Post-Cold War Era,* New York: Columbia University Press.

Tomlinson, Brian (2002) 'Defending Humane Internationalism: The Role of Canadian NGOs in a Security-Conscious Era', *International Journal* 57(2): 273–282.

United Nations Development Program (UNDP) (1994) *Human Development Report,* New York: United Nations.

Vankovska, Biljana (2007) 'The Human Security Doctrine for Europe: A View from Below', *International Peacekeeping* 14(2): 264–281.

Väyrynen, Tarja (2004) 'Gender and UN Peace Operations: the Confines of Modernity', *International Peacekeeping* 11(1): 125–142.

Wibben, Annick (2008) 'Human Security: Toward an Opening', *Security Dialogue* 39(4): 455–462.

Wyn Jones, Richard (1995) '"Message in a Bottle"? Theory and Praxis in Critical Security Studies', *Contemporary Security Policy* 16(3): 299–319.

Wyn Jones, Richard (1999) *Security, Strategy and Critical Theory*, London: Lynne Rienner.

Wyn Jones, Richard (2005) 'On Emancipation, Necessity, Capacity and Concrete Utopias', in Ken Booth (ed.) *Critical Security Studies and World Politics*, Boulder, CO: Lynne Rienner, pp. 215–236.

Youssef, Maisaa (2008) 'Suffering Men of Empire: Human Security and the War on Iraq', *Cultural Dynamics* 20(2): 149–166.

Zalewski, M. and C. Enloe (1995) 'Questions of Identity in International Relations', in K. Booth and S. Smith (eds) *International Relations Theory Today*, Cambridge: Polity Press, pp. 279–305.

8

WHY HUMAN SECURITY? THE CASE FOR RESILIENCE IN AN URBAN CENTURY

Peter H. Liotta and Aybüke Bilgin[1]

> We live in the age of the city.
> The City is everything to us – it consumes us, and for that reason we glorify it.
> *Onookome Okome*[2]

> We are eating our country, we are eating our earth, we are eating our children.
> *Thich Nhat Hanh*

By 2015 there will be six hundred cities on the planet with populations of 1 million or more, and fifty-eight with populations over 5 million. By 2025, according to the National Intelligence Council, there will be twenty-seven cities with populations greater than 10 million – the common measure by which an urban population constitutes a 'megacity' – and more recent estimates suggest there may be as many as thirty-seven megacities. With the rise of massive urban centers in Africa and Asia, cities that will matter most in the twenty-first century are located in less-developed, struggling states. A number of these huge megalopolises – whether Lagos or Karachi, Dhaka or Kinshasa – reside in states often unable or simply unwilling to manage the challenges that their vast and growing urban populations pose. There are no signs that their governments will prove more capable in the future. These swarming, massive urban monsters will only continue to grow and should concern the world.

If measures are not taken soon, some of these megacities will pose *the* most significant security threat in the coming decades. They will become havens for terrorists and criminal networks, as well as sources of major environmental depletion. They will serve as volatile natural laboratories where all the elements most harmful to international and human security are grown. Although there are significant differences in the cultures and histories of emerging megacities, from the dangerous streets of Karachi to the sprawling shantytowns of Lagos, basic similarities are dramatic. All have experienced recent and rapid population booms during unsettled periods in national histories, driven in large part by internal migration from depressed or chaotic rural districts. In each, municipal and national governments failed to either govern or provide for exploding urban populations. Continued failure seems preordained without external assistance.

Traditionally there have been two general approaches to understanding societies and states. One is the humanitarian or ecological perspective in which the focus is on society – how people live and are affected by war, pollution and economic globalization. The other is a realist perspective in which the focus is on the economic, political, and military relations among major powers such as the European Union, the United States, China, and Russia. What these traditional approaches underemphasize is the overlap and natural alignment between them. To understand the map of the future, we need to critically appreciate how astonishing population growth in cities – particularly fast-growing megalopolises in weak or failing states in Africa, the Middle East, and Asia – impacts ecology and ecosystems, human security, *and* the national security of Western states, as well as allies and trading partners.

For both better and worse, globalization and urban population growth have changed political and economic dynamics in ways that previous conceptions of how the world works cannot do justice. Now, we *must* examine how developments below the nation-state level – at the municipal level – affect how we see the world of the future. In making the case for human security and resilience in an urban century, we first address the theory and conceptual debate of the notions of security and how human security is a crucial centrality in that understanding; next, we provide two case examples of different challenges on different continents – yet in locations both intimately connected to globalization and the larger security context; finally, we present the argument for resilience through the human security lens in the urban challenge context.

From concept to contact: placing human security in theoretical context and its crucial role in the urban century

In 1905 only 10 per cent of the world's population lived in cities. Today over 50 per cent does. By 2030, likely much sooner, two out of three will live in cities, and 90 per cent of population growth will occur in cities of the developing world – what we should properly call the 'majority' world. This massive shift to urban landscapes has never occurred on such scale before in human history. Citizens flock to the city for opportunity, employment, healthcare, and education. Today one in six lives in cities with unhealthy air quality; one in fifteen has inadequate sanitation; one in thirty lacks access to safe drinking water.

In 1950 there was only one megacity on the planet: New York. In 1975 there were only three: Tokyo, New York, and Mexico City. Yet multiple, major and megacities in fragile states that have emerged in the last half-century have passed the tipping point. They have become overwhelmed, dangerous, ungovernable, and, remarkably, still grow.

What do we mean by security?

In the classical sense, security – from the Latin *securitas* – refers to tranquility and freedom from care, or what Cicero termed the absence of anxiety upon which the fulfilled life depends. Since the beginning of the twenty-first century, numerous governmental and international reports have focused on the terms 'freedom from fear' and 'freedom from want,' both of which emphasize a pluralist notion that security is a basic, and elemental, need.

Perhaps most widely touted among these reports – and one least put into practice – is the Canadian International Commission on Intervention and State Sovereignty's *Responsibility to Protect* (commonly referred to simply as 'R2P').[3] Based on the principle that sovereignty is not a privilege, but a responsibility, R2P focuses on preventing four violations that go beyond the traditional protection of borders: genocide, war crimes, crimes against humanity, and ethnic cleansing. R2P can be broadly broken down into three major conceptual aspects: (1) the state bears responsibility to protect its citizens and population from genocide, war crimes, crimes against humanity, and mass atrocities; (2) if the state fails at this responsibility, the international community must act with capacity-building measures, to include providing early-warning capabilities, mediating conflicts, strengthening security, and mobilizing standby forces; and (3) if the state patently fails to protect its citizens and conflict-avoidance measures are not working, the international community has the responsibility to intervene at first diplomatically, then more coercively, and, as last resort, with military force.

Although the phrase was taken up by the UN Secretary-General, it has never been put into action, largely for the failure to answer one essential question: does the 'Responsibility to Protect' mean the indiscriminate right to intervene? From this general – and Western – understanding of security, the human security concept centers on a concentration on the individual (rather than the state) and that individual's right to personal safety, basic freedoms, and access to sustainable prosperity. In ethical terms, human security is both a 'system' and a systemic practice that promotes and sustains stability, security, and progressive integration of individuals within their relationships to their states, societies, and regions. In abstract but understandable terms, human security allows individuals the pursuit of life, liberty, and both happiness and justice.

While one could find little to argue with in these principles – and their relevance to megacities and global insecurity – there are problems nonetheless. On the one hand, all security systems are not equal – or even very similar. Moreover, all such systems collectively involve codes of values, morality, religion, history, tradition, and even language. Any system that enforces human security inevitably collides with conflicting values, which are not synchronous or accepted by all individuals, states, societies, or regions. On the other hand, in the once widely accepted realist understanding, the state was the sole guarantor of security. Realists believe that security necessarily extends downwards from nations to individuals; conversely, the stable state extended upwards in its relationship to other states to influence the security of the international system. This broadly characterizes what is known as the anarchic order. The *responsibility* for the guarantee of the individual good – under any security rubric – has never been obvious.

Essentially cities, states, and regions, in a globalized context, can no longer afford to solely emphasize national security issues without recognizing that abstract concepts such as values, norms, and expectations also influence both choice and outcome. There are dangers in too closely following the precepts of one security concept at the expense of another. Some brief explanation of the concepts in Table 8.1 might prove useful. In essence, the distinctions move from a 'top-down' global emphasis to a 'bottom-up' individual focus.

National security represents the traditional understanding of security, to include the protection of territory and citizens from external threats – from other states, and, more recently, 'stateless' actors (which range from NGOs to terrorist networks). Hyperemphasis on state security, especially in the emergence of 'homeland security,' impacts the two following concepts of security, especially regarding the practice of individual liberties and the freedom to participate openly in civil society

'Parasitic security' is not synonymous with the more commonly used term 'societal security.' Rather, parasitic security is symbiotically linked to other security concepts. It often represents the narrow interests of specific communities, nations, or political action groups within a state. In its extreme form, it can lead to social stratification, the fracturing of 'common' interests, and xenophobia. Certainly, parasitic security played a role in the dismemberment of former Yugoslavia at the end of the Cold War. When 'citizens' began to identify with their nations and 'nationality' (Croat, Serb, Slovene, Bosniak, Kosovar) rather than with a larger identity, the state itself was doomed.

Human security – or, as we should more appropriately term it, 'security with a human face' – retains its focus on the individual, and remains an emerging concept. At its core, human

Table 8.1 Alternative 'security' concepts

Traditions and analytic bases	Security type	Specific security focus	Specific security concerns	Specific security hazards (threats/vulnerabilities)
Non-traditional	**Ecological Security**	The ecosystem	Global sustainability	Humankind: through resource depletion, scarcity, war, and ecological destruction
Traditional, Realist-based	**National Security**	Non-traditional	Sovereignty Territorial integrity	Challenges from other states (and 'stateless' actors)
Traditional and Non-traditional, Realist- and Liberal-based	**'Parasitic Security'**	Nations Societal groups Class/economic Political action committees/interest groups	Identity/ Inclusion Morality/Values/ Conduct Quality of life Wealth distribution Political cohesion	States themselves Nations Migrants Alien culture
Non-traditional, Liberal-, Marxist-based	**Human Security**	Individuals Humankind Human rights Rule of law Development	Survival Human progress Identity and governance	The State itself Globalization Natural catastrophe and change

security is about protecting people. Despite multiple, contending views that have emerged over human security since it gained new prominence in the 1990s – ranging from viewing human security as a radical departure from 'traditional' security forms, to a focus on moderate evolutionary changes to the existing security infrastructure and mandate – the central feature of most arguments addresses how best to both protect and empower people.[4]

With the fall of the Berlin Wall, it should have become clear that despite the macro-level stability created by the East-West military balance of the Cold War, citizens were not safe. They may not have suffered from outright nuclear attack, but they were being killed by the remnants of proxy wars, the environment, poverty, disease, hunger, violence, and human rights abuses. Ironically, the faith placed in the realist worldview, and the security it provided, masked the actual issues threatening the individual. The protection of the person was all too often negated by an over-attention to the state. Allowing key issues to fall through the cracks, 'traditional security' failed at its primary objective: protecting the individual. This new type of instability led to the challenging of the notion of traditional security by such concepts as cooperative, comprehensive, societal, collective, international, and human security. Although these concepts moved away from a focus on interstate relations, human security takes the most dramatic step by making the referent object not the state, society, or community, but the individual. This shift is meant to direct research and policy towards the actual issues threatening people's lives.

Emma Rothschild describes human security as one of four changes taking place in the concept of security. Beginning with the state, she sees security being brought down to the individual, brought up to the international system or supranational physical environment, broadened from a focus on the military to include the environment, society, and economy, and finally, diffused in all directions to include local governments, international agreements, nongovernmental organizations (NGOs), public opinion, forces of nature, and the financial market as sources of responsibility. Although not an explicit definition, this conceptualization provides an example of both how narrow the traditional paradigm has been, as well as how complex the expansion of the concept can become.[5]

Distinguishing threats and vulnerabilities

The following distinctions are contentious. In brief, however, we argue that not all security issues involve 'threats.' Rather, the notion of vulnerabilities is as serious to some peoples – and some cities – as the familiar 'threat' of armies massing at the borders, or barbarians at the gates. Admittedly, those who form policy and make critical decisions on behalf of states and peoples will continue to focus on aspects of traditional national security – or 'hard' security – in which military forces will play a preeminent role, as well as human security in which 'non-traditional' security issues may well predominate.

Commonly, a *threat* is an external cause of harm with identifiable consequences that may be immediate or at least visible on the horizon, which requires a near-term, tangible response. Military force, for example, has traditionally been sized against threats, to defend a state against an external aggression and to protect vital national interests. In some cases, such as Nigeria and Egypt, the state builds military power against an additional threat: domestic disorder or rebellion. The size of the U.S. and Soviet nuclear arsenals during the Cold War matched the perceived threat of global holocaust in the context of a bipolar, ideological struggle that was far greater then than in today's post-9/11 world. A threat is either *clearly visible* or *commonly acknowledged*. In short, for policy makers, a threat is something you can target.

Vulnerability, on the other hand, is a weakness or condition that *may* ultimately cause the kind of harm an unattended threat *will* cause. An instructive analogy may be in the field of counterterrorism where the threat is the existence of terrorists plotting to cause damage or kill people and the vulnerabilities are, for example, the high-value targets that are not guarded, parts of the telecommunications infrastructure that are not adequately protected by firewalls and encryption, and critical databases that are not backed up. This analogy is not exact, since social vulnerabilities such as severe overcrowding may not require an external agent such as a terrorist to call into being the harm that they have the potential to cause.

A vulnerability can be both internal and external in exerting complex influence. Human and economic geographers Hans-Georg Bohle, Karen O'Brien, and Robin Leichenko have addressed this 'double bind' of vulnerability in analyses addressing environmental and economic change and its impact on cities in particular.[6] Collectively they suggest that examining and assessing vulnerability is both relevant and necessary for policy issues. Vulnerability approaches can also identify regions and peoples at risk within the seven categories identified in the 1994 UNDP report: economic security, food security, health security, environmental security, personal security, community security, and political security.

A vulnerability – unlike a threat – is not clearly perceived, often not well understood, and almost always a source of contention among conflicting views. There are cases of long-term vulnerability and what we might term 'entangled vulnerabilities' which give rise to security concerns. Plausible entangled vulnerability scenarios might reasonably include the following:

- different levels of *population growth* in various regions, particularly between the developed and the majority world

- outbreak and rapid spread of *disease among* specific 'target' populations (such as HIV/AIDS and new strains of emerging contagions such as SARS or H5N1 influenza)
- significant *climate change*
- scarcity of *water* for drinking and irrigation and of other *natural resources* in specific regions
- decline in *food production, access, and availability*, and the need to increase imported goods
- progressing *soil erosion and desertification*
- increased *urbanization and pollution* in megacities around the globe
- lack of sufficient *warning systems* for natural disasters and environmental impacts – from earthquakes to land erosion.

These emerging vulnerabilities will not mitigate or replace more traditional hard-security dilemmas.

Both middle-power and major-power states, as well as the international community, must increasingly focus on long-term entangled vulnerabilities in order to avoid constant crisis response to conditions of extreme vulnerability. Granted, some have soured on the viability of the concept in the face of recent 'either with us or against us' power politics. At the same time, and in a bit more positive light, others have recognized the sheer impossibility of international power politics continuing to feign indifference in the face of moral categories. As Peter Burgess writes, 'for all its evils, one of the promises of globalization is the unmasking of the intertwined nature of ethics and politics in the complex landscape of social, economic, political and environmental security.'[7] While still not feasible to establish a threshold definition, it would be a tragic mistake to assume that national security and human security – both as concepts and as bases for policy decisions – are mutually harmonious rather than more often locked in conflictual and contested opposition with each other in the never-ending competition within governments and international organizations for budgetary resources.

Case in point: Kenya and Kibera's challenge

At first glance, Kenya would not be a state of major concern for chaos or failure – or even disruption. Since its break from British colonial rule in 1963, Kenya (even during the often dictatorial rule of Daniel arap Moi) was most often considered a stable, even prosperous, example for other African nations. With its population approaching 40 million people and with over forty-one different major ethnic groups, Kenya seemed a kind of prosperous example where – as was once true in former Yugoslavia – national identity could overcome religious, ethnic, cultural, and historic differences. As one native describes his country, Kenya, with 'its Anglicized urban population, modern cities, and relatively well-developed infrastructure, epitomized everything positive about Africa.'

The disastrous December 2007 presidential elections sharply illustrated that Kenya's stability was a fraud. In the election's wake, a national crisis ensued that resulted in political stalemate between the two contenders: President Mwai Kibaki and eventual prime minister Raila Odinga. Protests escalated into sectarian violence and destruction of property. Almost a thousand people died (often by machete mutilation or by burning, when tires were put on victims and set afire) and six hundred thousand were displaced. International mediation, with significant assistance from the United States, was necessary. Despite major constitutional reforms in 2010, rumors persist that weapons were being brought into divisive regions of Kenya in anticipation of the 2012 elections.

How could things have gone so wrong and been so deeply exposed in 2007 and 2008? Too many political, economic, and social injustices had been ignored or overlooked for far too long.

Perception and reality, essentially, merged: unless one were a member of the Kikuyu tribe, the largest and historically most ethnically dominant group, there was little to expect in terms of life improvement following the election of Kibaki to his first term in 2002. Certainly with ethnic Kikuyu gluttony bonding around the Kibaki administration, the poor were virtually ignored, witnessed only inflation as change, and lost all confidence in government. Some came to prefer the iron rule of Kibaki's predecessor, Moi.

Violence that emerged also exposed the truth that such protests could prove effective in bringing change. In a state where over 70 per cent of the population is under the age of thirty, protestors recognized that government was no longer an institution to be feared.[8] Post-election violence became an empowering event for many poor, disaffected Kenyan youths, who succeeded in controlling wide swathes of the country. In their aggressive expression, Kenyans found their first form of having a true democratic voice.

While some might think that this post-election uprising was simply an unfortunate bump in Kenya's history, we suggest otherwise. If one views Kenya's capital city of Nairobi (the fourth largest, and one of the fastest growing, cities in Africa) and its massive megaslum of Kibera as a case example of how cities can grow too far, too fast, it should be no surprise to witness frightening human outcomes as events boil over and erupt during its growth process. Nairobi has become a port of arrival. Whereas only 24 per cent of the population lived in urban centers in 1990, that figure had grown to one in three by 2000, with Nairobi now growing by 7 per cent each year. Most residents live in what are called 'informal settlements,' 50 per cent of the population lives below the poverty line, and most residents must find informal-sector activities (ranging from small trade to casual labor) to survive.

Sixty per cent of Nairobi's population – approaching two million residents – live in slums. Kibera, East Africa's oldest and largest slum, is a massive community of mile after mile of mud construction and corrugated roofs where one can dimly see the Nairobi city skyline in the distance. The 2009 Kenyan census claimed Kibera's population to be only 170,000 residents, whereas previous estimates range as high as 1 million. There is a likely explanation for such widely disparate population estimates. Kibera's residents lack any squatter property rights. Residents neither built their homes nor have any community control. Instead, they pay rent to often wealthy landowners, in theory, at least, they do not exist.

Piles of trash line every street and alley; sewage sluices run alongside water pipes, where the latter exist. Many residents spend half their meager monthly incomes to travel to 'the city' to hawk their goods. Unlike the hillside *favelas* of Rio, Kiberan mud homes are built in valleys, and in many cases you must walk down to enter houses. Although Nairobi ecotours bill Kibera as 'the world's friendliest slum,' it can be a dangerous place. While some still insist the slum is safe and secure, with over 50 per cent unemployment crime is rife – with high levels of rape and violence. (And, as we have seen, with gang acts that spill over into other communities.) Many members of the banned occult, political-religious, criminal Mungiki sect live in Kibera (with its largest base in the Mathare slum) and carry out violent acts with near impunity. The Mungiki were particularly active in the 2007 and 2008 post-election violence.[9] Compounding levels of violence and crime are the widespread use of cheap drugs and the drinking of the high-methanol local hooch known as *changaa*. Glue sniffing, which causes severe brain damage and death in many cases, is widespread among children.

Kibera, as with many slums in critical urban centers, is a point of arrival for many. Comprising almost twenty separate subcommunities split neatly in half by railroad tracks, Kibera represents the first 'taste' of the capital. Among its youth, more than half have migrated from other regions, especially rural areas. Sixty per cent of young girls claim they fear being raped, 50 per cent of youths describe living in fear of someone in their neighborhood, and young women have far fewer safety networks in their neighborhoods compared to boys.

A place known for cholera and other excrement-related diseases, Kibera is not just home to impoverished Kenyans. Its inhabitants also include middle class and civil servants; even the wealthy choose to live there. One resident Bilgin spoke with, originally from Uganda, confirmed that people live in Kibera because it is cheap – after all, you do not pay for electricity or water – and because there is a true sense of community. At the same time, you belong to a specific 'group' for purposes of security. But there are problems as well. Taxis, many of which have false plates, are often run by criminal gangs and control commutes to Nairobi proper (that is, for those who can afford the fare). HIV/AIDS rates are high, and many Nairobi prostitutes are residents of Kibera. It may sound like a nightmare. It is.

To the Kenyan government's credit, under an initiative from the United Nations Human Settlements Programme (commonly known as UN-HABITAT), attempts were made to eliminate current slums and replace them with high-rise apartment housing. Almost universally among Kiberans, this is unacceptable: they do not trust the government (which closed down and blocked off Kibera in the 2008 violence) and do not believe they can afford the costs of such housing, essentially turning 'horizontal slums into vertical ones.'[10] For many, though, Kibera is a place to make a stand – emblematic of slums in major urban centers of Africa and representing deep, enduring challenges that lie ahead.

Rio and the future favela

In October 2009, the *cidade maravilhosa* (marvelous city) of Rio de Janeiro – one of the most densely populated locales on earth – was named the site of the 2016 Summer Olympic Games. Bypassing stunned contenders such as Chicago, Madrid, and Tokyo, Rio emerged as the first city in South America to host an Olympic event and asserted its position as a major player on the world urbanization–globalization stage.

Within days violence had broken out across the city. Thirty-three people were left dead in the space of a few days and the unbridled optimism of the Olympic 'win,' which had left President Luiz Inácio Lula da Silva sobbing with happiness at its announcement, was shattered. Members of the dominant criminal gang in Rio, the Comando Vermelho (Red Command) had attacked a rival gang in the Morro dos Macacos ('Hill of Monkeys'). From the moments shots were first fired, everything – literally and figuratively – went downhill.

Nominally the attack was about control of drug trafficking – who controls what, who gets the profit, who is in charge. In reality, and as the governments of Rio and Brazil have been slow to adjust to, the real struggle is over turf. Increasingly sophisticated in organization and increasingly aggressive in their approaches to power, leaders of criminal networks use violence as means to secure territory and to eliminate competitors. This is no longer about the sale of drugs. The stakes are far higher now – and anyone who gets in the way dies.

Rio, among South American megacities, is not unique. In São Paulo, for example, Primeiro Comando da Capital ('First Capital Command') exercises similar authority, able to shut down the city for days at a time with drive-by shooting waves and public bus immolations. Over the past decades Rio (and São Paulo) has experienced extraordinary levels of violence. In 2008 there were 4,631 homicides in the Rio metropolitan area; New York City proper, by contrast, saw 523.

One of the most horrific incidents took place in early 2007 when carjackers forced a vehicle to the side of the road in a working-class neighborhood. The thieves motioned for the mother and her two children to exit the vehicle and move to the sidewalk. One of the children, a six-year-old boy, could not unlatch his seatbelt. The thieves took off – with the boy still hanging from the driver's-side rear door. He was dragged for four miles across the city, even as the driver violently swerved the car from side to side to shake his limp body loose. Eventually, they abandoned the car. The boy's corpse was still hanging from the seatbelt.[11]

With a population of 14 million, Rio is considered the cultural heart of Brazil. With roots deep in the heart of many *favelas*, Rio has seen a spike in violent – and organized – crime. Gangs have regularly attacked tourist sites, police stations, and buses, and act with impunity. Violence continues indiscriminate and unchecked. As one *favelada* confided to Liotta on the fate of most young men growing up in these ramshackle communities, 'They start young … usually around eleven years old … and they die young.'

Derived from the Brazilian equivalent for 'shantytown,' *favelas* (with inhabitants known as *favelados*) are common in the megacities of Rio de Janeiro and São Paulo. Characteristically *favelas* are both in the middle of cities and on the periphery. Lacking formal electricity or plumbing for sewers and drinking water, they are constructed from materials ranging from bricks to boards to garbage. *Favelas* are cramped and overcrowded – each a malignant culture rife with unrest and disorder, violence and insecurity – plagued by fetid sewage and rampant crime.

Favelas of Rio dominate the city's landscape. They rise just inland from the famous beaches of Copacabana and Ipanema. To wealthier Brazilians, of course, *favelas* are looked on as a disgrace and an embarrassment. Rio's middle- and upper-class residents sometimes see their nightmare becoming reality: the 'hills' – as *favelas* are known as – taking over the 'asphalt' – the developed parts of the city. Yet, with over six hundred *favelas* in Rio alone (with many of them bordering neighborhoods of the wealthiest residents), these communities have become a permanent feature of the Brazilian megacity landscape.

The *favela* of Cidade de Deus ('City of God') in Jacarepaguá, in the western zone of the city of Rio, was planned and executed by the state government of Guanabara as part of the policy to systematically remove *favelas* from the center of Rio. Many displacements came from Rocinha in a failed effort to reduce and ultimately remove the 'eyesore' of the first well-established *favela*. Founded in 1960, and shockingly portrayed in Meirelles's film, CDD (as it is known to residents) was intended to settle inhabitants in suburbs. Ironically, the city of Rio has now enveloped CDD and reached far beyond its boundaries; the City of God has, in effect, 'returned' to the heart of Rio. The *favelas* of Rio are now themselves *cities* of God.

Today, Rio's six hundred *favela* communities form the city inside the city, permanent features on the human landscape. Generations have grown there, and the 'hills' have conquered the 'asphalt.' With most residents living in extreme poverty, and with limited opportunities beyond what ingenuity can provide for, in neighborhoods where police most often refuse to patrol, the parallel power structures of *favelas* encompass highly organized, ferocious, and armed gangs that operate in lieu of normal government institutions. It may seem like chaos, but there is precision and control – and a power struggle going on – everywhere.[14]

Given the turmoil, no solution to the challenges of *favela* gangs and their security impact seems to exist. Action inside *favelas* by government agencies, especially by military forces, is hugely unpopular. Liotta interviewed a senior military officer who had operated inside several *favelas*. Ordered to lead a Marine helicopter raid into one of the most notorious communities, the officer related that he had little or no direction on how to conduct the raid other than to apprehend a specific list of individuals. When asked what the rules of engagement were for others not specifically targeted for arrest, he received vague advice. 'What should I do,' he asked for example, 'if a ten-year-old boy is holding a Kalašnikov in our face as we land?'

Specially trained police units often operate against drug gangs in *favelas* with tank-like armored vehicles, known as *caveirãoes*, which translates as 'big skulls.' Partially named for the symbol painted on the side of many of these vehicles – a skull pierced by a dagger with two crossed assault rifles in the background – the *caveirão* also represents the powerful symbolic failure of public security policy. As Amnesty International details in numerous reports, the symbolism is not lost on *favelados*. As one resident described it in agonizing frustration,

> Imagine an official armored vehicle, emblazoned with a skull and a sword, with police who come in shooting – first at the streetlights, then at the neighborhood's residents … this is the *caveirão*. An 11-year-old boy had his head torn off his body by shots which came from the *caveirão* – and we, the residents, still have to prove that it was the police.[13]

There have been attempts to bring 'softer' community policing efforts to communities. None has proven particularly effective. To the contrary, the *Christian Science Monitor* reports that most met with embarrassing results. In one experimental area, 'seventy per cent of the participating officers were accused of wrongdoing and removed … The project eventually fell apart and violence returned.'[14]

One effort touted as success as Rio marches toward its modest goal of securing forty *favelas* – out of six hundred – by the Summer Olympics is the *Unidade de Polícia Pacificadora* (UPP) or, more simply, the Peace Police. The goal is simple: to instill trust, even respect, for police where none previously existed and to transfer assurance security from gangs to good governance. The UPP official website proclaims its goals as:

> to bring police and population closer together, as well as to strengthen social policies inside communities. Even as Rio and São Paulo face enormous challenges from ever-expanding, and ever-more-accomplished, criminal networks, *favela* residents – caught in the crossfire between governments and gangs – manage to hang on, sometimes even prosper. While government must develop a more coherent strategy to confront more sophisticated crime, problems will continue to evolve and mutate. The solution is not found in placing forty thousand security personnel on the street during times of turmoil. Nor is the problem securing the city for its international esteem during the World Cup finals or for the Olympic Games. The real challenge for the state is human security. If the state cannot provide for the safety and security of its citizens, then meltdown slowly begins. Ever since Hobbes's *Leviathan,* this has been the basic expectation about what a state can guarantee for its citizens. Sadly, in Rio, the Leviathan state – providing basic security for citizens – does not exist for many residents.[15]

In 2011, Brazil eclipsed Britain and France to become the world's fifth largest economy. Rio – the spiritual, cultural, and political heart of Brazil – is a prime example of an international city in a state emerging as a major twenty-first-century power. Both the city and the state suffer and enjoy the benefits of urbanization and globalization. In almost every way, we have never been here before in human history. And it remains unclear how we, and residents of critical megacities around the globe, will emerge from the process.

Redrawing the map of the future: the case for resilience in an urban century

Despite the overwhelming challenges cities and those who live there face, there exists numerous examples of resilience and promise.

At the heart of such hope lies a basic sense of community and communal purpose. In massive cities, the ideal is to have such polity function as a magnet for education, employment, and public services, with access to justice and civil rights. In many locales, however, this has simply failed. When municipal governance fails, the community must take over. As Timothy Sisk writes:

> Resilient urban democracies are more likely to successfully manage and contain inter-group tensions that could lead to violence than are city authorities lacking legitimacy and the consent of the people. Strong systems of urban democracy diffuse values of tolerance, inclusion, accountability and citizen participation, deepening conflict resilience and broadening the basis of human security at the community level. Urban democracy can't be waged as a winner-take-all contest if it is to promote conflict resilience.[16]

Still, we do see cases of resilience. In Mumbai, for example, inadequate and corrupt police forces and inequitable access to policing services for the poor (especially women) has led communities to become directly involved in neighborhood policing through a system of more than two hundred *panchayats* that mediate local disputes and serve as intermediaries between slum residents and police. By harnessing community purpose *panchayat* representatives help moderate and settle disputes without resorting to a more formal legal system. The *panchayat* has improved police transparency and accountability, since police and police procedures face more public scrutiny.[17]

UN-HABITAT initiatives also point to ways in which improving slums builds human security capacity. Even modest efforts to improve slum conditions can equally improve social capital. In Nairobi's Korogocho slum, the Adopt-a-Light program, which promotes private sector sponsorship of streetlighting in busy areas, has affected public safety perceptions and fostered new relationships among residents, communities, and public institutions. In the bustling city of Durban, South Africa, involving traditional chiefs in policy planning helped defuse potential conflicts during the state's move from apartheid to democratic rule.

Allowing for democratic governance and participation, strengthening social capital and opportunities for access – especially access to scarce resources – and involving residents in municipal governance policy and decision making are crucial components in the quest for urban resilience.

As daunting as problems truly are, securing human security in an urban century is not a lost cause – yet.

The first steps towards meeting the challenges of megacities require recognizing the nature and severity of the problems. Initiatives to generate awareness and mobilize action include the following:

1 Take on the politics of plunder: governments and megacity leaders themselves – not foreign donors – should design projects and set agendas that focus on both physical and social infrastructure improvement and urban design and planning, as well as health and education improvement. Political leaders must be held accountable.
2 Invest in regional organizations: we must increase reliance on regional organizations to reduce the burden on the UN and delegate greater responsibilities to organizations that are closer to the scene than New York or Geneva. Regional organizations *can* play a crucial role in promoting economic growth among neighboring states and *can* promote stability through peacekeeping missions to member states. Regional organizations *can* be important sources of assistance in matters such as law enforcement or with problems such as natural disasters, pollution, and disease that know no borders.

3 Broker cooperative ventures for transnational missions.
4 Make aid work best, by bringing governments and NGOs together.
5 Mobilize and coordinate private sector contributions.
6 Harness remittances and microcredits and avoid their dangers.
7 Promote megacity-oriented civil society and civil-human security.
8 Establish 'charter cities,' whereby the UN, a regional organization, or an ad hoc coalition be given temporary responsibility for administering and reforming failed municipal agencies in select megacities.

In addition, 'micro-steps' required include:

- recognizing human rights as the cornerstone of security
- the use of microcredits, mechanisms to measure community-level progress
- drawing on community organizers and local NGOs as mediators or negotiator; improving child education
- community-level training for police; and enhancing civil-police cooperation.

Securing land reform in shantytowns and slums that so dominate the urban landscape in megacities is possible. In almost all megacities, slums are illegal settlements on public and, in some cases, private land, and the slum dwellers have no right to their homes. Some form of land reform, under which residents can acquire title to land they reside on, would stabilize the communities and promote socioeconomic growth.

Residents, simply, have a stake in and possess the incentive to improve community if they are only given privilege – and respect due them.

By establishing systems and mechanisms that promote bottom-up change in megacities, real change would happen. Some of this can be achieved by improving education and transportation systems so that residents acquire wider skills and manage to get to where the jobs actually are. Land reform could provide access to capital.

Brazil attempts to assert control over its notoriously ungoverned *favelas* in Rio de Janeiro and São Paulo – sending what amounts to massive force into neighborhoods to establish order and then set up what might become permanent outposts to maintain an effective presence. After decades of neglecting the violence, crime, and wretched living conditions in *favelas*, Brazil has begun taking these actions to prepare for hosting the 2014 World Cup and the 2016 Summer Olympics. Brazil has also been fortunate enough to enjoy dramatic economic growth in recent years and can now presumably afford to confront some social problems more seriously than it has in the past.

States with the most challenging human security-urbanization problems do not have the same levels of incentives or economic resources as Brazil – but they possess the need. The international community and effective regional identities may need to honestly determine what resources are required for security units to intervene in urban communities and consider if military forces may have to remain until 'local' units are prepared to step in and stabilize, secure, and sustain both humans and the city.

This *is* harsh prescription. But establishing human security and the rule of law inside urban environments is crucial to addressing the dangers residents face and the stability governments might lose

Right decisions to deal with urban insecurity must focus on the long view and not just the *next* crisis. To do so wisely requires strategic attention, strategic planning, and strategic investment. But by doing this, we provide the best hope for addressing problems that cities of the majority world – and through them, the rest of the world – now face.

Notes

1 P. H. Liotta's latest book is *The Real Population Bomb: Megacities, Global Security & the Map of the Future.* As a member of the United Nations Intergovernmental Panel on Climate Change, UN's IPCC, he shared the 2007 Nobel Peace Prize. Aybüke Bilgin is a doctoral candidate at Salve Regina University, focusing on women's development and rights.

2 Onookome Okome, 'Writing the Anxious City: Images of Lagos in Nigerian Home Video Films,' in *Under Siege: Four African Cities – Freetown, Johannesburg, Kinshasa, Lagos: Documenta11_Platform4,* moderated by *Okwui Enwezor* (Ostfildern, Germany: Hatje Cantz Verlag, 2003). Program outline and speakers are available in pdf form at: http://www.radiobridge. net/www/folder.pdf.

3 *The Responsibility to Protect: Report of the International Commission on Intervention and State Sovereignty* (Ottawa: International Development Research Centre, 2001), http://responsibilitytoprotect.org/ICISS%20Report.pdf (accessed 24 May 2013).

4 Though space does not allow further discussion, human security is hardly new. Its roots lie in Marxism and, indeed, Marx was not the first 'Marxist.' Rather, Plato was – or more appropriately Socrates, since the roots of dialectical analysis and social struggle for advancement begin here. (Liotta's former professor of Cornell – also his oddest and most beloved – the deconstructionist Jacques Derrida, would refer to Socrates as the greatest writer who ever lived, because he 'never wrote a word.')

5 Emma Rothschild, 'What is Security? The Quest for World Order,' *Dædulus: The Journal of the American Academy of Arts and Sciences,* June 1995, 124, 3: 53–98.

6 Bohle, H.-G (2001) 'Vulnerability and Criticality: Perspectives from Social Geography'. *IHDP Update* 2/01, 3–5. Leichenko, R.M. and K. O'Brien (2002) 'The Dynamics of Rural Vulnerability to Global Change: The Case of Southern Africa', *Mitigation and Adaptation Strategies for Global Change* 7(1):1–18.

7 'Commentary,' *Security Dialogue,* September 2004, 35, 3: 278.

8 The Kiswahili word for government is *serikali,* a combination of words *siri* (secret) and *kali* (fierce).

9 In Kikuyu, *Mungiki* means 'multitude' or 'united people.' Although we can identify no central doctrine, the Mungiki reject all things Western, including Christianity, as trappings of colonialism, favoring Kikuyu tradition over Kenya's modernization.

10 The average rent for a Kiberan resident is 600 Kenyan shillings a month – roughly $7.50. To move into high-rise Kiberan apartments is a considerable expense. While some single-bedroom housing in the Karanja Estates costs 2,000 Kenyan shillings a month, rents can go as high as 15,000 shillings for a three-bedroom in Kibera housing – an increase of 2,500 per cent from average rent and the equivalent of six months' salary for many. As of late 2010, construction had ceased, and it was unclear whether or not Kiberan apartment dwellers were paying any rent at all.

11 In this brutal carjacking in which the boy's body was left hanging from his seatbelt, the gang leader, twenty-three-year-old Carlos Eduardo Toledo Lima, was incarcerated under an open-regime prison system. When he failed to return to prison in late December 2006, no action was taken to locate him.

12 By the use of 'parallel power structure,' we mean that within *favelas* municipal governance often has no effective meaning; community governance runs parallel to, or in place of, outside influence.

13 '"We Have Come to Take Your Souls": The *Caveirão* and Policing in Rio de Janeiro,' Amnesty International, March 2006: AI Index: AMR 19/007/2006, http://www.amnesty.org/en/library/asset/AMR19/007/2006/en/1327a7a0-d454-11dd-8743-d305bea2b2c7/amr190072006en.pdf (accessed 24 May 2013).

14 Andrew Downie, 'Brazil Vows Olympic Security after Rio Violence: At Least 14 People Were Killed in Rio de Janeiro This Weekend, Including Two Policemen Who Died When Their Helicopter was Brought Down by Warring Drug Gangs,' October 18, 2009, *Christian Science Monitor,* http://www.csmonitor.com/World/Americas/2009/1018/p06s07-woam.html (accesssed 24 May 2013).

15 *Unidade de Polícia Pacificadora* website, http://www.upprj.com/ (accesssed 24 May 2013).

16 'Realizing the cosmopolitan ideal,' *Human Security for an Urban Century: Local Challenges, Global Perspectives,* 66, http://www.eukn.org/E_library/Security_Crime_Prevention/Security_Crime_Prevention/Human_security_for_an_urban_century_local_challenges_global_perspectives (accesssed 24 May 2013).

17 Sheela Patel, 'Community policing through police panchayats in Mumbai,' *Human Security for an Urban Century: Local Challenges, Global Perspectives,* Ottawa: Human Security Policy Division, Foreign Affairs and International Trade Canada, 2006, pp. 98-99.

PART II

Human security applications

9

VIOLENT CONFLICT AND THE INDIVIDUAL SECURITY DILEMMA

Mient Jan Faber and Martijn Dekker

Introduction

In the midst of a violent conflict, the search for human security is the first and foremost priority for every individual involved. However, one individual's quest for security may well endanger the security of others. People who are suffering from, or threatened by, violence, are confronted with numerous dilemmas when they seek to protect themselves and those around them. The way one acts when war breaks out, and the strategies one has to consider, differ from person to person. Where you live, which social or ethnic group(s) you are member of, your financial situation, and even your social capital – who do you know? – all influence your actions, the possibility of finding human security and, ultimately, your chances of survival. It is these difficult choices and the consequences thereof that are the ontological foundation for a critical analysis of human security initiatives in war situations – human security from below.

In order to illustrate our individual-centred approach to human security, we present you with an historical example of the personal dilemmas that arise when war breaks out. In the early days of World War II, as Hitler's expansionist thrust spread out over Europe, the Jewish populations of Germany's neighbours, Denmark and the Netherlands, were justifiably afraid of expulsion or persecution. In Denmark the German occupation was solely of a military nature, while in the Netherlands the Nazis also took over the state, since the Dutch government and Royal family fled the country and remained in the UK during the war. As a result most Danish Jews survived the war, while over a hundred thousand Jews from the Netherlands were massacred in German concentration camps. The main reason for this is that the Jews in Denmark were still protected by the Danish state, while the Dutch Jews, because of the absence of the Dutch government, were surrendered to the German Nazi regime. Although the Dutch Jews were mostly assimilated into society, and largely unarmed, self-protection against the German police forces or local collaborators was not a viable option, which meant that they had only three choices to improve their security; to flee, to hide, or to huddle together, hoping to be left alone. While fleeing abroad was difficult for many and hiding in plain sight did not provide a sense of safety, hiding somewhere else in the country was often seen as the only viable option, making them dependent on the behaviour of fellow citizens for their security.

The choice for offering a hiding place to Jews in your own home was not an easy one to make, as it significantly increased the insecurity of yourself and your family. It is estimated that

In The Netherlands between sixty and a hundred thousand people were engaged in providing hiding places to people – mostly for men trying to escape the so-called 'Arbeitseinsatz' (labour deployment) in Germany and for resistance fighters, and less for Jews – which is a considerable number, but still a small minority in a population of about ten million people. Obviously, the choice for becoming a resistance operative was dangerous, which is why only a small group was actively involved in actions aimed at sabotaging and hindering the occupying forces.

Wars and conflicts are difficult to be abstracted; each conflict has its own dynamics, which are largely determined by forces on the ground and shaped by decisions made by individuals. It is therefore that one of the tenets of human security, the challenge to the state-centric thinking of conventional, (neo-)realist-oriented, security studies, is of vital importance. Human security starts and ends with individual human beings.

Human security and critical security studies

We do not wish to delve deeper into the ontological and epistemological debates surrounding human security, which have been discussed in preceding chapters. However, before presenting our bottom-up approach to security, two conceptual remarks that shape *human security from below* have to be made. The first deals with the broadening of the traditional concept of security, which is termed *securitisation* by critical security scholars from the so-called Copenhagen School. They argue that by increasingly labelling certain phenomena as existential threats to the state, this 'designation of the threat as existential justifies the use of extraordinary measures to handle it' (Wæver 2004: 9). In other words, securitisation, i.e. expanding the concept of security, is a *speech act* meant to legitimise the use of force and to maintain or enforce beneficial power relations. It is therefore why many critical security scholars plead for a narrow approach to security, in the sense that it focuses on 'real threats' against 'real people' (Ibid.). But despite the many security scholars who plead for bringing the individual back to the centre of security analyses, the state often remains essential, at least in the sense that insecurity is perceived to occur at the level of actual people but the act of preventing or decreasing security problems is still attributed to state actors.

Therefore the second conceptual remark deals with the supposedly changed referent object of security. Despite being presented as a shift away from neo-realist security thinking, and thus a departure from traditional state security and signalling a human-centred approach, the idea of the state as main provider of human security remains pivotal. This state-centric propensity is exemplified by the policy-oriented and problem-solving tendencies inherent to human security thought, which renders it 'uncritical', working within existing political and institutional settings, and prevailing power-relations, rather than critically assessing them (Newman 2010). Solutions for human insecurity are devised in the hallways and conference rooms of cosmopolitan institutions like the United Nations, the European Union, the African Union and others, like NATO.

In this chapter we offer a critical view of the cosmopolitan peace project, and its use of human security as a guiding principle in particular. Although the R2P doctrine,[1] which was adopted by the UN General Assembly in 2005, is an admirable attempt to update the prevailing Westphalian sovereignty paradigm to a twenty-first-century, universalistic, moral obligation to protect every human being on the planet in spite of state borders, it remains rather doubtful whether a cosmopolitan approach will be an effective answer to elusive phenomena like new wars and international terrorism. We therefore share the critical stance towards human security, as voiced by critical security scholars like Krause (1998, 2004), Booth (2005, 2007) and Grayson (2008), amongst others, in the sense that its discourse is manoeuvring within, and 'uncritically' reinforcing, the prevailing status-quo of global power-relations. The main argument of this chapter is that a bottom–up, rather than a top–down approach is the only way forward to try to grasp contemporary, violent conflicts, and by doing so, we echo Newman's (2010) call for the development of so-called Critical Human Security Studies (CHSS).

Human security and new wars

Having said this, the question is: how to critically assess human security and look at it from the individual perspective? In a bottom–up approach, the first issue to be addressed is the situation on the ground in contemporary wars and conflicts. This involves a major discursive development in security thought which concerns an increased awareness of the supposedly changed nature of contemporary warfare. This change in security thought broadly commenced after the end of the Cold War and was linked to the drastic changes in international power relations.

Following the fall of the Berlin wall and the collapse of the Soviet empire, two prevailing representations of what the post-Cold War political arena would look like emerged, but despite there being arguments for both of them, the era did not herald the coming of a Kantian (1976) democratic peace, neither was the coming to an end of the bipolar world order the start of an increasingly chaotic and violent era, as suggested by Snow (1996), Huntington (1997), and Ogata et al. (2003).

Statistics do not support an increase in the number of conflicts; some even suggest a slight decrease (Newman 2004, De Wilde 2008). Violent conflict, as the ultimate manifestation of political struggle, has remained rather constant in occurrence (Heirman 2009), but some authors argue that the nature of conflicts did change. 'New wars' theory, advanced by Münkler (2005) and, most notably, by Kaldor (2001), became a principal theoretical paradigm to describe the dynamics of contemporary conflicts. According to new wars theory, the novelty of modern-day conflicts, compared to the more traditional inter-state wars that had been prevalent for the last few centuries,[2] revolves around six main features: the actors, motives, means, spatial context, impact or human suffering, and the political or war economy (Newman 2004).[3]

Much can be argued against new wars theory. All of the supposedly new characteristics attributed to contemporary conflicts have clearly been present in wars before, whether it concerns the involvement of private actors, the occurrence of intra-state (or civil) wars, the explicit targeting of civilians, the funding by non-state actors, or the importance of the illegal war economy (Hossein-Zadeh 2006) and the myriad small-scale criminals who benefit from conflict. Indeed, according to Newman it is not so much the characteristics of war that have changed themselves but rather our perception or, rather, awareness of them. 'Shifts in the causes, nature, and impact of war are more apparent than real' (Newman 2004: 179). This has much to do with the lack of detailed historical sources and, in contrast, the current abundance of available information and statistics on conflicts.

Although challenging 'a number of assumptions and theses' (Newman 2004: 186) related to new wars theory, Newman does, however, acknowledge its 'great service in deepening understanding of civil war'. It is exactly why human security is inextricably linked to new wars theory and why the latter is of vital importance, despite an apparent lack of empirical proof. On the one hand, new wars theory seeks an explanation for the chaotic and combustible mixture of identity politics, organised crime, terrorism and other gruesome forms of violence that characterise war, and on the other hand, CHSS for a considerable part builds on this theory, in the sense that it acknowledges that finding ways to provide security in contemporary conflicts does not start with looking at the current international, cosmopolitan institutions, or applying labels such as 'civil war', 'new war' or 'war of aggression' to conflicts, but that it has to commence with a deepening understanding of the unpredictability and chaos that constitute the reality on the ground.

The security fabric – self-protection, horizontal and vertical security

When the individual is the focal point of security, we have to take the instinctive need for human self-preservation as a starting point. According to Thomas Hobbes this human urge to self-preservation was in fact the only natural right. But, so reasoned Hobbes, while trying to preserve their individual power, men are forced to compete with their peers; the security of one person, or group of people, may well lead to the insecurity of others – a situation of anarchy.[4]

Hobbes' reasoning meant a radical departure from the peace paradigm that was dominant during the Middle Ages. Until that time, the prevalent thought, vocalised by Augustine and Thomas Aquinas amongst others, was that human beings were ultimately inclined to live peacefully together, by God's will (Dekker and Faber 2009). Hobbes, however, thus argued that a human being is in a constant and 'competitive struggle for power (...) or at least [struggling] to resist his powers being commanded by others' (1968: 37). In other words, people living in what he called the natural condition, were engaged in a war of all against all, *bellum omnium contra omnes* (Hobbes 1968). Indeed, security and freedom, although inextricably linked, are not interchangeable. Freedom is a prerequisite for feeling secure, but either too much or too little of it, will increase an individual's insecurity.

Hobbes' war of all against all has been pacified through a metaphorical contract between the citizens, in which they delegated the power to rule over them to the Leviathan, a large sea monster referred to in the Bible, by which he meant the sovereign or state.[5]

The latter guarantees the first a certain degree of freedom, but that freedom should not undermine the state's necessary security and ability to uphold law and order. As Baron de Montesquieu, founder of the *trias politica* theory, stated it in his *The Spirit of the Laws* (1989): 'Liberty is the right to do what the law allows (…) if a citizen could do what [the laws] forbid, it would be no longer liberty, because others would have the same powers.'

For this analysis we will depart from a negative, liberal interpretation of freedom, meaning that it equates the freedom from interference by the state and considers it inversely proportionate to state strength. While focusing on security, this implies that the more powerful a state and its security apparatus are, the more constraints they will place on the individual to provide for his or her own security, and, thus, the more people's (negative) freedom is curbed. Eventually, this will also negatively influence human security. When a state's security apparatus becomes too powerful, the legitimacy of the monopoly on the use of force declines among the people who do not benefit from the state's ubiquity. This means that the success of a state, expressed in its legitimacy, largely depends on finding the right balance between liberty and law enforcement, or, put differently, between individual freedom and security by government regulation (Zakaria 2007). But how does human security fit into this model?

Figure 9.1 is an (over)simplified representation of the state's power and its ability to place restraints on individual people's freedom. In this model, state power refers to the state's grip on the monopoly on the use of force. The word 'legitimate', as it was used in Weber's definition, is left out on purpose, while an authoritarian state may have an absolute monopoly on violence which may not be considered to be legitimate by part of the population.

The extreme ends of the axis are the violent state of nature as it was described by Hobbes and the totalitarian state as it was envisioned by George Orwell in his *1984*, respectively (Orwell 1990). For Hobbes, the ultimate answer to his *natural state,* in which there was no governing body, was the Orwellian state of repression, in the form of an absolute monarch.[6]

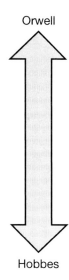

Figure 9.1 Hobbes–Orwell scale

States' positions in the graph obviously change over time. When we, for example, look at Iraq, we see that its position moved from a top position on the scale, with Saddam Hussein's pre-2003 strong Orwellian state apparatus, to a position on the lower end, with a very weak state and a new war raging, in 2006 and 2007. A brief study of this proposed model inevitably leads to the conclusion that human security, i.e. freedom from fear, is neither guaranteed in a Hobbesian nor in an Orwellian state.

In a stable state positioned somewhere in the middle of the Hobbes–Orwell scale, and where conflict is absent, it is usually clear which institutions are responsible for providing security; the police, intelligence, and the army. However, the Westphalian system of sovereign states, in which each state is responsible for its own citizens' security, is under pressure from both supranational as well as local processes, as is the realist ontology of state-centred security arrangements. But the apparently decreasing primacy of state power is a multilevel issue and does not only concern the hitherto international anarchic system in which each state is on its own and constantly in competition with others. It is also within states, traditionally considered to be 'black boxes' by neo-realists, who do not take states' domestic characteristics into account, that problems have become more prevalent and, at the very least, more visible. While large-scale inter-state wars have become quite rare, (cross-border) intra-state conflicts have gained prominence as the most common, and thus threatening, form of organised violence. Sub-state actors, from armed militias to full-fledged secessionist movements, also add to the multitude of processes that undermine the state's power and monopoly on the legitimate use of force.

The three different types of security provision and their related actors are:

1 Self-protection (of the individual, family, community, etc.)
2 Horizontal protection (protection of category 1 subjects by non-state actors of all kinds, like life-lines, humanitarian organisations, militant groups, etc.)
3 Vertical protection (protection by state-actors, including foreign states, UN, NATO, etc.).

    The first and most basic dimension of security, i.e. self-protection, may not sound that revolutionary but it does depart from conventional, state-centric security studies in the sense that states may not be able to provide protection to individual citizens and specific groups, and may even be a great source of insecurity.

The self and horizontal dimensions of security (1 and 2) are considered to be *human security from below*. In many instances, specifically in weak states or war situations, there is no balance of power between the security-providing agents, and the dynamics are continually changing. On the other hand, for several structural reasons, the dynamics between the actors within these three dimensions may be relatively static in stable democracies; this may also hold true for authoritarian regimes which successfully uphold a strict monopoly on the use of force.

To analyse these changing security dynamics within states, specifically those which are relatively unstable and prone to violent conflict, we use the so-called *security fabric*. The security fabric can be conceptualised as the composition of a definite territory in terms of its security architecture, meaning the actors involved, their (sometimes self-imposed) mandate and actual duties, territorial boundaries in which they operate and the level of influence they exert over that area, and their respective ethnic religious, social, and cultural affiliations. In short, the security fabric consists of the official state's security apparatus, from above, and non–state actors – security zones and communities –which provide human security from below.

In order to illustrate the variety of actors that influence the security dynamics, we have devised a number of security fabric ideal types. Figure 9.2 shows the security fabric in a stable, democratic society, in which security is mainly provided by the state but non-state actors are allowed to organise their own initiatives like neighbourhood watches, and security personnel in shopping malls.

Figure 9.3 depicts the security fabric of an authoritarian state and is also characterised by a relative stability. It is, however, a stability that is much more enforced. The width of the top arrow, representing the actors that are associated with human security from above, indicates that a much larger state security apparatus is needed, and simultaneously, human security from below is not tolerated as it is considered to be a threat to the state itself.

The opposite of a strong, authoritarian state is the failed state, as depicted in Figure 9.4. Failing, in this sense, means that the state is not able to uphold its monopoly on the use force in all of its territories. This may refer to a state that is confronted with a powerful secessionist movement but also to one that has to deal with various groups of non-state actors, such as rebel groups or armed militias, that have been able to challenge the state's security forces.

A failed state does not automatically mean that a war has broken out or that daily violence occurs. When, however, war breaks out, a major consequence is a drastic change in the security architecture of a territory; new actors emerge and the power-relations between them change continuously. This concerns both state- and non-state actors.

When international actors decide to intervene in an ongoing war, the security fabric will look something like Figure 9.5. It is a rather complex situation, in which various local and foreign actors, both state and non-state, compete for the power over certain territories, in order to establish a (local) monopoly on the use of force. The same goes for an inter-state war, in which foreign state-actors, in the form of an army, are also involved.

Often, in wartime, society is militarised, which means that the security apparatus of the state is not simply pre-occupied with fighting the enemy but also bolsters internal security, thereby trying to prevent security threats from within.

A last example of the security fabric ideal types is the imploded state, as seen in Figure 9.6. When the state's institutions, particularly the security apparatus, cease to exist, a chaotic and violent situation will ensue, in which rival non-state actors will compete for state power. This situation will last until one of the non-state actors is able to re-establish a central regime with a

Figure 9.2 Stable, democratic state

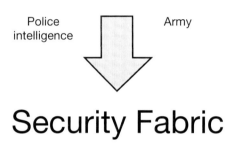

Figure 9.3 Authoritarian state

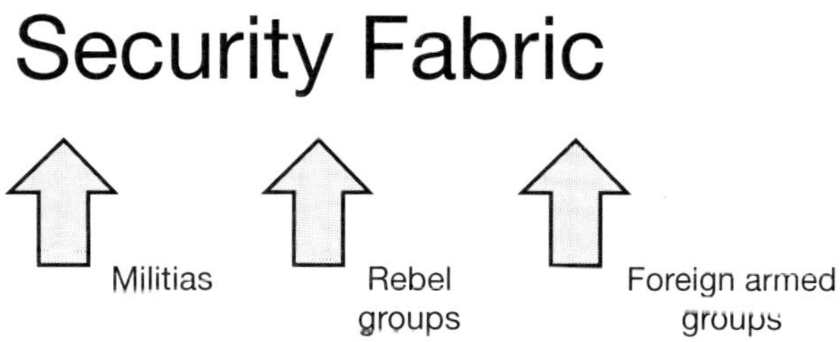

Security Fabric

Militias Rebel groups Foreign armed groups

Figure 9.4 The failed state

monopoly on the use of force, either alone or assisted by one or more foreign actors. Especially in the initial period of the new regime, the security fabric is likely to resemble that of a failed or weak state, as shown in Figure 9.4.

To sum up the above observations, whether a powerful local leader forms his own militia and starts to challenge the state's monopoly on the use of force (Figure 9.4), or if there is a peace-keeping mission deployed (Figure 9.5), or if a state implodes (Figure 9.6), the security fabric

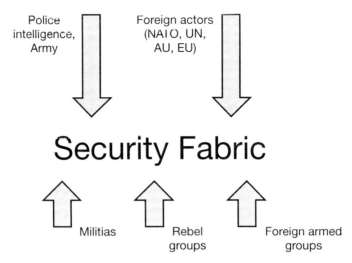

Figure 9.5 Civil war with peacekeeping mission deployment

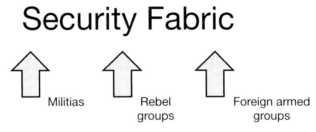

Figure 9.6 Imploded state

will change drastically. In the following paragraph we will focus specifically on the non-state actors, who are pre-occupied with what we term *human security from below.*

Human security from below

The first and foremost instinctual reaction to the outbreak of war is self protection. This starts with barricading your house and protecting yourself and your family, but may develop into considerable areas that are protected by armed groups. In Dekker and Faber (2009), areas in which not the state but non-state actors have taken responsibility for the provision of physical security are called *security zones.* The state's monopoly on the legitimate use of force has successfully been challenged. In many fragile states, these non-state actors have set up rather complex security structures, which are sometimes tantamount to pseudo-states. But also in so-called no-go areas in large cities, criminal gangs sometimes successfully keep the state's official security institutions from entering, roaming the streets with their own weapons.

If we conceptualise security zones as definite geographical areas in which the state's monopoly on the legitimate use of force has successfully been challenged by third parties, then churches, mosques or other buildings of religious significance may also be included, while in many cases they are regarded as sanctuaries, in which unauthorised entrance, let alone the use of weapons, is prohibited, even by official forces such as the police or army. Take for instance the Israeli army's reluctance to enter the Nativity Church in Bethlehem, as a result of which they decided to lay siege to the sanctuary for several weeks instead, in April and May 2002, when Palestinian militants had sought refuge there.

Self-organised security zones may emerge when state institutions are failing or perhaps even breaking down completely. Indeed, these zones are meant to fill in the gap that the state leaves, although the functions of these security zones will most likely develop simultaneously. We consider the first and foremost function of a security zone, to correspond with the most elementary need of people (in conflict situations), is the provision of physical security (Salomons 2006, Herrero 2005, Stokke 2006). It is therefore that many security zones will likely emerge as very rudimentary forms of self-protection – communities such as (extended) families that are seeking shelter together are a prime example of this. However, tribes and clans do already have broader functions and will enhance all of them, in particular providing security, in times of 'war'.

When a situation of protracted violence endures and a security zone (or a multitude of them) becomes more or less entrenched in the dynamics of conflict, the need for other services than providing physical security may emerge. It seems logical that when thousands of people are residing in a fortified area, shielded off from the outside world, the order on the inside also has to be maintained. In other words, the need for policing and basic forms of jurisdiction – rule of law – arises.

In war-torn Somalia, community-based security arrangements demonstrate a clear effort to preserve the rule of law. 'Neighbourhoods and towns have in some places organised the equivalent of "neighbourhood watch" systems, sometimes absorbing former young gunmen into paid protection forces' (Menkhaus 2003: 412). Although these arrangements seem 'hardly ideal, and sometimes engender local resistance, [they] do provide a more predictable security environment for local communities' (Ibid.). Furthermore, local jurisdiction in the form of sharia courts – although their rulings may be harsh, and therefore not of indisputable reputation – is widely acknowledged to have brought a certain stability in those areas and sense of security (Ibid.).

The harsh circumstances in which security zones emerge often have the consequence that the security zone's leaders have authoritarian tendencies, which means that the locally established monopoly on the use of force may lack legitimacy and is forcefully maintained. But although, to the outsider, it may seem a lawless micro society and even though the leaders may not be that benign – using extortion and fear in order to maintain their rule – there may well be strict rules and regulations that give the inhabitants at least, as Menkhaus calls it, a predictable security environment.

In many cases, security zones will dissolve when the conflict has ended. Only very well developed zones with a strong community sense, like for instance Iraqi Kurdistan, will remain, playing a vital role and become part of the (new) state's configuration. When regions have a traditional desire to secede from the state in which they live, wars may help them to reach their goal (Kosovo, Kurdistan, South-Ossetia, etc). In most other cases security zones will more or less dismantle themselves as soon as the war comes to an end.

Although there is often a clear relationship between a security zone and a group identity, the emergence of this connection does not always come about in an equal fashion. If we follow Eric Hobsbawm's line of reasoning (1990), in the sense that nationalism – the claim for the political autonomy of a community, based on a shared history and common destiny – followed state formation, then, in our case, the awareness of being a security community, follows the establishment of the actual security zone. This use of group identity, which can be referred to as identity politics, can indeed be employed by group leaders, in order to bolster the internal cohesion, especially when the own identity is pitted against one or more enemies. However, as we have mentioned earlier, in conflict zones, when identity is often the very reason for feeling insecure, the development of community sense is most likely to precede the actual formation of a security zone, or will develop simultaneously. If we look, for example, to the violence in the Gaza Strip, we see that Hamas had already developed a strong sense of community and gained a lot of goodwill because of numerous social programmes, long before they turned the Gaza Strip into their own self-organised security zone. With their current status in the Gaza Strip, Hamas is trying to provide human security in the traditional fashion, as a state, although their rule has strong authoritarian tendencies and polls suggest that their monopoly on the use of force lacks the legitimacy they aim for.

In northern Iraq, nine Christian villages have taken up arms and organised their own security zone. Traditionally already the home of many Iraqi Christians, the nine villages have now become a safe haven for many Christian refugees from all over Iraq. The Christian community in Iraq was targeted because of the very fact that they were Christians and not Muslims. Their group identity was a major source of insecurity but at the same time it gave them a sense of security to organise themselves together. The dynamics of intra-group cohesion and inter-group hostility reinforcing each other are unmistakable.

When speaking of social boundaries and communities and their connection with actual borders, one simply cannot ignore the brilliant standard work on nationalism, Benedict Anderson's *Imagined Communities* (2006). In his introduction Anderson conceptualises a nation as an 'imagined political community – and imagined as both inherently limited and sovereign' (2006: 6). Anderson explains that it is imagined because, except for small villages, members of communities will likely 'never know most of their fellow-members, meet them, or even hear of them, yet in the minds of each lives the image of their communion' (Ibid.). Furthermore, it is limited while each group (nation) has finite, though flexible boundaries, and is perceived to be sovereign because the idea of nationalism was born in the age of Enlightenment, when the universal claims of religion were contested and the formation of smaller geographical entities led to a longing for freedom through self-determination. Finally, the fact that nations are imagined as communities stems from the 'deep, horizontal comradeship' that constitutes them (Ibid.: 7).

When we try to translate this to our situation and combine it with our conceptualisation of security zones, and take the discussion above into consideration, we may say that security communities are groups of people, living within or across states, with clear, socially constructed borders, whose members with a (imagined) shared identity associate their security, and physical, as well as cultural and economic, well-being with membership of the community. Their shared identity may evolve around political affiliation, religion, kinship, geographical vicinity or any other unifying characteristic. What is more, group boundaries may intersect and membership of a group is certainly not mutually exclusive. The prevailing identity significantly depends on the context and is shaped by the dynamics of social conflict. A Christian Kurd may consider himself to be a Christian when attacked by a Kurdish Islamic group but, in a different context, identifies himself as being a Kurd, and may thus find himself on the same side as the aforementioned Islamic group, when the conflict is framed as being between Iraqis and Kurds.

In times of political turmoil, when identities can become entrenched, communities may develop a yearning for self-determination, after which they become a factor of importance. What is more, when the social borders are complemented with actual ones, and a guarded security zone is created, the foundations for a state-within-a-state are created, and identity politics may be put into effect with violent means.

War situations

In order to illustrate the intricate dynamics of wars, we will discuss two cases, civil war between Jews and Arabs, and old and new war in Iraq.

After the collapse of the Ottoman Empire, Great Britain and France divided the Middle East into so-called mandate states. These entities were temporarily ruled by the Western powers, while developing into independent states. The British Mandate of Palestine was not only home to a considerable majority of Arabs but part of it, as was sketched out in the Balfour Declaration of 1917, was also designated to be the place for a 'National Jewish Home'. Oscillating between the Jewish and Arab interests, the Britons were confronted by what may be referred to as a civil war between the two adversary groups. Up to today, the Jewish and Arab (now referred to as Palestinian) peoples remain in conflict over the territory of the former British Mandate of Palestine.

Currently, the state of Israel, as the epitome of the Jewish Home, outweighs the Palestinian Arabs militarily, politically and economically. Although the Palestinian Arabs have aspired for an independent state for decades, as yet they have not succeeded. Instead most of the territories that are now designated to become part of the future Palestinian state remain under Israeli control or occupation. One of the main reasons for the Jews' current powerful position can be traced back to the days of the British Mandate. While their horizontal organisation, of which security was a vital element, was very well developed, it not only resembled human security from above, as provided by the state-like Jewish Agency, it could also relatively easy be turned into an actual state.

The Palestinians now try to reproduce the Jewish strategy by continuously developing their own state institutions – of which, again, the security apparatus is a vital element – hoping to declare independence in the near future, whether unilaterally or not. Among the manifold difficulties the Palestinians face on this road to statehood are two major impediments. The first is that the course of history has led to a major disparity in power relations between the two adversaries. The Israeli state is such a powerful actor that the Palestinians can only secure their own state with the help of other states.

The second predicament concerns the internal divisions within Palestinian society. Both Gaza and the West Bank, which together are to become the future Palestine state, are ruled by rather authoritarian leaderships that are in competition with each other. By severely cracking down on political and clan-based security structures, human security initiatives from below, the two regimes, most notably Hamas in Gaza, have damaged the legitimacy of their rule. It follows that a viable Palestinian state – and a state that does not pose a threat to surrounding states – without proper support from Palestinian society at large, can only exist as an authoritarian regime. Despite the regional stability and security this would lead to, and the ensuing support of the international community, it would mean that many Palestinian individuals would definitely not enjoy human security.

In Iraq, which started as a rather conventional 'war of liberation', the coalition forces led by the US and UK, after abolishing most of the state's political institutions and security apparatus, quickly saw themselves confronted by a chaotic new war, in which ethnic, religious and communal groups all seemed to be fighting each other – a Hobbesian war, indeed.

During the rapidly emerging dangerous political vacuum, following the decisive invasion of Iraq, and on the request of the UN Security Council, the US and the UK agreed to run the country by themselves, until an Iraqi regime was deemed capable enough to take over. Paul Bremer was appointed the 'emperor' of Iraq, head of the Coalition Provisional Authority (CPA), with absolute powers. He arrived in Baghdad, in May 2003, and a short time later formed the

Interim Governing Council (IGC), a body of former resistance leaders. The IGC would, however, remain completely under control of Bremer's CPA. Indeed, the local leaders of the different sections of the Iraqi society were effectively sidelined, and instead a foreign occupation commenced. After the removal of Saddam, the keys of the state were not handed over to the locals, but the Americans and the British kept the keys for themselves. They, however, proved unable to provide security at all levels of society. What was happening on the ground within and between the various communities was out of the foreigners' reach. Different factions started to fight each other and (sometimes in cooperation with each other) to fight the occupiers. The Iraqi security fabric was quickly transformed from a powerful Orwellian state (led by Saddam Hussein) where practically all human security initiatives from below were suppressed, into a weak Hobbesian state (led by Paul Bremer, the US administrator of the Coalition Provisional Authority), in which horizontal security measures, in the form of armed militias and fortified security zones, mushroomed all over the country. The coalition forces proved unable to provide effective human security from above and instead became caught up between the rivalling groups providing horizontal security and, as such, increasingly mired in protecting themselves.

R2P: security fictions. The gap between security from above and below

According to conventional security theories, as well as most human security scholars, the first actor and foremost responsible actor for providing human security is the state, i.e. the complex of institutions that govern a people within a definite territory. This logically follows from the way the world is socially organised – in states – and rests on the assumption that states are responsible for the security of their people, which is actually one of the key reasons for the very emergence of states as such.

Another example of this type of actor are external states or multilateral coalitions of states that intervene to prevent massive violations of human rights, which occur because of either the lawlessness caused by weak state institutions or the oppressiveness of an authoritarian regime. The strategy of such interventions is that the traditional state's structures which should provide security are assisted – in the case of an operation labelled as 'R2P' – or bypassed without consent – in the case of a humanitarian intervention – in order to directly help the people in need. The reason for such courses of action is the fact that the state's security apparatus is not doing what it is supposed to do, i.e. actually providing security. In failed states this is characterised by a lack of control, because of which lawlessness and crime can prevail, while in oppressive states, the very security apparatus is used to control and oppress the population or specific groups of people.

In times of conflict, when human security from above can (apparently) no longer be relied upon, human security from below prevails; self-protection and horizontally organised forms of security emerge, as sub-state structures, like families (clans), political factions and militias (partly) take over the traditional role of the state as security provider, sometimes by establishing a localised monopoly on the use of force, a security zone. The longer these sub-state structures exist, the more difficult it becomes to neglect them, especially when they enjoy considerable popular support. Critical Human Security Studies specifically take these sub- or non-state actors into account.

While bypassing the state's official (human) security structures, external interventions often also bypass these sub-state actors. Despite the supposed prevalence of individuals over the state, human security from below initiatives, which are partly forms of transitional security but may well transform into entities in their own right in the political landscape of the state where the conflict is taking place, are often neglected. In fact, in most cases such initiatives are viewed as major obstacles (spoilers) on the road to restoring central power. But while violent conflict does not only leave physical scars, the social and security fabric also suffers severely, something that too often remains understated. The reconfiguration of the security fabric, which is a logical consequence of violent conflict, is interpreted as an unwanted temporary phase, in which local actors are undesired competitors, instead of a (temporary) countermeasure to the grave insecurity that characterises war, which many people who are confronted with the daily violence prefer over the absence of any order at all.

However, the prevailing strategy of the international community is often the cause of increased insecurity, where the central authority lacks legitimacy and is mistrusted because of either a weak state apparatus or abuse of power; initiatives from below provide more effective protection of their respective communities; providing security has created a certain position of power for the people responsible for it, which they are not likely to give up without coercion; and finally the emergence of different sub-state actors has shaped a complex web of power relations, which is not easy to break without changing community power relations, which in turn may lead to increased inter-community conflict.

It is a difficult paradox: while human security is conventionally seen as being provided by the state, the logical response to failing or oppressive states might appear to be intervention in order to establish a legitimate, capable and preferably democratic regime, but the monopoly on the use of force is challenged by the armed non-state actors who also search for human security that the international actors are supposed to provide.

A mediating and brokering role by external actors is important in containing intra-state conflict, but it may also imply choosing sides, as American soldiers did when they supported the Sunni-tribes in Iraq in their battle against al-Qaeda, which dominated some tribal areas. Only by acknowledging the role of all actors involved and the existing power relations between them, can security become inclusive. In other words, a true human security strategy should be based on an analysis of the security fabric and the existing power relations between the different security providers, sometimes aimed at taking away the zero-sum effect that characterises them, and sometimes choosing sides. Indeed, it should respect the prevailing situation on the ground, while a mere top-down approach to security and conflict resolution neglects the foundations of state-formation as the very means to achieve human security in the first place.

Notes

1   See for instance, International Commission on Intervention and State Sovereignty (2001).
2   Examples of *traditional* wars, as opposed to *new* wars, are the so-called 'cabinet wars' during the seventeenth and eighteenth centuries, the two *total* (or *world*) wars of the twentieth century, and inter-state wars like the Iran-Iraq war in the 1980s and the first Gulf War.
3   Herfried Münkler, who actually discerns only two major changes in the nature of warfare – the privatisation and the commercialisation of war and the divergence between military strategy and political reality (2005: 30) – adds that 'traditional' wars were formally declared and – after a decisive victory of either one of the warring parties or a political stalemate – concluded with a cease-fire or peace agreement, while new wars, in contrast, are not as clearly defined temporally.
4   On a global level, this phenomenon refers to what is called the 'Security Dilemma'. This concept, first coined by John Herz (1950), describes a process in which states improve their security by arming themselves, which at the same time leads to increased insecurity of other (surrounding) states. The arms race of the Cold War was an evident reflection of this.
5   This metaphorical contract was the outcome of a social contract designed by rational people living in a certain definite territory.
6   Although Hobbes himself favoured a liberal state, in which a large amount of individual, negative freedom was guaranteed.

References

Anderson, B. (2006) *Imagined Communities*. 2nd edition with new material. London: Verso.

Booth, K. (2005) 'Beyond Critical Security Studies', in Ken Booth (ed.) *Critical Security Studies and World Politics*. Boulder, Colorado: Lynne Rienner, pp. 259–278.

Booth, K. (2007) *Theory of World Security*. Cambridge: Cambridge University Press.

De Wilde, J. H. (2008) 'Speaking or Doing Human Security', in Monica den Boer & Jaap de Wilde (eds) *The Viability of Human Security. From Concept to Practice*. Amsterdam: Amsterdam University Press.

Dekker, M. and Faber, M. J. (2009) 'Winning the Hearts and Minds of the Foreign Protectors', in G. Molier & E. Nieuwenhuys (eds) *Reconstruction after Violent Conflicts*. Leiden: Brill Academic Publishers.

Grayson, K. (2008) 'The Biopolitics of Human Security', *Cambridge Review of International Affairs* 21, 3: 383–401.

Heirman, M. (2009) 'How Civilizations can Bridge Cultural and Religious Differences', in G. Molier & E. Nieuwenhuys (eds) *Reconstruction after Violent Conflicts*. Leiden: Brill Academic Publishers, pp. 25–48.

Herrero, J. L. (2005) 'Building State Institutions', in Gerd Junne and Willemijn Verkoren (eds) *Postconflict Development: Meeting New Challenges*. Boulder, Colorado: Lynne Rienner Publishers Inc.

Herz, J. (1950) 'Idealist Internationalism and the Security Dilemma', *World Politics* 2, 2: 157–180.

Hobbes, T. ([1651] 1968) *Leviathan*. Edited by C. B. Macpherson. Middlesex: Penguin Books Ltd.

Hobsbawm, E. (1990) *Nations and Nationalism since 1780: Programme, Myth, Reality*. Cambridge: Cambridge University Press.

Hossein-Zadeh, I. (2006) *The Political Economy of U.S. Militarism*. New York: Palgrave Mcmillan.

Huntington, S. (1997) *The Clash of Civilizations and the Remaking of the World Order*. London: Touchstone.

International Commission on Intervention and State Sovereignty (2001) *The Responsibility to Protect*. Ottawa: International Development Research Centre.

Kaldor, M. (2001) *New and Old Wars: Organized Violence in a Global Era*. Cambridge: Polity Press.

Kant, I. (1976 [1795]) *Zum Ewigen Frieden. Ein philosphischer Entwurf*. Stuttgart: Reklam.

Krause, K. (1998) 'Critical Theory and Security Studies. The Research Programme of "Critical Security Studies"', *Cooperation and Conflict* 33, 3: 298–333.

Krause, K. (2004) 'The Key to a Powerful Agenda, if Properly Delimited', *Security Dialogue* 35(4): 367–368.

Menkhaus, K. (2003) 'State Collapse in Somalia: Second Thoughts', *Review of African Political Economy* 18, 97: 405–427.

Montesquieu, C. L. de (1989 [1748]) *The Spirit of the Laws*. Translated by A. M. Cohler, B. C. Miller and H. S. Stone. Cambridge: Cambridge University Press.

Münkler, H. (2005) *The New Wars*. Cambridge: Polity Press.

Newman, E. (2004) 'The New Wars' Debate', *Security Dialogue* 35, 2: 173–189.

Newman, E. (2010) 'Critical Human Security Studies', *Review of International Studies* 36, 1: 77–94.

Ogata, S., Sen, A. K. et al. (2003) *Human Security Now: Final Report of the Commission on Human Security*. New York. Available online at: http://reliefweb.int/sites/reliefweb.int/files/resources/91BAEEDBA50 C6907C1256D19006A9353-chs-security-may03.pdf (accessed 14 May 2013).

Orwell, G. (1990 [1948]) *Nineteen Eighty-Four*. Middlesex: Penguin Books.

Salomons, D. (2006) 'Security: An Absolute Prerequisite', in Gerd Junne and Willemijn Verkoren (eds) *Postconflict Development: Meeting New Challenges*. Boulder, Colorado: Lynne Rienner Publishers Inc.

Snow, D. M. (1996) *Uncivil Wars: International Security and the New Internal Conflicts*. Boulder, CO: Lynne Rienner.

Stokke, K. (2006) 'Building the Tamil Eelam State', *Third World Quarterly* 27, 6: 1021–1040.

Wæver, O. (2004) *Aberystwyth, Paris, Copenhagen. New Schools in Security Theory and the Origins between Core and Periphery*. Paper presented at the ISA Conference. Montreal, March 2004.

Zakaria, F. (2007) *The Future of Freedom. Illiberal Democracy at Home and Abroad*. New York: W.W. Norton.

10

SECURITY AND DEVELOPMENT: CONTEXT SPECIFIC APPROACHES TO HUMAN INSECURITY[1]

Richard Jolly

Human security is a pioneering concept developed by the UN, first and notably in the Human Development Report (HDR) of 1994. Three key individuals led the way: Mahbub ul Haq, founder of the HDR and former Minister of Finance of Pakistan; and the distinguished economist-philosopher and Nobel laureate Professor Amartya Sen, an old friend of Mahbub ul Haq from their university days. The third person involved was Oscar Arias, twice President of Costa Rica and a leader who has often emphasized the benefits to a country of shifting expenditure from the military and weapons to education, health and other activities which directly benefit people.

The 1994 UNDP Human Development Report conceptualized human security as people-centred, multi-dimensional, interconnected and universal. It encompassed a shift from security of the state by means of military defence of borders to the security of people, using various measures to counter a diversity of chronic threats, which included: 'hunger, disease and repression and; protection from sudden and hurtful disruptions in the patterns of daily lives, whether in homes, jobs or communities' (UNDP 1994). The HDR report detailed the kind of actions required to respond to these problems, including measures of disarmament to free up resources to make the new actions possible. Oscar Arias provided a quantified proposal for reducing military spending in all countries, rich and poor, by 3 per cent a year, with part of the proceeds put into a Global Demilitarization Fund to be used for supporting the process of de-mobilization in developing countries. (Note that 3 per cent was more or less the rate at which world military spending was being reduced when Arias was writing and the rate of reduction from 1989–1996.)

Several reports on international policy followed which presented human security as a frame of reference for policy analysis and implementation. First and most significant was the Commission on Human Security (CHS), chaired by Amartya Sen and Mrs Sadako Ogata, who had been Executive Director of UNHCR from 1991–2001. This Commission produced the landmark study, *Human Security Now* (CHS 2003). Other significant formulations included the adoption of a human security framework in the report by the UN Secretary General Kofi Annan's 2004 *High Level Panel on Threats, Challenges and Change* (UN 2004), and in his subsequent report entitled *In Larger Freedom – Towards Development Security and Human Rights for All* (Annan 2005).

Despite this, attempts to re-define security along the broader lines proposed in the 1994 HDR report have met with a cautious or sceptical reception from academic and policy worlds. However, recent events have increased such insecurities and have made them felt worldwide: most notably, financial insecurities throwing whole countries into debt and recession, often with soaring levels of unemployment. To these have been added food insecurity and insecurities arising from climate change. Events in the United States since 2005 have demonstrated that no country is immune from such insecurities – whether in the form of major oil spills in the Gulf of Mexico which affected the livelihoods of fishermen, tourist operators and many others living along the coast or the ravages of Hurricane Katrina.

These examples give growing credence to basic points about the concept of human security: it is about people, it is a universal concern, its components are interdependent and it is easier to ensure through early prevention than later intervention. The global dimensions of human security have also become clearer: threats to environmental security from land degradation, deforestation – and of course the emission of greenhouse gases.

In light of these and other changes in the global context of security, the limited and cautious reaction to the concept of human security in 1994 and subsequently looks even more surprising. However, as Keynes (1936) remarked about economists' reactions to the General Theory:

> The ideas … are extremely simple and should be obvious. The difficulty lies, not in the new ideas, but in escaping from the old ones, which ramify, for those brought up as most of us have been, into every corner of our minds.

This chapter looks at advances in developing the concept and application of human security, from a development perspective, since it was first put forward. It uses two examples, firstly the UNDP's National Human Development Reports (NHDRs), as a tool for linking human development with security in specific national situations, and secondly the UN's Office for the Coordination of Humanitarian Affairs (OCHA) case studies of how to implement human security as an approach to development.

A human security perspective has been a main theme in some 20 of the 650 or so national-level human development reports, which have been prepared between 1991 and 2011, typically in one or other of three broad settings:

- by countries which have just emerged from conflict
- by countries facing elements of national (and in some cases, regional) insecurity as a result of military activity, and
- by countries in the midst of fundamental socio-political and economic transition.

It is in these cases that the UNDP's broad perspectives on human security have demonstrated their strength providing a frame for multi-dimensional analysis of insecurity.

A further example of how this kind of specific focus on people-centred security has gained support and can be translated into policy is the *Handbook on Human Security* issued by OCHA in 2008, which includes case studies of how the approach has been applied in countries as diverse as Kosovo, Moldova, El Salvador, Liberia, Myanmar and in two of Peru's remote rural communities in the foot of Andes. Reports on human security have been issued analyzing the insecurities affecting people in Thailand and in the Palestine Occupied Territories (UN OCHA 2008).

The chapter then goes on to elaborate the value added which a human security approach can bring to countries and internationally, and suggests practical answers to allay fears and doubts which some people and countries still harbour about using the concept in policy.

Two decades of progress in developing and applying the concept

The HDR 1994 described the concept of human security as follows: 'For too long the concept of security has been interpreted narrowly: as security of territory from external aggression, or as protection of national interests in foreign policy or as global security from a nuclear holocaust. It has been related more to nation states than to people' (UNDP 1994).

The HDR argued that the time has come for countries to focus on human insecurities as they affect the citizens of their countries – the worries of daily life, job insecurity, income insecurity, the risks of falling ill without medical treatment, insecurities arising from urban crime or gender violence. The setting for this change of emphasis represented by the 1994 Report was the obvious and increasing inadequacy of theoretical narratives which characterized international relations (IRs). The post-Cold War era demanded greater consideration for trans-national, intra-state factors and socio-economic conditions within the security calculus. A recognition of the analytical weaknesses of traditional and orthodox theories enabled a process of critical self-reflection, outside academia and within.[2]

The need to bring economic, social and environmental causes of conflict into the analysis of insecurity was articulated by the academics who later came to be known as the Copenhagen School (Knudsen 2001: 357), along with calls for widening of the levels of analysis to better explain causes and sources of insecurity in an increasingly destabilized international system.[3]

Human security had already emerged as one of the new alternative frameworks of analysis from this process of reflection. Mahbub ul Haq used the Human Development Reports to explore human security as a dimension of human development (UNDP 1993, 1994). James Busumtwi-Sam aligned human security to

> extended notions of security [which] attempt to broaden the scope horizontally by the inclusion or 'securitisation' of issues not confined to military threats (poverty, inequality, environmental degradation, human rights and so on) and deepen the domain vertically by shifting from a focus on the state/nation as the object of security to include the security of individuals and groups.
>
> *(Busumtwi-Sam 2002: 255)*

Caroline Thomas wrote that human security meant the provision of 'basic material needs' and 'emancipation from oppressive power structures – be they global, national or local in origin and scope' (Thomas 1999). Gary King and Christopher J. L. Murray's definition of human security through the rubric of development and poverty provided a further example of how contextualization was part of the concept's appeal. They defined 'an individual's human security as his or her expectation of years of life without experiencing the state of generalised poverty. Population human security is then an aggregation of individuals' human security' (King & Murray 2001–2002).

What each of these definitions had in common was the requirement to develop more context-related notions of insecurity, based on specific experiences, and develop policy responses based on this more nuanced understanding. Threats to socio-economic and political conditions, food, health, environmental, community and personal safety become part of the causes of insecurity and applying this framework suggests policy initiatives which reach beyond the traditional focus on military force, greatly reducing the emphasis on armies, if not replacing them altogether.

In this ideal setting, policies aimed at addressing human security become the aggregation of the various measures which are necessary in order to prevent or mitigate any and all of the individual factors which contribute to individuals' sense of their own insecurity. In practice, this means a need to focus on a core of insecurities within each specific context. A country-by-country approach, as set out in the UNDP-NHDRs, reveals what this core looks like. For example, attaining human security in Afghanistan will involve an across-the-board initiative including improving human rights, alleviating poverty, identifying and addressing basic needs, combating trans-national crime and introducing democratic governance. In the case of Nigeria, human security policies would emphasize protection from regional conflicts, socio-economic exploitation, civil unrest stemming from ethnic identities, poverty and public health issues such as HIV/AIDS and tuberculosis.

What the NHDRs also do is to acknowledge the importance of cross-cutting issues, of analyzing diverse security issues in a comprehensive way and developing policies aimed at prevention and protection. The linkages between different kinds of insecurity may be between terrorism and environment as in Afghanistan (UNDP 2004) or between urban development and health in East Timor (UNDP 2002a).

The NHDR Report on Human Security in Latvia (UNDP 2003) presents a practical example of the methodology which can be used to identify multiple forms of human insecurity in a particular country. The Latvian survey started with a randomized sample survey of 1000 adult men and women. Each person was asked about their perception of more than 30 specific threats – such as the threat of becoming seriously ill, of not being able to pay for medical care in the case of illness, of not receiving a pension large enough to live on, of falling victim to serious crime, of being physically abused at home. Men and women separately were asked to indicate whether or not they felt concern at each of these threats – and then to rate the degree of concern: whether they were not at all afraid, mostly not afraid, slightly afraid or very afraid.

The Latvian report provides an interesting and most useful ranking of the public perception of these threats. By far the most general causes of concern related to the risks of serious illness and of being unable to pay for or receive adequate treatment. Nearly four out of five persons put themselves in these categories. Next came the fears of having an insufficient pension or of being unable to support oneself. Two-thirds or more of those surveyed expressed these concerns. The third category related to being involved in an accident – or of being the victim of aggressive or unsafe driving practices. Over three-quarters expressed such concerns, with women indicating an even higher degree of concern than men. The fourth category related to being attacked on the street or being subject to theft – just over 60 per cent of respondents put themselves in this category, though falling victim to organized crime registered a slightly lower percentage.

Interesting differences also emerged with respect to threats felt by a smaller proportion of the population. Some seem a bit surprising – being 'emotionally abused by civil servants or police officers', was feared by two out of five people; or being 'in conflict with relatives or others over property issues' feared by one in five. Sexual assault was feared by two out of five women and by one out of five men. Nearly a third of women felt concern at being emotionally abused at work, about double the proportion of men – but a higher proportion of both feared losing the understanding and support of their colleagues. Being a victim of a terrorist attack was a fear felt by half the population and losing one's savings in a bank by a quarter.

In addition to personal threats, the Latvian report assessed public 'perception of general threats'. These included threats arising from the spread of narcotics, organized crime, HIV/AIDS – along with economic threats like rapid inflation, environmental damage for dumping hazardous waste, forest clearing and environmental pollution. All these categories were felt by over 80 per cent of the population. Two-thirds of those surveyed feared food poisoning and adding excessive preservatives in food. Global warming was a concern for over half the population along with nuclear threats. Ethnic or armed conflict in Latvia and the partial loss of Latvian sovereignty was less significant – though still a concern felt by more than a third of the population.

The value added of human centred-responses

Human security can add value to traditional concepts of security in at least four ways. Firstly, broader concepts of human security make decision-makers aware of risks and insecurities in other areas which require attention and action – often with higher priority than expenditures on traditional forms of responses to security. If broader and more appropriate policies are then adopted, value will be added by increasing the levels of security experienced by people in the country. There may also be added value in the use of better-directed public expenditure.

Secondly, broader concerns for people-centred security can also add value by generating greater public awareness of the broader range of threats to security and in turn for mobilizing their support for a better allocation of government resources and efforts to respond to these threats.

Thirdly, identifying threats and insecurities on a broader basis opens the way to value added from a more efficient use of resources – both of government resources and of resources and activities from private firms and non-government groups. In many countries, expenditures on the military amount to three or four per cent or more – with such expenditure often being ring-fenced and receiving special protection in budgets. A human security approach would analyze the contribution of various forms of action towards security of people – both military and non-military – apply cost–benefit principles to see which form of support added most value to the citizens of a country. Such analyses would not be easy, indeed often controversial. But potentially a redirection of such expenditures can add much value to the welfare and security of a nation's population.

Finally, there can also be added value in a human security approach at the international level. By shifting attention to people-centred securities, areas of regional or global action can be identified – to tackle diseases, to strengthen emergency preparedness, to respond to national disasters like earthquakes or floods, to diminish the risks of civil conflicts breaking out – or to help contain the consequences if they do. Such action can be classed as forms of global public goods, which all add value and usually more value than the costs to any individual country.

The future of human security policies

Clearly human security has come a long way in the last two decades. The concept has gained momentum, support from a number of developing country governments as well as from certain donors – Japan, Norway and Canada in particular. It has gathered international support from the Secretary General and others within the UN. Notwithstanding the progress and areas where value could be added, three sorts of doubt are often expressed.

Academic doubts: specialists in International Relations often emphasize political realism and find it difficult to break away from the belief that military systems are needed as a first priority of protection of national sovereignty, because national sovereignty is the fundamental building block of the international system.

Economists find the concept less problematic, emphasizing the way military expenditures still receive a major share of national resources and the benefits which could follow from a shift of resources from military uses to non-military uses directed to actions to diminish human insecurities.

Political doubts: some governments fear that ideas of human security may be used to justify intervention in developing countries. Some academics already argue that the theory of human security might globalize the problems of instability, making the West responsible for world security and leading to attempts to contain the risks of instability by various forms of influence or intervention in other countries. Some think that debate or analysis on security and development have already been so merged that the world now exists in a situation where security has been re-problematized and development has been securitized. Human security places a great deal of emphasis on blurring the boundaries between previously distinct spheres of practice, and in considering linkages between different types of threats to security, both in analysis and in the development of policy initiatives. This is a trend which has also been argued in a growing number of policy documents and other publications since the end of the Cold War. The UN Secretary General's High Level Panel on Threats, Challenges and Change puts it most clearly: 'Today, more than ever before, threats are interrelated and a threat to one is a threat to all. The mutual vulnerability of weak and strong has never been clearer' (UN 2004). The Panel's report elaborates:

> Development and security are inextricably linked. A more secure world is only possible if poor countries are given the chance to develop. Extreme poverty and infectious diseases threaten many people directly, but they also provide a fertile breeding ground for other threats, including civil conflict. Even people in rich countries will be more secure if their governments help poor countries to defeat poverty and disease by meeting the Millennium Development Goals. *(UN 2004)*

Operational doubts: Some have argued that if the causes of human security are cast so broadly, the concept does little more than rename as security risks problems which already have perfectly good names in their own right – and often programmes to deal with them. In this case, where can one draw the line, separating what is a problem of human insecurity and what are simply other problems? By not setting pre-determined boundaries and parameters, and considering anything and everything a risk to security, does the concept of human security leave policy makers without direction, and academics without clear analytical and comparative tools?

This particular objection highlights both the rigidity with which traditional concepts of security are understood in International Relations, as well, in contrast, as the fundamental and contemporary strengths that human security has to offer. In a state-centric model, security has very specific implications and connotations. Threats are assessed by their implications for structures, territorial boundaries and, most importantly, state 'interests'. But, as history has repeatedly shown, the interpretation of state interests often mimics the power and privileges of those in positions of economic and political advantage. In this situation, it is difficult to accept that securing the state ensures protection of all individuals and their interests.

Given the numerous challenges arising in the post-Cold War world, the state-centric model appears to be flawed, misdirected and outdated in its inability to respond effectively. The impacts of terrorism, disease and pandemics, globalization and environmental disasters on the state-centric international system increasingly demand that one give attention to alternative, broader assessments of security.

Broader definitions of security pose a practical and real issue – but again one which non-economists perhaps find more problematic than economists. Economists are used to tackling broad issues of choice and resource allocation – as when deciding how to allocate government spending across all the sectors of a national budget. The solution is not to limit the choice in advance by considering only one sector or by excluding some items from any consideration in principle. Instead, one should consider trade-offs, the relative merits or returns to each item compared to the others. Long ago, Robert McNamara, when President of the World Bank, demonstrated this approach when he considered US military expenditure and its contribution to US security. He concluded in a lecture in 1977 that the US was vastly over-spending on military means to security and greatly under-spending on other means.

There are answers to each of these doubts, mostly by recognizing that human insecurities must be defined

- in the context of each country
- by the government or by other groups or analysts of that country
- and that responsibilities for action to diminish insecurities and increase human security lie within the country
- help from abroad can at times be useful but only if and as requested.

These elements have generally been part of the UN's human security approach.

In conclusion, I would propose four actions – all of which in my view can and need to be taken – by countries, by regions and by the international system as a whole.

- More country analyses.

These should identify the forms of human insecurity which people identify as creating the most serious risks and fears in terms of their lives. The country situations analyzed in the UNDP NHDRs illustrate this point. These reports offer us new analytical traction by treating different elements of human security as part of an integral whole, rather than analyzing them separately. A 2007 study reviewed 13 NHDRs which dealt specifically with human security (Jolly and Basu Ray 2007). The reports covered the following countries: Afghanistan, Bulgaria, East Timor, Estonia, Kyrgyzstan, Latvia, Lesotho, Macedonia, Moldova, Mozambique, Philippines, Sierra Leone and the Solomon Islands. The review of these studies showed that most of the NHDRs did much more than give new names to old problems. Nor were the problems illustrated mono-dimensional; all had various aspects which were novel to traditional approaches to security and sometimes were pioneering in terms of the human security literature. Almost all the NHDRs showed links between military security, human security and development, emphasizing the interrelated nature of these dimensions.

In terms of policy recommendations the reports also illustrated the point that addressing the situations in these countries required action on a wide range of factors which affected both individuals and states, but that this action might encompass highly differentiated policy responses. For example, the Solomon Islands NHDR pinpointed the need to reshape education policies and, specifically, the content of school curricula, as one of the first steps to meaningful conflict prevention (UNDP 2002b). The Macedonian NHDR focused on strengthening health systems and environmental regulation as a means of addressing the security concerns of the citizens of the country (UNDP 2001). The Bangladesh Human Security Report considered an extensive set of justice-sector reforms to address the security needs of its population (UNDP 2002c) Through the human security framework, the multiplicity of both national and local experiences of insecurity was given greater consideration than what would have been found in traditional approaches to mitigating insecurity.

Such surveys need not be expensive – and certainly they are many times less costly than what countries spend on their military. Further, such reports might be supported by UNDP, the World Bank or another donor – and the results should certainly be made publicly available. Support for country-specific studies by OCHA, as in the Handbook drawing on the Latvian NHDR, would seem an important priority, especially if the study was undertaken by a national group or a national group working hand-in-hand with an international team. In countries which already have human security programmes, an outcome-evaluation can be made as to how well they have worked – and which parts of the population have benefited and why.

- More regional analyses

Regional reports are an important complement to national reports – and indeed can draw on the national reports, comparing the different rankings of human insecurities. These reports should also provide tables comparing the expenditures on the military with expenditures on other actions to diminish human securities – expenditures on employment, pensions, health, education and social protection.

- An international analysis of human security, military spending and development

Statistical documents of the form of Social Trends and Statistics have occasionally been produced by the UN Statistical Office – for instance the several pioneering statistical documents on women and gender. There is a strong case for producing a global statistical document on human security. This could show the results of different surveys of human insecurity, nationally and regionally. Where trend data was available, the document could show how human insecurities had changed over time. Data should also be provided on various forms of expenditure directed towards moderating or reducing human insecurities, including military expenditure, drawing on reputable sources such as Stockholm International Peace Research Institute.

- Establishment of training courses in the application of human security approaches

Many staff working for or with the UN in countries or in headquarters lack the expertise and perhaps confidence to give a lead in situations where human security should be central. Training courses could help prepare such people for these roles. Such courses should also help to provide a forum for discussion and debate on real-life situations of human insecurity and for exploring how best to react. OCHA might organize such courses, drawing also on other field agencies – in a way which helps to achieve a coordinated UN response.

Governments' motivations in introducing policies to prevent or mitigate the various forms of insecurity experienced by individuals in highly different settings will inevitably constitute another variable in the matrix of human security. Notwithstanding, analyses of human insecurity are still important as tools to critique government action, to press for a review of policy choices or to build coalitions for change in pressurising policy makers to address specific human security needs.

An approach to security based on threats, in which the relevant threats continue to be defined according to the interest of the state, can no longer be considered adequate. In today's world, the well-being of the individual requires a far more complex set of considerations than was considered necessary within earlier state-based definitions of security. The reason that, for an Afghani citizen, the specifics of security are radically different from those of a Latvian citizen, requires a re-formulation of the very definition of security.

The human security approach strives to contextualize this understanding of security in order to develop appropriate, relevant and effective policy responses. The NHDRs show that such a process is entirely possible, and shows us how a far more comprehensive picture of security needs, centred on the situations of individual citizens can guide more sophisticated policy choices than a state-based approach.

Notes

1   This chapter draws heavily on the NHDR review which the author undertook for UNDP with Deepayan Basu Ray in 2006 and the subsequent summary published in the *Journal of International Development*, 19, 457–472 (2007). I am grateful for the help of Mary C Martin in preparing this chapter.
2   For more information, see Walt (1991), Booth (1991), Homer-Dixon (1991), Walker (1997), Dalby (1997) and Buzan et al. (1998).
3   For further discussion, see Buzan et al. (1998) and Stoett (1999).

References

Annan K. (2005). *In Larger Freedom: Towards Development, Security, and Human Rights For All*, United Nations General Assembly, A/59/2005.

Booth K. (1991). Security and emancipation, *Review of International Studies* 17(4): 313–326.

Busumtwi-Sam J. (2002). Development and human security, *International Journal* 57(2): 253–272.

Buzan B., Wæver O., de Wilde J. (1998). *Security: A New Framework for Analysis*. Lynne Rienner Publishers: Boulder.

Commission on Human Security (CHS) (2003). *Human Security Now*. Communications Development Incorporated: New York.

Dalby S. (1997). Contesting an essential concept. In Krause K., Williams M. C. (eds) *Critical Security Studies: Cases and Concepts*, Borderlines Volume 8. University of Minnesota Press: Minneapolis.

Homer-Dixon T. F. (1991). On the threshold: environmental changes as causes of acute conflict, *International Security* 16(2): 76–116.

Jolly R., Basu Ray D. (2006). The human security framework and national human development reports: a review of experiences and current debates, *NHDR Occasional Paper 5,* Human Development Report Office, UNDP: New York.

Keynes J. M. (1936). *The General Theory of Employment, Interest and Money*. Macmillan: London and New York.

King G., Murray C. J. L. (2001–2002). Rethinking human security, *Political Science Quarterly* 116(4): 585–619.

Knudsen O. V. (2001). Post-Copenhagen security studies: desecuritizing securitization, *Security Dialogue* 32(3): 355–368.

Stoett P. (1999). *Human and Global Security*. University of Toronto Press: Toronto.

Thomas C. (1999). Introduction. In Thomas C., Wilkin P. (eds) *Globalisation, Human Security, and the African Experience*. Lynne Rienner: Boulder.

United Nations (2004). *The UN Secretary General's High-level Panel on Threats, Challenges and Change. 2004. A More Secure World: Our Shared Responsibility*. United Nations Press: New York.

United Nations Development Programme (1993). *Human Development Report*. Available at http://hdr.undp.org/en/reports/ (accessed 23 May 2013).

United Nations Development Programme (1994). *Human Development Report – New Dimensions of Human Security*. Oxford University Press: New York (2001).

United Nations Development Programme (2001). *Macedonia Human Development Report 2001: Social Exclusion and Human Insecurity in FYR Macedonia*. FYR Macedonia.

United Nations Development Programme (2002a). *East Timor National Human Development Report 2002: The Way Ahead*. Dili: East Timor.

United Nations Development Programme (2002b). *Solomon Islands Human Development Report. 2002: Building a Nation*. University of Queensland: Australia. 2002/2003.

United Nations Development Programme (2002c). *Bangladesh Human Security Report 2002: In Search of Justice and Dignity*. Bangladesh.

United Nations Development Programme (2003). *Latvian Human Development Report, 2002/3 (Human Security.)* Riga, Latvia.

United Nations Development Programme (2004). *Afghanistan National Human Development Report 2004: Security with a Human Face; Challenges and Responsibilities.* Army Press: Islamabad.

UN Office for the Coordination of Humanitarian Affairs (2008) *Human Security in Theory and Practice.* Available at https://docs.unocha.org/sites/dms/HSU/Publications%20and%20Products/Human%20Security%20Tools/Human%20Security%20in%20Theory%20and%20Practice%20English.pdf (accessed 23 May 2013).

Walker R. B. J. (1997). The subject of security, in Krause, K. and Williams M. C. (eds) *Critical Security Studies: Cases and Concepts.* Borderlines Volume 8. University of Minnesota Press: Minneapolis.

Walt S. (1991) The renaissance of security studies, *International Studies Quarterly* 35(2): 211–239.

11

HUMAN SECURITY IN THE R2P ERA

Lloyd Axworthy

Apologists for particular governments and for governments in general commonly argue, precisely, that they offer protection from local and external violence.

Charles Tilly[1]

It is sometimes good practice when one is heavily involved in the development or promotion of an idea to go back and sift through what had previously been written in order to evaluate just how far it has come. I wrote an article for *Global Governance* just over ten years ago.[2] It was written as a thought piece on how the last decade of the twentieth century offered the United Nations, as well as individual states, a new and different kind of security challenge from the bipolarity of the Cold War. Discussions around the maintenance of international peace traditionally focused on the state, because, as the Tilly quote expresses, with a monopoly over the means of violence, it is the state that assumes protection over its population.

But the model of a fully formed, modern state never really considered the era of decolonization, the emergence of non-state actors and the increasingly influential role of international organizations and corporations. Various states, hobbled by economic adversity, outrun by globalization, and hollowed from within by bad governance, had either lost the capacity, or simply the interest to provide this protection. This incapacity was particularly obvious in war-torn societies. The breakdown of the Cold War rigidities opened up a period of new thought about the basic assumptions regarding longer-term strategies and policy making. In the Canadian department of Foreign Affairs we examined, in particular, the intriguing argument contained in the United Nations Development Report (UNDP) in 1994 on human security to decide how a focus on the security of civilians could act as an equally relevant way of looking at the world.[3]

In the time since that first article articulating the Canadian approach to human security was written, the means by which the community of states operate together to provide greater peace, security and ultimately prosperity and well-being continues to evolve and the principles are being increasingly applied. This chapter will provide something of a bookend to that previous article, by revisiting the ideas it provided, but also by reflecting on the protection of civilians that has not only evolved into a stated doctrine, that of the Responsibility to Protect (R2P), but additionally that is being put into practice, as was witnessed this past year in Libya and later Syria.

Human security was born out of the understanding that the state, at times, can actually fail at its overarching role as protector. States have even, at times, come to be a major threat to their population's rights and welfare – or have been incapable of restraining the warlords or paramilitaries. Violent events in both Rwanda and Srebrenica in the 1990s demonstrated this stark reality far too clearly, driving us to broaden the focus of security beyond the level of the state and toward individual human beings, as well as to consider appropriate roles for the international system to compensate for state failure. This novel discourse on security represented a distinct shift in perspective. No longer were we limited to discussions of states' rights and national sovereignty. Protecting civilians, addressing the plight of war-affected children and the threat of terrorism and drugs, managing open borders, and combating infectious diseases are now part of the dialogue. These are the "problems without passports" as expressed by former UN Secretary-General Kofi Annan.[4]

While the explicit language that changed the security reference from state to civilian was reflective of the changing international context, the focus on people was definitely not. The recognition that people's rights are at least as important as those of states has been gaining momentum since the end of World War II. The legacy of the holocaust forced a serious examination of the place of international moral standards and codes in the conduct of world affairs. It also caused us to rethink the principles of national sovereignty. The Nuremberg trials acknowledged that grotesque violations of people's rights could not go unpunished. The United Nations Charter, the Universal Declaration of Human Rights, and the Genocide and Geneva conventions all recognized the inherent right of people to personal security. They challenge conventional notions of sovereignty when serious violations occur. Following suite, human security is an honest attempt to put people first and recognizes that their safety is integral to the promotion and maintenance of international peace and security. The security of states is essential, but not sufficient, to fully ensure the safety and well-being of the world's peoples.

Out of the violence of the 1990s came an urgent need to operationalize what was envisioned by human security. Elevating civilians as a primary security concern had been – up until then – outside the usual mandate of the UN. While the institution's original intent was to promote international peace, its framework had always been constrained by borders and collective state security. However, it was recognized in such cases as Angola and Sierra Leone, or in the aftermath of the Rwandan genocide, intra-state violence can have large-scale regional effects, spreading human suffering like a virus as fragile or weak borders are unable to contain the spread of violence.

This desire to hold individuals to account for state-sanctioned violence also made a compelling argument for a permanent court to judge crimes against humanity. In 1998, coalitions of like-minded states and NGOs produced the Rome Statute of the International Criminal Court (ICC). This court offered a significant new international institution in the battle against war crimes and genocide, a major step toward real international accountability.

Additionally, there was a need to work in partnership with civil society and the NGO community. NGOs can play a variety of important roles: they bring technical expertise and experience to the policymaking process from an on the ground perspective and often work with government to implement international agendas, and inform citizens about challenges and choices on the international agenda. They are excellent at mobilizing human and financial resources. Their activism is enhanced by information technology as groups have the capacity to reach audiences all over the world in an instant. Information systems have the ability to impact the politics and the application of human security, but the potential of this new tool is immense. The most obvious example of this has been the Ottawa Process, which ultimately led to the Anti-Personnel Mine Ban Convention.

The Ottawa Process led not only to an extraordinary gathering and collaboration of governments and international NGOs, and international organizations such as the International Committee of the Red Cross (ICRC), but also heralded the beginning of an information network of like-minded actors as a burgeoning new tool in world affairs. It was this collusion of events – the shift in focus to protecting civilians, along with the great aggregation of civil society efforts – that demonstrated how in this interconnected world, our own security is not only increasingly indivisible from that of our neighbors, but that individual human suffering is an irrevocable universal concern. While governments continue to be the important players, global economic integration and the ever growing power of the internet and its effects on communication have given an ever more significant role and a profile to those in business, civil society, and NGOs and intergovernmental organizations. Never has this more true than today. Barriers to entry onto the international stage have effectively been reduced, and today, with the advent of social media sites like Twitter and Wikileaks, the public are the watchdogs, and governments are to be held to account. New coalitions that result have produced new forms of diplomatic action. Coalition building among like-minded states and non-state actors is one dynamic element of this "new diplomacy."

The ICC and the Landmine Treaty are real world examples of how the international discourse on human security could effect change on the institutions and practice of global governance, all with the active participation of the Canadian government. They both also represented a new way of organizing support on the ground for international action, because both efforts were wholeheartedly supported by a coalition of NGOs who not only gave their explicit consent that these were the right actions to take, but they were also responsible for garnering widespread public support and maintaining momentum.

And yet, despite a rapid pace of change at the end of the last century, and the enthusiastic uptake, generally, of the human security ideal, there remained instances when conflict prevention diplomacy was either lacking or was totally inefficient. The work on human security in the new millennium would have to focus on how to fill this acknowledged gap in the provision of security at the highest levels, within the UN and in the function of the Security Council. It was realized that in cases of state neglect or the direct targeting of civilians through violent means, the international community must be prepared to end suffering. Deciding when intervention is warranted posed some very serious questions and required some very serious evaluation.

Actualizing the concept of human security requires all actors – states, international organizations, NGOs, and businesses – to act responsibly. This includes developing codes of conduct where appropriate, working to establish new international norms regarding the protection of peoples, and incorporating the human dimension into the work of international organizations. At the start of this century, the protection of peoples transformed into the most important issue for those of us who had been affected by the events of the 1990s. It became apparent that the framework for peace and security had become that much more disparate, sources and types of threats much more variable, and that the current international structure was wholly insufficient. Beyond navel-gazing, actions were taken to inject some of this new understanding of security into the dated operations of the United Nations.

The era of R2P

The UN – as the primary international governing body – was fashioned around the need to address interstate warfare and, in its first five decades, had little to say as far as civil war is concerned. As the previous section outlined, the language of human security represented a reaction in response to the rapidly changing international dynamic, whereby the greatest security concern rarely implicated borders, but exacted significant human cost and tragedy. But while human security is primarily described as an outcome of policy, it is much more than that – it is also a process, one which has led to significant changes at the level of the UN, but also in the international dialogue around the protection of civilians. The pathway forged by our human security approach led to a natural and logical outcome: that of a normative challenge to the precepts of state sovereignty. By working to advance the security and protection of individuals rather than state units – which is the gist of the human security approach – the coalition that grew out of the landmines treaty as well as the ICC had defined an alternative foreign policy paradigm.

Human security is considered as an alternative to a more traditional notion of security that focuses primarily on the state, but the truth is that they are more connected than appears obvious on the surface. More specifically, it fills in the gap where traditional security finds itself lacking. The end of the Cold War presented the world with a set of circumstances the UN and the Security Council were not yet able to adequately address, despite their mandate at securing peace. This is particularly obvious when one reflects on the failures of the UN system – as was the case in Kosovo, or more recently in Syria – understanding the space and application of human security as the logical outcome of these gaps in civilian protection allows for a reconciliation between perspectives.

However, an attempt at bridging this gap occurred in the development of the concept of the Responsibility to Protect. A question plagued me during my last years as minister of foreign affairs in Canada; if a new norm of humanitarian protection of people was to become a prime responsibility, one which should trump the old norm of national sovereignty, then what form of intervention was justified to enforce this standard and under what conditions could these actions be implemented? During that period we held a seat on the Security Council, having been elected in 1999 on a clear campaign commitment to advance the case for human security. When our turn as Chair of the Council came, we used the occasion to push for resolutions on the protection of civilians and hosted a series of roundtables on issues like the protection of women in Afghanistan. Our highlight was gaining support for a motion which culminated in the Secretary-General's Report on the Protection of Civilians in Armed Conflict.[5] The events in Kosovo in 1999 brought into question the means through which humanitarian intervention was to take place as well as the role of the UN in deciding upon this course of action. While UN approval is always the most desired method of proceeding, in the months and weeks leading up to the NATO bombing, we had been forced to decide, based upon our focus on the protection of civilians, whether or not we were prepared to put words into action.

It was this persistent question that led to our decision to launch a major global consultation on the issue of how to implement a framework of rules and procedures for addressing violence against civilians. This led to the gathering of fifteen experts under the Canadian sponsored International Commission on Intervention and State Sovereignty (ICISS) supported by Kofi Annan and the financial help of several American foundations. Their report, titled "The Responsibility to Protect," came out late in 2001, and it offered a transformative perspective that state sovereignty is based on the ability and interest of governments to protect their own citizens.[6] Even more interesting, the report suggested that, should a state not fulfill this requirement, the responsibility then fell on the international community to intervene in the matter. In principle, it worked to marry idea and action.

The ICISS report effectively offered an opportunity for human security in practice, and provided a framework through which to move forward with a focus on the protection of civilians, while redefining the role of sovereignty in the maintenance of international peace.

R2P pays homage to the human security approach in a number of fundamental ways. It focuses international attention and calls for action fashioned around where it is most needed – on the victim. It focuses on the responsibilities of sovereignty versus its privileges. Under the principle of R2P, it is no longer permissible for states to harm their populations with impunity. And finally, if for some reason a state is unwilling or incapable to protect its citizens, the responsibility then falls on the international community to do so.

What was particularly unique and innovative about the ICISS document was that it promoted the idea of R2P while arguing for military intervention as the least desirable option – to be considered as a last resort in only the most severe of circumstances. What is promoted above all else is prevention, a topic that is much too often neglected in the present debate. The report also offered up a number of tools in the foreign policy tool box to address humanitarian situations on the verge of crisis, some of them less political and generally more strategic than bullets, bombs, or fighter jets. The responsibility to provide protection for civilians was envisioned as so much more than the application of brute force. In fact, in order to avoid the use of military force, which is costly by any measure – including being politically untenable for most state leaders – the ICISS report established a trio of responsibilities: prevention, reaction and rebuilding – so that the safety and protection of civilians is at the forefront of decision-making.

Where prevention demands both root causes and direct causes of internal conflict be addressed well in advance, this pillar should form the foundation of any discussion around R2P. This prevention is directly linked to the concept of human security. When the *freedom from fear* and the *freedom from want* are both effectively provided and the state accepts its role in providing both of these freedoms, the need for external intervention is effectively removed. Unfortunately, it is the responsibility to react which gets the greatest attention.

The weakness in this approach is that when this responsibility becomes the priority, it becomes more difficult to move away from the ad hoc intervention approach that the world experienced in the mid-1990s. There unfortunately also tends to be propensity to focus on the military aspect of reaction, but the ICISS report promoted the application of appropriate measures based on the severity of the situation. The application of diplomatic means, sanctions, and the threat of international prosecution are always preferred over military intervention. When the most severe of situations demand a military reaction, the principles of just war (just cause, right intention, last resort, proportional means, and reasonable prospects) are applied to ensure that it is the most appropriate course of action. An ideal example of the peaceful resolution of an otherwise tragic event was when Kofi Annan successfully responded to post-election violence in Kenya in early 2008.[7]

Finally, the responsibility to rebuild tends to be the most neglected and most extended commitment and responsibility. Should all efforts at prevention prove useless and some form of intervention is employed, then it also becomes the responsibility of the interveners to provide full assistance with recovery, reconstruction, and reconciliation, particularly after the case of military involvement, and addressing the causes of the harm the intervention was designed to halt or avert. It should be this language – particularly in the prevention and rebuilding stages – that is used in discussions around R2P, in order to fend of criticisms of the concept, or to avoid doubts of the intention of the doctrine itself, separate from any dishonest intention of individual states. Such was the case with when the U.S. waged war in Iraq in 2003, falsely claiming humanitarian grounds, when the criteria for such actions under an R2P banner had so obviously been ignored.

The ICISS report came out to minimal fanfare, but it had caught the attention of enough political actors and representatives in the UN to make a significant leap forward, institutionally speaking, in September 2005. It was then that world leaders gathered together at a summit in

New York to review progress since the Millennium Declaration, adopted by all UN Member States in 2000. R2P was brought forward for consideration by the Secretary-General as part of a reform package. Earlier that year, Kofi Annan had argued in a report that a state's primary duty is to protect its citizens and should it fail to do so, it is up to the international community to step in.[8] For this reason, he implored member states to embrace R2P and accept the three pillars of responsibilities it stood for.[9] To the surprise of many, member states in attendance at the Global Summit unanimously adopted an Outcome Document that would forever place R2P under the auspices of the UN under paragraphs 138 and 139 of the World Summit Outcome Document. Member states committed themselves from then on to be:

> prepared to take collective action, in a timely and decisive manner, through the Security Council, in accordance with the Charter, including Chapter VII, on a case by case basis and in cooperation with relevant regional organizations as appropriate, should peaceful means be inadequate and national authorities manifestly fail to protect their populations from genocide, war crimes, ethnic cleansing and crimes against humanity.[10]

The eventual unanimous adoption of resolution 1674 affirming the 2005 World Summit document's commitment to R2P was preceded by six months of debate in the Security Council.[11] Despite the surprisingly positive outcome, the final words of the document strayed in some significant ways from the original intention of the ICISS report. For example, the range of threats to which R2P responded was narrowed considerably to the four listed above in paragraph 139, due to concerns over threshold criteria for intervention.

The narrowing of the concept also had the effect of switching the conversation away from a focus on protection to military intervention, which has muddied the waters and created some confusion around the framework. What gets lost in conversations about R2P is that it is a multi-pronged approach. Its intention is not simply to advocate for quick and dirty diplomacy by force. It is a framework through which force can be used, to protect human rights, but is neither necessary nor preferred. This reality has become particularly muddled with the NATO intervention in Libya in 2011 and associated controversy around the intended ends behind the use of military force.

Ultimately, what should not be neglected and which often goes under-appreciated in the analysis around the development of R2P is the incredible pace at which the language of its application as well as its adoption by the international community took place. Of course, it has faced its share of critics, no less in the 2009 General Assembly debate. However, in the world of diplomacy and international governance, such a bold and readily accepted change is a rarity. There is no denying that the success of the campaign to bring this forward in the UN came about through the culmination of a series of events following the Cold War that led to a reworking of how security was and should be understood. It can also be attributed to the thorough work of both the members of ICISS and the subsequent High Level Panel on Threats, Challenges and Change, in successfully delineating and outlining the new security context. It made sense from a foreign policy standpoint and reflected the changing reality and challenges the international community faces regarding threats to security, particularly the concerns of human security, which was evolving into a new international norm. The generally high degree of support for R2P was rather a surprise. Rather than the debate being a setback, it had the opposite effect, and served as a reaffirmation. Efforts could now turn to implementation. R2P is indeed emerging as a new norm, resetting limits on sovereignty, and a robust one at that.

The declaration changed forever the Westphalian model of state sovereignty. For the first time, an exception was made to the UN Charter's prohibition against international involvement in member states' domestic jurisdiction. The nuance is that R2P does not displace sovereignty as the source of authority in the world order, it serves to reaffirm and re-enforce it. It recognizes, however, that sovereignty gives rise not only to rights and privileges, but also to duties and obligations. Based on the human security framework, it provides the terms through which the members of the UN can fulfill their mandate to promote collective security, in a world of globalized threats.

If one looks back, therefore, on this series of events over 15 years, a very definite and positive arc can be traced. Despite skepticism and doubt, real progress has been made. There has truly been a continuous and relatively rapid evolution. We have concluded collectively that the old model of separate state authority simply cannot respond to the current generation of shared challenges. From the humble beginnings of an idea during the period following Kosovo, to casual conversations in the Foreign Affairs offices in Ottawa, to its adoption of a new international norm – there has truly been a continuous and relatively rapid evolution. We have acknowledged and accepted collectively that the old model of providing international security simply cannot respond to the current generation of shared challenges.

Since its adoption at the World Summit, the greatest progress forward in the evolving norm around the protection of civilians has occurred in the past year. The events of 2011, particularly the "Arab Spring," have come to shed light on the concept of R2P. Its application continues to face a series of challenges that threaten its legitimacy, but much of the critique is based on misunderstanding or a misapplication of the term. The intervention in Libya has further fostered these questionings by bringing R2P back into the spotlight, coming out from the shadows as a response to the violent reactions of Muammar Gadhafi, who had been president of Libya for over 40 years, against his own people. As a preliminary case for a UN-sanctioned application of the R2P principle, the overthrow of Gadhafi's regime and his sudden death have led many to question not only the legitimacy of the mission, but also whether or not this event will impinge on future efforts to intervene.

It should be argued, that despite the imperfections in its execution, the international collaborative intervention into Libya's revolution was a successful early example of the application of R2P and that it represents but another stepping stone in the further development of what Ruti Teitel calls "humanity's law," that is, a humanity-based framework for determining how we address conflict on an international level. She says,

> States may be good at protecting their own security, but in light of global threats, they cannot necessarily fully do the same when it comes to human security. Today the most menacing threats appear to be global in nature: terrorism, weapons of mass destruction, climate change, pandemics.[12]

This is an era for the development of new international norms and tools around human security, of which R2P is only one component. There are infinite possibilities available today in the development of a new global network that would help us achieve shared objectives. R2P offers principles that can accelerate humanity's efforts to pursue those objectives. R2P has become the basis for re-examining how the international community can challenge the foundations of state sovereignty in order to establish the tools to manage transcendent global problems or egregious internal threats to innocent people. It maintains that sovereignty, and the state itself, is a necessary concept in global governance, but with the benefits it brings, comes responsibility as well. It is here, by elevating the protection of individuals and groups as the primary reference for international efforts at peace and security, that the world continues the human security dialogue.

It is for this significant reason that more discussion needs to happen around developing the idea further. While ICISS came out of a reaction to the ad hoc nature of humanitarian intervention in the 1990s, the Arab Spring has revealed the multitude of challenges that remain ahead for the still-developing norm. One discussion that remains unfulfilled and is highlighted by the eerily similar context in Syria in 2013 to Kosovo in 1999 is the opportunity and justification for institutional reform in the UN. The UN experienced deadlock on the Syrian crisis, which at the time of writing had killed over 100,000 and threatened the stability of the region.

It was through the initial stalemate at the Security Council to authorize some form of negotiated intervention that led to the formation of a coalition and the bombing of Kosovo in 1999 by NATO. While the legitimacy of the intervention was questioned, the events truly appealed to a need to establish a set of criteria in which to engage in the protection of human security. There was a new demand being made on the UN in its international role, to that of humanitarian actor and legitimizing body of the provision of this public good. But it was highly desirable that the UN become the leader on this front, in order to shift away from the less than ideal series of events that led to the Kosovo bombing.

The truth remains that the UN Security Council is failing all too often to act out its post-Cold War commitment to provide safety and security and its credibility continues to erode. To allow this to continue is to increase the likelihood of more and more unilateral and multilateral action outside of the auspices of the UN, a truly dangerous trend if it were ever allowed to occur. I have written before, touching on the reasons why:

> proponents of human security consider multilateral institutions essential components of international order. In an era of heightened insecurity from a multitude of threats, international rules, cooperative arrangements, and a respect for international law are indispensable elements in the protection of individual rights and security. As both an architect and conveyor of international rules and norms, the UN is seen not simply as a *recommended* path towards security but a fundamental *prerequisite* of international peace, justice, and stability.[13]

Following from this acknowledged weakness, another question that is raised has to do with the Russian and Chinese veto on Syria. No question that this has set back the UN's credibility. There has to be a response to this quandary. Again, it seems appropriate to refer back to the original ICISS report. One of those ideas is working to create a "code of conduct" by the permanent members to refrain from using the veto on initiatives that are designed to protect people and apply R2P principles.[14] While not a perfect solution, it would offer a midway point between the current status quo – which is threatening the legitimacy of council – and total reform, which would be difficult to say the least. The term applied in the report is "constructive abstention" and it remains under-explored as an option. Those who discount it are caught in a myopic insider's view of what is acceptable to the P-5, instead of looking at the broader necessity of UN reform and change.

Additionally, it is upon the foundations of human security and the protection of civilians that R2P should remain focused, for it is much better to design consensus and collaboration around a final objective such as this one, than limit discussions to military intervention. As Allan Rock and I have written in the past, there remains an entire tool-box of application that remains under-explored in the specific context of R2P practice.[15] For example, the ICISS report promoted the idea of a UN-specific stand-by force, which would take on the role of intervening where NATO has in the past.

One very important development in the effort to deepen the capacity of R2P is the increasing interest in the concept by the emerging nations like India, Brazil, Indonesia and a coterie of African and Latin American states. The Brazilian idea of "Responsibility While Protecting" is complementary to the original R2P concept, and several southern states are exploring the basic question of how it can improve the ability of states themselves to provide protection or even how R2P can be applied more thoroughly through regional associations.[16] The work in ECOWAS is also a good example.[17] This shows increasing buy-in from the emerging states, rather than a rejection or indifference. They should be welcomed as key players in its continued refinement and application.

Ultimately, instead of continuing to focus on whether or not R2P is here to stay, it would seem to be much more effective use of the brilliant academic and policy minds of our time to begin to formulate and unpack other more innovative ways in which R2P could be applied. Considering the rapid pace in which the norm of sovereignty as responsibility has already taken hold, if we are bold enough as to look beyond civilian conflict and 10 or 15 years into the future, under what other circumstances could we utilize this tool of civilian protection? I often refer to Kofi Annan's "problems without passports." By this I mean threats that we face as humanity, and fail to recognize borders. These are real challenges to human security such as pandemics, natural disasters, and climate change. It is the evolving concept of collective security that is unique to understanding human security. The common experiences of individuals across borders and not solely within borders and the opportunity to discover innovative and cooperative solutions to these threats is what makes the concept of security unique in this century.

Today more than ever, the changing nature of threats does not discriminate between states based on population size, geographic advantages, or military might, they affect states on the level of the individual, the community, and can be destabilizing and destructive. The economic challenges since 2008 demonstrate the need for a collaborative response. The rapid quality and depth of this divergence in security concerns should not go underappreciated. The shift away from military collaboration to coordinated responses to non-state threats is an enormous leap forward to undergo in less than two decades. It reflects the new era of security concerns that I referred to in my original essay.

Regardless of the title in which it falls, the truth is, there is a pressing need for solutions developed through a framework that is as global as the problems that confront us. Although R2P itself is uniquely and solely intended to deal with protecting populations from large scale preventable deaths, when R2P is "unbundled" and its component principles examined, it becomes clear that those principles might help address other problems that engage humanity as a whole, which I have addressed previously.[18] Again, this is with the intention of eliminating the need to respond to calamities in an *ad hoc* nature and to ultimately ensure the safety and security of people everywhere. A significance not to be understated.

To quote Sir Martin Gilbert,

> Since the Peace of Westphalia in 1648, non-interference in the international policies even of the most repressive governments was the golden rule of international diplomacy. The Canadian-sponsored concept of "responsibility to protect" proposed the most significant adjustment to national sovereignty in 360 years.[19]

Notes

1 Charles Tilly, "War making and state making as organized crime," in *Bringing the State Back In*, ed. Peter B. Evans et al. (Cambridge: Cambridge University Press, 1985), p. 169.

2 Lloyd Axworthy, "Human security and global governance: putting people first," *Global Governance,* 2001, 7: 19–23.

3 United Nations Development Program (UNDP), *Human Development Report 1994* (New York: Oxford University Press, 1994), p. 22.

4 Kofi Annan, "Problems without passports," *Foreign Policy,* 1 September 2002.

5 UN, *Report of the Secretary-General to the Security Council on the Protection of Civilians in Armed Conflict,* S/1999/957, 8 September 1999.

6 International Commission on Intervention and State Sovereignty (ICISS), *The Responsibility to Protect* (Ottawa: International Development Research Centre, 2001).

7 Roger Cohen, "African genocide averted," *New York Times,* 3 March 2008.

8 UN, *Report of the Secretary-General on the Protection of Civilians in Armed Conflict,* S/2005/740, 2005.

9 UN GAOR, 59th Sess., UN Dox. A/59/2005 (21 March 2005), para. 135.

10 UN General Assembly, *2005 World Summit Outcome,* A/60/L.1, 20 (September 2005), para. 139.

11 Alex. J Bellamy, "The Responsibility to Protect – five years on," *Ethics & International Affairs,* 2010, 24: 145.

12 Ruti Teitel, *Humanity's Law* (New York: Oxford University Press, 2011), p. 212.

13 Lloyd Axworthy, "Human security: an opening for UN reform," in Richard M. Price and Mark W. Zacher (eds) *The United Nations and Global Security,* (New York: Palgrave Macmillan, 2004), p. 246.

14 ICISS, *The Responsibility to Protect,* p. 51.

15 Lloyd Axworthy and Allan Rock, "R2P: a new and unfinished agenda," *Global Responsibility to Protect,* 2009, 1: 54–69.

16 UN, "Letter dated 9 November 2011 from the Permanent Representative of Brazil to the United Nations addressed to the Secretary-General," A/66/551–S/2011/701, 2011.

17 Thelma Ekiyor, "ECOWAS Conflict Prevention Framework (ECPF)," *A New Approach to an Old Challenge.* West Africa Civil Society Institute Op-Ed, 2008.

18 Axworthy and Rock, "R2P: a new and unfinished agenda" (2009).

19 Sir Martin Gilbert, "The terrible 20th century," *The Globe and Mail,* 31 January 2007.

12

HUMAN SECURITY AND WAR

Jennifer Leaning

Introduction

The argument advanced in this chapter is that human security, the essential social expression of human attachment, is at once highly vulnerable to the ravages of war and tightly linked to all efforts to prevent and mitigate its effects. The buildup to war is often influenced by erosion in human security. The period during the war may be marked by sustained assaults on human security, particularly if the warring parties make no effort to limit harmful effects on civilians. The period of transition out of war is a particularly pivotal time in which attention to issues of human security may promote or degrade efforts at stabilization and recovery. It is argued here that recognition of the pivotal role that human security plays during pre, intra, and post-conflict periods is foundational to local, national, and international policies that seek to prevent war, mitigate conflict, and help post-war societies recover.

This argument is based on empirical and theoretical strands from the social sciences, history, psychology, public health, and international law. It is buttressed and supported by data gathered from contemporary settings and by informed observation of recent and current conflict and post-conflict settings.

Human security

The notion of human security arises from an analysis of the world that establishes people, rather than nation-states, as the central repositories of value, meaning, and authority. The roots of this analysis can be traced to the early days of the Enlightenment.[1] The notion surfaced in international policy deliberations with the 1983 Palme Report, *Common Security*,[2] which argued that the nuclear arms race missed the point, that the real security of the world rested on whether people themselves, in every country, felt that their own social, economic, and political needs were being met. Human security, as a term and as an aspiration, received prominent attention in the 1994 UN Development Report[3] and has been extensively explored in the scholarly and policy literature that provided momentum for the international effort that in 2003 produced the UN-sponsored Human Security Report.[4] The wide-ranging essays in this last report establish through empirical and theoretical discussion that governments and the international community must shift from a dominant emphasis on accumulation of arms and elaboration of international political arrangements to efforts that strengthen the foundations of livelihoods and social enterprise that make people healthy and comfortable within their own communities and regions.

The concept of human security invoked here is tightly linked to this discussion. It moves the focus more intensely to the psycho-social dynamics of individuals and communities, and looks in particular at these dynamics in societies in transition from oppression or conflict. This focus is based on the recognition that human beings share common psycho-social needs of identity, recognition, participation, and autonomy.[5] Another fundamental need – for attachment – applies as well.[6]

These human needs obtain regardless of economic status or political stability but are muted or submerged when people are in absolutely desperate circumstances, such as in the immediate settings of famine or gross physical insecurity. Once minimum survival needs have been met, however, these needs will surface and demand engagement. People will seek to be seen for who they are, will need to feel that they belong, will ask to be heard, and will begin to make claims and assert agency. These dynamics, which can be assessed at both the individual and community level, will exert enormous influence over the extent to which external assistance of any kind can be absorbed and integrated into the local setting to good effect. The case for this approach to human security was first advanced as an analytic guide to agencies engaged in post-conflict settlement and recovery activities.[7] That guide included a detailed discussion of metrics and means of assessing key components of human security.

The three main components of this concept of human security involve a sense of home, a link to community, and a positive sense of the future, or a sense of hope. The component of home captures many aspects of the human need to forge and maintain proximity to those in whom we invest our physical and psychological safety and to establish and maintain identity. Home harbors records and memories of interactions with loved ones as well as sensations and feelings regarding attachment to a particular place. The concept of home may be forced into elasticity, however, as war or disaster forces people to leave their ancestral burial plots, their farms or villages, the experience of a stable and dear landscape and night sky. The family unit, even in flight or exile, may provide the assurance and support that individuals need in order to maintain their sense of who they are and where they belong.

The component of community in this definition of human security includes the need to be recognized and to be able to participate in the larger world. The meaning of community coheres around relationships, some of which are based on personal relationships or extended kinship ties but many of which are built through familiar, secure, and repeated interactions with a broad range of independent actors. To varying degrees, all people yearn to take part in such networks, in order to meet their individual and family lists of needs, expectations, and desires. If land is to be bought or sold, a marriage to take place, food to be purchased or bartered, some form of community is required. The essential element in these relationships is impersonal trust, achieved through repetitive and predictable transactions. Communities built on homogenous identity lines, however, may prove antagonistic when facing outsiders, and communities built on established lines of wealth and class may prove fractious if sudden shifts in horizontal inequalities disturb long-held assumptions and stabilities. In the human security model advanced here, community is a fraught concept, filled with promise of social and economic diversity but also known to produce deadly animosities.

The human need for autonomy is captured in the stance towards the future. People with a positive sense of the future will strive to achieve a sense of agency through time, to construct their own future in ways that will expand their sense of wellbeing and capacity. People with a negative sense of the future will not make investments for the long term and may take high risks for short-term gain. Assessing this component of human security entails identifying aspects of hopefulness in behavior or attitude, such as saving for educational expenses of children. In its negative mode, people may make decisions based on a high discount rate, where what appears to be destructive or wasteful behavior may in fact derive from a profound sense of despair about what the future may hold.

The human need to love and trust is embedded in our psycho-biology, according to studies in both the neurosciences and psychology. As described by proponents of attachment theory, the unwanted separation from and loss of our attachment figures can introduce a range of disturbances in the subsequent ability of a person to trust, find solace, and create meaning in life.[8] Wherever sought in empirical studies, it has been found that ruptures in family units and destruction of close relationships caused by disaster and war introduce profound and lasting feelings of grief and despair.[9]

This model of human security has great relevance to the approach that the international community takes to populations that have just emerged from war, oppression, or major disaster. Without an understanding of underlying psycho-social dynamics of human security, it is possible to ask too much of people in the early phase, when they are bereft and lack a sense of home and belonging. It is possible to distribute resources in ways that aggravate underlying community hostilities or to flood a community with resources it cannot yet legitimately absorb and regulate. And it will be easy to dismiss high-risk behavior as simply that, without realizing the lack of hope that lies behind it. Deploying this human security model involves assessing individuals and groups along these parameters of home, community, and sense of the future and then adjusting the flow of inputs and expectations to meet people where they are, rather than where the international community might wish them to be.

Impact of war on human security

The immediate impact of war upon society is usually assessed in terms of numbers of military dead, numbers of civilians forced into flight, extent of infrastructure destroyed, and short-term economic costs. Estimates of civilian mortality in conventional wars and current intra-state wars are highly variable and speculative, always incomplete, and accomplished long after the fact, since no formal institution has ever been assigned responsibility for ongoing, contemporaneous enumeration of non-combatant deaths. Yet civilian deaths in wartime can often far exceed military deaths, and the immediate and enduring consequences of these losses, in terms of human security, has not been plumbed.

Longer-term impacts of war include an elaboration of these quantifiable elements (military mortality, forced migration, destruction of the built environment, and economic costs) along with discussion of less quantifiable factors such as destruction or contamination of the natural environment, longer-term economic effects, and social, political, and psychological consequences.[10] Enumerating these longer-term impacts often prove in themselves to be very drawn out inquiries. It may take decades before participants begin to write deeply and honestly about their memories of events and their views of what has been lost or gained. Even more years may transpire before archives are opened or retrieved and national census and accounting systems are developed or re-instated.

In many parts of the world, attempts to assess both short- and longer-term impacts are severely hampered by the inadequacy of record keeping during the pre-war period and by the widespread destruction of records brought about by the war itself. During the conflict and for months to years after the ceasefire it may be that the only information available for understanding the situation of civilians derives from surveys conducted by humanitarian organizations and international institutions, such as the United Nations and the International Committee of the Red Cross (ICRC).

The following brief review of the impact of war on human security examines social and psychological aspects that are not immediately or easily quantifiable. The extent of these negative qualitative consequences is directly related to the intensity and duration of what we might call a continuum of suffering, an imposition of loss and a contribution to atrocity that is felt across all sectors of the population, combatant and non-combatant alike.

The burden of loss

Long and intense wars, particularly those associated with aerial bombardment or repeated ground assaults over the same terrain, cause great urban and environmental destruction. Vast stores of accumulated wealth, culture, and history disappear. Assessments by the U.S. Strategic Bombing Survey of war damage in Germany (conducted in 1945–1946)[11] and in Japan (conducted in 1945–1947)[12] contain estimates of numbers of destroyed buildings and major structures, but do not convey the sweeping loss of centuries of recorded and constructed products of civilized activity (libraries, museums, religious structures, gardens, archives, statues).

The reconstruction process, which may be supported by the victors (as in post-war Europe and Japan) or may not be (as in the USSR), creates its own pattern of new wealth and new debt. But many things and places cannot be recreated or replaced. And the list of what has been lost is always incomplete.

For example, no accounting has ever been done of the impact of the 1991–1992 shelling of Mogadishu. This beautiful and urbane coastal city, resplendent in flowering shrubs and trees, abundant in restaurants and cultural sites reflecting an Italian gloss on centuries of Arab and African commerce, was utterly and pitifully transformed in the space of three punishing months to a rubble-filled landscape of concrete and sand, stripped of all services, devoid of capacity for social life. In the twenty years since, unremitting conflict and instability throughout Somalia have shredded attempts at governance and blocked international aid. The city remains a squalid jumble of ad hoc settlements and minimal amenities and across the land millions are fleeing a famine judged at least as bad as that which haunted the years 1990–1992.

A more recent example of the impact of long and intense conflict can be seen in Afghanistan in 2002, as it emerged from 23 years of fighting first the Soviet invasion and then a civil war. Most of the irrigation and water works, virtually all of the bridges and tunnels, many of the roads, and large sections of the major cities were all damaged or destroyed. Explosive remnants of war dating from the start of the war with the Soviet Union were scattered throughout the countryside and the cities that saw heavy conflict. Estimates were that over four million people lived in land-mine affected areas.[13] Of the estimated population of 20 million, over 20 per cent (four million) were forced by the conflict to seek refuge in Iran, Pakistan, or elsewhere; another 2 million were estimated to have been displaced throughout the country. Between one and two million people were thought to have been killed. In late 2001 and early 2002, the cities filled up with people who had fled the conflict in rural areas. The alleys and edges of the streets were packed with makeshift shelters for the homeless and the beggars, many of them war widows, orphans, and amputees. The major museums and libraries had been sacked, the carefully culti- vated gardens of the elite razed in the battles for different sections of the cities. The orchards and vineyards of the main agricultural lands had been cut down for firewood. Because of rural flight from the land, a severe three-year drought, and destruction of all built waterworks, agricultural production was at a minimum. Serious shortages of food and shelter were felt throughout the country. Over the last ten years, characterized by ongoing counterinsurgency warfare laced with extraordinary investments in nation-building by the international community, the majority of refugees have returned and arguably some progress has been made in urban areas in all parameters of human security. Yet these gains are uncertain, the ruin and rubble persist in many quarters, and life for ordinary people still carries marked unpredictability and risk.

The international community welcomes the occasion of a cease-fire, whenever and wherever it can be obtained. When the fighting is brought to a close, however, people emerge from shelters or return from afar to confront unremitting ugliness. The tidal disorder of war has obliterated the expected divide between construct and space, between settlement and nature. The eye cannot escape the rubble of buildings, the bombed-out streets, the sheer absence of everything. Huge holes and breaches in the ruins recall where treasured landmarks used to stand, even the rubble has been stripped of pipes and wires, glass, trim, and tires. In the countryside, the paths and fields are littered with abandoned and stripped down tanks or jeeps. Forests are shorn, mountainsides gouged out, military forts and installations mar the horizons, and the earth is not safe to tread on for fear of mines and munitions.

It is a struggle for people to move past these sensory perceptions and the feelings they evoke. In Afghanistan, women and older men were particularly vocal about the waste that war had brought, the destruction of everything they had loved and that had given life meaning. They expressed strong anger at the men, including their own men, who had persisted in the madness of conflict over the previous two decades, and in this time had driven the country into something ghastly and decimated, a place from which they recoiled as they had to remain.[14]

These reactions echo ones that are only now being assembled, arising from the (now elderly) stunned citizens who gazed at the demolished cities and towns of post-war Germany. In the years that followed, as Sebald notes in an account of these feelings, people repressed their bleak dismay and outrage, acquiescing to the sweeping world consensus that whatever had happened to Germany and the Germans was well deserved. Repression and denial were also necessary defenses against the horrors of what people had seen and experienced. Yet sixty years later, the emotional and cognitive reality of those times for the immediate survivors is finally beginning to surface.[15]

Although we are beginning to note and even look for these feelings of dislocation and alienation as relevant aspects of the psychological costs of war, we have not yet formulated the ways to identify these feelings systematically on a population basis. Nor have we developed the methods to measure their relative influence, in terms of life choices and behavior through time, for either individuals or groups.

The layered experience of loss in war includes the disruption and disorientation of flight and return. Flight from war may take people to distant havens where the culture and the environment are completely different from what is familiar and loved. Even forced dislocation to another part of one's country means leaving particular dwellings, gardens, landscapes, and burial grounds. In the immediate transition, when survival of oneself and one's family is at stake, forced migrants make do and accommodate. But as time goes on and return either becomes impossible or becomes a trip back to a place that has ceased to exist except in memory, the sorrow at what cannot be recovered begins to seep in. We underestimate, at risk of missing immensely important aspects of human wellbeing, the extent to which human beings, even those in industrialized and urban societies, retain attachments to particular places.

This forced migration not only breaks the bonds that people have to their homes and their land but leads to new and often alienated settlement upon return. When we look at countries where war was waged at least in part on their own territories, as in postwar Europe or Japan, or as in more recent conflicts, a consistent finding appears to be rapid and pronounced urbanization. In the Soviet Union, by 1961, sixteen years after World War II, the majority of the population had moved into urban areas.[16] It is estimated that postwar Angola has over 50 per cent of its population in the coastal capital of Luanda.[17]

This urbanization does not necessarily reflect positive individual choice. Rural areas may be depopulated, mined, devoid of employment opportunities. Going to the cities is the only option, and to some a very unwelcome one, despite the surface bustle of international activity and new investment. Only the older urban squatters in large towns in Angola even dimly remember their farms, villages, and ancestral cemeteries, hundreds of miles in the interior, made inaccessible by years of war and rampage, now still out of reach because of land mines, unpassable roads, and economic ruin in the region. The preponderance of Angolans, those under 30 years of age, many of whom were born and grew up as refugees, have no memories and scant knowledge of their country from earlier times. In Afghanistan as well, it is the older Afghan workmen, filling thin stoves with firewood for Kabul residents, who grip thick cords of grapevine, remnants from vines that took 30–40 years to grow, and lapse back on their knees, recalling what life had been like when they were young, the grapevines standing, and the wars not begun.

War also imposes a set of demographic changes upon the surviving population. Most of these involve loss, as in physical and mental disability among veterans and affected civilians, loss of spirited and brave leaders (killed or forced into exile), and general attrition in labor force and skills that comes from sheer population loss. For men, the intra-war mobilization of women into the workplace can be perceived as a loss, and when postwar societies reverse that gender shift, the return from the workplace to home can appear to be a loss for women. Much has been written about these issues, particularly in relation to the two major world wars of the twentieth century. It suffices to note that these demographic factors are at play as well in the less well studied internal and civil wars that have occurred since 1945.

The burden of atrocity

The breakdown of distinction between warrior and civilian, home front and battle front, characterizes many of the current non-state or intra-state conflicts. This breakdown of distinction has also occurred in many so-called conventional wars, past and present, at different phases of these wars and in different locations where they have been waged.

Conflict analysts who note this loss of definitive boundary between civilians and combatants in past or current wars agree that the causes are multiple but emphasize different factors as major determinants.[18] In the major conventional wars of the twentieth century, atrocity-laden campaigns against civilians are seen as arising from formal command authorization or in the final stages of long and brutal struggles, where command authority had broken down or dissipated under the stress of events. In current intra-state wars, or in the case of insurgencies launched within nation-state wars (Iraq, Afghanistan), some analysts cite lack of training or disciplined command structures among non-state armed groups who have not benefited from the indoctrination given to formal military forces. Others discern a deliberate disregard for doctrine of international humanitarian law (IHL), in service of a strategy that privileges assault on civilian populations. This assault in turn can spring from several motivations: the need to cause people to flee and empty the land, because without supply lines and communication systems these armed groups cannot secure and hold a populated area; or the direct animus of ethnic cleansing, wherein the aim is not the capture of territory but the expulsion of stigmatized peoples. In the years since September 11, 2001, some analysts of transnational groups describe the tactics of terror based on tenets of radical Islam, according to which the killing of those deemed infidels is not a transgression of international norms but a duty of the truly faithful. Other analysts emphasize the dynamics of asymmetric warfare, where unless non-state actors break the rules of distinction, they face overwhelming odds against the military forces of modern states equipped with high-tech weapons in an electronic battlefield.

It is possible that wars with the most destructive effects on human security are those where bounds between civilian and combatant status are not drawn or are consistently violated. Home is invaded, community torn asunder, the future marred by guilt, anger, loss, and fear. In these wars, where communities are split along communal lines (race, religion, language, ethnicity), individuals and groups targeted on the basis of their communal characteristics are forced to undergo a profound disorientation in their sense of social stability, trust, and personal identity. For the targets of attack, what once seemed safe and taken for granted (a neighbor's smile, a courtesy at the market) turns into a lethal connection. To be recognized is to be at risk. The foundations of one's world slip away.

Wars laced with atrocity consume much social capital. Large numbers of people, victims and perpetrators, find it difficult to resume their lives for years after the ceasefires and peace accords. Guilt, humiliation, fear, rage, denial, and rejection may haunt the perpetrators. The victims carry their own versions of these feelings. Talent and energy are drained from the postwar project of reconstruction.

The feelings and memories may find other avenues of expression. Analysts speak of the 'trauma story,' a communal construct of what happened and what may lie ahead.[19] This story is tied to experience but elaborated to confer meaning, explanation, and exculpation for the side that tells and conveys it. Often these stories are mirror images of each other, one told by perceived victim (but perhaps perpetrator to the other); the other told from the other point of view. The traumatic event may lurk in past centuries (for modern Serbs and Kosovar Albanians it is the 1389 Battle on the Field of Blackbirds) or in recent history (for India and Pakistan, it is the 1947 Partition; for radical anti-U.S. Islamists it is the first Gulf War). Regardless, the trauma story serves to drive a wedge between communally defined groups and freeze-frame their interpretation of all subsequent events.

Hence human security may remain out of reach for generations.

Human security and policies relating to conflict

Pre-conflict situations

Despite significant advances in the scholarly and policy communities, the characterization of a society as entering a 'pre-conflict phase' has proved to be troublesome. Indicators of early warning can identify societies that are at risk but have not been shown to have marked predictive power.[20] However, sufficient work has been done, by economists and political scientists in particular, to suggest that the human security concept has real theoretical and policy application to efforts at identification of risk and stabilization of trends.

The human security concept asks that we focus on individual capacities and human life, in the context of promoting an individual's active engagement with networks of support and communication. Human security thus rests on certain types of capacities and capabilities that successfully support group resilience and coping. These constructive relationships need not just be cooperative – in fact, many of the most successful are those that enhance competition. Certain kinds of rivalries (markets, democratic elections, for instance) are healthy components of a society whose individuals feel grounded at home, equipped to be at ease in their communities, and at least moderately confident of their future.

The challenge in pre-war settings is to identify those destructive tensions and ties that lead to conflict, rather than to productively cooperative or competitive social behaviors. This challenge requires attention to three questions: what are the tensions that can be seen as de-stabilizing; what changes in the environment, circumstances, or relationships will introduce or aggravate these tensions; and finally, what different groups are likely to be involved, or coalesce, in relationship to these tensions. In other words, who will stand to win or lose with regard to exogenous or endogenous change?

Many of these societies that engender 'pre-conflict' scrutiny are very poor and among the world's most vulnerable (in terms of withstanding economic or political shocks). They are staggering under the burden of educating growing numbers of young people and finding ways to integrate them into stagnant or collapsing economies. This demographic 'youth bulge' is often referenced as a source of human insecurity and a risk factor for future war.[21] Other societies in this risk category, however, may lie in the more middle range of the human development index but contain within them traditions of hierarchy, discrimination, and social exclusion that entrench a trajectory of economic growth and power for only the elite, or only a few groups. Both categories of societies are likely to suffer from an absent or insufficiently developed set of regulatory and administrative systems that apply equally and fairly to all members of the society. Even if a modicum of material goods is available, there may be major and dysfunctional gaps in the way these societies have adopted the rule of law.

These anticipatory assessments of vulnerabilities, risk, and resilience are necessary to make when granting aid, introducing development strategies, or supporting existing leaders and power structures.[22] Human rights abuses have human security implications and ill-advised measures intended to shore up human security can badly backfire. Infusion of resources with the aim of promoting human security (schools, health care, roads, investment and market opportunities) may differentially benefit those who already hold power or status and thus intensify or solidify discriminatory or abusive structures and behaviors. This added burden on the vulnerable or marginalized may accelerate their growing sense of human insecurity.

Informed attention to home, community, and sense of the future – the psycho-social human security perspective – invokes issues of dignity, equity, and voice. What conditions and fears do excluded groups express or experience? What instances of direct or indirect harm have occurred to certain groups in these societies that can be examined in terms of harbingers of potential trends and escalations? Here is where a close reading of competing communal narratives becomes most valuable. Grievances from past conflicts, especially those that have pitted groups within a society against each other or have engaged communal identities across nation-states, can be sustained for decades and even centuries. These sustained fault lines, if not deftly and directly addressed during times of relative stability, will provide fissionable material in times of crisis or rapid change. Hence human security policies in the pre-conflict period must aim to support training and diffusion through all sectors of society, including the military, in the norms of human rights and international humanitarian law.

An indicator of risk of future conflict is whether the society has recently already been involved in war.[23] Although this indicator is derived from a macro-political analysis of large data sets, it could be argued that much of its empirical validity is rooted in the psychological dynamics of human insecurity. This indicator also reflects the historical finding that wars based on communal dynamics or ancient grievances can last for a very long time, exhaust material and human assets, and give rise in the post-conflict period to pervasive violence, humiliation, and annihilation of community self-respect. These wars are very difficult to recover from. For these reasons, an important aspect of human security strategy in the pre-conflict period is to maintain a high priority on policies aimed explicitly at conflict prevention and conflict mitigation.

The human security perspective, in the pre-conflict situation, thus suggests a mix of promotional and restraining strategies. Positive strategies include those that promote individual and group attachment to constructive activities of cooperation or competition. Negative strategies are those that reduce, block, or restrain the introduction or development of destructive group relationships.

It is outside the scope of this chapter to address the many examples of efforts that have been made in the field of conflict prevention. Successful use of preventive diplomacy, including deployment of preventive forces, took place when the international community intervened during the 1990s to restrain mass violence in Burundi and to forestall the spread of the Yugoslav conflict into Macedonia.[24]

Conflict situations

The terrible impact of war on civilians and combatants can be mitigated by a range of measures that reduce brutality and atrocity, limit assaults on civilians, minimize destruction of civilian assets, and create strong disincentives for grave violations of international law.[25] These measures fall into several main categories: 1) training of formal and non-state militaries, to the extent access can be obtained, throughout the duration of the war; 2) tactical use of incentives and disincentives in securing compliance with IHL in the field setting; 3) monitoring and reporting of formal and informal military interactions with civilian populations; 4) maintaining human contact with the outside world by humanitarian aid; 5) application of international diplomatic (and, at the extreme) military force, with the aim of bringing about a rapid ceasefire; and 6) creation of deterrence effect through enforcement of judicial procedures at the state and international level against individuals alleged to have committed war crimes.

A wide range of state and non-state actors have roles to play in carrying out these various measures. The International Committee of the Red Cross is a crucial agent for the first four measures, the result of its assigned tradition of engagement with combatants on all sides and monitoring of the conduct of hostilities. To the extent that formal military from outside nations are involved, their behavior and reporting functions have the potential to restrain unlawful acts on the part of non-state actors. Humanitarian and human rights NGOs serve a critical function by providing a normative and empathetic connection with the international community. The relatively small niche afforded in international humanitarian law for the delivery of relief supplies and medical aid also creates the opportunity to bear witness, report on the hardships and atrocities, and convey the message that the outside world cares about what is happening to the local, ordinary people trapped inside the cauldron of hostilities.

In wars of the 1990s, in the period between the collapse of the Cold War and the launch of the war on terror, the humanitarian role in protecting civilians from harm proved particularly robust.[26] The space for humanitarian action, the so-called humanitarian niche, expanded in the areas where the great powers left (the war zones of Angola, Mozambique, and Sudan) and where international forces were absent, late, or ineffective (the conflicts in Somalia, Bosnia, Rwanda, and Kosovo)[27] During these years, humanitarian NGOs, working with the humanitarian agencies of the UN and the ICRC to build upon their collective experience from the 1980s response to famine and disaster, established a reasonably coherent approach to the support of refugees and internally displaced people (IDPs) in war-torn areas. This approach, at its best, gave practical life to the key tenets of international law. Weapons were not allowed in hospital zones and clinic areas; refugee camps were disarmed; medical personnel were trained; health care protocols were developed. Attention to human rights and individual dignity began to thread through programs, so that best practices were designed to reduce and respond to gender-based violence; broad-gauged psycho-social support programs were introduced when settlements were considered sufficiently safe; and activities to promote child welfare and education became part of the standard mix of services in the more stable areas.

Much effective action can also be taken from outside the conflict zone on the part of civil society actors working with their own governments and the international community. Mobilizing grass-roots and elite demands for international diplomatic engagement (in terms of UN resolutions and public and private state communications) may prove influential (as it did in Somalia, Bosnia, Kosovo, and South Sudan). The content and tone of this diplomatic engagement are pivotal, in that carrots as well as sticks should be imaginatively entertained. Whatever measures are considered, their application needs to be specific and targeted, since non-state armed groups are less vulnerable to state-based sanctions but can be reached through pressure or positive incentives directed at the nation-states who grant these groups resources, sanctuary, and political support.

The threat of prosecution for war crimes may have marked deterrence effect if that threat can be carried out in a practical human time frame. Meeting that condition requires adequate funding and staffing of the International Criminal Court and sustained political support for this level of resource commitment on the part of the international community. It also requires that nation-states invigorate their own domestic law to create obligatory channels of cooperation and compliance.[28]

In the abstract, it is straightforward to argue that such measures, if implemented, could be seen to help sustain human security in war. Home, in terms of ties to family and place, is central to the human security concept. In war, if the distinction between civilian and combatant has broken down or been deliberately discarded, home becomes one of the first targets. Community is crushed when war breaks out and pits identifiable groups and individuals, previously linked in forms of social networks, against one another. The notion of community turns ever more terrifying, however, when it becomes evident that people and groups whom one had trusted turn out to betray that trust in violent and vicious attacks on oneself and one's family. And for all but the few who celebrate its onset, war blocks all paths to previously envisioned futures. It forces a confrontation with the present or a retreat into the past. The urgency of survival drains the capacity to dream. The longer the war continues, and the more extensive its destruction of beloved built structures, repositories of cultural memory, and treasured landscapes and vistas, the more alienated the population comes from its future life in that terrain. A positive sense of the past carries people into the future. When that past is obliterated and its landmarks gone, the future becomes a far more uncertain place.

But in practical terms, the record is incomplete when it comes to assessing whether or not the particular measures discussed above have been shown to make much difference on the ground, for a given specific conflict. Seasoned humanitarian aid officers, policy makers, and academics have their own long list of positive anecdotes, even narratives and analyses.[29] What is inescapably evident to those who have witnessed war and efforts to mitigate its effects is that for some people, for some time, these forms of support and intervention have made a huge difference. Perhaps that is as much as can be hoped for. War is a terrible enterprise for all involved and efforts to diminish its reach can at best be accomplished only at the margins.

Post-conflict situations

A critical fallacy in thinking about war is to assume that when a ceasefire has taken place the war is then 'over.' The English language reinforces this error by providing few alternatives to words and phrases like 'post-conflict, postwar, aftermath, reconstruction, recovery, rehabilitation, demobilization, disarmament, de-mining.' At least the word 'de-mining' is a gerund, connoting a sense of ongoing process.

The reality of war is that the immediate period after the ceasefire contains all the embers for a future re-kindling of violent hostilities. An uncertainty characterizes this period, for which no working definition exists. Descriptive characteristics of this phase, which usually extends for weeks or months after the ceasefire agreement, include the fact that open fighting has ceased, there is some appreciable improvement in civilian security; and local leadership is starting to emerge. Spontaneous refugee return is beginning, people are already flocking to the cities to find work with the international humanitarian and peace-keeping agencies, and prices for food, housing, and petrol are beginning to soar.

The situation, depending upon the nature of the preceding war, is marked by mass population dislocation, high levels of insecurity for the population, possibly high levels of insecurity for members of the international community and those who work for them, widespread destruction of infrastructure, and a burden of unaddressed loss and atrocity.[30]

The overall goal for the local leadership and for the international community must be to agree upon the objectives of the stabilization and reconstruction efforts and the strategy for achieving them. A human security perspective would suggest an inclusive and participatory approach oriented towards restitution of safety, livelihoods, and local empowerment.[31]

That said, the threat of reversion to violence is very high in this early period and regardless of process, a set of essential early measures must be quickly put into motion, in a sequence that attends to the psychological dynamics of the people and their leaders. In actuality, many of these measures are not introduced when needed or in proper sequence, and the grey time between war and peace, the post-conflict 'transition' period, often extends into years.

These essential measures begin with shoring up security, an operational imperative but also extremely important from the human security perspective. People need to feel safe before they can begin to seek out steps back to a semblance of normal life. The main threats to security in the immediate post-ceasefire period are from armed groups, criminal elements, and weapons dispersed among members of the general population. Military or police forces must be deployed to maintain weapons-free civilian zones, guard public buildings and sites where resources are stored, organize traffic flows, and patrol streets and highways. Local or international police are usually more tolerated by the general population than military units and usually have the more appropriate training to maintain law and order. The task of disarming armed groups and collecting weapons from members of the public often requires months and should proceed under the command of the military, as part of the extended ceasefire and subsequent peace agreement.

As soon as physical insecurity has been reduced to a tolerable level, the authorities should proceed to provide basic human survival needs to the general civilian population (water, shelter, food, essential medical care). In this process, particular attention must be given to the protection and care of those populations that are most vulnerable. These populations will vary depending on the war context but usually include orphans, widows, amputees and other physically disabled people, and stigmatized groups at risk of reprisal or hostile attack.

The next steps that must be accomplished in a matter of months are almost all measures that derive from and reinforce a human security model.

1 Policies relating to refugee and IDP return can either fully support the human security concept of home or rapidly vitiate it. Family tracing and reunification must be a priority. Giving people goods, seeds, and tools will be helpful but attention must also be carefully tuned to issues of coping mechanisms and capacity building. During these first few months, the authorities and relief workers must recognize that the majority of people are not likely to be especially good at problem solving, taking the initiative, or self-mobilization. Their entire fund of emotional and cognitive energy will be expended in the daily struggle for

survival, adjusting to shifting and often alien circumstances, accommodating new or changed returnees, and managing their own feelings and memories.

An important factor in refugee and IDP return is the extent to which the land they left can readily be reclaimed. In many postwar situations, records have been lost or were based only on face-to-face witnessing and oral contracts. In the years since people fled, others may have moved in. Usually there are issues relating to the rights of widows to use, inherit, or transfer land. This question of land tenure becomes more bitter and complex the longer the conflict has gone on (as in Afghanistan, South Sudan, and Angola) and can be complicated, not improved, by government policies on land redistribution and relative de-mining priorities attached to commercial or elite vs. subsistence land holdings (as in Angola).

2 De-mining, notwithstanding the social competition behind identification of priority areas, is a critical element in creating a stable sense of home. It is well accepted that people will either not return or not return as large family groups if landmines or unexploded ordnance (explosive remnants of war, ERW) are known to exist in their own family plots, along the customary paths and roads, and at key intersections and bridges. The risk profile of local people varies within and between countries but it is also a well-accepted fact that for people to return to their homes, at minimum their entire village and farming area must have all sites of ERW contamination identified and all places where people actually live, farm, and routinely travel must be thoroughly de-mined. One stray accident with animal or human consequences will set back resettlement for a considerable period of time.

3 Closely linked to de-mining operations is the effort to repair roads and bridges and set up communication systems. These must also be high priority tasks in this post-ceasefire setting. The problems of transport and communication can appear completely disabling to all other actions that the international and local communities try to put into motion. One cannot get to outlying areas to assess problems or deliver services. One cannot meet with people in nearby locales because travel times are extremely long (hours to days) and very unpredictable (traffic jams, a new collapse in an unstable road bed). One cannot make phone calls. Mobility, of people and ideas, is essential to all aspects of planning and operations. In these months after the fighting has stopped, mobility turns out to be the major bottleneck.

From the human security perspective, this problem of mobility is central to the recreation of community. Local people need to come together in some form of meetings and other participatory processes to talk about their concerns, make short-term plans, and organize cooperative work projects, such as clearing rubble or restoring wells. Re-starting basic markets relies on people bringing goods or produce to sell and others coming forward to buy or barter. These activities of engagement require some form of predictable transport and interactive communications. The lack of traversable roads and communication systems similarly grind down efforts of the international community to encourage these local activities as well as carry out their own operations. Hours of time and gallons of petrol are wasted each day trying to drive from one town to another, or driving across towns to find out if someone is at home, in the office, somewhere else, or en route to the meeting that is now 3 hours late and has only one-third of expected participants. Those NGOs and international players that rely on internal radio communication can deliver brief and linear messages but as useful as this mode is it is no substitute for face-to-face gatherings of people from different sectors and local groups.

Early post-conflict settings are notorious for traffic jams, operational inefficiencies, high levels of frustration, and recurrent confusion and misunderstanding among all parties. These issues are often direct results of, or certainly aggravated by, the difficulties of getting roads and phones to work.

4 An over-arching determinant of community attitude, however, is the strategy and methods used for identifying needs and distributing resources. Health posts, schools, hospitals, administrative buildings, housing, and other essentials for community life will have been destroyed or substantially depleted. Whenever outside aid comes in to help with reconstruction at this phase, the potential for splitting groups within communities along hostile competitive lines must be anticipated, identified, and dealt with on an ongoing basis. The task of seeking opinion and reaching out to different groups in an unfamiliar community via intermediaries and translators is time-consuming, hazardous, and essential.[32] Several factors, in addition to the difficulty of the task, conspire to reduce the likelihood that agencies will take it on. Everyone has a sense of urgency and everyone tries to respond to the pent-up impatience of all actors to see tangible improvements in a very short time frame. In the rush to accomplish something tangible, this important task of assessing and dealing with fissiparous community dynamics often gets pushed aside.

5 In the longer run, those in charge of the reconstruction process must make every effort to introduce some administrative regularity into the functions of daily life. These administrative structures serve at the local level to create the rudimentary elements of the rule of law: complaint procedures, detention centers, consistent definition and implementation of sanctions and punishments, requirements regarding commercial and banking transactions, some form of legitimate adjudication system. These structures will support a constructive pattern of individual and group behavior and allow a productive mix of social and economic activities to take hold.

6 Throughout these early days and months, the authorities and the humanitarian community must remain alert to underlying psychological dynamics in the civilian population. Beneath the surface people will be dealing with feelings of guilt, anger, humiliation, and revenge. Families will be struggling to integrate members who have been away for years; returning neighbors may view each other with suspicion or outright certainty of previous atrocity. Social and legal processes for dealing with serious abuses committed during the conflict will not have been defined or set up during this period, leaving it up to local communities how they might deal with identified or suspected perpetrators. These concerns, if not dealt with as soon as is possible in a coherent, transparent, and participatory mode, will prove destructive to the longer-term re-knitting of community relationships and development of forward momentum towards the future.

Examples of successful human security strategies in this context include the vigorous de-mining efforts in Angola, which provide a sense of physical security and safety to the population, employ local people, and open up land for resettlement; and extensive road and bridge reconstruction in Kosovo, which supported a return to intra-country commerce and communication. Save the Children UK has launched a global effort to provide education to the estimated 39 million conflict-affected children who have had their schooling severely disrupted by years of war and forced migration. Their 2007 report notes considerable progress in enlisting children and promoting stability and wellbeing in their school programs.[33] Increasing use of community and regional radio transmission has proved a robust means of keeping people in urban as well as rural areas informed and up-to-date about political and social issues that affect their lives.[34]

This section on post-conflict policy has focused on the first weeks and months of international and local activity. If the measures outlined above are introduced in a timely and reasonably effective manner, the potential for the longer-term work, including local capacity building[35] and conflict resolution,[36] appears much greater. However, clambering out of war takes much longer, on a human scale, than descending into it. In many ways, Europe and parts of Asia are still dealing with the repercussions and consequences of World War II. It is not difficult to identify the themes in U.S. social and political life that date directly from the Vietnam War or even from the U.S. Civil War of the mid-nineteenth century.

Conclusion

At the geopolitical level, there may be a warrant for some wars, at some times. A human security perspective, however, describes war as an almost generic process of calamitous damage and imperfect repair. Every war is different, yet each yields, to those who look for it, a recognizable pattern of human connection and loss. At each juncture, in the turning towards war, in the midst of war, and in the final turning away, there are opportunities to enhance the connection and mitigate the loss. We must acknowledge, however, that whatever might be done in these modes, there is always a negative balance. War takes away more than can be given back.

Notes

This chapter was originally published in *Risking Human Security: Attachment and Public Life*, edited by Marci Green (published by Karnac Books in 2008), and is reproduced with kind permission of Karnac Books.

1　Rothschild, E. What is security? *Daedalus* 1995, 124: 53–98.
2　Independent Commission on Disarmament and Security Issues. *Common Security: A Blueprint for Survival*. Simon and Schuster. New York, 1982.
3　United Nations Development Program. *Human Development Report*. UNDP. United Nations. New York, 1994.
4　Commission on Human Security. *Human Security Now*. Communications Development Inc. New York, 2003.
5　Amoo, S. The challenges of ethnicity and conflicts in Africa: The need for a new paradigm. *UNDP Emergency Response Division*. United Nations. New York, 1997.
6　Green, M. Introduction. In Green, M., ed. *Risking Human Security: Attachment and Public Life*. Karnac Books, Ltd. London, 2008: xiii–xxix.
7　Leaning J., Arie S. *Human Security: A Framework for Assessment in Conflict and Transition*. Working Paper Series Vol 11, No. 8. Harvard Center for Population and Development Studies. Cambridge, MA, September 2001.
8　Cozolino L., Walker MD. The social construction of the human brain. In Green, M., ed. *Risking Human Security: Attachment and Public Life*. Karnac Books, Ltd. London, 2008: 1–18.
9　Marris, P. Attachment and loss of community. In Green M., ed. *Risking Human Security: Attachment and Public Life*. Karnac Books, Ltd. London, 2008: 21–33.
10　Laquer W. *Europe since Hitler: The Rebirth of Europe*. Penguin Books. New York, New York, 1984.
11　United States Strategic Bombing Survey. *Summary report, European War, September 30, 1945*: 15. Available: http://www.anesi.com/ussbs02.htm (accessed 10 June 2013).
12　United States Strategic Bombing Survey. *Summary report, Pacific War, 1 July 1946*: 17. United States Government Printing Office. Washington, D.C., 1946.
13　Fruchet P., Kendellen M. *Landmine Impact Survey of Afghanistan: Results and Implications for Planning*. March 7, 2006. Available: http://maic.jmu.edu/journal/9.2/focus/fruchet/fruchet.html (accessed 13 August 2013).
14　Holleufer G., Leaning J., Briton N. *Report to the ICRC on the People on War Project. Afghanistan Country Report*. Unpublished. Harvard School of Public Health. Boston, 2000.
15　Sebald WG. *On the Natural History of Destruction*. Random House. New York, 2003: vii–x; 3–104.
16　Judt T. *Postwar: A History of Europe since 1945*. Penguin Books. London, England, 2005: 385.
17　Jenkins P., Robson A., Cain J. Local responses to globalization and peripheraliztion in Luanda, Angola. *Environment and Urbanization* 2002, 14: 115–127.

18 Kaldor M. *New and Old Wars: Organized Violence in a Global Era*. Stanford University Press. 2nd edn. Stanford, California, 2007.

19 Volkan V. D., Itzkowitz N. *Turks and Greeks: Neighbours in Conflict*. Eothen Press. Cambridgeshire, England, 1994: 7–10.

20 International Commission on Intervention and State Sovereignty. *The Responsibility to Protect*. International Development Research Centre. Ottawa, Canada, 2001: 21.

21 Goldstone J. A. Demographic change and the sources of international conflict. In: Weiner M., Russell S. S., eds. *Demography and National Security*. Berghahn Books. New York, 2001: 62–108.

22 Collier P., et al. *Breaking the Conflict Trap: Civil War and Development Policy*. World Bank and Oxford University Press. Washington, D.C., 2003.

23 Harff B. No lessons learned since the Holocaust? Assessing risks of genocide and political mass murder since 1955. *Am Pol Sci Rev* 2003, 97: 57–73.

24 Gurr T. R. Early-warning systems: From surveillance to assessment to action. In Cahill K. M., ed. *Preventive Diplomacy: Stopping Wars Before They Start*. Basic Books. New York, 1996: 130–132.

25 Leaning J., Arie S., Holleufer G., Bruderlein C. Human security and conflict: a comprehensive approach. In Chen L., Leaning J., Narasimhan V., eds. *Global Health Challenges for Human Security*. Global Equity Initiative, Harvard University. Harvard University Press. Cambridge, MA, 2003: 13–30; Jones B. D., Cater C. K. From chaos to coherence? Toward a regime for protecting civilians in war. In Chesterman S., ed. *Civilians in War*. Lynne Rienner. Boulder, Colorado, 2001: 237–262.

26 Bruderlein C, Leaning J. New challenges for humanitarian protection. *BMJ* 1999, 319: 430–435.

27 The tragedy for Chechnya is that it was held thrall to US–Russian relations during this period. For political and military reasons the conflict was consigned by the international community to the Russian sphere of influence, and in the anarchy of the first war (1994–1996) became a no-go zone for international humanitarian involvement.

28 Ratner S. R., Bischoff J. L., eds. *International War Crimes Trials: Making a Difference*. Proceedings of an international conference held at the University of Texas School of Law. November 6–7, 2003. The University of Texas at Austin School of Law. Austin, TX, 2004.

29 For informed but very different views of the humanitarian field, see: Kennedy D. *The Dark Sides of Virtue: Reassessing International Humanitarianism*. Princeton University Press. Princeton, 2004; Minear L. *The Humanitarian Enterprise: Dilemmas and Discoveries*. Kumarian Press. Bloomfield, CT, 2002; Rieff D. *A Bed for the Night: Humanitarianism in Crisis*. Simon and Schuster. New York, 2002; Terry F. *Condemned To Repeat? The Paradox of Humanitarian Action*. Cornell University Press. Ithaca, NY, 2002; Overseas Development Institute. *Aid and War: A Response to Linda Polman's Critique of Humanitarianism*. May 2010. Available: http://www.odi.org.uk/resources/download/4835.pdf (accessed 12 June 2013).

30 Medecins sans Frontières. *World in Crisis: The Politics of Survival at the End of the Twentieth Century*. Routledge. London, 1997: 100–203.

31 World Bank. *Post-conflict Reconstruction: The Role of the World Bank*. The World Bank. Washington, D.C., 1998.

32 Anderson M. B. *Do No Harm: How Aid Can Support Peace – or War*. Lynne Reinner. Boulder, Colorado, 1999.

33 Save the Children UK. *Rewrite the future –One Year On*. Available: http://www.savethechildren.org.uk/resources/online-library/rewrite-the-future---one-year-on (accessed 13 August 2013).

34 Fraser C., Estrada S. R. *Community Radio Handbook*. UNESCO. Paris, 2001. Available: http://www.odi.org.uk/resources/download/4835.pdf (accessed 12 June 2013).

35 Smillie I., ed. *Patronage or Partnership: Local Capacity Building in Humanitarian Crises*. Kumarian Press. Bloomfield, CT, 2001.

36 Byrne S., Irvin C. L., eds. *Reconcilable Differences: Turning Points in Ethno-political Conflict*. Kumarian Press. Bloomfield, CT, 2000.

13

HUMAN SECURITY AND NATURAL DISASTERS

Dorothea Hilhorst, Alpaslan Özerdem and Erin Michelle Crocetti

This chapter explores the nexus between human security and natural disasters. As of today, the framework of human security has not had much explicit translation in relation to natural disasters. However, as this chapter will elaborate, the framework is highly relevant, and may indeed become more central in the years to come. Human security is an integrative concept that combines ideas on human development, human needs and human rights (Gasper, 2010: 29). This fits well with the current thinking on natural hazards that views disasters as the combined outcome of hazards and vulnerability.

Until the Second World War, disaster risk reduction, mainly through water management, was hazard-oriented and seen as a matter for engineering. In the twentieth century optimistic modernism led to the 'hydraulic mission' (Turton and Ohlsson, 1999). The state controlled water resources and 'developed' the basin with mega-structures for flood protection and water retention. Embankments and barriers were built in order to tame the rivers and safeguard life and livelihoods of the population behind the dikes. In the 1960s this hazard-oriented paradigm became complemented by social science perspectives. Gilbert White (1986 (1960)) proposed that people should be given a greater range of options, which would make them consider leaving or avoiding high-risk areas. This so-called behavioural paradigm coupled a hazard-centred interest in the geo-physical processes underlying disaster with the conviction that people had to be taught to anticipate it.

The 1983 landmark publication of *Interpretations of Calamity from the Viewpoint of Human Ecology* edited by Kenneth Hewitt argued that structural factors such as increasing poverty and related social processes accounted for people and societies' vulnerability to disaster. This signalled the beginning of a vulnerability paradigm that understands disasters as the interaction between hazard and vulnerability (O'Keefe et al., 1976). Disaster risk reduction would then entail the transformation of social and political structures that breed poverty and the social dynamics that serve to perpetuate it (Heijmans and Victoria, 2001), from the local to the international level (Wisner et al., 2004). The vulnerability paradigm brought along increasing attention to the role of disaster-affected people and their communities in disaster risk reduction (Anderson and Woodrow, 1989). Community-based disaster risk reduction became a widely advocated approach. Since the 1990s, the understanding of disasters again shifted to emphasize the mutuality of hazard and vulnerability to disaster due to complex interactions between nature and society. In this view, hazards are increasingly the result of human activity. This has the important implication that vulnerability might not just be understood as how people are susceptible to hazards, but can also be considered as a measure of the impact of society on the environment (Oliver-Smith and Hofmann, 1999; Hilhorst, 2004).

Human security can easily be aligned to the current understanding of disasters. Disaster risk reduction seeks to integrate the immediate needs of disaster victims with risk reduction measures and structural development as a means to reduce disaster vulnerability. Like human security, it thus aims to integrate needs and development, and encompasses concerns for individual survivors of disasters with the need to develop more disaster-resilient communities, societies and global relations.

The next section of this chapter reviews some of the normative frameworks pertaining to natural disasters and asks what they mean in terms of human security. The following part of the chapter reviews the debate whether natural disasters could be considered grounds to evoke the Responsibility to Protect. We then address the question how current discourses around human security find translation in rights-based approaches in disaster response. This specifically looks into the experiences of disaster response following the 2004 tsunami in Sri Lanka. We conclude that there is room for expanding human security thinking into disaster response, and that until now human security thinking has not found systematic translation in disaster risk reduction efforts. While human security is very promising as a framework to guide disaster risk reduction, its translation and value in practice is yet to be established.

Frameworks regulating natural disaster response

To understand the potential of the idea of human security in disaster risk reduction, it is important to embed this discussion in the different frameworks that regulate disaster response. Disaster response is the realm of governments, civil society, disaster managers and humanitarian agencies. They each represent domains with their own frameworks and standards. In the first place, there are national laws and frameworks. Each country has disaster response mechanisms that are more or less embodied in law. These national frameworks are outside the scope of this chapter. We will also not focus on the bodies of institutionalized practices that govern local responses and knowledge on disasters. As human security represents an international frame, we introduce here a few of the international frameworks disaster response fits into.

Humanitarian principles and international humanitarian law

The classic humanitarian principles are associated with the foundation of the Red Cross and the emergence of International Humanitarian Law (IHL). The International Committee of the Red Cross (ICRC)'s status is secured in International Humanitarian Law, with the important implication that signatory parties must protect the humanitarian space that ICRC needs to access people in need. To live up to its designated role, ICRC has formulated four basic principles that guide humanitarian action. The principle of humanity is defined as 'the desire to prevent and alleviate human suffering wherever it may be found'. The principle of impartiality states that the Red Cross movement makes no discrimination as to nationality, race, religious beliefs, class or political opinions. The principle of neutrality says that the Red Cross may not take sides in hostilities or engage at any time in controversies of a political, racial, religious or ideological nature. The principle of independence states that the Red Cross must always maintain its autonomy in relation to its donors.

Due to their affinity with IHL, it has been questioned whether the humanitarian principles should also pertain to natural disasters in peacetime (of course many disasters do happen in conflict areas as well). If these would not be applicable, there have been discussions whether there is a gap in international legal instruments in relation to natural disasters. The World Disaster Report 2000 signalled the discussion and raised the question whether it would be opportune to develop an international disaster response law (IFRC, 2000: 145–157).

International refugee law and Internally Displaced Persons

Like International Humanitarian Law, the Convention of Refugees as well as the (legally softer) guidelines for Internally Displaced Persons are not drafted with the situation of natural disaster displaced people in mind. As will be elaborated further in the next part of the chapter, this may raise questions whether disaster-affected persons should have similar entitlements as conflict-related refugees, or whether perhaps alternative arrangements should be put into place.

Norms, codes and standards

ICRC and UNHCR have a special status in international law. The provision of aid to crisis-affected populations has, however, become the concern of thousands of agencies. Besides, the classic principles did not reflect any guidelines on how to provide quality support in humanitarian crises. This led to the initiative of a Code of Conduct for Disaster Relief situations. The Code concerns the Red Cross movement and humanitarian NGOs. It was published in 1994, and welcomed in 1995 by states at the 26th International Conference of the Red Cross and Red Crescent. The Code brings together the classical humanitarian principles of humanity, independence, (a watered down version of) neutrality and impartiality, along with modern principles derived from the development aid sector: accountability, partnership, participation and sustainability (Hilhorst, 2005). Although the Code is not restricted to conflict situations, it can be considered an elaboration of the classic principles and hence its applicability in disaster situations has occasionally been questioned (Walker, 2005). Soon after, the Code was followed by the initiative of the Sphere Standards.

The Sphere standards clearly pronounce the introduction of a rights-based approach in humanitarian aid, as they set minimum standards that humanitarian crisis-affected people are entitled to. The Sphere standards, and the numerous interagency norms that have followed since,[1] bring about a new positioning of humanitarian agencies vis-à-vis rights. Whereas humanitarian assistance set out as an expression of the desire to save lives, a voluntary gesture, increasingly humanitarians are called upon to account for the professional delivery of services, turning them into duty-bearers. This is legitimized by pointing out that humanitarians are obliged to deliver relief, because they raise funds on behalf of people in need. The introduction of rights-based language alters the conception of recipients of aid, away from vulnerable and needy victims to right-holders entitled to a decent level of services. Many agencies engaged in direct service delivery profess to the importance of rights-based approaches but the translation in practice is still evolving, and there seem to be many different interpretations of what a rights-based approach means and in what ways it differs with a more strict humanitarian paradigm.

Hyogo Framework for Action

The Hyogo Framework for Action (HFA) was adopted by 168 Member States of the United Nations in 2005 at the World Disaster Reduction Conference, which took place just a few weeks after the Indian Ocean Tsunami. The HFA was preceded by the UN's International Decade for Natural Disaster Reduction; this did not lead to much attention and concerted action, unlike the HFA which has quickly become a living document. The HFA outlines five priorities for action, and offers guiding principles and practical means for achieving disaster resilience. The first is to ensure that disaster risk reduction is a national and a local priority with a strong institutional basis for implementation. This has been translated in national multi-stakeholder disaster reduction committees in many countries. The other priorities are to identify, assess and monitor disaster risks and enhance early warning; to use knowledge, innovation and education to build a culture of safety and resilience at all levels; to reduce the underlying risk factors; and to strengthen disaster preparedness for effective response at all levels. The HFA has contributed to more coordinated action, and has made disaster risk reduction a matter of inclusion, bringing together government, non-government and science at national and international levels. The International Secretariat of Disaster Reduction regularly organizes the Global Platform for Disaster Risk Reduction, bringing together these different actors. The HFA does not explicitly adopt a rights-based language in relation to disasters. As the Hyogo Framework for Action emphasizes, a paradigm shift is required, from emergency response to holistic disaster risk management. Ad hoc disaster responses are not adequate; instead a holistic and integrated approach is required which incorporates awareness-raising, preparedness, mitigation and response. As such, the HFA is holistic and inclusive, yet displays a technocratic rather than a rights-based approach to disaster risk reduction.

Human rights protection in situations of natural disasters

The only framework that specifically addresses the rights of disaster-affected people are the Operational Guidelines and Field Manual on Human Rights Protection in Situations of Natural Disaster, by the Inter-Agency Standing Committee (IASC). The IASC is an inter-agency forum for coordination, policy development and decision-making in humanitarian assistance, recognized as such by General Assembly Resolution 48/57. The guidelines were developed after the 2004 Tsunami, that 'highlighted the need to be attentive to the multiple human rights challenges that persons affected by such disasters may face. All too often their human rights are not sufficiently taken into account' (UN IASC, 2006). The box below gives a condensed version of the Guidelines' understanding of human rights protection during disaster relief. The guidelines were produced in 2006 and further developed into a pilot manual in 2008. The specific use and usefulness of the guidelines still needs to be established.

We may conclude from this exposé that there are few international frameworks pertaining specifically to natural disasters. The applicability of legal instruments and codes of conduct developed for humanitarian action is sometimes questioned. On the other hand, this discussion glosses over the fact that many disasters actually happen in conflict situations (Buchanan-Smith and Christoplos, 2004; Bhavnani, 2006; Spiegel et al., 2007; Nel and Righarts, 2008). Besides, it can be stated that in practice agencies refer to these principles and standards as well during natural disasters. There are even fewer instruments that specifically take a rights-based approach to disasters. The Sphere standards make no exception for natural disasters and are thus considered applicable. There is only one instrument – the IASC guidelines – specifically referring to the human rights of disaster-affected people. The idea of human security may thus be highly relevant to natural disaster situations, yet is until now little explicitly applied in the field.

The next part of this chapter explores whether it would be feasible to apply the Responsiblity to Protect to natural disasters with a specific reference to the 2008 Nargis Cyclone case study in Myanmar. We then bring out some ramifications of a rights-based approach to disaster by focusing on the case of Sri Lanka, where the government has been instrumental in promoting rights-based approaches in disaster response.

The Guidelines' understanding of human rights protection during disaster relief (condensed)

1   Those affected by natural disasters remain entitled to the protection of international human rights. At the same time, they have particular needs which call for specific protection.
2   The primary duty and responsibility to provide such protection and assistance lies with the national authorities of the affected countries.
3   Protection is not limited to securing the survival and physical security of those affected by natural disasters. Protection encompasses all relevant guarantees – civil and political as well as economic, social and cultural rights – attributed to them by international human rights and, where applicable, international humanitarian law.
4   In all cases States have an obligation to respect, protect and fulfil the rights of their citizens and of the people living in their territory.
5   States therefore have an obligation to do everything within their power to prevent and/or mitigate the potential negative consequences that natural hazards may wreak.
6   UN agencies, international and national NGOs and other relevant international actors have an essential role to play in advocating on behalf of the rights of the victims. In addition, they can assist governments in their efforts and strengthen national capacity to protect rights.
7   Where the capacity and/or willingness of the authorities to meet their responsibilities are insufficient, the international community needs to support and supplement the efforts of the government and local authorities.
8   Protection activities of the international actors can be responsive, remedial or environment building.

Source: Protecting Persons Affected by Natural Disasters, IASC Operational Guidelines on Human Rights and Natural Disasters (UN IASC, 2006)

Responsibility to Protect and natural disasters[2]

One of the domains in which the human security idea has been translated into action is in the Responsibility to Protect (R2P). In this section we will explore whether R2P would be applicable to natural disasters. We then elaborate the case of Myanmar, where during cyclone Nargis in 2008 this possibility was actually considered.

The Responsibility to Protect rests on two basic principles: first, that sovereignty implies responsibility, namely a responsibility of each and every state to protect its population from suffering; and second, where a population is suffering serious harm and the state in question is unwilling or unable to halt or avert such harm, the responsibility to protect falls to the international community (ICISS, 2001a). In 2005 the UN World Summit endorsed the collective international responsibility to protect populations from genocide, war crimes, crimes against humanity and ethnic cleansing.[3] Resolution 1674 on 28 April 2006 of the Security Council 'reaffirmed' its 'readiness' to adopt appropriate steps, 'where necessary' for the responsibility to protect (Bellamy, 2009a).

The Responsibility to Protect is in line with the relatively new focus on human rights and the rights of internal populations to be protected from suffering. Whilst state sovereignty is crucial to the maintenance of good international relations its inviolability is no longer applicable in relation to human suffering as a result of war, insurgency, repression or state failure. The crucial aspect in the R2P philosophy is the shift in focus from sovereignty as *control* to sovereignty as *responsibility* (ICISS, 2001b; Luck 2009). This responsibility has three parts: a responsibility to *prevent* occurrences that will endanger individuals, a responsibility to *react* should these events actually occur and finally a responsibility to *rebuild* after events have occurred. If states fail to uphold these responsibilities (either through unwillingness or inability) then responsibility falls on the international community (Bellamy, 2009b).

As the UN endorsement has limited its areas of responsibility to the four categories of genocide, war crimes, crimes against humanity and ethnic cleansing, the question has been asked as to whether the international community should not also invoke the R2P in response to natural disasters. After all, if disaster-affected people are dying simply because they cannot get any relief aid due to their state's political decisions, then should not that also be considered as a 'crime against humanity'? It is also important to note that the initial ICISS proposal included environmental and natural disasters as possible events that would give the international community a right to intervene if the state fails to protect its citizens. Moreover, according to Thakur (2008):

> there is no difference between large numbers of people being killed by soldiers firing into crowds or the government blocking help being delivered to the victims of natural disasters. To the extent that R2P is rooted in solidarity with victims of atrocity crimes, the sophistry of the distinction between a lakh killed by troops or through deliberate government neglect is morally repugnant.

The discussion whether to apply R2P in natural disasters became real with the event of cyclone Nargis in Myanmar in 2008.

Cyclone Nargis in Myanmar

Category 3 Cyclone Nargis hit the Union of Myanmar on 3 May 2008, affecting 50 townships in the Ayeyarwaddy division including Yangon (Rangoon), the country's largest city. In its wake Nargis left a streak of destruction, loss of life and internal displacement. It was the worst natural disaster to occur in Myanmar and the most devastating cyclone in Southeast Asia since 1991 (Tripartite Core Group, 2008). Though the actual death toll may never be known, the Tripartite Core Group – comprising the UN, the Association of Southeast Asian Nations (ASEAN) and the Burmese Government – claim the official death toll as of June 24, 2008 as 84,537 with 53,836 missing and 19,359 injured, though other commentators estimated the actual death toll to be closer to 140,000 (Belanger and Horsey, 2008).[4] Furthermore, around 2.4 million people were at risk in its aftermath from further hardship, suffering, disease and death in a possible 'second wave' of humanitarian disaster (UN News Centre, 2008).

The international community – UN humanitarian bodies, individual governments and a plethora of NGOs – was quick to offer its help and to support the ruling junta in Myanmar to provide relief to the victims. The junta, however, was not as willing to accept aid as the international community had hoped, refusing to accept the presence of foreign personnel in the country (other than those who were already there through long established aid links) and only willing to accept relief supplies if transported on civilian ships. Any hope of docking foreign navy ships in Myanmar was quickly quashed, as the regime was highly suspicious of the inter-national community's intentions with the provision of relief aid (BBC, 2008a; BBC, 2008b; *The Times*, 2008).

With the regime's initial reaction it is important to note that the nature of the Myanmar state made it very difficult to accept overseas aid. As a military regime it relies on what – to western observers – is a very peculiar sort of legitimacy. First, there is a mutual alienation of state and society, which has manifested itself so many times in terms of the brutal violence used by its security forces against pro-democracy demonstrators. Second, the priority of self-preservation by the regime has meant that there is a huge divide between the military elite and masses living in poverty. Third, the state has a chauvinistic nationalist insistence on self-reliance and it tells its citizens that they must give up or suspend their political rights and in return the state will look after them and provide for them (Taylor, 2009). Therefore, after the cyclone disaster, it seems that the state in Myanmar might have considered the acceptance of overseas aid as a possible threat to their paternalistic relationship with the poor masses. Overall, though the junta claimed it was more than able to supply aid to the cyclone's victims it soon became apparent that they could not, or would not, clearly expressing its priorities by holding the previously scheduled 10 May constitutional referendum as planned, merely a week after the cyclone tore its way through the country (BBC, 2008c).

Even after the UN Secretary General Ban Ki Moon met with Senior General Than Shwe, the Head of State of Myanmar, on 23 May and an agreement was reached that Myanmar would open its borders to a full scale international humanitarian operation actual progress was not encouraging (BBC, 2008a, 2008d).[5] It is true that aid workers capable of improving the situation on the ground in Myanmar such as logistics and communication experts were then allowed access, but further complications stifled their progress. According to a representative from the World Food Programme, aid workers' movements were severely restricted with most only being allowed access to the city of Yangon and not allowed access to the delta region which suffered the most severe damage (BBC, 2008e). On top of all this, the BBC reported that the junta was even hostile to the local population supplying urgently needed supplies to their suffering neighbours, demanding that they return home (BBC, 2008f).

All of these difficulties caused great criticism by the international community. During a UN General Assembly session for example, Jean-Maurice Ripert, the French ambassador to the UN, warned that the Myanmar government's refusal to allow aid to be delivered to those who needed it 'could lead to a true crime against humanity'. Significantly, he used the language of R2P and continued: 'Hundreds of thousands of lives are in jeopardy and we think that the primary responsibility of the government of Myanmar (Burma) is to help and open the borders so that the international aid could come into the place'. Moreover, some political figures such as Bernard Kouchner, a veteran humanitarian worker and Foreign Minister of France, called for an enforcement of the R2P principle and to pursue humanitarian inter-vention, claiming that the people of Myanmar are the victims of a double scourge: on the one hand, they are suffering from the direct effects of a natural disaster and on the other, from the aftershocks of a political disaster (BBC, 2008g; Kouchner, 2008).[6] These suggestions never made it officially to the Security Council and hence were not taken to decision. Their significance lies in the fact that they did consider applying R2P in the case of natural disaster. It remains the question, however, whether it would be suitable to apply R2P in natural disasters. The question recurred during the January 2010 *Implementing the Responsibility to Protect* conference, where it proved to be a highly sensitive issue and a primary concern for a number of member states in the UN.[7]

Is R2P a suitable framework for natural disasters?

It is important to consider a number of potential shortcomings with the application of R2P in the context of natural disasters. First, like the main approaches to humanitarianism, R2P may indicate the willingness of the international community to take action to protect human life. However, question marks remain as to whether R2P can be applied universally. Within the constraints of *Realpolitik* it is highly unlikely that the international community will apply this principle each time it needs to be invoked. The history of international intervention, whether justified in terms of collective security or humanitarian aims, is prone to decisions that seem arbitrary and inconsistent. The R2P principle, although 'progressive' in its recognition of humanitarian imperatives, still faces geo-strategic realities whether applied to political mass human rights violations or the fall-out of natural disasters.

Second, it should also be noted that what R2P advocates is similar to the concept of 'new humanitarianism'. As a backlash to the 'classical humanitarianism' protected by the traditional principles of neutrality, impartiality and independence of the ICRC, the new humanitarianism advocates a human rights perspective in the provision of humanitarian aid, and argues that relief aid should be more than just saving lives but also seek possible ways of addressing the root causes of conflicts and disasters. For the new humanitarianism, neutrality in terms of not taking sides in order to ensure access to disaster-affected populations would be a fallacy. However, the logic of new humanitarianism means that humanitarian actors make a number of assumptions. For these actors (who are usually western), these assumptions are usually neutral (the primacy of human rights, the primacy of the individual, the purity of humanitarian motives, etc.) On the other hand, for many other non-western actors, these foundational assumptions upon which R2P rests are deeply political and ethnocentric, and are likely to be a source of suspicion in the future.

Third, within the current international system with the UN and its Security Council structures, it is also unlikely that the use of R2P in the context of natural disasters will have any chance of gaining legality. This is due to the political quagmire that would arise from the opposition of one of the five permanent members of the Council if a Security Council Resolution was called for to invoke Charter VII and take military action against a sovereign state. Therefore, even if natural disasters were to become one of the possible contexts for the invoking of R2P in the future, there would likely be a legality-legitimacy conundrum.

Finally, the use of the R2P principle in the context of natural disasters may not be practical and effective at all. In the aftermath of a natural disaster if relief assistance is not provided in the first three to seven days, then the chances of saving lives through search-and-rescue and emergency assistance are often slim. Even for the prevention of possible communicable diseases or further environmental hazards, assistance needs to reach the needy in the first two–three weeks after a disaster. Therefore, time would be a highly critical factor for the effectiveness of assistance. Although the use of macro-level diplomacy also requires time, even without trying to get the approval of the UN Security Council, a military intervention would demand more time for planning and to achieve its objectives. It is very likely that by the time the military intervention was undertaken and even if it were successful, it could be too late for those populations affected by that disaster.

On the other hand, if the principle of R2P is considered not only in the context of 'reacting' but also 'rebuilding', then there would be a stronger argument for intervention. As the timeliness of assistance would have more flexibility with reconstruction, it might be argued that R2P can be invoked in situations where disaster-affected people would be deliberately prevented from benefiting and achieving the rebuilding of their lives and livelihoods.

The experience of post-conflict and disaster reconstruction around the world shows, however, that the international community is not likely to have sufficient compassion, resources and political will to consider the invoking of the R2P principle in order to 'rebuild' disaster-affected societies.

Disaster risk reduction, security and human rights in Sri Lanka

Post-conflict Sri Lanka presents a case study of a country where rights-based approaches have been adopted in the Disaster Risk Reduction (DRR) programming of some humanitarian agencies and government actors. However, as we shall see, real-time challenges of governance, funding and human security limit the effectiveness of these initiatives. Lessons learned from reconstruction and risk reduction campaigns following the 2004 tsunami have yet to be methodologically considered, leaving some communities still marginalized and vulnerable. The militarized political stabilization of the country (Goodhand, 2010) has left humanitarian actors in some areas shifting their interest from emergency aid to longer-term development and working to align their actions with the new goals and agendas of the state. This context presents emerging opportunities to mainstream rights-based approaches and considerations of security into existing DRR programming across the country.

There is a crosscutting relationship between disaster risk, human security and human rights in Sri Lanka, with those most at risk to disasters also being the majority of those marginalized, in insecure settings and lacking in protection of their most basic rights. The Government of Sri Lanka has publicly established the importance of recognizing this linkage through the creation of its Ministry for Disaster Management and Human Rights and is signatory to multiple international agreements on human rights and security. The efforts of the Ministry, and the Sri Lanka Disaster Management Centre, are largely in support of promoting good governance strategies regarding DRR, but are still working to effectively operationalize rights-based approaches in policy and in practice, particularly at the community level.

Challenges to the protection of human rights in Sri Lanka in disaster contexts, particularly in the aftermath of the tsunami, have been documented. The 2006 survey on the Human Rights Impacts of Post-Tsunami Policies conducted by the Disaster Risk Management Unit's Human Rights Commission of Sri Lanka (see UNDP, 2005) noted discriminatory and corrupt practices of aid and reconstruction efforts in multiple districts. Rights infringements suffered by tsunami affected populations were also clearly highlighted by Satkunanathan, in the Sri Lankan State of Human Rights Report of 2006: 'Many human rights of tsunami affected persons have been violated, compromised or subject to strain as a result of both the immediate effects of the tsunami as well as the manner in which relief, rehabilitation, reconstruction and reintegration programmes have been carried out over the past year' (2007: 49). The State of Human Rights Report further recorded that these violations extended beyond the context of the tsunami, and included infringements on 'the right to equality, life, liberty and security of person, information, participation in public affairs, access to justice, a livelihood, an adequate standard of living, privacy, health, education, home and shelter, a clean and healthy environment and development' (ibid: 49–50).

The importance of incorporating considerations of security and the use of rights-based approaches in Sri Lanka extends beyond the impacts of both the tsunami and civil conflict. Sri Lanka is frequently exposed to multiple hazards which have different implications on specific rights. Drought infringes rights to food, life and social security, whereas flooding infringes the right of access to education and shelter. Pollutants and chemical hazards infringe rights to health and environmental, economic, social and cultural development. Violence against women in Sri Lanka has been proven to increase during disaster contexts (Fisher, 2010), as do poverty levels, reliance on insecure livelihoods, and health and food insecurity. Through reducing risk to disasters, a community's right to security would thus be protected. Conversely, by not supporting communities in building effective DRR strategies, the rights of these communities could be considered to be flagrantly violated. Even in a post-conflict Sri Lanka, therefore, rights and human security considerations must be consistently and effectively incorporated into DRR efforts.

In response to the tsunami, many agencies have consciously adopted a rights-based framework in their DRR activities. Research into DRR practices has revealed that this is not without challenges. Common issues surrounding effective DRR initiatives include limited funding and resources and a lack of sharing lessons regarding good practices as well as failed initiatives. Such challenges extend to rights-based DRR efforts, but can be met with the willingness of members of communities of practice. By building partnerships not only for DRR, but for rights-based approaches, agencies can increase the effectiveness of their initiatives as well as share financial, knowledge and social resources which may otherwise be lacking to them. These partnerships can also ensure that care is taken in responsible DRR, and that risk reduction efforts themselves do not undermine the rights of Sri Lankans. In some areas of Sri Lanka, after the tsunami, decisions on re-zoning and relocation violated the participatory rights of individuals in decision-making processes on the choices of locations for communities, as dictated by Article 14 (1h) of the 1978 Sri Lankan Constitution (which provides that 'every citizen is entitled to – the freedom of movement and of choosing his residence within Sri Lanka'). The development of partnerships in rights-based DRR can therefore serve to raise awareness of existing commitments and flag possible challenges for sustainable and effective operations even beyond risk reduction which may otherwise not have been identified.

Existing commitments and expertise

In this post-conflict setting, commitments to national and international agreements relating to human rights and security need to be revisited, and efforts to meet these obligations by both state and non-state actors can be supported from the local level up by building community capacity to reduce disaster risk and therefore enhance overall security levels. Areas which have been heavily impacted by decades of conflict can strengthen DRR efforts in other areas of the country by sharing perspectives on sustaining resilience and managing vulnerability levels even during periods of insecurity. Long-term development and livelihood projects now have more potential to be undertaken within partnerships and in a more equitable manner across regions and ethnic groups, though humanitarian organizations are already facing the challenge of scaling back on projects as funding deadlines for conflict and tsunami-specific programming are reached.

Agencies who adopt a rights-based approach to DRR can support the monitoring and evaluation activities necessary to determine how well international protocols on human rights and security are being addressed on local levels, as well as generally promote awareness on human rights and security issues in at-risk communities. The launching of IASC's Operational Guidelines on Protecting Persons in Natural Disasters in 2006 and subsequent publications of field manuals on human rights in disaster contexts can guide these efforts and be used to help operationalize discussions on rights-based approaches in DRR which until now have only been theoretical for some post-conflict communities.

As rights-based approaches are grounded in the notion that citizens should be protected by their government from disaster and security risks to the most significant extent possible, attention needs to be paid to ensure that the state has both the political will and resources necessary to meet the needs of their population. Under the new Human Rights Protection guidelines (IASC, 2008), the responsibilities of the state include not only assisting with response and recovery, but also include prevention, obliging governments including that of Sri Lanka to mainstream rights-based approaches to risk reduction and not only response and recovery. Where necessary, assistance can be accepted by state actors to build resources, capacity and interest, but this needs to be considered as a transitional approach to DRR. Non-state actors should be considered wherever possible to be important but supportive actors for rights-based approaches to DRR. Communities also should be able to assume ownership of activites at the local level, with the support and coordination of state players. Spheres of responsibility should be clearly established, with information on who is to be held accountable for planned activites being made available to communities and local officials as well as other non-state and state actors. Clear lines of communication and agency, to address grievances and share information, also combat the flow of misinformation which can erode trust, develop opportunities to learn from different levels of actors, establish clearly lines of responsibility for various stages of activites and foster overall practices of good governance that can be upheld by partners even in post-event environments.

Though the field of DRR is still emerging, indigenous ways to manage risk in Sri Lanka have a long heritage. Agencies fostering rights-based approaches to DRR should do so in alignment with local coping mechanisms for risk they have experienced over extended periods of time. Those populations facing different forms of risk, including displaced populations affected by conflict, also have experiences (ways to manage the loss of livelihoods, social capital, physical infrastructure, lands, etc.) which can be used to build coping capacities for disasters. Examples of mechanisms that could be shared include considerations for planning evacuation routes, the inclusion of disabled and elderly populations on risk maps and civil society groups who are able to quickly and efficiently organize volunteers. Marginalized populations in Sri Lanka are consistently also least represented by institutions involved in DRR. From homeless or transient groups to IDPs, communities displaced due to conflict, disasters or socio-political reasons are often omitted from DRR programming as well as data on risk and statistics on numbers of people impacted by specific events. For rights-based approaches to DRR to meet their needs, agencies can ensure that these groups have representation in relevant networks and access to more formal sources of information.

Agencies adopting rights-based approaches to DRR can find their overall initiatives not only reducing risk but also bolstering the capacity of existing formal groups in Sri Lanka operating on human rights and/or disaster management. Structures such as Sri Lanka's Disaster Risk Management Unit and the Human Rights Commission of Sri Lanka already have significant capacity which can be used to monitor DRR activities and develop rights-based approaches that are suitable to the knowledge and needs of individual communities. Partnerships between these institutions and development agencies can extend the sustainability of a wide variety of programming. This use of existing expertise and structures can also frame agency mainstreaming of rights-based approaches to DRR as a transitionary (not a revolutionary) approach that does not require venturing into unfamiliar territory, but rather unites existing practices and addresses and provides support for already prevailing situations.

Moving forward

Supporters of DRR in Sri Lanka, including the Government itself, have succeeded in laying the groundwork for risk reduction activities, but further work is still needed to ensure activities are operationalized in an equitable and inclusive manner. State and non-state actors can build upon existing disaster management efforts and post-tsunami projects by using a rights-based approach to DRR that is aligned with national strategies and considerate of continued security issues. This strategy will further promote the principle of equality, strengthen levels of human security and development and also ensure that Sri Lankan communities have access to the support, information and protection not only that they need to survive, but also that they are entitled to as citizens.

Conclusion

In this chapter we have explored the nexus between the human security framework and natural disasters. In the first part of the chapter, we have demonstrated the relevance of the human security framework for natural disaster response. Human security, as understood by Des Gasper, is an integrative concept that brings together ideas on human development, human needs and human rights (Gasper, 2010: 29). This fits well with the current thinking on natural hazards which views disasters as the combined outcome of hazards and vulnerability. It therefore seeks to integrate the immediate needs of disaster victims with risk reduction measures and structural development as a means to reduce people's vulnerability to disasters.

On the other hand, we have also outlined how notions of human security have so far found little expression in natural disaster response. Disaster response is governed by a number of international regulations, including international humanitarian law, humanitarian principles, human rights, codes of conduct and even refugee law. These instruments have principally been developed in the framework of violent conflict and their applicability to natural disaster contexts in peacetime is therefore sometimes questioned or ambiguous. Especially for the case of natural disasters, there is the Hyogo Framework for Action, which is holistic and inclusive, yet does not have an explicit human rights framework. The *IASC Operational Guidelines on Human Rights and Natural Disasters* are the only instrument that specifically addresses the nexus between human rights and natural disasters, yet this instrument is still in its infant phase.

We have then explored whether one of the hallmarks of human security, namely the *Responsibility to Protect,* would be applicable for natural disaster situations. The discussion was triggered by responses to cyclone Nargis in Myanmar. Apart from the fact that the inclusion of natural disasters in the framework of R2P is a far-fetched possibility in today's world, we also listed some major problems we would foresee in evoking R2P for natural disasters. The final part of the chapter elaborated on the use of a rights-based framework in disaster response in Sri Lanka. The case illustrates that the nexus between human rights and natural disasters may be more elaborate at country-level than would perhaps be expected considering the thin discussions and instruments generated internationally. It also shows how effectively incorporating a rights-based approach in DRR still encounters many challenges. The analysis shows how these approaches are still in the conceptual phase and are currently more defining the horizon of disaster risk reduction than being firmly translated in practice. The latter can perhaps serve as a general conclusion to the chapter. While human security is very promising as a framework to guide disaster risk reduction, its translation and value in practice is yet to be established.

Notes

1 See http://www.humanitarianinfo.org/iasc/.
2 This section is based on Özerdem (2010) 'The "responsibility to protect" in natural disasters: another excuse for interventionism? Nargis Cyclone, Myanmar' in *Conflict, Security & Development,* 10 (5): 693–713.

3   The UN World Summit took place on 14–16 September 2005 and covered issues related to a wide
    range of critical global concerns from terrorism and development to peacebuilding, human rights and
    responsibility to protect.
4   The majority of those missing people are now considered as dead, bringing the death toll to 140,000.
5   Senior General Than Shwe is also Commander-in-Chief of the Tatmadaw and chairman of the State
    Peace and Development Council (SPDC) since 23 April 1992.
6   This was not actually surprising as Kouchner has always argued the necessity of *droit d'ingerence* which
    can be rendered in English as the right for intervention, and it should be noted that he was one of the
    leading figures who actively advocated and supported the humanitarian intervention in Kosovo.
7   The 'Implementing the Responsibility to Protect' Conference was organized by The Stanley
    Foundation on 15–17 January 2010.

References

Anderson, M. B. and Woodrow, P. J. (1989) *Rising From the Ashes: Development Strategies in Times of Disaster*,
    Boulder: Westview Press.
BBC News. (2008a) 'Will Burma Keep its Word on Aid'. Available: http://news.bbc.co.uk/1/hi/world/
    asia-pacific/7417203.stm (accessed 15 July 2008).
BBC News. (2008b) 'US Aid Ships to Leave Burma'. Available: http://news.bbc.co.uk/1/hi/world/asia-
    pacific/7435188.stm (accessed 15 July 2008).
BBC News. (2008c) 'Burma Approves New Constitution'. Available: http://www.bbc.co.uk/1/hi/world/
    asia-pacific/7402105.stm (accessed 15 July 2008).
BBC News. (2008d) 'UN Head Pressures Burma's Leader'. Available: http://news.bbc.co.uk/1/hi/world/
    asia-pacific/7415873.stm (accessed 15 July 2008).
BBC News. (2008e) 'New Challenges for Delta Aid Workers'. Available: http://news.bbc.co.uk/1/hi/
    world/asia-pacific/7432874.stm (accessed 15 July 2008).
BBC News. (2008f) 'Burmese Dodge Junta to Supply Aid'. Available: http://news.bbc.co.uk/1/hi/world/
    asia-pacific/7409834.stm (accessed 15 July 2008).
BBC News. (2008g) 'France Angered by Burmese Delays'. Available: http://news.bbc.co.uk/1/hi/world/
    asia-pacific/7405998.stm (accessed 15 July 2008).
Belanger, J. and Horsey, R. (2008) 'Negotiating humanitarian access to cyclone-affected areas of
    Myanmar: a review', *Humanitarian Exchange Magazine*, 41. Available: http://www.odihpn.org/report.
    asp?id=2964 (accessed 11 January 2009).
Bellamy, A. (2009a) 'Realizing the Responsibility to Protect', *International Studies Perspectives*, 10(2):
    111–128.
Bellamy, A. (2009b) *Responsibility to Protect: The Global Efforts to End Mass Atrocities*, Cambridge: Polity
    Press.
Bhavnani, R. (2006) *Natural Disaster Conflict*, Cambridge, Massachusetts: Harvard University.
Buchanan-Smith, M. and Christoplos, I. (2004) 'Natural disasters amid complex political emergencies',
    HPN Exchange Magazine, Issue 27. Available: http://www.odihpn.org (accessed 20 May 2013).
Fisher, S. (2010) 'Violence against women and natural disasters: findings from post-tsunami Sri Lanka',
    Violence Against Women, 16(8): 902–918.
Gasper, D. (2010) 'The idea of human security', in K. O'Brien, A. St Clair and B. Kristoffersen (eds)
    Climate Change, Ethics and Human Security, Cambridge: Cambridge University Press, pp. 23–27.
Goodhand, J. (2010) 'Stabilising a victor's peace? Humanitarian action and reconstruction in eastern Sri
    Lanka', *Disasters*, 34, Issue Supplement s3: s342–s367.
Heijmans, A. and Victoria, L. P. (2001) *Citizenry-based & Development-oriented Disaster Response: Experiences
    and Practices in Disaster Management of the Citizens' Disaster Response Network in the Philippines*, Quezon
    City, the Philippines: Center for Disaster Preparedness.
Hewitt, K. (1983) *Interpretations of Calamity from the Viewpoint of Human Ecology*, The Risks & Hazards
    Series, Boston: Allen & Urwin Inc.
Hilhorst, D. (2004) 'Complexity and diversity: unlocking domains of disaster response', in G. Bankoff, G.
    Frerks and D. Hilhorst (eds) *Mapping Vulnerability: Disaster, Development and People*, London: Earthscan,
    pp. 52–67.
Hilhorst, D. (2005) 'Dead letter or living document? Ten years code of conduct for disaster relief',
    Disasters, 29(4): 351–369.

ICISS (2001a) *The Responsibility to Protect: Research, Bibliography, Background*, Ottawa: International Development Research Centre.

ICISS (2001b) *The Responsibility to Protect*, Ottawa: International Development Research Centre.

IFRC (2000) *World Disaster Report*, Geneva: International Federation of Red Cross and Red Crescent Societies.

Kouchner, B. (2008) 'Burma'. Available: http://www.ambafrance-uk.org/Bernard-Kouchner-on-Burma-disaster.html#sommaire_3 (accessed 28 August 2008).

Law and Society Trust (2007) *Sri Lanka: State of Human Rights 2006 – The Tsunami and its Aftermath*, Colombo: Law and Society Trust, pp. 20–46.

Luck, E. C. (2009) 'Sovereignty, choice, and the responsibility to protect', *Global Responsibility to Protect*, 1(1): 10–21.

Nel, P. and Righarts, M. (2008) 'Natural disasters and the risk of violent civil conflict', *International Studies Quarterly*, 52: 159–185.

O'Keefe, P., Westgate, K. and Wisner, B. (1976) 'Taking the "natural" out of natural disasters', *Nature*, 260 (15 April): 566–567.

Oliver-Smith, A. and Hofmann, S. (eds) (1999) *The Angry Earth: Disaster in Anthropological Perspective*, New York and London: Routledge.

Özerdem, A. (2010) 'The "responsibility to protect" in natural disasters: another excuse for interventionism? Nargis Cyclone, Myanmar', *Conflict, Security & Development*, 10(5): 693–713.

Parliament of the Democratic Socialist Republic of Sri Lanka (1978) *The Constitution of the Democratic Socialist Republic of Sri Lanka*. Colombo: Department of Government Printing.

Spiegel, P. B., Phuoc, L., Ververs, M. T. and Salama, P. (2007) 'Occurrence and overlap of natural disasters, complex emergencies and epidemics during the past decade (1995–2004)', *Conflict and Health*, 1, 2.

Taylor, R. (2009) *The State in Myanmar*, Singapore: NUS Press.

The Times (2008) 'UN Chief Ban Ki Moon to Meet Burma's "Senior General" Than Shwe'. Available: http://www.timesonline.co.uk/tol/news/world/asia/article3976806.ece (accessed 1 July 2008).

Thakur, R. (2008) 'To invoke or not to invoke R2P in Burma', *The Hindu*, 20 May 2008. Available: http://www.hindu.com/2008/05/20/stories/2008052054140800.htm (accessed 15 June 2008).

Tripartite Core Group. (2008) *Post Nargis Joint Assessment*. Comprised of representatives of the Government of the Union of Myanmar, the Association of South-east Asian Nations and the United Nations.

Turton A. R. and Ohlsson, L. (1999). *Water Scarcity and Social Stability: Towards a Deeper Understanding of Key Concepts Needed to Manage Water Scarcity in Developing Countries*, SOAS Occasional Paper.

United Nations Development Programme (2005) *The Report on People's Consultations on Post Tsunami Relief, Reconstruction and Rehabilitation in Sri Lanka: July–September 2005*. Colombo, Sri Lanka: Disaster Relief Monitoring Unit, Human Rights Commission of Sri Lanka, UNDP and Colombo University Community Extension Centre.

United Nations Inter-Agency Standing Committee (2006) *Protecting Persons Affected by Natural Disasters – IASC Operational Guidelines on Human Rights and Natural Disasters*. UNIASC. Washington DC: Brookings-Bern Project on Internal Displacement.

United Nations Inter-Agency Standing Committee (2008) *Human Rights and Natural Disasters: Operational Guidelines and Field Manual on Human Rights Protection in Situations of Natural Disaster*. Pilot Version (March 2008). UNIASC. Washington DC: Brookings-Bern Project on Internal Displacement.

UN News Centre. (2008) 'More Than 1 Million Cyclone Victims Have Received Aid, says UN'. Available: http://www.un.org/apps/news/story.asp?NewsID=26896&Cr=myanmar&Cr1= (accessed 1 July 2008).

Walker, P. (2005) 'Cracking the code: the genesis, use and future of the Code of Conduct', *Disasters*, 29: 323–336.

White, G. F. (1986 (orig. 1960)). 'Strategic aspects of urban floodplain occupancy', in B. Wisner, P. Blaikie, T. Cannon and I. Davis (2004) *At Risk: Natural Hazards, People's Vulnerability and Disasters*, 2nd edn, London: Routledge.

Wisner, B., Blaikie, P., Cannon, T. and Davis, I. (2004) *At Risk: Natural Hazards, People's Vulnerability and Disasters*, 2nd edn, London: Routledge.

14

FOOD AND HUMAN SECURITY

Robert Bailey

Introduction

Secure access to food is crucial for human security. Without food, a person cannot live more than a few weeks. Alongside water, food is our most basic need. A hungry person's capacity for work is reduced, threatening their economic security. Malnourishment makes people more susceptible to disease. It impairs child development, stunts growth and reduces educational attainment.

An individual's food security is threatened if sufficient food is physically unavailable, or if sufficient food *is* physically available but unaffordable. As well as being physically and economically accessible, food must be socially accessible: of an appropriate form and consistent with the particular cultural preferences of the individual. Finally, if malnutrition and ill health are to be avoided food must provide essential nutrients. These requirements lead to the most widely used definition of food security adopted at the 1996 World Food Summit that 'food security exists when all people, at all times, have physical and economic access to sufficient, safe and nutritious food that meets their dietary needs and food preferences for an active and healthy life'.[1]

Paradoxically, in a world that produces more than enough food to feed everyone, food security is far from universal. The Food and Agriculture Organization of the United Nations (FAO) estimated the number of hungry people in the world was 850 million between 2006 and 2008 – a little under one in seven of humanity.[2] These people face chronic undernourishment: an inability from one day to the next to source sufficient calories and nutrients for themselves and their families.

Meanwhile food crises continue to impose extreme hunger on some of the poorest and most vulnerable populations in the world. Though temporary in nature and localized in impact, these humanitarian disasters bestow horrific costs upon their victims including the destruction of livelihoods, acute malnutrition, and in the worst cases death. In 2011, 13 million people were affected by a food crisis in the Horn of Africa, with famine declared in regions of Somalia. In West Africa, 10 million were affected by a crisis in 2010 and over 18 million by a second crisis in 2012.

This chapter will examine chronic and acute food insecurity as they exist in the world today and consider how environmental, demographic and economic trends are likely to affect food security in the future. Its core argument is that food insecurity, whether chronic or acute, is primarily a result of government failures. The resources to end global hunger exist, the political will to do so does not.

Chronic food insecurity

Chronic food insecurity is a major impediment to achieving universal human security. According to the World Food Programme (WFP), hunger-related deaths each year outnumber those for AIDS, malaria and tuberculosis combined (Sheeran, 2008). But the costs of chronic food insecurity extend far beyond lives lost. Undernourished people are more susceptible to illness, and less able to work, earn and produce. Chronic food insecurity is a trap. By limiting people's potential to participate in economic, social and political spheres of life, persistent undernourishment limits their ability to achieve human security.

People are chronically food insecure because they lack power. They lack the economic power to access food at affordable prices. They lack the political power to force governments to respond. Chronic hunger is therefore concentrated among the poor and marginalized. This means hunger is predominantly female. Women are estimated to account for over 60 per cent of chronically hungry people (Pinstrup-Andersen and Cheng, 2007). In many developing countries, when food is scarce, women and girls are usually the first to go without due to discriminatory traditions and social structures. These same factors conspire against them as workers, entrepreneurs and farmers, ensuring they systematically receive lower wages, fewer opportunities and less access to resources than their male counterparts.

Power structures also mean hunger is predominantly rural. Worldwide, about 80 per cent of hungry people are thought to live in rural areas, where poverty and political marginalization are greatest (Sanchez et al, 2005). In a cruel irony, they are surrounded by the means to produce food, and yet they go without.

Governments have a long track record of neglecting rural populations in the developing world. Political scientists have explained this in terms of urban bias, whereby governments prioritize the needs of urban populations which mobilize more rapidly and effectively when discontented. Urban bias may go further than simple neglect of agriculture if governments actively pursue policies that transfer wealth from rural to urban areas, for example by imposing agricultural price controls to ensure cheap food in cities (and low prices for farmers). This has been compounded by a common view held by many developing country governments that farming is backward and that industrial projects should be prioritized. Despite agriculture being the largest economic sector in many poor countries and crucial to the livelihoods of the poorest people, it typically accounts for a remarkably small fraction of government expenditure, about 4 to 6 per cent in Africa for example (Fan et al, 2009).

The rural poor in developing countries are also penalized by the governments of industrialized countries, which provide hundreds of billions of dollars every year in support for their own farmers. This makes it hard for farmers in developing countries to compete, and acts as a powerful disincentive for developing country governments to invest in their own agricultural sectors.

Industrialized country governments have also neglected the rural poor in developing countries. Over the last two decades, they have drastically cut back on their aid to agriculture, the share of which in official development assistance (ODA) declined from over 20 per cent in 1983 to less than 4 per cent in 2006 (Bailey, 2011).

The effect of these policies of penalization and neglect, in developed and developing countries alike, has been to undermine agricultural development and perpetuate the prevalence of hunger in rural areas. Yet despite this, slow progress was made for a number of decades:

the FAO's estimate of the number of hungry people worldwide declined slowly until the mid-1990s, when it fell below 800 million for the first time. Sadly this was not to last. The trend went into sharp reverse in the run-up to the 2007/8 food price crisis, which saw steep rises in the international prices of staple foods (Bailey, 2011). In the 18 months between January 2007 and June 2008 the FAO cereal price index rose 78 per cent. This was followed by a second price spike within three years, when the same index rose 77 per cent in the 12 months from April 2010 to April 2011. A third spike followed in 2012, which saw record prices for maize and soybeans in the wake of a severe drought in the Midwest breadbasket of the USA.

For the poorest people, who may spend between half and three-quarters of their incomes on food, sudden price rises on this scale are devastating. People are forced into short-term coping strategies with long-term consequences. Families forgo meals and healthcare. Assets are sold and new debts taken on. Children are taken out of school. Households and communities are shattered as people are forced into migration. As human security is diminished, so vulnerability to the next shock increases, precipitating a downward spiral of decreasing human security and increasing vulnerability.

The risk of more price spikes is real and present. International food prices are expected to remain high and volatile over the next decade (FAO-OECD, 2011). A number of different factors have been identified as contributing to higher food price volatility. Low levels of agricultural commodity stocks mean that supply or demand shocks result in dramatic price spikes, as reserves are not available to smooth consumption or release onto markets when prices begin to climb. Oil price movements have fed into food prices through the cost of fertilizers and transport, and through the intermediating effect of biofuel policies, which make food a substitute for oil. Some commentators have also blamed financial speculation via commodity derivatives, although this remains highly contested (Tangermann, 2011).

One of the most serious problems has been government imposed agricultural export controls, designed to keep food within national borders but with the inevitable consequence of taking supply out of the international market and driving-up prices further. For governments worried about the possibility of protests at the price of food, these policies may make sense in the short-run, but collectively they are disastrous. Each restriction increases prices, erodes confidence, and increases the chance of the next. During the 2007/8 price spike, in a giddying escalation of beggar-thy-neighbour policies, over thirty governments imposed export restrictions on their agricultural sectors. Those that lose the most from these policies are people in poor, food-importing countries. But in the longer run those countries imposing controls may also lose as well: their farmers will be penalized and more reluctant to invest, and their trading partners may seek alternative, more reliable, sources of supply.

Perhaps the most troubling source of volatility has been the biofuel policies pursued by many developed countries, in particular the USA and EU. As well as transmitting price volatility from oil markets to food markets as described above, these policies have also introduced significant new sources of demand for food, driving up prices and contributing to the decline in stock levels. What is more, this demand arises from policies that mandate the use of biofuels irrespective of how high food prices rise: it is perfectly inelastic. This leads to higher price spikes and imposes the burden of adjustment on food consumers, among who the poorest will suffer the greatest declines in purchasing power.

The threats posed by biofuels to food security are well accepted. In 2011, a group of ten international organizations including the World Bank, FAO, WFP, International Monetary Fund and the Organization for Economic Cooperation and Development presented a report to the G20 recommending the dismantling of biofuel support as a way to address food price volatility (FAO et al, 2011). Their advice was however ignored because governments were not prepared to confront the domestic special interests that profit from biofuel support measures; in particular their powerful farm lobbies.

Biofuel policies are certainly not the only factor driving food price volatility; they may not even be the most significant, but they are perhaps the most egregious. They exist primarily for the benefit of a small number of sectoral interests, yet have profound implications for human security. Governments chose to implement these policies, and could choose to dismantle them, but they do not.

Acute food insecurity and food crises

Acute food insecurity arises when people suffer a drastic reduction in their ability to access food. Food crises are extreme in impact and short-term and regional in scope. They often follow a particular chronology, beginning with failed rains leading to a poor harvest, after which household food reserves are run down, assets such as livestock are sold off, income opportunities decline, and the terms of trade for the most vulnerable decline precipitously, pushing the real price of food out of reach. People may be left acutely food insecure until the next harvest comes – often a period of four to five months known as the hunger gap – during which time malnutrition may climb rapidly. In the worst cases mortality rates, particularly among infants, also increase sharply.

The time taken from failed rains to crisis peak may be several months: plenty of time to undertake early interventions such as cash transfers, nutrition support, fodder distributions and veterinary services designed to shore-up livelihoods and prevent the downward spiral into destitution and starvation. In recognition of this, and following repeated crises in Africa during the 1980s and 1990s, famine early warning systems have been established to monitor vulnerable regions, most notably in the Sahel and Horn of Africa.

Early warning systems have proven to be highly effective, often warning of crises months in advance. But too often early warning does not translate into sufficient early action because governments are slow to respond. Delay is often politically preferable to action. For example, in crisis-affected countries, politicians may be reluctant to acknowledge an emergency for fear it may adversely affect perceptions of their governments among domestic populations or the international community, where famine is often equated with government failure. Meanwhile donor governments, when taking decisions on whether to fund humanitarian action, tend to prioritize foreign policy considerations and domestic factors – such as whether the crisis is likely to make the headlines – over humanitarian needs (Bailey, 2012).

All of these factors were evident during the 2011 crisis in the Horn of Africa. In Ethiopia, the national government revised down early assessments of humanitarian need. These subsequently had to be revised back up, resulting in avoidable delay. In Kenya, where the crisis was concentrated among politically marginalized pastoralist communities, the government was particularly slow to declare an emergency. In Somalia, Western donors withheld emergency funds as part of their anti-terror strategies, specifically to avoid the risk that aid was captured by Islamist insurgents operating in the country. It was not until famine was declared and the story broke that funding was released at scale.

As well as being late, emergency responses are often inappropriate; routinely compromised in order to benefit interest groups in donor countries. Food aid is often tied, meaning donors insist it is provided in-kind, as food grown by their farmers, processed by their agribusinesses and freighted by their shipping companies. Sourcing food locally, or providing hungry people with cash when food is available but too expensive, is very often faster, cheaper and better for the livelihoods of local farmers and market traders.

As a result of government failures to recognize problems and intervene quickly and appro-priately, far more people are affected by food crises than need be the case. Human security is diminished, and populations are left more vulnerable to the next shock. This is government failure by neglect, though note that failure can be absolute: the complete absence of government in Somalia meant the 2011 food crisis became a famine there, but remained less devastating in neighbouring Ethiopia and Kenya where national responses, although late, were at least possible.

Food crises can also arise due to government actions to penalize certain groups. Famine, the most severe categorization of food crisis, is often the result of pernicious government failures – of active decisions to take food from populations that need it, or block the delivery of food to those that are starving. This is government failure by penalization, and it has a long and shameful history.

The Ukrainian famine of 1932–33 occurred despite a bumper harvest, as a result of Soviet policies to collectivize farms and extract an agricultural surplus. Similar policies were behind the horrific Chinese famine of 1958–61, when central planners seized grain for urban and industrial centres, starving the farmers in the process. Perversely, death rates were highest in the regions with highest per capita food production. The Biafran famine of 1967–70 was the result of a war persecuted by Nigeria following the smaller state's secession, and in particular the Nigerian government's decision to blockade food and medical supplies. The Ethiopian famine of 1984–85, which led to the famous Live Aid concert, was triggered by drought, but its roots lay in the disastrous policies of the Marxist Derg government, which again sought to extract an unsustainable agricultural surplus from farmers, prioritized a war against neighbouring Eritrea, and responded to the crisis by forcibly relocating affected communities and blocking humani-tarian relief less it should fall into the hands of separatist rebels in the worst affected regions.

The role of government failure in famine was famously pointed to by Amartya Sen, who asserted that famine is not the result of a shortage of food, but essentially a lack of *access* to food. Sen (1981) argued that famines are usually the result of a precipitous decline in 'exchange entitlements' – adverse shifts in the terms of trade between food and household endowments such as livestock prices or wages. Famines are distributional in nature, arising when political, social and economic systems place available food out of the reach for certain socioeconomic groups. Governments can actively create these conditions, by waging war, taking food from people, or impeding the movement of food or people. Or they can fail to intervene should some other event, such as a drought or economic shock, place the price of food beyond people's reach. Sen's most famous insight is that famines do not occur in functioning democracies (Sen, 1999). A government that is fully accountable to its citizens cannot risk failure on the scale of famine.[3]

Food security and current trends

A number of environmental, social and economic trends have significant implications for both chronic and acute food insecurity and human security more broadly.

Population growth

Alarmism about population growth is not new. In 1798, Thomas Malthus penned his famous *Essay on the Principle of Population*, arguing that population must increase more rapidly than food production, and that famine and poverty are the inevitable result. Needless to say, he was proved wrong. Food production has not only kept pace with, but exceeded, population growth, as agricultural land has expanded and rapid increases in productivity have followed from new technologies such as those of the Green Revolution, a globally coordinated effort to develop and expand the use of high-yielding varieties of wheat, rice and maize, synthetic fertilizers and pesticides and new irrigation and farm management practices.

Despite this astounding success, Malthusian concerns have resurfaced. In 2011, global population passed 7 billion people, and is projected to reach 9.3 billion by 2050 and 10.1 billion by 2100 in the UN's medium variant scenario (UNESA, 2010). Though this represents a slowing of global population growth, it is still a lot more mouths to feed. What is more, there are signs that the Green Revolution is running out of steam: global cereal yields are flatlining, and despite slowing itself, population growth is now the faster.

More troubling is the prospect of where population growth will occur. High fertility is associated with low human security and high poverty, and in particular a lack of access to education and appropriate healthcare for women. Population growth is therefore concentrated in the poorest and most food insecure regions of the world.

Economic development

Economic development within emerging economies is leading to higher incomes and contributing to improved food security, at least among those households participating in growth. This in turn is leading to growing consumer preferences for meat, dairy and processed foods, the result of which is increased demand for basic foods such as grains and oilseeds, used for animal feed. Alongside biofuels, this is the main demand-side explanation for tighter global commodity markets and low stocks. It sharpens the challenge posed by declining yield growth on the supply side, and contributes to upward pressure on food prices.

Taken together, by 2050 economic development and population growth are expected to have increased demand for food by 70 per cent above 2009 levels, and up to 100 per cent in developing countries (FAO, 2011b). Today, people are hungry not because of an overall shortage of food, but because of inequalities of access. Tomorrow, unequal access may become compounded by inadequate supply.

Two other important points follow from this. First, the pace of urbanization in developing countries means that poverty and hunger is increasingly an urban problem. Universal food security will not be achieved by focusing exclusively on the rural poor. Second, the shift in diet that occurs as middle classes emerge in developing countries can bring new health challenges familiar to populations in industrialized countries, such as obesity, heart disease and diabetes.

Environmental constraints

Slowing yield growth is not the only supply-side challenge. The amount of arable land per head has almost halved since 1960 (Bailey, 2011). Estimates of the amount left vary according to judgements as to the acceptable limits of cropland expansion given other concerns such as deforestation, displacement of local communities and biodiversity loss. The indications are however that there is not much more. Most of what remains is in Sub-Saharan Africa and South America and of increasingly marginal quality. One study estimates global expansion in arable land of only 5 per cent by 2050, driven almost entirely by expansion in Sub-Saharan Africa and Latin America (Bruinsma, 2009). Another major review of sustainable farming simply concluded that 'we should work on the assumption that there is little new land' (Foresight, 2011).

Water, the lifeblood of agriculture, is also becoming a scarce resource. Agriculture already accounts for 70 per cent of global freshwater use, and by 2030 agriculture's demand for water may have increased by 30 per cent (Foresight, 2011). In addition demand for water from industrial, energy and municipal uses is growing rapidly, as countries develop and urbanize.

So we must learn to grow more with less. And in doing so, we must emit less as well. Agriculture is one of the biggest sources of greenhouse gases – possibly approaching a third of global emissions once land-use change is included. Other significant agricultural sources of greenhouse gases are nitrogen-based fertilizers and cattle. Avoiding catastrophic climate change will require new patterns of food production and consumption.

Climate change

As well as being a driver of climate change, agriculture is also increasingly a victim. The potential of extreme weather to reduce harvests and destabilize markets is well known. In 2010, a heatwave in Eastern Europe devastated wheat production in Russia with output down more than 30 per cent on the year before. The government responded by imposing export controls, followed by Ukraine (which had also been affected) and Pakistan, precipitating vertiginous rises in international prices: by April 2011, wheat prices were 85 per cent higher than a year earlier. A year later, the worst drought in over half a century to hit the Midwest United States devastated corn and soybean harvests and sent international prices back onto an upward trajectory.

In a future of higher demand and struggling output, international food prices will be even more vulnerable to the kinds of extreme weather events climate change is making more likely. One piece of research modelled the impacts of extreme weather events on international food prices in 2030, and found for example that a North American drought could see international maize prices spike by 140 per cent (Carty, 2012).

Droughts and floods may imperil human security further by causing localized food crises, destroying livelihoods and assets and increasing the incidence of disease. In some regions, evidence suggests that climate change is already leading to an observable increase in the frequency and severity of extreme weather (IPCC, 2012). In the future, such events will become increasingly important threats to food and human security, resulting in natural disasters, regional food crises and international price spikes.

Climate change is not only changing weather at the extremes, it is also changing average temperature and precipitation patterns. Climate trends may already be reducing output: one study estimated that between 1980 and 2008, global maize and wheat production had declined by 3.8 per cent and 5.5 per cent respectively, compared to a counter-factual without climate change (Lobell et al, 2011). The modellers found temperature rises to be wiping out the gains from technology and from higher concentrations of atmospheric carbon dioxide.

The creeping changes in seasons that result from rising temperatures and shifting rainfall patterns make it harder for farmers to know when best to sow, cultivate and harvest their crops (Jennings and Magrath, 2009). This is having a particularly serious impact upon the poorest farmers, who lack the access to credit, insurance and technology needed to help them better manage these risks.

The food security outlook is therefore challenging. Environmental, demographic and economic trends mean that food production must be rapidly transformed so that we can produce more food, use resources more efficiently, produce fewer emissions and build resilience to climate change. And if we are serious about improving human security then this must be done in an inclusive way, which creates sustainable livelihood opportunities for the rural poor.

The challenge is immense, but there are reasons to be hopeful. Human ingenuity has an excellent track record of innovation in response to resource scarcity and we should not repeat Malthus's mistake in dismissing this. Existing technologies in agriculture and energy can already go a long way towards meeting these challenges if they are adopted broadly and quickly. There are obvious opportunities for investment. Consider agriculture, where yields in the poorest countries are often a tiny fraction of those achieved in the West. Expanding poor farmers' access to land, water, technologies, credit, infrastructure and markets will not only boost food production, but dramatically increase human security by focusing investment on some of the poorest and most vulnerable people in the world.

The problem is that none of this will happen at the speed and scale needed unless governments act decisively and concertedly. Industry needs strong signals to abandon fossil fuels and invest in low carbon technologies, yet governments continue to subsidize fossil fuels more than renewables by something like a factor of six to one. The Green Revolution was premised upon significant public funding to create global public goods in the form of agricultural technologies; transforming agricultural production to improve human security requires a similar boost in public funding for agricultural R&D. Investment will not flow to Sub-Saharan agriculture without government interventions: to create public goods such as infrastructure, weather data and extension services, to undertake land reform, and to correct failures in finance markets.

Conclusion

Food security is crucial to human security. Yet in a world that produces enough to feed everyone, almost one person in seven is hungry. And in a world in which the capacity, technology and resources exist to properly predict and prevent food crises, starvation remains. Environmental, economic and social trends point to a potentially worsening picture: a world where today's inequalities are exacerbated by tomorrow's scarcities.

Food insecurity can have many proximate causes such as weather or economic events, but ultimately it can always be traced back to government failures. Governments may fail by neglect, for example turning a blind eye to a gathering food crisis, or withdrawing public support for agriculture in poor countries. Or they may fail by penalization, for example by taking food from people that need it, or pursuing policies such as biofuel support, that diminish vulnerable people's access to food.

If food insecurity can be traced to government policies that either neglect or penalize the vulnerable, it follows that reform of these policies, alongside new policies to support and protect the vulnerable, can enhance food security. Industrialized countries can untie food aid and remove their support for biofuels. Developing country governments can adopt and enforce policies that ensure women's equal access to resources and opportunities. And in partnership with donors and multilateral institutions, they can invest in their farmers and expand policies to improve access to food and build resilience to shocks, such as social protection programmes and disaster risk reduction.

Unfortunately correcting government failure is not a simple technocratic exercise. Governments fail the hungry not out of incompetence, but because their political calculus subordinates the needs of the hungry to the interests of other groups or other priorities. Empowering people, so that they are better able to act on their own behalf, engage in political processes, assert their rights and hold governments to account, is essential to correcting government failures and fundamental to ensuring food security.

Notes

1   Rome Declaration on World Food Security, Rome, 13 November 1996. Available HTTP: http://www.fao.org/docrep/003/w3613e/w3613e00.htm (accessed 12 September 2012).

2   See FAO (2011a). Note that estimates for more recent years, of 925 million undernourished people in 2010 and 1,023 million in 2009 (FAO, 2010) have been withdrawn as the methodology for these estimates is currently being revised.

3   Note that this assertion is not universally accepted (see for example Rubin, 2009). In particular, differences of opinion related to definitional issues as to what constitutes a famine and what constitutes a functioning democracy.

Bibliography

Bailey, R. (2011) *Growing a Better Future: Food Justice in a Resource Constrained World*, Oxford: Oxfam International.

Bailey, R. (2012) *Famine Early Warning and Early Action: The Cost of Delay*, Chatham House Programme Report, London: Chatham House.

Bruinsma, J. (2009) *The Resource Outlook to 2050: By How Much Do Land, Water and Crop Yields Need to Increase by 2050?* Paper presented at the FAO Expert Meeting on How to Feed the World in 2050, 24–26 June, Rome.

Carty, T. (2012) *Extreme Weather, Extreme Prices: The Costs of Feeding a Warming World*, Oxfam Issue Briefing, Oxford: Oxfam International.

Fan, S., Babatunde, O. and Lambert, M. (2009) 'Public Spending for Agriculture in Africa: Trends and Composition', ReSAKSS Working Paper No. 28, Washington D.C.: International Food Policy Research Institute.

FAO (2010) *The State of Food Insecurity in the World 2010*, Rome: Food and Agriculture Organization of the United Nations.

FAO (2011a) *The State of Food Insecurity in the World 2011*, Rome: Food and Agriculture Organization of the United Nations.

FAO (2011b) *The State of the World's Land and Water Resources for Food and Agriculture*, Rome: Food and Agriculture Organization of the United Nations.

FAO, IFAD, IMF, OECD, UNCTAD, WFP, the World Bank, the WTO, IFPRI and the UN-HLTF (2011) *Price Volatility in Food and Agricultural Markets: Policy Responses*, Rome: Food and Agriculture Organization of the United Nations.

FAO-OECD (2011) *Agricultural Outlook 2011–2020*, Paris: OECD.

Foresight (2011) *The Future of Food and Farming, Final Project Report*, Foresight Project, London: Government Office for Science.

IPCC (2012) *Special Report: Managing the Risks of Extreme Events and Disasters to Advance Climate Change Adaptation*, A Special Report of Working Groups I and II of the Intergovernmental Panel on Climate Change, Cambridge: Cambridge University Press.

Jennings, S. and Magrath, J. (2009) *What Happened to the Seasons?*, Oxfam Research Report, Oxford: Oxfam GB.

Lobell, D., Schlenker, W. and Costa-Roberts, J. (2011) 'Climate Trends and Global Crop Production Since 1980', *Science*, 333, 6042: 616–20.

Pinstrup-Andersen, P. and Cheng, F. (2007) 'Still Hungry', *Scientific American* August 2007.

Rubin, O. (2009) 'The Merits of Democracy in Famine Protection – Fact or Fallacy?', *European Journal of Development Research*, 21: 699–717.

Sanchez, P., Swaminathan, M. S., Dobie, P. and Yuksel, N. (2005) *Halving Hunger: It Can Be Done*, report of the UN Millennium Project Task Force on Hunger, London: Earthscan.

Sen, A, (1981) *Poverty and Famines: An Essay on Entitlement and Deprivation*, Oxford: Clarendon Press.

Sen, A. (1999) *Development as Freedom*, Oxford: Oxford University Press.

Sheeran, J. (2008) 'The Silent Tsunami: the Globalization of the Hunger Challenge', keynote address to the Peter G. Peterson Institute for International Economics, Washington D.C., 6 May 2008. Available: http://www.wfp.org/eds-centre/speeches/silent-tsunami-globalization-hunger-challenge-keynote-address-peter-g-peterson-i (accessed 12 September 2012).

Tangermann, S. (2011) *Policy Solutions to Agricultural Market Volatility: A Synthesis*, Issue Paper No. 33, Geneva: International Centre for Trade and Sustainable Development.

UNESA (2010) *World Population Prospects, the 2010 Revision*, New York: United Nations.

15

NAVIGATING THE 'NATIONAL SECURITY' BARRIER: A HUMAN SECURITY AGENDA FOR ARMS CONTROL IN THE TWENTY-FIRST CENTURY

Deepayan Basu Ray[1]

Conventional arms control has long been a subject of intense debate in forums like the United Nations, regional security organisations, and for bilateral discussions between countries. This is largely because arms control processes speak to the very core of security policy for all UN member states. Negotiations on control regimes tend to compel states to undertake a complex balancing act between robustness of treaty demands versus universal appeal and consensus amongst all negotiating partners. In light of this tension, it is not difficult to see why arms control initiatives often fail to produce strong and comprehensive frameworks to deal with the scope and breadth of the problems at hand. This is as much a reflection of the inflexibility of governments to compromise on issues which they believe are vital to the interests of national security, as it is a complex calculus of economic interests, trade and strategic relations, and genuine defence concerns.

The single largest hurdle for effective arms control regimes is that of national security – which tends to evoke very strong responses from state authorities in all corners of the world. Officials responsible for safeguarding national security have the unenviable task of identifying all threats to the state, and devising effective policy and institutional responses to address these threats. During the Cold War, this was a relatively straightforward exercise – the dominant threat was either neighbouring states or regional/global superpowers. In the early part of the twenty-first century however, this calculus has changed radically. Intra-state tensions and conflict dominate the security dialogue, and the distinction between combatants and non-combatants is often (deliberately) blurred by the warring parties. Moreover, individual perceptions of insecurity are also being paid greater attention by policy makers and analysts alike. For example, survey data from UNDP's 1994 Human Development Report on human security finds that rather than the traditional threats associated with perceptions of insecurity (attack by foreign armed forces, nuclear and other mass-destruction attacks, etc.), individuals experience greater insecurity from issues that affect their daily lives – poverty, inadequate (or non-existent) social protection mechanisms, weak rule of law, low absorptive capacity to sudden onset shocks or disasters, and poor governance mechanisms (UNDP, 1994). That said, these concepts have not necessarily been reflected in the dominant security discourse – which still aims to mitigate threats to national borders and institutions from external actors. In effect, there is a growing disjunction between the dominant discourses of national security and the actual drivers of insecurity that are destabilising countries and regions.

This has major consequences on the ways in which states operate in the multilateral system of international cooperation – particularly around arms control initiatives. When national security imperatives dominate the debate around arms control issues, they tend to generate systems that are without universal appeal, contain few obligations on states to change their behaviour, and rarely achieve 'security' – be it conceived as national or human, or both. And yet, the desire to develop such regimes is inevitably motivated by experiences of situations where a fundamental deficit in (or weakness of existing) controls has lead to civilian casualties and the creation of humanitarian crises.

This chapter seeks to explore how the concept of human security can help to overcome 'national security' barriers in order to develop arms control regimes that are fit for purpose in the twenty-first century – i.e. a global architecture that is capable of protecting lives and livelihoods.

First, this chapter explores the experiences of developing and implementing landmark conventional arms control mechanisms over the past sixty years. It explores the rationale, the characteristics, and the context in which these agreements take shape, and attempts to identify blockages and challenges that have affected the adherence and impacts of arms control mechanisms. Next, this chapter unpacks the concept of national security as it is relevant to arms control processes – who we are speaking about, what is at stake and what issues are being debated, and finally why these issues are important and/or dominant. The chapter then considers the operational and functional challenges on arms control processes, using the preparatory meetings and negotiations for the July 2012 Diplomatic Conference for the Arms Trade Treaty as an illustration of the convergence of political, economic, and security agendas. Finally, the chapter concludes by examining how a human security lens could add value to arms control processes, and how this approach could assuage national security concerns at the same time.

In essence, the chapter argues that if a wider concept of security forms the basis of debate for arms control measures in multilateral fora, the outcomes of these deliberations would deliver tangible human security improvements – and by consequence, strengthen national security.

'Effective' arms control – feasible or utopian?

It appears to be conventional wisdom that one of the most effective ways to prevent the outbreak or contain the lethality of conflict or armed violence is to make access to the tools of violence a difficult prospect. The United Nations has certainly embedded this issue into the core of its work – with the UN General Assembly's First Committee dedicated to discussing matters of international peace and security in general, and developing global mechanisms for disarmament and arms control.[2] A number of landmark treaties have taken shape in this forum, including the Chemical Weapons Convention (CWC), the Biological Weapons Convention (BWC), the Nuclear Non-Proliferation Treaty (NPT), the UN Programme of Action on Small Arms and Light Weapons (PoA), and the Convention on Certain Conventional Weapons (CCW). On some occasions, under the leadership of certain states, a number of processes of multilateral arms control have also taken place outside the auspices of the UN, and these include the 'Landmines Ban Treaty', and the Cluster Munitions Convention (CMC).

Broadly speaking, arms control processes deliver three different types of outcomes. Firstly, they take the form of outright bans on certain types or categories of weapons, e.g. the Landmines Treaty. Secondly, they take the form of regulatory frameworks that limit or control access/production/usage of certain types or categories of weapons, e.g. the Treaty on the Non-Proliferation of Nuclear Weapons (NPT) or the UN Programme of Action on small arms and light weapons (PoA). Thirdly, they take the form of disarmament treaties which seek to demobilise and reduce stockpiles of certain types or categories of weapons, e.g. Strategic Arms Reduction Treaties – START.

In practice, these agreements seek to prevent armed conflict between (and more recently, within) states by reducing stockpiles of arms and ammunition, and, in some cases, preventing the acquisition of certain types of weapons platforms. These processes tend to be accompanied by transparency and confidence building mechanisms, in order to minimise suspicion. Although the motivation to begin deliberations is often humanitarian (for example the CCW or the CMC), the end result tends to reflect an overwhelming desire to achieve a degree of strategic parity, and to remove the incentives to engage in arms races.

However, more often than not, these regimes concentrate power in the hands of those that already have it. The evidence for this is rife in the nuclear arms control arena, where emerging nuclear powers like India have deliberately positioned themselves outside the treaties because they believe that the regimes are inherently biased – they prevent the acquisition of these arms on the one hand, but do nothing to reduce existing stockpiles in the hands of the nuclear powers.[3] When the concentration of power is explicitly addressed in the treaty text of conventional arms control regimes, the world's biggest manufacturers, users, and stockpilers tend to stay out of the mechanism. The Cluster Munitions Convention is a good example of this, as it does not include the US, China, Russia, Pakistan, India, and Israel, who are among the largest producers and users in the world (Reliefweb, 2011).

That said, the very idea of arms control is an appealing mechanism to proponents of human security. Be it expressly articulated, or inferred though analysis and assessment, the rationale for conventional arms control regimes has always been broadly consistent with the principles of human security – i.e. to prevent the uncontrolled proliferation of the tools of violence. One of the reasons that the humanitarian rationale is eroded in these agreements during negotiations is because these mechanisms are debated in chambers and forums where expanded notions of security are often dismissed entirely, or undermined by supposed operational concerns like bureaucratic and technical efficiency.[4] Effectively, the potential for improvements in human security remains subordinate to implementation mechanisms and political will – both of which are weak.

Many developing countries face a real existential and/or territorial threat from internal and external sources today. From organised crime to armed militias, resource-based conflicts to persistent political disharmony between neighbours, a plethora of threats manifest themselves into 'hot' and 'cold' conflict in all corners of the world. According to data from the Global Burden of Armed Violence (GBAV) report 2011, an estimated 526,000 people are killed each year as a result of lethal violence (Geneva Declaration Secretariat, 2011: 1). These conflicts have a number of roots – and many can be traced back to the legacies of colonialism and cold-war interference/alliances. The history, experiences, and results from the cold-war era proxy wars, the contested borders, and the engineered social orders and hierarchies in post colonial societies remain fresh in the minds of politicians and strategic analysts in many developing countries. As a result, the need to acquire 'hard power' capabilities to deter potential aggressors remains the most common elucidation of national security.

The focus of national security in most countries has been based on preventing armed aggression by predominantly external actors (Davidson, 2011: 1) – though in a number of cases, armed internal actors are also a major source of national insecurity (see Kaldor, 2007; Duffield, 2007; and Nightingale, 2008). The assumption by the state authorities is therefore to ensure that the security and defence forces are equipped and resourced to address a range of threats – a common theme in most publicly accessible national security strategies.[5] Though many countries recognise that elements like poverty, inequality, climate change, and poor governance have a very negative impact on national security, the significant thrust of the national response is still based on strengthening the hard power capacity to deter negative consequences. Defence policy is seen to be the most trusted means of addressing national security concerns (see Malik and Kanwal, 2006). As a result, the overwhelming majority of policy and practice around national security issues tends to focus on defence policy and capital expenditure on military and internal security establishments.

Based on current evidence however, there is little justification for this approach of securing the state. Disaggregated data from the GBAV reveals that only 10 per cent of all victims of lethal armed violence originate in conflict situations. The vast majority (more than 75 per cent – or 396,000 deaths per year) occur as a result of 'intentional homicides', often as a result of organised crime or gang activity (Geneva Declaration Secretariat, 2011: 4). It would be absurd to propose that tanks, aircraft carriers, or helicopter gunships could provide an appropriate means of deterrence to this kind of insecurity – and yet this is what the majority of state expenditure is allocated to over the world. According to the World Bank 2011 World Development Report (WDR), 'Lower Middle Income' countries allocate on average 16.1 per cent of their central government expenditure for the military (World Bank 2011: 337). When this is juxtaposed with the Bank's assertion that no fragile or conflict affected state has met any of the MDGs and is unlikely to do so before 2015, it is an important proxy for the opportunity cost of investment in the defence sector. Therefore, the evidence suggests that the calculus of national security as a function of external threats is somewhat inadequate given the overwhelming evidence about the source of insecurity.

Despite this evidence, governments continue to conflate national security and defence policy into one agenda. In so doing, they confer extraordinary levels of privilege on defence establishments. For instance, defence budgets, allocations, and expenditure are not subject to the same degree of public scrutiny and debate as other areas of government expenditure. In fact, detailed debate of budget allocations, transparency around procurement procedures and results, and parliamentary and/or citizen oversight mechanisms are either actively suppressed, or discouraged in the name of national security. Furthermore, this lack of transparency is often accompanied by a relatively high degree of suspicion by state authorities of anyone proposing alternative narratives of national security, or demanding greater clarity on defence expenditures.

What this creates is a system where (a) the drivers of insecurity are incorrectly/inadequately identified, (b) the finite resources of the state are spent/allocated towards activities which do not necessarily make the country or the citizens qualitatively safer, (c) there is complete autonomy of the security sector to dominate the political and strategic decision-making infrastructure, and (d) the defence industry often enjoys an unhealthy closeness with ministries of defence and other relevant government departments. In practice, these factors narrow the scope of what state officials consider to be drivers of security, and consequently, the kinds of strategies necessary to preserve/create security. Unsurprisingly, this has an affect on international arms control mechanisms, because the assumptions through which states approach the negotiating table are – fundamentally – inadequate. It would be a folly to expect defence manufacturers to lobby for a wider conceptualisation of insecurity given the sheer amount of money that hangs in the balance of such a policy decision.[6]

The privilege afforded to the defence establishment should not be overlooked when considering the issue of national security. By invoking strategic secrecy, defence establishments have been able to frequently prevent transparency and parliamentary oversight in their operating budgets and capital expenditure activities. For example, unpublished research conducted by SIPRI has found that as much as 8 per cent of Nigeria's 2008 national budget was dedicated to secret items relating to national security, and information was presented to the legislature in such a highly aggregated figure that there simply were no details to debate (Perlo-Freeman, 2010). Nigeria is not alone – this lack of disclosure can be found to some degree in nearly every country.

There are four broad consequences of the 'national security' exception on defence and security policy-making and expenditure. Firstly, without adequate scrutiny of defence budgets, extra-budgetary mechanisms are used to facilitate non-accountable transactions and procurements of arms and ammunition. One need only recall the extraordinary amounts of money that the US government spent on the war in Iraq through the US since 2003.[7] Furthermore, the Costs of War project at Brown University finds that 'because the Pentagon does not competently account for appropriations to it, according to decades of reports from the Government Accountability Office and the Department of Defense's own Inspector General, we have no reliable assurance of how, or even where, the funds were actually spent' (Costs Of War, 2011).

Secondly, and related to the first point, national security exceptions weaken reporting requirements for expenditure and procurement, and are often reinforced by discretionary laws, rules, and regulations which legitimate these inadequate practices. For example, Russian arms companies are restricted by the degree to which they can voluntarily disclose information on defence contracts because of the 1993 Law of the Russian Federation on State Secrets. 'This law provides that the information on the foreign economic activities of the Russian Federation, disclosure of which can cause damage to the security of the country, is considered a state secret' (Irkut, 2010: 10). In effect, Russian law prevents transparency on commercial activities on the premise that doing so would threaten the national security of the state.

Thirdly, national security considerations can also affect the development and articulation of comprehensive Defence Policy frameworks, which are vital for safeguarding against ad-hoc and non-strategic budgeting and procurement. Defence policy frameworks like white papers are as yet not the norm in the majority of the countries of the UN, and participatory processes to develop these policy positions are rarer still. When these strategic documents do exist, they are themselves subject to state secrecy, and therefore not shared widely, or in some cases, implemented effectively. India is a good example, where despite concerted efforts to develop five-year and ten-year defence plans, 'Ad-hocism is the order of the day, leading to knee-jerk responses and haphazard planning' (Malik and Kanwal, 2006: 7).

Finally, national security exceptions enable and condone systemic and institutional corruption, which in turn acts to undermine accountability and efficiency efforts. Table 15.1 below illustrates this point – states which score poorly on corruption indices tend to have high military expenditures, and do not have a strong track record of submitting reports to transparency frameworks like the UN Register on Conventional Arms (UN Register).

Table 15.1 illustrates the impacts of the national security exception on defence, security, and socio-economic conditions in a country. When countries place a premium on the health of their defence sector and the military, a number of consequences can be observed. For instance, none of the countries identified in the table have submitted reports on their defence procurement and exports to the UN Register in 2010 – a voluntary mechanism.[11] All of these states have also spent a large portion of their central budgets on military expenditure during the same period, at least over 10 per cent. Finally, nearly all of these states have scored poorly on Transparency International's Corruption Perception Index over the same period.

Table 15.1 Non-reporters to the UN Register on Conventional Arms in 2010

	Military expenditure as per cent of central government expenditure[8]	*CPI rank*[9]	*CPI score*[10]
Colombia	20.9%	78	3.5
Jordan	19.2%	50	4.7
Georgia	18.1%	68	3.8
Armenia	16%	123	2.6
Uganda	15.8%	127	2.5
Burkina Faso	10.3%	98	3.1

Other key non-contributors to the UNRCA in 2010 include: Egypt, China, Israel, Iran, DPR Korea, Cuba, Indonesia, Myanmar, Libya, Syria, UAE, and Saudi Arabia.

The cumulative impact of invoking the national security exception therefore is stark indeed. When defence policy and acquisitions are conducted without clear political direction and adequate coordination of defence plans and economic development, there is a constant risk of ad-hoc procurement, poor reporting, and no incentive to be transparent on allocation processes. These consequences are in themselves reinforcing – by encouraging non-transparent and non-accountable practices, the subject of national security itself becomes the explicit privilege of a select few within the polity.

The particularities of the definition of national security therefore have a major impact on arms control initiatives, as governments tend not to voluntarily constrain their ability to purchase/develop arms. Effective arms control mechanisms can prevent potential aggressors from acquiring certain weapons and systems – at the very least, this principle underpins most current examples of multilateral arms control. However, most states recognise that by preventing the acquisition universally, the architecture restricts the defence options for all signatory states. This conundrum often is responsible for weakness in adherence of treaty requirements, non-universal membership, or unambitious and ineffective frameworks.

'National Security' and the trade in conventional arms

Arms control issues are often framed publicly in the language of security. There are however a number of other key factors that determine the success or failure of an arms control regime, not the least of which is the economic implications. There are considerable financial vested interests in the fortunes of the global arms industry. SIPRI estimated global military expenditure to amount to well over US$1.6 trillion in 2010 (SIPRI, 2011). Some US$40 billion of this total is the net-worth of the trade in conventional arms for the same year (ibid.). Defence manufacturers are therefore very valuable to their national economies. For example, US sales totalled in excess of US$28 billion in 2010, representing a sizeable share of the country's GDP (SIPRI, 2011). It is thus logical to expect that arms control mechanisms that seek to ban the production and use of certain weapons, or even regulate the sale and transfer of weapons and systems, may be opposed simply on economic grounds by certain actors.

Some initiatives are framed as inherently humanitarian – the Convention on Cluster Munitions explicitly recognises in its preamble that 'cluster munition remnants kill or maim civilians, including women and children, obstruct economic and social development' (CMC, 2008: 1). Yet others are framed in the language of hard security and confidence building – as the Strategic Arms Reduction treaties on ballistics missiles between the US and the USSR/ Russian Federation have demonstrated over the years. Still others are framed in the language of armed violence reduction and peacebuilding, as demonstrated by the UN Programme of Action on Small Arms and Light Weapons.

The ongoing negotiations on a prospective Arms Trade Treaty (ATT) however aims to conflate all of these perspectives into one framework. This has generated some of the most complicated negotiations to date on conventional arms control within the UN, whereby governments have to grapple with all aspects of the trade in conventional weapons. This has ranged from debates around the scope of the treaty (which weapons/systems are included), the types of transfers of arms (loans, exports, etc.), the criteria by which an exporting state will feel it appropriate to sell the arms to a potential buyer (e.g. risk assessment of corruption, human rights violations, etc.), legal jurisdiction and considerations of extra-territoriality, national systems of control and oversight in importing countries, reporting and transparency, and international assistance mechanisms. As a result, nearly every prevalent threat to national security has been introduced into the debate at some point by countries at the negotiating table.

The negotiations have thus far produced a Draft Treaty (UN, 2012b) following a four-week Diplomatic Conference that took place over July 2012. The Conference failed to produce an agreement – the result of a set of rules of procedure which were based on consensus for the final text rather than an outcome document being voted on by the delegations. This effectively afforded every delegation a veto in the proceedings, and allowed each country to safeguard their individual national security concerns over and above all collective concerns of humanity. The invoking of national security by countries has therefore impacted significantly on the discussions for the ATT.

For example, the Draft Treaty suggests that the right to self defence – as enshrined by the UN Charter Article 51 – also includes a national prerogative to manufacture, import, export, transfer, and retain conventional arms for self-defence purposes and security needs.[12] The implication of a treaty that enshrines this expanded notion of the right to self-defence to be synonymous with the right to sell arms is a monumental shift in international relations. It will set a precedent that could do more harm than good – as it is entirely conceivable that arms deals to inappropriate destinations could be legitimated under the guise of a charter-protected right.

Another example of where national security conditions are hindering progress on the ATT negotiations is around specific elements of the prospective treaty such as the scope and criteria. There are still objections to the inclusion of ammunition into the scope of what the ATT would seek to cover. Leaving aside for a moment the absurdity of a control regime for guns that doesn't include the very bullets that make these instruments lethal, it is widely accepted that small arms and light weapons are responsible for more civilian casualties and fatalities every year than any other weapon or system.[13] As a result, the ammunition necessary for these arms must fall into the same control regime as the weapon itself. This notwithstanding, there has been resistance to the suggestion for inclusion of ammunition on strategic and bureaucratic grounds.[14] There is a latent fear that inclusion of ammunition into a control mechanism could compromise the security of military operations, defence policy, and the security of partners/allies – as it would present a good proxy for the strategy and capacity of the armed forces in question.

Another suggestion for the prospective treaty calls for transfer of arms to only be authorised once the exporting country is assured that the arms/ammunition will not have a negative impact on human rights, humanitarian law, or socio-economic development of the importing country.[15] There has been considerable objection to this collection of risk assessment criteria, on the grounds that they are subjective and prone to political manipulation – thereby having a negative impact on national security of the importing country.[16] The conundrum of course is that in order for the treaty to be effective – i.e. preventing abusers of human rights and humanitarian law from gaining access to their tools of violence – it needs to have very strong risk assessment criteria. On the other hand, it is precisely the strength of these criteria that could potentially present threats to national security, as it may prevent states from acquiring the means of self-defence. Unfortunately though, experience from voluntary or non-binding mechanisms has shown repeatedly that initiatives without legal obligations do little to change the status quo and spur positive change. In fact, given the political and/or economic magnitude in certain cases, even certain legally binding obligations have been overridden. For example, despite the existence of the European Code of Conduct/Common Position on Arms Transfers, European countries still exported arms to repressive regimes around the world on a number of occasions (Vranckx et al., 2011: 3). At the very least, on these occasions, the space has been created by legal obligations to call on these states to account for their decisions – as civil society organisations have done recently with two revealing reports on controversial exports (see Vranckx et al., 2011).

Some apprehension has also been expressed about reporting requirements for the prospective ATT.[17] This is rooted not only in capacity constraints – i.e. the bureaucracy simply does not have the skills, resources, or capacity to meet additional reporting requirements – but also in an unwillingness to be completely transparent about arms transfers.[18] Unsurprisingly, objection to this requirement has come from states who have not submitted annual reports to the UN Register with any regularity – if any at all. In a similar vein, a number of countries have also objected to corruption as risk assessment criteria for arms transfers[19] – which is broadly consistent with previous analysis in this chapter.

As these examples from the ongoing negotiations on the prospective ATT have illustrated, multilateral arms control mechanisms are often unable to navigate the national security considerations of countries. Either the initiative results in a regime powerless to obligate a particular type of behaviour, or it lacks the support of the key players in order for the architecture to be effective. In effect, given the constraints of the current geo-political and strategic interests, a wholesale paradigm shift in the way in which national security and arms control is conceived of is necessary. The reasons for arms control initiatives are not being questioned here – the humanitarian imperative is as compelling a rationale as any other. It is however the process by which this change is realised that is inherently problematic. It is here that a human security perspective could be of particular importance and merit.

The human security agenda and its implications for effective arms control

As this chapter has illustrated, the practice of security making has been alarmingly narrow in scope, catering almost exclusively to military and defence policy needs as a means of addressing national security. This approach is particularly problematic because in recent years, individuals and communities have endured far greater levels of insecurity than the nation state. Since only 'one in every ten of all reported violent deaths around the world occurs in so-called conflict settings or during terrorist activities', there is ample proof to suggest that most existing calculations of national security are missing the mark quite considerably (Geneva Declaration Secretariat, 2011: 1). The composite elements of the human security agenda offer policy makers an alternative conceptualisation of national security. A human security perspective seeks to shift the referent object of concern for policy makers from the state and its institutions, to the individual citizen and their immediate communities. The state is still central to the equation, the shift is merely in *who* is secured by the actions of the state. This is because the state remains the only legitimate authority to use force and possess the tools of violence, although primarily for the purposes of defence and the maintenance of law and order.[20] Furthermore, there are contexts where persistent insecurity will require the sustained engagement of the formal security sector in order to create conditions where peace and long-term socio-economic development can take root. Arms control mechanisms must reflect a nuanced understanding of the interface between legitimate security needs and socio-economic development, so as not to block transactions that could help states legitimately address the drivers that undermine development.

The UNDP was the first to explicitly articulate the concept of human security through the Human Development Reports in 1993 and 1994. Many academics, analysts, and policy makers have since opined on the dimensions, characteristics, and features of the concept, generating a rich and diversified debate on the subject. Some of the key elements to have emerged from this debate is that human security can broadly be characterised as a people-centred, multi-dimensional, inter-connected and universal approach. Human security analysis takes the context as the starting point. It seeks to identify the relevant concerns, and only then define the core of high-priority policy responses rather than choosing an action from a pre-determined set of options (Jolly and Basu Ray, 2007: 461). This is the point at which arms control mechanisms find the greatest resonance with human security objectives. The concept of arms control is, as already suggested, broadly consistent with the principles of human security. In seeking to limit access to the tools of violence, arms control mechanisms offer a practical application of human security in action.

There are three ways in which a human security perspective can add value to arms control processes. Firstly, a human security approach to effective conventional arms control would deliver an architecture where responsible governments could address legitimate security and defence concerns, whilst ensuring their actions were broadly consistent with other governance responsibilities like social protection and service delivery. Secondly, control regimes informed by an individual-centric approach would help shape systems that were acutely sensitive to the impacts of arms on individuals and communities, and their enjoyment of socio-economic development, security, and human rights. Finally, a human security approach would strive to deliver maximum transparency and accountability, and generate mechanisms that were malleable enough to (re)focus attention on actual threats. This is particularly important because insecurity is rarely a static phenomenon – shocks and stresses are constantly redefined with the passage of time.

In an ideal situation, the cumulative impact would result in the development of a very robust architecture that could respond to the multiplicity of drivers of insecurity experienced by individuals and communities. This in turn would have significant positive impacts on the perceptions of national security. It would also be better at recognising that the aggregate security of individual citizens of a state is in fact a better proxy for national security than the majority of current formulations which are skewed in favour of the state, its territorial borders, and its institutions. However, it is worth qualifying that the biggest challenge to this conceptualisation of effective arms control is that in order for this agenda to deliver successfully, it would require near-universal acquiescence to this calculus of national security. Suffice to say, this is a tall order – consensus on high standards in multilateral initiatives is perhaps one of the toughest outcomes to secure. Still, the merit of this approach is that it helps to identify what the highest possible standard actually looks like, and that is an important exercise in and of itself.

Conclusions

As this chapter has illustrated, national security and arms control processes have been debated in very narrow terms – the list of threats and policy options have been limited at best. This has contributed to the lack of comprehensive success in conventional arms control initiatives. By introducing human security considerations into the frame, it may be possible to broaden the debate on national security and deepen the engagement of different actors into the discussions. This will be very important because of the prevailing tendency of governments to operate in silos on issues like arms control – which have governance implications well beyond that of national security.

The privilege afforded to actors responsible for national security has also been identified as a major impediment to successful multilateral arms control issues. The political, economic, and institutional vested interests of the defence-industrial complex are considerable, and cannot be underestimated. But this privilege comes at a steep price. It helps shape a national security narrative that is disconnected with the reality. This is where a human security perspective can help to find common ground – between a meaningful recognition of the drivers of insecurity for individuals and communities, and the resource requirements of the national defence and security establishments. The sheer net financial value of the latter has helped to overshadow the former – but the relationship is undeniable. If the policy focus leans too heavily on one side, it will have profound implications for perceptions of insecurity. A human security perspective will help to ensure that adequate attention is paid to both considerations – and that in turn should deliver an emancipated conceptualisation of national security. In such conditions, arms control initiatives premised on human security approaches cannot but succeed.

Afterword

Prior to this publication being launched, the United Nations convened the Final Conference on the Arms Trade Treaty in March 2013. The conference could not achieve consensus on the final draft, with Iran, Syria, and North Korea blocking agreement. A group of states immediately took the draft text forward to the UN General Assembly. On 2 April 2013, with a vote of 156 in favour, 22 abstentions, and 3 opposed, the UN Arms Trade Treaty was overwhelmingly adopted. Subsequently, on 3 June 2013 – the first day the treaty opened for signature – 71 states signed on to the treaty, which included some of the largest arms producers like the UK, Germany and France; and the emerging exporters like Mexico and Brazil. Encouragingly, in its statement on the day of the ATT Signing Ceremony, the US government registered its intent to sign the treaty once all the official translations were in conformity.

The Text of the Arms Trade Treaty (as adopted by the General Assembly) can be found online at: http://www.un.org/disarmament/ATT/docs/ATT_text_(As_adopted_by_the_GA)-E.pdf (accessed 12 June 2013).

Notes

1 The views and opinions expressed in this chapter are expressly the author's own, and should not be attributed to any other institution or organisation.
2 General Assembly of the United Nations, 'First Committee: Disarmament and International Security', http://www.un.org/en/ga/first/ (accessed 17 May 2013).
3 Statement made by Ms Arundhati Ghose, Ambassador/ Permanent Representative of India to UN Offices at Geneva, in the Plenary of the CD on 20 June 1996 (New Delhi: Ministry of External Affairs, Government of India, 1997)
4 A number of delegations have made statements during arms control negotiations which suggest that issues such as poverty, corruption, or human rights are either inappropriate for discussion, better dealt with in other forums, or very difficult to meaningfully implement. For example, Vietnam and Malaysia state that issues such as development, corruption and poverty are better dealt with in other forums, and should not be debated in the negotiations for the Arms Trade Treaty (UN, 2012a, pp. 59 and 113). India's statement at the 2010 Biennial Meeting of States for the UNPoA notes that 'The correlation between lack of development and small arms proliferation has not been convincingly demonstrated',

and suggesting that this issue remains too contentious for discussion within the PoA forum (Gill, 2010). On the issue of including development as a criteria for arms transfers, Canada has intimated that it 'is not convinced that including such criteria in an ATT would be workable' (Government of Canada, 2011). A similar rationale was used by the US delegation on the issue of including ammunition in the ATT, which US representatives suggested was 'hugely impractical' (Countryman, 2012).

5 For example, see US National Security Strategy (President of the USA, 2010), pp.17–27; UK Strategic Defence and Security Review (Cabinet Office, 2010b) and the UK National Security Strategy (Cabinet Office, 2010a); Brazil's National Strategy for Defence (Ministry of Defence, 2008); and Sierra Leone Defence White Paper (Ministry of Defence, 2003). A compendium of defence and security policies can also be found at MERLIN (http://merln.ndu.edu/whitepapers.html) and the Stimson Centre's SSR Bibliography (http://www.stimson.org/images/uploads/research-pdfs/Practice_notes_bibliography_11dec09_FINAL.pdf)

6 The top five contractors to the US government in 2010 were representatives of defence industries – Lockheed Martin Corporation; The Boeing Company; Northrop Grumman Corporation; General Dynamics Corporation; and Raytheon Company. Together they accounted for US\$102 billion in contracts in 2010 alone. Put in context, the Department of Defence was the single largest source for contracts in the US in 2010 (FPDS, 2011).

7 The *Costs of War* project at Brown's University estimates that DoD Appropriations for the Iraq War between 2003 and 2011 are in excess of US\$757 billion (Wheeler, 2011: 2).

8 World Bank (2011) 'World development indicators'.

9 Transparency International (2011), *Corruption Perceptions Index 2011*, London, http://cpi.transparency. org/cpi2011/results/ (accessed 17 May 2013).

10 The CPI scores countries on a scale of 1–10, with 10 representing a very clean, open, non-corrupt society. Only 46 (26 per cent) of all the 178 countries ranked scored 5.0 or higher in 2010. Ibid, p. 3.

11 Reporting against the categories of the register have been steadily declining since 2001 when a record high 126 countries submitted reports. In 2010, a mere 61 countries submitted reports (UN, 2011: 1).

12 The Preamble of the Draft Treaty recognises the 'legitimate political, security, economic and commercial rights and interests of States in the international trade of conventional arms' (UN, 2012b: 1). Please also refer to statements by Argentina, Bangladesh, Brazil, Canada, China, Egypt, India, Indonesia, Philippines, and Trinidad and Tobago from the February and July 2011 Preparatory Committee for the ATT, http://www.un.org/disarmament/convarms/ATTPrepCom/Statements. html (accessed 17 May 2013).

13 The GBAV finds that 'Guns are increasingly the weapon of choice of gangs and groups engaged in organized crime' (Geneva Declaration Secretariat, 2011: 101). The majority of these weapons are Small Arms and Light Weapons, as noted by the UN Office for Disarmament Affairs (UNODA, 2012). This dynamic has been recognised by the UN, and a number of General Assembly resolutions that (a) recognise the scale and depth of the problem, and (b) resolve to collectively act to overcome the destructive capabilities of SALW – for example: A/RES/66/4/ (http://undocs.org/A/RES/66/4/).

14 Some countries have suggested that the sheer number of bullets produced every year would make control mechanisms very onerous. An estimated 10–14 billion rounds of ammunition are produced each year – and some states have argued that it is practically very difficult to place effective control mechanisms over such massive quantities. It is worth noting that the global trade in ammunition is an estimated USD\$1.77 billion annually – and is more valuable than the trade in firearms (Greene, 2006; Anders, 2006).

15 Please refer to statements by Australia, Costa Rica, Kenya, Nigeria, Trinidad and Tobago, and UK from the February 2011 Preparatory Committee for the ATT, http://www.un.org/disarmament/convarms/ ATTPrepCom/Statements.html (accessed 17 May 2013).

16 Please refer to, for example, statements by the Arab Group, China, Egypt, India, Iran, and the Russian Federation from the February 2011 Preparatory Committee for the ATT, http://www.un.org/disar-mament/convarms/ATTPrepCom/Statements.html (accessed 17 May 2013).

17 Indeed, the Draft Treaty does not make provisions for national reports to be made public (UN, 2012b: 6–7). Please also refer to statements by Brazil, Canada, India, and Israel from the February and July 2011 Preparatory Committee for the ATT, http://www.un.org/disarmament/convarms/ ATTPrepCom/Statements.html (accessed 17 May 2013).

18 The Draft Treaty makes exemptions on reporting for all information deemed by the reporting state to be 'commercially sensitive' or could compromise national security (UN, 2012b: 7).

19 Please refer to, for example, statements by Argentina, Brazil, Canada, China, and India, and from the February and July 2011 Preparatory Committee for the ATT, http://www.un.org/disarmament/convarms/ATTPrepCom/Statements.html (accessed 17 May 2013).
20 Article 51 of the UN Charter recognises a state's right to self defence in the instance of an armed attack.

References

Anders, H. (2006), 'Ammunition: the fuel of conflict', Oxfam International Briefing Note, http://www.oxfam.org/sites/www.oxfam.org/files/ammunition.pdf (accessed 27 June 2010).

Cabinet Office (2010a), 'A strong Britain in an age of uncertainty: the National Security Strategy', London, http://www.cabinetoffice.gov.uk/sites/default/files/resources/national-security-strategy.pdf (accessed 17 May 2013).

Cabinet Office (2010b), 'Securing Britain in an age of uncertainty: the Strategic Defence and Security Review', London, http://www.direct.gov.uk/prod_consum_dg/groups/dg_digitalassets/@dg/@en/documents/digitalasset/dg_191634.pdf (accessed 17 May 2013).

Cluster Munitions Convention (2008), 30 March 2008, Dublin, Ireland, http://www.clusterconvention.org/files/2011/01/Convention-ENG.pdf (accessed 17 May 2013).

Costs of War project 'Pentagon Budget', Watson Institute, Brown University, http://costsofwar.org/article/pentagon-budget (accessed 17 May 2013).

Countryman, T. (2012) 'Positions for the United States in the Upcoming Arms Trade Treaty Conference', Stimson Centre, Washington DC, 16 April 2012, available at: http://www.state.gov/t/isn/rls/rm/188002.htm (accessed 17 May 2013).

Davidson, J. (2011), *Prevention in the National Security Context*, Opening Keynote, Prevention Regimes and Strategies Workshop, Global Public Policy Academic Group, Naval Postgraduate School, Monterey, CA, 15 August 2011, http://www.nps.edu/Academics/AcademicGroups/GPPAG/Docs/PDF/Researchper cent20andper cent20Publications/Davidsonper cent20Speech.pdf (accessed 17 May 2013).

Duffield, M. (2007), *Development, Security and Unending Wars: Governing the World Order of Peoples*, Polity Press, Cambridge.

Federal Procurement Data System – FPDS (2011), *Top 100 Contractors Report*, https://www.fpds.gov/downloads/top_requests/Top_100_Contractors_Report_Fiscal_Year_2010.xls (accessed 17 May 2013).

Geneva Declaration Secretariat (2011), *Global Burden of Armed Violence – Lethal Encounters*, Cambridge University Press, Cambridge, http://www.genevadeclaration.org/measurability/global-burden-of-armed-violence/global-burden-of-armed-violence-2011.html (accessed 17 May 2013).

Gill, A.S. (2010) 'Statement by Amandeep Singh Gill, Counsellor (Disarmament), Permanent Mission of India to the Conference on Disarmament', 4th Biennial Meeting of States (BMS) on the Implementation of the UN programme of Action to Prevent, Combat and Eradicate the Illicit Trade in Small Arms and Light Weapons in All Its Aspects; New York, 14-18 June, 2010, available at: http://www.poa-iss.org/BMS4/1NationalStatementsBMS4/India-E-BORD.PDF (accessed 17 May 2013).

Government of Canada (2011) 'Statement by the Delegation of Canada – Arms Trade Treaty Prepcom – July 14, 2011', New York, July 2011, available at: http://www.un.org/disarmament/convarms/ATTPrepCom/Documents/Statements-MS/PrepCom3/2011-July-14/2011-07-14-Canada-EL.pdf (accessed 17 May 2013).

Greene, O. (2006), 'Ammunition for small arms and light weapons: understanding the issues and addressing the challenges', in S Pézard and H Anders (eds.) *Targeting Ammunition: A Primer*, Small Arms Survey, Geneva.

Irkut (2010), *Consolidated Financial Statements for the Year Ended 31 December 2009*, Moscow, http://www.irkut.com/common//img/uploaded/IRKUT_IFRS_2009.pdf (accessed 17 May 2013).

Jolly, R. and Basu Ray, D. (2007), 'Human security – national perspectives and global agendas: insights from national human development reports', *Journal of International Development*, 19: 457–472.

Kaldor, M. (2007), *Human Security: Reflections on Globalization and Intervention*, Polity Press, Cambridge.

Malik, General V. P. and Kanwal, Brig. G. (2006), *Defence Planning in India*, Observer Research Foundation, http://www.observerindia.com/cms/export/orfonline/modules/policybrief/attachments/py050120_1162534133844.pdf (accessed 17 May 2013).

Ministry of Defence (2003), *Defence White Paper: Informing the People*, Government of Sierra Leone, Freetown, July, http://merln.ndu.edu/whitepapers/SierraLeone.pdf (accessed 17 May 2013).

Ministry of Defence (2008), *National Strategy of Defence – Peace and Security for Brazil*, http://www.defesa. gov.br/projetosweb/estrategia/arquivos/estrategia_defesa_nacional_ingles.pdf (accessed 17 May 2013).

Nightingale, K. (2008), *Shooting Down the MDGs – How Irresponsible Arms Transfers Undermine Development Goals*, Oxfam International, Briefing Paper 120, http://www.oxfam.org/sites/www.oxfam.org/files/ bp120per cent20Shootingper cent20downper cent20theper cent20MDGs_FINALper cent01Oct08. pdf (accessed 17 May 2013).

Perlo-Freeman, S. (2010), *Case Studies for the ATT*, SIPRI unpublished research commissioned by Oxfam GB.

President of the United States of America (2010), *National Security Strategy*, Washington, http://www. whitehouse.gov/sites/default/files/rss_viewer/national_security_strategy.pdf (accessed 17 May 2013).

ReliefWeb (2011), *Lebanon: Meeting Bolsters Cluster Munitions Convention*, 22 September 2011, http:// reliefweb.int/node/448249 (accessed 17 May 2013).

SIPRI (2011), Military Expenditure Database, http://milexdata.sipri.org, (accessed 17 May 2013).

United Nations – UN (2011), *United Nations Register of Conventional Arms: Report of the Secretary-General*, 66th Session of UN General Assembly, 12 July 2011, A/66/127, http://www.un.org/ga/search/ view_doc.asp?symbol=A/66/127 (accessed 17 May 2013).

United Nations (2012a), Compilation of Views on the Elements of an Arms Trade Treaty, United Nations Conference on the Arms Trade Treaty, New York, A/CONF.217/2, http://www.un.org/ga/search/ view_doc.asp?symbol=A/CONF.217/2&Lang=E (accessed 17 May 2013).

UN (2012b) *Draft treaty text submitted by the President of the ATT Conference on 26 July 2012.* (A/ Conf.217/CRP.1), available at: http://www.un.org/ga/search/view_doc.asp?symbol=A/CONF.217/ CRP.1&Lang=E

UNDP (1994) *Human Development Report 1994.* New York: Oxford University Press.

UN Office for Disarmament Affairs (UNODA) (2012), *Small Arms*, New York, 2012, available at: http:// www.un.org/disarmament/convarms/SALW/ (accessed 17 May 2013).

Vranckx, A. (ed.) (2010), *Rhetoric or Restraint: Trade in Military Equipment under the EU Transfer Control System – A Report to the EU Presidency*, Academia Press, Gent, 2010, http://eugrasp.eu/fileadmin/ user_upload/rhetoric_or_restraint_.pdf (accessed 17 May 2013).

Vranckx, A., Slijper, F. and Isbister, R. (2011), *Lessons from MENA: Appraising EU Transfers of Military and Security Equipment to the Middle East and North Africa*, Academia Press, Gent, November 2011, http://www.saferworld. org.uk/downloads/pubdocs/Lessonspercent20frompercent20MENApercent20Novpercent202011.pdf (accessed 17 May 2013).

Wheeler, W. T. (2011), 'Unaccountable: Pentagon spending on the post-9/11 wars', *Costs Of War Project*, Watson Institute, Brown University, 23 June 2011, http://costsofwar.org/sites/default/files/ articles/39/attachments/Wheelerper cent20Pentagonper cent20Spending.pdf (accessed 17 May 2013).

World Bank (2011), *World Development Report: Conflict, Security, and Development*, Washington, http:// wdr2011.worldbank.org/sites/default/files/pdfs/WDR2011_Full_Text.pdf (accessed 17 May 2013).

16

ADJUSTING THE PARADIGM: A HUMAN SECURITY FRAMEWORK FOR COMBATING TERRORISM

Cindy R. Jebb and Andrew A. Gallo

Introduction[1]

In his last speech at the United States Military Academy at West Point as the Secretary of Defense in February 2011, Robert M. Gates warned the Corps of Cadets that while we cannot know with absolute certainty what the future of warfare will hold, we know that it will be exceedingly complex, unpredictable, and unstructured. Matter-of-fact, he asserted:

> When it comes to predicting the nature and location of our next military engagement … our record has been perfect. We have never once gotten it right, from the Mayaguez to Grenada, Panama, Somalia, the Balkans, Haiti, Kuwait, Iraq, and more – we had no idea a year before any of these missions that we would be so engaged.[2]

Given the dynamic nature of the environment in an era of complex local, regional, and global change, it is helpful to consider a new paradigm with a set of guiding principles that the U.S. military might leverage in its operations. Specifically, a *human security framework* for combating terrorism provides a multi-dimensional approach that offers decision-makers a set of useful tools to employ in the operational environment.

Before we examine security and terrorism, there are some macro-level truths that we must first acknowledge. First, Clausewitz's basic premise – that war is a continuation of politics by other means – is a useful foundation upon which we can build. This enduring principle ought to be a touchstone as the United States searches for a paradigm that will help guide national security in a dangerous world. Second, we believe that Secretary Gates aptly describes the current complex reality:

> In recent years the lines separating war, peace, diplomacy, and development have become more blurred, and no longer fit the neat organizational charts of the 20th century. All the various elements and stakeholders working in the international arena – military and civilian, government and private – have learned to stretch outside their comfort zone to work together and achieve results.[3]

For the U.S. military, this reality means that it must be prepared to operate effectively across a range of operations, many of which will consist of a complicated mixture of lethal and nonlethal actions designed to affect not only military conditions, but also political, economic, social and other conditions within a given operational area.[4] Counterterrorism is but one small part of this continuum of military operations – stability and reconstruction, peacekeeping, counter-insurgency, humanitarian relief, counterterrorism, and even conventional war-fighting – that must be integrated, valued, and understood. Furthermore, there must be an equally under-stood common purpose at all levels and across the continuum. The military must not only synchronize its own actions, it must also effectively strive for unity of effort toward achieving a common goal with civilian organizations and non-U.S. military organizations in the operational area. The non-linear, fast-changing nature of security environments requires that all leaders embrace the reality of these complex operations.

Past approaches have limited our ability to effectively anticipate, understand, and operate in these complex environments. In fact, such approaches have constrained our ability to under-stand the problem, and in many cases reduced our thinking to binary dyads, such as we-they; us-them; peacekeeping-counterterrorism; and military-non-military.[5] While the world appears much simpler when viewed in such a binary manner, it causes security professionals to under-state or miss the important contextual dynamics necessary for accurately assessing problems and capitalizing on opportunities.

Military leaders must not only be able to solve nuanced, unstructured problems; they must also be able to identify new problem sets, and this is increasingly more challenging. In regards to terrorism, it is not sufficient to just understand the complicated structure of Al Qaeda; one must also understand its growing complexity – how it is morphing, influencing, and connecting to other groups and individuals globally, regionally, and locally. Many of these types of challenges require a multi-dimensional approach, with the military in a supporting role. Subsequently, military leaders must be open to forming new teams that reflect diverse perspectives and approaches whatever the operation, guided by a common purpose and a unity of effort.

How do we prepare in such a world? The first step is to acknowledge a common starting point, definitions, and achievable outcomes. The first part of this paper will do just that. Then, we will offer a human security framework, which provides a comprehensive, contextual lens required for understanding threats, vulnerabilities, and opportunities, while providing the basis for posing important questions at the local level, anticipating second and third order effects of potential actions or decisions, and managing expectations of outcomes. This perspective helps us understand trade-offs and risks, given the desire for stability, redefined. Third, we provide a new way to reconsider the paradigm and we offer a set of guiding principles, which we argue adheres to Clausewitz's definition of war in today's and what can be reasonably anticipated in future, security environments. While the Nation's budget stringency, reality and fatigue of U.S. operations in Iraq and Afghanistan will influence strategy, we must resist the temptation to let both budget and/or fatigue constraints dictate that strategy. Instead, a clear-headed approach that focuses on human capital across the government and the military in particular will be our greatest asset as we approach twenty-first century challenges that have already – in one short decade – surprised everyone.

Unpacking concepts

In the spirit of Clausewitz – understanding that war is a continuation of politics – democracy has been at the forefront of how we think about, articulate, and craft strategy. In fact, the most recent U.S. national security strategies from 2006 and 2010 state, respectively:

It is the policy of the United States to seek and support democratic movements and institutions in every nation ... In the world today, the fundamental character of regimes matters as much as the distribution of power among them.[6]

The United States supports the expansion of democracy and human rights abroad because governments that respect these values are more just, peaceful, and legitimate. We also do so because their success abroad fosters an environment that supports America's national interests.[7]

Of course *democracy means many things to many different people*. Many theorists and political scientists highlight the importance of the culture of democracy. Gabriel Almond and Sidney Verba discuss societal virtues that form the foundation for a democracy: trust, tolerance to diversity, competence of an empowered citizenry to affect politics, and allegiance towards the regime. Larry Diamond emphasizes that 'The quality of democracy also depends on its levels of freedom, pluralism, justice and accountability.'[8] Of course Samuel Huntington questions the importance of the nature of the regime:

The most important political distinction among countries concerns not their form of government but their degree of government. The differences between democracy and dictatorship are less than the differences between those countries whose politics embodies consensus, community, legitimacy, organization, effectiveness, stability, and those countries whose politics is deficient in these qualities.[9] (emphasis added)

Fareed Zakaria warns us that *democratic transitions are dangerous* when he wrote in 1997 that:

Far from being a temporary or transitional stage, it appears that many countries are settling into a form of government that mixes a substantial degree of democracy with a substantial degree of illiberalism ... *As we approach the next century, our task is to make democracy safe for the world.*[10] (emphasis added)

Yet, Amartya Sen argues that freedom is instrumental for development – 'Development is indeed a momentous engagement with freedom's possibilities.'[11] All of these ideas from the national security strategies to democratic theorists and economists suggest that there are *risks that must be acknowledged and understood* so that policy makers may be able to decide if risks are unacceptable or take the necessary steps to mitigate them. These same policy makers must shoulder the burden of these risks as opposed to soldiers and innocent civilians.

Let us now shift to the problem of terrorism.[12] Bruce Hoffman, in a discussion at West Point, shared that while terrorist organizations are dangerous, the real danger is the possibility of the political movements that they can spark among populations. The Princeton Project refers to terrorism as a 'global insurgency with a criminal core' that should be addressed by a 'counter-insurgency that utilizes a range of tools.'[13] These two views are important for two major reasons. First, they highlight the crisis of legitimacy found in many parts of the world where people are also suffering from grave human insecurities. Second, they suggest that terrorism is not merely a military problem, but one that must be addressed primarily with non-military means.

How should members of the international community address terrorism? How do policy makers know which terrorist organizations to address and how best to address them? These questions can only be addressed in a cooperative or collaborative manner, understanding that there can be different perceptions of the nature of terrorism. While we might agree that groups that target innocent civilians are terrorists, we might also agree to note that their political motivations could have roots in real grievances. This is not to say that real grievances justify indiscriminate violence, but it does provide some space to make real gains to either delegitimize the terrorist group or legitimize state actions that address real grievances.

The first step to understanding the contextual basis of legitimacy is understanding security from the individual's point of view. This *human security* perspective opens up the security aperture in important ways.[14] When the UN presents aggregate data such as one billion people who lack access to clean water, two billion people who lack access to clean sanitation, three million people who die from water related diseases annually, 14 million (including 6 million children) who die from hunger annually, and 30 million people in Africa alone who die of HIV/AIDS, it primarily describes and reflects myriad human insecurities and the increasing global gap between the haves and the have-nots.[15]

While there are some commonalities among underdeveloped regions, they are far from all alike. One commonality, however, is that many of these transnational forces are directly harmful to people, do not recognize borders, and are particularly harmful to susceptible regions that are already suffering.

Human security is a concept that both describes these conditions and provides an approach to better understand their effects. The UN recognized this approach in a 1994 document:

> The concept of security has far too long been interpreted narrowly: as security of territory from external aggression, or as protection of national interests in foreign policy or as global security from the threat of nuclear holocaust. It has been related to nation-states more than people … *Forgotten were the legitimate concerns of ordinary people who sought security in their daily lives.* For many of them, security symbolized protection from the threat of disease, hunger, unemployment, crime [or terrorism], social conflict, political repression and environmental hazards. With the dark shadows of the Cold War receding, one can see that many conflicts are within nations rather than between nations.[16] (emphasis added)

Clearly, not all areas face the same insecurities or combination of insecurities that the UNDP categorizes in terms of economic, food, health, environmental, personal, community, and political.[17] As we have witnessed in our increasing global world, these insecurities frequently have diffuse global effects, such as migrations, reverberations in Diaspora communities, environmental impacts, and even the exportation of terrorism.[18] *The human security paradigm should remind strategists that they must approach issues holistically and empathetically; this painstaking analysis, patience, and tenacity is imperative to reach a set of realistic, achievable outcomes that are the result of understanding the problem, possible opportunities, and the identification of trade-offs and risks.*

Realistic, achievable outcomes

An effective human security framework and a set of guiding principles must be oriented on achieving realistic outcomes. While these outcomes will likely vary in time and place, failing to establish realistic, achievable ends will result in unfocused policies and the eventual loss of political will. It is often understood that a primary national interest is fostering a stable world order. Our national security strategies suggest that encouraging democracy would in fact lessen the *prevalence* of terrorism.[19] It is what we hope for in Iraq and Afghanistan. What does that mean exactly? Ralf Dahrendorf explains *stability as the sum of two key components: effectiveness and legitimacy.* He argues that for governments to work *two things have to be present: effectiveness and legitimacy. Effectiveness is a technical concept. It simply means that governments have to be able to do things which they claim they can do...they have to work. Legitimacy, on the other hand, is a moral concept. It means that what governments do have to be right ... A government is legitimate if what it does is right both in the sense of complying with certain fundamental principles, and in that of being in line with prevailing cultural values.*[20] (emphasis added)

Legitimacy, therefore, must be rooted in the people, not imposed. What this central concept suggests is that the means of attaining stability is all the more critical and achieving stability requires tireless efforts, perseverance, and tenacity. Small changes over time will make a difference. The United States and the international community must invoke strategic patience, while learning how to better tap non-military capital in ways that will make a difference. For the United States, this may require restructuring and properly resourcing its interagency process, so that the United States may effectively leverage all aspects of its power, such as diplomatic, economic, financial, agricultural, and commercial influences. Monitoring progress will be difficult but essential as policy makers, politicians, academics, business, nongovernmental organizations, and military leaders forge an adaptable way ahead.

Rethinking security

Diagnosing the problem

Tony Blair suggests that the first step in determining whether to intervene anywhere is to *diagnose the problem*.[21] Key to this process is to *understand* and *value* the *local* perspective. Understanding the problem often means that we must learn from past studies, bring forward important lessons, and re-evaluate assumptions. Bruce Hoffman notes that our failure has been an inability or perhaps an unwillingness to learn from the past:

> This inability to absorb and apply, much less even study, the lessons learned in previous counterinsurgency campaigns is a problem that has long afflicted the world's governments and militaries when they are confronted with insurgencies. Guerrilla Groups and terrorist organizations, on the other hand, learn lessons very well.[22]

To effectively diagnose the problem, one must understand that often there is a 'conflict eco-system' at play.[23] If you do not understand that eco-system, affecting change in one area may produce unwanted change in another. Thus as we think about the dynamic terrorist threat, it is a threat that is set against or exists in an eco-system. David Kilcullen, for example, addresses the many differences between the classical insurgent and the modern insurgent, dispelling many assumptions, given this complex 'conflict eco-system' that harbors numerous insurgent groups.[24] Therefore, it is important to rethink security – for whom, from whom, by whom, and with what means to better understand this eco-system.[25]

The human security framework sheds light on the importance of the local perspective as well as providing possible alternative courses of action. For example, while international terrorism may be a U.S. priority, local terrorism may not be the most pressing security problem for the host nation or its people. In many areas that are suffering from grave human insecurities, there are far more pressing issues that affect daily survival. Moreover, a foreign force's presence in a country, just by virtue of being there, changes the security environment. The infrastructure, whether it is new roads, bridges, or electric grids, that the military provides enables the population but also the adversary. Our actions may inadvertently create winners and losers. Even just moving vehicles may disrupt activities. Clearly, the simple acts of showing respect, reciprocity, and trust are extremely important at the individual engagement level. But even such acts grow tired in a country that is occupied by liberators. This empathic understanding is important.

We must also acknowledge that we may inadvertently be acting as an antibiotic, creating resistant strains of bacteria. Are our actions aiding the adaptability and resiliency of al-Qa'ida? Our traditional counterterrorism lens does not account for how we may actually be inadvertently providing the engine of innovation for AQ. If so, how do we respond? How do we become more networked versus hierarchical so that we ensure that we adapt ahead of our adversaries? Moreover, it is imperative that our behavior is guided by our values. Mistreatment or disrespect of local people may fuel insurgents or terrorist groups. In fact, detention centers can have generational effects.

Given that our adversaries are constantly adapting, it is important that we take a holistic approach in our study of these groups. In order to more comprehensively understand how to combat terrorism, we should understand the factors that lead to terrorism's resiliency. Often these factors are counterintuitive. One terrorist group whose survival depends on its unique resiliency mechanisms is al-Qa'ida in the Arabian Peninsula (AQAP). Common western assumptions regarding AQAP's resiliency consider the source of that resiliency to be a product of a weak Yemeni state and a tribal network that supports the group's existence. However, a recent Combating Terrorism Center (CTC) report suggests that rather than a weak Yemeni state and a supporting tribal network, the real source of AQAP's resiliency is the existence of a core group of leaders, a policy that avoids the indiscriminate killing of civilians, a sophisticated information operations effort, and a coherent strategy with nuanced rhetoric.[26] Additionally, while the recent deaths of Anwar al-'Awlaqi and Samir Khan have been touted as significant victories in the fight against AQAP, the CTC report suggests that America's focus on English-speaking AQAP members like these often comes at the expense of a deeper understanding of the terrorist group's local strategy and operations.[27] This example demonstrates the importance of understanding local dynamics as well to grasp the resiliency of an adversary group. An in-depth look at a different insurgent group, the Haqqani network, again reveals the importance of a holistic approach, one that strives to understand the local, regional, and global dynamics. A recent CTC report suggests that the counterterrorism community has failed to appreciate 'the global character of the Haqqani network and the central role it has played in the evolution of al-Qa'ida and the global jihadi movement.'[28] These two examples demonstrate that hard, deliberate, and continuous study is needed to properly diagnose the problem.

Assessing progress

This complex, uncertain, and unstructured environment presents a challenging landscape to assess progress. *Assessments* for understanding the building of legitimacy cannot be quantified; the assessment relies on the qualitative insights of the observer, which we tend to marginalize. Many times progress does not occur in a linear fashion, so an overreaction to backsliding may exacerbate the situation. For example, as a country democratizes and a terrorist group sees the window of opportunity closing, there may actually be a spike in violence. For Spain during the late 1970s and early 1980s, this was the case with ETA. Spain's continuing adherence to democratic principles allowed it to contain and marginalize ETA, while furthering the state's legitimacy.[29]

It is also extremely difficult to assess adversaries, for example AQ, which requires hard and continuous study as it constantly changes. A Combating Terrorism Center publication suggests the importance of assessing AQ across five dimensions: in terms of its power to destroy, power to inspire, power to humiliate, power to command, and power to unify.[30] AQ, while an organization of global goals and reach, is able to influence local contexts through inspiration messaging, such as Western humiliations of Muslim people.[31] Moreover AQ is diverse, which allows it to adapt to changing circumstances especially through mergers with other groups. 'These mergers not only serve as a force multiplier for al-Qa'ida, but they also effectively lower the barriers of entry ... creating increased opportunity and access for participation.'[32]

Arguably, it is difficult to study adversaries, especially terrorist groups like AQ, because as Bruce Hoffman notes:

> All terrorist movements throughout history have presented themselves as monoliths: united and in agreement over fundamental objectives, aims, strategies, tactics and targets. Too often their opponents succumb to such fiction and therefore fail to seize a critical opportunity to identify and exploit opportunities: by deepening existing and creating new sources of dissension, widening emergent ideological fault lines and driving wedges within movements based on internal disagreements. This approach of undermining terrorist groups from within has arguably been missing from the conduct of the war on terrorism.[33]

Moreover, it is difficult to distinguish among bandits, terrorists, smugglers, thugs, and perhaps other illicit activities that support people's livelihoods. Yet, by not distinguishing among them, there is grave risk of applying a strategy that might exacerbate the problem, misunderstand risks, or engage the wrong people.

Capitalizing on opportunities

Of course when we only look for threats, we miss *opportunities*. Empowering people through economics has come to the forefront in conflict-prone societies. General David Petraeus identified money as even more effective than ammunition in the campaigns in Iraq and Afghanistan when in the right hands.[34] This new dimension of military activity – expeditionary economics – suggests that grave human insecurity in many areas is a result of very little effective economic activity. There are some tools that the military has that may help it act as the paramedic before the civilian experts are able to assist with long term economic development.[35] Having said this, it is important to take the time to identify what economy does exist. What is currently being produced? How is it produced? And who benefits? There may be existing businesses that could be supported, and perhaps even local entrepreneurs.[36] These same observations along social structures, informal leaders, and formal leaders highlight existing power structures that may help with transitional efforts to alleviate human insecurities while addressing alternative ways forward.

Many practitioners and scholars rightfully question the practice of the west helping the rest. Answers can be found locally or from other non-western societies. In fact, General Petraeus' first observation in his article is regarding the importance of empowering the local people. He cites T.E. Lawrence: 'Do not try to do too much with your own hands.'[37] Collaboration between international and local communities is important to build local stakeholders on projects that are jointly planned and relevant. While the United States and its allies want and ought to help states counter terrorism, this help cannot be at the expense of the local people or such that real grievances are ignored.

What we have also found through our expeditionary economics work and other research is that women must be empowered; it cannot be an afterthought, but integral to any strategy designed to help societies stabilize and prosper. It is interesting to note David Galula's reasoning for empowering women. He says, 'Reflecting on who might be our potential allies in the population, I thought that the … women, given their subjugated condition, would naturally be on our side.'[38]

Interestingly, the UNDP's Arab Development Report cited the Arab world as suffering from three deficits: 'the freedom deficit; the women's empowerment deficit; and the human capabilities/knowledge deficit relative to income.'[39] In several countries in Africa, women's empowerment also rises to the fore as an important way ahead. Education of women directly affects human security factors, such as health, good agricultural practices, fertility rates, and child mortality rates. Educated women tend to ensure that their children are educated.

Trade-offs and managing risks

In the search for solutions we are confronted with uncomfortable realities. Brian Fishman and Assaf Moghadam ask uncomfortable questions regarding AQ. If it is not achieving its strategic goals how does it remain operationally capable? And if it is operationally capable, why isn't it achieving its strategic objectives? While it would seem that its internal divisions would necessarily make AQ weaker, why is it so resilient? How do we understand these divisions and what do they matter? What this discussion potentially suggests is that the best we can do is contain terrorist groups, marginalize them, and prevent them from inspiring, fueling, and supporting mass movements.

With every choice, there are trade-offs that must be acknowledged. This is a critical balance that must be struck as states weigh the trade-offs between liberty and security. The danger, of course, is to shift so much that governments and societies no longer reflect those values that define and guide them. The challenge is to find the right balance in a world faced with the transnational nature of dire security issues.

When urgent action must be taken, it is easier to operate unilaterally. The trade-off, depending on the situation, is the legitimacy of such actions. This is an especially careful consideration for the International Coalition as it assists Iraqi and Afghan security forces. The quick solution to what may appear to be urgent security actions may prompt, for example, a U.S. unit to take unilateral action, but of course such action may serve to de-legitimize the very forces they are charged to assist. Moreover, insurgents and terrorists try to provoke governments to take harsh retaliatory measures through violent actions. The trade-offs between urgency and legitimacy must be carefully weighed.

Of course, the adversary is also making such choices that we must understand, which is difficult. Martha Crenshaw distinguishes between terrorists who have an effect in the security environment, but not necessarily success, that is in producing the desired outcome. To evaluate a terrorist group's effect, one must just observe outcomes, but to assess the group's success, one must understand intentions.[40] The international community must also distinguish between having an effect, but not necessarily a desired effect or success. This is the balance between having a quick win in the short term, but realizing that it might undermine a longer term strategic goal.

Re-sizing the paradigm

Traditionally, we apply military solutions to security problems, especially when we have a narrowed view of security. The old saying, of course, is when all problems are viewed as nails, no need to use anything but a hammer. As noted earlier, the majority of security challenges do not fall cleanly in the traditional kinetic category. The human security framework highlights this reality by shedding light on the transnational, multi-faceted, and multi-dimensional nature of the security environment. As we rightly apply a human security lens and 'see' more comprehensively the multidimensional nature of security challenges, it is imperative that we re-assess roles and missions of militaries. Specifically, if war is a continuation of policy through other means as Clausewitz reminds us, then how do we bring to bear an integrated approach across all dimensions of power, while realizing that the non-linear and complex nature of the security environment requires overlapping jurisdictions of responsibility as Secretary Gates so plainly and eloquently states?

And no one nation can address the challenges that quite frankly face all of humanity. The human security approach calls for the sharing of intelligence, knowledge, and perspective in order to facilitate an integrated strategy in support of policy. As discussed earlier, one of the challenges is to identify *early* the indicators of terrorism, insurgency, or opportunity. The earlier the better to detect and take action. This is very difficult, but in order to shape the future, one must be open to different possibilities by not only sharing information, but applying different perspectives on the issues. Moreover, collaboration between international and local communities is important to build local stakeholders on projects that are jointly planned and relevant. While the United States and its allies want and ought to help states counter terrorism, this help cannot be at the expense of the local people or such that real grievances are ignored. This point does not suggest that everywhere there is terrorism the international community must embark on a full-out nation-building effort. Quite the contrary, in fact. If terrorism is deemed a national and international security threat, there are options and combinations of kinetic and non-kinetic approaches that can simultaneously address the terrorists kinetically, while holding state leaders accountable, and addressing the human insecurities in society. By fully diagnosing the problem in context and partnering among agencies internal to the U.S. government, local stakeholders, and the international community, a more cost-effective early approach is better than waiting until open conflict and war occurs at great costs. In other words, we offer a re-thinking of the tools to address what has been recognized as a security environment that presents primarily non-military challenges. And while the military must accept its role in this non-traditional context, it is time that the United States and the international community capitalize on the enormous but not yet fully tapped non-military elements of power that reside in the U.S. government, society, and international community.

Guiding principles

From this discussion, we offer guiding principles that inform strategic direction. We deliberately do not offer a highly detailed, cookie-cutter approach; the security environment demands otherwise. However, the human security lens facilitates some guiding principles that could best help inform not only decisions on whether to intervene but how to intervene with a better understanding of realistic outcomes. In fact, while these guiding principles hold whether they are in place at the highest levels of government or at the small military unit level, they are mostly aimed at the U.S. military.

- *Diagnose the problem*: admittedly, this is Tony Blair's first step, but we offer that the human security lens enables the right questions not only to best understand the changing dynamic of a terrorist organization but the context in which it is operating to include the regime and its leaders, as well as all the environmental factors that affect human survival and dignity.

- *Identify opportunities*: again, the human security approach facilitates the questions that highlight the economic, political, religious and societal landscape to include informal leaders. This process leads to empowering local stakeholders, to include women.
- *Collaboratively determine achievable outcomes*: while achieving national interests, the United States and the international community must view outcomes empathetically and in partnership with local stakeholders. In other words, there must be an empathetic understanding of the legitimacy formula as well as an understanding of the level of state effectiveness. It is too easy to impose our own views on such matters. Moreover, as the security environment changes, we must be willing to reassess outcomes.
- *Acknowledge that assessments are hard*: assessments are critical, but must also be acknowledged as difficult. Quantitative assessments do not adequately describe progress, given the non-linear nature of complex situations, and at worse, they could incentivize adverse behavior. For example, the tendency for western governments is to see progress even at the expense of empowerment. Subsequently, it is important that assessment criteria be established collaboratively to more firmly establish partnerships among local stakeholders to best achieve both legitimacy and effectiveness.
- *Understand trade-offs and manage risk*: the human security paradigm highlights trade-offs, especially if there are losers and winners involved in certain decisions. There may be trade-offs between short-term and long-term gains and between unilateral action and collaborative action. The important point is to acknowledge those trade-offs to better understand the risks involved to not only ensure informed decisions but better prepare for second and third order effects.
- *Be ready for full-spectrum operations*: the military must be ready for full spectrum operations in any situation. Even within a short span of distance, one local area may require immediate kinetic operations, while an adjoining area may require a non-kinetic approach. Given the short- and long-term uncertainties, the best hedge for now and in the future is competence across the full spectrum. It is upon this imperative that we focus the last guiding principles, developing aspects of our profession, individually and collectively.
- *Be self-aware*: the actions a military takes, even with the best intentions, may have adverse effects, especially if those actions include occupying another country. Units and service members affect the security environment; adversaries adapt, while over time the local populations can become weary.
- *Value human capital*: the imperative of full spectrum competence under complex and uncertain conditions require a diverse set of talents that must be valued. As the U.S. military engages in talent management, it must ensure that the professional requirements of its members align with the personnel bureaucracy that manages recruitment, retention, employment, and development.[41]
- *Continually professionalize ourselves and assist with professionalizing other militaries*: the military must ensure that its members continue to have the experiences, education, and training required to successfully face the complex challenges today and in the future. Second, the positive impact that the U.S. military has had professionalizing other militaries should not be under-estimated. Some argue that the U.S. military's impact on the Egyptian and Tunisian militaries greatly influenced those militaries' positive response to their societies during the Arab Spring.[42] Finally, build upon the interagency and coalition partnering that has occurred over the last decade. Educate and train alongside these partners.
- *Prepare future leaders both at home and abroad*: the challenges facing future leaders require strategic thinkers who embrace the warrior ethos and are guided by moral-ethical principles. In short, the United States and its allies require leaders of character. This point may seem

self-evident, but it is worth stating explicitly in the midst of budget stringency. And, the current programs at the Service Academies, War Colleges, and ROTC not only educate and develop the U.S. officer corps, but their international programs achieve tremendous effects around the world.[43] As our Secretary of Defense recently stated at West Point, we cannot expect our officers to succeed in these environments, unless we provide them with the right experiences, education, and incentives.[44] There is too much at stake to do any less.

It is sobering to know that fifty years ago, President Eisenhower remarked

> We face a hostile ideology global in scope, atheistic in character, ruthless in purpose, and insidious in method. Unhappily the danger it poses promises to be of indefinite duration. To meet it successfully, there is called for, not so much the emotional and transitory sacrifices of crisis, but rather those which enable us to carry forward steadily, surely, and without complaint the burdens of a prolonged and complex struggle – with liberty the stake. Only thus shall we remain, despite every provocation, on our charted course toward permanent peace and human betterment.[45]

Such a challenge requires strategic patience, perseverance, and tenacity. When peace-loving nations galvanize their efforts and commitment, much can be done. Freedom prevailed before over such an adversary and will again.

Notes

1 This work reflects the views of the authors and not the views of the U.S. government, Department of Defense, the U.S. Army, or West Point. The authors would like to thank several scholars in the Department of Social Sciences to include the Combating Terrorism Center, especially Michael Meese, Reid Sawyer, Liam Collins, Nelly Lahoud, Arie Perliger, Gabe Koehler-Derrick, Alex Gallo, Don Rassler as well as P.H. Liotta, Angelica Martinez, Assaf Moghadam, and Mark Crow. All have discussed portions of this paper especially as Cindy Jebb prepared several speeches and talks regarding this topic.

2 Robert M. Gates in a speech to the United States Military Academy on Friday, 25 February 2011, available online 1 March 2012 at http://www.defense.gov/speeches/speech.aspx?speechid=1539.

3 Robert Gates, 15 July 2008, Washington D.C. as cited in Mark Crow, 'Senior Conference XLVI, Bridging the Cultural Divide: NGO–Military Relations in Complex Environments,' Senior Conference Paper, 28–30 May 2009, West Point, New York.

4 Army doctrine refers to these operations as 'full-spectrum operations,' FM 5-0 (26 March 2010).

5 See Azza Karam, 'Transnational Political Islam and the USA: An Introduction,' in *Transnational Political Islam: Religion, Ideology and Power*, ed. Azza Karam (London: Pluto Press, 2004), p. 2.

6 The National Security Strategy, The White House, March 2006, 1.

7 The National Security Strategy, The White House, May 2010, 37.

8 The discussion about civic culture is from Gabriel A. Almond and Sidney Verba, *The Civic Culture: Political Attitudes and Democracy in Five Nations* (Princeton: Princeton University Press, 1963), p. 490. For a concluding discussion see pp. 473–505 as recounted in Cindy R. Jebb, P. H. Liotta, Thomas Sherlock, and Ruth Beitler, *The Fight for Legitimacy: Democracy vs. Terrorism* (Westport: Praeger Security International, 2006), pp. 7–8. The quotation is from Larry Diamond, 'The Global State of Democracy,' *Current History* 99, 641 (December 2000): 414.

9 Samuel P. Huntington, *Political Order in Changing Societies*, (New Haven: Yale University Press, 1968), p. 1.

10 Fareed Zakaria, 'The Rise of Illiberal Democracy,' *Foreign Affairs,* 76, 6 (November/December 1997): 24 and 43.

11 Amartya Sen, *Development as Freedom* (New York: Anchor Books, 1999), p. 298.

12 For a full discussion on the definition of terrorism, see Cindy R. Jebb, P. H. Liotta, Thomas Sherlock, and Ruth Beitler, *The Fight for Legitimacy: Democracy vs. Terrorism* (Westport: Praeger Security International, 2006), pp. 3–5.

13 Please see Cindy R. Jebb, Peter H. Liotta, Thomas Sherlock, and Ruth Beitler, *The Fight for Legitimacy: Democracy vs. Terrorism* (Westport: Praeger Security International, 2006), pp. 3–7, for a discussion on perceptions and definitions of terrorism. Bruce Hoffman's definition is from Bruce Hoffman, Lecture at West Point, April 2004; the Princeton Project reference comes from G. John Ikenberry and Anne-Marie Slaughter, *Forging a World of Liberty Under Law: U.S. National Security in the 21st Century*, The Woodrow Wilson School of Public and International Affairs, Princeton University, 27 September 2006: p. 9.

14 Note that this section is modified from Cindy R. Jebb, Laurel J. Hummel, Luis Rios, and Madelfia Abb, 'Human and Environmental Security in the Sahel: A Modest Strategy for Success,' in *Environmental Change and Human Security*, eds. P. H. Liotta et al. (The Netherlands: Springer Books, 2008), pp. 343–353.

15 'Part One: Towards a New Security Consensus,' *Report of the High-Level Panel on Threats, Challenges, and Change to the Secretary General*, available at http://www.un.org/secureorld/report.pdf (accessed 23 January 2006), p. 17. And as cited in Jebb et al., 'Human and Environmental Security,' p. 346.

16 United Nations Development Program (UNDP) Report, 1994, 3, pp. 22–23, as quoted by P. H. Liotta, *The Uncertain Certainty* (Lanham, Lexington, 2004), pp. 4–5.

17 UNDP, UN Development Report, Ch 2, 'New Dimensions of Human Security,' pp. 22–25 as cited in P.H. Liotta and Taylor Owen, 'Sense and Symbolism: Europe Takes on Human Security,' *Parameters* 36.3 (Autumn 2006): 90.

18 Also see Tedd Gurr, 'Why Minorities Rebel: Explaining Ethnopolitical Protest and Rebellion,' in *Minorities and Risk: A Global View of Ethnopolitical Conflicts* (United States Institute of Peace: October 1997), pp. 123–138 and Robert Kaplan, 'The Coming Anarchy,' *The Atlantic Monthly*, 273, issue 2 (February 1994): 44–76.

19 Jebb et al., *The Fight for Legitimacy*, 6.

20 Ralf Dahrendorf, 'On the Governability of Democracies,' in *Comparative Politics: Notes and Readings*, eds. Roy C. Macridis and Bernard Brown (Pacific Grove, California: Brooks/Cole Publishing Company, 1990), pp. 285–286. Also see Jebb et al., *The Fight for Legitimacy,* p. 7.

21 Tony Blair, 'Doctrine of the International Community,' in speech delivered to the Chicago Economic Club, 22 April 1999.

22 Bruce Hoffman, 'Foreword in David Galula,' *Pacification in Algeria:1956-1958,* available online 1 March 2012 at http://www.rand.org/pubs/monographs/2006/RAND_MG478-1.pdf, p. iii.

23 David Kilcullen, 'Counterinsurgency Redux,' available online at http://www.au.af.mil/au/awc/awcgate/uscoin/counterinsurgency_redux.pdf (Accessed Aug 13, 2013)

24 Kilcullen, 9–10.

25 This notion of security was discussed by P. H. Liotta in a presentation at West Point, New York, 11 January 2011.

26 Combating Terrorism Center, 'A False Foundation? AQAP, Tribes and Ungoverned Spaces in Yemen,' *Harmony Program*, (September 2011): 10.

27 Ibid.

28 Combating Terrorism Center, 'The Haqqani Nexus and the Evolution of al-Qa'ida,' *Harmony Program,* (July 2011): 2.

29 For more on this case, see Cindy R. Jebb, 'The Fight for Legitimacy: Liberal Democracy Versus Terrorism,' *The Journal of Conflict Studies*, XXIII, 1 (Spring 2003): 126–152.

30 Combating Terrorism Center, 'Al-Qa'ida's Five Aspects of Power,' *CTC Sentinel* 2, 1 (January 2009): 1.

31 Ibid., 2.

32 Ibid., 4.

33 *Self-Inflicted Wounds: Debates and Divisions Within al-Qa'ida*, eds. Brian Fishman and Assaf Moghadam, Combating Terrorism, West Point, 4.

34 David H. Petraeus, 'Learning Counterinsurgency: Observations from Soldiering in Iraq,' *Military Review* (January–February 2006), 4.

35 Jeff Peterson and Mark Crow, Senior Conference Paper, West Point, 2011.

36 See Mark Crow, 'Economics and Counterinsurgency,' a briefing to 10th Mountain Div, March 2011.

37 Petraeus, 3.

38 Hoffman cites Galula, vi.

39 *The Arab Human Development Report 2002: Creating Opportunities for Future Generations* (New York: United Nation's Human Development Programme), p. 27.

40 Martha Crenshaw, 'Terrorism in the Algerian War,' in *Terrorism in Context* (University Park: The Pennsylvania State University Press, 2001), p. 475.

41 See Talent Management Series beginning with: Casey Wardynski, David S. Lyle, and Michael Colarusso, *Towards a U.S. Army Officer Corps Strategy for Success: A Proposed Human Capital Model Focused Upon Talent*, Strategic Studies Institute, April 2009.

42 Nelly Lahoud, David DiMeo, Cindy Jebb, Arie Perliger, Ruth Beitler and John Ringquist, *The Arab Spring: An Investment in Durable Peace*, 29 June 2011, White Paper, West Point, New York.

43 Ibid.

44 Secretary of Defense Robert M Gates speech delivered 25 February 2011 to the Corps of Cadets at West Point, New York.

45 President Dwight D. Eisenhower, 'Farewell Address to the Nation,' 17 January 1961.

PART III

Human security actors

17

THE UNITED NATIONS AND HUMAN SECURITY: BETWEEN SOLIDARISM AND PLURALISM

Edward Newman

Human security appears to be at the heart of much of the UN's work. The organization's Charter, its humanitarian programmes and agencies, and the normative ideas it promotes all appear to point towards a people-centred worldview, and the modern human security movement owes much to a UN report which popularized the concept in 1994. However, there is a paradox in the UN's association with human security, and this has implications for the operationalization of human security more broadly.

Human security, taken to its logical conclusion, holds 'critical' implications for the way politics and economics are organized: it challenges the values and institutions which currently exist as they relate to human welfare, and it questions the interests that are served by these values and institutions. Above all, human security is solidarist in a cosmopolitan sense: it implies moral obligations towards humans across borders, and that free and secure individuals are the foundation of peace and security between and within states.[1] Yet, in reality, the UN is in many ways inherently quite conservative. Instead of taking a 'critical' approach to human security, it attempts to promote human security within the existing political, legal and normative constraints of the 'real world'. It promotes and protects state sovereignty in a conventional Westphalian way. In addition, instead of being truly solidarist, the UN – at least at the level of states – embraces a pluralist view of international politics and humanity. That is, it promotes the idea that order in international society is based upon cooperation and rules amongst independent sovereign states, and norms including non-interference. According to this, there is no consensus on issues of justice and rights, and – except in extreme circumstances – differences amongst states must be tolerated.

There are certainly interesting developments in the twenty-first century which suggest that the UN, as a collectivity and as an actor, is moving closer to a meaningful role as a promoter and agent of human security – such as the human protection agenda, and the broadening definition of security that is being embraced throughout the organization – even though this is not necessarily expressed in the language of 'human security'. However, the commitment of the UN to human security seems to be limited in fundamental ways as a result of its nature and structure. Can these tensions be reconciled? Are policy-oriented human security initiatives inevitably undermined by their co-option into statist agendas? Is the radical, emancipatory promise of the concept of human security blunted when it is exposed to policy, or can policy-oriented human security initiatives have a positive impact from within?

Human security

In its broadest sense, human security seeks to place the individual as the referent object of security, rather than – although not necessarily in opposition to – constructions such as state sovereignty and 'national security'. In broad terms human security is 'freedom from want' and 'freedom from fear': positive and negative freedoms and rights as they relate to fundamental individual needs.[2] Human security is normative; it argues that there is an ethical responsibility to re-orient security around the individual, and much human security scholarship is therefore explicitly or implicitly underpinned by a solidarist or cosmopolitan commitment. Some human security scholarship also seeks to present explanatory arguments concerning the nature of security, deprivation and conflict. In addition, many scholars and practitioners working on human security emphasize the policy orientation of this approach; they believe that the concept of human security can and should result in policy changes which improve the welfare of people.

Growing interest in human security since the early 1990s can be seen within a particular historical and social context which saw challenges to the narrow, state-centric, militarized national security paradigm which had dominated academic and policy thinking for decades. This background is well documented elsewhere and need not be examined closely here.[3] There is no uncontested definition of, or approach to, human security; very few supporters of the concept would describe it as a 'paradigm' (although it has been described as such).[4] Like most non-traditional security approaches, human security – as a starting point – challenges orthodox neorealist conceptions of international security. Scholars of human security argue that for many people in the world – perhaps even most – the greatest threats to 'security' come from internal conflicts, disease, hunger, environmental contamination or criminal violence. And for others, a greater threat may come from their own state itself, rather than from an 'external' adversary. Human security thus seeks to challenge attitudes and institutions that privilege so-called 'high politics' above individual experiences of deprivation and insecurity. This is not to presume that human security is necessarily in conflict with state security; the state can and should be a key provider of security in ideal circumstances. Human security does, however, suggest that international security traditionally defined – territorial integrity – does not necessarily correlate with human security, and that an over-emphasis upon state security can be to the detriment of human welfare needs. So, traditional conceptions of state security are a necessary but not sufficient condition of human welfare. The citizens of many states that are 'secure' according to the traditional concept of security can be personally perilously insecure to a degree that demands a reappraisal of the concept of security.

Human security also raises important implications for the evolution of state sovereignty. Traditionally, state sovereignty and sovereign legitimacy rest upon a government's control of territory, state independence and recognition by other states. The role of citizens is to support this system. The human security approach reverses this equation: the state – and state sovereignty – must serve and support the people from which it (in theory) draws its legitimacy. The concept of 'conditional sovereignty' has therefore – in theory at least – taken on a renewed importance through human security: the international legitimacy of state sovereignty rests not only on control of territory, but also upon fulfilling certain standards of human rights and welfare for citizens. As a corollary, the sovereignty of states that are unwilling or unable to fulfil certain basic standards may be questionable. All approaches to human security agree that the referent of security policy and analysis should be the individual, but they disagree about which threats the individual should be protected from, and what means should be employed to achieve this protection.

Human security, policy, and the UN

Engagement with policy, and a desire to change security policy in 'progressive' ways, is at the heart of the human security movement: the community of scholars and practitioners, including civil society, working to promote individuals and communities as the beneficiary of security analysis and practice. However, some critical approaches to human security – and some critical scholars who challenge the concept of human security – are sceptical of 'policy oriented' approaches to human security. Indeed, some scholars have argued that the mainstreaming of human security in the UN and in other national and international contexts does not represent a paradigm shift in favour of human emancipation; it has even reinforced existing power structures and relationships.[5] According to this line of reasoning, human security can never overcome its central paradox: it apparently calls for a critique of the structures and norms that produce human insecurity, yet the ontological starting point of most human security scholarship and its policy orientation endorse and perpetuate these structures and norms. Some scholars have sought to explore ways in which the human security concept can remain intellectually challenging but also policy-relevant, but for many observers this is an uncomfortable duality.[6]

From a mainstream, policy-oriented, perspective, human security is naturally at the heart of much of the UN's work. The Charter sanctifies 'We the peoples' and reaffirms faith in fundamental human rights, the dignity and worth of the human person, and the equal rights of men and women. It emphasizes justice and social progress and better standards of life in larger freedom. The popularity of the concept since the 1990s – at least in the policy world – is partly attributable to the work of the UN Development Programme and other UN agencies. Indeed, UNDP's 1994 Human Development Report was a milestone in the international evolution of human security and it successfully disseminated the concept to a global audience.[7]

The civil, political, social and economic rights embodied in the major human rights instruments codified or promoted by the UN represent an elaborate framework of international human rights.[8] In addition, a wide range of UN agencies and programmes work directly on enhancing the health and welfare of humans, including the World Health Organization, the Food and Agricultural Organization, the UN Development Programme, the High Commissioner for Refugees, and the High Commissioner for Human Rights. Other developments also seem to strengthen this commitment to human security. The Millennium Development Goals, adopted by the UN General Assembly in 2000, provide a human-oriented path to peace and development including the eradication of extreme poverty and hunger, the achievement of universal primary education, and the promotion of gender equality. This was complemented by the Global Compact, launched in 2000 to 'give a human face to the global market.'[9]

Some institutional developments arguably also illustrate the growing support for human security – in name or ethos – within the UN. For example, the Office of the Special Representative for the Prevention of Genocide and Mass Atrocities, the Special Representative of the Secretary-General for Children and Armed Conflict, the Special Adviser to the Secretary-General on Gender Issues and Advancement of Women, and a Special Adviser for the 'Responsibility to Protect'.

The normative leadership of some senior UN officials – including the Secretary-General – has also arguably strengthened the human security focus, even when this has been controversial. Kofi Annan championed the ideas of human security and individual sovereignty, concepts that can be in tension with norms of state sovereignty.[10] The UN has also incubated the *Responsibility to Protect* (R2P) idea. Before and after the release of the 2001 R2P report middle powers such as Canada sought to use UN forums to promote various visions of human security, and the concept itself has been the subject of a number of thematic debates in the UN. This has been very significant. In arguing for a 'modern' understanding of state sovereignty in the context of changing norms the R2P report has had a huge impact on debates related to peace and security and individual rights.[11] The momentum of R2P – which began as a human security initiative, despite the efforts made to separate the two concepts in subsequent years – has been quite remarkable. The R2P concept has been the subject of a report of the Secretary-General to the General Assembly, and a debate amongst UN member states.[12] The UN Secretary-General's High-level Panel on Threats, Challenges and Change also endorsed the R2P concept throughout its pages. More significantly, the 2005 World Summit Outcome document, agreed amongst UN member states, contains an explicit endorsement of R2P.[13]

Although many analysts and governments prefer to distance R2P from human security, by many definitions of human security the use of military force to prevent war crimes, crimes against humanity and genocide is clearly relevant. Therefore, recent UN resolutions and decisions on the protection of civilians appear to point towards a greater UN engagement with the R2P – and thus the human security – concept. After being endorsed at the UN World Summit in 2005, it has featured in a number of UN resolutions. UN Security Council resolution 1973, passed on 17 March 2011, authorized member states to take all necessary measures to protect civilians under threat of attack in Libya. UN action in Côte d'Ivoire in 2010 also suggested that the 'protection agenda' – a central human security principle – was becoming more robust at the UN. According to Bellamy and Williams, resolution 1973 broke new ground as the first time that the Security Council had authorized the use of force for human protection purposes against the wishes of a functioning state; 'international society is now explicitly focused on civilian protection'.[14]

The UN reform process and a number of landmark reports and initiatives also appear to illustrate that foreign policy thinking at the UN has internalized key human security messages (at least in substance, if not always expressed explicitly as 'human security'). In November 2003, UN Secretary-General Kofi Annan observed that 'the past year has shaken the foundations of collective security and undermined confidence in the possibility of collective responses to our common problems and challenges. It has also brought to the fore deep divergences of opinion on the range and nature of the challenges we face, and are likely to face in the future.' He announced a High-level Panel on Threats, Challenges and Change (HLP) made up of various luminaries, including political leaders. The Panel's report provided something of an endorsement of the human security approach.[15] Indeed, one half of the HLP report's definition of a security threat reflects the human security concept: 'any event or process that leads to large-scale death or lessening of life chances and undermines states as the basic unit of the international system.'[16] The report focused upon six clusters of security threats: economic and social threats, including poverty, infectious disease and environmental degradation; inter-state conflict; internal conflict, including civil war, genocide and other large-scale atrocities; nuclear, radiological, chemical and biological weapons; terrorism; and transnational organized crime. Clearly, the first and third of these clusters emphasizes areas of concern that are central to the human security argument.

A further aspect of the HLP report that supports the human security movement was its emphasis upon the inter-connections amongst security challenges, whether traditional or human: 'Every threat to international security today enlarges the risk of other threats.'[17] Thus, human deprivation, malnutrition and disease can have negative repercussions for more conventional security issues. The report argued that international terrorist groups prey on weak states for sanctuary, and that poverty, infectious disease, environmental degradation and war feed on one another. The idea of interconnections amongst security challenges comes through particularly well in the following passage, which also embraces the human insecurity dimension:

Civil war, disease and poverty increase the likelihood of State collapse and facilitate the spread of organised crime, thus also increasing the risk of terrorism and proliferation due to weak States and weak collective capacity to exercise the rule of law. Preventing mass-casualty terrorism requires a deep engagement to strengthen collective security systems, ameliorate poverty, combat extremism, end the grievances that flow from war, tackle the flow of infectious disease and fight organised crime.[18]

The sections of the HLP report relating to state sovereignty are more or less also in line with the human security ethos: 'It clearly carries with it the obligation of a State to protect the welfare of its own people …'[19] As a corollary, the report also acknowledges that this 'responsibility to protect' conditions modern ideas of sovereignty; in situations where a state is unable or unwilling to fulfil basic standards of human rights, that responsibility may shift to the international community.

A further key report of the UN was the Secretary-General's reform report *In Larger Freedom*, which also endorses the 'responsibility to protect' concept. The report states that 'the time has come for Governments to be held to account, both to their citizens and to each other, for respect of the dignity of the individual, to which they too often pay only lip service.'[20] It continues,

> If national authorities are unable or unwilling to protect their citizens, then the responsibility shifts to the international community to use diplomatic, humanitarian and other methods to help protect the human rights and well-being of civilian populations. When such methods appear insufficient, the Security Council may out of necessity decide to take action under the Charter of the United Nations, including enforcement action, if so required.[21]

A key thrust of this report is that development, security and human rights are mutually dependent:

> Not only are development, security and human rights all imperative; they also reinforce each other. This relationship has only been strengthened in our era of rapid technological advances, increasing economic interdependence, globalisation and dramatic geopolitical change. While poverty and denial of human rights may not be said to 'cause' civil war, terrorism or organised crime, they all greatly increase the risk of instability and violence. Similarly, war and atrocities are far from the only reasons that countries are trapped in poverty, but they undoubtedly set back development. Again, catastrophic terrorism on one side of the globe, for example an attack against a major financial centre in a rich country, could affect the development prospects of millions on the other by causing a major economic downturn and plunging millions into poverty. And countries which are well governed and respect the human rights of their citizens are better placed to avoid the horrors of conflict and to overcome obstacles to development.[22]

Interestingly, some authors have suggested that human security has effectively been dropped from the UN agenda, and that human security is a failed concept within the UN. As Martin and Owen have observed, the human security concept within the UN has been problematized by its ambiguous relationship with human rights and human development, and its conceptual overstretch.[23] Some of its earlier supporters – such as Canada – have lost interest in the concept of human security as an explicit foreign policy framework. Other states are more openly sceptical of the concept. The language of human security is therefore not so visible in recent key UN documents, especially in comparison with the Kofi Annan years, in which, for example, the Secretary-General gave prominence to the idea in the 2000 report *We the People*.[24] However, even though some key reports have not explicitly referred to human security – because the concept is undoubtedly sensitive amongst some UN member states – this does not mean that the fundamental concept is not present in the UN. This is surely human security in everything but name: 'We will not enjoy development without security, we will not enjoy security without development and we will not enjoy either without respect for human rights.'[25] The High Level Panel Report preferred to focus on a new form of collective security rather than 'human security', but the message is similar. Moreover, there certainly are still UN initiatives and programmes that are explicitly couched in the language of human security, most obviously the Secretary-General's 2010 report on the topic.[26]

Of course, the reports of the HLP and the Secretary-General are not a demonstration of – or even a commitment to – action on the part of the governments of the world. Nevertheless, they do reflect an emerging normative consensus, and are not completely divorced from the 'real world' of policy. After all, the Secretary-General's report was drafted, with specific policy recommendations, with governments in mind, and often in consultation with UN member states. Yet only governments can accept or reject the proposals, not international civil servants. We saw an indication of the response of UN member states in the form of the statements of the high-level plenary meeting of the General Assembly, which took place in September 2005 and included an endorsement of 'human security as a means to empower people.'[27] It also endorsed the theoretical thrust of those earlier reports in stating that 'development, security and human rights form the indispensable foundations for collective security and well-being' and that development, security and human rights are mutually dependent and reinforcing.[28] In line with this, the report demands an end to impunity and recommends steps for promoting international accountability.

The final 2005 World Summit Outcome maintained much of this message, including the interrelationship between development, security and human rights, which is a theme which explicitly runs through the whole declaration. The declaration gives prominence to the fundamental importance of development and the Millennium Development Goals – as expected – but it is in areas related to human rights and governance that the declaration is interesting from a human security perspective. The emphasis upon promoting good governance and, explicitly, democracy, is progressive. It was not so long ago that a UN role in the process of democracy and democratisation was considered to be controversial, given the sensitivities that exist in international politics towards anything that implies intervention or an encroachment upon state sovereignty. The 2005 World Summit Outcome promoted democracy as a universal value and emphasized the idea that 'democracy, development and respect for all human rights and fundamental freedoms are interdependent and mutually reinforcing'.[29]

A number of other developments illustrate the apparent movement towards the UN's adoption of the human security concept in more practical ways. The UN Trust Fund for Human Security was established in 1999 with the aim of 'promoting human security through the protection and empowerment of people and communities threatened in their survival, livelihood and dignity', mainly based upon resources donated by Japan.[30] Since 1999, the Trust Fund has committed over 350 million dollars to human security projects in over 70 countries.[31] The Human Security Unit was established in 2004 in the United Nations Office for the Coordination of Humanitarian Affairs to 'integrate human security in all UN activities'.[32] The unit is involved in allocating the trust fund resources to worthy programmes and initiatives, and disseminating and promoting activities on human security, with the emphasis upon translating the human concept into 'concrete' programmes which improve the lives of people on the ground. Following the 2005 World Summit the UN hosted the launch of the Friends of Human Security, a group of states interested in promoting the concept.

Such diplomatic niceties do not always have a great deal of meaning in reality, and the Summit Outcome did water down the messages of the High Level Report and the Secretary-General's 'In Larger Freedom' report. However, these reports, and even the Summit Outcome, go beyond the usual UN banalities in their promotion of human security ideas. Above all, the explicit endorsement in the Summit Outcome of the Responsibility to Protect, and the frequent reference to the concept in subsequent years, is a step forward for UN member states.

The paradox

It would appear that the UN is a key actor in promoting the human security idea, translating human ideas into policy and providing a forum for state leadership in human security initiatives – even if such activities are not necessarily undertaken within the specific language of 'human security'. However, there is a paradox. Thinking about human security in and around the UN reflects a tension between 'problem solving' and 'critical' approaches, and this exposes some uncomfortable home truths about the whole concept of human security, especially as it relates to policy. As Robert Cox has famously suggested, problem-solving approaches take prevailing social and power relationships and the institutions into which they are organized as the given framework for actions. In contrast, critical approaches call these into question, and question how institutions emerged and are maintained.[33] If human security is to be a meaningful challenge to orthodox security ideas and practices, it must essentially be critical in outlook.

In reality, the UN – both in terms of institutional programmes and intergovernmental action – does not take a critical approach to human security. It reflects, defends and works – as a collective group of states and an international civil service – within the existing norms and institutions and seeks to address human security within this 'reality'. The UN essentially works within a problem-solving approach to human security, and this will always impose severe limitations upon its promotion and protection of the concept, especially when human security conflicts with institutions such as sovereignty or the free market. Despite the good work done by committed individuals within various programmes and initiatives, the structural constraints mean that it is unlikely that the UN can act as an agent of fundamental transformation or emancipation. UN human security programmes adopt a policy-oriented approach which attempts to improve human welfare within the political, legal and practical parameters of the 'real world', assuming the integrity of prevailing policy approaches and norms. The UN's human security initiatives do not *fundamentally* question existing structures and institutions of power, gender, and distribution in relation to economic and political organization. The UN, while in some ways promoting the individual as the referent object of security even when this is in tension with the state, is more likely to see a strong state as a necessary requirement for individual security, even though many member states of the UN have dubious human rights records.

Human security at the UN also demonstrates a tension between cosmopolitan solidarist and pluralist values. As an organization based upon sovereign states, the UN reflects a pluralist view of international politics, and this has implications for its approach to human security. The pluralist view of international society emphasizes the sanctity of sovereign states, mutual recognition, and non-interference into the jurisdiction of other states. Pluralism essentially tolerates different value systems and does not make judgements about different forms of justice and rights. A pluralist view of international relations therefore emphasizes the rules of coexistence which sustain international order and peace amongst states, rather than issues of justice within states. Pluralists argue that this is in the interests of international peace and security, which is also in the interests of the citizens of states.

Within this pluralist worldview, there can clearly be a tension between order and justice. The citizens of certain states may be deprived of individual human rights and needs, but since international order is based upon an international society of states which accept rules of cooperation and co-existence, this deprivation is (except in the most extreme circumstances) tolerable, or rather it is a domestic issue. It is primarily the responsibility of states – not international actors – to serve the interests of their citizens (even though many states will not or cannot). The legal, political and moral obligations of governments must be to their own citizens; this obligation does not extend across borders, because this would be practically and morally impossible.

According to pluralism, there may be, therefore, a tension between justice – or human security – and international order, but it is in everyone's interests that international order is prioritized. To ignore this would threaten the basis of interstate order (which is the highest goal) by opening the door to wars of intervention, or to ride roughshod over relativist cultural or political rights. This is also in line with the legalist view of international politics. Clearly, the UN has moved beyond this absolutist vision of pluralism; a range of activities and initiatives, including the organization's conditional endorsement of R2P, indicates that the 'domestic' concerns of member states – relating to human rights, conflict and governance – are no longer off the international agenda. However, the pluralist view of international politics is fundamentally embodied in the UN. The UN Charter and a plethora of landmark resolutions champion self-determination and sovereignty as a fundamental norm – even above human rights – and this is in tension with the cosmopolitan values of human security. The UN is therefore inherently quite conservative. It promotes and protects state sovereignty in quite a conventional Westphalian way which arguably lags behind normative and empirical changes occurring on the ground and in civil society.

Human security, 'critical' theory, and solidarism

Human security is fundamentally 'critical' and solidarist, and the structure of the UN – both in terms of member states and UN programmes – essentially obstructs it from taking such an approach.

A critical approach questions – and if necessary challenges – the institutions of 'reality'. A critical approach to human security raises questions about existing policy assumptions and the interests they serve, and this may lead us to challenge existing constructions, such as state sovereignty, 'high politics', the liberal market economy, and the 'national interest'. Critical approaches question or challenge prevailing structures of power and power relations, and also prevailing discourses or ways of thinking. Clearly, a critical approach to human security that challenges fundamental ideas such as state sovereignty and free market economics is not at home at the United Nations.

If human security is ultimately 'solidarist', then there are also obviously limitations to the UN's pluralist approach to human security. A pluralist international system based upon non-interference allows human rights abuses and extreme differences of welfare amongst humans behind the legal shield of sovereignty. For solidarists, the legitimacy of states, and the international system, is tied to justice for individual people. Ultimately, a human security outlook would view international relations as a cosmopolitan society of humans, not of states. According to this, universal justice, transcending state boundaries, can and does exist.

Thus, according to the solidarists, governments have a moral responsibility not only to the protection and defence of the citizens of their own countries, but also to the citizens of other countries. Solidarists therefore conclude that 'states that massively violate human rights should forfeit their right to the treated as legitimate sovereigns, thereby morally entitling other states to use force to stop the oppression.'[34] In order to be legitimate, an international system must uphold minimum standards of common humanity. 'State sovereignty' is a social construction; it is not a natural or inevitable phenomenon; it can therefore be challenged on moral grounds.

Even with the apparent endorsement of R2P, these ideas are not embodied in the United Nations, as an organization based upon principles of sovereignty and non-interference. Therefore, from a 'critical' and a solidarist perspective, there are real (structural) limitations to the UN's commitment to human security. It is true that actors – individuals and organizations – can work in the interests of human security even within such constraints and the value of this must not be downplayed. No one, for example, questions the commitment of staff in organizations such as the UN Development Programme, the World Health Organization, the Food and Agricultural Organization – and many others – to alleviate deprivation and human insecurity in the world. The impact of this work, moreover, improves the lives of millions of people in the developing world.

However, despite the UN's apparent commitment to human security, the limitations are obvious. UN member states acquiesce in the face of huge differences in income and welfare around the world; commitment to the realization of the Millennium Development Goals is a woeful indicator of the fundamental unwillingness of states to address deprivation in the developing world. Despite the higher profile of issues of human rights on the UN agenda, there is a remarkable tolerance of human rights abuses inside member states, despite the reformulation of the UN's human rights apparatus. The failure of UN member states to formulate a rigorous framework for addressing civil war and even genocide – whilst preferring ad hoc, case-by-case approaches to such challenges – is also symptomatic of the UN's embodiment of 'international society'.

Martin and Owen rightly observe that the primary lesson of the problematic UN experience with human security is that 'institutionalization cannot compensate for poor conceptualization'.[35] This is certainly true, but the constraints within which the UN works can more fundamentally be attributed to the UN's pluralist and 'problem-solving' approach, at the level of governments and also international civil servants. Of course there is concern for poor, malnourished and oppressed people. But the solutions are considered from the perspective of existing norms and policy assumptions as the starting point, and through a pluralist view of politics which sees stable states as the foundation of international society – not individuals. The UN's lowest-common-denominator approach to human security expressed in the Secretary-General's 2010 report – no doubt designed to assuage the concerns of some member states – observes that 'Human security is based on a fundamental understanding that Governments retain the primary role for ensuring the survival, livelihood and dignity of their citizens. It is an invaluable tool for assisting Governments in identifying critical and pervasive threats to the welfare of their people and the stability of their sovereignty'.[36] The report does not (because it separates the Responsibility to Protect from human security) consider the possibility that governments may not be willing or able to address critical and pervasive threats to human welfare; it clearly sees state sovereignty and governments as the essential framework for promoting human security. It calls for 'people-centred' approaches to security and wellbeing without considering the structural factors which result in deprivation and insecurity.

This points to a fundamental challenge – that has relevance far beyond the UN – in attempting to apply the human security concept to policy. The human security concept focuses on the needs of individuals as a priority for security policy, but in order to have an impact, the concept must to a large degree work within existing policy frameworks – it must influence or be internalized by policy elites whose interests are not necessarily served by new security ideas or practices. For this reason, it is within existing policy frameworks and assumptions that human insecurities have emerged. For critical social scientists this tension undermines the credibility of the human security concept as a means of emancipating vulnerable people and addressing deprivation. For this reason, the manner in which human security has been adopted in various national and international policy circles – including the UN – is deeply troubling for some critical scholars. According to this, human security is, in theory and practice, not a radical, emancipatory paradigm shift; it has been willingly co-opted by states but in reality has little positive impact upon policy.[37] Seeing human security described in the UN Secretary-General's report as a 'tool for governments' does lead one to wonder if the concept of human security should still be seen – as it once was – as a radical alternative to orthodox models of security.[38]

In contrast, other scholars interested in human security hold out hope that the promotion of the idea of human security in policy contexts can have a net benefit and is therefore a worthwhile pursuit.[39] Can this fundamental tension be reconciled? Does the structure and normative foundation of the UN obstruct it from playing a genuine role in promoting and protecting human security?

Conclusion

Aside from the tensions between solidarism and pluralism and between 'problem-solving' and critical approaches, there are other political reasons why the UN is limited in promoting and protecting human security. There are fundamental disagreements about how progress in human welfare should be promoted, and also problems over the interventionist connotations. Indeed, there are connotations of 'human rights imperialism', and some observers associate human security with the Western agenda of promoting (or imposing) 'liberal' values.[40] This is illustrated by the association between human security and humanitarian intervention and the changing norms regarding state sovereignty and human rights. Referring to the 1999 'humanitarian intervention' into the former Yugoslavia, Lloyd Axworthy, Canada's former foreign minister, stated that

> the crisis in Kosovo, and the Alliance's response to it, is a concrete expression of this human security dynamic at work … The concept of human security establishes a new measure for judging the success or failure of national and international security politics, namely: do these policies improve the protection of civilians from state-sponsored aggression and civil, especially ethnic, conflict?[41]

Even the UN Secretary-General, Kofi Annan, known to support the human security idea, described a 'developing international norm in favour of intervention to protect civilians from wholesale slaughter and suffering and violence'.[42] This approach to human security has alienated the concept from many UN member states.

There have also been concerns that the policy community's use of the human security idea is distorting its true meaning. For example, the Philippine government's 2007 Human Security Act is essentially an 'anti-terror law' which would warrant special counter-terrorism measures and – according to critics – encroach upon human rights. Less controversially, the EU has embraced the human security concept for some of its external relations issues – including peacekeeping – but this is an application which nevertheless raises connotations of a 'liberal' vision of how the world should be organized.

The consequence of this has been that – in the UN and elsewhere – the human security concept has been controversial. Some governments in the developing world – which, in theory, is meant to be the primary beneficiary of human security ideas – have been noticeably cool towards human security ideas, because they tend to see it as a northern, liberal movement with interventionist connotations. The speeches made during the UN General Assembly thematic debate on human security on 22 May 2008 were an illustration of the ambivalence of many states towards the concept.[43] This ambivalence comes not only from ideological disagreement, but also the feeling that human security is a distraction that allows states to publicly 'commit' to a progressive idea without addressing the underlying and fundamental sources of insecurity and deprivation. As Martin and Owen have observed, this has resulted in something of a retreat by the UN in the explicit use of the human security concept.[44]

However, the tensions between solidarism and pluralism and between 'problem-solving' and critical approaches form a more fundamental challenge for the UN in the area of human security. At present the UN's commitment to human security is contingent or possibly ambivalent. It shows signs of leadership in human security (sometimes amongst states or groups of states, sometimes by international civil servants) and achieves progress but this is always contingent on the nature of the inter-state environment that the UN embodies. As long as the UN is embedded in a (fairly orthodox) Westphalian conception of international relations, the tensions will remain. Indeed, in some ways, the attention to human security ideas is a reflection, like the 'security-development nexus', of enlightened self-interest in the context of the new security agenda. In this sense powerful states see challenges in the developing world – state failure, conflict and poverty – as a non-traditional threat to their own security, rather than a 'human security tragedy' that needs to be addressed for its own sake.[45] Indeed, there is little evidence that states pursue human security initiatives when that would be contrary to their interests, traditionally conceived. The dilemmas of human security at the UN are reflected in public policy more generally. Can the UN move to a post-Westphalian future which would embrace solidarist aspirations? The paradox and tensions can be addressed (but probably never overcome) in a number of ways, but these solutions will not be supported by scholars across the whole range of different approaches to human security.

Fundamentally, a mobilization of cosmopolitan humanitarianism at the public level would bring about a transformation in public politics which might genuinely promote the human security movement within the UN. But this is surely difficult to achieve. Enlightened leadership by states and groups of states, in partnership with non-governmental organizations, can achieve progress that has a net benefit for individuals. For example, the Human Security Network, and leadership initiatives that were seen in Canada's Security Council performance under the theme of human security can achieve modest human security breakthroughs. The ban on anti-personnel landmines, the Jubilee 2000 developing world debt forgiveness movement, and the international criminal court are some examples. Yet surely there will always be limitations to 'statist' human security initiatives.

This raises a fundamental problem for human security as a movement. Can 'policy-relevant' human security ideas ever be meaningful if they, by necessity, must work within – and thus endorse – existing policy frameworks? Some critical scholars are highly sceptical of the policy orientation of the concept for this reason; 'the moment where human security might have served as a heterodox challenge to mainstream security practices has passed, and the concept has itself become a new orthodoxy'.[46] In contrast, others suggest human security can remain a radical theoretical concept with policy relevance, albeit within constraints.[47] The bottom line is that human security must, amongst other things, expose the structural pathologies in economics and politics which give rise to terrible human suffering and deprivation. Unfortunately, the mainstreaming of human security within the UN, whilst achieving some incremental successes, fails on this important point. This points to a tension – amply exposed at the UN – between human security as an intellectual concept and as a policy orientation.[48]

The human security movement – in both its intellectual and policy incarnations – may need to more directly confront the internal inconsistencies which exist within the concept, and especially its policy applications. This involves accepting the constraints which exist in approaching human security and policy, and being more conscious of structural 'realities' as a starting point. In policy terms, human security could hardly be called a paradigm-shifting or emancipatory movement; at best, it would be an incremental, contingent process within an imperfect system. Would this undermine the credibility of human security as a theoretical concept? There is no satisfactory answer. Clearly, however, there are fundamental differences between the theoretical concept of human security and its policy application.

Notes

1 Buzan uses solidarism to describe international societies with a high degree of shared norms, rules and institutions among states, where there is cooperation over a wide range of issues – including human rights – which goes far beyond coexistence. See Barry Buzan, *From International to World Society? English School Theory and the Social Structure of Globalisation*, Cambridge: Cambridge University Press, 2004. However, solidarism has also been used to specifically describe a cosmopolitan project as a part of these shared international norms, and it is with this meaning that the concept is used in this chapter.

2 S. Neil MacFarlane and Yuen Foong-Khong, *Human Security and the UN: A Critical History*, Bloomington: Indiana University Press, 2006; *Human Security Now: Commission on Human Security*, New York: United Nations, 2003; Shahrbanou Tadjbakhsh and Anuradha Chenoy, *Human Security: Concepts and Implications*, London: Routledge, 2006; Edward Newman, 'Human security and constructivism', *International Studies Perspectives*, 2, 3, 2001.

3 Fen Osler Hampson, *Madness in the Multitude: Human Security and World Disorder*, New York: Oxford University Press, 2001; Shahrbanou Tadjbakhsh and Anuradha Chenoy, *Human Security: Concepts and Implications*, London: Routledge, 2006; Caroline Thomas, *Global Governance, Development and Human Security*, London: Pluto, 2000; Edward Newman, 'Human security', in Robert A. Denemark ed., *The International Studies Encyclopedia*, Oxford, Blackwell, 2010.

4 Hampson, *Madness in the Multitude*, p. 12.

5 David Chandler, 'Human security: the dog that didn't bark', *Security Dialogue*, 39, 4, 2008; Annick T. R. Wibben, 'Human security: toward an opening', *Security Dialogue*, 39, 4, 2008.

6 Edward Newman, 'Critical human security studies', *Review of International Studies*, 36, 1, 2010.

7 United Nations Development Program, *Human Development Report 1994*, New York: Oxford University Press, 1994.

8 These are, for example, the Universal Declaration of Human Rights, and the nine core human rights instruments: International Convention on the Elimination of All Forms of Racial Discrimination; International Covenant on Civil and Political Rights; International Covenant on Economic, Social and Cultural Rights; Convention on the Elimination of All Forms of Discrimination against Women; Convention against Torture and Other Cruel, Inhuman or Degrading Treatment or Punishment; Convention on the Rights of the Child; International Convention on the Protection of the Rights of All Migrant Workers and Members of Their Families; International Convention for the Protection of All Persons from Enforced Disappearance (not yet into force); and the Convention on the Rights of Persons with Disabilities. In addition to the International Bill of Rights and the core human rights treaties, there are many other universal instruments relating to human rights, covering the following areas of protection: the right of self-determination; prevention of discrimination; rights of women; rights of the child; rights of older persons; rights of persons with disabilities; rights related to detention or imprisonment; social welfare, progress and development; marriage; right to health; right to work and to fair conditions of employment; freedom of association; slavery, slavery-like practices and forced labour; rights of migrants; nationality, statelessness, asylum and refugees; war crimes and crimes against humanity, including genocide; and humanitarian law.

9 *Secretary-General Proposes Global Compact on Human Rights, Labour, Environment, in Address to World Economic Forum in Davos*, UN Press Release SG/SM/6881, 1 February 1999.

10 Kofi Annan, *Speech of the UN Secretary-General to the General Assembly*, 20 September 1999. New York: United Nations.

11 *The Responsibility to Protect. The Report of the International Commission on Intervention and State Sovereignty*, Ottawa: International Development Research Centre, 2001, p.8.

12 UN General Assembly, *Implementing the Responsibility to Protect: Report of the Secretary-General*, 12 January 2009, A/63/677.

13 Resolution adopted by the General Assembly, 2005 World Summit Outcome, 24 October 2005, A/RES/60/1, paragraphs 138–140.

14 Alex J. Bellamy and Paul D. Williams, 'The new politics of protection? Côte d'Ivoire, Libya and the responsibility to protect', *International Affairs*, 87, 4, 2011: 826.

15 United Nations, Secretary-General's High-level Panel on Threats, Challenges and Change, *A More Secure World: Our Shared Responsibility*, New York: United Nations, December 2004.

16 *A More Secure World*, p. 2.

17 *A More Secure World*, p. 14.

18 *A More Secure World*, p. 16.

19 *A More Secure World*, p. 17.

20 United Nations, Secretary-General, *In Larger Freedom: Towards Development, Security and Human Rights for All*, New York: United Nations, 21 March 2005, para. 132.

21 Ibid., para. 135.

22 Ibid., para. 16.

23 Mary Martin and Taylor Owen, 'The second generation of human security: lessons from the UN and EU experience', *International Affairs*, 86, 1, 2001: 212–216.

24 Kofi Annan, *'We the Peoples'*, *Report of the Secretary-General*, New York: United Nations, 2000.

25 Ibid., para. 17.

26 General Assembly, *Human Security. Report of the Secretary-General*, 8 March 2010, A/64/701. See also, UN Office for the Coordination of Humanitarian Affairs, *Human Security-Related Initiatives and Activities by UN Agencies, Funds and Programmes*, New York: OCHA, 2007; and Human Security Unit, *Human Security in Theory and Practice: Application of the Human Security Concept and the United Nations Trust Fund for Human Security*, New York: Office for the Coordination of Humanitarian Affairs, United Nations, 2009.

27 United Nations, The President of the General Assembly, High-level Plenary Meeting of the General Assembly September 2005 (July 2005 draft).

28 United Nations, The President of the General Assembly, High-level Plenary Meeting of the General Assembly September 2005 (July 2005 draft), para. 115.

29 2005 World Summit Outcome (draft resolution referred to the High-level Plenary Meeting of the General Assembly by the General Assembly at its 59th session), 20 September 2005, para 135.

30 Trust Fund Overview, http://www.unocha.org/humansecurity/trust-fund/un-trust-fund-human-security, accessed May 2013.

31 Human Security Trust Fund, http://www.unocha.org/humansecurity/trust-fund/un-trust-fund-human-security, accessed May 2013.

32 Human Security Unit, http://www.unocha.org/humansecurity/human-security-unit/about-human-security-unit, accessed May 2013.

33 Robert Cox, 'Social forces, states and world orders: beyond international relations theory', *Millennium*, 10, 2, 1981.

34 Nicholas J. Wheeler, *Saving Strangers: Humanitarian Intervention in International Society*, Oxford, Oxford University Press, 2000, pp. 12–13.

35 Mary Martin and Taylor Owen, 'The second generation of human security: lessons from the UN and EU experience', p. 220.

36 General Assembly, *Human Security. Report of the Secretary-General*, 8 March 2010, A/64/701, p. 1.

37 David Chandler, 'Human security: the dog that didn't bark', *Security Dialogue*, 39, 4.

38 General Assembly, *Human Security. Report of the Secretary-General*, 8 March 2010, A/64/701, p. 1.

39 Edward Newman, 'Critical human security studies', *Review of International Studies*, 36, 1, 2010; Shahrbanou Tadjbakhsh and Anuradha Chenoy, *Human Security: Concepts and Implications*, London, Routledge, 2006.

40 See, for example, Uwe-Jens Heuer and Gregor Schirmer, 'Human rights imperialism', *Monthly Review*, 49, 10, 1998; Perry Anderson, 'Force and consent', *New Left Review*, 2, 17, 2002; I. Mgbeoji, 'The civilised self and the barbaric other: imperial delusions of order and the challenges of human security', *Third World Quarterly*, 27, 5, 2006.

41 Lloyd Axworthy, 'NATO's new security vocation', *Nato Review*, Winter 1999.

42 Kofi Annan, *Speech of the UN Secretary-General to the General Assembly*, 20 September 1999. New York: United Nations.

43 Thematic Debate on 22 May 2008 *General Assembly Thematic Debate on Human Security*, http://www.un.org/ga/president/62/ThematicDebates/humansecurity.shtml, accessed May 2013.

44 Mary Martin and Taylor Owen, 'The second generation of human security: lessons from the UN and EU experience', pp. 212–216.

45 See Sandra J. MacLean, David R. Black and Timothy Shaw (eds), *A Decade of Human Security: Global Governance and the New Multilateralism*, London, Ashgate, 2006; Ryerson Christie, 'Critical voices and human security: to endure, to engage or to critique?', *Security Dialogue*, 41, 2, 2010.

46 Ryerson Christie, 'Critical voices and human security, p. 170. See also Alex J. Bellamy and Matt McDonald, '"The utility of human security": which humans? What security? A reply to Thomas and Tow', *Security Dialogue*, 33, 3, 2002.

47 Edward Newman, 'Critical human security studies'; Shahrbanou Tadjbakhsh and Anuradha Chenoy, *Human Security: Concepts and Implications*.

48 Taylor Owen, 'The critique that doesn't bite: a response to David Chandler's "Human security: the dog that didn't bark"', *Security Dialogue*, 39, 4, 2008: 450.

18

JAPAN AND NETWORKED HUMAN SECURITY

Yukio Takasu

It is perhaps not well known outside of Japan that human security is an extremely popular subject in Japan. On the part of the government, successive Japanese political leaders have confirmed their strong commitment to promote human security in the world. At the UN Millennium Summit in September 2000, the theme of which was "The United Nations in the Twenty-first Century," Japanese Prime Minster Yoshiro Mori emphasized the importance of human security in order to make the twenty-first century human-centered, and stated Japan's intention to promote the concept as a pillar of its foreign policy. At the UN General Assembly and the high-level Security Council meeting in September 2010, Prime Minister Naoto Kan reaffirmed that Japan would continue to contribute to international efforts to protect vulnerable people and states from a human security perspective.[1]

Despite changes of government and parties in power, Japanese governments have consistently upheld the promotion of human security as one of the pillars of its foreign policy. Japan is the only country that appoints an ambassador exclusively dedicated for this purpose.[2] It seems there is no sign of the government's interest weakening.

At the academic level, I can safely state (although there is no comparable global statistical data yet) that there is no other country than Japan which has so many university courses, scholars, and students in human security. Japan's academic consortium of human security comprising of 12 universities developed into the Japan Academic Society on Human Security Studies in September 2011. Almost every week, conferences and workshops are organized throughout Japan on themes related to human security.

I have been personally involved in every step of Japan's initiatives on human security since their inception at the end of the 1990s until now, most recently as permanent representative of Japan to the United Nations and subsequently as Ambassador in charge of human security. In this chapter, I would like to discuss Japan's human security initiatives, the thinking behind them and challenges and future direction to be taken.

When and how Japan's initiative started

The idea of attaching importance to the value of the individual is as old as human history. What is new in human security initiatives over the last couple of decades is that they are placed at the centre of diplomacy and security policy.

Human security is generally understood as the effort to address global problems – such as conflict, poverty, refugees, human rights violations, pandemics, infectious diseases, public health, crime, terrorism, the environment – from the viewpoint of ensuring the life, livelihood, and dignity of the individual. It needs to be emphasized that these global issues are in themselves nothing new. The concept of human security, however, focuses on the individual rather than the state – in other words, a different approach that emphasizes individual perspective. An approach that emphasizes ensuring the individual's life, livelihood, and dignity adds a moral dimension to actions by the international community.

Underlying the increased importance placed on the individual is the dramatic acceleration of transnational flows of people, goods, money, and instant communication accompanying the advance of globalization, the proliferation of challenges that individual countries, however powerful militarily or economically, cannot solve alone, and qualitative changes in these challenges. Another important factor is that since the end of the Cold War, new types of internal conflicts caused by ethnic, religious, and other differences have increased, making it difficult to ensure people's lives, livelihoods, and dignity solely on the basis of the traditional concept of national security, that is, the state protecting its citizens and territory.[3] A third major factor is that the tide of democratization that has swept many parts of the world in the wake of the Cold War has made it more important than ever for states to ensure that they respond to the will of the people; today national progress is measured by the state's ability to realize people's individual potential and enrich their lives.

The 1994 *Human Development Report* of the UN Development Program addressed human security as an important concept in the post-Cold War era. However, the far-sighted visions the report presented to address uncertainties of employment, income, and crimes through a comprehensive concept of human security were not translated into concrete policy action either by the 1995 UN summit for social development, nor by any member state until Japan took it up as a major policy objective at the time of the Asian financial crisis of 1997–98.

During this crisis many Asian countries that had hitherto enjoyed smooth economic growth found themselves suddenly facing rising unemployment and poverty and unable to safeguard people's access to education and medical care; this led to an awareness of the necessity to carry out nation-building while putting in place a safety net for society as a whole rather than simply focusing on policies for the socially vulnerable. In addition to providing assistance from the viewpoint of human security for Asian countries reeling from the crisis, then Japanese Prime Minister Keizo Obuchi took the initiative of organizing the Intellectual Dialogue on Building Asia's Tomorrow in December 1998 in Tokyo, articulating a policy of promoting human security. This initiative, with its emphasis on freedom from want, represented a more comprehensive approach to human security than simply freedom from fear in time of conflict.[4] Subsequently, the Intellectual Dialogues in Singapore and Thailand, an international conference on human security in Mongolia and a workshop on human security in China in the aftermath of the financial crisis spread understanding of and support for this broad-based Japanese concept in Asian countries.

Japanese leaders felt strongly that some of the approaches the international financial institutions then took would exacerbate the situation and presented an alternative human-centered approach, coining it human security. At a time of financial crisis, their recommendations to reduce budget deficits and cut subsidies resulted in the severe curtailment of social expenditures, such as health and education, creating irrevocable setbacks in tackling infectious diseases and reducing illiteracy. Japan's development policy places importance on human resources development and prioritizes education and health in resource allocation.

From this point of view, Japan extended bilateral support for a social safety net to those Asian countries which suffered from the sudden downturn. Japan also proposed creating a Fund for Asia Pacific countries, which eventually led to the Cheng Mai Initiative: an arrangement for mutual support among participating countries such as Malaysia, Chile, Indonesia, and Thailand. Economic interdependence had developed so deeply in the region that these initiatives were considered essential for the sound recovery of the Asian economy but they were also important for Japan's own economic growth.

In fact, Japan's initiative to focus on the security of the individual at a time of economic downturn coincided with the paradigm change taking place in the overall security architecture in the post-Cold War world with intensifying globalization. As the Asian financial crisis was evolving, another turning point that made the concept of human security a focus of international attention was the human tragedies in Rwanda and the former Yugoslavia. The international community found itself faced with the question of how to respond when people's lives were threatened in countries where effective governance had collapsed.

The paradigm change for rethinking the concept of security and the importance of a human security perspective can be summarized as follows:

- The security agenda must be broadened beyond conventional state–state politico-military security to transnational insecurities of the individual and peoples.
- A state alone can no longer provide sufficient protection against imminent threats.
- Sovereignty entails obligations and duties to one's own people and to other sovereign states.
- The utility and limitation of force must be complemented by other non-military means.

Japanese human security initiatives

The UN Trust Fund for Human Security (UNTF) (1999–2013)

As a part of its effort, Japan considered it important to finance a project which aimed to help vulnerable people at a global level. In March 1999 the Japanese government contributed to the establishment of the UN Trust Fund for Human Security, providing ¥9 billion for multi-sector projects in Thailand, Kosovo, East Timor, and elsewhere in less than 18 months. The initial contribution was made with the expectation that others would follow. But Japan has continued to contribute to the UNTF for Human Security every year without interruption. The total contribution by Japan has now reached US $346 million and supported 190 projects in over 60 countries and regions. These projects are all implemented by UN funds and programs, in partnership with civil society, NGOs and local entities with identifiable benefits to the human security of people and communities in the fields of health care, primary education, extreme poverty, sudden economic downturn, natural disaster, refugees and Internally Displaced Persons, people facing discrimination, and national reconciliation.

The Commission on Human Security (CHS) (2001–03)

UN Secretary-General Kofi Annan's April 2000 report on the upcoming Millennium Assembly, "We the Peoples: The Role of the United Nations in the Twenty-first Century," emphasized a human-centered viewpoint and proposed an approach based on a similar standpoint to that promoted by Japan. The Group of Eight (G8) Kyushu–Okinawa Summit in July 2000 also emphasized the individual dimension in addressing such issues as infectious diseases, crime, drugs, poverty, and education. At the end of July the Japanese government organized the International Symposium on Human Security, whose participants included such intellectuals as

Nobel Laureate Amartya Sen and former UN High Commissioner for Refugees Sadako Ogata. At the symposium, it was emphasized that human security was not an abstract concept but a practical necessity to be used as a tool for bringing about specific actions. In translating the concept into actions, the Japanese government considered it important to develop a common understanding on human security and to formulate a policy framework for all stakeholders. They should include not only the public sector such as government and international organizations but also civil society, and the private sector. At the Millennium Summit Prime Minister Mori announced Japan's intention to support the establishment of an international commission on human security, with the participation of world-renowned opinion leaders.

In forming the Commission as an independent body, and throughout its work, every effort was made to coordinate as closely as possible with UN Secretary-General Kofi Annan in selecting its members, determining the scope of work and the line of recommendations. With the blessing of the Secretary-General, the Commission on Human Security was formally launched in January 2001, with Ogata and Sen as co-chairs. Through intensive work and a series of regional hearings, the Commission's Report, '*Human Security Now*' was completed and presented to the Secretary-General in May 2003.[5] The CHS came up with a working definition of human security: "To protect the vital core of all human lives in ways that enhance human freedom and human fulfillment." In essence, it is based on the belief that a human being is entitled to live a healthy, dignified, fulfilling life, irrespective of where he or she is born; not only protected from insecurities but empowered to develop ability to the maximum extent possible. This is the conviction to which Japan is wholeheartedly committed.

The CHS advocated a human-centered, integrated, multi-sector approach, seeking to address conflict, poverty and human rights violations simultaneously and recommended a policy framework for 10 priority actions, most of which have been implemented by now.

The most important contribution the CHS made, in my view, was the equal emphasis it placed on empowerment as on protection. It is recognized that the potential of so many people is wasted or untapped, to the detriment of not only their own fulfillment but of society as a whole. A human security approach should reflect the need to improve this situation.

Initiatives outside the United Nations

The report *Human Security Now* was well received and had a major impact globally; many governments adjusted policy in line with its recommendations. Japan was also instrumental in the effective follow-up of the recommendations of the CHS at bilateral, regional and global levels. As an example of a national effort, Japan revised its ODA Charter, and created a new grant aid program for enhancing human security. The Japan International Cooperation Agency (JICA) also established guidelines for selecting and formulating and implementing its assistance program, reflecting a human-centered, integrated approach as recommended by the CHS. Many other governments, most notably, Canada, Sweden, Switzerland, and Thailand, also attached importance to human security in their foreign policy.

Regionally, a series of hearings and workshops by the Commission helped to raise understanding of this concept and after the completion of the Report, several regional organizations updated their security doctrines. For instance, the Organization of American States (OAS) special meeting in October 2003 agreed a declaration on strengthening human security including freedom from want. The African Union (AU) Peace and Security Commission and peacebuilding conference stressed the importance of a human security approach. The AU has incorporated human security in its vision of a united and strong Africa in its Non-aggression and Common Defense Pact. In the Asia Pacific region, APEC and ASEAN have been actively engaged with human security in pandemics, natural disasters and cross border drug trafficking.

Japan has promoted cooperation and organized specific programs and workshops with many European countries as well as with the EU and OSCE. The Barcelona Report in September 2004 was an important contribution to the development of European security strategy in the new security paradigm.[6]

Initiatives in the United Nations

UN Secretary-General Kofi Annan established in 2004 the Advisory Committee on the UN Trust Fund for Human Security chaired by Mrs Sadako Ogata, to advise him on the use of the trust fund in line with the recommendations of the CHS. In this way, a linkage was established so that CHS recommendations would be followed up through activities to be financed by the UNTF.

Secretary-General Kofi Annan's high-level panel submitted a report as an input to the 2005 UN Summit. The report did not explicitly mention human security but covered the same ground as the CHS and formulated a series of recommendations under freedom from want, freedom from fear, and freedom to live in dignity.[7]

On the basis of the Report of the High-level Panel, Japan played a leading role in moves to include a reference to human security in the 2005 UN Summit Outcome document. The negotiation among member states resulted in the following consensus paragraph.

> We stress the right of people to live in freedom and dignity, free from poverty and despair. We recognize that all individuals, in particular the vulnerable people, are entitled to freedom from fear and freedom from want, with an equal opportunity to enjoy all their rights and fully develop their human potential. To this end, we commit ourselves to discuss and define the notion of human security in the General Assembly.[8]

Responsibility to Protect

In this connection, it is relevant to refer to the concept of the responsibility to protect which was also included in the 2005 UN Summit Outcome document but in the section on human rights. This concept was the product of a Canadian initiative of the International Commission on Intervention and State Sovereignty (ICISS) (2000–01).[9] In fact, Japan was invited to participate earlier in the Human Security Network (HSN) which had been promoted by Canada and Norway and now in the work of the independent commission, but declined on both occasions because of the latter's emphasis on humanitarian intervention and Japan's fundamental reservation on use of force without the authorization of the Security Council. It is certainly a great challenge for the international community to be confronted with taking effective measures against gross violations of human rights in conflict, particularly if the Security Council is unable to agree a common line of measures. Japan believed, however, that the measures taken should conform to the principles and procedures established within the United Nations. It is especially important to uphold the principle of adherence to the UN Charter in the case of measures entailing use of force.

The high-level panel of the Secretary-General basically endorsed the recommendations of the ICISS. And the General Assembly reached the following agreements in the 2005 Outcome document:[10]

- State sovereignty implies the responsibility to protect its people from genocide, war crimes, ethnic cleansing and crimes against humanity.
- Where the State is unwilling or unable to halt serious harms to its people, the international community has the responsibility to protect by appropriate peaceful means.
- As an exception, military action by the international community is warranted to protect from those crimes.
- The use of force will be permitted only with the authorization of the UN Security Council in accordance with the Charter.

Thus, through intensive negotiations in the General Assembly, two important qualifications were made to this concept. The first was to limit the scope of applying the Responsibility to Protect to four types of most serious violations: genocide, war crimes, ethnic cleansing, and crimes against humanity. The second was the confirmation that the use of force would be permitted only with authorization of the UN Security Council. From the Japanese point of view, the latter confirmation is crucially important because Japan has serious misgivings regarding the use of force in the name of humanitarian intervention or responsibility to protect without authorization by the Security Council.

Both concepts – human security and responsibility to protect – in the UN 2005 Outcome document address the common challenges of individual insecurity where the state alone is unable to cope with and provide sufficient protection.

However, at least in the UN context, both are clearly delineated.

Human security places a focus on empowerment of the vulnerable and enhancement of social capital and is more preventative. The use of force is not envisaged in human security as accepted in the UN.[11]

The Friends of Human Security (FHS)

After the 2005 UN Summit Outcome document reaffirmed the principle that the use of force was to be regulated in accordance with the UN Charter, Japan's concern about some countries, which focused solely on freedom from fear and the use of force, was largely dissipated. Japan was then ready to support the broader scope of human security and took the initiative to combine different streams of efforts and resources on human security to make major impacts on UN activities. At the ministerial meeting of the Human Security Network in Bangkok in May 2006, at which Japan participated as a guest for the first time, Japan presented a proposal to create a forum to promote collaboration among various initiatives, which was strongly supported. The HSN, on its part, moved to broaden its scope to include challenges on freedom from want.

Japan invited Mexico to co-chair the Friends of Human Security, an informal group of Member States and international organizations to collaborate in mainstreaming human security in the UN. The first meeting of representatives of 30 countries took place in October 2006 at UNHQ and has met regularly semiannually since then. The objectives of the FHS are to make a human security approach better reflected in UN activities, and promote collaboration among interested countries and agencies. The first meeting of the FHS agreed that members should pursue collaboration on the basis of a common understanding of human security, in line with the definition provided by the Commission on Human Security. Over the years the partici-pating members have expanded to more than 100 countries and identified the implementation of MDGs, humanitarian activities, peacebuilding, and protection of civilians as priorities.

The strength of the FHS is its flexibility; under the framework of the FHS, interested countries will collaborate to achieve common objectives. For instance, members of the FHS extended support to the initiative on a UN General Assembly draft resolution on the protection of children in conflict. A similar initiative was made by interested members to ameliorate the impact of climate change on small island countries. Thus, the FHS provides a forum to facilitate a coalition of the willing on certain themes of global impact. It is now an established practice for the HSN to invite co-chairs of the Friends of Human Security to its annual ministerial meeting.

As a follow up to the 2005 Outcome document, the FHS took the initiative of organizing an informal debate on human security in the General Assembly in 2007 to broaden the support of human security, and requested the endorsement of the SG-designate Ban Ki-moon and the President of the General Assembly. Thereafter, the initiative of the FHS resulted in a formal debate at the UN General Assembly in 2008 with a view to adopting a resolution. The FHS has been instrumental in mobilizing political support and in seeking a common understanding on human security in the UN General Assembly.

Why Japan is the main promoter of human security in the world

As described earlier, Japan's human security initiative came originally from the political leadership of Foreign Minister and later Prime Minister Keizo Obuchi who took it as his personal agenda. As a compassionate political leader, he signed the land mine treaty, announced a program for no land mine victims at Ottawa in December 1997, and played a leading role in ratifying it at unusual speed, despite reservations within the government. In the wake of the Asian financial crisis in 1998, he advocated an alternative approach to deal with the plight of vulnerable people. Surin Pitsuwan recalled the conversation he, as the Foreign Minister of Thailand, had with the then visiting Japanese Foreign Minister Obuchi, in which the latter inquired how people could cope with cuts in health and education services due to budget deficit reduction.[12] Obuchi believed that particularly in an economic downturn, social expenditures should be given a high priority, otherwise, the long-term implications of economic stringency would irreparably affect the healthy growth of the younger generation.

Obuchi passed away unexpectedly in May 2000 and the post of prime minister was taken over by Yoshiro Mori, who committed himself to carry on Obuchi's initiative and reaffirmed at the 2000 UN Millennium Summit Japan's firm determination to promote human security. It is important to stress that there is bipartisan political support for human security across the Democratic Party, Liberal Democratic Party, and New Komeito Party, which is unusual in Japanese politics.

The core of strong supporters in and outside government is also an important factor in Japan's continued commitment. They have consistently advocated Japan's leadership and influenced political leaders. Obuchi's advisors such as Keizo Takemi in the Diet, and the late Tadashi Yamamoto in civil society, have been instrumental in ensuring the continuity. Sadako Ogata has actively engaged in her capacity as the president of JICA and also as chair of the Advisory Board of the UN Trust Fund. The author has been involved himself throughout the process in different capacities in the Foreign Ministry and in the UN.

Most importantly, the concept of human security is deeply rooted among the Japanese people, reflected in Japanese universities and NGOs. Such popular interest has influenced the government and political parties. Strong interest in human security derives from the historical experiences the Japanese people have undergone through the devastation that militarism brought and reconstruction after the end of the Second World War. The concept fits the psyche of the Japanese. The 1946 Constitution of Japan starts with the preamble:

> We, the Japanese people, desire to occupy an honored place in an international society striving for the preservation of peace, and the banishment of tyranny and

245

slavery, oppression and intolerance – from the earth. We recognize that all peoples of the world have the right to live in peace, free from fear and want. – We pledge our national honor to accomplish these high ideals and purposes with all our resources.

Article 25 of the Constitution stipulates that all Japanese nationals shall have the right to maintain the minimum standards of healthy and cultured livelihood. Such high goals have been a guiding principle for the Japanese people to pursue human-centered reconstruction efforts, placing high priority on the development of human resources.

Recent development in the UN

Despite general acceptance of human security's relevance and added value to the work of the UN, the absence of an agreed definition/common understanding of human security in the UN had hampered its application beyond project activities of UN Agencies and Programs supported by the UN Trust Fund for Human Security. In order to mainstream human security in UN activities and to establish it as an international norm and value of behavior, it is essential to achieve legitimacy by reaching a definition/common understanding in the UN General Assembly. With this recognition, Japan has placed its main efforts in recent years on broadening the area of agreement and seeking a convergence of views among member states on the definition/common understanding of the concept.

Primarily initiated by Japan and like-minded countries such as Jordan and Switzerland, five formal and informal debates took place in the General Assembly between 2008 and 2012. In 2010 Japan took an initiative to request the Secretary-General Ban Ki-moon to present his first Report on Human Security in April 2010,[13] and succeeded in adoption of the first GA resolution on human security in July 2010, thus establishing a strong basis for further elaboration of this concept.[14] The Secretary-General appointed the author as his Special Advisor on Human Security in December 2010 to facilitate consultation among member states.

Through these debates at the UN General Assembly, it has become clear that major concerns by certain member states on the notion of human security are related to its relation with national sovereignty, and the possibility of military intervention in the name of human security. A human security approach addresses the root causes of insecurity and helps the government to reduce the weakness of its institutions, thereby supporting exercise of sovereignty.[15] Human security should be pursued in accordance with the UN Charter and nowhere has it authorized violation of sovereignty nor military intervention. As mentioned earlier, unlike the Responsibility to Protect, the use of force is not envisaged.

Another concern was expressed from an opposite direction: excessive emphasis on human security may lead to neglecting the importance to maintain military strength for self-defense. This is clearly to misunderstand human security. Emphasis on human security comes from recognizing the increasing global tendency that traditional politico-military state security is no longer sufficient to protect people. The pursuit of human security is complementary to national security and self-defense, which is the basic function of a state. States have still a major role to play in a globalized world, and where a state is unable to provide a minimum level of security protection, the individual can hardly live in peace.

A more serious and legitimate concern is that if human security means almost everything related to human activities, it is too broad to have a meaningful basis for action. An answer to this would be that we should establish selected priority areas that are most urgent and serious to the international community and then focus efforts on these areas.

Through these debates and consultations led by Japan and Jordan, a convergence of views has finally emerged on a common understanding on human security largely on the basis of the proposal contained in the second report by the Secretary-General on human security.[16] The General Assembly adopted a resolution on human security by consensus on 10 September 2012.[17] It is a significant milestone. It marks the first time the General Assembly has agreed on a common understanding on human security since Japan organized the CHS in 2001 and UN discussions began in 2005. It paves the way for formally applying human security within the work of the United Nations system.

What changes has the HS approach brought about?

It is recognized that the security of an individual cannot be achieved by national security alone but must be complemented by human security. This is most acutely felt where the authority in power does not take sufficient action to protect or in an extreme case attacks its civilian population. People-centered, comprehensive, context-specific and preventive approaches have presented added value in addressing various insecurities.

In conflict and emergency situations, a human security approach aims to improve the protection of civilians and victims, irrespective of their legal status; to enforce effectively humanitarian and human rights standards, and to acknowledge and deal with sub- and non-state actors. Those improvements are essential in addressing intra-state conflict.

In post-conflict situations, a human security approach is to fill the institutional and financial gaps from humanitarian assistance to economic recovery; to integrate a peacebuilding strategy, addressing conflict and poverty in an integrated manner; to promote co-existence and recon-ciliation by providing practical opportunities for people belonging to different ethnic groups to cooperate; and to strengthen capacities of local authorities and good governance.

For sustainable development and growth, this approach attaches importance to social capital, the achievement of inclusive development not only at national level but also at community and individual level; it places emphasis on empowerment and preparedness of people, respecting equity and human dignity, in tackling global issues and extending development and other assis-tance, and it seeks to raise the profile of climate change impact as a threat to security.

In particular, I consider MDGs/post-2015 development agenda and peacebuilding are the high priority areas for application of a human security approach, reflecting global interest and Japan's strength and expertise.

Achieving the MDGs and addressing post-2015 development goals require first of all, on the part of developing countries, self-help efforts, appropriate domestic policies and resources, capacity building, and sustained commitment.[18] Such sense of ownership must be supported by partnerships of donor communities and international organizations, with a human security perspective.

National and aggregate approaches and the focus on inputs not on outputs have proved to be insufficient to achieve MDGs and inclusive and equitable development. Another illustration of shortcomings of the conventional approach to focus on aggregate and input is the case of the so-called 20/20 initiative. At the 1995 World Summit for Social Development in Copenhagen, it was agreed that developing countries would allocate 20 per cent of their national budgets and developed countries 20 per cent of external assistance respectively, to education, medical services, and other social development expenditures. But do outlays of 20 per cent really mean that a country has met this objective? If 20 per cent of the budget is earmarked for education but is used largely to pay for heating school buildings, the target has not yet been met from a human security viewpoint. There is a need for further specific actions.[19] A high priority in the MDG and post-2015 development agenda should be placed on primary education and vocational training. Empowering the young and vulnerable, and particularly those in refugee and IDP camps, is another case where delay means an opportunity lost forever. Amartya Sen has stated that "the process of development is not primarily one of expanding the supply of goods and services, but one of enhancing the capability of people."[20] This was precisely the conviction that pushed forward Japan's development and was the goal of Japan's nation-building. The utmost effort should be put into enhancing educational opportunities for women in developing countries, who have been deprived of such opportunities for socio-cultural reasons, since achieving primary education for all will reduce disparities between men and women, and have a great impact on development as a whole.

Another area where a human security approach can make a noticeable difference will be peacebuilding. A major source of global instability comes from the weak governance and fragile situation in conflict-related countries, in particular in border areas, which have become hotbeds for terrorism, international crime, and drug syndicates.

Post-conflict peacebuilding is defined by the UN Secretary-General as "an activity to identify and support structures which can strengthen and solidify peace,"[21] in other words, how to prevent a relapse into another cycle of conflict. Most of the bottom billion people live in conflict or post-conflict situations; the list of twenty countries with the highest mortality of children under five largely overlaps with countries in conflict or post-conflict situations.[22] The OECD/Development Assistance Committee (DAC) has appropriately defined peacebuilding as [the] "means to create the sustainable environment for human security in [a] post-conflict situation."[23]

It is a prerequisite in post-conflict situations to restore and maintain basic safety, to reform the security sector, and to establish the rule of law and justice. Measures to protect civilians are still far from satisfactory. But equally important is to empower the people, irrespective of which side of the border they are, and to create changes in everyday quality of life, livelihood, deliver public goods and services. Human security approaches could be a valuable tool to focus on the social and economic stability along border areas of countries in conflict. It was also an innovation to include energy as one of five priorities in the integrated peacebuilding strategy for Sierra Leone, despite strong reservations initially expressed from conventional thinkers.[24]

Future directions

The human security concept will have real significance when it is applied to concrete cases and contributes to making visible changes on the ground. Bringing about broad-based human security requires the understanding and involvement of not only public sector – national government, the UN and its agencies – but also a wide range of other actors: international financial institutions, regional organizations, civil society, nongovernmental organizations, business, academia, and the media.

The major challenge before us is to what extent human security is not only a relevant but also an effective norm for formulating frameworks of action or guidelines for public or private actors. I would suggest the following proposals to promote such progress.

Firstly, it is important to mainstream a human security perspective in addressing major domestic concerns and to help make a vibrant and tolerant society in Japan. Japan has advocated human security so far primarily as a concept in supporting developing countries or countries in conflict overcoming their insecurities. Taking the initiative in building a global society in which all people can live together in peace and safety, whatever their ethnicity, religion, and culture, Japan should continue to lead in creating a tolerant society that values harmonious coexistence with other cultures. However, the great East Japan Earthquake and the Fukushima nuclear power plant accident on 11 March 2011 forced us to rethink the concept of human security. There are acute needs for protecting human survival and dignity even in an advanced country like Japan. The domestic challenges confronting contemporary Japanese society need to be increasingly tackled from a human security perspective: the vulnerable victims of tsunami and nuclear accidents, aging population, social welfare, health insurance system, foreign workers, and refugees. Japan may be able to present prescriptions for such challenges, as the fastest aging society in the world.

Secondly, Japan should take a lead to form an international alliance of human security for strengthening partnership and collaboration among civil society organizations. In promoting a human security approach as global norms for public as well as private actors, it is essential to bring forward active participation of NGOs, scholars and researchers, foundations, youth organizations, labor unions, the media, etc. Civil society organizations play an essential role in putting ideas into practice and also as a pressure group on public policy makers. With a view to forming a global alliance on human security in the future, we should build upon the ongoing collaborations, for instance, on global health or peacebuilding among research institutions and foundations through organizing joint research and symposia. Global networking of academic scholars on human security should be further promoted.

Thirdly, it is essential to strengthen the partnership with private corporations, which have a determining influence on the success or failure of addressing global challenges. Improved access to affordable medicine for infectious diseases such as GAVI, control of illicit trade of natural resources are made possible with active participation of private corporations. It is not always easy to pursue, in a compatible manner, development of resources and preservation of nature and livelihood of indigenous people in the development area. However, this must be done and many worthwhile initiatives from a human security point of view are being taken, such as the cool earth initiative, biodiversity offset initiative, and the Yasuni-ITT initiative in Ecuador.[25] Corporate social responsibility and the UN Global Compact are important initiatives for private enterprises themselves to promote sound and vibrant economic and productive activities as good members of society. Such private initiatives could broaden the scope of activities to human security and peacebuilding in the future.

In conclusion, human security will provide important norms or codes of conduct for all stakeholders for ensuring global security and human dignity in an increasingly interdependent world. The historical experiences of Japan since the Second World War to reconstruct and develop with a strong human-centered focus demonstrate the value and validity of human security approach. If every act and decision in daily life reflects the perspective of security and dignity of the individual, and human security is used as an important tool for evaluating every act and decision, we will be able to live in a more peaceful, prosperous and just world.

Notes

1 Statements by Prime Minister Naoto Kan at the Summit meeting of the UN Security Council, 23 September 2010 and at the UN General Assembly, 24 September 2010.
2 Japanese government has appointed an Ambassador in charge of human security since 2006. Thailand has established the ministry of social development and human security; the 2008 Constitution of Ecuador has adopted human security to build sustainable peace; some governments have divisions of human security.
3 Mary Kaldor, *New and Old Wars*, Cambridge, Polity Press (1999).
4 *The Asian Crisis and Human Security: An Intellectual Dialogue on Building Asia's Tomorrow*, Tokyo, JCIE and ISESA (1998).
5 *Human Security Now*, New York, Commission on Human Security (2003).

6 *A Human Security Doctrine for Europe*, The Barcelona Report of the Study Group on Europe's Security Capabilities, September 2004.

7 UN Secretary General, *In Larger Freedom: Towards Development, Security and Human Rights for All* (A/59/2005, March 2005).

8 2005 World Summit Outcome document, paragraph 143, of A/RES/60/1.

9 The Report of the International Commission on Intervention and State Sovereignty (ICISS), December 2001.

10 2005 World Summit Outcome document, paragraphs 138-140, A/RES/60/1.

11 Statement by Yukio Takasu, Permanent Representative of Japan to the UN on the Responsibility to Protect at the UN General Assembly, 24 July 2009.

12 Based on an interview with the author, 21 October 2010.

13 The Report of the UN SG on Human Security, A/64/701, April 2010.

14 UN General Assembly Resolution A/RES/64/291, 16 July 2010.

15 The Report of the UN SG on Human Security, A/64/701(paragraphs 20–22).

16 The Report of the UN SG on Human Security, A/66/763, April 2012.

17 The UN General Assembly Resolution, A/RES/66/290, 10 September 2012.

18 The UN General Assembly Resolution, A/RES/65/1 at the High-level Meeting on the MDGs, 22 September 2010.

19 UNICEF, *Report on Progress for Children*, September 2010 and *Narrowing the Gap to Meet MDG Goals*, 7 September 2010.

20 Amartya Sen, *Development as Freedom*, Oxford, Oxford University Press (1999).

21 UN SG Boutros Boutros-Ghali, *The Agenda for Peace*, Report of the UN Secretary-General 17 June 1992, available at: http://www.unrol.org/files/A_47_277.pdf (accessed 17 May 2013).

22 UNICEF *Annual Report 2006*; Afghanistan, Angola, Burkina Faso, Burundi, CAR, Chad, Côte d'Ivoire, DRC, Equatorial Guinea, Ethiopia, Guinea, Liberia, Niger, Nigeria, Mali, Rwanda, Sierra Leone, Somalia, Swaziland, and Zambia.

23 OECD/DAC, *Principles for Good International Engagement in Fragile States and Situations*, April 2007.

24 UN Peacebuilding Commission, Sierra Leone Peacebuilding Cooperation Framework, 3 December 2007.

25 Statement of President of the Republic of Ecuador, Rafael Correa, at the high-level dialogue on climate change of UN General Assembly, 24 September 2007.

19

THE EUROPEAN UNION AND HUMAN SECURITY: THE MAKING OF A GLOBAL SECURITY ACTOR

Javier Solana

Human security has been an important part of the rapid developments in the external relations of the European Union and its role in contributing to global security in the first decade of the twenty-first century. But it was a concept which did not speak its name. When we talk about human security and the EU, the most apparent problem is that officially it did not exist as a distinct policy or as a label for an external mission. Rather, it was an approach which informed and guided what the EU did, and which could be inferred from the aims of its policies and the methods it used to achieve them.

Three key ideas and one event drove the EU's increasing activity in ensuring global security after September 11 2001. The drivers were first the need to develop a collective response to the challenges of the post Cold-war era, and to the threat posed by international terrorism. The EU also had to react to crises in many parts of the world, from Asia to Africa and to Europe's nearest neighbourhoods in North Africa, the Middle East, the Balkans and the Caucasus, which threatened European interests. Rather than acting alone, EU member states had to show that by combining their efforts and resources they could create a powerful and positive new element in international diplomacy and security.

Secondly, Europe had to represent a distinctive form of action. The EU was not a nation state. It was a peace project which grew from a legacy of war, but it was not set up to provide traditional forms of security and defence, which meant protecting territory and sovereignty. It could act without the classical motivations of defending borders and territorial rights, in order to promote peace, democracy and human rights. It could do so using instruments and resources which were also different from national armies. It offered security through negotiation, governance assistance, rule of law measures and economic aid. In wars where there is no longer a front line and the sources of conflict are deep rooted, we have learned that there is no simple division or sequencing between military and civilian assistance.

Our capabilities had to allow us to respond to a conflict cycle of prevention, management and reconstruction deploying for not only the military phase of crisis management but also civilians to deal with stabilisation and reconstruction efforts according to the demands of each crisis on the ground.

During the first decade of the new century this meant going beyond the EU's civilian tools and deploying soldiers in Africa for the first time as part of its crisis management operations. This way of security also meant supporting international law and agreements and working in close co-operation with other partners such as the United Nations, NATO, the African Union as well as the United States.

The final driver which influenced the development of the EU as a global security actor was the need to be able to operate autonomously. Even when established security providers such as NATO were unable or unwilling to intervene, as was the case in Africa, the EU needed to be able to step in, with both hard and soft forms of security assistance. To do so, it needed not only capabilities on the ground but also strategic planning and operational capacities, an institutional framework and the confidence and public support to implement them.

One event which crystallised all these factors was the invasion of Iraq in 2003. It saw Europe divided between those states who supported the US-led invasion and who had joined the 'Coalition of the Willing', and those who were opposed to military action. Our ability to contribute to promoting peace and functional politics was at risk because of the deep and damaging differences between member states. The fault line, dubbed by US Defense Secretary Donald Rumsfeld as 'Old Europe/New Europe' was never quite that clear cut; however, major member states of the European Union, such as Britain and Spain, emerged on a different side to others such as Germany and France, while candidate countries which were then waiting to join the EU – such as the Czech Republic and Poland – also supported the invasion, and added to a sense of division and fracture in Europe.

Against this background the idea began of publishing a document which would put in written form a security strategy for the EU. The intention was to go beyond simple platitudes or a lowest common denominator approach, and try to define a doctrine which would command consensus and which represented how we, as Europeans, could and should behave in a post-September 11 world. The strategy expressed and encompassed our wish to act collectively, distinctively and autonomously.

It was a significant step also in defining a European identity, through setting out a core set of values, convictions and experiences that together form a composite sense of who we are as Europeans. At the time there were elements of a European model to be found in how we organised our societies and interacted with the wider world, but through our security and external policies we had another much more visible opportunity to create cohesion between member states and to present a European view in a rapidly changing world.

What you do on the international stage is also a function of your identity; of how you define yourself and the values you seek to promote abroad. Identity becomes a problem when there is no identity, particularly in situations of crisis and turbulence, when established ties of social cohesion are eroding or breaking down. There was a need for a European responsibility of a different kind than the Enlightenment civilization mission. In the light of this new responsibility the concept of a European identity is problematic since it conjures up images of a European unity and a fiction of peace and concord as well as strength and power (Strath 2002: 396).

A new active Europe had to function as a mediator and a bridge-builder in a global world.

The Enlightenment quest for improvement and mastery, with a fundamentalist and totalising core, would in this 'new activism' scenario be transformed into a communications specialism, based on a readiness to listen to other views and promote dialogue among them (Strath 2002: 397). Its role lay in trying to harmonise these ideas of self – and concretely in bringing together the worlds of diplomats, soldiers and development experts.

What are the elements of this European approach? Compassion with those who suffer; peace and reconciliation through integration; a strong attachment to human rights, democracy and the rule of law; a spirit of compromise, plus a commitment to promote in a pragmatic way a rules-based international system. All these elements have been an intrinsic part of establishing Europe as a responsible power.

The relationship between identity and foreign policy works in both directions. Foreign policy is a way to express your identity. But acting together on the world stage is also a way to progressively shape and enhance a common identity. Identities are not static. They change with different experiences. The very fact of acting together, and generating shared successes and the occasional failure was likely to ensure that our reflexes would converge; and from this, the idea of a European identity would become less elusive and more concrete.

The European Security Strategy (ESS), which was presented to the European Parliament in December 2003, was a blueprint for us to act together despite the differences over the war. At the same time, it was inspired by more than just the row over Iraq: it was also intended to set out how we saw the future of conflict and conditions for peace globally. It also drew together the lessons learned by a decade of experience in the Balkans and from other conflicts which had occurred since the fall of the Berlin Wall.

By virtue of the mandate delivered by the European Council of Cologne in 1999, the European Union undertook crisis management in terms of humanitarian and evacuation tasks, peace keeping and armed interventions in order to manage crises. The Cologne council also decided on the necessity of having credible military forces, and the capacity to act and react when necessary to international crises. This was the basis on which the European Union embarked on developing both military and political structures. The Strategy of 2003, entitled 'A Secure Europe in a Better World', set the tone for these and other rapid developments in the EU's role over the next decade. And by 2010 we had mobilised more than 70,000 people from soldiers to policemen, judges, tax inspectors and economists on 20 external missions.

The document had the benefit that it was written by a small group of people: Robert Cooper for the English version, Nicole Gnesotto in French and Christoph Heusgen who worked on the German text. It was concise, clear and readable, not at all a classic document of European bureaucracy. However, it required us to navigate complicated issues with individual member states, such as the position of the nuclear forces of the UK and France, and to do this certain states were approached bilaterally to seek their approval of the entire text rather than having committees go through it paragraph by paragraph.

The core of the ESS was based on established norms such as multilateralism, the importance of the rule of law and good governance and human rights. It was distinctive by its significant difference in relation to the US security strategy, the 2002 version of which had explicitly committed the US to pre-emptive strikes against states or non-state actors which were deemed to threaten national security (USS 2002). In Europe the aim was to use a different terminology. Hence the determination to set out what we saw as forms of 'preventative' rather than pre-emptive security policy, and this was a theme which ran through the text of the ESS, and which also worked when translated into the EU's many different languages.

At the time, the European Union had no concept of human security. The ESS did not mention the term but it set in train an evolutionary process and allowed the introduction of innovative operational practices which would later be described as human security (HSSG 2004, 2007; Kaldor, Martin and Selchow 2007, Owen and Liotta 2006, Matlary 2008). When the original document was reviewed by the European Council at the end of 2008, the Report on the Implementation of the European Security Strategy explicitly used the term 'human security' to describe the European Union's security policies. This was perhaps symbolic, but nevertheless the fact that it was present showed how far the EU had come (European Parliament 2008).

More importantly, sympathy for human security had grown rapidly and its ideas had become increasingly embedded in the way EU institutions operated, in the EU's external policies, readiness to act and in the nature of the EU missions. The EU had begun to show what could be done in crisis management. This meant comprehensive approaches, working in partnership and respecting international law, but it also meant putting human beings at the heart of security.

Events also propelled the EU forward: as well as the war in Iraq, there was the continuing challenge of rebuilding the countries of the former Yugoslavia, of acting in Africa, sometimes in very difficult circumstances such as in Congo and Chad where we mounted military missions, and in Aceh in Indonesia when there was a peace negotiation and civilian mission following the December 2004 tsunami.

Firstly, these crises triggered a demand for more action by the international community, and specifically by the European Union. This demand was matched by a willingness of European citizens to become involved: not just to promote our material interests or because we risked being eclipsed by big powers of today or of tomorrow. The popularity of external policies, which was evident consistently in opinion polls, was also part of Europeans' wish to defend 'a certain idea of Europe' in a more fragmented world.

Secondly, these crises required the EU not only to act collectively but to intervene in ways which did not follow the pattern of classic security interventions. In some cases these interventions saw member states which had previously shunned participation in security issues taking the lead in operations, such as Ireland leading forces in Chad or Germany in the Democratic Republic of Congo.

The EU was breaking new ground in combining different aspects of security. For example, in Aceh it used the humanitarian crisis triggered by the tsunami to start negotiations about a peace treaty and begin to forge relationships between parties on the ground which contributed to a new environment of security. In Haiti the EU was also present after the earthquake.

There were very few conceptual approaches at the time which could give depth to what had been elaborated in the European Security Strategy in 2003. The premise was that war was no longer possible in the political sense; there was a need to approach security in a way which ruled out the classical ideas about the use of force. The rules of international politics were also changing. Globalisation had produced a double power shift: towards multipolarity, which meant taking into account the relative weights of new major players, such as China, Russia, India, as well as the US. It was also a shift away from states – to markets, NGOs, media and individuals. This meant we had to view international relations from a different standpoint.

It had to be clear that war was no longer on the agenda and the classic form of state-to-state security was no longer valid. These ideas needed to be put forward within the United Nations and in our partnerships with other international bodies. The EU also had to prove to our partners the added value of working together. Both because of what the European Union could offer, collectively, and because of who the EU was and what it stood for.

In 2003 as part of the work on the European Security Strategy we also started to share ideas about the future nature of conflict with outside experts. I asked Mary Kaldor to convene a group of practitioners and academics to look at the European Union's security capabilities. The Study Group which resulted was something of a ginger group. Its report proposed a doctrine of Human Security, a response force and a new legal framework to put into practice its claim that: 'the most appropriate role for Europe in the twenty-first century would be to promote human security' (HSSG 2004). The group's Barcelona Report defined human security as representing a departure from the state as the referent of security, and towards an emphasis on protecting individuals and communities. The aim of human security was: 'to protect the vital core of all human lives in ways that enhance human freedoms and human fulfilment', and puts the focus of security policies clearly on the 'needs of people in severe insecurity' (Glasius and Kaldor 2005: 67).

This built on the conceptualisations proposed by the Commission on Human Security, but it combined a narrow view of security, meaning freedom from fear with the broader perspective meaning freedom from want which came from the UN interpretation. The Human Security doctrine proposed by the Barcelona Report was based on five principles and these helped to explain what human security could mean for the EU. These were: the primacy of human rights, legitimate political authority, a bottom-up approach, effective multilateralism and a regional focus.[1]

However, the problem we faced with human security was that there was not a good definition which could be used. Member states found it difficult to know what we were talking about if we referred to human security. Nevertheless, there was the feeling that the EU had to produce documents and behave in ways which were consistent with this idea of putting human beings at the centre of our policies, rather than focusing on having a good definition. And to mobilise people to act. The operational aspects were key. The manner in which the Member States acted was the most important consideration.

This collective action contributed to building not only the European Union's capabilities, but also coherence among the different forms and representations of European foreign policy. People were not going to be convinced about a collective European security and defence policy (ESDP) by talking about it. It was imperative to put it into practice.

However, human security received strong backing from The European Parliament and from the European Commission, particularly during the period in office of the Commissioner of External Relations, Benita Ferrero-Waldner, a longstanding proponent of the concept (European Commission 2005). In 2008, two parties in the Parliament proposed an amendment to the Committee of Foreign Affairs' Kuhne Report on the implementation of the ESS, to include an emphasis on the concept of human security, with the objective of initiating 'a robust political mandate enabling it to act effectively in crises'.

The backing of some member states was also important in this period to promoting the concept of human security. The Presidency of the European Union, until the reforms of the Lisbon Treaty in 2007, was a key institution for member states to advance their own interests within the EU and became an important vehicle for advancing human security ideas. Sweden and Finland both used their presidencies to promote initiatives on ESDP, and the Spanish presidency of 2007 provided another opportunity for a meeting to stimulate debate about a human security approach. It helped make possible the successor to the Barcelona Report, the Madrid Report of the Human Security Study Group. Subsequent presidencies in Slovenia and the Czech Republic also helped the spread of ideas beyond the Council and the European Commission and among member states.

Between 2003 and 2009 sympathy towards the human security idea grew rapidly. There was a strong sense of learning by doing and that the EU was constructing itself by its own actions. This was much more important than fighting for a definition which in any case risked becoming bogged down in bureaucracy.

Our experiences led us in two directions: firstly, to develop the European Union's capabilities to be able to act decisively and autonomously; secondly, towards a manner of acting which we could call human security. In this period it was very important to develop military capabilities, and to have uniforms on our team. Civil–military co-ordination, and how to combine these two kinds of instrument, was a complicated rather than a controversial process, but it was part of being able to define what the EU was and how it would respond to the challenges we faced.

This development brought problems which were not just operational and logistical, but also cultural and political. The EU had the possibility of autonomous action but the only basis on which it could act was the culture of Berlin Plus, which meant using NATO resources for operations which were carried out solely by the EU. However, in moments when NATO would not act, for example in Africa, it mattered that the European Union had the capability to do something. Yet this meant two very different cultures. The European Union was not NATO. It was a political institution with military means. We had a reputation for soft power, not fighting. However, if we wanted to do crisis management in a serious way, we had to have military in the same building as civilians, but this represented a big cultural shift and a tense negotiation with the Americans. Yet it was crucial to making Europe prepared for autonomous action.

From the EU's perspective, Brussels could be used for strategic planning but was not suitable for operational headquarters. Among member states there were very few – Britain, France, Germany, possibly Spain and Italy – who could support this kind of operational organisation. The problem was that for the Americans, the Berlin Plus formula was the only way that the EU could act and this meant using NATO facilities. Our intention was not to have operational headquarters for their own sake but we recognised that there would be moments when NATO would not want to be involved and that if the EU was to step in, it needed an independent planning, strategic and operational centre. Eventually it was agreed to set up a facility at Tervuren, south of Brussels.

The second important development alongside capabilities was how the EU would act in crisis management operations. On the ground, for example in Chad, military capabilities were used to create and operationalise concepts of human security. The same was true in the Democratic Republic of Congo. In both cases it was demonstrated not only that EU member states could act collectively despite an apparent reticence of individual states such as Germany to intervene externally, but also that they could deliver a comprehensive type of crisis management, using different kinds of instruments. We were learning by doing. Successful implementation required that the EU was able to move from theory to practice and from practice to theory.[2]

Aceh, which was a civilian mission, was the best example of this flexibility and combination of different kinds of assistance. Georgia was another excellent example of a hybrid mission: a police operation organised from Brussels under the leadership of a civilian commander. In Georgia the EU demonstrated that it could act decisively and quickly. It took less than two weeks to mobilise a monitoring mission from the moment when an agreement was signed with the Russians in Moscow, which meant they would withdraw their troops from South Ossetia after the conflict of August 2008. Although it was criticised as ineffectual, the simultaneous conduct of high-level peace talks in Geneva about how to resolve the conflicts in the south Caucasus, with EU action on the ground, was an important contribution which the EU was able to put together better than any other actor.

In other interventions we were less successful in implementing human security. Although human security was the basis of EU operations in Kosovo, which saw the largest European external mission ever deployed in the form of EULEX – the 2008 law and order mission – Serb opposition made it difficult to fulfil our mandate and it showed that the politics also needs to be right if the European Union is to implement successfully its vision of security.

In Afghanistan the experience has been positive in the sense that the Germans and the French are both present – something that did not happen in Iraq – but at the same time Afghanistan has not been a crisis management operation. The EU has made a useful contribution to building a functioning state bringing aid, people and willingness. Europeans have deployed 30,000 troops – more than they ever did in Bosnia. The European Police (EUPOL) mission focuses on civilian policing and training the trainers. This presence is important, as part of defending Afghanistan from the threat of terrorism. And this has been acknowledged by our partners. But it has been difficult to persuade European public opinion of the benefits of this operation, and it is difficult to describe it as human security.

However, Afghanistan demonstrated the importance of one of the principles of the Human Security doctrine elaborated by the Study Group, that of regional focus. As the Barcelona Report noted: 'New wars have no clear boundaries … Indeed most situations of severe insecurity are located in regional clusters' (HSSG 2004: 13). In Afghanistan it has been demonstrated that we need a regional focus because of the importance of neighbouring countries such as Pakistan and their interest in promoting stability. This is something that the EU has recognised in its security policies and its presence in Afghanistan (Cassar 2009).

Another human security principle is a bottom-up approach. Only local people can produce politics which work for them. We as foreigners can help but it is ultimately the responsibility of populations on the ground, even though the consequences of failed politics reverberate internationally. In helping people to mobilise, it is fundamental to organise a better meeting between the EU's role as a policy-maker, acting from the top down, and the power of the people. This is also true if we want to ensure European citizens' support for the EU's external policies and a new tier of action so that it can be done both bottom up and top down.

Future potential: developing a human security approach to EU external relations

Crises in many parts of the world continue to present Europeans with the challenge to act to save lives, improve conditions in which people live and to contribute to security on a regional and global level. The EU has also tried to use human security to promote a different perspective on other types of security problems, in addition to conflicts. Climate change is one example of both a threat to stability and a threat multiplier which exacerbates tensions and instability and underpins other trends. It has the potential to overburden states and regions which are already fragile and spark new forms of conflict. The outcome of climate change is not just the risk of new humanitarian disasters or 'natural' catastrophes but political and security risks which would also directly affect European interests. Moreover, in line with the concept of human security, it is clear that many issues related to the impact of climate change on international security are interlinked, requiring comprehensive policy responses. For example, the attainment of the Millennium Development Goals would be at considerable risk because climate change, if unmitigated, may well wipe out years of development efforts (European Union 2008).

If climate change is an example of a 'new' type of security threat which provokes the EU to act, power relations between major states echo a more traditional form of international politics, but one where new approaches are also needed. In June 2008 Russian president Dmitri Medvedev put forward a proposal for a new European security architecture. He sought to re-construct relations between Russia and 'The West' on the basis of a European Security Treaty focusing on issues such as borders and the use of military force. This overture provided an opportunity to revive the EU-Russia relationship but with the added challenge of expanding classic understandings of the nature of security to include material, as well as physical security; and to include contemporary areas of concern, such as energy security, the impact of the financial and economic crisis, the environment and transnational crime (HSSG 2010).

The concept of human security encompasses the three baskets which made up the 1975 Helsinki Accords which were pivotal in creating a security dialogue with Russia during the Cold War. The third basket is about the security of individuals and communities, the second basket about material security and the life threatening risks arising from poverty and natural disasters, which require economic, scientific and cultural co-operation to manage and control. The first basket of Helsinki was about military security and this now requires thinking about how to make people feel safe through the rule of law and governance and not war-based measures. Therefore there is a modern twist to the 1975 agreement with Russia and human security offers a way for the EU to reframe a security compact and architecture to include Russia in making the European neighbourhood, and beyond, a safer place.

Human security offers a different lens through which to understand some of the key elements of European security. For example, conflicts in the Balkans or the Caucasus have become flashpoints for disagreements between Russia and the West and tend to be considered in geo-political terms or in terms of ethnic rivalry. Instead, Russia and the EU could start from a human security perspective and focus on how to end the conflicts in a way that enhances the human security of all the people living in those areas. Energy security is also framed in geo-political terms. A human security approach to energy would mean working together to ensure universal access to energy supplies, to combat climate change through energy efficiency and diversification, and to foster the stability and development of suppliers, who are excessively dependent on oil rents.

Instead of focusing on future military attacks, a human security approach would put much more emphasis on so-called non-traditional threats such as the spread of drugs, organised crime, terrorism, or natural and man-made disasters. And instead of trying to counter the rise of emerging powers, Russia and the EU should cooperate to strengthen global solutions to the global challenges of our time (Kaldor and Solana 2010).

The financial crisis of 2008 and the eurozone crisis of 2011 presented Europe with new and unexpected challenges about their commitment to each other as well as how they could act responsibly to tackle global problems. The first decade of the twenty-first century saw damaging rifts between European states over the War on Terror and the invasion of Iraq. The second decade began with a fracture over economics and finance. Yet Europeans still have the potential to play a decisive role in a world where power is fluid, where the relative influence of different players is uncertain but certainly changing. Leadership is required to seize this potential, as is a commitment to a new way of doing things, and a clear language which expresses our core values. State relations can never again be based on the possibility of war. The rule of law and common institutions must shape our future, as well as a concern for the lives of human beings everywhere. Human security has helped define such a European vision of politics in an age where we are constantly challenged by new and unfamiliar threats, and it should continue to guide our actions.

Notes

1 A sixth was added later: clear and transparent strategic direction.
2 See CIDOB, available at http://www.cidob.org/en/news/security_and_world_politics/javier_solana_ and_mary_kaldor_discuss_human_security_in_madrid (accessed 5 June 2013).

References

Cassar, A. (2009) 'European Union aid to Pakistan: steadily on the rise' *EUISS Analysis*, December, available at http://www.iss.europa.eu/uploads/media/EU_aid_to_Pakistan.pdf (accessed 30 September 2011).

European Commission (2005) *B. Ferrero-Waldner, 'Remarks to the joint meeting of the Foreign Affairs and Defence Committees of the European Parliament and of National Parliaments'*, European Parliament, Brussels, 5 October.

European Parliament (2008) *Report on the Implementation of the European Security Strategy and ESDP*, European Parliament Committee on Foreign Affairs, 15 May.

European Union (2008) *Climate Change And International Security*, paper from the High Representative and the European Commission to the European Council, available at http://www.consilium.europa.eu/uedocs/cms_data/docs/pressdata/en/reports/99387.pdf (accessed 30 September 2011).

Glasius, M. and Kaldor, M. (2005) 'Individuals first: a human security doctrine for the European Union', *Internationale Politik und Gesellschaft (IPG)* 1, p. 67.

HSSG (2004) *A Human Security Doctrine for Europe*, the Barcelona Report of the Study Group on Europe's Security Capabilities, available at http://eprints.lse.ac.uk/40209/ (accessed 5 June 2013).

HSSG (2007) *A European Way of Security*, the Madrid Report of the Human Security Study Group, available at http://eprints.lse.ac.uk/40207/ (accessed 5 June 2013).

HSSG (2010) *Helsinki Plus: Towards a Human Security Architecture for Europe*, the first report of the EU-Russia Human Security Study Group, available at http://www2.lse.ac.uk/internationalDevelopment/research/CSHS/humanSecurity/HelsinkiPlusEnglish.pdf (accessed 5 June 2013).

Kaldor, M. and Solana, J. (2010) 'Time for the human approach'. Open Democracy.net, 15 November, available at http://www.opendemocracy.net/od-russia/mary-kaldor-javier-solana/time-for-human-approach (accessed 30 September 2011).

Kaldor, M., Martin, M. and Selchow, S. (2007) 'Human security: a new strategic narrative for the EU', *International Affairs* 83, 2: 273–288.

Liotta, P. H. and Owen, T. (2006) 'Symbolic security: the EU takes on human security', *Parameters. The Journal of the US Army War College* 36, 3: 85–102.

Matlary, J. (2008) 'Much ado about little: the EU and human security', *International Affairs* 84, 1: 131–143.

Strath, B. (2002) 'A European identity: to the historical limits of a concept', *European Journal of Social Theory* 5: 387–401.

USS (2002) *United States Security Strategy*, available at http://georgewbush-whitehouse.archives.gov/nsc/nss/2002/nss5.html (accessed 5 June 2013).

20

THE PAN-AFRICANIZATION OF HUMAN SECURITY

Thomas Kwasi Tieku

Introduction

A distinctive characteristic of the African Union (AU) is the emphasis it has placed on human security, defined as the protection of people and communities, rather than of states, from violence and imminent danger. No international organization has embellished its binding agreements, key policy documents, treaties, memoranda of understanding, plans of action, mission and vision statements, communiqués, conventions, declarations and decisions with human security ideas more than the AU. Human securitization of AU appears to be at odds with post-September 11 2001 institutional development which often prioritized traditional military security issues. Indeed, traditional security seems to have regained its preeminent position in the post-9-11 international system. Most international institutions and structures that emerged post-9-11 provided privileged positions to counterterrorism and military security issues. Traditional security became a priority area in the assistance program of aid agencies and international organizations such as the United Nations assumed leadership roles in the promotion of traditional military and counterterrorism. Yet, the AU, which was inaugurated a few months after September 11 2001 terrorist attacks on the United States of America, kept faith with its human security approach to continental cooperation and interstate interactions in Africa. So how and why did human security become a central feature of the African Union? What challenges has the Union faced in its effort to make human security the only security doctrine in town?

The chapter argues that human security ideas entered into the practice of Pan-Africanism as part of a broader continental, institutional and normative shift in Africa in the early 1990s. The ideational shift was predicated on the idea that traditional understanding of security has contributed in impoverishing the African continent. A new understanding of security centered on the individual might help Africa deal with security and economic predicaments. The Kampala Movement and policy entrepreneurialship of the then Secretary General of the Organization of African Unity, Salim Ahmed Salim, are largely credited for undermining the attraction of traditional security ideas among the African ruling elite and for introducing human security as a persuasive alternative to fill the intellectual void which emerged. The ideational shift led to the formation of the African Union as an instrument for the promotion and socialization of human security ideas at the interstate level. Almost all the decisions, declarations and protocols that African leaders adopted in the first eight years since the formation of the AU had strong human security undertones. The AU is, however, facing tremendous challenges in promoting its human security agenda. The Arab spring, which led to the toppling of two major financers of the AU, and the support the international community gave to Libyan rebels have turned human security from a darling idea to almost a taboo subject in the corridors of the AU.

The argument of the chapter is organized into four sections. The first section sets a context for the analysis, noting that the formation of the African Union was informed, in part, by human security concerns. It is followed by an outline of ideas of human security as they may be said to exist in the AU, teasing out the human security elements in key AU documents. The third part of the article examines AU institutions promoting human security. The fourth section examines challenges the AU faces in its efforts to convince the African elite that they should accept the human security doctrine as the desirable norms and guiding principles in their states.

Pan-Africanism in practice: from the OAU to the AU

African leaders created the AU on May 26, 2001 to reflect a shift in the focus of the Pan-African project.[1] Pan-Africanism as practised within the institutional framework of the Organization of African Unity (OAU) focused primarily on legitimizing and institutionalizing statehood in Africa. Protection of states and governing regimes in Africa became the referent of Pan-Africanism. As part of the efforts to protect and consolidate the African state, the Charter of the OAU committed African governments to a treaty that contained some of the strongest clauses that defend and hold together key elements of juridical sovereignty ever to be embodied in any international organization (Clapham 1996). The Charter also put in place only institutions, rules and administrative mechanisms that strengthened sovereign prerogatives and the territorial integrity of African states. Many institutional restrictions were imposed on the OAU Secretariat to prevent it from becoming a supranational entity.

The institutionalization of the state across the African continent meant that Pan-Africanism needed a new focus and meaning. A new generation of Pan-Africanists led by the eminent South African Nelson Mandela and the shrewd Tanzanian diplomat Salim Ahmed Salim made conscious efforts in the 1990s to give a new meaning to Pan-Africanism. They felt that Pan-Africanism needed to deal with challenges facing ordinary Africans, rather than those encountered by broader entities such as states and regimes (Mandela 1994; Salim 1990). They identified three main challenges: namely, security threats, underdevelopment and the impact of international political economic forces (Salim 1995). These three major issues informed the creation of the AU and the drafting of its legal text, called the Constitutive Act of the African Union (CA). To provide a framework for dealing with human insecurity, the CA empowers the Union to prevent, manage and resolve conflicts on the continent (Powell and Tieku 2005).[2] The hope is that the AU will create conditions in which peace may prevail on the African continent, to make continental Africa a 'zone of peace.' African leaders also felt that regional economic integration could provide a basis for sustainable development; as a result, the CA provides the legal and institutional framework for African states to integrate their economies (African Union 2001). Last, the AU is designed to assist African governments in managing international issues effectively. As part of the move to enhance Africa's role in the international system, in July 2003 in Maputo in Mozambique, African leaders asked the AU Commission 'to set up a negotiating team (…) headed by [an] experienced person to negotiate on behalf of all Member States the fundamental issues that are being negotiated in the World Trade Organization (WTO)' (African Union 2003).

These three core areas drive the work of the 17 institutions that make up the AU (Cilliers 2003). Of those, the key ones are the African Heads of State and Government (Assembly), the

Executive Council, the Permanent Representative Committee, the Pan-African Parliament (PAP), AU Commission, Peace and Security Council, the Pan-African Court of Justice, the Economic, Social and Cultural Councils (ECOSOC), the African Central Bank, the Investment Bank and the Monetary Fund. In theory, the Assembly provides policy directions, including the human security agenda for the Union. In practice, though, the AU Commission and the Peace and Security Council have taken the center stage in shaping the AU human security agenda. The AU human security objectives entail creating conditions for individuals to satisfy their basic needs. These include, first, working to provide the social, economic, political, environmental and cultural conditions necessary for the survival and dignity of the individual; second, striving to create conditions for the protection of and respect for human rights and good governance; and third, trying to guarantee for each individual the opportunity to fulfill his/her full development (African Union 2005a). This understanding of human security informs the AU's work in the areas of peace, security, political governance and economic development.

AU human security agenda

The AU human security agenda in the areas of peace and security is clearly expressed in Article 4(h) of the Constitutive Act of the African Union. Article 4(h), which empowers the Union to intervene in the affairs of a member state in order to 'prevent war crimes, genocide and crimes against humanity,' was inserted into the CA, as a number of informed writers on the CA have eloquently argued, with a view to protecting ordinary people in Africa from abusive governments (Malan 2002; Cilliers and Sturman 2002; Kioko 2003).[3] To provide an operational arm to this specific human security element, the AU made room for the creation of an African Standby Force charged with the task of intervening militarily in states for humanitarian purposes (African Union 2001). The condition laid down for human security intervention under the AU 'goes "beyond" the provision made for intervention in the internal affairs of a country in the UN Charter' (Schoeman 2003). The CA has actually set lower thresholds for intervention than those outlined in any international legal code (Weiss 2004). The specification of *war crimes, genocide, and crimes against humanity* by the drafters of the CA as grounds for intervention has provided a clearer set of criteria for the Union to intervene in a state for human security purposes. The AU, unlike other international organizations, does not necessarily require the consent of a state to intervene in its internal affairs in situations where populations are at risk. That is, the OAU's system of complete consensus has been abandoned. Under the AU, a decision on the part of a two-thirds majority of the Assembly is required for intervention purposes (Powell and Tieku 2005). The AU used the two-thirds majority principle to arrive at the decision to deploy a peacekeeping force to monitor a ceasefire in Burundi in April 2003. The Assembly also used the principle to decide on the mission to the Darfur region of Sudan in the summer of 2004. The AU also approaches economic development from a human security perspective. The development agenda in Articles 3 and 4 of the CA is intended to create conditions necessary for sustainable development to take place. As part of the sustainable development agenda, the AU commits its Member States to ensuring balanced economic development, to promoting gender equality and good health, and to working towards eradicating preventable diseases (Articles 3 (j) and (n); 4(l) and (n)).

The AU has adopted an approach to political governance in Africa that is human security-centered inasmuch as the CA commits Member States of the AU to promoting 'respect for the sanctity of human life' (Article 4(o)). Article 4(i), moreover, makes it clear that African people have a 'right to live in peace.' Article 3(h) of the CA, therefore, commits Member States to a path where they will 'promote and protect human and peoples' rights in accordance with the

African Charter on Human and Peoples' Rights and other relevant human rights instruments.' It is also significant that 3(g) enjoins member governments to promote democratic principles and institutions, popular participation and good governance. This provision in the CA is important for the AU human security agenda, because it is generally understood in the human security research community that democratic development is a critical aspect of human security (Hammerstad 2005). The decision to exclude from the AU states whose governments came to power through unconstitutional means therefore advances the human security agenda. The strength of the human security ideas embedded in the CA begs the question of how and why these human security doctrines entered into the discourse, agenda, documents and programs of the AU.

Pan-Africanism and human security

Human security entered into the discourse of Pan-Africanism in the early 1990s. It was initiated by the Kampala Movement and Salim Ahmed Salim (Deng and Zartman 2002). The Kampala Movement was an initiative of civil society groups that met in Kampala in Uganda in the early 1990s to develop a regime of principles regarding security, stability, development and cooperation for Africa. At the heart of the principles, widely known as the CSSDCA, was a conscious effort to redefine security and sovereignty, and to demand certain 'standards of behaviour ... from every government [in Africa] in the interest of common humanity' (Obasanjo and Mosha 1992: 260). The Movement demanded that African leaders redefine their states' security as a multi-dimensional phenomenon going beyond military considerations to include economic, political and social aspects of the individual, the family and the society. In the view of the Movement, '[t]he concept of security must embrace all aspects of society ... [and the] security of a nation must be based on the security of the life of the individual citizens to live in peace and to satisfy basic needs' (Obasanjo and Mosha 1992: 265).

On security, the CSSDCA package aimed at influencing African leaders to treat security as both a human security issue and an interdependent phenomenon.[4] As a human security issue, it proposed that '[t]he concept of security must embrace all aspects of society ... [and that the] security of a nation must be based on the security of the life of the individual citizens to live in peace and to satisfy basic needs' (AHG/Decl.4 (XXXVI)). As an interdependent phenomenon, it urged African leaders to see the security of their states 'as inseparably linked to that of other African countries.' This not only implies that the maintenance of security anywhere in Africa is a collective responsibility of all African states, but also suggests that sovereignty no longer offers the protection behind which African leaders can conceal abuse of their citizens.

On stability, the CSSDCA set the criteria for judging the solidity of African states, suggesting that it should be grounded in liberal principles, such as respect for the rule of law, human rights, good governance and the participation of African citizens in public affairs. On cooperation and development, the package did not contain anything distinctly different from previous proposals submitted to the OAU. The majority of issues discussed under the cooperation and development sections essentially reiterated the traditional rhetorical Pan-African ideals, such as African solutions for African problems and the importance of integration for Africa's development, among others.

The emphasis the reforms laid on the effective participation of civil society in cooperation and development programs brings to Pan-Africanism an essential missing link. Indeed, the CSSDCA urged African leaders not only to involve regional and grassroots civil society organizations in the continental decision-making process, but also to allow nongovernmental groups to act as the main engine for dealing with security, stability, development and cooperation issues. In addition, they established a clear relationship between development and cooperation and also declared that the 'security, stability and development of every African country is [*sic*] inseparably linked' to that of other African states (Africa Union 2002). This meant that successful management of security, stability and development requires a continental approach. The CSSDCA called on African leaders to develop 'a common African agenda based on a unity of purpose' to confront Africa's security, stability and development challenges (Africa Union 2002: 27).

The human security document was submitted to African leaders for integration into the OAU framework in early 1991. The OAU convened a meeting of African governments to discuss it in May 1991 in Kampala in Uganda. The leaders who attended agreed in principle in the Kampala Declaration to explore the possibility of integrating the ideas into the OAU in another meeting in June 1991 in Abuja in Nigeria. The CSSDCA was not adopted during the Abuja summit because of opposition by Libya's Muammar Ghaddafi, Sudan's Omar Hassan Ahmed el-Bashir and Kenya's Daniel Arap Moi (Deng and Zartman 2002). The leaders suspended discussions on the document and, indeed, on human security indefinitely.

Although the OAU leadership rejected the CSSDCA, the Kampala initiative provided the platform for Salim Ahmed Salim to place human protection on the OAU's agenda. The specific elements of the human protection agenda formed part of a broader policy initiative articulated in a document called *The Political and Socio-Economic Situation in Africa and the Fundamental Changes Taking Place in the World*, which the Assembly of the OAU adopted as a Declaration on July 11, 1990 (Salim 1990). The Declaration recognized that the end of the Cold War had fundamentally changed the geopolitics of the world, and that African governments needed to adopt specific measures to adapt to the new world order. It further argued that African states would henceforth have to do things on their own; there would be no geo-strategic basis for outside powers to protect Africans. It therefore called on the leaders to revive indigenous continental protection initiatives. More specifically, the Declaration urged the OAU leadership to develop a framework for preventing, managing and resolving conflicts, since there would be no rationale for the international community to keep peace and promote human rights in Africa in the post-Cold War era.

The Declaration opened the space for Salim, during the OAU summit in July 1991 in Abuja in Nigeria, to propose to the Assembly a framework to create a mechanism for the OAU to prevent, manage and resolve conflicts in Africa. The mechanism was not just for the order-maintaining purposes that many writers tend to emphasize; it had a broader goal of protecting ordinary Africans from imminent danger. The Assembly adopted the mechanism in principle, and instructed the OAU Secretariat to hold consultations with Member States and to revise the proposal to reflect 'the views, comments and proposals of Member States' (AHG/Decl. 1 XXVIII). A much watered-down version of the mechanism was adopted by the Assembly in Cairo, Egypt in June 1993 (Ibok 1999). Some governments in Africa, in particular the governments of Daniel Arap Moi of Kenya and Lansana Conté of Guinea, ensured that the provisions in the draft framework that placed emphasis on human protection and proposed the delegation of powers to the OAU Secretariat to protect ordinary Africans from state abuse were removed. The extensive revisions of the draft framework by African governments largely explain why the mechanism that was approved during the OAU summit in Cairo in June 1993 adopted a traditional security approach. Nevertheless, Salim's initiative set in motion serious discussions within the OAU leadership on the need for the OAU to play a central role in protecting ordinary Africans from imminent threats.

The former South African President, Nelson Mandela, pushed further the human security discussions on June 13, 1994 when he asked African leaders to empower the OAU to protect

African people and to prevent African governments from abusing the sovereignty of states (Mandela 1994). The call emboldened the OAU Secretariat to initiate a series of reform processes between 1995 and 1998 that were aimed at structuring the OAU in order to make it focus on human security concerns (Salim 1995, 1997). It also, in 1998, encouraged the Secretariat to submit, and the Assembly to adopt, three key human security issues. The first sought to make the promotion of 'strong and democratic institutions' a key objective of the OAU (AHG/Decl. XXXV). The second excluded from the OAU states 'whose Governments came to power through unconstitutional means,' and the third gave the OAU the mandate to assist military regimes that may exist on the African continent in moving towards a democratic system of government. The election of Olusegun Obasanjo, who was a key figure in the Kampala Movement, as president of Nigeria encouraged the OAU Secretariat to embellish OAU documents and policies with human security doctrines. Obasanjo himself made it a top priority to set in motion the process of integrating the CSSDCA into the OAU (Deng and Zartman 2002: xv).

The decision to create the AU in September 1999 provided a good opportunity for the Nigerian and the South African governments to support the OAU Secretariat in merging human security doctrines with Pan-African ideas. The strategy adopted by the Secretariat aimed to encourage the delegations that negotiated the legal treaty of the AU to codify as principles of the AU some of the ideas in the CSSDCA while simultaneously working with African leaders to ensure the adoption of the CSSDCA as a working document of the AU. The then Assistant Secretary General in Charge of Political Affairs, Said Djinnit, and the Acting Legal Counsellor of the OAU, Ben Kioko, played instrumental roles in making the delegations adopt the human security ideas found in Articles 3 and 4 of the CA and that were discussed in the previous sections of this chapter. As a step towards making African leaders adopt the CSSDCA, the Secretariat, with the strong backing of the Nigerian government, convened a ministerial meeting in May 2000 to discuss ways to integrate the CSSDCA into the AU/OAU. The Report of the ministerial meeting that was prepared by the Secretariat was approved by the OAU summit in Lomé in July 2000. African leaders agreed to use the CSSDCA as norms and guiding principles of security, stability, development and cooperation in a Memorandum of Understanding in July 2002 in Pretoria in South Africa. Though the Memorandum of Understanding added many traditional security concerns to the CSSDCA, it retained most of the human security principles.

Institutional mechanisms for promoting human security

The Memorandum of Understanding paved the way for the Secretariat to create a unit within the OAU to coordinate CSSDCA activities. The CSSDCA unit is now called the African Citizens' Directorate (CIDO). More crucially, it opened the space for the AU Commission to try to institutionalize human security ideas in Africa, which it is doing through civil society channels. The CIDO is building coalitions around, and engineering consensus on, human security within the civil society groups. The office of the Chair Person of the AU Commission, the Political Department, the Peace and Security Department and the Legal Affairs Department are also using state channels, such as the Assembly of Heads of State and Government, the Council of Ministers and the Permanent Representative Committee, to convince the African ruling elite to accept human security doctrines.

The African Citizens' Directorate (CIDO)

The CIDO was originally established in 2001 as the implementation directorate of the CSSDCA. The Nigerian government, which provided the resources for the creation of the directorate, wanted the unit to focus primarily on integrating the CSSDCA ideas into all documents of the AU. The AU Commission gave the CIDO the additional responsibility of facilitating civil society engagement with the AU. As part of its efforts to engage civil society with the AU organs and process, in 2001 the CIDO developed an annual conference of indigenous African civil society and the AU. The CIDO usually invites over 50 civil society groups in Africa to attend these conferences, which are normally held prior to AU summits. About five conferences have been held since the first AU-civil society meeting was held in June 2001. The conferences have turned out to be a good place for the AU Commission to sell AU programs, projects and agendas to civil society groups. The CIDO is using the conferences to create awareness about AU's work and persuade the civil society groups to integrate AU's policies, including the human security agenda, into their advocacy activities and promote them in their states. Because the CIDO was established to promote CSSDCA and the AU human security agenda, the discussions of all past AU-civil society conferences have been dominated by human security issues. The head of the CIDO, Jimmi Adisa, has taken full advantage of the AU-civil society conference to create awareness and update civil society groups about the CSSDCA and AU human security activities. The CIDO is also promoting the human security agenda in the intellectual and diaspora communities. The head of CIDO has taken advantage of the CIDO civil society mandate to sell the human security agenda at two big conferences to selected African intellectuals and Africans in the diaspora. The first conference was held in October 2004 in Senegal, and the second was held in July 2006 in Brazil.

Challenges to AU human security promotion

The AU human security agenda is impressive on paper but many of the ideas the AU seeks to implement are abstract in nature, difficult to operationalize and even harder to implement. One of the distinctive markers of the AU human security agenda is the acceptance of the idea that an African state can claim to have security not only when individual citizens live in peace but also when their basic needs are satisfied. The concept of peace is not only loaded but it is a tall order for African states, such as Democratic Republic of Congo where banditry, rape, and lawlessness appear to be widespread and Somalia which is often used as a classic case to illustrate failed state thesis in mainstream scholarship, to even aspire to achieve negative peace. It will at the minimum require disbarment, demobilization and integration of former combatants into mainstream society. But as well-equipped international organizations such as the United Nations and North Atlantic Treaty Organization (NATO) have found out in places like Burundi, Côte d'Ivoire, Sierra Leone and Afghanistan, DDR 'is a complex process … and many DDR programmes stall or are only partly implemented' (UN 2009). Indeed, NATO had difficulty implementing the DDR mandate in the Afghanistan mission.

The AU human security agenda revolves around the practice of rule of law, respect for human rights and consolidation of democracies in African societies. But as Hawkins (2009) tells us, the definitions of these concepts are 'not entirely open ended' and they mean different things to different people. Certainly Libya, Egypt and Algeria – three of the five countries who contribute 75 per cent to AU's operational budget – do not share AU's interpretation of these concepts. The Algerian President in particular has often warned African leaders to take a cautious approach, arguing that sovereignty is the last frontier and the only protection Africans have in a highly unequal and selfish world.[5] While Algeria has not been able to prevent the AU Commission from inserting human security ideas in almost every AU document, it is hard to see where the AU Commission will get the money to translate them into concrete actions. Libyan and Egyptian new leaders have shown little interest in human security ideas and South African and Nigerian interests in human security have gone down since Presidents Obansajo and Mbeki left office. Most keen observers of AU politics do not expect current governments of South Africa and Nigeria to stand firmly behind the human security principles embedded in AU should the Algerian government purge future AU documents of any human security pretensions. There are strong indications that future AU documents will contain little human security ideas. The ultra conservative AU's Permanent Representative Council (PRC), composed of Ambassadors from AU member states, has repositioned itself as the vanguard of traditional realist understanding of security following the just ended NATO's military campaign in Libya. The PRC members will use the gate keeping powers they have to prevent any human security oriented document from going through.

Some member states of the AU are also unhappy about the space the CIDO has opened for civil society to participate in AU activities. The states that opposed the integration of the CSSDCA into the OAU in the early 1990s remain uncomfortable with the human security agenda. It is perhaps the case that these leaders are opposed to AU's promotion of human security doctrines because it renders their regimes vulnerable. They have however succeeded in creating the impression in AU leadership circles that the human security and the CSSDCA process are nothing but vehicles for promoting Western values in Africa. A number of African leaders such as President Bashir seem to think that the introduction of human security language and doctrines into the work and documents of the AU is a conscious effort by Western governments and institutions to use the AU as an instrument to pursue their cultural colonialism project.

The anti-human security leaders in the AU leadership have asserted their influence primarily because the unwavering support human security enjoyed in the Assembly of the AU during the early days of the AU has waned considerably. Strong supporters of the CSSDCA, such as Obasanjo and Mbeki, are no longer in power and their successors are less keen on human security. The ambivalent attitude of the supporters of human security has allowed the anti-human security leaders in the Assembly to move to curb its influence in recent AU documents. For instance, the African Union Non-Aggression and Defence Pact which was recently developed took a minimalist human security approach. Compared with the original draft of the Common African Defence and Security Policy that was developed in the early days of the AU, this follow-up document (i.e. the African Union Non-Aggression and Defence Pact) paid human security scant heed. The minimalist human security orientations of recent policy documents of the AU attest to the increasing influence of the anti-human security elements in the AU leadership. The increasing visibility of the anti-CSSDCA elements in the AU leadership raises the question: does human security have a future within the AU?

In addition, the CIDO human security promotion through civil society groups is also facing serious problems. The anti-human security governments in Africa are undermining CIDO's ability to meet with civil society groups. These governments usually do not cooperate with the CIDO to convene the AU-civil society conferences when they host the AU summits. The Libyan and the Sudanese governments failed to give the CIDO the necessary logistical and political support to convene AU-civil society conferences prior to the summits in Sirte in June 2005 and in Khartoum in January 2006.

The AU-civil society conferences have also come under attack. Some of the big non-governmental organizations (NGOs) operating in Africa have started to question their relevance. They are unhappy with the CIDO's engagements with African civil society, and claim that the civil society groups invited to these conferences are neither representative of civil society organizations in Africa nor given the opportunity to contribute to the work of the AU. A recent report by some of the NGOs sums up their concerns:

> [T]he quality of the debate [during AU–civil society conferences] is often poor, with a lack of substance, and there are some concerns that the forums are rather used to endorse decisions that have already been taken than to provide a real opportunity for civil society organisations to influence decision-making at the summit... In addition, the criteria applied by CIDO in selecting participants to attend forums are not clear; many of those who are invited are quite closely connected to governments, and there have been cases where self-funded participants have been excluded from the meetings, even though they would appear to fulfill the qualifications to attend.
>
> *(AfriMAP, AFRODAD, Oxfam 2007)*

The paucity of opportunities civil society gets to shape AU agenda may discourage civil society groups from adding AU human security initiatives to their work.

The CIDO unit itself is seriously understaffed. Besides Jimmi Adisa, the head, there is only one person working full-time. It is also poorly equipped. The institutional capacity of CIDO is weak in part because it was envisioned to be a mere coordinating unit. The Department for Political Affairs (PDA) and Department for Peace and Security (DPS) were supposed to manage major aspects of human security projects. But both institutions have serious capacity deficiencies. The current structure of the AU Commission allows the PDA to recruit nine full-time professionals of which five are required to work on issues relating to democracy, governance, human rights, elections issues and the other four have responsibilities over humanitarian, refugee and internally displaced affairs. As of the time of writing, three of the nine were not in post and none of the six professionals who have been recruited are experts on human security. The DPS is relatively well equipped as its staff complement is three times that of the PDA. The problem is that the department has been suffering from high turnovers as many of its most competent officials continue to be poached by other international organizations such as the UN. The DPS in particular and the AU in general have become training grounds for the UN. The lure of bigger pay and less work made some of the ardent Pan-Africanists and senior professional staff at the DPS abandon the AU for the UN.[6] It has become an open secret that many people in the AU aspire to move to a more lucrative even if lowered-ranked position in the UN. The other problem with both departments is that they are generally perceived as elitist institutions whose activities are often inaccessible to civil society groups.

Both departments have serious financial challenges with the DPA in the more difficult position. The DPA's activities are funded mainly through the extremely unreliable annual contributions made by AU member states. African governments have carried the terrible habit of serially defaulting in the payment of annual contributions. While the situation is not as bad as the OAU era, there are far too many governments in Africa who are just happy to free ride. On average, less than 50 per cent of statutory contributions are paid on time every year. Even in better times such as in 2005, the AU was only able to collect just 57 per cent, representing US$36 million out of US$63 million of assessed contributions. This money was supposed to cover the 2005 budget of around US$158 million, representing US$63 million for operations and US$95 million for programs. The statutory contributions paid in that year could not even cover the US$63 million operating budget. The AU sought to change the situation in 2005 by developing new funding formulae which has made five African States – Algeria, Egypt,

Libya, Nigeria and South Africa – contribute 75 per cent to AU's operational budget. But as AU Commissioner for Economic Affairs, Maxwell Mkwezalamba, observed in 2006, the new funding formula is unsustainable (Maxwell Mkwezalamba 2006). The shift to an 'ability-to-pay system' has moved AU from the realm of solidarity politics, a core value and a unique feature of Pan-Africanism, to the area of *realpolitic*. There is a fear that the five states will use their financial contribution to control the AU similar to the way the permanent members of the Security Council control the UN system. The current leaders of the five paymaster generals of the AU are at best indifferent to human security and at worst hostile. While the new Libyan and Egyptian leaders have not shown any interest in the AU human security agenda, Algeria, Nigeria and South Africa consider human security or protection of civilians as a new regime change language. The NATO bombings of Libya have turned human security from a darling idea to a taboo subject in the corridors of the AU.

Conclusion

This chapter sought to show that the AU has taken a center stage in the promotion of human security in Africa. The AU drew on the work of the civil society movement in the early 1990s to develop a Pan-African version of human security that comprises principles of security, stability, development and cooperation in Africa. This conceptualization of human security is meant not only to give a new perspective on the doctrines; it provides creative ways of making the concept acceptable in Africa. Member States of the AU approved the CSSDCA in 2000 in Lome, Togo, and the OAU Secretariat and the AU Commission made serious efforts to integrate it into the work of the AU. Institutions of the AU Commission, such as the Peace and Security Department and the Political and Legal Affairs Departments, have translated the doctrines into AU documents and work. They have used the insights of the CSSDCA to enrich AU binding agreements, key policy documents, treaties, memoranda of understanding, plans of action, mission and vision statements, communiqués, conventions, declarations and decisions. Almost all decisions, declarations and protocols that the leadership of the Union adopted after the formation of the AU have some element of human security.

The integration of human security doctrines into AU binding agreements and other documents is significant in part because legalization at the continental level is one of the most important components of institutionalization of ideas and doctrines and in part because it provides a basis for the incorporation of the doctrines into national laws and policies. It also strengthens the hands of organizations and actors promoting human security in African states to influence their governments to pursue human security policies. Legalization of the doctrines would at least make African governments careful in using these human security ideas for rhetorical purposes only.

The AU has moved to persuade the African elite to adopt human security as a guiding principle. The AU Commission has mandated the African Citizens' Directorate to pursue socialization and institutionalization processes. The African Citizens' Directorate is doing this by creating awareness among civil society groups about the AU human security agenda and activities. The hope is that the civil society groups will integrate the AU human security work into their advocacy activities and then promote it in their states. The African Citizens' Directorate has encountered serious challenges in its efforts to institutionalize human security. A number of African governments are undermining CIDO's work, tacitly undercutting its ability to meet with civil society groups. The CIDO also faces serious institutional and human resource challenges. It is understaffed and under-resourced. There is also the real danger that the entire human security agenda is going off the radar screen of the AU. The Arab Spring has toppled major financiers of the AU. The new Libyan and Egyptian leaders have not shown any interest in the AU human security agenda, and Algerian, Nigerian and South African governments consider human security or protection of civilians as a new regime change language. Indeed, the NATO bombings of Libya seem to have taken away any appetite AU political leaders had for promoting human security at the state level.

Notes

1 26 May, 2001 is recognized as the official date that the AU came into existence because it was the date that the Constitutive Act of the African Union entered into force. It was exactly thirty days after the deposit of the instrument of ratification by two-thirds of the member states of the OAU, as provided for in Article 28 of the CA.
2 The new security architecture, which is managed by a newly created fifteen-member Peace and Security Council (herein referred to as PSC), calls for the development of a rapid reaction force, an African Standby Force (ASF), to be fully developed by the year 2010. The ASF will build on the military capabilities of the regional economic communities in Africa to develop the ASF. Note that the new security regime had already undertaken its first peacemaking operations called the African Mission in Burundi (AMIB). AMIB was an integrated mission made up of 3500 contingents drawn mainly from South Africa, Mozambique and Ethiopia deployed by the AU in April 2003 to monitor a ceasefire in Burundi. On 21 May 2004, the United Nations Security Council passed a resolution to take over the mission after AMIB had stabilized and created conditions conducive for peacekeeping operations. It has also deployed another mission to the Darfur region of Sudan.
3 The article has been amended to include intervention to 'restore peace and stability' and in response to 'a serious threat to legitimate order.'
4 This section draws on Tieku (2004).
5 President Boutifleka of Algeria used the phrase 'the last frontier.' Quoted in Adonia Ayebare, 'Regional Perspectives on Sovereignty and Intervention,' *Discussion Paper of ICISS Round Table Consultation*, Maputo, 10 March 2001. Available online at http://web.gc.cuny.edu/icissresearch/maputu.htm (accessed on 2 March 2004).
6 Prominent DPS figures who moved from AU to UN included former Commissioner for Peace and Security and one time the number two person in the Pan-African organization Said Djinit, former head of Conflict Management Division Sam Ibok, and former information analyst Musifiky Mwanasali.

Bibliography

African Union. 2001. *The Constitutive Act.* Addis Ababa: African Union Publication.
—2002. African Union, *Memorandum of Understanding on Security, Stability, Development and Cooperation.* Durban.
—2003. *Declaration of the Heads of State and Government of the African Union on the Fifth WTO Ministerial Conference at the Second Ordinary Session.* Assembly of the African Union Second Ordinary Session 10–12 July 2003, Maputo, Mozambique. Addis Ababa: African Union Publication.
—2005a. *Declaration of the Heads of State and Government of the African Union on the Fourth Ordinary Session of African Union*, Addis Ababa, Ethiopia.
—2005b. African Union, *Non-Aggression and Common Defence Pact.* Available from: http://www.africa-union.org/root/AU/Documents/Treaties/text/Non%20Aggression%20Common%20Defence%20Pact.pdf (accessed 1 March 2007).
—2006. Report on the elaboration of a framework document on Post Conflict Reconstruction and Development (PCRD), Banjul, The Gambia.
AfriMAP, AFRODAD, Oxfam. 2007. *Towards a People Driven African Union: Current Obstacles and New Opportunities.* Available from: http://www.soros.org/resources/articles_publications/publications/people_20070124/au_20070124.pdf (accessed 1 March 2007).
Cilliers, J. 2003. A summary of outcomes from the 2002 OAU/AU summits in Durban. *Institute for Security Studies Occasional Paper,* 76.
Cilliers, J. and Sturman, K. 2002. The right intervention: enforcement challenges for the African Union.

African Security Review, 11(3). Available from: http://www.issafrica.org/pubs/ASR/11No3/Cilliers. html (accessed 4 March 2007).

Clapham, C. 1996. *Africa and the International System: The Politics of State Survival.* Cambridge: Cambridge University Press.

Deng, F. M. and Zartman, I. W. (eds). 2002. *A Strategic Vision for Africa: The Kampala Movement.* Washington, D.C: The Brookings Institution Press.

Hammerstad, A. 2005. *AU Commitments to Democracy in Theory and Practice: An African Human Security Review.* South African Institute of International Affairs, Monograph, 2005. Available from: http://www.africanreview.org/forum/docs/feb04partmeet/saiia1.pdf (accessed 2 March 2007).

Hawkins, D. 2009. Protecting democracy in Europe and the Americas. *International Organization,* 62 (Summer): 373–403.

Ibok, S. 1999. *The OAU Mechanism for Conflict Prevention, Management and Resolution.* Addis Ababa: Organization of Africa Unity Publication.

Kioko, B. 2003. The right of intervention under the African Union's Constitutive Act; non-interference to non-intervention. *International Review of the Red Cross,* 85: 807–825.

Malan, M. 2002. *New Tools in the Box? Towards A Standby Force for the African Union.* Johannesburg: Institute of Security Studies.

Mandela, N. 1994. *Statement of the President of the Republic of South Africa at the OAU Heads of State and Government Summit.* Tunisia. Available from: http://www.anc.org.za/ancdocs (accessed 4 March 2007).

Mkwezalamba, Maxwell (2006) Statement on the Occasion of the Opening of the Meeting of Governmental Experts on Alternative Sources of Financing the African Union, African Union, Addis Ababa, available at: http://www.africa-union.org/root/UA/Conferences/Mai/EA/29mai/WELCOME%20STATEMENT%20%20Alternative%20source%20of%20funding.pdf.

Obasanjo, O. and Mosha, F. G. N. (eds). 1992. *Africa Rise to the Challenge: Conference Report on the Kampala Forum.* Abeokuta/New York: Africa Leadership Forum.

Powell, K. and Tieku, T. K. 2005. The African Union and The Responsibility to Protect: Towards a Protection Regime for Africa? *International Insights,* 20(1&2): 215–235.

Salim, A. S. 1990. *The Political and Socio-Economic Situation in Africa and the Fundamental Changes Taking Place in the World.* Addis Ababa: Organization of Africa Unity Publication.

—1995. *The Report of the Secretary-General to the Special Session of the Council of Ministers on Economic and Social Issues in African Development.* Addis Ababa: Organization of Africa Unity Publication.

—1997. *Introductory Note to the Report of the Secretary-General to the Thirty-third Ordinary Session.* Addis Ababa: Organization of Africa Unity Publication.

Schoeman, M. 2003. *The African Union after the Durban 2002 Summit.* Available from: http://www.teol.ku.dk/cas/nyhomepage/mapper/Occasional%20Papers/Schoeman_internetversion.doc (accessed 4 March 2007).

Tieku, T. 2004. Explaining the clash and accommodation of interests of major actors in the creation of the African Union. *African Affairs,* 103: 249–267.

United Nations Organization. 2009. *Disarmament, Demobilization, and Reintegration Resource Centre.* Available from http://www.unddr.org/what-is-ddr/introduction_1.aspx (accessed 4 June 2013).

Weiss, T. G. 2004. The sunset of humanitarian intervention? The Responsibility to Protect in a unipolar era. *Security Dialogue,* 35(2): 135–153.

21

HUMAN SECURITY AND EAST ASIA

Paul Evans

Of the new approaches to security in East Asia in the past two decades, human security remains the most controversial. The idea that the individual must be at least one of the referent points in answering the eternal questions of security for whom, from what, and by what means has been criticized as an alien Western import, analytically problematic, vague, morally risky, unsustainable, and counterproductive. It is far less controversial when applied to development issues and has spawned a conceptual cousin, the idea of "non-traditional security" that has found wide acceptance.

The geo-politics of China's rise and regional responses overlap with unresolved territorial disputes, competitive arms acquisitions, cyber clashes, national rivalries, and intra-state conflicts to provide a full agenda of national security concerns for the region. But parallel to these concerns has been the recognition in academic, governmental, and civil society circles that disaster relief, communicable diseases, illegal migration, climate change, and environmental sustainability are legitimate and recurring security issues that need attention.

Asian debates at the intellectual and policy levels have revolved around two divergent streams of thought about human security – a broader one focusing on multiple dimensions of human well-being and a narrower one focusing on the specific threats of protection of individuals in situations of armed conflict. Both mirror debates, norms, and practices in other parts of the world. But while human security has global resonance, its development and future in East Asia have some distinctive characteristics.

Two meanings of human security

In East Asia as elsewhere there are frequent disagreements about the nature and meaning of human security – its what and how – but far fewer on its why and when. Advocates regularly point to changes in the post-Cold War security environment; the increasing significance of intra-state as compared to inter-state conflict; the emergence of a new form of diplomacy that connect states, international institutions, and civil society actors; and deepening globalization that brings with it new information networks and media capacity that highlight violence, natural disasters, and other human vulnerabilities in powerful ways.

At the core of human security approaches are three core assumptions:

1 that the individual (or the individual in a group or community, say, ethnic Karens in Myanmar) is one of the referent points (or in some formulations *the* referent point) for security;
2 that the security of the individual or the group is subject to a variety of threats of which military threats from outside the state are only one and often not the most significant;
3 that there is a possible tension between the security of the individual and that of the nation, the state, and the regime even recognizing the state has prime responsibility for the protection of the individual.

Framed this way, human security raises a challenge to traditional conceptions of national security by changing the referent point and introducing issues and means that extend beyond conventional security strategies. Philosophically, it raises hard issues of conscience, obligations beyond borders, development, and domestic legitimacy. Politically, it raises questions about sovereignty, intervention, the role of regional and global institutions, and the relationship between state and citizen. Insecure states almost always mean insecure citizens. But strong and secure states do not necessarily mean secure citizens. As noted in the *Human Security Report*, in the past century more people have been killed by their own governments than by foreign armies.[1]

Human security thinking quickly fragmented into different approaches on how broadly to define the threats, how to prioritize them, and whether to emphasize the complementarity or tension between the state and the individual. If security is the absence of anxiety upon which the fulfilled life depends, how many human anxieties need to be assuaged? And by what means? The answers to these questions have been bundled in several ways. Two were seminal.

Echoing the initial formulation of the 1994 Human Development Report, the most elaborate variant of the broad or holistic approach appeared in the work of the Commission on Human Security, supported by the Japanese government and co-chaired by Sadako Ogata and Amartya Sen. Its final report stated that the aim of human security is "to protect the vital core of all human lives in ways that enhance human freedoms and human fulfillment" and "protecting people from critical (severe) and pervasive (widespread) threats and situations." This meant creating systems that "give people the building blocks of survival, livelihood and dignity."[2]

The substantive chapters dealt with situations of violent conflict, refugees and internally displaced persons, recovery from violent conflict, economic security, health, knowledge, skills, and values. The report explicitly aimed to connect issues of protection, rights, development, and governance. And it conceived of human security in a comprehensive sense of dealing with situations of both violence and deprivation.

The second approach has emphasized a narrower band of issues, focusing on protection of individuals and communities in situations of armed conflict and other forms of organized violence. Sometimes labeled the freedom-from-fear approach, the focus is on human security *in extremis*, usually in the context of intra-state violence and occasionally in the context of state-directed violence. Adherents do not deny that there are multiple threats to human well-being but for reasons of analytical clarity and operational focus concentrate on one species of threat. They have argued that institutions and networks for addressing issues of development already exist and that what is needed is a concentration on a specific set of threats and the creation of political will and practical instruments for addressing them. Human security, it is claimed, can make the biggest difference in one of two ways: if it keeps squarely focused on issues like protection of refugees, women, and children in conflict zones, humanitarian intervention, peacekeeping, post-conflict peacebuilding, conflict management, prevention, and resolution, and lawless societies; or if it zeroes in on an even narrower set of issues including genocide and mass atrocities.

The seminal expression of the logic of the narrow approach was outlined by the International Commission on Intervention and State Sovereignty (ICISS) in its October 2001 report, *The Responsibility to Protect* (often cited as R2P).[3] Against the background of contested humanitarian interventions (and non-interventions) in Somalia, Sierra Leone, Rwanda, Bosnia, and East Timor, the ICISS was a response to the request by Kofi Annan for the international community to forge a consensus on the principles and processes for using coercive action to protect people at risk.

The ICISS report explicitly eschewed the vocabulary of "humanitarian intervention" and "the right to intervene" and instead focused on the needs of people requiring assistance by framing the issues of sovereignty and intervention in terms of the responsibility to protect. It identified a series of core principles that connected state sovereignty, obligations under the UN Charter, existing legal obligations under international law, and the developing practice of states, regional organizations, and the Security Council. It extended the responsibility to protect to include the responsibility to prevent, to react, and to rebuild when faced with human protection claims in states that are either unable or unwilling to discharge their responsibility. And it provided a precise definition of the just cause threshold as well as precautionary principles, right authority, and operational principles. It did allow for interventions without consent in extreme cases.

The report made a direct connection between R2P and the broader conception of human security. Treating human security as "indivisible," it argued that "issues of sovereignty and intervention are not just matters affecting the rights or prerogatives of states, but they deeply affect and involve individual human beings in fundamental ways." Focusing on the most vulnerable, it underlined that forces inside a country could often pose more significant threats on a daily basis to life, health, livelihood, personal safety, and human dignity than external aggression.

International reactions to R2P as a norm and policy framework have been varied and heated, with the main theaters of action being in Africa and in the United Nations. Kofi Annan's *High Level Panel on Threats, Challenges, and Change* declared "a collective international responsibility to protect" and characterized the R2P as "an emerging norm." His own report (*In Larger Freedom,* 2005) advanced the R2P as a component of collective action for shared development and governance, rather than as a global peace and security strategy.[4]

The effort to institutionalize the norm culminated at the UN World Summit of 2005. The Summit Outcome Document (A/Res/60/1, 2005), notably paragraphs 138 and 139, stated that it was the state that had the primary responsibility for providing for and protecting its own citizens. The international community's responsibilities, on the other hand, were substantially qualified, to focus upon assistance to states meeting their responsibilities to protect citizens. Should a state "manifestly fail" in its responsibilities, the international community has an obligation to undertake peaceful means to protect populations from the designated perils in Chapter VI, on a "case by case basis and in cooperation with relevant regional organizations," and further to *consider* [italics added] military action should peaceful means be inadequate. This could only occur with UNSC approval and be restricted to four kinds of transgressions: genocide, war crimes, ethnic cleansing, and crimes against humanity.[5]

In July 2009, Ban Ki-moon's report "Implementing the Responsibility to Protect" directed to the UN General Assembly focused heavily on prevention and capacity building. In practice, the Security Council has been reluctant to invoke the term when authorizing peacekeeping missions, though the recent success in Côte D'Ivoire may be a landmark development.

Asian reactions and formulations

While human security has a significant Asian pedigree – the initial UNDP report in 1994 was written by a Pakistani with an Asian audience in mind – it continues to receive a mixed welcome. In general terms, Japanese-led activities that have focused on the broad understanding of human security have been largely uncontested, though they were initially difficult to distinguish from conventional development issues. They did produce several regional champions including Tadashi Yamamoto, Kim Dae-jung, and Keizo Obuchi. The Asian financial crisis in 1997 underlined the reality that two decades of economic growth and state-building had not eliminated severe vulnerabilities for large numbers of Asians and the growing role of non-state actors as alternative service providers and participants in the policy process.

In the context of regional governmental institutions, the phrase has been used intermittently by political leaders and bureaucrats, albeit with no agreed definition. It appeared in the final report of the East Asia Study Group[6] and has been used repeatedly in ASEAN circles (though never formally endorsed by ASEAN), usually in the context of the need to address a range of non-traditional security issues, including environmental degradation, illegal migration, piracy, communicable diseases, and transnational crime. In a politically understandable but intellectually confusing synthesis, it was used after 9/11 in the Asia Pacific Economic Cooperation forum, with specific reference to dismantling terrorist groups, eliminating the danger of weapons of mass destruction, and confronting other direct threats to security including communicable diseases, protection of air travelers, and energy security.[7]

In track-two circles, the broader meaning is scarcely controversial but is most often framed around a variety of non-traditional security issues.[8] The MacArthur Foundation provided a major grant to the Centre for Non-Traditional Security Studies at the Rajaratnam School of International Studies in Singapore and the Centre has become a major hub for research and discussion. Other universities and think tanks have launched research projects and teaching programs with a similar focus.

The broader approach to human security is compatible with most formulations of comprehensive security, resonates with the needs-oriented approach of many Asian governments, is flexible in including both individuals and communities as the referent of security, and connects well to developmental issues and indigenous traditions of human dignity. The replacement of nationalism by performance is key to the legitimacy of most regimes and this puts more pressure on governments to address basic human needs and protection.[9] As argued by Rizal Sukma in the context of the fall of the Suharto government, "While it might be presumptuous to argue that the emphasis on human security will automatically ensure political and economic stability, one can make a reasonably strong claim that ignoring it will definitely serve as a recipe for disaster."[10]

The narrower approach continues to generate intense debate, much of it focused on R2P. The most important instrument for regional advocacy has been the Australia-based and funded Asia Pacific Centre for the Responsibility to Protect. In 2010 the Council for Security Cooperation in Asia Pacific commissioned a study group on R2P that produced a significant report. As determined and persistent as its external and internal advocates have been, getting governmental and intellectual support for R2P continues to be an uphill battle. Unlike Africa, only two countries (Japan and Mongolia) have integrated human security as a key pillar of their foreign policy, and there is little indication that principal regional organizations, including ASEAN, will do so in the near future.[11]

Almost all Asian governments, India being a notable exception, showed a willingness to support the norm as it took form in the 2005 World Summit report and have been supporters of the protection of civilians agenda embedded in various peacekeeping operations around the world. R2P had been vilified in the package presented by the ICISS because of sovereignty concerns and the prospect of intervention without consent. WS 2005 was a turning point in that it emphasized state responsibility for its citizens while guaranteeing that through a Security Council veto China could ensure domestic consent.

Asian states have been very reluctant to see R2P principles applied in their home countries or their region. They continue to believe that they are the best (and perhaps only) providers of security and tenaciously guard the principles of Westphalian absolute sovereignty and noninterference in domestic affairs. One analyst concludes that many states in Southeast Asia "still see the broader R2P norm as a potential threat to sovereignty and regime security, and as such have not internalized many of its key aspects," adding that "there is as yet no single government *inside* Southeast Asia that is a strong supporter of R2P" and only one country, the Philippines, can be seen as a consistent advocate.[12] Another argues that Southeast Asian governments are tacitly committed to a new conception of state sovereignty based on responsibility even as they are ambivalent about its application to Southeast Asia on the "assumption that conflicts in the region are not of the nature or intensity to warrant R2P's invocation."[13] Some believe that the mass atrocities and crimes that R2P addresses are not likely to occur in their own backyard.

It would be a mistake to view these regional norms and attitudes as static. Regional reactions to the genocide in Cambodia in the 1970s were very different than reactions to the violence in East Timor in 1998–1999. In the context of Cambodia, there was virtually no discussion within ASEAN of the need for external intervention and virtually no sympathy for occasional Vietnamese arguments that its intervention was motivated by humanitarian impulses. In the context of East Timor in 1999, while Indonesia and ASEAN insisted upon Indonesian consent before authorizing a military intervention, there were frequent demands for swift international action, including the use of military force, by citizens and top political leaders in several Southeast Asian capitals.

At the regional level, ASEAN, the ASEAN Regional Forum have not adopted R2P as regional doctrine or norm, though aspects of the broader conception of human security, especially non-traditional security issues, have been regular subjects of attention.

Thailand

Thailand was one of the first countries in Southeast Asia to give strong governmental support to human security in both its broad and narrow configurations. It set up a domestic Ministry of Development and Human Security, became an enthusiastic member of the Human Security Network, and participated in peacekeeping and humanitarian assistance operations headed by the UN in Burundi, Kosovo, East Timor, and Sudan. Several of its leading Democrat politicians, especially Surin Pitsuwan who served as a member of ICISS and later became the Secretary General of ASEAN, were strong advocates of developing and applying the doctrine globally and regionally. The commitment was reversed with the change of government in 2005. Like Canada a year later under a new Conservative government, Thailand backed away from the concept and phrase, steadfastly maintaining that the insurgency in the southern part of the country and, later, the Red Shirt protests and their suppression in 2010 were domestic affairs outside the purview of the R2P. According to one recent assessment, domestic political turbulence combined with the unresolved conflict in the southern part of the country to reverse official thinking. The new emphasis was on non-interference in Thai domestic affairs and a shift from intervention to prevention in international settings.[14]

Officials and academics have criticized the initial ICISS report and the subsequent UN discussions from several angles ranging from its specific elements to underlying philosophy.

For many, the American intervention in Iraq and the NATO intervention in Libya diminished support for the doctrine of R2P.

Japan

The one major country in East Asia that has made human security a consistent mainstay of its foreign policy is Japan. Japanese intellectuals and policy makers proposed as early as 1979 the idea of "comprehensive security" that extended beyond military and defense issues and included economic well-being, natural disasters, and energy. In 1998 Prime Minister Obuchi used the term "human security" with particular emphasis on protecting vulnerable peoples. His government created the $200 million Trust Fund for Human Security at the UN, and his successors provided support for the Commission on Human Security.

Subsequent Japanese governments have continued to use the concept. A recent review of Japanese thinking and practice outlines its multiple strands and the close embrace of both the broader and narrower interpretations of the concept that now ranges from poverty alleviation and public health through to conflict prevention, post-conflict assistance, long-term peace efforts, and even military intervention in situations where other means fail. Japan did not join the Human Security Network championed by Canada and Norway but did take the initiative in 2006 in establishing the Friends of Human Security Forum in the UN which meets twice a year. In its aid programming, it used the concept to address freedom from fear and freedom from want, protection and empowerment of people and support for dealing with global risks, especially in the areas of health and medicine. And in the wake of the March 2011 triple disaster in Japan, it has been applied with increasing frequency inside Japan in the context of disaster response and relief.[15]

Japan has supported UN-led efforts to define and promote R2P along with other measures to protect civilians in situation of armed conflict. Japanese policy makers have been less concerned than other Asian states that R2P provides a pretext for unilateral intervention. They supported the World Summit declaration but on what one Japanese analyst describes as a "passive" basis. In Japan, as elsewhere, internal debates have been substantial, tied to alternative visions of Japanese foreign policy and international identity, factional politics, and calculations about advancing other Japanese priorities including a permanent seat on the Security Council and avoiding agonizing internal debates about dispatching the Self Defence Forces to conflict zones. Revisions under Ban Ki-moon to R2P that acknowledged the value of the broad Japanese approach opened up a window for Japanese participation without major troop commitments or lifting restrictions on the operations of Japanese troops overseas. "Thus Japan no longer views R2P as a threat to human security doctrine, but also sees little incentive to play a bigger role in mainstreaming R2P."[16]

China

Until the late 1990s the term human security was virtually unknown to Chinese academics and is still only rarely used by officials in formal meetings or by the media. The situation has changed in two main respects. First, some of the domestic aspects of human security, including environmental concerns, natural disasters, and social security, now receive frequent attention in official and online media. Second, human security overlaps with some of the key elements of China's "new security concept," issued in 1997, that promotes cooperative action to address pressing transnational issues. Preferring the idea of non-traditional security to human security, Chinese officials in November 2002 co-signed The Joint Declaration of ASEAN and China on Cooperation in the Field of Non-Traditional Security Issues related to illegal drugs, people smuggling, trafficking in women and children, piracy, terrorism, arms smuggling, money laundering, international economic crime, and cybercrime.[17]

Turning to the pointy end of human security – protection of individuals in situations of violent conflict – directly tied to the concepts of sovereignty and intervention, Chinese responses since 1997 have been increasingly fluid and complex. There remain vocal proponents of a strict interpretation of the principles of sovereignty and non-interference, stressing the Five Principles of Peaceful Coexistence, emphasizing article 3(4) of the UN Charter, preferring humanitarian assistance to humanitarian intervention, advocating strict neutrality in peacekeeping, and seeing ulterior motives in the practice of intervention. They echo deeply embedded views in China about past humiliations; fears of potential interventions in Taiwan, Tibet, and Xinjiang; and a political philosophy that focuses on the nation rather than the individual and that separates human safety from what now is called human security.

Chu Shulong pointed out in 2002 that "the Chinese leadership will continue to defend fundamental national sovereignty rights, but at the same time, the pressure of global trends means they will become more flexible and accepting toward relatively new concepts of security, including human security," adding that "the Chinese recognize that in times of integration and globalization, nations and peoples around the world will gain more than they will lose from changing their traditional positions on national security."[18] In a 2002 report, Allen Carlson observed that "many Chinese elites have now come to accept the general legitimacy of multi-lateral intervention to resolve particularly prominent humanitarian crises" and that "China has become a reluctant participant in the international trend toward questioning the sanctity of state sovereignty and expanding the international community's right to intervene."[19]

A decade later the contradictions and complexity are even more apparent. In what one scholar identifies as a combination of acceptance and resistance to the R2P approach,

> China has adeptly avoided directly challenging what it perceives to be the Western normative order underpinning R2P in a manner that might repudiate China's self-professed responsible engagement in UN peacekeeping arrangements. At the same time, China has leveraged its relationship with like-minded states to limit the prospect of R2P directly undermining its resistance to nonconsensual intervention, or to utterly discredit its commitment to enhancing civilian protection through political negotiations rather than enforcement measures.

Rather than obstructing R2P, China has contested and shaped its development. It no longer contends that humanitarian crises are strictly internal affairs of sovereign states but instead that "protection is best achieved through political settlements rather than coercive protection measures."[20]

After initial opposition to non-consensual and unauthorized interventions in Iraq, Yugoslavia, Somalia, Rwanda, Haiti, and Kosovo and to the ICISS report, Chinese officials endorsed the limited version of R2P agreed upon at the World Summit in 2005. Importantly, R2P, for China, was established as a concept, rather than a norm or a principle of international relations, and, therefore, in the words of two observers, had to "be interpreted and applied in a prudent and accurate manner, assessed in individual cases, not abused, and restricted to the four specific threats outlined in the World Summit document." China's response to the crises in Darfur, Burma, and, more recently Syria, has closely followed this logic.[21]

This amounts neither to outright acceptance nor rejection of the R2P. Currently, China only supports collective action against individual states that have failed to protect their populations in extremely serious cases and when China's political interests coincide with the other members of the UNSC. China supported the establishment of UNAMID, the joint United Nations-African Union (AU) peacekeeping mission in Darfur, yet opposed the attempts to collectively address the situation in Myanmar. More recently, China supported a NATO mission to protect civilians in Libya, but later objected to authorizing one for Syria. China has been willing to use its influence in order to pressure governments for a solution to their humanitarian crises and secure their consent to intervention. And it has become one of the major contributors of troops to the UN peacekeeping operations including engineering units in Darfur, civilian police in East Timor, and military observers in Western Sahara.

China has shifted from being a norm taker to a norm maker in regional and global settings, attempting to make intervention and the use of force more compatible with its interests and preferences. It has operated as "a conservative force in the R2P debate," notes a recent study, but is not blocking discussion or trying to unravel the 2005 WSO consensus. It has thus found a way to continue supporting the norms of state sovereignty and non-interference at the same time that it supports international actions linked to humanitarian catastrophes and mass violence that can be interpreted as threats to peace and security.[22]

Though other East Asian countries may not have similar diplomatic influence, the basic pattern is similar. The normative underpinnings of human security have been largely accepted even as its application in specific contexts has not. This may sometimes align with Western interests and perspectives but rests on a different philosophic foundation. In the words of Gregory Chin and Ramesh Thakur, "China is interpreting Western Enlightenment principles through a Confucian lens of governance that stresses an essential unity between citizens and state, rather than giving primacy to human rights as claims against the state."[23]

Conclusion

The defining characteristic of East Asia is its diversity – in history, culture, religion, languages, civilizational underpinnings, levels of economic development, and regime types. Yet as a region, it is at the center of world economic growth, increasingly economically interdependent, linked to global supply and value chains, and slowly constructing a regional institutional architecture in a distinctive way that eschews political integration, diminution of sovereignty, and that is premised on the belief that high levels of cooperation can be achieved with low levels of institutionalization. It still is troubled by a significant number of intra-state conflicts and no shortage of flashpoints but has been successful in reducing the incidence and prospect of inter-state war and building increasingly effective states.

Security discourse and practice are shifting but not in ways that completely converge with the "Enlightenment" principles described by Thakur and Chin. Rigid concepts of sovereignty and non-interference have been softened but not jettisoned. It is no longer imaginable that Pol Pot-style genocide of the 1970s could be ignored or tolerated. Yet most Asian states have been very reluctant to focus regional and global attention on the dynamics of intra-state war. The instruments of preventive diplomacy developed and applied in Europe have been very slow to find acceptance. What has been accepted is that domestic instabilities and vulnerabilities need special attention by the states in which they are occurring. For many analysts, even a bad government can do this better than no government or a government imposed through outside intervention.

For all these reasons, East Asia is important in the future evolution of human security thinking and practice. It is significant as a brake on liberal-inspired conceptions of a well-functioning security order and at the same time is an incubator of creative ideas including non-traditional security that focus on significant trans-national problems. Non-traditional security thinking is distinctive because it is intentionally ambiguous about whether the state is the primary or only force capable of addressing the human security problems of the region and whether there is a fundamental tension between states and their citizens. As the most vulnerable region in the world to a myriad of natural disasters, it may be that the biggest chapter in security cooperation will focus on environmental degradation and the adaptation to climate change.

Providing for the well-being and security of civilians is no longer controversial. How this is to be achieved is a work in progress.

Acknowledgements

This article draws heavily on my earlier essay, "Human security and East Asia: In the beginning," from *Journal of East Asian Studies*, 4, 2. Copyright © 2004 by the East Asia Institute. Used with permission by Lynne Rienner Publishers, Inc.

My thanks to Akiko Fukushima and Brian Job for their advice and Minami Orihara for translation of Japanese materials.

Notes

1 *Human Security Report 2005: War and Peace in the 21st Century*, p. VIII. Available at http://books.google. ca/books?id=rSIrNeFWIfcC&printsec=frontcover&dq=human+security+report&hl=en&sa=X&ei =xMCjUbqgBaH7igLGmYGICg&ved=0CDkQ6AEwAA#v=onepage&q=human%20security%20 report&f=false. Accessed 27 May 2013.
2 Commission on Human Security, *Human Security Now: Protecting and Empowering People* (New York: CHS, 2003), p. 4.
3 International Commission on Intervention and State Sovereignty, *The Responsibility to Protect* (Ottawa, November 2001). The report and the supplementary volume, Research, Bibliography, and Background, are available at http://responsibilitytoprotect.org/ICISS%20Report.pdf. Accessed 26 May 2013.
4 Both reports plus eight others from the UN are available at http://responsibilitytoprotect.org/index. php/publications. Accessed 28 May 2013.
5 Available at http://responsibilitytoprotect.org/index.php/publications. Accessed 27 May 2013.
6 East Asia Vision Group Report 2001, "Towards an East Asian Community," 2001. Available at http://www.mofa.go.jp/region/asia-paci/report2001.pdf. The phrase "human security" also appeared in the second EAVG report in November 2012, though more frequently was covered by the term "non-traditional security." See http://www.mfa.go.th/asean/contents/files/asean-media-center-20130312-112418-758604.pdf. Both reports were accessed on 27 May 2013.
7 APEC Leaders' Declaration, "Bangkok Declaration on Partnership for the Future," October 21, 2003. Available at: www.apec.org. Accessed 27 May 2013.
8 See David Capie and Paul Evans, "Non Traditional Security," in *The Asia-Pacific Security Lexicon*, 2nd edn (Singapore: Institute of Southeast Asian Studies, 2007), pp. 173–178.
9 Amitav Acharya, "Human Security: East Versus West," *International Journal* (Summer 2001), pp. 444–451.
10 Rizal Sukma, "Indonesia," in Pranee Thiparat (ed.), *The Quest for Human Security: The Next Phase of ASEAN?* (Bangkok: Institute of Security and International Studies, 2001), p. 62.
11 CSCAP Memorandum No. 18, "Implementing the Responsibility to Protect,"September 2011. Available at: http://www.mfa.go.th/asean/contents/files/asean-media-center-20130312-112418-758604.pdf. Accessed 27 May 2013.
12 David Capie, "The Responsibility to Protect Norm in Southeast Asia," *The Pacific Review*, 25, 1, March 2012, pp. 76 and 82.
13 Mely Caballero-Anthony, "The Responsibility to Protect in Southeast Asia: Opening Up Spaces for Advancing Human Security," *The Pacific Review*, 25, 1, March 2012, p. 114.

14 Keokam Kraisoraphong, "Thailand the Responsibility to Protect," *The Pacific Review*, 25, 1, March 2012, pp. 6 and 22.

15 Akiko Fukushima, Ningeng no anzenhosho: Gurobaru ka surs tayor na kyoi o seisaku furemuwaku [*Rethinking Human Security: Responding to Emerging Global Threats*], Tokyo: Chikura shobo, 2010.

16 Jun Honna, "Japan and the Responsibility to Protect: Coping with the Human Security Diplomacy," *The Pacific Review*, 25, 1, March 2012, pp. 97 and 107.

17 The Joint Declaration is available at http://www.vifindia.org/document/2002/joint-declaration-of-asean-and-china-on-cooperation-in-the-field-of-non-traditional-security-issues. The subsequent "Plan of Action," dated 12 October 2011, is available at http://www.asean.org/communities/asean-political-security-community/item/plan-of-action-for-the-memorandum-of-understanding-between-the-association-of-southeast-asian-nations-asean-and-the-government-of-the-people-s-republic-of-china-on-cooperation-in-the-field-of-non-traditional-security-issues. Both documents accessed 27 May 2013.

18 Chu Shulong, China and Human Security (Vancouver: Program on Canada-Asia Policy Studies, North Pacific Policy Paper no. 8, 2002), p. 25. Available at http://www.iar.ubc.ca/programs/pastprograms/PCAPS/pubs/nppp8_final.pdf. Accessed 27 May 2013.

19 Allen Carlson, "Protecting Sovereignty, Accepting Intervention: The Dilemma of Chinese Foreign Relations in the 1990s" (New York: National Committee on United States–China Relations, China Policy Series No. 18, September 2002), pp. 3, 29, 32.

20 Sarah Teitt, "The Responsibility to Protect and China's Peacekeeping Policy," *International Peacekeeping*, 18, 3, June 2011, pp. 299 and 311.

21 Brian Job and Anastasia Shesterinina, "China as a Global Norm-Shaper: Institutionalization and Implementation of the Responsibility to Protect," in Alexander Betts and Phil Orchard (eds), *Implementation and World Politics: How International Norms Change Practice* (Oxford, Oxford University Press: forthcoming, 2014).

22 Rosemary Foot and Andrew Walter, *China, the United States and Global Order* (Cambridge: Cambridge University Press, 2011), p. 52.

23 Gregory Chin and Ramesh Thakur, "Will China Change the Rules of Global Order?," *The Washington Quarterly*, 33/4, 2010, pp. 119–138.

PART IV

Human security tools

22

AN ECONOMIST'S PERSPECTIVE ON HUMAN SECURITY

Syed Mansoob Murshed

This chapter addresses two dimensions of human security: freedom from want and freedom from fear. It examines the first by focusing on economic growth. Differences in growth rates over the last two centuries have produced the present disparities between rich and poor countries. Growth also constitutes the principal avenue for poverty reduction. With regard to the freedom from fear, the chapter looks at violence as an alternative economic activity to peaceful production. It then examines what economics can contribute to the understanding of the causes of civil war and why peace agreements to end war are so notoriously fragile. The chapter concludes by looking at the relationship between globalisation and conflict, bearing in mind that civil war is not the only form of violent organised internal conflict, and the fact that the relationship between economic progress and human security may be non-linear.

The origins of the concept of human security can be traced back to the basic needs concepts of the 1970s, and Amartya Sen's (1985) capability approach, which finally took shape in the notion of human development in the 1990s (see Streeten 1993). Essentially, it marked a move away from narrow concepts of welfare based purely on consumption. Based on this, we have the human development index for most countries, at both the national and regional levels, which is an unweighted average of per-capita income, health and educational attainment.[1] Human security represents an accretion to the concept of human development embedding rights to safety and security. This development, at the turn of the millennium, was motivated by the greater recognition of nature of civil war, which until about a decade ago was a subject not normally analysed by development economists. As indicated, there is now a widespread acceptance of the poverty-conflict nexus (Collier et al. 2003), whereby endemic poverty exacerbates the risk of internal violent conflict as poverty lowers the opportunity cost of the violent over the non-violent (negotiated) option in dispute settlement. In turn, violent internal wars help to perpetuate poverty through the collateral damage that war engenders, and because internal war is believed to retard poverty reducing (or pro-poor) growth. Thus, the earlier concept of human development needed further extension and elaboration so as to incorporate individual and collective safety and security. Consequently, human security may be characterised as human development combined with political and social freedoms; above all individual and collective safety and security. It encompasses economic as well as personal (or group) security and rights.

Two dimensions of human security could be addressed by the economist: freedom from want and freedom from fear.[2] The first refers to the quality of life, and economics is rich in approaches to this, many of which go beyond the simple utilitarian paradigm; making the epithet that economics is 'the gospel of Mammon' rather unfair. The crudest form of the utilitarian approach states that (cardinally immeasurable) utility emanates from consumption. One can, of course, incorporate non-hedonistic or altruistic components into an individual utility function, such as the utility of one's children, as well as solidarity with a cause. Societal welfare is maximised when the sum of individual utilities are maximised. This, in turn, leads to the two fundamental welfare theorems in mainstream economics which are associated with the concept of *efficiency*. A competitive equilibrium is Pareto efficient, and a Pareto optimal allocation is also a competitive equilibrium. Pareto efficiency, in the strictest sense, implies that one person cannot be made better off by re-allocation without making at least another person worse off. It also means that changes that make some better off without making any others worse off should be implemented. But it raises problems of equity. In a two-person society, for example, Pareto efficiency is compatible with one person having everything and another person nothing, something that is repugnant to most sensibilities. Consequently, in economics, we are used to separating issues relating to efficiency from normative matters pertaining to *equity*.

Besides utilitarianism we also have Sen's (1985) capability approach which states that well-being emerges from capability, examples of which could be the twin freedoms from want and fear. Capabilities are related to entitlements, that could include security; but exchange entitlements or participation in the market are very much part and parcel of 'entitlement'. Rawls' (1971) maximin principle is, perhaps, less well known. Allocation and choice under this rule maximises the utility of the least fortunate member (or group) in society.

The latest challenge, from within economics, to crude measures of well-being based principally on hedonistic consumption comes from behavioural economics which emphasise the psychological basis of choice. Individual preferences are not just about maximising utility in consumption, but contain innate and socially (hence institutionally) determined preferences that may contradict choice which is principally based on narrow self-interested (current and future) consumption.[3] Unlike in traditional economics where preferences were exogenous (or given) to the analyst, I am referring to preferences that are endogenous to, and shaped by, economic, political and social institutions (Bowles 1998). Preferences (and choices) may also be related to personal histories of violence and trauma. Akerlof and Kranton (2000) also demonstrate how individuals can derive utility from behaviour and actions appropriate to their own group's identity and norms, as well as similar behaviour by other members of the group one identifies with. Earlier work by Boulding (1956) about individual self-image and the effect of various stimuli in framing one's image is remarkably similar to the tenets of the currently fashionable behavioural economics.

The second section of the chapter examines freedom from want by focusing on economic growth. Differences in growth rates, particularly over the last two centuries, have produced the growing disparities between rich and poor countries, which is the principal factor underlying the current state of underdevelopment. By choosing to focus on growth I may be regarded as an unreconstructed utilitarian. Growth, however, creates possibilities for greater happiness, well-being and security. Without growth, citizens cannot exercise capabilities. Growth also constitutes the principal avenue for poverty reduction. In poor countries mere acts of income or asset distribution can only serve to make all people equally poor. This does not mean, however, that no attention should be paid to distribution, as perceptions about unfair distribution across groups can promote conflict, as we shall see in sections 3 and 4. Section 2 also analyses the role of institutional functioning in explaining the determinants of long-term growth and growth failure. As the opening line of Tolstoy's novel Anna Karenina pithily points out: "Happy families are all alike; every unhappy family is unhappy in its own way."

Section 3 concentrates on the freedom from fear. It begins by looking at violence as an alternative economic activity to peaceful production. It then examines what economics can contribute to the understanding of the causes of war. The problem of transnational terrorism is also analysed. I also examine reasons as to why peace agreements are so notoriously fragile.

Section 4 provides a synthesis, indicating the possible links between globalisation and conflict, along with a sketch of the new forms of conflict that are appearing. It also develops the idea that both under-development and development can produce large-scale violent conflict. Thus, the relationship between economic progress and human security may be non-linear, implying that the association between the two is at times positive and at other times negative.

The lack of economic growth and the freedom from want

Freedom from want in low-income countries, where poverty is endemic, can only ensue in the long run from economic growth. This is because growth enlarges the economic pie and creates the necessary pre-conditions for economic well-being. Granted, this is not sufficient for the freedom from want, which also depends on other mechanisms including the distribution of income. As far as growth is concerned Table 22.1 suggests that recent growth rates of real income per-capita have been low, and even negative, for many developing countries, particularly in sub-Saharan Africa and Latin America in the 1980 to 2000 period. In Africa, in particular, the last two decades of the twentieth century were associated with huge development failure. Not only did incomes decline, but also other indicators of inclusion and well-being also deteriorated. This includes the return of old diseases such as tuberculosis, the AIDS pandemic, stagnating maternal mortality and literacy rates. On the other hand, developing countries in East Asia, and more recently in South Asia, have been doing well.

Historically also, disparities between rich and poor countries have been growing in the last two centuries. UNDP (1999) reproduces figures to show that the gap in average income between the richest and poorest nations was only 3:1 during the dawn of the industrial revolution in 1820, rising to 11:1 by 1913. More recently, it grew to 35:1 in 1950, rising slightly to 44:1 by 1973. After the commencement of the present round of globalisation, this figure has acquired a staggering magnitude of 72:1. The lack of economic growth, and the increasing disparity between rich and poor nations, undermines human security from the standpoint of the freedom from want and other human capabilities.

What are the long-term determinants of growth? The new growth theory suggests that many factors can raise the productivity of the inputs (capital and labour) that enter the production process. Initially, the stress was put on the development of human resources or human capital. Lately, consideration is also being given to other over arching factors that might help explain long-term growth, or more importantly, growth failure. These include geographical location, culture and institutional functioning; see Murshed (2010, chapter 2) for a survey. In this section I shall focus mainly on the role of certain types of natural resource rents in retarding growth in the long run and poor institutions, both of which are inter-connected.

Besides the adverse macroeconomic effects on international competitiveness of natural resource booms,[4] there are political economy arguments as to why resource booms or a substantial dependence[5] on mineral resource exports can retard long-run growth, (Murshed 2010: 29–52). Natural resource rents of a certain type (oil, gas, or mineral rents, for example) are more readily captured, compared to profits from manufacturing or traditional agriculture; the presence of substantial rents of this type can make corruption, predation and rent-seeking

Table 22.1 GDP per capita (1995 constant US$) growth rates

Area/Country	Annual average GDP growth % 1960–1970	Annual average GDP growth % 1970–1980	Annual average GDP growth % 1980–1990	Annual average GDP growth % 1990–2000	Annual average GDP growth % 2000–2006
All developing	3.1	3.3	1.2	1.9	5.7
East Asia & Pacific	2.9	4.5	5.9	6.0	8.6
South Asia	1.8	0.7	3.5	3.2	7.0
Latin America & Caribbean	2.6	3.4	−0.8	1.7	3.1
Sub-Saharan Africa	2.6	0.8	−1.1	−0.4	4.7

Source: World Development Indicators, World Bank

a more attractive entrepreneurial option. This incentive is greater the weaker the environment of law and contract enforcement following societal upheavals. A related problem concerns the allocation of entrepreneurial talent, as analysed in Murphy, Shleifer and Vishny (1991). The idea is that talent can focus either on production or predation. This decision is a function of the relative returns to these two activities. By the same token, in countries where good institutions are already well established, in Norway for example, the appearance of substantial natural resource rents does not necessarily cause problems. Also, resource abundance has not historically caused adverse effects in countries such as the USA, Canada and Australia.

Acemoglu, Johnson and Robinson (2005) contend that good economic institutions (property rights and the rule of law) are required for growth in the longer term. Economic institutions are a product of political systems and processes. These authors argue that growth-promoting institutions are more likely to materialise in the context of settings that constrain the arbitrary exercise of political power (democracy), where there is a broad-based interest in property rights implying less inequality, and if there are fewer rents that can be appropriated by a small political elite. Recent empirical studies also confirm the independent importance of institutions in determining economic performance as measured by the levels of per-capita income. Easterly and Levine (2003) present evidence based on cross-country econometrics that a mineral natural resource endowment, a poor geographical (tropical) location and an excessive mortality rate (disease burden) retard economic development but via institutions of governance. Similarly, bad economic policies and choices also hinder economic development via institutional quality. Consequently, institutions and institutional functioning are the crucial link between resource endowments, geography, policies on the one hand and economic outcomes on the other hand. A similar line of reasoning is presented in Rodrik, Subramanian and Trebbi (2004).

There is now a consensus that institutions, in the shape of the framework of governance, respect for property rights, contract and law enforcement, the rule of law and administrative capacity, matter a great deal if a country is to be successful in its quest for growth and development. The current economic literature points to several sources of institutional determination, some of which may be related to natural resource endowment.

Authors such as Acemoglu, Johnson and Robinson (2001) date poor (or good) institutional determination to the pattern of colonialisation at least a century ago. They distinguish between two types of colonies. The first group corresponds to parts of the new world settled by European migrants, as in North America and Australasia. The second group refers to tropical developing countries, today's third world. The idea is that better institutions, especially property rights and the rule of law, were embedded in the first group.[6] In the second category of colonial countries, an extractive pattern of production was set up. This extractive and exploitative pattern of production is also the legacy of colonialisation, malign colonialisation in these cases. Clearly, this pattern was more prevalent in some parts of the world, particularly in Africa and Latin America; the Belgian Congo is cited as the worst example. The latter's contemporary counterpart, the Democratic Republic of Congo (DRC), has probably the worst growth experience on record. As the extractive state is expropriatory and predatory, bad institutions emerge and become entrenched even after independence, and a predatory equilibrium emerges. The important question that remains unanswered is why does de-colonialisation, and the opportunities it provides for policy changes, not alter the destiny of an extractive economy? It does in some, but not others. Secondly, despite the salience of the colonial phase in history, many developing nations have had a collective experience prior to, and after, colonialisation that must have also shaped institutions. In East Asia, South Asia, the Middle East and North African regions of the developing world, well-functioning institutions of good governance existed well before the advent of colonialisation, and European colonial powers merely adapted pre-existing administrative institutions. The work of Acemoglu, Johnson and Robinson (2001) is therefore mostly applicable to sub-Saharan Africa, Latin America and the Caribbean.

Another strand of the literature builds on the link between inequality and mineral type resource endowment (Easterly 2007). Commodity endowments of the mineral or plantation variety tend to depress the middle-class share of income in favour of elites, as in Latin America. The idea is that these elites in turn use their power, identical with the forces of the state, to coerce and extract rents. When different groups compete with each other for these rents, the rent-seeking contest can lead to even more perverse and wasteful outcomes than when elites collude. The important point made by Easterly (2007) is that small elite-based societies do not have a stake in the long-term development of the land. Unlike in middle-class dominated societies, publicly financed human capital formation and infrastructural development falls by the wayside, hence depressing growth prospects. The reason is that mass education promotes growth, although it eventually leads to power shifting away from elite groups through demands for democracy. The important point is that a tiny oligarchy may be the most disinclined to redistribute income.

Violent internal conflict and the freedom from fear

We are used to viewing war as something that happens between nation states. Today's conflicts mostly occur between groups within the same country, and in the *developing* world. Conflict is also a major cause for the persistence of poverty, which in turn is also a cause of conflict (Collier et al. 2003).

Are these violent conflicts fundamentally irrational, and couldn't the differences underlying these disputes be settled peacefully? Sadly, conflict may be the product of rational decisions, even if it is only of a bounded or myopic rational choice variety. It is important to understand that violence is an alternative to peaceful production as a form of economic activity. Francis Edgeworth, writing in the late nineteenth century, distinguished between consent – and its absence – in human economic interaction:

The first principle of Economics is that every agent is actuated only by self-interest. The workings of this principle may be viewed under two aspects, according as the agent acts *without*, or *with*, the consent of others affected by his actions. In wide senses, the first species of action may be called *war*; the second, contract.

(Edgeworth 1881: 16–17)

In securing an income, humanity has a choice between production and predation, the relative returns being in part determined by the cost of 'swords' relative to 'ploughshares'. The institutional environment, the quality of law and contract enforcement also determine this choice. Criminal activity, whether taking the form of extortion or theft, is only one aspect of the economics of violence. War, especially civil war, also has an economic dimension. Hirschliefer (1995) models anarchic inter-group warfare using non-cooperative game theory, in a setting reminiscent of the primitive conflict over resources between neighbouring communities. Similarly, Grossman (1991) models rebellion against a tax-farming state, where individual choices are predicated upon the relative returns to farming or working for the state or rebelling against it. The main characteristic of these rational choice approaches is the notion of expected utility; the returns (sometimes negative) are the sum of the pecuniary value of various activities weighted by their subjective probability.

In the new rational choice literature on civil war, a distinction is often made between *grievance,* a motivation based on a sense of injustice in the way a social group is or has been treated; and *greed,* an acquisitive desire similar to crime, albeit on a much larger scale.[7] In many ways the former refers to intrinsic motivation, and the latter to an extrinsic or pecuniary incentive to go to war. These motives are not entirely separate in practice, and change as conflict progresses. Addison, Le Billon and Murshed (2002) present an analytical game-theoretic model of civil war where greed and grievance exist simultaneously in the midst of poverty.

There is a long-standing position that relative deprivation (Gurr 1970), which refers to a feeling of being left behind in the midst of generalised progress, fuels internal violence.[8] Identity is also crucial to intra-state conflict. This is due to the collective action problem, as discussed in Olson (1965). It is difficult to mobilise large groups to undertake collective action, because of mutual mistrust, monitoring difficulties and the free-rider problem. Ethnic identities, whether based on race, language, religion, tribal affiliation or regional differences, may serve as a more effective amalgam for the purposes of group formation, compared to other forms of difference such as socioeconomic class. The formation of enduring identities is therefore central to mobilising groups, including the machinations of conflict entrepreneurs who organise men to fight each other. Conflict cannot proceed without the presence of palpably perceived group differences, or grievances, which may have historical dimensions. Frances Stewart (2000) has introduced the notion of *horizontal inequality*, the inequality between groups, rather than the inequality within an ethnically homogenous population (vertical inequality). Here more enduring (or hard to change) dimensions of inequality (Tilly 1998) compared to relatively more transient causes of inequality (like current income) are crucial, such as the manner in which certain groups are discriminated against, simply because of their ethnic characteristics, rather than their other personal attributes.

More often than not, horizontal inequalities and/or relative deprivation take the form of high asset inequality, discriminatory public spending across groups and unequal access to the benefits of state patronage, such as government jobs. Furthermore, state failure in providing security and a minimal level of public goods often force individuals to rely on kinship ties for support and security.

Discussion of greed as a motive for conflict arises mainly in the context of natural resource endowments in Africa, and has been popularised, for example, by the work of Collier and Hoeffler (2004). Capturable natural resource rents, such as alluvial diamonds in Angola and Sierra Leone, can result in contests over the right to control these, some of which take the form of warfare, but also criminality and corruption in other instances. Ross (2004) points out that lootable gemstones and illegal narcotics help to finance and perpetuate civil war, as they are a major source of profit for some of the competing groups. Their presence does not, however, robustly explain why civil wars begin in the first place but why they may last longer as a ready source of finance is available. Ross (2004) also finds that oil and gas revenues significantly contribute to secessionist wars.

The greed versus grievance dichotomy can provide a useful beginning to the discussion of the causes of conflict. But for these forces to take the form of large-scale violence there must be other factors at work, specifically a failing 'social contract' and conflict triggers. A functioning social contract, and the concomitant institutions that distribute income and resolve disputes, can prevent the violent expression of greed or grievance (Murshed 2002, 2010). The degeneration of a viable social contract that resolved disputes without recourse to large-scale violence is the sufficient cause for the outbreak of conflict, and in the extreme can lead to a failed or collapsed state (as in Somalia, for example). Furthermore, the outbreak of conflict always requires triggers, both internal and external. External triggers involve support and succour from an outside power; internal triggers refer to events that induce parties to abandon peaceful negotiation in favour of outright war. Addison and Murshed (2006) indicate that a social contract could contain three dimensions. The first is *political* (the rules that govern political representation, consultation and decision-making), the second consists of *moral* values (the rules that govern personal conduct and society's sense of justice) and the third is *economic* (the rules that govern production, exchange, distribution and government intervention).

Transnational terrorism, and the strategy of conducting a 'war on terrorism' to combat it, is a form of 'new' war. Here intrinsic motivation, which often takes the form of the collective sense of humiliation, plays a greater role; therefore deterrence against terrorists may backfire if it hardens their resolve to resist, as modelled by Addison and Murshed (2005). Perpetrators of terrorist acts are not often uneducated and poor, unlike in the case of civil wars where the soldiery is often drawn from the ranks of the impoverished whose alternative gainful employment prospects are scant. In fact, education can act as an indicator of reliability in acts such as suicide bombing. Terrorism requires individuals to express solidarity with an intrinsic cause or value, where the notion of pecuniary gain associated with greed in the case of civil wars is totally irrelevant. From the viewpoint of individual choice, suicide bombing may be a rational act as explained by Wintrobe (2006). This is because the individual has made an all or nothing choice between solidarity to a cause and individual autonomy. An all or nothing choice involves a 'corner solution' to a utility maximisation problem. In this situation changing relative prices (increasing deterrence) has little impact on individual choice, which is another way of saying that deterring terrorism will not succeed in preventing people from committing to their cause, even if the success rate of individual acts of terrorism diminishes.

Conflict resolution is more difficult when the intrinsic motivation to fight is strong, as is the case in secessionist wars and certain forms of terrorism. It is also difficult to sustain peace when parties feel tempted to resume warfare so as to enable them to continue looting valuable resources. The commitment problem to an agreed peace treaty is also a serious problem. This difficulty arises when it is in the interest of one or either side to renege on the promise of peace, and the actions that peace involves. In that situation, commitments lack credibility. Sometimes agents or groups cannot commit credibly because there are no institutions or mechanisms upon which to anchor promises. For governments, this is more likely in the context of weak state capacity, as it is difficult for a state to guarantee pledges when its own legitimacy and power base is fragile.

An important aspect of the commitment problem is the very high discount rates, or the short time horizons of the parties involved (Addison and Murshed 2002). In situations of poverty and high uncertainty, agents strongly prefer a dollar today to a dollar tomorrow. Although the absolute value of future peace may be much higher than that of continued warfare, the present value may be much lower when the discount rate is high and there is an impatience to consume. The same argument can be applied to reputation, a factor that is key to the credibility of peacemaking. Breaking an agreement damages *future* reputation, but with a high enough discount rate it might pay to renege because the cost comes in the future. Each failure of the peace process raises the discount rates of the belligerents, thereby increasing the difficulty of making peace. Given the tarnished reputations of belligerents it is even harder to establish credible peace. The problem is particularly apparent in Africa where most indicators of political risk are substantially greater than elsewhere in the world. Solutions lie in directly increasing the cost of reneging on peace agreements, devising commitment technologies through institutional innovation and improving the quality of peacekeeping forces.

Conclusions

In this essay I have attempted to argue that human security as broadly understood in economics could encompass elements of the freedoms from want and fear. What I have discussed are some of the necessary conditions for these freedoms, which emanate respectively from growth and the prevention of violent internal conflict. Freedom from want has been the traditional subject matter of economics, and includes a wide-ranging understanding of utility and welfare. The freedom from fear or insecurity is something development economists have been increasingly paying attention to, as it is recognised that economic policy cannot be formulated or conducted independent of the political and security environment. Furthermore, the potential for conflict and civil war in retarding growth and development are also accepted.

Development and human security imply the maximisation of growth and the minimisation of conflict. The latter objective also requires that growth is not too unequally distributed. Institutions and institutional functioning are central to both these goals, as they promote growth and prevent conflict. As Rodrik (1999) emphasises, countries with weak institutions of conflict management, as well as high income inequality are less able to withstand economic shocks and experience growth failure. Moreover, growth and conflict are related in other ways. Countries with low per-capita income are more prone to conflict (see Collier et al. 2003), and nations in conflict have their growth potential curtailed. Although poor institutional quality can both retard growth and promote violent internal conflict, its effect on these two phenomena are not symmetric. Not all countries that are growth failures descend into large-scale internal violence. Similarly, although most nations experiencing conflict do have a poor record in terms of economic growth, several others do not, such as in East Asia (Indonesia), South Asia (Nepal, Sri Lanka) and Latin America (Colombia). History is not bereft of examples of growth and conflict prevention success via good institutions against the odds, when the wrong kind of endowment and geography had existed, such as in Botswana (rich in mineral resources) and Singapore (tropical location with a high initial settler mortality rate). Ultimately, conflict prevention requires the presence of a set of institutions governing economic distribution, political participation and social norms that result in the non–violent resolution of inter-group disputes. I refer to these mechanisms as the social contract.

The number of civil wars peaked in 1991 when 52 wars occurred in 38 countries, but by 2007, this number declined to 34 wars in 25 countries (Gleditsch 2008). Along with this, associated conflict fatalities are also declining. However, the number of Muslim countries experiencing civil war as a proportion of all civil wars is rising. Civil (and inter-state) war incidence is on the wane, but other forms of violent conflict may be rising, and these do not always involve the state as a direct participant. Moreover, the new types of conflict often occur in countries and contexts of 'development', and where growth and success in globalisation is taking place. An example would be the various Maoist insurgencies in India that take place in the overall national context of growth and success in a globalised economy.

A variety of lacunae remain in conflict studies. First, and foremost, is the complex and non-linear relationship between development and economic progress and conflict risk. Both severe underdevelopment and rapid economic progress can produce conflict risk. The former is associated more with the risk of civil war, the latter usually with mass violent protest and localised rebellion that does not fundamentally undermine the position of the state. Bates (2001) gives us historical examples when increased prosperity first increased violence before further economic progress slowed it down. The reason is increased affluence initially produced haves and have-nots, and the insecurity of the latter increased violence. But further increases in living standards could not be sustained except via relative peace and the emergence of new rules of the game governing production and distribution.

Attention has to be focused on the distributional consequences of growth. New sources of tension arise in our globalised world because of rising food and fuel prices which intensify existing grievances against the state, burdens of servicing international debt and through the relative deprivation felt because of the ever widening gap in living standards between rich and poor countries. The losers from increased globalisation which widens the gulf between the 'haves and have-nots' sometimes transform their protests into violent insurgencies. Rapid globalisation, especially in the form of increased international trade and inward foreign investment, has increased income differences between skilled and unskilled workers all over the world (Mamoon and Murshed 2008), and income inequality generally (Milanovic 2011). The reason is that the race to acquire international competitiveness, a zero sum game, requires real wage compression relative to labour productivity, something that has been skewed towards the relatively unskilled worker in the past three decades. In many developing societies, rural hinterlands have been particularly disadvantaged; where it is combined with ethnic differences with the majority of the state's population, this relative backwardness can constitute a recipe for violent (Maoist style) insurgencies. The important point is that such relative deprivation can take place even when the nation's aggregate economic performance is impressive, and growth is both positive and buoyant. Moreover, there are ethnic or communal conflicts where groups compete over dwindling environmental resources, such as those utilised in agriculture (Homer-Dixon, 1999) or other contestable endowments like land. Many of these ethnic conflicts do not include the state as a direct participant.

Secondly, we have the non-linear impact of increased democratisation on conflict risk (Hegre et al. 2001). Mature democracies are peaceful, but democratic transitions enhance the chances of violent conflict. Although there has been a marked shift towards democracy in most developing countries since the end of the Cold War, and most have adopted the multi-party electoral system to form governments, they still lack adequate constraints on the executive and their electoral systems are fraught with imperfections, making them *anocracies* rather than democracies. An anocracy has characteristics of both democracy and autocracy; most developing countries fall into this category, raising conflict risk. This means we have to have a nuanced take on the role of institutions, eschewing the naive institutional fundamentalism that pervades the mainstream thinking about long-term development nowadays.

Thirdly, greater emphasis has to be put on detailed case studies of local conflict. This means a deeper understanding of local economic conditions and social capital. Household surveys, if intelligently designed, can also yield deeper psychological insights on how the trauma of violence affects economic behaviour, as well as gauging the contribution of group identity and group grievances to any future conflict risk. The role of intrinsic motivation in joining movements, particularly the part played by an individual's identification with the cause of a disadvantaged group that he belongs to, deserves much more than the scant and passing attention that it has hitherto received in the rational choice literature on conflict. The study of sectarian (or communal) conflicts in countries such as India, Indonesia and Nigeria, as well as cultural conflict with Muslims in Europe, deserves more sophisticated research. In the ultimate analysis, conflict resolution has always ubiquitously required justice, not just the justice that is in the interest of the stronger.

Finally, with regard to the achievement of peace, even an idealist philosopher like Immanuel Kant (1795) considered war to be the natural state of man. In that respect, he shared the perspective of the English philosopher Thomas Hobbes (1651). According to Hobbes, the state of nature was characterised by anarchy akin to perpetual war;[9] each man taking what he could with no basis for right or wrong. Life was: 'solitary, poor, nasty, brutish and short'. Consequently, it was in the interest of individuals to surrender their individual freedom of action to an absolute ruler in return for personal security and rule-based interactions in society. Kant was concerned more with preventing war between nations. That would require the simultaneous adoption of a republican constitution by all nations, which *inter alia* would check the war-like tendencies of both monarchs and the citizenry; the *cosmopolitanism* that would emerge among the comity of nations would preclude war, implying a confederation amongst such nation states (*foedus pacificum*).[10] Kant's notion of cosmopolitanism is also applicable to divided and factionalised nation states. Both thinkers were concerned with mechanisms that would engender peace. In other words, peace has to be achieved through deliberate design.

Notes

1 It has to be pointed out that per-capita income and the other two indicators of the human development index (health and education) are highly correlated, in other words they go together; richer countries tend to have better educational and health outcomes in most cases.

2 These are the last two of the four freedoms enunciated in President Franklin Delano Roosevelt's state of the union address to Congress on 6 January 1941, see http://www.Fdrlibrary.marist.edu/od4frees.html (accessed on 29 June 2005).

3 One may trace the conventional view of welfare in economics to Jeremy Bentham's utilitarianism using an exogenous pleasure-pain principle from which individuals derive utility. Societal welfare is the sum of all individual welfare, leading to the greatest good of the greatest number principle. It has to be remembered, however, that another great utilitarian, John Stuart Mill, who may be regarded as a linear disciple of Bentham, wrote 'it is better to be a human being dissatisfied than a pig satisfied; better to be Socrates dissatisfied than a fool satisfied' (Mill 1863), thus contradicting simplistic interpretations of the pleasure–pain principle.

4 Here I am referring to booms in mineral and fuel (oil and gas) sectors, and in countries where there is a substantial export dependence on these types of commodities.

5 It is important to distinguish between resource abundance and dependence, as many countries rich in natural resources (the United States for example), do not depend on them for export.

6 The authors argue that the mortality rate amongst Europeans is what determined whether Europeans settled a colony or not.

7 The expression greed disguised as grievance was coined by Paul Collier.

8 Mention of this factor is made in Aristotle's *Politics*.

9 *Bellum omnium contra omnes*, or war by all against all.

10 Arguably, the ideal behind the European Union is in the spirit of Kant's thinking.

References

Acemoglu, Daron, Simon Johnson and James A. Robinson (2001) 'The Colonial Origins of Comparative Development: An Empirical Investigation', *American Economic Review*, 91(5): 1369–1401.

Acemoglu, Daron, Simon Johnson and James A. Robinson (2005) 'Institutions as the Fundamental Cause of Long-Run Growth', in Philippe Aghion and Steven Durlauf (eds), *Handbook of Economic Growth* 1(1), Amsterdam: Elsevier, pp. 385–472.

Addison Tony and S. Mansoob Murshed (2002) 'Credibility and Reputation in Peacemaking', *Journal of Peace Research*, 39(4): 487–501.

Addison Tony and S. Mansoob Murshed (2005) 'Transnational Terrorism as a Spillover of Domestic Disputes in Other Countries', *Defence and Peace Economics*, 16(2): 69–82.

Addison, Tony and S. Mansoob Murshed (2006). 'The Social Contract and Violent Conflict', in Helen Yanacopoulos and Joseph Hanlon (eds), *Civil War, Civil Peace*, Oxford: Currey, pp. 137–163.

Addison, Tony, Philippe Le Billon and S. Mansoob Murshed (2002) 'Conflict in Africa: The Cost of Peaceful Behaviour', *Journal of African Economies*, 11(3): 365–386.

Akerlof, George and Rachel E. Kranton (2000) 'Economics and Identity', *Quarterly Journal of Economics* 115(3): 715–753.

Bates, Robert H. (2001) *Prosperity and Violence*, New York: Norton.

Boulding, Kenneth E. (1956) *The Image: Knowledge in Life and Society*, Ann Arbor: University of Michigan Press.

Bowles, Samuel (1998) 'Endogenous Preferences: The Cultural Consequences of Markets and Other Economic Institutions', *Journal of Economic Literature*, 36(1): 75–111.

Collier, Paul and Anke Hoeffler (2004) 'Greed and Grievance in Civil Wars', *Oxford Economic Papers*, 56(4): 563–595

Collier, Paul, Lani Elliot, Håvard Hegre, Anke Hoeffler, Marta Reynal-Querol and Nicholas Sambanis (2003) *Breaking the Conflict Trap: Civil War and Development Policy*, World Bank, Oxford University Press.

Easterly, William (2007) 'Inequality Does Cause Underdevelopment', *Journal of Development Economics*, 84(2): 755–776.

Easterly, William and Ross Levine (2003) 'Tropics, Germs and Crops: How Endowments Influence Economic Development', *Journal of Monetary Economics*, 50: 3–39.

Edgeworth, Francis Y. (1881) *Mathematical Psychics*, London: C Kegan Paul.

Gleditsch, Nils Petter (2008) 'The Liberal Moment Fifteen Years On', *International Studies Quarterly*, 15(4): 691–712.

Grossman, Herschel I. (1991) 'A General Equilibrium Model of Insurrections', *American Economic Review*, 81(4): 912–921.

Gurr, Ted R. (1970) *Why Men Rebel*, Princeton: Princeton University Press.

Hegre, Håvard, Tanja Ellingsen, Scott Gates and Nils Petter Gleditsch (2001) 'Towards a Democratic Civil Peace? Democracy, Civil Change, and Civil War 1816–1992', *American Political Science Review* 95(1): 17–33.

Hirshleifer, Jack (1995) 'Anarchy and its Breakdown', *Journal of Political Economy*, 103 (1), 26–52.

Hobbes, Thomas (1651) *Leviathan*, reprinted 1998, Oxford: World Classics, Oxford University Press.

Homer-Dixon, Thomas F. (1999) *Environment, Scarcity, and Violence*, Princeton: Princeton University Press.

Kant, Immanuel (1795) *Perpetual Peace and Other Essays on Politics, History and Morals*, reprinted 1983, Indianapolis: Hackett Publishing.

Mamoon, Dawood and S. Mansoob Murshed (2008) 'Unequal Skill Premiums and Trade Liberalization: Is Education the Missing Link?', *Economics Letters*, 100(2): 262–266.

Milanovic, Branko (2011) *The Haves and the Have Nots*, New York: Basic Books.

Mill, John Stuart (1863) *Utilitarianism*, available from Google books www.books.google.co.uk (accessed 20 February 2012).

Murphy, Kevin, Andrei Shleifer and Robert Vishny (1991) 'The Allocation of Talent: Implications for Growth', *Quarterly Journal of Economics*, 106(2): 503–530.

Murshed, S. Mansoob (2002) 'Civil War, Conflict and Underdevelopment', *Journal of Peace Research*, 39(4): 387–393.

Murshed, S. Mansoob (2010) *Explaining Civil War: A Rational Choice Approach*, Cheltenham: Edward Elgar.

Olson, Mancur (1965) *The Logic of Collective Action*, Cambridge MA: Harvard University Press.

Rawls, John (1971) *A Theory of Justice*, Cambridge MA: Harvard University Press.

Rodrik, Dani (1999) 'Where Did All the Growth Go? External Shocks, Social Conflict, and Growth Collapses', *Journal of Economic Growth*, 4(4): 385–412.

Rodrik, Dani, Arvind Subramanian and Francesco Trebbi (2004) 'Institutions Rule: The Primacy of Institutions over Geography and Integration in Economic Development', *Journal of Economic Growth*, 9(2): 131–165.

Ross, Michael L. (2004) 'What Do we Know About Natural Resources and Civil Wars', *Journal of Peace Research*, 41(3): 337–356.

Sen, Amartya (1985) *Commodities and Capabilities*, Amsterdam: North Holland.

Stewart, Frances (2000) 'Crisis Prevention: Tackling Horizontal Inequalities', *Oxford Development Studies*, 28(3): 245–262.

Streeten, Paul (1993) 'From Growth via Basic Needs to Human Development: the Individual in the Process of Development', in S. Mansoob Murshed and Kunibert Raffer (eds), *Trade, Transfers and Development*, Aldershot: Edward Elgar, pp. 16–33.

Tilly, Charles (1998) *Durable Inequality*, Berkeley: University of California Press.

Tolstoy, Leo (1877), *Anna Karenina*, New York: Random House (2000).

UNDP (1999) *Human Development Report – 1999*, New York: United Nations Development Programme.

Wintrobe, Ronald (2006) 'Extremism, Suicide Terror and Authoritarianism', *Public Choice*, 128(1): 169–195.

23

FROM CONCEPT TO METHOD: THE CHALLENGE OF A HUMAN SECURITY METHODOLOGY

Mary Martin and Denisa Kostovicova

Introduction

One area which has received less attention in the decade and a half since human security emerged as a field of inquiry and policy application is that of methods and methodology. While critical thinking about security has sought to change understandings and produce new analytical perspectives, it has relied largely on methods of inquiry and decision-making which are rooted in established conventions about the nature of security, its objects and goals. Where human security has attempted to challenge conventions, it has done so by reframing conceptual pillars of security including rethinking the nature of threats and causes of vulnerability, redefining the referent objects of security, and proposing a securitisation of everyday life. It has also set out a normative vision, in which human needs as well as affective factors such as dignity and control as well as agential power and actorness are part of the security agenda. Human security has made a novelty of privileging 'who?' and 'what?' questions, in focusing on individuals within security problematics, but has paid less attention to the methodological implications and imperatives of reorientating security away from its classical roots in state sovereignty, towards the local, individual and personal (Kostovicova et al. 2012).

In this chapter we begin by reviewing how human security has affected discussions of methods. We then explore further the operational challenges which the concept poses to researchers and policy-makers, and we set out the case for pursuing methodology as a way of better understanding and locating human security in the field.

Human security and existing methodologies: quantitative and qualitative perspectives

Methodology is understood as an encompassing term referring 'to those basic assumptions about the world we study, which are before the specific techniques adopted by the scholar undertaking research' (Fierke 2004: 36; also Pouliot 2007: 360). A methodology comprises a set of epistemological and ontological requirements that in turn formulates its own scientific standards and truth conditions – or put differently 'criteria of proof and demonstration' (Hacking 2002: 189). Research methods will flow from the researcher's framework of reasoning, as well as how s/he approaches ontology and epistemology. While the same methods may be shared by various methodologies, the methodology adopted will determine what are the most appropriate methods and concrete tools of inquiry, while for the practitioner, methodology is also the starting point for shaping consistent policy responses and will influence the choice of both practical approaches and relevant resources.

The failure to apply suitable investigative tools is part of the gap in understanding human security, which has contributed to its being dismissed as fuzzy and imprecise and therefore of limited policy utility (Paris 2001). Critics who contend that the concept is a product of excess normative reasoning have overlooked the possibility that more appropriate research methods might be instrumental not only in applying the concept, but in providing greater definition and empirically grounded clarity in understanding it, and that there is a link to be explored, between methodology and conceptualisation (Kostovicova et al. 2012).

Meanwhile the challenge for human security is to devise research practices and policies which are consistent with the deemed conceptual shift from the security of states to that of individuals and communities, but which do more than merely pay lip service to this change.

The methodological response to the emergence of a new security agenda has been to pursue the shift which reconceptualises the nature of insecurity. Researchers have attempted to capture threat multiplicity and vulnerability, as conceptual focus has moved from defending the state and protecting borders to the dangers faced by individuals, from natural disasters to poverty, under-development and aspects of conflict. The fundamental tenets of human security including the dualism between 'fears and wants' (Tadjbakhsh and Chenoy 2007), or deprivations versus needs, led researchers in two different methodological directions, based on the assumed distinction between observable harms and speculative aspirations. Quantitative methods concentrated on trying to identify and measure novel forms of insecurity to distinguish them from conventional forms of security data, as well as developing proxies for these various forms. Qualitative methods involving interviews and perception studies attempted to filter available data through the prism of individualised experiences.[1] In many cases human security methodology sought to combine the two, as it attempted to counter criticisms of conceptual fuzziness through making use of what might be regarded by some as more rigorously scientific quantitative data, while also allowing room for the subjective experience of insecurity. Examples of this include the Palestinian Human Development Report 2009/10, which applied a human security lens, and aimed 'to integrate public opinion and perceptions wherever possible'. A consultative process was also critical for compiling the human security survey (UNDP 2010: 14).

The discussion around the definition of civil wars, and battle-deaths as an appropriate way of measuring them, is an example of how human security has impacted upon methodological debates, particularly in applying quantitative approaches. The Uppsala Conflict Data Programme which is widely used by a number of subsidiary indices defines conflict as: 'a contested incompatibility that concerns government and/or territory where the use of armed force between two parties, of which at least one is the government of a state, results in at least 25 battle-related deaths in a year.'[2]

While the debate focused on appropriate thresholds of fatalities to justify the label of a civil war, and limitations such as unreliable sources and statistical hazards of measuring populations, the datasets were also challenged at a more fundamental level for framing violence to individuals in familiar terms such as the number of fatalities and the period of hostilities, rather than including other measures which denoted extreme vulnerability. For critics, this kind of measure fails to adjust the analytical horizon and allow for a wider interpretation of insecurity and conflict (Spagat et al. 2009).

In trying to combine highly different datasets researchers were challenged to be able to provide a robust identification of long-term generic risk factors for violence, rather than an explanation of why specific conflicts happened (Human Security Centre 2003). The need for extra analytical purchase on observed data becomes a recurring theme in the attempt to do justice to the ambitions of human security in capturing both objective (in)security and the subjectivity of the human factor. Merely recording events and phenomena, however broad, satisfies the first ambition but underproblematises the second.

In the case of the civil war datasets, a human security approach suggested that account be taken of obvious manifestations of danger such as battle deaths, and in addition collateral effects such as illness, famine, physical and material insecurity. What was missing from this broad approach, however, was a way of identifying how multiple threats might be correlated and how violent conflict might fuel disease or economic hardship. Human security researchers also sought to highlight elements of desirable well-being, such as access to education, participation in democratic processes and so on, beyond elements of freedom from fear (King and Murray 2001: 601).

The application of the human security framework in national settings has already proven its analytical value. This is illustrated by an introduction of a concept of 'securitability' in the National Human Development Report (NHDR) in Latvia, including a range of other novel insights into people's perceived vulnerabilities as in the NHDR in Afghanistan, Bangladesh and Macedonia, as highlighted in chapter 10 in this volume.

Whichever theoretical model of insecurity is adopted, there are difficulties in obtaining relevant data. Many indicators that could be considered appropriate are particularly vulnerable to being reported in inaccurate, inconsistent or biased ways. Comparisons are likely to be problematic, for reasons of different data collection environments in different countries or regions, while the act of comparison itself may be meaningless.

Aggregation into composite indexes raises problems which include underspecifying with too few indicators, assigning inaccurate relative weighting to different variables, double counting and confusion about conceptual categories of indicators, and compounding individual measurement errors across the whole index. Researchers investigating human insecurity in Afghanistan used four indicators: deaths from armed conflict, human rights violations, refugees and internally displaced persons (IDPs) and natural and technological disasters. They noted that the indicators were descriptive rather than evaluative, inasmuch as they captured dimensions of past events rather than assessments of (present) capacities to respond to particular threats. Moreover each indicator raised a specific set of problems relating to sources, definition and comparability. To take just one example, civilian deaths in Afghanistan as counted in one dataset reflected

> discrepancies (which) may be attributed to such factors as differential motives of the various sources, and variations in adopted definitions of 'civilian': specifically, whether families of Taliban and Al Qaeda members are counted as civilian.[3]

Beyond this, it is worth noting that quantitative measures do not escape criticisms of subjective interpretation, on the one hand, or concerns about the credibility of either estimated or actual data. The research group on Afghanistan noted the presence of anecdotal information alongside quantitative statistics, for example in the reporting of human rights violations. A more obvious manifestation of this dilemma was the controversy which erupted in 1991 when the United Nations Development Programme (UNDP) ranked countries according to a human freedom index. The group of 77 states objected to criteria for the index which included freedom for homosexuality, denouncing the measure as lacking in cultural sensitivity (Barsh 1993).

Initiatives such as the Human Security Index, the Human Development Index and the Human Security Report attempt empirical measurement by taking pre-selected, theorised components of broad vulnerability. A prototype Human Security Index released in 2008–9 draws together over 30 categories of data in a series of sub-indices on economic, social and environmental concerns. It tries to measure personal and community impacts by capturing effects such as hardship, vulnerability, empowerment and sustainability. The problems faced by the prototype included finding adequate data particularly on aspects such as equitability and inclusiveness, as well as sufficiently diversified indicators of racial, ethnic, religious, age-based and other 'dis'ability-based forms of security.

Similarly, the Global Peace Index assembles data on domestic and international conflict, and societal safety and security from 149 countries. It is composed of 23 qualitative and quantitative indicators, suggested by an international panel of experts, which reflect levels of military expenditure, relationships between states, human rights situations and so on. The GPI claims to deliver 'a snapshot of relative peacefulness among nations while continuing to contribute to an understanding of what factors help create or sustain more peaceful societies' (GPI 2010).

The act of measurement which is integral to exercises such as the Human Development Index and the Generalised Poverty Index is problematic for human security in several ways: large-scale indices are predicated on the availability/collectability of data, as well as how successfully they lend themselves to data aggregation and comparability. They seek validation through the global reach of datasets, the number of countries covered as well as the depth of sub-thematic indices, which allows them to claim comprehensiveness and which allows for comparability across countries and regions (GPI 2010). Yet not only is measurement dependent on a pre-determined idea of what should be measured (Owen 2008), most measures of insecurity do not explore hierarchies between different sub-indicators, although the statistical background to compiling them encompasses myriad decisions made at each point about the relative importance of the different components. In addition, measurement indices often ignore certain types of vulnerabilities/capabilities because they are not objective factors inasmuch as they have different meanings for different people, or because the data is simply not available (Tadjbakhsh 2005 :18).

Large-scale indices pursue breadth at the expense of generating meaningful local data which can guide more targeted and therefore effective policy. They do not probe the complex hinterland of lived experiences of security at the individual and local level, by showing how plural sources of insecurity interact, the ingredients of violence, how it affects different people differently to what degree, or what the implications of it are on the social fabric of communities. As Justino et al. point out, questionnaires used in standard household surveys in countries affected by violence and conflict rarely feature questions which ask about the causes and consequences of violence in the lives of those affected by violent conflict. When they do, there is a lack of systematic implementation of the findings nor are there consistent comparisons across different settings (Brück et al. 2010).

As Owen notes, this has not only normative connotations in overgeneralising the severity of threat some individuals face, but has operational implications too. The broader the definition of harms, the more difficult meaningful measurement becomes because both aggregation and differentiation between each of the autonomous variables become more difficult the more indicators are included (Owen 2002, 2008). In addition, complete data are unlikely to be available or reliable, and dangerous and harmful conflict environments, where the need for such data is greatest, are likely to yield the least dependable results. Thus the dilemma highlighted by Owen is between narrow and feasible methodologies or overstretched ones which are impossible to implement and/or inaccurate.

One solution proposed by Owen is a spatial mapping approach: rather than relying on national level data, he suggests shifting perceptions of space, and measuring insecurity at the local level. The threats identified would be regionally and locally relevant, they could be aggregated by using space as a common denominator, and issues of data integrity would be addressed by balancing the subjectivity of individuals with the advantages of local knowledge combined with disciplinary experts (Owen 2008).

Such an approach measures both the plurality of harms, and by grouping them within spatially defined localities, begins to address the inter-relatedness of different forms of (in)security. In common with many methodological approaches based on human security, the step from conceptualising (in)security to subsequently determining the cultural and institutional conditions for states of peace, and trying to achieve them makes assumptions about linkages and cause/effect dynamics which are themselves not unproblematic. Unless these assumptions are also systematically identified, challenged and tested, something goes missing in all stages from the collection of data, to analysis and assessment, through to end use and implementation.

A human security audit represents an attempt to fuse quantitative and qualitative approaches, identifying diverse threats in order to then manage them. It is a device which links analysis to possible solutions. It is potentially transformative, because it is performed in order to 'know better what one should care about, what it is in one's power to do, and what crises are looming' (Bajpai 2000). However, an audit implies that an external 'expert' will be required to carry out this assessment, prioritise the threats and then undertake the action required. The linguistic connotations of 'auditor' suggest a distinction between the expert who is measuring on the one hand, and what or whom is being examined. While the audit carries no specific prescription of how this information might be obtained, it presumes a discourse of difference and distance. Individuals are rendered doubly passive and objectified in the face of attacks on their personal safety and/or well-being, not only by the techniques of control designed and deployed by others to rescue them, but also by the processes of gathering knowledge about their insecurity (Kostovicova et al. 2012).

Although significant work has been done to translate human security into quantitative techniques, including the design of indicators as part of a broader attempt in the social sciences to record and understand political, social and economic phenomena (Davis et al. 2011), the chief limitation of existing quantitative methods in terms of human security is their ability to integrate an individual perspective into contexts of insecurity: either statistically through the way they handle data collection and aggregation, or conceptually in under-representing the personal dynamic in the security problematic. How to handle subjectivity and agency are not only questions to which quantitative approaches have limited answers; frequently such questions are not raised at all.

Qualitative approaches on the other hand are validated by their assumed appropriateness in capturing both the breadth and depth of insecurities experienced 'on the ground,' in contrast to data collection carried out by surveys. They provide further explanatory information beyond statistical or 'headline' data and help to contextualise vulnerability. The focus on individuals' own accounts of their attitudes, motivations and behaviour has strengths in that 'individuals are interviewed in sufficient detail for their results to be taken as true, correct, complete and believable reports of their views and experiences' (Hakim 2000: 36), including the conduciveness of that data to establishing connections and patterns of association between different factors. However, qualitative approaches are often seen as overly subjective-interpretative, placing generous licence in the hands of the researcher analyst to read too much into sources or draw conclusions based on personal biases (cf. Schnabel and Krummenacher 2009: 9). Self-reported data are liable to be dismissed for validating 'fleeting emotional states' rather than producing 'enduring evaluations (Alkire, 2005: 224; Schnabel and Krummenacher, 2009: 9).

The trap of methodological individualism also beckons in reifying the personal at the expense of understanding how social relations and the contextualized operation of agency affect qualitative accounts by individuals and groups (Cramer 2002). For all these reasons, subjectivity, and the nature of individual agency in fragile contexts, needs to be part of the ontology of security as well as how we investigate and understand it.

Methods for obtaining and analysing information accept and assume a distance between the researcher/outsider and the local individual, and a hierarchy which places the balance of power in the interrogative relationship between them firmly on the side of the researcher, as we have illustrated in the case of the human security audit. Indeed the lack of emphasis on questions of 'how' knowledge about security is constructed, and acted upon, has been seen as largely unproblematic (Kostovicova et al. 2012). Methodological nationalism which assumes the nation state as the frame of reference has affected not only conceptual views of security but clouded the means by which it is researched and operationalised. Firstly, it has obscured a view of transnational communities, encouraging the belief that they are a novel product of globalisation instead of something which was always there, which we need to rediscover (Wimmer and Glick Schiller 2002: 301). It has also blocked our view of the individual's perspective of security. By disaggregating the idea of the nation-state as the reference framework for security, a human security analysis seeks to reinstate 'the perceptions and lived experience of real people and their communities rather than abstract states' (Thomas 2007: 117). Accordingly, a key characteristic of human security is a bottom-up perspective. However, attempts to probe the bottom-up perspective are still in their infancy.

A bottom-up perspective has been used as shorthand for consultation with the locals, be they representatives of the state or civil society (Kostovicova and Bojicic-Dzelilovic 2011: 94–98). However, if a bottom-up approach is to be conducive to obtaining human security data and tightening the conceptual understanding of human security, we suggest that it should include a re-balancing of power between locals and outsiders, and between those suffering insecurity and those who seek to address it. It is important to recognise that sustainable security can only be achieved in the end by those who suffer insecurity. Outsiders can assist but they cannot supply security unilaterally. Unlike traditional security approaches, human security also contains an explicitly normative and emancipatory aspect. It inaugurates an ethical rupture, in that it 'offers a definition of an end point towards which all politics have to strive, i.e. the ethics of ultimate ends, which holds a transformatory potential for actors and institutions at all levels of international governance' (Tadjbakhsh & Chenoy 2007: 20). Individuals and communities are not merely a point of reference for thinking about insecurity and its remedies, they should be the active subjects and not just passive objects of attempts to re-establish security. In this respect, research into human security could benefit from ethnographic and participatory methods, not only because of research that presumes understanding of the local context, but also because of its preoccupation with the relationship between the researcher and research subjects.

Overcoming the division between the researcher as the outsider and the research subject, who is the insider, is a key challenge facing social scientists in using the ethnographic method. Most importantly, this division affects the construction of knowledge in the issue area under study. Therefore, much attention in ethnographic research is given to recognising and overcoming biases, which may be political, cultural, ethnic, racial, etc., as well as knowledge gaps (Hirsch 2008). At the same time, the research process is geared towards capturing the perspective of the subject comprehensively and accurately. As Bayard de Volo and Schatz (2004: 267) put it, ethnographic methods seek 'to uncover emic (insider) perspectives on political and social life and/or ground-level processes involved therein'. This process is not without its challenges, including the establishment of truth and objectivity (Borneman and Hammoudi 2009: 9). The position of an insider researcher, who conducts research 'at home', and is, therefore, equipped with 'local' knowledge that does not require cultural translation (cf. Maranhã and Streck 2003), is not free of problems, either. In fact, his or her knowledge can be taken as an impediment, while 'closeness' lends itself to interpretation as political bias and partisan affiliation (O'Reilly 2009: 109–117). A bottom-up approach seeks to capture local voices, while benefiting from 'being there', a key concept to ethnographic enquiry based on immersion in 'foreign' environments. Similarly, Read proposes a term 'site-intensive methods' (SIM) to refer to 'the collection of evidence from human subjects within their own contexts, their interaction with which informs the study just as the researcher's own questions do' (Read 2006: 10). Operationalising the bottom-up approach in human security ultimately could benefit from ethnographic sensibilities with which the researcher approaches the field and knowledge.

Unlike ethnography, participatory research does more than this. It also addresses the structural relationship between power and knowledge and recognises that conventional processes of knowledge production entail deep-seated inequalities – even (sometimes, especially) between insiders (Cornwall and Jewkes 1995). In post-conflict contexts and environments where societies are conflicted along ethnic lines, knowledge seeking inevitably involves vulnerable and marginalised people. Studies that seek empirical data from such targets run a spectrum of risk from doing nothing to challenge or redress the inequalities that contribute to vulnerability and marginalisation, to positively aggravating divisions. The traditional power of the researcher towards those who have knowledge consists of framing questions, selecting and sifting data and interpreting it in ways which not only reflect the researcher's bias but which also reproduce the asymmetry between marginalised and vulnerable people and others. It also risks entrenching inequitable social relations between different communities (Heron and Reason 2008; Grant et al. 2008). Therefore, capturing the local perspective depends on neutralising some of these inherent power imbalances by providing the space and opportunity for all voices to be heard including those often marginalised because of their lack of social status, education or discursive skills. A participatory methodology, using techniques of debate and discussion rather than interrogation, allows participants greater opportunity to voice their position and attitudes in their own, rather than others' terms, and it reaches beyond the focus group methodology of much traditional research to encompass the knowledge that remains untapped. In sum, research is a relational process, in that the interaction between the researcher and the researched leads to the (co)-constitution of knowledge. Such an approach incorporates elements of collaborative ethnography: it emphasises co-operation and reciprocity, as part of interaction with others within their local context. The research process 'moves collaboration from its taken-for-granted background and positions it on center stage' (Lassiter 2005).

The concepts of emancipation and empowerment that are integral to human security should also be rethought in the context of research ethics. Researchers in conflict-affected areas must consider whether and how their research is directly relevant and how it impacts on the people it involves (Ross 2009: 183). The transformative potential of human security is conventionally expressed in the improvements of observable indicators, such as violence on the sharp-end or employment figures on the soft-end of human security. The affective aspect of (in)security has been largely left unexplored despite the prominence of the feeling of dignity in the human security paradigm. By contrast, the scholars of conflict and intervention have begun to engage rigorously with the role of emotions to 'more validly capture[s] the reality of conflict' (Petersen 2011: 298; cf. Keen 2012: 195–234). Understanding lived experience of insecurity including its affective dimension could contribute to capturing the meaning of human security more comprehensively. At the same, it can provide additional guidelines for practice as to what needs to be restored for human security to be achieved. The affective dimension of subjectivity is related to cognition. Ellis and Flaherty point out 'there is an emotional horizon for cognition because, in large measure, people think about the same things they care about' (Ellis and Flaherty 1992: 4). At the same time, emotional, cognitive and physical experiences as aspects of subjectivity are interconnected (Ibid). The affective aspect of human security adds additional perspective on subjective experience of (in)security best captured by the 'worm's eye view' of security concerns as opposed to the 'bird's eye view' offered by survey (Hakim 2000: 36). But, accounting for emotions in a holistic explanation of human security raises additional methodological challenges. Here human security research can draw on interpretive methods that acknowledge emotionality throughout the research process, including 'in the lives of those who are studied' and 'the observations that are gathered' (Denzin 1989: 30). Furthermore, this method also goes towards shifting power from the researcher to the researched, in that it 'accords others the full range of human agency, including legitimating others' local knowledge – their own expertise in their own lived experience' (Yanow 2006: 70).

Lastly, a human security method could draw on the idea of reflexivity to be found notably in the work of Beck et al. (1994) and of Bourdieu (1990). For these social theorists, reflexivity is essential to uncover the intellectual and political biases of the observer/researcher/analyst. It is a means by which they might 'critically interrogate their own interested actions as cultural producers' (Eagleton-Pierce, 2011: 806). Stuvøy (2010) integrates subjective interpretation in the research methodology in order to validate subjects' views and perceptions in the production of security. However, even for Stuvøy (Ibid), research subjects remain no more than the source of data that are subject to interpretation in human security terms by a reflexive researcher. However, reflexivity can be key to engaging individuals and groups actively in the research and inquiry process, rather than relegating them to a subordinate position. In this under-standing of reflexivity, the research subjects themselves interpret their own understandings of security within the research process. Kostovicova et al. (2012) demonstrate how dialogue as a research tool enables this process, and allows and equips the researched to understand their security situation 'anew' by seeing it in different light. Inquiry into human security requires that the researcher is concerned not just empirically with individuals and groups as sources of knowledge and knowing, but also normatively enabling them to influence the production of that knowledge. Otherwise, thinking of individuals only in terms of a referent of security, i.e. as 'those on whose behalf action is being taken' (McCormack 2008: 124), rather than as agents as well, forfeits the promise of emancipation and empowerment built into the human security framework. In other words, to live up to the prominent claim of being emancipatory, human security research and methodology need to construct people as active agents when analysing vulnerability and attempting to produce security; and each person's individual experience of insecurity is valid and constitutive of generalized notions of human security, without falling into a trap of methodological individualism (Kostovicova et al. 2012).

Scholars have begun to question static and universal assumptions of security, and posit it as a site of 'shifting political imaginaries and practices' (Bubandt 2005: 276–277; cf. Hudson, 2005; Grayson, 2008). Such actor-oriented and vernacular approaches pave the way for rethinking methodologies. Yet this still leaves underexplored the question of how situated individuals and their personal capacity to act come together in practice. This is to go further than producing nuanced and authentic evidence of the complexity of threat and vulnerability. The distinc-tiveness of human security in comparison to traditional approaches lies in the fact that both the means and the ends of security are important – *how* people are made secure matters as much as the fact that they are protected both materially and physically (Kaldor et al. 2007: 279). A consequence of this distinctiveness is that the position of individuals, including their capacity to articulate their lived experience of security issues, merits more attention within the research, and would enrich both the understanding of the concept as well as its operationalisation by policy-makers and scholars alike (Kostovicova et al. 2012). Such an approach to the methods appropriate to researching human security would engage with the notion of positionality, reflexivity and ultimately ownership of the knowledge of human security. It would be underpinned by rethinking where the power lies in the research process. MacLean (2006: 13) notes that conscious recalibration of power differences between us as researchers and our human subjects, may 'not only improve the quality of our data collection and analysis but also invigorate our own everyday lives with a new level of democracy.'

Conclusion

The challenge of human security methodology remains that studying insecurity and developing responses to it both risk falling into the very trap the proponents of human security condemn in classic approaches – the use of old tools to tackle new problems. One size does not fit all and simply adapting conventional approaches to data or the use of traditional policy envelopes in an attempt to extend the security horizon to encompass individuals contains operational and ethical risks, and more profoundly it misunderstands the full implications of the human security concept.

If human security is to realise its potential to present an alternative paradigm of security, then critical conversations have to include methods of both knowledge production and policy implementation which respect more than just the superficial differences between this concept and conventional understandings of security. The task for methodology is to capture the 'messiness' and inchoate nature of security at the personal and local level, while at the same time opening up processes of knowledge production and policy implementation which allow subjective accounts to be acknowledged and considered valid.

Notes

1   For a comprehensive review of different methods see: Taylor Owen (2002) 'Body count: rationale and methodologies for measuring human security', *Human Security Bulletin* 1(3): 17.
2   See http://www.pcr.uu.se/research/UCDP/ (accessed 15 May 2013).
3   Project on Defense Alternatives, http://www.comw.org/pda/0201oef.html# (accessed 10 June 2013). Conetta, Carl (January 2002) *Strange Victory: A Critical Appraisal of Operation Enduring Freedom and the Afghanistan War*, http://www.slashdocs.com/iyiwwh/project-on-defense-alternatives-strange-victory-carl-conetta-jan-2002.html (accessed 29 May 2013).

References

Alkire S. (2005) 'Subjective quantitative studies of human agency', *Social Indicators Research* 74(1): 217–260.
Bajpai, K. (2000) 'Human security: concept and measurement', *Kroc Institute Occasional Paper #19:OP: 1*, August 2000.
Barsh, R. L. (1993) 'Measuring human rights: problems of methodology and purpose', *Human Rights Quarterly* 15(1), February: 87–121.
Bayard de Volo, L. and E. Schatz (2004) 'From the inside out: ethnographic methods in political research', *PSOnline*, www.apsanet.org, April: 267–271.
Beck, U. (1994) 'The reinvention of politics: towards a theory of reflexive modernization', in Beck, U., Giddens, A. and Lash, S. (eds) *Reflexive Modernization: Politics, Tradition and Aesthetics in the Modern Social Order*, Cambridge: Polity Press, pp. 1–55.
Beck, U., Giddens, A. and Lash, S. (eds) (1994) *Reflexive Modernization: Politics, Tradition and Aesthetics in the Modern Social Order*, Cambridge: Polity Press.

Borneman, J. and A. Hammoudi (2009) 'The fieldwork encounter, experience and the making of truth', in John Borneman and Abdellah Hammoudi (eds) *Being There: The Fieldwork Encounter and the Making of Truth*. Berkeley: University of California Press, pp. 1–24.

Bourdieu, P. (1990) *The Logic of Practice*. Cambridge: Polity Press.

Brück, T., P. Justino, P. Verwimp and A. Avdeenko (2010) *Identifying Conflict and Violence in Micro-Level Surveys*, HiCN Working Paper 79, July, available at www.hicn.org (accessed 10 August 2011).

Bubandt, N. (2005) 'Vernacular security: the politics of feeling safe in global, national and local worlds', *Security Dialogue* 36(3): 275–296.

Cornwall, A. and R. Jewkes (1995) 'What is participatory research?', *Social Science and Medicine* 41(12): 1667–1676.

Cramer, C. (2002) '*Homo economicus* goes to war: methodological individualism, rational choice and the political economy of war', *World Development* 30(11): 1845–1864.

Davis, K., B. Kingsbury and S. Engle Merry (2011) 'Indicators as a technology of global governance', *International Law and Justice Working Papers* 2010/2 Rev (August 2011). Global Administrative Law Series; available at: http://ssrn.com/abstract=1583431 (accessed 5 May 2012).

Denzin, N. K. (1989) *Interpretive Interactionism*. Newbury Park, London and New Delhi: Sage Publications.

Eagleton-Pierce, M. (2011) 'Advancing a reflexive international relations', *Millennium: Journal of International Studies* 39(3): 805–823.

Ellis, C. and M. G. Flaherty (1992) 'An agenda for the interpretation of lived experience', in Carolyn Ellis and Michael G. Flaherty (eds) *Investigating Subjectivity: Research on Lived Experience*. Newbury Park, London and New Delhi: Sage Publications.

Fierke, K. (2004) 'World or worlds? The analysis of content and discourse', *Qualitative Methods* 2(1): 36–39.

GPI (2010) Institute for Economics and Peace, *Global Peace Index. Methodology, Results and Findings,* available at: http://www.humansecuritygateway.com/documents/IEP_GPI2010_MethodologyResultsFindings.pdf (accessed 9 February 2011).

Grant, J., G. Nelson and T. Mitchell (2008) 'Negotiating the challenges of participatory action research: relationships, power participation, change and credibility', in Peter Reason and Hilary Bradbury (eds) *Handbook of Action Research: Participative Inquiry and Practice*. London: Sage.

Grayson, K. (2008) 'Human security as power/knowledge: the biopolitics of a definitional debate', *Cambridge Review of International Affairs* 21(3): 383–401.

Hacking, I. (2002) *Historical ontology*. Cambridge, Mass: Harvard University Press.

Hakim, C. (2000) *Research Design: Successful Designs for Social and Economic Research*. London and New York: Routledge, 2nd edn.

Heron, J. and P. Reason (2008) 'The practice of co-operative inquiry: research "with" rather than "on" people', in Peter Reason and Hilary Bradbury (eds) *Handbook of Action Research: Participative Inquiry and Practice*. London: Sage.

Hirsch, E. (2008) 'Knowing, not knowing, knowing anew', in Narmala Halstead, Eric Hirsch and Judith Okely (eds) *Knowing How to Know: Fieldwork and the Ethnographic Present*. New York and Oxford: Berghan Books, pp. 21–37.

Hudson, H. (2005) 'Doing security as though people matter: a feminist perspective on gender and the politics of human security', *Security Dialogue* 36(2): 155–174.

Human Security Centre (2003) 'Mapping and explaining civil war: what to do about contested datasets and findings'. Workshop report, Oslo 18–19 August, 2003.

Kaldor, M., M. Martin and S. Selchow (2007) 'Human security: a new strategic narrative for Europe', *International Affairs* 83(2): 273–288, p. 279

Keen, D. (2012) *Useful Enemies: When Waging Wars is More Important than Winning Them*. New Haven and London: Yale University Press.

King, G. and C. Murray (2001) 'Rethinking human security', *Political Science Quarterly* 116(4): 585–610.

Kostovicova, D., M. Martin and V. Bojicic-Dzelilovic (2012) 'The missing link in human security research: dialogue and insecurity in Kosovo', *Security Dialogue* 43(6): 569–585.

Kostovicova, D. and V. Bojicic-Dzelilovic (2011) 'External statebuilding and transnational networks: the limits of the civil society approach', in Denisa Kostovicova and Marlies Glasius (eds) *Bottom-up Politics: An Agency-Centred Approach to Globalization*. Basingstoke: Palgrave Macmillan, pp. 93–111.

Lassiter, L. E. (2005) *The Chicago Guide to Collaborative Ethnography*. Chicago and London: The University of Chicago Press.

MacLean, L. M. (2006) 'The power of human subjects and the politics of informed consent', *Qualitative Methods* 4(2): 13–15.

Maranhã, T. and B. Streck (eds) (2003) *Translation and Ethnography: The Anthropological Challenge of Intercultural Understanding*. Tucson: The University of Arizona Press.

McCormack, T. (2008) 'Power and agency in the human security framework', *Cambridge Review of International Affairs* 21(1): 113–128, p. 124.

O'Reilly, K. (2009) *Key Concepts in Ethnography*. London: Sage.

Owen, T. (2002) 'Body count: rationale and methodologies for measuring human security', *Human Security Bulletin,* 1(3).

Owen, T. (2008) 'Measuring human security: methodological challenges and the importance of geographically-referenced determinants', in Peter Liotta (ed.) *Environmental Change and Human Security: Recognizing and Acting on Hazard Impacts*. Springer NATO Science Series, pp. 35–64.

Paris, R. (2001) 'Human security: Paradigm shift or hot air?', *International Security* 26(2): 87–102.

Petersen, R. D. (2011) *Western Intervention in the Balkans: The Strategic Use of Emotion in Conflict*. Cambridge: Cambridge University Press.

Pouliot, V. (2007) '"Sobjectivism": Towards a constructivist methodology', *International Studies Quarterly* 51(2): 359–384.

Read, B. L. (2006) 'Site-intensive methods: Fenno and Scott in search of a coalition', *Quantitative Methods*, Fall: 10–13.

Ross, A. (2009) 'Impact on research of security-seeking behaviour', in Chandra Lekha Sriram et al. (eds) *Surviving Field Research: Working in Violent and Difficult Situations*. London and New York: Routledge, pp. 175–188.

Schnabel, A. and H. Krummenacher (2009) 'Towards a human security-based early warning and response system', in Hans Gunter Brauch, U. Oswald Spring et al. (eds) *Facing Global Environmental Change: Environment, Human, Energy, Food, Health and Water Security Concepts*. Berlin-Heidelberg: Springer-Verlag.

Spagat, M., A. Mack, T. Cooper and J. Kreutz (2009) 'Estimating battle deaths', *Journal of Conflict Resolution* 53: 934–950.

Stuvøy, K. (2010) 'Human security research practices: conceptualizing security for women's crisis centres in Russia', *Security Dialogue* 41(3): 279–299.

Tadjbakhsh, S. (2005) *Human Security: Concept, Implications and Application for Post-Intervention Afghanistan*, Etudes du CERI, No. 118, September. Paris: CERI Sciences Po.

Tadjbakhsh, S. and A. Chenoy (2007) *Human Security: Concepts and Implications*. London: Routledge.

Thomas, C. (2007) 'Globalization and human security', in Anthony McGrew and Nana K. Poku (eds) *Globalization, Development and Human Security*. Cambridge: Polity, pp. 107–131.

UNDP (2010) *Investing in Human Security for a Future State*, The Palestinian Human Development Report 2009/10.

Wimmer, A. and N. Glick Schiller (2002) 'Methodological nationalism and beyond: nation state building, migration and the social sciences', *Global Networks* 2(4): 304–334.

Yanow, D. (2006) 'Neither rigorous nor objective? Interrogating criteria for knowledge claims in interpretive science', in Dvora Yanow and Peregrine Schwartz-Shea (eds) *Interpretation and Method: Empirical Research Methods and the Interpretive Turn*. Armonk, New York and London: M.E. Sharpe, pp. 67–87.

24

HUMAN SECURITY MAPPING

Taylor Owen

Why measure human security?

Up until the end of the Cold War, what we now refer to as 'traditional security' or 'national security' dominated the field of international relations. In this view, the state was responsible for the preservation of territorial integrity, domestic order and international affairs. 'Security' generally meant the protection of the state from external attack, nuclear proliferation, international espionage and internal rebellion. In response, the security and defense infrastructure was tailored to address threats through military buildup, nuclear stockpiling and foreign intelligence.

While the security policy and apparatus of many countries remain focused on preserving national sovereignty, today's reality is that most deaths are not a result of interstate war. Instead, disease, violence, natural disasters and civil conflict are the leading causes of preventable premature mortality as we enter the twenty-first century (see Table 24.1). This rapid evolution in primary threats has prompted a substantial shift in relevant security issues and thinking. This includes both a widening of the potential array of security threats as well as a broadening of the security mandate from a narrowly focused national perspective to one focusing on human and community-based requirements.

We can expect the broadening of security threats to continue as the complex adaptive systems from which people and communities are threatened – global environmental change, disease spread, impoverishment, violence from non-government forces – continue to evolve at a rapid pace. These changes coupled with a security infrastructure that is slow to change, national in scope and hierarchical, suggests that the gap between security threats and the capacity to ameliorate these threats will grow even larger in the years to come. Clearly, there is an urgent need to address this disconnect between the theory and mechanisms of the traditional security paradigm and the majority of harms that people and communities face.

One alternative to traditional security, human security, shifts the focus of the concept from the state to the individual and community. Whereas a security threat was once something that threatened the integrity of the state, under the *human security* rubric, it is the set of harms that threatens the integrity of the individual and community. This shift in the referent of security provides an expanded set of threats resulting in a more inclusive and comprehensive security paradigm. However, the concept of human security poses some difficult analytic and policy problems, namely, how does one distinguish and prioritize threats if all possible harms to

Table 24.1 A global death registry, 2000

Cause of death	Global death totals
Interstate war	10,000
Internal and internationalized internal conflict	90,000
Disasters	65,000
Homicide	730,000
Communicable disease	18,000,000

Source: Disasters (EM-DAT, 2000); war, homicide and suicide (Krug et al., 2002); communicable disease (WHO, 2001)

individuals are deemed security concerns? *If traditional security is overly restrictive, human security risks is expansive and vague.*

While the validity of the normative interpretation of human security is relatively uncontested, at least among proponents of the concept, its analytic utility is fiercely debated. It is one thing to say that individuals are at risk from a much wider array of threats than the current security paradigm addresses – it is quite another to identify, measure and assess these many possible harms. Central to this debate are the parameters with which one selects human security threats. If, for example, a broad definition of human security is used, all threats that could potentially harm an individual must be included. A global assessment using this criteria is impossible. Quite simply, people can be harmed by such of vast array of threats that complete coverage is conceptually, practically and analytically impossible. Practitioners have circumvented this reality using two qualifiers in their measurement attempts – researcher and data defined threat identification. Both arbitrarily limit the included threats to those falling under categories such as violence, human right abuses, or health. More importantly, both marginalize the very core principle of the human security concept, that actual insecurity must drive our response mechanisms.

The question of whether or not human security should be measured is contested. Critics raise a number of objections.

First, measuring implies a predetermined definition. What is included in the measurement necessarily provides a de facto list of what is and is not a human insecurity. For those who are hesitant to limit human security to one definition, this is problematic.

Second, the term 'measuring' in itself implies a degree of certainty that the existing data do not warrant. Moreover 'objective' and 'subjective' measures may be contradictory. Subjectively, opinion polls indicate that people in developing countries fear violence more than disease. Objectively, however, mortality statistics tell us that by far the greatest threat is disease. How such contradictory assessments might be combined into a broad measure is not clear. A final consideration is that organizations often become defined by their measuring methodology. For example, regardless of other extensive and varied academic work, the International Institute for Sustainable Development (IISD) and the UNDP's Human Development Report (HDR) are arguably known best by their measuring indices. Although this isn't necessarily bad, it can distract from other important work being done, especially if early flawed research results are released.

Despite the above concerns, the measurement of human security should be undertaken for the following four reasons. First, measurement helps define the often ambiguous concept of human security. Second, measurement can reveal patterns that would not otherwise be observed. A substantial measurement exercise will inevitably help identify and locate human insecurities. Studying the relationships between multiple insecurities could reveal chains of causality and cumulative impacts not currently recognized, articulated or quantified.[1] Third, in the positivistic social sciences – with the goal of determining causal and correlative relationships – measurement is seen as essential. Fourth, measurement provides 'objective' evidence of trends that can be of great value in policymaking and political debate and can influence public and media perceptions of the issue in question.

Human security mapping

A central challenge in the measurement of human security is how can a measure stay true to the broad nature of human security – viz, not leave out any serious threat harming individuals – but also limit or refine our included threats to a manageable and measurable list?

In addition to the usual requirements of providing more reliable data in an efficient and timely manner, advancing the policy relevance of human security measures requires addressing two fundamental limitations associated with previous approaches. The new method must:

- move away from a standardized set of input indicators to a set which focuses only on those threats which are of critical importance in a specific region or nation, and
- re-orient the scale to the sub-national level to capture and monitor locally dispersed threats to human security.

Methodology

> Human Security is the protection of the vital core[2] of all human lives from critical and pervasive economic, environmental, health, food, political and personal threats.

The above definition articulates a general conceptualization of human security. By itself, however, it does little to indicate what the threats are, who they are affecting and where they are of concern. Without this qualifying information, critics rightly point out that the broad concept of human security has little theoretical grounding or policy relevance (Paris, 2000; Krause, 2000; Foong Khong, 2001).

With this in mind, I have developed a combination of grounded empirical and qualitative research and a Geographic Information System (GIS) approach that facilitates the collection, organization and spatial analysis of human security information.

This methodology takes a sub-national approach to data collection and analysis. The method isolates 'hotspots' of aggregated insecurity and determines spatial correlations between rarely compared security threats.

This methodology also engages the paradox of measuring human security: that the broader the conceptualization used, the greater the difficulty of establishing a consistent metric. It does so by addressing the problems associated with aggregating differing data types. By building the methodology around the spatial reference of data a common denominator is created – space – allowing for direct aggregation and analysis without creating a subjective nominal scale.

Also critical is the methodology's focus on identifying local hotspots rather than creating a national index. Although many global indices point policy makers to underdeveloped or insecure countries,[3] none isolate specific regional vulnerability within these countries.

This coarse resolution arguably contributes to poor, nationally ubiquitous development policy and a lack of meaningful correlation analysis between harms.

Critics of human security rightly point out that it would be impossible to collect data for all imaginable human security threats for every location in the world. Past measures have responded by limiting the list of considered threats. This limiting is often driven by data availability (requiring global coverage) and inevitably leaves out important harms.

This new methodology takes a different approach. By recognizing that there is no difference in a death from a gun or a disease, it lets a threshold of severity guide the list of included threats (Owen, 2004).

Stage one: threat assessment

By shifting the focus of vulnerability from the state to the individual, human security attempts to incorporate what are traditionally considered development concerns into the realm of security studies – focusing on threats such as natural disasters, communicable diseases, dire poverty, human trafficking or landmines rather than nuclear or interstate war. This shift in focus, however, presents a potentially unmanageable mandate. Critics have pointed out that if all potential harms are included, the concept is elusive and analytically indeterminate (Mack 2002). Although this may be true if attempting to measure all possible harms in all places in the world, by controlling the location of the study, the list of relevant harms is limited significantly and the use of a GIS makes the spatially referenced data amenable to analysis.

The first stage of the methodology, therefore, seeks to determine from grounded empirical and qualitative research what specific threats affect a particular country or region. This can be achieved in a number of ways. Ideally, regional experts in each of the six categories[4] of security would be interviewed and asked whether there are any issues that would qualify as human security threats in their region – threats that present a critical and pervasive vulnerability to the vital core. By way of illustration, for the environment, this could be an extreme flood, or for personal threat, this could be a high risk from landmines. There are no limits to the number of threats in any category as the only criterion is that they surpass the threshold of human security.

The most important point about this stage of the methodology is that it has reduced a seemingly endless list of threats (anything that can seriously harm an individual) down to only those that in practice affect a particular country or region. By shifting scales from the national to a local focus, human security becomes a manageable concept, going from hundreds of threats, down to a handful.

Figure 24.1 is a visualization of stage one. For each of the six human security subsystems, boxes a, b, and c represent threats chosen by the experts. The vertical lines separating the subsystems demonstrate the isolation of the raw data within disciplines.

Stage two: data collection and organization

Now that the human security threats affecting a country or region have been determined and classified, data detailing them must be collected. These data can be both quantitative and qualitative, but all must have a spatial dimension. Ideally, the data sets collected will detail the indicator that best represents each specific threat. The indicators are chosen and the data collected using local researchers, the NGO community, government ministries and international organizations. There will of course be some overlap with the experts consulted in stage one. A key to this stage is data availability. It is argued that the challenge is best addressed by

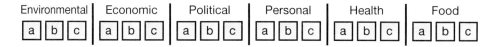

Figure 24.1 Stage one diagram: threat assessment

looking at the sub-national level, by using disciplinary experts and by focusing only on relevant threats, those that surpass the human security threshold.

The concept of subsidiarity[5] is particularly important to the feasibility of the data collection process. Although information on all threats will not be available for all areas, the data are likely to cluster in the scale and regions in which they are relevant. For instance, if a flood affects only region x of a country, there will not necessarily be relevant hydrologic data for region y.

Once data sets detailing each threat are collected, they are organized in a Geographic Information System (GIS) by their spatial reference. This reference can either be a political boundary, a coordinate or a grid space. What is important is that there is a link between specific threat severity and location, or space.[6]

At this point, we can now determine the level of threat for any point in our study region for any of the initial threats.

Table 24.2 depicts an example of the Stage Two data organization. The spatial reference does not have to be the same for all threat data sets. In the final table, however, all data will be disaggregated down to match the set with the finest resolution.

Stage three: data visualization and analysis

The final stage of the methodology is to map and analyze the spatially referenced threat data. For each of the determined threats, we now have data sets detailing the location and severity of the threat within the country. As all information is linked to a spatial reference (e.g., province, city, coordinate etc.) each threat can be mapped using a Geographic Information System. This process involves three steps: base map creation, hotspot analysis and functional analysis.

Base maps are created in the GIS by linking threat data sets to digital boundary maps using their like spatial reference.[7] Once this is done, each threat can be mapped. These base maps are called layers and will be the foundation for the subsequent spatial analysis (see Figure 24.2).

Although at this point each data set represents the total range of severity for each threat, this methodology is designed to isolate where each threat is most severe. This is done by first classifying the data based on their natural breaks.[8] This process produces a map for each threat showing where the threat severity is 'high', 'medium' or 'low.'

Hotspots are regions of aggregated human insecurities. They are places that experience multiple 'high' level human security threats. Although a country as a whole may experience many different threats, these threats are often regionally dispersed – different areas afflicted by different harms to different degrees of severity. In some locations, however, these threats overlap. Presumably, a person in a region suffering from five high level threats will be less secure than someone in a region with only two threats.[9]

Hotspots are found by first separating only the regions with 'high' levels of insecurity in each of our threat severity maps. All of these maps can then be overlaid[10] to show the regions subject to multiple high levels of human insecurity – how many 'high' rankings a spatial unit has received.

In Table 24.3 it is clear that province 5, with 6 high security threats is less secure than say province 2, with only one high security threat.

Table 24.2 Example of stage two table

Province Name	Economic			Health		
	Threat A	Threat B	Threat C	Threat A	Threat B	Threat C
1						
2						
3						
4						
5						
...						

Table 24.3 Example of stage three

Province Name	Economic			Health			Hotspot Count
	Threat A	Threat A	Threat B	Threat C	Threat B	Threat C	
1	1	1	2	2	2	0	3
2	1	1	1	2	0	1	1
3	2	0	0	2	0	1	2
4	0	0	0	2	0	2	2
5	2	2	2	2	2	2	6
...							

Human security hotspot analysis is useful for a number of reasons. First, conceptually, hotspots demonstrate the necessity of using a broad conception of human security. They clearly show that people remain insecure while not at war, and that within their border they may be suffering from a much wider range of possible threats than the traditional human security paradigm suggests.

Second, spatially aggregating varying data sets facilitates a degree of interdisciplinary analysis that is rarely achieved. By way of illustration, although many people know where floods are harming people, and many people know where poverty is worst, few people know both. Also, difficulties of data aggregation and cross discipline communication often hinder well-meaning broad analysis. By limiting subjective decisions on the relative severity of various threats to the early discipline-specific first stage (threats assessment), the analysis limits subjective data aggregation

Third, hotspot analysis has practical utility for development and humanitarian relief efforts. The logistical benefits of knowing exactly what harms are affecting which region of a country are clearly evident. In addition, having all the information in a GIS allows for easy access to large data sets that generally do not get shared, let alone used widely within the development community.

Results – Figure 24.3 provides an example of part of the above methodology as it was implemented through a trial in Cambodia.[11] It outlines the threat assessment, data collection and spatial analysis stages for two of the six human security subsystems – economic security and health security. The process is divided into 7 stages which are briefly outlined below and in Figure 24.3.

Province Boundary Shapefile

GIS Code	Province	Area	Perimeter
1	Barteay Meanchey	6054204712	535684.9
2	Older Meanchey	6681936370	556668.9
3	Somreap	10663661754	638385.1
4	Preah Vihear	13655706155	713819.8
5	Stueng Treng	12076709457	702785.5
6	Battambang	11803125596	684479.7
7	Palin	1102792730	171511.7

Joined with Domestic Violence data table

GIS Code	Province	Domestic Violence Rate
1	Barteay Meanchey	12.3
2	Battambang	8.9
3	Kampong Cham	16.8
4	Kampong Chhnang	19.8
5	Kampong Speu	2.7
6	Kambong Thom	13.4
7	Kampot	11.1

Results in Combined Table (linked by GIS Code)

GIS Code	Province	Area	Perimeter	Domestic Violence Rate
1	Barteay Meanchey	6054204712	535684.9	12.3
2	Battambang	6681936370	556668.9	8.9
3	Kampong Cham	10863661954	638385.1	16.8
4	Kampong Chhnang	13655706145	713819.8	19.8
5	Kampong Speu	12076709457	702785.5	2.7
6	Kambong Thom	11803125598	684479.7	13.4
7	Kampot	10002792730	171511.7	11.1

Which can then be thematically mapped

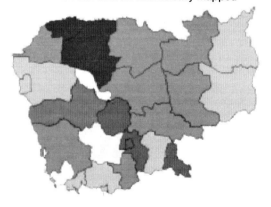

Figure 24.2 Diagram of spatial joining process

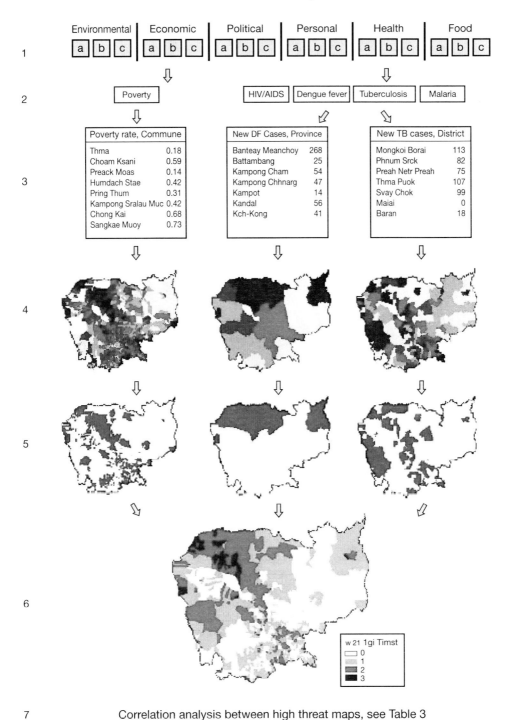

Figure 24.3 *Diagram of methodology*

1 Human security is first conceptually divided into six subsystems following the United Nations Development Program's (UNDP) categorization (UNDP, 2004).
2 The relevant Cambodian threats for each of the threat subsystems were determined. Sixty interviews were conducted in Phnom Penh with experts spanning the six human security categories. They were asked what, if any, concern within their area of expertise would qualify as a threat to human security. For example, for economic security, poverty was the threat and for health security, HIV/AIDS, malaria, dengue fever and tuberculosis were the threats.

In order to simplify the demonstration of the methodology, from this point on we will follow poverty, dengue fever and tuberculosis from data collection to final correlation mapping. Again, in the full Cambodia study, 12 threats were identified and measured.[12]

1 Indicators that best represented each of these threats were then determined by consulting disciplinary experts and the spatial data necessary to measure them were collected. For poverty the indicator chosen by the Cambodian experts was percentage of population below the poverty line calculated as monetary equivalent of calorie intake collected at the commune level. For tuberculosis the indicator was number of cases per 100,000 collected at the regional district level. And for dengue fever the indicator was the number of cases per 100,000 collected at the provincial level. These data were then joined to the spatial databases of the boundary GIS files enabling them to be mapped.
2 The data sets were classified by their natural breaks in order to define high, medium and low threat areas.
3 High threat areas were isolated and mapped on their own. This is important as human security involves a threshold of severity. Human security is threatened when the worst of all the possible threats are at their highest levels in a particular location.
4 All three high threat maps can now be overlaid to find hotspots of aggregated insecurity. In Figure 24.3, the scale of this hotspot map ranges from 0 to 3 high threats in any one commune.
5 Finally, spatial functional analysis can be conducted between pairs of human security threats. Taking the three examples from Figure 24.3, the national probability of being exposed to a high poverty, TB and dengue fever threat was calculated. For example, out of a possible 1,626 communes, 451 have a high poverty threat (more than 65 per cent of the population below the poverty line), meaning all else being equal, there is a 27 per cent probability of a commune having a high poverty threat.

The threat determination and data collection stages have shown that data are available to document a wider range of indicators at a finer resolution than has been suggested in some of the academic literature. Also, that given a degree of institutional collaboration, meaningful collection and organization of broad ranging indicators is possible. Support for a broader definition of human security and the possibility of its rigorous analysis is thereby provided.

For development practitioners in Cambodia, this methodology has clearly pointed to regions that are subjected to the aggregated impact of multiple human insecurities. In the example given here, there are regions that suffer from poverty, TB and dengue fever, but also regions that suffer from two or all three of these threats simultaneously. Regions with three human insecurities are clearly less secure than those with two, one or no high level human security threats. Policy and decision makers should find this added spatial resolution of assistance especially for coordination of work between NGOs with separate but ultimately overlapping interests.

Conclusions

Considering the multi-scaled characteristics of human security (conceptual, definitional, and practical) is a critical step in taking the referential shift of human security seriously. The implications of this shift must be understood if the concept is going to effectively drive policy and gain its rightful place in the international security discourse.

With this in mind, human security hotspot analysis is useful for a number of reasons. First, conceptually, hotspots demonstrate the policy utility of human security. They clearly show that people remain insecure while not at war (countering traditional security), and that within their border they are suffering from a wide range of possible threats.

Second, the practical utility of knowing exactly which harms are affecting which regions of a country are clearly evident for the policy and development community. In addition, having such information in a GIS allows for easy access to vast amounts of data that may be of tremendous value to, and may not otherwise be shared by, policy makers, practitioners and humanitarian operations.

Third, hotspots are an effective means of presenting large amounts of information to the public and to the policy-making community. This process is replicable in any region or country and can provide varying levels of detail. The human insecurity of a region can be displayed as one final map for the media, as a summary report for the policy community, or as its base data for academics.

This new methodology leads to the following clear policy recommendations.

Capture the relevant threats only. For policy to effectively target the most vulnerable, clear information on only what is harming people is essential. Measures that include data on all possible threats to all people in all places divert attention away from the acute harms needing immediate action.

Draw on local knowledge. A vast amount of valuable expertise and threat information exists at the local level. Local researchers and development workers, not only international theoretical frameworks, should be consulted as to what the relevant threats are.

Use sub-national data where available. Once the focus is shifted from world coverage to specific regions, a vast amount of local, sub-national data becomes available. These data should be used at its most detailed level in order to capture the critical spatial variation within each threat. Aggregation to the national level will likely distort the validity of threat data.

Human security should inform humanitarian assistance. Development and humanitarian assistance policy should target a more specific level than the state, be tailored to locally relevant threats and must be more reflexive to rapid changes in insecurity levels and causes. A local level human security assessment team, dispatched prior to international operations, would greatly increase the targeting of specific vulnerabilities and assist collaboration between actors in these complex environments. On-going monitoring and updating of the process would allow for real-time anticipation of rising insecurity levels.

As the nature of insecurity evolves, so too must our security mechanisms. This means addressing issues such as poverty, communicable disease, environmental disasters and the proliferation of small arms with the same vigor we once used to counter the nuclear threat and to secure the Cold War balance of power. To do this, however, we need sophisticated mechanisms for clearly identifying the complex nature of vulnerability. Using the concept of human security and modern GIS mapping technologies, the proposed methodology makes the most of existing local knowledge and points policy makers to the many and complex regionally relevant threats to people's security.

Notes

1 A good example is the UN skepticism that the levels of warfare had declined in the 1990s, until this downward trend was proven wrong by data from the Universities of Maryland and Uppsala, and in the 2005 Human Security Report.
2 For a discussion of the concept of 'vital core' see CHS (2003).
3 For example, the Human Development Index and The Human Poverty Index.
4 The threats falling under Community Security, the 7th category of the UNDP conceptualization (UNDP, 1994), were deemed insufficiently harmful to cross the threshold of insecurity.
5 The notion that problems be addressed at the relevant or most appropriate scale. Commonly used in relation to central political administrations only performing functions that are subsidiary to essential local functions. This is particularly important in this methodology as data for different threats must be represented using different scales and data types. This is the benefit of using spatial data and also the reason why we need to break data into classes before aggregating together.
6 This is ideally a standardized GIS code linked to a particular boundary. This is often not available, however, and the data will often need to be recoded. A feasible but timely process.
7 The databases are connected using the 'join' function in ArcGIS.
8 There are many other ways that data can be classified. For a detailed description see Slocum (1999). We chose natural breaks because we are only looking for the range in the data where the threat is most severe, the entire range of the data being relatively unimportant to us. It is also conceptually elegant. As our primary collaborators are development workers and policy makers, there is no need to over-complicate what is simple stage of our methodology.
9 It is of course possible that an indicator for one system will also be relevant to another. This will result in a degree of spatial statistical interdependence between variables. However, as the hotspot analysis only includes the worst of the threats at their highest level, we feel that there is enough independence in each indicator to warrant separate categorization. However, in subsequent work, we have statistically analyzed the relations between the threats. As this work requires much more detailed data rather than generalities regarding threat 'degree', we keep the data sets in their cardinal format and build explanatory multivariate regression models.
10 For a description of 'overlaying' see Bernhardsen (1999).
11 This study was conducted from November 2002 to January 2003 based at the Cambodian Development Research Institute (CDRI) in Phnom Penh.
12 Poverty, flooding, droughts, malaria, TB, dengue fever, HIV/AIDS, domestic violence, gun injuries, landmines, human rights violations, village level violence.

References

Bernhardsen, T., 1999, *Geographic Information Systems: An Introduction.* (2nd Edition), Chichester, John Wiley.
Commission on Human Security, 2003, *Human Security Now.* Final Report to the Human Security Commission (2002–2003), CHS, New York.
EM-DAT, 2000, EM-DAT: OFDA/CRED International Disasters Data Base.
Foong Khong, Y., 2001, Human Security: A Shotgun Approach to Alleviating Human Misery? *Global Governance* 7: 231–236.
Krause, K., 2000, *Une Approche Critique de la Sécurité Humaine.* Programme d'Études Stratégiques et de Sécurité International, Institut Universitaire de Hautes Études Internationales, Genève.
Krug, E. G., Dahlberg, L. L., Mercy, J. A., Zwi, A. B. and Lozano, R., eds, 2002, *World Report on Violence and Health.* Geneva, World Health Organization, p. 4.
Mack, A., 2002, *Feasibility of Creating an Annual Human Security Report*, Program on Humanitarian Policy and Conflict Research, Harvard University, February 2002.
Owen, T., 2004, Human Security – Conflict, Critique and Consensus: Colloquium Remarks and a Proposal for a Threshold-Based Definition. *Security Dialogue*, 35 3.
Paris, R., 2000, Human Security: Paradigm Shift or Hot Air? *International Security* 26: 87–102.
Slocum, T., 1999, Thematic cartography and visualization. Upper Saddle River, NJ: Prentice Hall.
United Nations Development Program, 1994, *New Dimensions of Human Security. Human Development Report.* New York, Oxford University Press, pp. 22–25.
World Health Organization, 2001, *World Health Report 2001.* Geneva, WHO, p. 114.

25

HUMAN SECURITY: IDEA, POLICY AND LAW

Gerd Oberleitner

Since it made its first appearance in the 1994 UNDP Human Development Report,[1] the concept of human security has gained considerable significance in scholarly debates as well as in global policy and practice. Human security has fertilized debates in many academic disciplines, first and foremost the social sciences, international relations theory, defence, security and peace studies. The concept has been taken up in policy circles and has been formulated and prioritized as a foreign policy goal by some small- and middle-power countries, acting in networks of like-minded states such as the Human Security Network or the Friends of Human Security. It has been refined in expert meetings such as the Commission on Human Security.[2] Human security has brought together civil society initiatives[3] and has made its way into international organizations, first and foremost the United Nations, where a number of key documents refer to human security.[4]

Over the years, the concept has moved from an idea to a political project and to a foreign policy agenda or 'political leitmotif'.[5] While these manifestations of human security along with its potential as an advocacy tool and analytical framework have been thoroughly debated, the legal and normative implications of human security have received less attention. As an academic discipline, international law has been reluctant to respond to the rise of human security and neither the idea nor the practice of human security have attracted widespread interest among international legal scholars. While various subject matters and fields of international law, most notably international human rights law, have been examined with regard to the emergence of human security,[6] the potential impact of human security on established international legal concepts as well as the guidance which the concept may provide for the further development of international law as a whole remain largely unexplored.[7]

Consequently, a number of important questions remain unanswered: what is the legal dimension of human security? Are human security concerns already covered by international law, and if so, how? Is there already an international 'human security law' in all but the name? Which areas of international law are particularly prone to and responsive to the concept of human security, and why? How would a 'human security approach' affect law-making, law enforcement and international institutions? Can the theory and practice of international law support and underpin the concept of human security? Is international law the appropriate tool for fostering human security, or is it in its present state rather an obstacle to human security?

International law, the UN Charter and security

Although the quest for a universally agreed definition of human security has led nowhere the essential elements of human security are sufficiently well understood to consider the legal aspects of the concept, analyze international law from a human security perspective and discuss the possible impact of human security on international law. What human security does, in a 'vertical' move, is to deepen the understanding of security by positioning the security of individual human beings (as opposed to states or borders) as the ultimate goal.[8] In this sense, human security is concerned with the kind of security people seek in their everyday lives rather than with the security of abstract entities such as the state. The concept suggests that the individual human being is the ultimate beneficiary of security rather than the state, that the kind of security which really matters to the individual is a comprehensive security in every-one's life, and that in order to achieve such security individuals must be both protected and empowered.[9] In doing so, human security can connect with those elements of international law which implement a concern for individual human beings and groups into an otherwise state-centred legal system.

In a 'horizontal' move, the concept broadens security by bringing together, in a compre-henisive fashion, threats and risks which go beyond national security concerns. Human security is interested in the complexity and interlinkages of threats and risks – natural disasters, refugee flows, economic and financial downturns, volatile food prices, human rights violations, armed conflicts and so on – and seeks to develop responses to non-conventional and trans-national threats against which the protection of borders and the preservation of territorial integrity do not provide adequate protection. Finally, human security views security not as a matter of state interest but rather as a common interest or common concern of the international community.[10] In doing so, it borrows from worldviews such as Franklin D. Roosevelt's ideas of 'freedom from want' and 'freedom from fear' and, ultimately, from international human rights law in which these ideas have found their expression. Because human security relies on human rights to give concrete meaning and normative substance to its propositions, the concept introduces the value and language of human dignity – as spelled out in international human rights law – into discourses on security.

Even though human security can be anchored in international legal developments and may find support in existing norms the concept is, at the same time, at odds with international law with its predominantly state-centred approach. International law understands security primarily as national or state security; as the security of states as the primary subjects of international law which are built upon the principles of territorial integrity and sovereignty. This is what the Charter of the United Nations has in mind when it speaks of the UN's principal purpose of maintaining international peace and security.[11] Consequently, the Charter understands security as safety from the use of armed force between states.[12] The supreme interest of the state in its survival, even if it comes at the expense of the destruction of a major part of its population (as epitomized in the strategic planning of nuclear wars) characterizes the extreme form of such an approach where the security of the state supersedes the fate of individuals.[13] While the UN Charter, in 1945, opened the doors for 'internationalizing' security (by allowing states to act collectively and, if necessary, with the use of force to uphold or restore international peace and security under Chapter VII of the Charter) and thus acknowledged a common interest of states in international security, it still retained the understanding that it is the security of states, not individuals, which matters.

Human security challenges such a state-centred approach to security by shifting the focus towards the individual and by basing security on common values rather than singular interests.

This vertical move from the state down to the individual means that any legal framework which provides security for abstract entities (the state or the nation) but ignores the security (i.e. the well-being, safety and dignity) of individual human beings misses the point: from a human security perspective, there is no secure state with insecure people living in it. While such an approach does not *per se* question the rights of states under international law nor does it downplay the legitimate interest which states have in their security, it means that the intrinsic moral value of individual security is to be rated at least as high, or higher, than the instrumental value of the state. As a consequence, state security, together with the means to achieve it, need to be measured against the security of the individual as the ultimate beneficiary.[14] What human security calls for is that the state – in addition to providing protection from external aggression or military attack – has to create an environment which allows for the well-being and safety of the population as an equally important goal. Human security means thus 'shap[ing] a security paradigm that captures the need to reach out in defence of people as well as states, and that can orchestrate and steer our endeavours in both directions.'[15]

Human security acknowledges that the state, its structures and institutions are important means to protect individual security but argues that the existence of such structures and institutions is not a goal in itself nor is the fact that they are secured a sufficient benchmark for human security. Given that human security seems to suggest that security is a common concern or a kind of global public good the enjoyment of which is not limited but extends potentially to everyone, security becomes egalitarian and universalist in the sense that it pertains to all persons and not just to privileged sections of society.[16] Such a cosmopolitan view of security finds its normative underpinning in international human rights law with its equally universal appeal.

The predominance of state security in international law is, however, only one side of the coin. As far as the UN Charter is concerned, maintaining the stability and survival of a state-centred international order is indeed the overarching goal under the rubric of international peace and security. But while the preservation of territorial integrity, sovereign equality and political independence, together with the principle of non-interference in internal matters (as laid down in Article 2 of the Charter) remain essential elements to achieve this goal, the Charter contains a second fundamental concept, namely the protection of human rights as contained in Article 1(3).[17] The question which of these two principles should prevail when they clash was for long answered in favour of the principles of territorial integrity and non-intervention. Since the end of the Cold War, however, significant changes have led to a more complex and fragile balance of the two concepts. Human security can build on this second pillar of the Charter's understanding of security as it is ultimately geared towards protecting individuals from threats as well as to empower them to secure their own life and guarantee their livelihood. It thus resonates, in a modern fashion, with the twin concerns of the UN Charter: providing (inter-national) stability and guaranteeing human rights. A human security approach means reading these two potentially conflicting purposes of the UN afresh and positioning them more firmly on the same level so that the ultimate goal of the UN to provide for a world in which both states *and* individuals are secure can stand out more clearly.[18]

The UN Charter is not the only international document to rely on human security. Other (regional) legal regimes reflect human security, too. A basic commitment to a broad concept of human security has been identified, for example, in the Treaty of the European Union, where Article 21 lists as the Union's foreign policy objectives the preservation of peace, conflict prevention, strengthening international security, consolidation and support for democracy, rule of law, human rights and principles of international law.[19] The Non-Agression and Common Defence Pact of the African Union of 2005, to name another example, explicitly refers to human security. The Pact defines human security and relies on the concept to develop a framework under which the African Union may intervene or authorize intervention to prevent or address situations of aggression.[20]

Sovereignty, non-state actors and civil society

While the perception of security as people-centred, comprehensive, interlinked and guided by shared values – as put forward by human security – is not alien to international law and is reflected in legal texts, the rise of human security is also a challenge to international law. The concept can have an impact on the future development of international law, not only in selected fields which are particularlary reflective of the human security approach but also with regard to the role and rights of states under international law. Their sovereignty is the fundamental premise on which international law rests, and safeguarding the state and its constituent elements, its borders as well as its institutions and laws is of paramount importance. Human security, however, deconstructs state sovereignty and puts the individual at the centre so that it can be effectively protected and empowered to cope with threats to life, livelihood and dignity. The concept sees the sovereign nation no longer seen as the ultimate referent of security or the sole provider thereof and argues that 'the state is no longer able to monopolize the concept and practice of security'.[21]

This is not a new insight as far as international law is concerned; indeed, much of the academic writing in the field revolves precisely around the issue of sovereignty and human security merely fuels the debate. Reconciling the demands of human security with international law's focus on sovereignty may work out in different ways. On the one hand, human security and sovereign states are not incompatible because 'human security is best guaranteed in the sovereign state which is governed under the rule of law with full respect for the human rights and the fundamental freedoms of those who reside in its territory'.[22] This is also the view expressed firmly by the General Assembly when it states that '[t]he advancement of human security requires strong and stable institutions. Among these, Governments retain the primary role in providing a rules-based system …'.[23] Yet, arguing that individuals' rights are at least as important as those of states, as promoters of human security do,[24] questions such traditional approaches to state sovereignty. On the one hand, state sovereignty and the ability of individual states to manage large-scale crises are questioned by complex threats such as pandemics, natural disasters and climate change which transcend borders and necessitate joint responses by states. On the other hand, the state itself can be a threat to the human security of individuals and unaccountable and corrupt national security institutions, police forces and law enforcement officials are a major source of insecurity in many countries.[25] Such a human security critique of sovereignty builds on other discourses on sovereignty, most notably the idea of individual sovereignty and the perception of sovereignty as responsibility. In a well-known contribution to this debate, UN Secretary-General Kofi Annan has described the shift from territorial sovereignty to individual sovereignty in the following terms:

> State sovereignty, in its most basic sense, is being redefined – not least by the force of globalisation and international cooperation. States are now widely understood to be instruments at the service of their peoples, and not vice versa. At the same time, individual sovereignty – by which I mean the fundamental freedom of each individual, enshrined in the charter of the UN and subsequent international treaties – has been enhanced by a renewed and spreading consciousness of individual rights. When we read the Charter today, we are more than ever conscious that its aim is to protect individual human beings, not to protect those who abuse them.[26]

The changing nature of sovereignty is accompanied by the rising importance of an increasing range of stakeholders which participate in international relations and in the creation, interpretation, application and defence of international norms, standards and principles. As much as they contribute to fostering human security such non-state actors also have the capacity to create insecurity and armed non-state groups and transnational organized criminal organizations are among the most potent threats to human security.[27] The debate on the role and accountability of non-state actors takes place in international law, e.g. on the human rights obligations of transnational corporations which provide blueprints for regulating their conduct in line with the demands of human security. On the other hand, non-state humanitarian actors, civil society movements and development organizations are important contributors in humanitarian crises; in the case of failed states, they may indeed remain the only institutions capable of delivering security.[28]

Coexistence, cooperation and intervention

Human security suggests integrated and cooperative responses to threats and thus accompanies the move from an international legal order concerned merely with securing the peaceful coexistence of states towards an international law of global cooperation. When human security argues that security ought to be realized in multilateral settings and through cooperative efforts it necessarily relies on international law as the appropriate framework for facilitating and guiding international cooperation and emphasizes the importance of international institutions. The development of the concept in cross-regional networks of like-minded states and in the UN confirms this approach. The Organization for Security and Cooperation in Europe (OSCE) may serve as another example of an organization which has abandoned the principle of strict non-interference when it comes to the promotion of human rights and democracy (the 'human dimension' in OSCE parlance) and instead adopted a holistic view of security and a community-oriented approach which combines security issues with humanitarian questions.[29]

While the call for international cooperation is likely to find support by many states, the interventionist streak of human security has been received less favourably. With a view towards threats against the life of individuals and the existence of groups, such as genocide, crimes against humanity or gross human rights violations, the International Commission on Intervention and State Sovereignty, set up in 2000 on the initiative of Canada, relied explicitly on human security as a constituting element of the responsibility to protect.[30] Human security is indeed 'interventionist': as a foreign policy goal by some states it was meant to be a pragmatic and action-oriented approach to solving crisis situations and to counter threats.[31] And given that it emphasizes individual and group security over an unquestioned understanding of state sovereignty, it is not a concept which allows standing passively aside when massive and pervasive threats disrupt individuals' lives and impede societies' development.

This, however, does not mean that human security postulates a right to unilateral military intervention. The UN General Assembly, for example, considers that the use of force is not at all envisaged in the human security concept.[32] Indeed, human security emphasizes cooperation over unilateralism and asks for considering an array of non-military approachs to solving crises. It has thus been argued that human security could more productively be used to divert the debate over humanitarian intervention away from the unhelpful dichotomy between human rights and sovereignty and instead place the risk of harm to individuals at the centre of analysis.[33] Furthermore, any intervention – military or not – would still be faced with the constraints of human security, namely that any action must be measured against the impact it has on the security of those on whose behalf an intervention is carried out. As a result, when military force is used in 'human security missions', the close link between human rights and human security will force a reassessment and upgrading of human rights in the design and conduct of such missions. This is, in turn, likely to restrain the use of military means beyond what is expected by, for example, international humanitarian law which accepts civilian deaths and destruction of civilian property as long as it is not excessive in relation to the military advantage achieved – an advantage which is measured in terms of national and not necessarily human security.

Regulatory frameworks for human security

It has rightly been observed that many, if not all, of the items on the 'human security agenda' – from the protection of civilians in armed conflict, children's rights, the spread of small arms and light weapons, drug trafficking, terrorism, arms trade, transnational organized crime, poverty, infectious diseases, environmental degradation, internally displaced persons and more – have been addressed by international law through a variety of binding and non-binding legal instruments.[34] Indeed, none of these threats is unknown to international law. One should not conclude, however, that the fact the international law deals with such threats means that it always approaches them in a way that fosters human security.

The fields in which international law has come closest to providing regulatory frameworks based on considerations of human security are perhaps international human rights law, international humanitarian law, peace operations, small arms and light weapons, terrorism and organized crime and the protection of displaced persons. These areas may stand here as representative of the way in which human security matters to international law and, in turn, international law invokes many of the core ideas of human security. But other areas, too, are suitable candidates for exploring a human security approach in a more comprehensive and broader fashion – development, climate change, environmental degradation and global health concerns, to name a few.[35] While the former category of global concerns is representative of a narrow understanding of human security (the 'freedom from fear'), the latter areas invite for yet more research and debate from a human security perspective so as to better understand how a comprehensive approach to human security will impact on international legal developments.

International human rights law

Various fields of international law are particularly close to human security because they deal with the kind of interdependent risks and threats to which human security seeks to respond but the relationship between international human rights law and human security is special. Promotors of human security have repeatedly stressed this point and have argued that human rights constitute the normative backbone of human security.[36] Human rights and human security share many of the same concerns: both postulate that people matter and sovereignty is not absolute when it comes to human dignity. Through their common roots in Roosevelt's 'freedom from fear' and 'freedom from want' and their emphasis on protecting and empowering individuals they both position the individual firmly at the centre. The human rights movement has many decades ago begun to transform the state-centred international law into a legal regime which acknowledges the individual as rights-holder, similar to what human security calls for today.

Different from human security, however, international human rights law comprises a developed body of norms, standards and principles which protect individuals and groups from human rights violations, seeks to prevent such violations, provides avenues of redress for victims and aims at empowering individuals and communities. Human rights provide the strongest legal underpinning of human security and can give content, structure and clarity to a concept which suffers from analytical uncertainties but the relationship between the political concept of human security and the legal regime of human rights remains precarious and the two are by no means synonymous.[37] Human rights also cover and respond to many issues on the human security agenda so that the latter may appear redundant. But human security has also comparative strengths: it is broad and flexible enough to cover situations not sufficiently regulated by international human rights law, such as threats by non-state actors or natural disasters, and invoking human security instead of human rights obligations may be a promising advocacy tool in some situations.[38]

Armed conflict, international humanitarian law, forced displacement

The fate of civilians caught in armed conflict has been identified as a prime focus of human security from the outset.[39] International humanitarian law – the set of rules developed since the 1860s to limit the means and methods which can lawfully be applied in armed conflict and to protect the wounded, shipwrecked, prisoners of war, civilians and the civilian population and civilian property from the consequences of warfare – can thus be seen as a first expression of human security. The great range of humanitarian law treaties, first and foremost the four Geneva Conventions of 1949 and the two Additional Protocols of 1977,[40] establish a legal framework which protects from a variety of threats to life, livelihood and dignity in specific settings, i.e. in international and non-international armed conflicts and in situations of occupation.

Some of the more recent additions to international humanitarian treaties echo the spirit of human security more specifically. The most prominent example of a human security approach in creating a normative framework for the protection of civilians is the Ottawa Convention on anti-personnel mines.[41] The Convention reflects many essential traits of the human security debate: it was driven by like-minded small- and middle-power states in an open and cooperative process together with civil society actors and with a clear focus on the human impact of the use of this particular type of weapon in terms of the death toll among civilians as well as with regard to long-term consequences for affected communities. The protocol on child soldiers to the Convention on the Rights of the Child can also be seen as an example of such 'human security treaties'.[42] The same can be said for the most recent addition to the range of humanitarian law treaties, the Convention on Cluster Munitions, both for the treaty's substance as well as for having been realized in a similar way as the landmine convention.[43]

However, international humanitarian law constantly balances the humanitarian concern for civilians with the principle of military necessity.[44] In doing so it creates a perpetuous stream of calculations on how much destruction civilians have to endure as 'collateral damage' in attacks which are otherwise deemed lawful. While the consequences of such attacks may be dramatic in terms of human security they may still be perceived acceptable under international humanitarian law. Examining international humanitarian law through a human security lens may thus have a profound impact on military operations because the concept prioritizes the protection of people over pursuing military objectives. Military operations for the purpose of enhancing human security will therefore have to allow for more scrutiny on whether the means are adequate to the end. And because human rights are so important in the concept of human security they will also have to be invoked more frequently in armed conflict.

Forced displacement, whether caused by armed conflict or driven by other sources, is another area in which human security is at stake. The 1951 Geneva Convention on the Status of Refugees has been criticized (from a human security perspective) for its state-centred approach[45] but the Guiding Principles on Internal Displacement, drafted in 1997 by the (then) Representative of the UN Secretary-General on internally displaced persons, Francis Deng, express human security more clearly.[46] They bring together human rights law, international humanitarian law and refugee law in a set of guidelines for the more effective protection of internally displaced persons and thus reflect the comprehensive approach to analyzing and proposing solutions to multi-faceted problems which human security suggests.

Terrorism, organized crime, small arms and light weapons

The importance of human security in responding to terrorism and organized crime is increasingly better understood, including the value of holistic approaches to countering terrorism and organized crime, the search for their root causes and the need for effective legal and operational responses based on considerations of human security, human rights and the rule of law.[47] The core legal document on organized crime, the Convention against Transnational Organized Crime and its protocols[48] create a comprehensive web of obligations, including the drafting of national laws on money laundering, corruption, obstruction of justice, illicit arms trade and trafficking in human beings, extradition, law enforcement cooperation, training and technical assistance.

The campaign against small arms and light weapons is another example of a human security approach. The problem of small arms and light weapons has largely escaped the attention of international disarmament and arms control negotiations with their focus on state security. The negative consequences of the availability of and trade in small arms and light weapons were not considered as serious enough to merit international regulation and their primary use by non-state actors against individuals made them invisible on the radar-screen of international law for too long. The (lawful) acquisition of small arms may have little or no impact on national security but the freedom to possess and use small arms can pose a threat to human security which might well necessitate action by the state.[49] The campaign on small arms and light weapons has led to the creation of an expanding international normative framework of regional and universal treaties which fed into the UN Programme of Action adopted at the 2001 UN Conference on the Illicit Trade in Small Arms and Light Weapons in All Its Aspects.[50]

The UN Security Council, peace operations and peace-building

When it comes to operationalizing the concept of human security, the institutions of international law clearly matter. But do the existing institutions of international law provide the kind of 'protective and empowering infrastructure'[51] which proponents of human security are asking for? This is a question which pertains first and foremost to the UN Security Council. As it stands, the Council seems often more an obstacle to human security than a mechanism for enhancing it, and attempts to reform it have so far changed little.[52] In 1999, Mahbub ul-Haq, one of the creators and leading thinkers of human security, had proposed the creation of a Human Security Council with three principal goals: providing leadership in tackling global economic crises, establishing a comprehensive early-warning mechanism for internal conflicts and violence, and strengthening the UN efforts in the area of development.[53] This was obviously too utopian a concept. For decades, the Council's interpretation of international peace and security revolved around state security while its attempts to respond to situations of human insecurity, from gross human rights violations to the effects of armed conflicts on civilians, remained haphazard and unpredictable. But even though the Council does not explicitly embrace the concept of human security it is gradually accepting that international security is threatened when the security of individuals is in jeopardy.[54] The manner in which the Council now invokes human rights and international humanitarian law in its resolutions demonstrates how it seeks to break away from a purely statist perspective of security towards guaranteeing the security of individuals in a more comprehensive, consistent and predictable way. During its membership in the Council from 1998–2000 Canada sought to introduce human security into the Council's actions on the protection of civilians in armed conflict and the trafficking in small arms and 'blood diamonds' in Angola.[55] In 2000, Security Council resolution 1325 on women, peace and security linked a gender perspective on human security with human rights, humanitarian law, international criminal law, refugee law, the spread of HIV/Aids and UN peacekeeping activities in a holistic framework.[56] In 2009 Security Council resolution 1894 on the protection of civilians in armed conflict applied human security principles, albeit without explicit reference to the concept.[57] Effectively and sustainably mainstreaming human security into the assessment, planning, implementation and evaluation of all the Council's peace operations and peace-building efforts is, however, still a task ahead.[58]

Conclusion

When human security is seen as a set of principles, policies and strategies aimed at placing the individual human being at the centre of attention, protecting it from the most pervasive threats to life, livelihood and dignity and empowering it to use all its capabilities, then international law can be a strong, albeit precarious, ally. Many of the underlying issues of human security are not new to international law: the shifting perception of security, the focus on the individual, the waning of state sovereignty, the rise of new actors, the problem of intervening in humanitarian crises, the prevention of genocide and mass atrocities, and more. International law and its institutions have accumulated experience in some of the areas of the human security agenda. Human security can build on those elements of international law and on legal doctrines and normative precedents which put the individual at the centre of concern, first and foremost in the fields of international human rights law, international humanitarian law and refugee law.

Some core elements of international law – the way in which it postulates the rule of law, legal accountability, international cooperation and the enforcement mechanisms which it offers – resonate strongly in terms of human security. When human security provides the conceptual framework then international law is the 'toolbox' in which there are means to realize, operationalize and institutionalize the concept. And anchoring human security concerns in international law also remedies the volatile nature of human security as a policy which may come and go as governments change, resources dwindle and political priorities shift.

While a number of normative developments in different areas of international law can be seen as an expression of the human security agenda and, where effective, may serve as examples for realizing human security in normative regimes, human security remains, at the same time, at odds with fundamental principles of international law as it presently stands. International law's emphasis on state security, state sovereignty and non-intervention in domestic affairs may serve international stability but often comes at the cost of obstructing human security. Human security provides arguments for further developing international law from a law of coexistence towards a law of cooperation and further on to a law which recognizes common values as the core of a constitutionalist view of the international order. Acknowledging the importance of human security may have repercussions for the role of non-state actors in international law as both providers of and a threat to human security, initiate the creation of new instruments for conflict prevention and conflict management, bring separate fields of international law closer together and assist in assigning an appropriate place for the individual human being in the international legal framework. Human security thus challenges international law to become more in line with the needs and realities of today's globalized and interdependent world which comprises a multitude of actors and faces interlinked threats and risks.

Notes

1 United Nations Development Programme, *Human Development Report 1994: New Dimensions of Human Security*, available at http://hdr.undp.org/reports/global/1994/en (accessed 8 October 2012).

2 See Commission on Human Security, *Human Security Now*, 2003, available at http://ochaonline.un.org/humansecurity/CHS/finalreport/index.html (accessed 8 October 2012).

3 Human security concerns figure prominently on the agenda of, for example, the Coalition for the International Criminal Court, see www.iccnow.org (accessed 8 October 2012) or the International Campaign to Ban Landmines, see www.icbl.org (accessed 8 October 2012).

4 Prominent among them are the *Millennium Report* of 2000, available at http://www.un.org/millennium/sg/report (accessed 8 October 2012), p. 46, and the report *In Larger Freedom*, available at http://www.un.org/secureworld (accessed 8 October 2012). In the 2005 UN *World Summit Outcome Document* states committed themselves to discussing and defining the notion of human security, see UN General Assembly resolution UN Doc. A/RES/60/1, para. 143. In 2010, the General Assembly agreed to discuss how to best mainstream human security in United Nations activities and to request a periodic report on this matter by the UN Secretary-General, see United Nations, *Human Security. Report of the Secretary-General*, UN Doc. A/64/701 (8 March 2010), para. 72.

5 Sascha Werthes and David Bosold, 'Caught between Pretension and Substantiveness – Ambiguity of Human Security as a Political Leitmotif', in Tobias Debiel and Sascha Werthes (eds), *Human Security on Foreign Policy Agendas: Changes, Concepts and Cases*, Duisburg: INEF Report 80, 2006, pp. 22–38.

6 See, e.g., Bertrand Ramcharan, *Human Rights and Human Security*, The Hague: Kluwer, 2002; David Petrasek, 'Human Rights "Lite"? Thoughts on Human Security', *Security Dialogue*, 2004, 35: 59–62; Wolfgang Benedek, 'Human Rights and Human Security: Challenges and Prospects', in *L'etat actuel des droits de l'homme dans le monde. Défis et perspectives*, Alice Yotopolous-Marangopolous (ed.), Paris: Pedone, 2006, pp. 95–109; and Gerd Oberleitner, 'Human Security', in David P. Forsythe (ed.), *Encyclopedia of Human Rights*, Oxford: Oxford University Press, 2009, 2: 486–493.

7 Exceptions include Hisashi Owada, 'Human Security and International Law', in Ulrike Fastenrath, Rudolf Geiger, Daniel-Erasmus Khan, Andreas Paulus, Sabine von Schorlemer and Christoph Vedder (eds), *From Bilateralism to Community Interest. Essays in Honour of Judge Bruno Simma*, Oxford: Oxford University Press, 2011, pp. 505–520; Barbara Tigerstrom, *Human Security and International Law – Problems and Prospects*, Oxford: Hart, 2007; Gerd Oberleitner, 'Human Security – A Challenge to International Law?', *Global Governance*, 2005, 11(2): 185–203; Matthias C. Kettemann, 'The Conceptual Debate on Human Security and its Relevance for the Development of International Law', *Human Security Perspectives*, 2006, 3(1): 39–52.

8 See, e.g., Lloyd Axworthy, 'Human Security and Global Governance: Putting People First', *Global Governance*, 2001, 7(1): 19–23.

9 See, e.g., Sadako Ogata and Johan Cels, 'Human Security – Protecting and Empowering the People,' *Global Governance*, 2003, 9(3): 273–282.

10 See Tigerstrom, *Human Security and International Law* (supra note 7), p. 72.

11 Art. 1(1) Charter of the United Nations: 'The purposes of the United Nations are: to maintain international peace and security, and to that end: to take effective collective measures for the prevention and removal of threats to the peace, and for the suppression of acts of aggression or other breaches of the peace, and to bring about by peaceful means, and in conformity with the principles of justice and international law, adjustment or settlement of international disputes or situations which might lead to a breach of the peace.'

12 See Nigel D. White, *The United Nations System. Toward International Justice*, Boulder: Lynne Rienner, 2002, p. 49.

13 See Tigerstrom, *Human Security and International Law* (supra note 7), p. 64.

14 Ibid., p. 51.

15 Sverre Lodgaard, *Human Security: Concept and Operationalization*, available at http://www.cpdsindia.org/conceptandoperationalization.htm (accessed 8 October 2012).

16 Tigerstrom, *Human Security and International Law* (supra note 7), p. 52.

17 Art. 1(3) Charter of the United Nations: 'promoting and encouraging respect for human rights and for fundamental freedoms for all without distinction as to race, sex, language or religion ...'

18 This is also the position taken by the General Assembly, see United Nations, *Human Security. Report of the Secretary-General*, UN Doc. A/64/701 (8 March 2010), para. 21.

19 See Markus Möstl, 'The European Way of Promoting Human Security in Crisis Management Operations: A Critical Stocktaking', in: Wolfgang Benedek, Matthias Kettemann and Markus Möstl (eds), *Mainstreaming Human Security in Peace Operations and Crisis Management. Policies, Problems, Potential,* New York/London: Routledge, 2010, pp. 148–149; and in greater detail Mary Martin and Mary Kaldor (eds), *The European Union and Human Security: External Interventions and Missions,* London: Routledge, 2009.

20 Art. 1(k) African Union Non-Agression and Common Defence Pact (adopted 31 January 2005): 'Human Security means the security of the individual in terms of satisfaction of his/her basic needs. It also includes the creation of social, economic, political, environmental and cultural conditions necessary for the survival and dignity of the individual, the protection of and respect for human rights, good governance and the guarantee for each individual of opportunities and choices for his/her full development'.

21 Lodgaard, *Human Security: Concept and Operationalization* (supra note 15), p. 4.

22 Hans Correll, *From Territorial Sovereignty to Human Security,* address to the annual conference of the Canadian Council of International Law, 1999, available at www.un.org/law/counsel/ottawa.htm (accessed 8 October 2012).

23 United Nations, *Human Security. Report of the Secretary-General* (supra note 4), para. 20.

24 See, e.g., Axworthy, 'Human Security and Global Governance: Putting People First' (supra note 8), p. 19.

25 See, for example, on the role of the national security sector as both a threat and a provider of human security, Paul Heinbecker, 'Human Security: The Hard Edge', *Canadian Military Journal,* spring 2000: 11–16.

26 Kofi Annan, 'Two Concepts of Sovereignty', *The Economist,* 18 September 1999.

27 See, e.g., Claude Bruderlein, *The Role of Non-State Actors in Building Human Security,* Geneva: Centre for Humanitarian Dialogue, 2000.

28 See Claude Bruderlein, 'People's Security as a New Measure of Global Stability', *International Review of the Red Cross* 83, 2001, 842: 361.

29 See Gerd Oberleitner, 'The OSCE and Human Security', *Security and Human Rights,* 2008, 1: 64–72.

30 See *International Commission on Intervention and State Sovereignty: The Responsibility to Protect,* available at www.responsibilitytoprotect.org/ICISS%20Report.pdf (accessed 8 October 2012).

31 See Don Hubert, 'An Idea that Works in Practice', *Security Dialogue,* 2004, 35: 351–352.

32 United Nations, Human Security. *Report of the Secretary-General,* UN Doc. A/64/701 (8 March 2010), para. 23.

33 Tigerstrom, *Human Security and International Law* (supra note 7), p. 195.

34 Ibid., pp. 60–61.

35 On human development and human security see Shahrbanou Tadjbakhsh and Anuradha M. Chenoy, *Human Security. Concepts and Implications,* London: Routledge, 2007, pp. 98–122; on health and human security, see Tigerstrom, *Human Security and International Law* (supra note 7), pp. 166–192.

36 See Commission on Human Security, *Human Security Now* (supra note 2), p. 10.

37 See Gerd Oberleitner, 'Porcupines in Love: The Intricate Convergence of Human Rights and Human Security', *European Human Rights Law Review,* 2006, 6: 588–606.

38 See Tigerstrom, *Human Security and International Law* (supra note 7), p. 208.

39 See, e.g., Commission on Human Security, *Human Security Now* (supra note 2), pp. 20–39.

40 Convention (I) for the Amelioration of the Condition of the Wounded and Sick in Armed Forces in the Field; Convention (II) for the Amelioration of the Condition of Wounded, Sick and Shipwrecked Members of Armed Forces at Sea; Convention (III) relative to the Treatment of Prisoners of War; Convention (IV) relative to the Protection of Civilian Persons in Time of War (all adopted 12 August 1949); Protocol Additional to the Geneva Conventions of 12 August 1949, and relating to the Protection of Victims of International Armed Conflicts; and Protocol Additional to the Geneva Conventions of 12 August 1949, and relating to the Protection of Victims of Non-International Armed Conflicts (both adopted 8 June 1977).

41 Convention on the Prohibition of the Use, Stockpiling, Production and Transfer of Anti-personnel Mines and on Their Desctruction (adopted 18 September 1997).

42 Optional Protocol to the Convention on the Rights of the Child on the involvement of children in armed conflict (adopted 25 May 2000).

43 Convention on Cluster Munitions (adopted 30 May 2008).

44 The principle of proportionality allows for civilian damage not excessive to the anticipated military advantage, see Art. 51 Protocol Additional to the Geneva Conventions of 12 August 1949, and relating to the Protection of Victims of International Armed Conflicts (adopted 8 June 1977): 'Among others, the following types of attacks are to be considered as indiscriminate: […] an attack which may be expected to cause incidental loss of civilian life, injury to civilians, damage to civilian objects, or a combination thereof, which would be excessive in relation to the concrete and direct military advantage anticipated.'

45 See Gary G. Troeller, 'Refugees, Human Rights and the Issue of Human Security', in Edward Newman and Oliver P. Richmond (eds), *The United Nations and Human Security*, Basingstoke: Palgrave, 2001, p. 78.

46 United Nations, *Guiding Principles on Internal Displacement. Report of the Representative of the Secretary-General, Francis Deng,* UN Doc. E/CN.4/1998/53/Add.2, Annex.

47 See, for example, Wolfgang Benedek, 'The Human Security Approach to Terrorism and Organized Crime in Post-Conflict Situations', in Wolfgang Benedek, Christopher Daase, Vojin Dimitrijevic and Petrus van Duyne (eds), *Transnational Terrorism, Organized Crime and Peace Building*, Palgrave: London, 2010, pp. 3–16; and Wolfgang Benedek, 'Human Security and Prevention of Terrorism', in Wolfgang Benedek and A. Yotopoulos-Marangopoulos (eds), *Anti-terrorist Measures and Human Rights,* Leiden: Brill, 2004, pp. 171–183.

48 Convention Against Transnational Organized Crime; Protocol to Prevent, Suppress and Punish Trafficking in Persons, Especially Women and Children; Protocol against the Smuggling of Migrants by Land, Sea and Air (all adopted 15 November 2000); and Protocol against the Illicit Manufacturing of and Trafficking in Firearms, their Parts and Components and Ammunition (adopted 31 May 2001).

49 See in greater detail Tigerstrom, *Human Security and International Law* (supra note 7), pp. 141–145.

50 Inter-American Convention Against the Illicit Manufacturing of and Trafficking in Firearms, Ammunition, Explosives, and Other Related Materials of 1997 (adopted 14 November 1997); Protocol to the UN Convention on Transnational Organized Crime on the Illicit Manufacturing of and Trafficking in Firearms, Their Parts and Components and Ammunition (adopted 31 May 2001); ECOWAS (Economic Community of West African States) Convention on Small Arms and Light Weapons, Their Ammunition and Other Related Materials (adopted 14 June 2006).

51 Ogata and Cels, 'Human Security – Protecting and Empowering the People' (supra note 9), p. 276.

52 See Emma McClean, *Security Council Reform: The Case for Human Security?*, 2006, p. 64, available at http://www.nottingham.ac.uk/shared/shared_hrlcpub/HRLC_Commentary_2006/McClean.pdf (accessed 8 October 2012).

53 Mahbub ul-Haq, 'Global Governance for Human Security', in Majid Tehranian (ed.), *Worlds Apart: Human Security and Global Governance,* London: Tauris, 1999, p. 88.

54 See Dwight Newman, 'A Human Security Council? Applying a "Human Security" Agenda to Security Council Reform', *Ottawa Law Review,* 1999–2000, 31(2): 213–241.

55 See Lloyd Axworthy, *Navigating a New World: Canada's Global Future,* Toronto: Alfred A. Knopf, 2003, p. 237.

56 UN Doc. S/RES/1325 of 31 October 2000.

57 UN Doc. S/RES/1894 of 11 November 2009.

58 See Wolfgang Benedek, 'Mainstreaming Human Security in United Nations and European Union Peace and Crisis Management Operations: Policies and Practice', in Wolfgang Benedek, Matthias Kettemann and Markus Möstl (eds), *Mainstreaming Human Security in Peace Operations and Crisis Management. Policies, Problems, Potential*, Routledge: London, 2010, pp. 13–31.

CONCLUSION

Taylor Owen and Mary Martin

The twenty-year history of the concept of human security has undoubtedly been contentious. Born as a challenge to the dominant state-based security paradigm, it has struggled for definitional clarity, been appropriated for a wide range of policy and activist campaigns, used as the foundation for major international reports, re-imagined as a lens for critical security studies, measured and mapped.

This volume has sought to bring some clarity and definition to this arc: to show how the seemingly disparate uses of the concept can be organized and thought of as more than the sum of their parts. We feel that viewed in these four categories (concepts and context; global policy challenges; actors and applications; and methodologies, tools and approaches), the history of human security is not only rich in content, but makes sense as a discipline of study and action. The concept of human security, despite setbacks, is a success story.

Despite human security's achievements this volume reveals real challenges for the concept. Challenges that we feel should be addressed by those who use and study human security.

First, on the concept itself. It is certainly the case with human security that definitions matter. How one defines the bounds of concept necessarily affects which issues fall under its purview, what policy space the concept engages, which actors use it, and what institutions and norms the concept is positioned within. Definition matters. And it is clear that a lack of definitional clarity, while in some respects liberating for the myriad of activists who have used the concept, has limited the widespread institutional adoption of human security.

In some respects the Human Security Commission was a turning point in this definitional debate. By keeping the concept very broad, and intrinsically overlapping with the concept of human development, the Commission made it more difficult for organizations like the United Nations to adopt human security as a policy-guiding concept. Struggling with definitional uncertainly, the EU went some distance in articulating a clearer version of the concept, but ultimately did not adopt it to the extent that the norm entrepreneurs within the institution sought.

And this reveals the underlying conceptual tension in a concept that seeks to both shift the referent of security away from the state and to the individual, while at the same time being a policy tool for guiding the actions of the state. While states such as Japan and Canada have at times adopted the concept, they surely have done so in order to promote their own interests. And when scaled to state-based institutions such as the United Nations, it is very challenging to define the collective state interest in devolving, to any degree, the power of the state. In many ways, the concept has failed to overcome this tension. Human security, despite some isolated policy success, has always been more comfortable in theory than in practice.

Which leads to the second section of the volume and a study of what policy challenges have been articulated and acted on in the name of human security. The group of topics (landmines, humanitarian intervention, food security, arms control, counter-terrorism) is both broad, but also notable in its connection to traditional areas of security concepts. And so at the core of these uses of the concept lies a question: are such collaborations between human and traditional security possible and on what terms? For radical proponents of human security, however normative and holistic the framework the authors set out, it heralds a slippery slope at the end of which the concept's critical credentials are bound to be subverted. The counter-terrorism agenda threatens to do more than acknowledge or co-exist with human security. By co-opting it, it squeezes any room for a revision of practice and power. As in other policy domains such as natural disaster management and arms control, the potential of human security for overturning classical approaches and producing better policy responses is still being explored. At stake is a wholesale reframing of global challenges from hunger to weapons proliferation, terrorism and natural disasters, including climate change. Human security is in this sense, problem-solving. The extent to which it can recast these challenges in people-centric terms, and devise a role for states in which they are both constrained and mobilized, will determine whether the concept offers policy solutions which are radically different or simply rearrangements of traditional prescriptions

While all of these issues clearly fall under the banner of human security, the question remains whether there is something common that binds them; a common element on which the concept can grasp, which creates a whole that is greater than the sum of its parts? It also must be noted that the ICISS report on the Responsibility to Protect in many ways became the policy manifestation of the narrow, violence-based articulation of human security. By doing so, however, it relegated the concept to a far more limited policy discourse than many had envisioned – namely, the military response to large scale acts of violence.

The third section, on the UN, EU, Japan, Asia and Africa, further demonstrates the numerous tensions over the policy implementation of the concept. What the chapters in this section also show, however, is the fragility of human security as a politically convenient/expedient narrative. Deprived of charismatic policy entrepreneurship, the commitment to human security has waned in almost all cases except in Japan. The African Union faces challenges in promoting its human security agenda, not least because, as Thomas Tieku says, the Arab Spring has turned it 'from a darling idea to almost a taboo subject in the corridors of AU'. It has been expunged from official communications in the Canadian ministry of foreign affairs, and less dramatically its visibility in the EU declined with the succession of Catherine Ashton as High Representative in place of Javier Solana.

Finally, attempts to develop economic, legal, indicator and map-based measures for human security also reveal but the breadth of the concept, as well as how important clear articulation of the bounds of the concept is for its implementation. How one defines the concept instrumentally determines what is and is not measured. Policy makers and academics using these measures then base action and analysis on these models.

A recurring theme amongst these measures is the mutual constitution of *praxis* and *lexis* – the link between what is done to initiate human security policies and the conceptualization of human security. The more one delves into the implications of human security ideas for practical action, the stronger sense and meaning is derived about what human security actually is. The story of human security has been an ebb and flow between academic theorizing, policy scepticism, intellectual contestation and practitioner enthusiasm. At times, the Academy has driven the discourse forward, only to be overtaken by policy makers and practitioners whose initial doubts and wariness about yet another new security concept have been swept aside by the imperative of having to come up with new responses to intractable global issues.

In conclusion, a few overarching comments can be made about the historical arc of the concept of human security captured in this volume.

First, the evolution of the concept has been significantly shaped by events. Its adoption by both state and non-state actors is highly contextualized within the wider global policy debates. For example, the Iraq war shaped the EU's engagement; the Asian financial crisis effected Japan's; and the timing of the birth of R2P, mere days after 9/11, played a significant role in it becoming the standard bearer of the concept.

Second, it is important to reflect on what is new about the concept. How much of the human security discourse has really been shaped by the actual security needs of the individual or how much about a societal need, or the needs of the states and state-based institutions that have adopted it, or even the theoretical needs of researchers? It is worth keeping front of mind that it is generally not individuals who are doing human security but institutions acting in their name.

Third, human security has taken root in different policy silos and disciplinary settings but there has also been cross-fertilization between different discourses and actors. This encouraging of interdisciplinarity, across institutional silos, between disparate activists organizations, and through academic fields of study, may be one of the principal achievements of the concept.

Finally, we have to acknowledge the role of key individuals in promoting and defining the concept. Looking at the discourse on human security as a twenty-year global project, spanning governments, NGOs, international instructions and academic disciplines, what is overwhelmingly clear is that a relatively small group of norm entrepreneurs gave this concept life by acting in its name. These include Amartya Sen, Sadako Ogata, Prime Minister Keizo Obuchi, Javier Solana, Ferrero Waldner, Lloyd Axworthy. Without them, it is clear that the concept would have had a very different and far more limited life than the one it has had, and the one we ultimately sought to summarize and highlight in this volume.

INDEX